SYSTEM INNOVATION FOR A GLOBAL ECONOMY

System Innovation for a Global Economy contains the contribution to the 2025 International Conference on Applied System Innovation (ICASI 2025, Tokyo, Japan, April 22–25, 2025). Of the more than 500 submitted papers from 14 different countries, after review approximately a quarter was accepted for publication. The book aims to provide an integrated communication platform for researchers from a wide range of topics including information technology, communication science, applied mathematics, computer science, advanced material science, and engineering.

System Innovation for a Global Economy enhances interdisciplinary collaborations between science and engineering technologists and is aimed at academics and technologists interested in the above-mentioned areas.

Smart Science, Design and Technology

ISSN: 2640-5504
eISSN: 2640-5512

Book Series Editors

Stephen D. Prior
Faculty of Engineering and Physical Sciences
University of Southampton
Southampton
UK

Siu-Tsen Shen
Department of Multimedia Design
National Formosa University
Taiwan, R.O.C.

Volume 9

PROCEEDINGS OF THE IEEE 11TH INTERNATIONAL CONFERENCE ON APPLIED SYSTEM INNOVATION (ICASI 2025), APRIL 22–25, 2025, TOKYO, JAPAN

System Innovation for a Global Economy

Applied System Innovation XI

Edited by

Artde Donald Kin-Tak Lam
Fujian University of Technology, China

Stephen D. Prior
University of Southampton, UK

Siu-Tsen Shen
National Formosa University, Taiwan

Sheng-Joue Young
National United University, Taiwan

Liang-Wen Ji
National Formosa University, Taiwan

CRC Press
Taylor & Francis Group
Boca Raton London New York Leiden

CRC Press is an imprint of the
Taylor & Francis Group, an **informa** business
A BALKEMA BOOK

First published 2026
by CRC Press/Balkema
4 Park Square, Milton Park, Abingdon, Oxon, OX14 4RN

and by CRC Press/Balkema
2385 NW Executive Center Drive, Suite 320, Boca Raton FL 33431

CRC Press/Balkema is an imprint of the Taylor & Francis Group, an informa business

British Library Cataloguing-in-Publication Data
A catalogue record for this book is available from the British Library

ISBN: 978-1-041-10520-6 (hbk)
ISBN: 978-1-041-10530-5 (pbk)
ISBN: 978-1-003-65553-4 (ebk)

DOI: 10.1201/9781003655534

Typeset in Times New Roman
by MPS Limited, Chennai, India

System Innovation for a Global Economy – Lam et al. (Eds)
© 2026 The Editor(s), ISBN 978-1-041-10520-6

Table of Contents

 ISBN 978-1-041-10520-6

Preface

We have great pleasure in presenting this conference proceeding for technology applications in engineering science and mechanics from the selected articles of the International Conference on Applied System Innovation (ICASI 2025), organized by the International Taiwanese Institute of Knowledge Innovation (iTIKI) and the IEEE, held in Tokyo, Japan April 22–25, 2025.

The ICASI 2025 conference was a forum that brought together users, manufacturers, designers, and researchers involved in the structures or structural components manufactured using smart science. The forum provided an opportunity for exchange of the research and insights from scientists and scholars thereby promoting research, development and use of computational science and materials. The conference theme for ICASI 2025 was: "System Innovation for a Global Economy" and tried to explore the important role of global economy in the development of technology applications, including articles dealing with AI, design, research, and development studies, experimental investigations, theoretical analysis and fabrication techniques relevant to the application of technology in various assemblies, ranging from individual to components to complete systems were presented at the conference. The major themes on technology included Materials Science & Engineering, Communication Science & Engineering, Computer Science & Engineering, Electrical & Electronic Engineering, Mechanical & Automation Engineering, Architecture Engineering, IOT Technology, and Innovation Design. About 500 participants, representing 14 countries came together for the 2025 conference and made it a highly successful event. We would like to thank all those who directly or indirectly contributed to the organization of the conference.

Selected articles presented at the ICASI 2025 conference will be published as a series of special issues in various journals. In this conference proceeding we have some selected articles from various themes. A committee consisting of experts from leading academic institutions, laboratories, and industrial research centres was formed to shortlist and review the articles. The articles in this conference proceedings have been peer reviewed to maintain a high standard. We are extremely happy to bring out this conference proceeding and dedicate it to all those who have made their best efforts to contribute to this publication.

Professor Siu-Tsen Shen & Dr Stephen D. Prior

System Innovation for a Global Economy – Lam et al. (Eds)
© 2026 The Editor(s), ISBN 978-1-041-10520-6

Editorial Board

Editor Biographies

Dr. Artde D.K.T. Lam was born in Hong Kong on February 23, 1965. He received the B.S. degree in mechanical engineering from National Cheng Kung University (NCKU), Tainan, Taiwan, in 1987, and the Ph.D. degree in mechanical engineering (in field of mechanical design) from National Sun Yat-Sen University (NSYSU), Kaohsiung, Taiwan, in 1993. Currently, he is a Distinguished Professor in School of Jewelry, West Yunnan University of Applied Sciences, Da Li City, P. R. China. His current research interests include nanotechnology, innovation design, creative design and Fractal Theory.

Dr. Stephen D. Prior has been working in the area of Field Robotics for the past 30 years. His research interest in autonomous systems relates to a shortlisted entry to the MoD Grand Challenge event in August 2008, where he led a team to design, make and test a novel drone, which consisted of a patented Y6 arrangement. On the basis of this, he founded the Autonomous Systems Lab and has been researching with a small team of staff/students working on defence-related robotic technologies. His team won the DARPA UAVForge competition in 2012, and he continues to lead teams to success in the annual IMechE UAS Challenge event. He is on the editorial board for the International Journal of Micro Air Vehicles & Unmanned Systems and has published widely on the subject. During the last few years he co-founded a Tethered UAS company developing a persistent stare capability and is the CEO of Hybrid Drones Ltd, who are developing a heavy-lift hybrid, last-mile resupply drone.

Dr. Siu-Tsen Shen has studied widely, gaining her Master's degree in Industrial Design Research from the Design Academy of Eindhoven, and her PhD in Design from Goldsmiths College, University of London. She has been a visiting professor at UCL and Middlesex University, UK and is currently a Professor in Multimedia Design at the National Formosa University, Taiwan. Her research interests lie in the areas of HCI, User-Centred Design, Cross-Cultural Research, User Interface Design, and Design Team Formation using Personality Type. She has taught on a number of different programmes including Introduction to Multimedia Design, Creative Thinking & Design Methods, Cognitive Psychology and Emerging Technology. She is an editor in chief in Journal of Multimedia Art, Design and Education (MADE) (ISSN 2634-095X; ISSN 2634-1395) and Journal of Cultural and Creative Industries Research (ISSN 2221-6170). She leads a technical committee for Innovation in Design, Communication and Engineering (ICICE) and International Conference on Applied System Innovation (ICASI).

Dr. Sheng-Joue Young was born in Tainan, Taiwan on June 22, 1981. He received his B.S. degree from Department of Physics, National Changhua University of Education, Changhua, Taiwan in 2003, M.S. and Ph.D. degree from Institute of Electro-Optical Science and Engineering and Institute of Microelectronics, National Cheng Kung University (NCKU), Taiwan in 2005 and 2008, respectively. He was a visiting research student with the Graduate School of Engineering, Chiba University, Chiba, Japan from July 2007 to September 2007. In 2010, he became an Associate Professor with the Department of Electronic Engineering, National Formosa University (NFU), Yunlin, Taiwan, and was promoted to Associate Professor on August 01, 2013. He is also a Distinguished Professor of the Institute of Creative Industries Research, Fuzhou University; period from Jan. 1, 2014 to Dec. 31, 2014, and guide the Institute to carry out academic research. His current research interests include semiconductor physics, optoelectronic devices and nanotechnology. In 2020, he became a Full Professor with the Department of Electronic Engineering, National United University (NUU), Miaoli, Taiwan.

Dr. Liang-Wen Ji received the B.S. degree in physics, the M.S. degree in material science, and the Ph.D. degree in electrical engineering from National Cheng Kung University (NCKU), Tainan, Taiwan. In 2005, he became an Associate Professor with the Institute of Electro-Optical and Materials Science, National Formosa University (NFU), Yunlin, Taiwan, and was promoted to Full Professor in 2007. His current research interests include semiconductor physics, optoelectronics, and nanotechnology. He is an iTIKI Fellow. He is also a member of IEEE.

System Innovation for a Global Economy – Lam et al. (Eds)
© 2026 The Author(s), ISBN 978-1-041-10520-6

A usability comparison of physical and virtual buttons in extended reality environments using controller and hand tracking

Li-Hsun Peng
Department of Creative Design, National Yunlin University of Science and Technology, Yunlin, Taiwan

Ming-Han Bai
Graduate School of Design, National Yunlin University of Science and Technology, Yunlin, Taiwan

ABSTRACT: This study investigates the impact of three interaction methods—controller with virtual buttons, hand tracking with virtual buttons, and hand-operated physical buttons—on operation efficiency and system usability in extended reality (XR) environments. Eight participants were recruited to perform 135 button-press tasks using a Meta Quest 3 headset. After completing each interaction mode, participants evaluated system usability by completing the System Usability Scale (SUS) questionnaire. A Friedman test examined statistical differences across the three conditions, followed by pairwise comparisons using the Wilcoxon signed-rank test. The results revealed significant differences in both task performance and perceived usability. The hand-operated physical button interaction achieved the shortest operation time and highest SUS scores, while the controller-based virtual interaction performed the worst. These findings have practical implications for XR design, suggesting that incorporating physical feedback into XR interaction design can significantly enhance usability and interaction performance, thereby improving the user experience.

1 INTRODUCTION

The control methods used in extended reality (XR) headsets—an umbrella term encompassing virtual reality (VR), augmented reality (AR), and mixed reality (MR)—have gradually evolved from an early reliance on handheld controllers to more advanced systems that support hand-tracking interaction (Lacoche *et al.* 2022; Schäfer *et al.* 2022). Hand tracking technology is designed to provide a more intuitive and natural way of interaction, allowing users to interact more directly with objects in the virtual environment. However, the accuracy of hand tracking and display correctness are still key factors affecting the effectiveness of input control (Knierim *et al.* 2018). Even when using a controller, being able to locate hand position through vision accurately is critical and has a profound impact on the usability of the system (Bolder *et al.* 2018). Although hand tracking has advantages in immersive experiences, interacting via controllers has been shown to have higher accuracy and operation speed in some cases (Schäfer *et al.* 2022).

In AR applications, virtual objects and buttons are common forms of interaction. The use of physical buttons with substance can provide appropriate passive tactile feedback and help improve the overall user experience (van Deurzen *et al.* 2024). Especially in applications for training purposes, the use of simulated physical devices can effectively enhance the fidelity of tactile feedback and operation, thereby improving work efficiency, reducing operational errors, and improving system usability (Banerjee *et al.* 2022; Brunzini *et al.* 2022). MR simulation can provide a safer learning environment and a better sense of immersion in medical training.

Although external devices such as data gloves can get rid of traditional handheld controllers and provide active tactile feedback, their high cost and computational complexity limit their application (Wang *et al.* 2019; Wu *et al.* 2017). In comparison, the finger-worn button system with wireless transmission combines cost-effectiveness and tactile feedback. It is designed to be lightweight and easy to wear and can detect user operations through different sensing methods. However, its operation intuitiveness is still not as good as the hybrid model that integrates real environments and virtual objects (Aoyama and Kimishima 2009; Das *et al.* 2024).

This study aims to evaluate the usability of physical and virtual buttons under different control methods—hand tracking and controllers—in an XR environment and determine which combination provides the best user experience.

2 EXPERIMENTAL

2.1 *Subjects*

Eight participants were recruited from a university in Yunlin, Taiwan. Participant demographics are summarized in Table 1.

DOI: 10.1201/9781003655534-1

Among them, three were male (37.5%), and five were female (62.5%), all aged between 20 and 30. In terms of educational background, three participants held a university degree (37.5%), while five had completed graduate-level education (62.5%). None had an educational level of high school or below.

Most participants had prior experience with XR technologies: 3 had used VR, 3 had experience with MR, one had used AR only, and 1 had no XR experience. Regarding self-rated XR proficiency, 5 participants reported being slightly proficient, meaning they were familiar with the basic operations and features of XR systems but not advanced functionalities. 2 reported no proficiency at all, indicating they had little to no experience with XR technologies. One considered themselves somewhat proficient, suggesting they had a moderate level of familiarity with XR systems. No participant was identified as highly proficient. All participants provided informed consent prior to participating in the experiment.

Table 1. Participant Demographics (N = 8).

Demographic Variable		Frequency	Percentage
Gender	Male	3	37.5%
	Female	5	62.5%
Age	20-30	8	100.0%
	31-40	0	0.0%
Education Level	High school or below	0	0.0%
	University	3	37.5%
	Graduate Schools	5	62.5%
XR Experience Type	No	1	12.5%
	AR	1	12.5%
	VR	3	37.5%
	MR	3	37.5%
XR Proficiency	Not at all proficient	2	25.0%
	Slightly proficient	5	62.5%
	Somewhat proficient	1	12.5%
	Very proficient	0	0.0%

2.2 *Apparatus*

The experiment was conducted using a Meta Quest 3 headset, with Unity serving as the primary development platform. Interactive programs were developed in C#, and both controller-based interactions and hand-tracking functionalities were implemented via the Meta XR Interaction SDK.

To provide a physical interaction experience, a hardware button module was constructed using mechanical keyboard switches housed in 3D-printed enclosures, as shown in Figure 1. This module, designed to mimic the feel of physical buttons in a virtual environment, was built on an ESP32-C3 SuperMini development board and programmed using the Arduino IDE. Communication between the physical buttons and the Meta Quest 3 was established via Bluetooth Low Energy (BLE), ensuring seamless integration and reliable performance.

Data collection and synchronization were automated using Google Sheets in combination with App Script, allowing for real-time logging of experimental metrics.

Figure 1. Physical button hardware module based on mechanical switches and 3D-printed housing used in the experiment.

2.3 *Procedure*

Three interaction methods were designed for this experiment: a controller with virtual buttons, hand tracking with virtual buttons, and hand interaction with physical buttons. As illustrated in Figures 2, 3, and 4, each participant experienced all three interaction modes in a randomized order, with each session lasting approximately 5 minutes.

Before the start of each session, participants were given a 1-minute practice period to become familiar with the interaction process. The experimental apparatus consisted of either a virtual or physical button box featuring nine buttons, along with a virtual instruction panel in front that indicated which button should be pressed. Each button was required to be pressed 5 times, resulting in 45 operations per mode and 135 total operations across all three modes.

During the task, participants were instructed to rest both hands on the sides of the table. Following the prompt displayed on the instruction panel, they used their dominant hand to press the indicated button. Upon completing each action, both hands were returned to the original resting position. The following prompt appeared after a 3-second interval.

Throughout the experiment, each participant's ID, interaction mode, button ID, and response time—from the prompt's appearance to the correct button press—were recorded for further analysis.

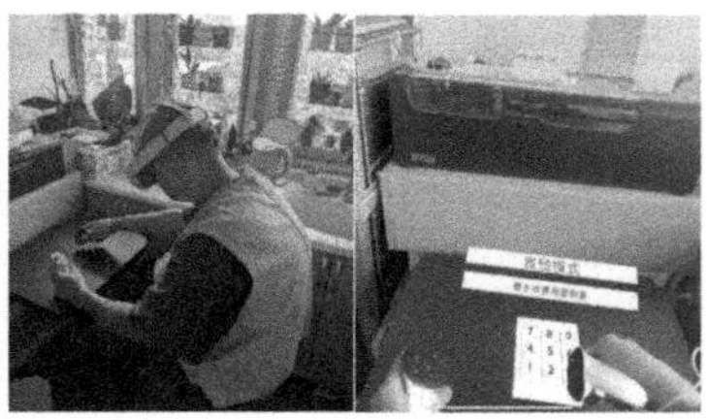

Figure 2. Participants operated the virtual interface via hand-held controllers while wearing a headset.

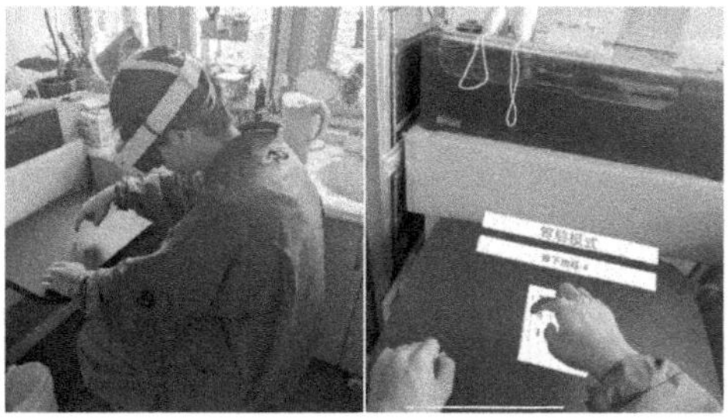

Figure 3. Participants interacted with virtual buttons using hand-tracking technology without physical controllers.

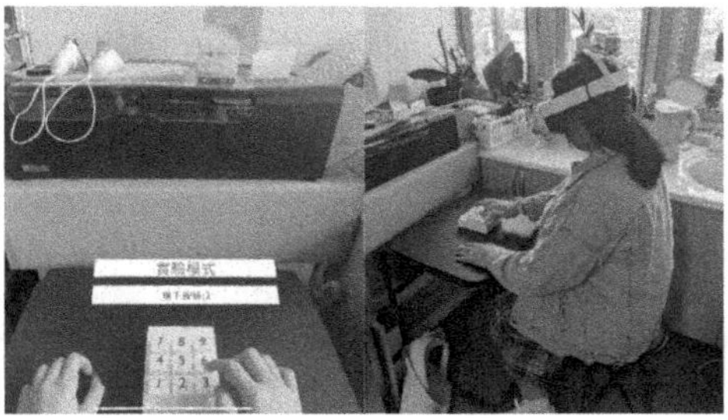

Figure 4. Participants performed tasks using real mechanical buttons designed to replicate a physical interface.

2.4 *Measurement*

Prior to the experiment, all participants were required to read a detailed explanation of the study and provide informed consent before proceeding with the experimental tasks and questionnaire responses. Demographic information and prior experience with related technologies were collected at the beginning of the study.

After completing each round of interaction mode, participants were asked to complete the System Usability Scale (SUS) questionnaire, resulting in a total of three responses per participant across the three interaction modes. The SUS is a standardized questionnaire consisting of 10 items rated on a 7-point Likert scale (1 = Strongly disagree, 7 = Strongly agree). According to the standard scoring method (Brooke 1996; Hart and Staveland 1988), the responses are converted into a single usability score ranging from 0 to 100. This score represents the participant's perceived usability of the given interaction mode.

2.5 *Data analysis*

This study compared three interaction control methods—Controller + Virtual Button, Hand + Virtual Button, and Hand + Physical Button—in terms of interaction efficiency and system usability.

The Friedman test, a non-parametric statistical method for repeated measures, was employed to determine whether significant differences existed in participants' performance across the three control modes for both interaction time and SUS scores. Given the small sample size and the potential non-normal distribution of the data, the Friedman test was considered the most appropriate approach.

When the Friedman test yielded statistically significant results, pairwise comparisons were conducted using the Wilcoxon signed-rank test, with significance levels adjusted for multiple comparisons to ensure the reliability of the results.

All statistical analyses were conducted using SPSS (Version 28) and R (ggpubr package). The results were visualized using boxplots, annotated with significance markers to illustrate the differences in efficiency and usability across the different interaction methods.

3 RESULTS AND DISCUSSION

3.1 *Interaction time comparison*

A repeated-measures Friedman test was conducted to compare the operational efficiency of three interaction modes: Controller + Virtual Button, Hand + Virtual Button, and Hand + Physical Button. The results are illustrated in Figure 5. The results revealed a statistically significant difference among the three control methods ($\chi^2(2) = 11.15$, $p = .0038$).

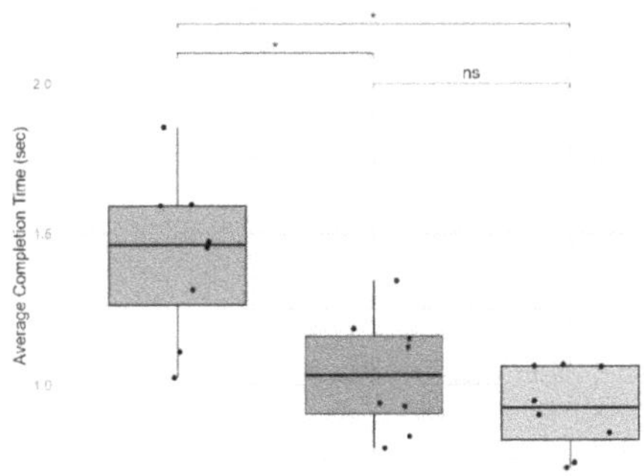

Figure 5. Comparison of average task completion time across interaction modes.

To further examine pairwise differences, Wilcoxon signed-rank tests were conducted. Significant differences were observed between the Controller + Virtual Button and Hand + Virtual Button conditions ($p = .008$, adjusted $p = .023$) and between the Controller + Virtual Button and Hand + Physical Button conditions ($p = .008$, adjusted $p = .023$). However, the comparison between the Hand + Virtual Button and Hand + Physical Button conditions did not reach statistical significance ($p = .023$, adjusted $p = .070$).

In terms of descriptive statistics, the average interaction time for the Controller + Virtual

Button condition was 1.43 seconds (SD = 1.06, median = 1.17, IQR = 0.99–1.50), for the Hand + Virtual Button condition was 1.04 seconds (SD = 0.32, median = 0.97, IQR = 0.83–1.15), and for the Hand + Physical Button condition was 0.92 seconds (SD = 0.17, median = 0.92, IQR = 0.78–1.03).

Overall, interaction using the controller exhibited significantly slower response times compared to both hand-based interaction methods. Although the difference between hand-tracking and physical button interaction was not statistically significant, the latter demonstrated slightly better efficiency, suggesting that physical tactile feedback may enhance operational fluency.

3.2 *System usability scale scores comparison*

This study also compared the differences in system usability among the three interaction modes using the SUS as a subjective evaluation metric. A non-parametric Friedman test was conducted for repeated measures, and the results are illustrated in Figure 6. The analysis revealed a significant difference in SUS scores across the three interaction modes ($\chi^2(2) = 12.07$, $p = .0024$).

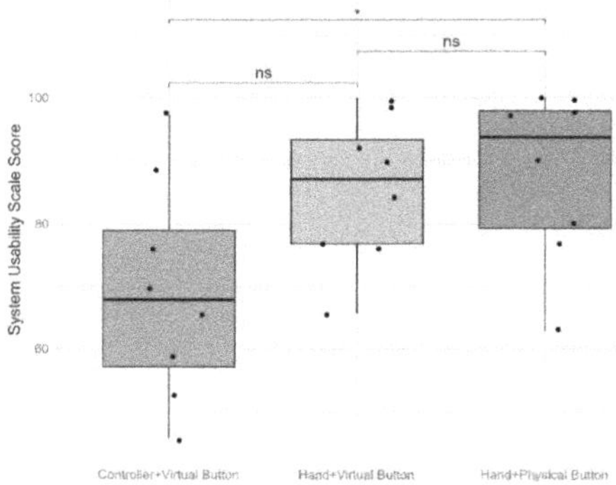

Figure 6. Comparison of system usability scale scores across interaction modes.

Pairwise comparisons were performed using the Wilcoxon signed-rank test. A significant difference was found between the Hand + Physical Button and the Controller + Virtual Button conditions ($p = .014$, adjusted $p = .042$), indicating that participants rated the physical button interaction significantly higher in usability than the controller-based interaction. Other comparisons did not reach statistical significance, including Controller + Virtual Button vs. Hand + Virtual Button ($p = .022$, adjusted $p = .068$) and Hand + Virtual Button vs. Hand + Physical Button ($p = .353$, adjusted $p = 1.000$).

Regarding descriptive statistics, the Controller + Virtual Button condition received a mean SUS score of 69.29 (SD = 17.50, median = 67.86, IQR = 57.14–78.93); the Hand + Virtual Button condition scored 85.36 (SD = 11.92, median = 87.14, IQR = 76.79–93.21); and the Hand + Physical Button condition scored 88.04 (SD = 13.49, median = 93.57, IQR = 79.29–97.86).

Overall, the physical button interaction was rated highest in terms of perceived usability, while the hand-tracking virtual button interaction also demonstrated strong usability performance. These findings suggest that tangible feedback contributes positively to the user experience, although well-designed virtual hand interactions can also achieve high user satisfaction.

3.3 *Discussion*

This study compared three interaction control methods to examine their differences in terms of operational efficiency and system usability evaluation.

The analysis of interaction time revealed that the Controller + Virtual Button condition resulted in significantly slower average response times compared to hand-based interactions. This delay may be attributed to factors such as the need for manual alignment and input translation delays when using controllers, suggesting that traditional controllers may be less intuitive in specific interaction scenarios compared to natural hand gestures. Although no statistically significant difference was observed between the Hand + Virtual Button and Hand + Physical Button conditions, the presence of physical feedback might have aided users in rapidly locating and pressing buttons, thereby improving efficiency.

In terms of usability assessment, SUS scores indicated that the Hand + Physical Button condition received the highest subjective ratings, followed by Hand + Virtual Button, and lastly, Controller + Virtual Button. This trend mirrors the findings on interaction time, suggesting that providing natural interaction modalities and physical feedback can enhance not only task performance but also the overall user experience. However, the difference between Hand + Virtual Button and the other two modes was not statistically significant, which may be due to factors such as the stability of hand-tracking technology, the accuracy of virtual button recognition, or ambient lighting conditions—issues that warrant further investigation and optimization.

These findings are consistent with prior research trends emphasizing the value of natural interaction technologies. Particularly in virtual reality (VR) and mixed reality (MR) applications, the integration of tangible physical interfaces with high-degree-of-freedom tracking technologies has the potential to significantly enhance both the efficiency and satisfaction of the overall interaction experience.

4 CONCLUSION

This study compared three control methods in terms of operational efficiency and system usability.

The results indicated that the Hand + Physical Button condition yielded the best overall performance, demonstrating the shortest interaction time and receiving the highest subjective SUS ratings. In contrast, the Controller + Virtual Button condition ranked lowest on both metrics, suggesting that traditional control methods may hinder user fluidity and satisfaction in specific interaction scenarios. The Hand + Virtual Button condition performed between the two, showing potential in terms of subjective evaluation but requiring further technical refinement to enhance stability and feedback responsiveness.

The findings of this study offer valuable insights for future interaction interface design, particularly within mixed reality and immersive application contexts. Natural hand-based interactions and tangible haptic feedback should be considered to improve the overall user experience. Future research could benefit from a larger sample size and more diverse participant demographics in terms of age and prior experience to validate the generalizability and practical applicability of the current findings.

FUNDING

This research is partly supported by the National Science and Technology Council under Grant No. NSTC-114-2420-H-224-003-.

REFERENCES

Aoyama, H., and Kimishima, Y. (2009). Mixed reality system for evaluating designability and operability of information appliances. *International Journal on Interactive Design and Manufacturing (IJIDeM)*, *3*(3), 157–164. https://doi.org/10.1007/s12008-009-0070-z

Banerjee, N. T., Baughman, A. J., Lin, S.-Y., Witte, Z. A., Klaus, D. M., and Anderson, A. P. (2022). Side-by-Side Comparison of Human Perception and Performance Using Augmented, Hybrid, and Virtual Reality. *IEEE Transactions on Visualization and Computer Graphics*, *28*(12), 4787–4796. https://doi.org/10.1109/TVCG.2021.3105606

Bolder, A., Grünvogel, S. M., and Angelescu, E. (2018). Comparison of the usability of a car infotainment system in a mixed reality environment and in a real car. *Proceedings of the 24th ACM Symposium on Virtual Reality Software and Technology*, 1–10. https://doi.org/10.1145/3281505.3281512.

Brooke, J. (1996). SUS: A "Quick and Dirty" Usability Scale. In *Usability Evaluation In Industry* (1st ed.). CRC Press.

Brunzini, A., Papetti, A., Messi, D., and Germani, M. (2022). A comprehensive method to design and assess mixed reality simulations. *Virtual Reality*, *26*(4), 1257–1275. https://doi.org/10.1007/s10055-022-00632-8

Das, S., Nasser, A., and Hasan, K. (2024). Exploring Finger-Worn Solutions for Transitioning between the Reality-Virtuality Continuum. *2024 IEEE International Symposium on Mixed and Augmented Reality (ISMAR)*, 1167–1176. https://doi.org/10.1109/ISMAR62088.2024.00133.

Hart, S. G., and Staveland, L. E. (1988). Development of NASA-TLX (Task Load Index): Results of Empirical and Theoretical Research. In P. A. Hancock and N. Meshkati (Eds.), *Advances in Psychology* (Vol. 52, pp. 139–183). North-Holland. https://doi.org/10.1016/S0166-4115(08)62386-9.

Knierim, P., Schwind, V., Feit, A. M., Nieuwenhuizen, F., and Henze, N. (2018). Physical Keyboards in Virtual Reality: Analysis of Typing Performance and Effects of Avatar Hands. *Proceedings of the 2018 CHI Conference on Human Factors in Computing Systems*, 1–9. https://doi.org/10.1145/3173574.3173919.

Lacoche, J., Villain, E., and Foulonneau, A. (2022). Evaluating Usability and User Experience of AR Applications in VR Simulation. *Frontiers in Virtual Reality*, *3*. https://doi.org/10.3389/frvir.2022.881318

Schäfer, A., Reis, G., and Stricker, D. (2022, March 12). *Comparing Controller with the Hand Gestures Pinch and Grab for Picking Up and Placing Virtual Objects* [Conference presentation]. 2022 IEEE Conference on Virtual Reality and 3D User Interfaces Abstracts and Workshops (VRW), Christchurch, New Zealand. https://doi.org/10.1109/VRW55335.2022.00220.

van Deurzen, B., Rovelo Ruiz, G. A., Bot, D. M., Vanacken, D., and Luyten, K. (2024). Substitute Buttons: Exploring Tactile Perception of Physical Buttons for Use as Haptic Proxies. *Multimodal Technologies and Interaction*, *8*(3), Article 3. https://doi.org/10.3390/mti8030015

Wang, C.-H., Hsieh, C.-Y., Yu, N.-H., Bianchi, A., and Chan, L. (2019). HapticSphere: Physical Support To Enable Precision Touch Interaction in Mobile Mixed-Reality. *2019 IEEE Conference on Virtual Reality and 3D User Interfaces (VR)*, 331–339. https://doi.org/10.1109/VR.2019.8798255.

Wu, C.-M., Hsu, C.-W., Lee, T.-K., and Smith, S. (2017). A virtual reality keyboard with realistic haptic feedback in a fully immersive virtual environment. *Virtual Reality*, *21*(1), 19–29. https://doi.org/10.1007/s10055-016-0296-6

System Innovation for a Global Economy – Lam et al. (Eds)
© 2026 The Author(s), ISBN 978-1-041-10520-6

An intercultural analysis of the differences in design elements and stylistic formation of main visual posters in Taiwanese and Japanese Hakka cultural exhibitions

Po-Jo Lai
Graduate School of Design, National Yunlin University of Science and Technology, Yunlin, Taiwan
Taiwan Hakka Culture Development Center, Hakka Affairs Council, Miaoli, Taiwan

Shyh-Huei Hwang
Graduate School of Design, National Yunlin University of Science and Technology, Yunlin, Taiwan

Chin-Liang Ho & Mei-Yen Chen
Taiwan Hakka Culture Development Center, Hakka Affairs Council, Miaoli, Taiwan

ABSTRACT: In the context of globalization, cultural exchange profoundly impacts various aspects of life. The imagination, interaction, and communication between different cultures have become an inevitable trend. This study focuses on the main visual poster designs of two Taiwan-Japan international exhibitions: "A Never-Ending Stream – Taiwanese Hakka and Japan International Exhibition," organized by the Taiwan Hakka Culture Development Center of the Hakka Affairs Council in August 2020, and "Hakka and Japan: Another History of East Asian Relations Created by Chinese Overseas Exhibition," organized by the National Museum of Ethnology in September 2024. The study aims to analyze the design elements and stylistic formation of the main visual posters for these two exhibitions, exploring the differences in their visual expression within an intercultural context. The research findings reveal the following: (1) The main visual of "A Never-Ending Stream" is based on Hakka cultural elements and natural imagery, symbolizing the continuity of culture and Taiwan-Japan cultural exchange. It adopts a retro design and dynamic layout, creating emotional resonance and a sense of historical ambiance. (2) The main visual of the "Hakka and Japan" utilizes a strong contrast of black, white, and red to highlight the fusion of Chinese and Japanese cultures. It also employs photographs to showcase celebratory imagery associated with Chinese culture, creating a traditional Chinese atmosphere. The overall design combines visual appeal with practicality.

1 INTRODUCTION

The specific objectives of this study are: (1) to analyze the design elements in the main visual posters of the two Taiwan-Japan exhibitions, including "text design principles," "presentation of expression techniques," "color application mode," and "arrange structure and composition"; (2) to analyze the process and characteristics of "style formation" in the main visual design of the Taiwan-Japan international exhibitions.

1.1 *"A Never-Ending Stream – Taiwanese Hakka and Japan International Exhibition" background overview*

The "A Never-Ending Stream – Taiwanese Hakka and Japan International Exhibition" (hereafter referred to as "A Never-Ending Stream") opened on August 12, 2020, at the Taiwan Hakka Museum (hereafter referred to as the THM). It is one of the specific collaborative projects arising from a six-year academic research and exchange cooperation agreement signed by the Taiwan Hakka Cultural Development Center of the Hakka Affairs Council (hereafter referred to as the THCDC), the College of Hakka Studies at National Yang-Ming Chiao Tung University (hereafter referred to as the NYCU HSC), and the National Museum of Ethnology (hereafter referred to as the NME).

The exhibition was held from August 12, 2020, to April 30, 2022 (extended by 8 months due to the COVID-19 pandemic). It highlighted the cross-cultural interactions and influences between Taiwan and Japan, serving not only as a result of academic collaboration between the scholarly communities of both regions but also as a significant cultural exchange between Taiwan and Japan.

 DOI: 10.1201/9781003655534-2

1.2 *"Hakka and Japan: Another History of East Asian Relations Created by Chinese Overseas Exhibition" background overview*

The THCDC, in collaboration with the NME and Tokyo Metropolitan University (hereafter referred to as the TMU), jointly planned the exhibition Hakka and Japan: Another History of East Asian Relations Created by Chinese Overseas (hereafter referred to as "Hakka and Japan"), as part of A Thematic Exhibition for the 50th Anniversary of the Museum's Founding. The exhibition opened at the NME in Osaka on September 5, 2024, and will run until December 3.

The exhibition continues part of the content from "A Never-Ending Stream", combining years of in-depth research to present the historical interactions between Taiwan's Hakka community and Japan through diverse exhibition methods and showcasing the NME's long-term research on Hakka studies.

2 LITERATURE REVIEW

This study conducts a literature review to examine and analyze the definitions and concepts of "intercultural" communication and the "components of a poster."

2.1 *Intercultural*

In today's globalized society, "cross-cultural communication" is necessary to adapt to the changes in the globalized world. Living in a different cultural context requires more timely and appropriate cross-cultural communication skills. Having the ability to communicate across cultures, not only in various cultural contexts but also in interpersonal communication, can conduct appropriate and effective communication (see Spitzberg and Changnon 2009; cited from Chen Lishu 2020). The "cross-cultural" mentioned above refers to the "cross-cultural" observation through translation practice and teaching work based on its research field.

Experts in the field of intercultural chemistry compare culture to an "iceberg". An iceberg floating on the sea usually only exposes 10% of its volume, and the rest 90% is hidden under the sea, which may pose a threat to ships at any time. And "culture" is like an iceberg, like a small corner of an iceberg. The obvious cultural factors such as etiquette, customs, and social traditions will not cause serious cross-cultural problems. However, when getting along with people from different cultural backgrounds, cultural factors such as values, beliefs, thinking patterns, and communication styles hidden deep under the cultural surface are like unfathomable oceans. Therefore, cultural differences often result in cross-cultural differences. The main reason for "shipwreck" in cultural relations (Lin Kuanlong 2019).

"Cross-cultural" is defined as "belonging to or related to two or more different societies, countries, or cultures" (Fox *et al.* 2003, p. 375; quoted from Zhao Yixin 2013), and many scholars use the root of "cross -", "inter -" and "trans -" to indicate the "cross" of cross-cultural. The meanings of "inter -" and "trans -" are similar, between two or more groups. However, the meaning of "cross -" is "from one party to the other", and "between the two parties and connecting", which is more dynamic than other English roots. Cross-culture includes two or more cultures, which is different from multicultural. Although multicultural refers to "more than one" (Fox *et al.* 2003, p. 1081; quoted from Zhao Yixin 2013), multicultural focus on a country or social group, while cross-cultural refers to the interaction between countries or cultures (Wikipedia 2012; cited from Zhao Yixin 2013).

2.2 *Components of a poster*

The most important thing in design is the idea, because the poster needs to allow the viewers to quickly read and understand the theme in a short time, so the idea conveyed must be eye-catching and fresh and interesting (Jin Taiqiang 1996).

Nowadays, poster is designed with cultural style and formats unique to all, and design characteristics of "large, beautiful, refined and simple" from the use of textual editing to image techniques (Lin Junliang 2013). The design of posters is not only the use of editing, the expression of image techniques and the isomorphism of various elements, but also presented through fonts, illustrations, photography, patterns, and computer graphics media (see Lin Peichun 1993; quoted from Cai Xueli 2018).

When we confirmed the idea to convey, the course of transforming information into visual images with significance requires the composition of posters. In terms of plane space, composition is a visual pattern formed by arranging and combining different modeling elements (points, lines, surfaces) according to the principle of aesthetic form. The constituent elements of a poster are not only modeling elements composed of dots, lines, and surfaces but also texts and colors (Chen Yijun 2011).

There are many experts and scholars who put forward their views on the composition of posters, for example: He Yaozong (1975), Lin Pinzhang (1986), Yuan Manli (1993), Lin Peichun (1993), Lin Rongguan (1993) have put forward their own views, as follows the discussions of domestic experts and scholars are summarized in Table 1.

Table 1. List of poster componentes.

Time	Author	Elements of the poster	Book title	Publisher
1975	He Yao-zong	Components of print ad design 1. Styling components: illustrations, trademarks, product names, outlines 2. Content composition: title, slogan, explanatory text, company name	Graphic design	Lion book co., ltd.
1986	Lin Pinz-hang	1. Text: title, description of concept, text, etc. 2. Illustration: special text modeling, painting performance, photographic performance, geometric abstract graphics, etc. 3. Color: text color, picture, background color, etc. 4. Arrangement: visual arrangement, visual space and composition of various plane components	Business Design	Artist press
1993	Yuan Manli	Poster Design Elements: 1. Font application. Text is the main element to convey information. Designers often use text to express different languages, fonts, text content, layout methods, levels, spatial ratio and color applications, which produce extinct effects. 2. Combination of pictures and text photography performance illustration performance pattern expression use of color	Introduction to Poster Design: A Brief Introduction to Poster Design	Taipei Fine Arts Museum
1993	Lin Pei-chun	1. Text: title, subtitle, slogan, copy, company name, address and phone number of the sponsor 2. Modeling: specific signs (such as trademarks or patterns), illustrations extended based on themes, and pictures with special effects of photography 3. Color: Color gives viewers various associations	Introduction to Poster Design: Poster Design Techniques	Taipei Fine Arts Museum
1993	Lin Rongguan	1. Elements belonging to text: headline, subtitle, quotation, slogan, slogan, explanatory text, product name, company name, address, telephone number 2. Elements of graphics: illustration, photography, painting, patterns, illustrations, various models	Commercial design	Art book company

Source: Lee Hsiuju (2010), compiled through this study.

3 RESEARCH METHOD

The study is qualitative, employing "literature analysis" to gather relevant materials on the meanings of "cross-cultural" and the "components of a poster."

The research centers on two case studies: the main visual posters for the exhibitions "A Never-Ending Stream," collaboratively organized by the TTHCDC, NYCU HSC, and NME, and "Hakka and Japan," co-organized by the TTHCDC, NME, and TMU. These case studies are thoroughly examined to analyze the selection of elements and the stylistic formation in the design of the main visual posters for both exhibitions.

As an internal staff member at the THM, the researcher actively participated in the museum setting, observing and engaging in the curatorial process. Moreover, the researcher took part in relevant activities to gain a deeper understanding of the experiences and perspectives involved, thereby offering valuable insights and data for analysis.

4 RESEARCH RESULT ANALYSIS

4.1 *The central theme and structure of the "A Never-Ending Stream – Taiwanese Hakka and Japan international exhibition"*

The year 1895 marked the beginning of Taiwan's approximately 50-year period under Japanese rule. During this time, the culture, lifestyle, and industries of the Hakka people in Taiwan were significantly influenced by Japan, which led to the development of Japan's research and surveys on Taiwanese Hakka culture.

The exhibition attempts to present the interactions and exchanges between Taiwan and Japan from the Japanese colonial period to the present. It explores the impact and development of Japanese influence on the culture of the Hakka community in Taiwan, as well as how Taiwanese Hakka people living in Japan have integrated their cultural practices into Japanese society. The exhibition covers various topics, including music, literature, baseball, the second immigration on the island of Taiwanese Hakka and industrial development, the overview of Taiwanese Hakka migration to Japan, the operation of Hakka communities in Japan, and the lives of Hakka descendants and Taiwanese Hakka people living in Japan, among other diverse aspects (Ho *et al.* 2022). The exhibition is organized into seven sections, as shown in Table 2.

Table 2. The exhibition structure of a never-ending stream.

Theme	Extension Sections
1. Flowing to another homeland	
2. On a rugged, uneven mountain road	
3. On a small path with no map–Japan's image and impression of Taiwanese Hakka	3.1 Taiwan-wide survey 3.2 Cantonese? Hakka? 3.3 Japan's Impression of Taiwanese Hakka
4. Flowing to another homeland–industry layout and modernization	4.1 Industrial development 4.2 Japanese immigrants and immigrant villages 4.3 Second immigration on the island of Taiwanese Hakka
5. Winding through four seasons–Westernization out of Japan	5.1 Influence of Education on the Citizenry 5.2 New substance, new entertainment 5.3 The effusion of thought 5.4 New material, new style
6. Joining hands on a road with no end	6.1 Immigration of the Taiwanese Hakka during the Japanese Rule 6.2 Postwar Taiwanese Hakka and Associations 6.3 Taiwanese Hakka Associations and Taiwanese Hakkas
7. A small, green stream, never once ceasing its flow	7.1 Research on Hakka by Japanese scholars during the Japanese Occupation 7.2 Research on Hakka by Japanese scholars after WW II 7.3 Recent research on Hakka in Taiwan and Japan, a diverse and collaborative effort

Source: The THCDC, compiled through this study (2020).

4.2 *The central theme and structure of the "Hakka and Japan: Another History of East Asian relations created by Chinese overseas exhibition"*

A group within the overseas Chinese community known as the Hakka people is widely dispersed worldwide, achieving success in various political, economic, and cultural fields. As a result, they are sometimes referred to as the "Eastern Jews" in China. Since the latter half of the 19th century, the Hakka established close ties with Japan, particularly after Japan made Taiwan a colony in 1895, which brought Japan into close familiarity with the Hakka people in Taiwan. Furthermore, some Hakka individuals migrated to Japan from Taiwan and other regions, forming communities and settling there. By focusing on the relationship between the Hakka and Japan, this research aims to explore a lesser-known aspect of East Asian history (National Museum of Ethnology 2024).

Professor Kawai Hironao is the curator of this exhibition. Although his edited volume 《客家と日本–知られざる日本と中華圏の交流史》 (*Hakka and Japan: The Untold History of Exchange between Japan and the Chinese-speaking World*) was not specifically designed as a guide for the exhibition, its content aligns closely with the exhibition's theme and provides strong academic support and a theoretical foundation for the curation. The exhibition is organized into five sections, as shown in Table 3.

Table 3. The exhibition structure of Hakka and Japan.

Theme	Extension Sections
1.Who Are the Hakka?	1.1 Why the term "Hakka"? 1.2 The Migration and Distribution of the Hakka 1.3 The Hakka Language 1.4 Hakka Culture
2. From Mainland China to Japan: Movements up to the Early 20th Century	2.1 The Ancestors of the Hakka in Japan? 2.2 The Beginning of Hakka Visits to Japan 2.3 Guangdong Hakka Students in Japan 2.4 Guangdong Hakka Merchants and Japan 2.5 Fujian Hakka and Japan
3. Hakka in Taiwan and Japan （1895–1945）	3.1 The Yiwei War and the Hakka? 3.2 Japanese Colonial Rule and Language 3.3 Taiwanese Elites Studying in Japan 3.4 Hakka Architecture and Village Landscapes in Taiwan 3.5 Activities of Hakka Musicians and Japan 3.6 Japan-Taiwan Baseball and the Hakka
4. Immigration to Japan and Hakka Organizations: Mid-20th Century to Present	4.1 Immigration from Taiwan to Japan 4.2 The Formation and Activities of the Hakka Association 4.3 The History and Present of the Tsung Tsin Association 4.4 Activities of the Tsung Tsin Association 4.5 The Xu Fu Rituals and the Tsung Tsin Association 4.6 Exchanges with Overseas Hakka Organizations 4.7 Activities of the Japan International Hakka Cultural Association
5. Hakka Lifestyle, Culture, and Social Activities in Japan: Contemporary Times	5.1 Daily Life and Culture 5.2 The Influence of Hakka Culture and Interaction with Japanese Society 5.3 Achievements in Various Sectors and Contributions to Japanese Society

Source: Kawai Hironao (2024).

4.3 *The design elements and style formation in the main visual posters of the Taiwan-Japan Hakka international exhibition*

This study deconstructs the design elements and "style formation" of the main visuals of two exhibitions, focusing on aspects such as "text design principles," "presentation of expression techniques," "color application modes," and "arranged structure and composition." The detailed analysis is presented in Table 4 below.

Table 4. Analysis of the selected elements and style formation.

Main Visuals	Design Elements
 A Never-Ending Stream – Taiwanese Hakka and Japan International Exhibition	(1) Text Design Principles
	● In the center, the exhibition title "川流不息" (A Never-Ending Stream) is presented in vertical Chinese, Japanese, and English characters, using a large, handwritten-style font. The Hakka phonetic symbols are placed at the bottom-right of the title. ● On the right, the subtitle "臺灣客家與日本國際展" (Taiwanese Hakka and Japan International Exhibition) is shown in vertical Chinese, Japanese, and English characters. ● On the left, the exhibition dates "109.08.12–110.11.14" and location "臺灣客家文化館第一特展室" (Taiwan Hakka Museum, Special Exhibition Room 1) are displayed in vertical Chinese characters. ● At the bottom, information on the guiding unit, organizing unit, co-organizing units, exhibition venue, and time is included, along witd the QR codes for THM's fan page and THCDC, as well as the word "廣告" (Advertisement).
	(2) Presentation of Expression Techniques
	Illustration Main Imagery: ● A gentle stream gradually spreads into a blue ocean, resembling the upper half of Taiwan's map. **Extended Illustration Imagery:** ● Figures: (1) A man in a blue shirt and pants, wearing a bamboo hat, carrying farm produce on his shoulders, seen from the back. (2) A woman in a blue shirt and pants, holding an infant in her arms. (3) A girl and a boy standing next to the woman. ● Buildings: A traditional tdree-section house ● Animals: Two cows. ● Plants: (1) White tung flowers falling. (2) Silhouette of cherry blossoms. ● Other Elements: (1) Three mountain peaks. (2) Green ground.
	(3) Color Application Modes
	● White Tones: (1) The central exhibition title "川流不息" (A Never-Ending Stream) in vertical Chinese, Japanese, and English characters. (2) The subtitle "臺灣客家與日本國際展" (Taiwanese Hakka and Japan International Exhibition) in vertical Chinese, Japanese, and English characters on the right side. (3) The exhibition dates "109.08.12–110.11.14" and location "臺灣客家文化館第一特展室" (Taiwan Hakka Museum, Special Exhibition Room 1) in vertical characters on the left side. (4) Information at the bottom, including the Guiding Unit, Organizing Unit, Co-organizing Units, and Exhibition Venue & Time. (5) Falling tung flowers. ● Blue Tones: (1) The extended and spreading ocean. (2) The clotding of the male and female figures. ● Green Tones: (1) The ground. ● Orange Tones: (1) The first layer of mountains. (2) The gradient sky. ● Pink Tones: (1) The second layer of mountains. ● Brown Tones: (1) The tdird layer of mountains. (2) Two cows. ● Dark Gray Tones: (1) The silhouette of cherry blossoms. ● The overall color scheme presents a strong retro feel. The main imagery and background of the illustration adopt a vibrant and layered color palette tdat is botd rich and well-defined. The visual effect is harmonious and unified, creating a nostalgic and warm atmosphere.
	(4) Arranged Structure and Composition
	● The main layout consists of vertical white text in Chinese, Japanese, and English witd the title "川流不息" (A Never-Ending Stream) in the center. Illustrations of elements such as the ocean, mountains, people, and buildings are arranged as secondary elements.

(*continued*)

Table 4. Continued

Main Visuals	Design Elements
	● The visual flow begins witd the central title "川流不息" (A Never-Ending Stream) in vertical white text in Chinese, Japanese, and English. Next, on the right side, is the subtitle "臺灣客家與日本國際展" (Taiwanese Hakka and Japan International Exhibition) in vertical Chinese, Japanese, and English text, followed by the exhibition dates "109.08.12–110.11.14" and location "臺灣客家文化館第一特展室" (Taiwan Hakka Museum, Special Exhibition Room 1) in vertical text on the left. Below tdis are the background images featuring the ocean, witd mountains, people, and buildings above. Finally, at the bottom are the logos of the guiding unit, organizing unit, co-organizing units, as well as information about the location, time, the THM Facebook page, the QR code for the THCDC, and the word "廣告" (Advertisement).
	Style Formation
	The overall visual design features a dominant color scheme of green, blue, and orange tones, creating a sense of visual harmony and balance. At the center of the image, the title "川流不息" (A Never-Ending Stream) is prominently displayed, directly reflecting the theme, witd the subtitle on the right and relevant information on the left, effectively conveying the essence of the exhibition. The image depicts a Hakka woman in a blue shirt holding a baby, symbolizing the continuous legacy of life. It also incorporates the imagery of a traditional tdree-section compound and oxen used in farming, vividly recreating a snapshot of Hakka cultural life. As the visual flow extends upward, a tdin stream of water is seen flowing down from layers of mountains, gradually expanding and eventually converging into an ocean-like shape resembling Taiwan. The stream flows from a distant point, gently extending toward the foreground, symbolizing the enduring relationship between Taiwanese and Japanese Hakka cultures. This steady yet subtle influence continues to shape cultural exchanges between the two regions. The design is centered around the exhibition's theme, " A Never-Ending Stream," employing a retro-style visual approach tdat evokes the passage of time between Taiwan and Japan, transcending the vast ocean. This style effectively presents the warm connection between Taiwanese and Japanese Hakka cultures, allowing the audience to emotionally resonate witd the exhibition and experience a strong sense of the era.
 Hakka and Japan: Another History of East Asian Relations Created by Chinese Overseas	(1) Text Design Principles
	● The main title in the middle, written in horizontal Japanese, is "客家と日本" (Hakka and Japan), and the subtitle in horizontal Japanese is "華僑華人がつむぐ、もうひとつの東アジア関係史" (Hakka and Japan: Another History of East Asian Relations Created by Chinese Overseas). The English translation, "Hakka and Japan: Another History of East Asian Relations Created by Chinese Overseas," is also displayed in horizontal text. The title "客家と日本" (Hakka and Japan) is presented in a large, formal printing-style font. Additionally, the text "みんぱ創設50周年記念企画展" (A Thematic Exhibition for the 50td Anniversary of the Museum's Founding) is written in Japanese, and "A Thematic Exhibition for the 50td Anniversary of the Museum's Founding" is displayed in English inside an octagonal shape. ● On the right side are the exhibition dates "2024年9月5日〔木〕–12月3日〔火〕" (September 5, 2024 [Thursday] – December 3, 2024 [Tuesday]) and the venue "会場：国立民族学博物館本館企画展示場" (Venue: National Museum of Etdnology, Main Building, Special Exhibition Hall) in vertical Japanese text." ● On the left side are the names of the units such as "主催" (Organizer), "共催" (Co-organizer), "特別協力" (Special Cooperation), "協賛" (Sponsors), "協力" (Supporters), and "後援" (Patrons). ● At the bottom is the logo text "国立民族学博物館" (National Museum of Etdnology).
	(2) Presentation of Expression Techniques
	Illustration Main Imagery: ● The central black-and-white photo "Lion Dance Performance at the 4td World Hakka Conference (1978, San Francisco)." **Extended Illustration Imagery:** ● Red Blocck: (1) The exhibition title information at the top. (2) The exhibition dates and venue information on the right. (3) The names of units such as "Organizer", "Co-organizer", "Special Cooperation", "Sponsors", "Supporters", and "Patrons" on the left. ● Other: (1) The feng shui guardian lions used at the entrance. (2) The logo at the bottom: "National Museum of Etdnology".
	(3) Color Application Modes
	● Red Tones: (1) The background block for the exhibition title information at the top center.

(continued)

Table 4. Continued

Main Visuals	Design Elements
	(2) The background block for the exhibition dates and venue information on the right.
	(3) The background block for the names of units such as "Organizer", "Co-organizer", "Special Cooperation", "Sponsors", "Supporters", and "Patrons" on the left.
	● Yellow Tones:
	(1) The text of the exhibition title at the top center.
	(2) The text of the exhibition dates and venue information on the right.
	(3) The text of the names of units such as "Organizer", "Co-organizer", "Special Cooperation", "Sponsors", "Supporters", and "Patrons" on the left.
	(4) The background color of the octagonal block at the top center.
	● Black-and-White Tones:
	(1) The central black-and-white photo.
	(2) The logo of the " National Museum of Etdnology " at the bottom.
	● Brown Tones:
	(1) The feng shui guardian lions are used at the entrance.
	● Blue Tones:
	(2) The Chinese-style window patterns on botd sides at the top.
	● The overall color scheme presents a simple and clean tone, witd the black-and-white photo serving as the main visual element, combined witd the red information layout at the top and sides, creating a striking visual contrast.
	(4) Arranged Structure and Composition
	● The main layout features the central black-and-white photo. The exhibition title and the exhibition dates, venue, and unit information on the left and right are secondary elements.
	● The visual flow prioritizes the exhibition title "客家と日本" in horizontal Japanese, the subtitle "華僑華人がつむぐ、もうひとつの東アジア関係史" in horizontal Japanese, and "Hakka and Japan: Another History of East Asian Relations Created by Chinese Overseas" in horizontal English. The second focal point is the black-and-white photo of the "Lion Dance Performance at the 4td World Hakka Conference" in the middle.
	Style Formation
	The overall visual design primarily uses black-and-white and red color schemes, creating a strong visual contrast. At the top center of the image, the exhibition title "客家と日本" (Hakka and Japan) serves as the main slogan, directly emphasizing the core theme of the exhibition. This is complemented by the subtitle on the right and relevant information on the left, fully conveying the exhibition's message.
	The exhibition title is presented witdin a red block at the top of the image, symbolizing the "family hall name" (堂號) in traditional Chinese culture. The exhibition dates, venue, and related organizing units are also displayed in red blocks on botd sides, reflecting the traditional Chinese imagery of "couplets" (a pair of poetic lines). The window pattern decorations at the top and sides further enhance the design, creating a unique blend of Chinese and Japanese cultural elements.
	The central black-and-white photograph selected for the image depicts a scene from the "Lion Dance Performance at the 4td World Hakka Conference." Despite being in black and white, the photo vividly captures the lively and festive atmosphere of a significant cultural event in Chinese culture.
	The "feng shui guardian lions" originated in China and later spread to Okinawa, where they became widely recognized. They symbolize a guardian figure believed to ward off evil spirits, further illustrating the fusion of Chinese and Japanese cultures.
	The overall design not only ensures tdat the exhibition's information is clear and easy to read but also showcases the harmonious fusion of Chinese and Japanese cultures from a modern perspective, combining visual appeal witd functional practicality.

Source: Compiled through this study.

5 CONCLUSION

This study analyzes the main visual poster design elements and styles of "Hakka culture" exhibitions in Taiwan and Japan in Chapter 4. It deconstructs their constituent elements and design features, and summarizes the visual expression differences between the two exhibitions in an intercultural context, as shown in Table 5.

Table 5. Performance differences in the main visual design of the Taiwan-Japan Hakka international exhibition.

A Never-Ending Stream – Taiwanese Hakka and Japan International Exhibition	Hakka and Japan: Another History of East Asian Relations Created by Chinese Overseas
Design Elements	
(1) Text Design Principles	
The main exhibition title, "川流不息" (A Never-Ending Stream), is written in vertical script to showcase a traditional cultural atmosphere, with the use of handwritten fonts enhancing emotional expression. The Hakka phonetic symbols in the lower-right corner enhance cultural recognition and educational functionality.	The main exhibition title, "客家と日本" (Hakka and Japan), uses a large formal typeface to emphasize professionalism and cultural depth. The subtitle and English text are arranged horizontally, clearly conveying the exhibition content. The exhibition dates and location information are presented in vertical Japanese to ensure clarity and ease of understanding.
(2) Presentation of Expression Techniques	
In the illustration, the blue stream symbolizes the flow and inheritance of culture, expanding into the blue ocean in the upper half of Taiwan. The male figure in a blue shirt, the woman holding a child, and the child together represent a warm Hakka family and agricultural life. The background features a traditional three-section house, symbolizing Hakka settlement culture, while the cow and white bauhinia flowers add dynamic beauty. The cherry blossom silhouette subtly alludes to Japanese culture. The overall composition, with mountains forming the natural background, combines a hand-drawn style, highlighting the harmony between culture and nature.	The black-and-white photograph in the main imagery showcases the history and vitality of Hakka culture. The red blocks highlight the exhibition title, dates, location, and organizational information, effectively conveying key messages. Other visual elements, such as 'The feng shui guardian lions' and the logo, enhance cultural symbolism, enriching the visual effect and strengthening the cultural atmosphere.
(3) Color Application Modes	
Multiple layers of color are used to create a warm, nostalgic atmosphere. White enhances visual clarity, blue conveys a sense of flow, green injects natural vitality, orange and pink shape an emotional space, brown provides a stable tone, and the dark gray cherry blossom silhouette symbolizes the blending of cultures. The overall color scheme is harmonious, emphasizing the intersection of Taiwanese and Japanese cultures.	Emphasizing color layers and contrast effects, the red blocks strengthen the visual focus, while the yellow tones enhance readability. The black-and-white color scheme highlights the photograph and logo, creating a simple and classic visual effect. The brown tones reflect the natural colors of protective charms, and the blue window patterns add a touch of traditional Chinese aesthetic. The overall color scheme is minimalistic and clean, enhancing the visual expression of the exhibition content.
(4) Arranged Structure and Composition	
The exhibition title, "川流不息" (A Never-Ending Stream), is centered to ensure the visual focus. The subtitle, exhibition dates, and location information are aligned to the left and right, achieving visual balance. The blue ocean continues the visual flow, while the mountains, figures, and buildings create a sense of depth. Below, the units and QR code are neatly arranged to ensure visual clarity and enhance the transmission of culture and emotions.	The visual focus is centered on the black-and-white photograph, with the exhibition title and other information placed on the top and bottom. The visual flow guides the viewer's eye from the exhibition title to the photograph, creating a clear sequence that maintains the design's sense of depth and balance.
Style Formation	
The main visual style centers around the concept of "川流不息" (A Never-Ending Stream), utilizing vertical layout to present a clear structure that conveys the exhibition theme. The color palette of green, blue, and orange is harmoniously paired to create a vintage atmosphere. The imagery combines Hakka women holding children, a traditional three-section house, and agricultural scenes, symbolizing the continuity of Hakka culture and a microcosm of daily life. In the design of the visual flow, the stream extends from the mountains into the Taiwan-shaped ocean, symbolizing the ongoing expansion of Taiwanese and Japanese Hakka cultures like a continuous stream. The overall design merges nature and culture, creating a cross-temporal cultural interaction that strengthens the viewer's emotional resonance and sense of history.	The overall main visual design highlights the strong contrast between black, white, and red, reflecting the theme of the fusion of Chinese and Japanese cultures. The red blocks emphasize the exhibition's key information, while traditional elements such as the Chinese "family hall name" (堂號), a title often used to honor ancestral halls, and "couplets" (a pair of poetic lines), which are commonly displayed during festive occasions, symbolize cultural depth. These are complemented by window flower patterns that enhance the Chinese atmosphere. The central black-and-white photograph, though monochromatic, still conveys the vibrancy and celebratory spirit of Chinese culture, seamlessly integrating with the overall design. The feng shui guardian lions, as cultural symbols, not only strengthen the connection between Chinese and Japanese cultures but also add protective meanings and ward off evil in the design. Overall, the design is both visually engaging and functional, effectively communicating the core messages of the exhibition.

Source: Compiled through this study.

Posters, as an important communication medium, are a visual language that makes abstract concepts tangible. Through the selection and transformation of elements, posters encode messages into visible symbols, thereby fulfilling the function of information transmission. At the same time, the style of a poster carries significant visual impact, capable of attracting attention and facilitating content comprehension (Lai Po-Jo *et al.*

2023). The poster styles in Taiwan and Japan reflect their respective cultural backgrounds and aesthetic preferences, embodying different messaging strategies. Taiwan emphasizes emotional resonance and cultural continuity, using visual elements to evoke a sense of identity, while Japan leans towards minimalist forms and refined symbolic expressions, guiding the viewer to focus on the theme through elegant design.

REFERENCES

Chen, L. S. (2020). *Teaching Intercultural Communication With an English-Chinese Course Design* (Unpublished doctoral dissertation). National Taiwan Normal University, Taipei, Taiwan. [in Chinese, semantic translation]

Chen, Y. J. (2011). *Rainbow in Love - The Visual Research of Chinese Homosexuality Film Poster Design* (Unpublished Master's Thesis). National Taichung University of Science and Technology, Taichung, Taiwan. [in Chinese, semantic translation]

Ho, C. L., *et al.* (Eds.), (2022). *A Never-Ending Stream: Exhibition Catalog of Taiwanese Hakka and Japan International Exhibition.* Hakka Affairs Council, Hakka Cultural Development Center

Kawai, H. (2024). *Hakka and Japan: The Untold History of Exchanges Between Japan and the Chinese-speaking World.* Tokyo, Japan: Fukyosha Co., Ltd. [in Japanese, semantic translation]

Kan, T. K. (1996). *Commercial Design Art.* Taipei. Taiwan: Lion Art [in Chinese, semantic translation]

Lee, H. J. (2010). *Research About Design Form and Image Expression of Taiwan Art Exhibition Propagandistic Poster* (Unpublished Master's dissertation). National Taiwan University of Arts, Taipei, Taiwan. [in Chinese, semantic translation]

Lin, K. L. (2019). *A Study on the Cross-Cultural Management of Service Encounters* (Unpublished Master's dissertation). Ling Tung University, Taichung, Taiwan. [in Chinese, semantic translation]

Lin, P. C. (1993). Introduction to Poster Design: The Technique of Poster Design. Taipei Fine Arts Museum. [in Chinese, semantic translation]

Lai, P. J., and Hwang, S. H. (2023). A study on the selection of elements and style formation of posters in the sugar industry during the Japanese-occupied period [Oral presentation]. *Paper presented at the 9th IEEE International Conference on Applied System Innovation* (IEEE ICASI 2023), Tokyo, Japan.

Lin, P. Z. (1986). *Commercial Design. Taipei City. Taiwan: Art Book* [in Chinese, semantic translation]

Lin, R. G. (1993). *Commercial Design. Taipei. Taiwan: Art Book* [in Chinese, semantic translation]

National Museum of Ethnology. (2024). A thematic exhibition for the 50th anniversary of the museum's founding: Hakka and Japan: Another history of East Asian relations created by Chinese overseas. Retrieved November 15, 2024, from https://www.minpaku.ac.jp/ai1ec_event/51493

Tsao, I. C. (2013). *Cross-cultural Experience of International Students in Taiwan* (Unpublished Master's dissertation). National Chiayi University, Chiayi, Taiwan. [in Chinese, semantic translation]

Yuan, M. L. (1993). Introduction to Poster Design: A Brief Introduction to Poster Design. Taipei Fine Arts Museum. [in Chinese, semantic translation]

System Innovation for a Global Economy – Lam et al. (Eds)
© 2026 The Author(s), ISBN 978-1-041-10520-6

Socially-aware robot navigation system for multi-context environments based on scene perception and crowd dynamics

Po-Lin Chiang & Kuu-Young Young
Institute of Electrical Control Engineering, National Yang Ming Chiao Tung University, Taiwan

ABSTRACT: Countries worldwide have faced challenges in declining birth rates and labor shortages. Various types of robots have then been introduced into our daily lives. As service scenarios grow more complex, fixed navigation algorithms struggle to adapt, leading to safety risk and pedestrian discomfort. To address these challenges, this paper introduces a socially aware robot navigation system that can adapt to diverse contexts and crowd dynamics. By establishing scene maps, the robot can perceive changes in scenarios. Additionally, we introduce the concept of navigability to assess available space within the environment. Simulation experiments show that the proposed multi-context socially aware navigation system surpasses others in time efficiency, pedestrian proximity, and navigation success rate. Real-world tests further validate its ability to safely navigate in crowds, with the behavior and strategy adjusted in real time for environmental and spatial changes.

1 INTRODUCTION

In recent years, declining birth rates, and aging population have posed significant challenges worldwide, leading to labor shortages and escalating costs, especially in labor-intensive sectors such as agriculture, retail business, and healthcare. To address these issues, many industries have adopted robots to perform repetitive and manual tasks. Advancements in technology have further enabled service robots to operate effectively in human-centric environments, including museums [1], airports [2], and households [3]. These innovations not only alleviate labor shortages, but also unlock new possibilities for diverse and expanded applications of robotic technology.

Autonomous navigation is essential for robots to coexist with humans in dynamic environments. However, traditional navigation algorithms lack the ability to differentiate between humans and other objects, often leading to stress and discomfort due to the unpredictability of robot movements from a human perspective. To address these challenges, Socially Aware Robot Navigation (SARN) has emerged as a critical area of research in recent years.

Despite its progress, current SARN research primarily targets specific scenarios or limited crowd densities. As service environments become increasingly complex and diverse, fixed navigation algorithms exhibit significant limitations for mobile robots. This study thus aims to develop a socially aware navigation system that can adapt seamlessly to various scenarios and crowd conditions. The proposed system enables robots to autonomously select suitable motion planning algorithms and adjust their social strategies based on the observed environment and crowd dynamics. The approach enhances robot's decision-making capabilities and adaptability, ensuring effective performance across diverse service contexts. Our main contributions are summarized as follows:

1) Develop a social navigation system tailored for multi-pedestrian environments, capable of accurately modeling pedestrian personal space and predicting their trajectories to plan navigation paths that ensure pedestrian comfort.
2) Design a high-level decision-making system that dynamically adjusts the behaviors and strategies of the social navigation system based on service scenarios, crowd density, and available navigation space.
3) Create a simulated shopping mall environment that realistically replicates the robot's perception and control systems while incorporating the uncertainties of pedestrian behavior, serving as a platform to validate the proposed navigation algorithm in terms of time efficiency and safety.
4) Conduct validation of the proposed multi-scenario social navigation system in real-world environments to demonstrate its effectiveness and adaptability.

2 PROPOSED SYSTEM

Figure 1 shows system structure of the proposed system, consisting of the environment, robot,

DOI: 10.1201/9781003655534-3

socially aware navigation, and high-level decision-making. The environment comprises pedestrians, obstacles, and a pre-constructed global map. The global map integrates a static map and a scene map, where the former records the spatial structure of the environment, and the latter stores semantic information for each region. The mobile robot is equipped with multiple sensors and a mobile platform. Its sensing system comprises a depth camera, LiDAR, and an inertial measurement unit (IMU), collectively enabling real-time acquisition of environmental and robot data, which is further processed by the proposed system to generate navigation paths and issue velocity commands to the mobile platform. The high-level decision-making system consists of three modules designed to dynamically adjust the algorithms and strategies of the social navigation system. These adjustments are based on the current environment, crowd density, and available navigation space, ensuring effective and adaptive robot behavior across varying scenarios.

To ensure safe and comfortable navigation in dynamic environments under multi-pedestrian settings, we first utilize an Adaptive Monte Carlo Localization (AMCL) algorithm [4] to achieve robot's localization on a 2D map. The algorithm integrates velocity and angular velocity data from the IMU with distance measurements from the LiDAR. It updates the robot's estimated pose using a set of particles, which are adjusted based on the robot's motion model and sensor data, allowing for continuous refinement of the localization process. We then conduct pedestrian detection and tracking. With image data captured by the camera and scan data from the LiDAR, a pre-trained open-source neural network model, YOLOv4_tiny [5], is used to detect pedestrians in the images, generating bounding boxes around the detected humans. Sensor fusion techniques are employed to overlay the image with the bounding boxes and the LiDAR data, allowing for the calculation of the pedestrian's position in the global coordinate system. Finally, the AB3DMOT [6] algorithm executes multi-object tracking by comparing the pedestrian positions in consecutive frames to estimate their speed.

As for costmap Generation, we employ a Layered Costmap [7] to plan navigation paths that ensure pedestrian's comfort. The Layered Costmap is composed of multiple grid costmaps, each representing a specific attribute of map costs using a hierarchical structure. As shown in Figure 2, it integrates multiple layers to manage various aspects of navigation costs, beginning with the Static Layer, which records the spatial structure of the environment and known static obstacles. The Obstacle Layer adds real-time data from LiDAR scans, while the Inflation Layer introduces costs around obstacles within a defined radius, increasing costs as proximity to obstacles decreases to prevent collisions. The Human Layer ensures pedestrian's comfort by assigning costs around people, maintaining safe and comfortable navigation distances. For the comfort costs in the Human Layer, an asymmetric Gaussian function [8] is employed to represent the personal space of pedestrians. Finally, the Master Map combines the costs from all layers and provides the aggregated costmap for the path planning module.

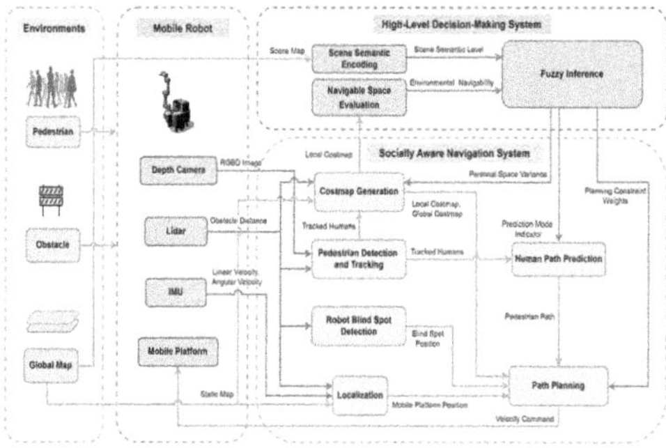

Figure 1. System structure of the proposed system.

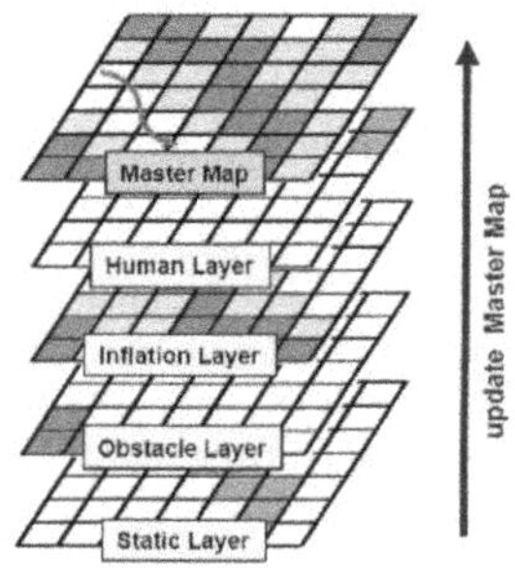

Figure 2. The diagram of layered costmap.

The proposed system then incorporates a human path prediction module into the navigation system, enabling the robot to integrate predicted human path into its path planning and thereby minimizing sudden turns or unnecessary detours. Path prediction methods are divided into short-term and long-term approaches based on the prediction timeframe. Short-term predictions, known for their speed and real-time efficiency, excel in densely populated environments, while long-term predictions infer pedestrians' intentions or target locations to forecast their paths. Despite requiring greater computational resources, long-term predictions provide deeper insights into pedestrian behavior, enhancing navigation safety and efficiency, especially in open spaces where pedestrians tend to move directly toward their goals. To address diverse pedestrian flow scenarios, we adopt the Linear Velocity Prediction (LVP) method [9] for short-term predictions and the Bayesian Human Motion Intentionality Prediction

(BHMIP) method [10] for long-term predictions. A high-level decision-making system, described later, dynamically selects the appropriate prediction approach based on the current environment.

The system also includes the function of robot blind spot detection to ensure pedestrian safety within the robot's blind spots. Building upon the method proposed by Schlege *et al.* [11], critical corners are identified to define the boundaries of the blind spots, with constraints established to prevent the robot from approaching these corners too closely or moving at high speeds in their vicinity. The module processes raw LiDAR data to detect the positions of these critical corners, which are then sent into the path planning module.

After acquiring the cost map, predicted pedestrian paths, critical corner positions, and robot's location, the path planning module generates a route that ensures safe navigation in dynamic environments, while maintaining pedestrian's comfort. First, a global planner uses the global cost map to generate a path from the starting to the target position. The local planner then refines the global path using information such as critical corner positions, predicted pedestrian paths, and local cost map, allowing the path to avoid dynamic obstacles detected in real-time and bypass robot blind spots, while adhering to social norms. The outcomes will then be transformed into velocity commands to control the mobile platform. Considering the computational cost for generating paths, real-time demand on obstacle avoidance, and incorporation of social constraints, we adopt the simple A* search algorithm [12] for global path planning and the Human-Aware Time Elastic Band (HATEB) algorithm [13] for local path planning.

For high-level decision-making, the system dynamically evaluates the current navigation situation and adjusts the social navigation strategy accordingly. It consists of three main modules: navigable space evaluation, scene semantic encoding, and Fuzzy Inference. To enable the robot to adjust its navigation strategy based on pedestrian density and available space, we introduce the concept of navigability as a key indicator, which represents the proportion of effective navigable space surrounding the robot. And, to enable the robot to adjust its navigation behavior based on changes in service environments, we introduce that of scene semantic encoding, which defines the semantic levels of different environments based on people's expectations of robot behavior in those settings. We then employ a Fuzzy Inference System (FIS) to evaluate environmental navigability and scene semantic levels, enabling real-time adjustments to social navigation algorithms and strategies. This FIS comprises five inputs and five outputs. The inputs include environmental navigability obtained from the navigable space evaluation module and the four semantic levels defined in the scene semantic encoding module. These inputs are fuzzified into membership degrees and then processed through the fuzzy inference mechanism, where they are matched with fuzzy rules. These values are subsequently input into the social navigation system, allowing for dynamic adjustments to its algorithms and strategies.

3 SIMULATIONS AND EXPERIMENTS

The performance of the proposed socially-aware robot navigation system was first evaluated through simulations of a mobile robot performing patrol and restocking tasks in a large shopping mall. To replicate these tasks, the shopping mall environment was modeled by using Gazebo [14], which features domains such as warehouses, corridors, and store areas. We intended to test system's adaptability to varying domains and ability to display suitable navigation behaviors accordingly. The open-source pedestrian simulation library PedSim ROS was utilized to simulate pedestrian movements, offering a realistic depiction of dynamic human behavior in real-world settings. And, a variety of navigation scenarios were designed within the simulation environment.

We compared the performance of the proposed system with two other navigation systems (System 1 and System 2). System 1 employed A* for global path planning and TEB [15] for local path planning, where TEB considered only the robot's kinematic constraints without accounting for pedestrian comfort. System 2, proposed by Teja *et al.* [16], as a multi-context socially aware navigation system, also used A* for global path planning, but adopted HATEB [13] for local path planning. It considered predicted pedestrian trajectories and incorporated social constraints to optimize robot's navigation path, while it only dealt with personal spaces for stationary pedestrians. The evaluation metrics included path length, navigation time, minimum distance to pedestrians, and navigation failure rate, which was classified into collisions with pedestrians or obstacles and stagnation, defined as the robot remaining in the same position for over 10 seconds.

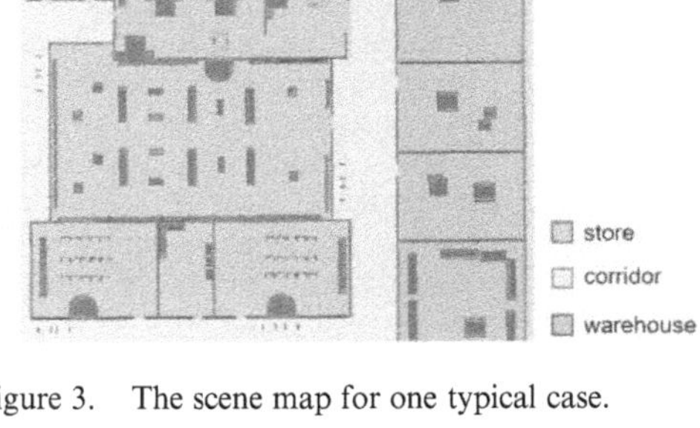

Figure 3. The scene map for one typical case.

Table 1. Results of performance evaluation.

Methods	Elapsed time (s) (avg.)	Path Length (m) (avg.)	Min distance (m) (avg.)	% Failure (% collision, % timeout)
System 1 [14]	X	X	X	100.0 (100.0,0.0)
System 2 [15]	387.70	**52.87**	0.38	35.0 (25.0, 10.0)
Our System	**292.84**	55.65	**0.57**	**0.0 (0.0, 0.0)**

We conducted a series of simulations in environments with densely populated pedestrians. Figure 3 shows the scene map for one typical case. During the simulation, the robot needed to go from the store area, traverse the corridor, and ultimately reach the target location in the warehouse to complete a pick-up task. The robot began at the initial position, navigated through a narrow space between two stationary pedestrians by considering their personal spaces and slowing down its speed to ensure safe passing. It then encountered a moving pedestrian approaching from the side, and consequently decreased its speed to maintain a safe distance. Next, the robot paused near the store exit to let a pedestrian pass before proceeding. It entered the corridor by following the social norm of passing on the right, and then crossed to the opposite side to prepare to enter the warehouse. Upon encountering an incoming pedestrian, the robot speeded up to avoid infringing on the pedestrian's intimate space. Finally, the robot successfully arrived at the target location with all these behavior adjustments through the proposed system.

Table 1 lists the results of performance evaluation between Systems 1 and 2 and our proposed system. System 1, which only considered robot's motion constraints and treated pedestrians as static obstacles, failed the navigation task under this pedestrian-dense environment. System 2, despite accounting for personal space, assigned excessively large space to stationary pedestrians and lacked dynamic adjustment, leading to unsatisfactory navigation, with 10% of tests in timeouts and 25% in collisions during pedestrian crossing. In contrast, the proposed system efficiently managed the personal spaces for both stationary and moving pedestrians, ensuring a safe distance and minimizing risk. The integration of a high-level decision-making system allowed dynamic adjustment of personal space based on environmental navigability, ensuring smooth navigation even in dense crowds. Additionally, the system adapted to environmental changes by considering blind-spot pedestrians in the store, adhering to the social norm of passing on the right in corridors, and increasing speed in the warehouse for efficiency. These actions contributed to the superiority of the proposed system over the other two.

To validate the feasibility and effectiveness of the proposed system in real-world applications, we conducted experiments on our school building, with the environment set up to emulate a shopping mall similar to that in the simulations. The pedestrian flow and spatial constraints were also carefully arranged to create realistic variations, enabling us to evaluate system's ability to adapt its navigation strategies to different environmental conditions. Throughout task execution, the pedestrian path prediction module adapted to changes in navigability. In areas with high navigability, such as the shopping zone and warehouse, the system used long-term predictions to anticipate pedestrian's intentions, thereby improving robot's understanding of pedestrian dynamics. In areas with lower navigability, short-term predictions were employed to respond more promptly to sudden pedestrian movements. The experimental results demonstrated the potential of the proposed system for real-world applications.

4 CONCLUSION

In this paper, we have developed a social-aware robot navigation system capable of adapting to various environments and crowd dynamics. The system establishes a social navigation framework suitable for multi-pedestrian environments, enabling precise personal space planning for pedestrian's comfort. A high-level decision-making system has been designed to dynamically adjust the algorithms and strategies of the social navigation system based on the current environment, crowd density, and available navigation space, ensuring effective and adaptive robot behavior across varying scenarios. Simulations and experimental results have demostrated its effectiveness, ensuring that the robot can navigate safely and efficiently in complex environments, which also paves the way for possible applications in real-world senarios.

ACKNOWLEDGMENT

This work was financially supported in part by the National Science and Technology Council, Taiwan.

REFERENCES

[1] Thrun S. *et al.*, (1999), MINERVA: A second-generation museum tour-guide robot, *IEEE International Conference on Robotics and Automation.*

[2] Triebel R. *et al.*, (2015), SPENCER: A socially aware service robot for passenger guidance and help in busy airports, *International Conference on Field and Service Robotics.*

[3] Marder-Eppstein E., Berger E., Foote T., Gerkey B., and Konolige K., (2010), The office marathon: Robust navigation in an indoor office environment, *IEEE International Conference on Robotics and Automation.*

[4] Wasisto I., Istiqomah N., Trisnawan I. K. N., and Jati A. N., (2019), Implementation of mobile sensor navigation system based on adaptive Monte Carlo localization, *International Conference on Computer, Control, Informatics and its Applications.*

[5] Bochkovskiy A., Wang C. Y., and Liao H., (2020), Yolov4: Optimal speed and accuracy of object detection, ArXiv:2004.10934.

[6] Weng X., Wang J., Held D., and Kitani K., (2020), 3D Multi-object tracking: A baseline and new evaluation metrics, *IEEE/RSJ International Conference on Intelligent Robots and Systems.*

[7] Lu D. V., Hershberger D. and Smart W. D., (2014), Layered costmaps for context-sensitive navigation, *IEEE/RSJ International Conference on Intelligent Robots and Systems.*

[8] Su C. Y., Wang H. C., Ko C. H., and Young K. Y., (2023), Development of an autonomous robot replenishment system for the convenience store, *Electronics*, vol. 12, no. 8, pp. 1940.

[9] Kollmitz M., Hsiao K., Gaa J., and Burgard W., (2015), Time dependent planning on a layered social cost map for human-aware robot navigation, *European Conference on Mobile Robots.*

[10] Ferrer G. and Sanfeliu A., (2014), Bayesian human motion intentionality prediction in urban environments, *Pattern Recognition Letters*, vol. 44, pp. 134–140.

[11] Schlegel K., Weissig P. and Protzel P., (2021), A blind-spot-aware optimization-based planner for safe robot navigation, *European Conference on Mobile Robots.*

[12] Hart P. E., Nilsson N. J., and Raphael B., (1968), A formal basis for the heuristic determination of minimum cost paths, *IEEE Transactions on Systems Science and Cybernetics*, vol. 4, no. 2, pp. 100–107.

[13] Khambhaita H., and Alami R., (2020), Viewing robot navigation in human environment as a cooperative activity, *Springer Proceedings in Advanced Robotics.*

[14] Koenig N. and Howard A., (2004), Design and use paradigms for Gazebo, an open-source multi-robot simulator, *IEEE/RSJ International Conference on Intelligent Robots and Systems.*

[15] Roesmann, Feiten W., Woesch T., Hoffmann F., and Bertram T., (2012), "Trajectory modification considering dynamic constraints of autonomous robots," *German Conference on Robotics.*

[16] Teja P.S. and Alami R., (2020), HATEB-2: Reactive planning and decision making in human-robot co-navigation, *IEEE International Conference on Robot and Human Interactive Communication.*

System Innovation for a Global Economy – Lam et al. (Eds)
© 2026 The Author(s), ISBN 978-1-041-10520-6

Traditional Chinese Hunan locks

Kuo-Hung Hsiao
Exhibition Division, National Sciemce and Technology Museum, Kaohsiung, Taiwan

Jian-Liang Lin
Science Education Division, National Sciemce and Technology Museum, Kaohsiung, Taiwan

ABSTRACT: Locks are mechanical devices to achieve security that have been used worldwide for millennia. Traditional Chinese locks can generally be categorized as stationary wooden locks or portable metal locks. Wooden locks, which were the earliest locks in use, can be further classified as bolt locks and pin tumbler locks. Unlike traditional Chinese wooden locks, metal locks could be moved and used on a variety of objects, including doors, boxes, cabinets, and chests. Metal locks can generally be categorized as combination locks or spring locks. Spring locks were the most widely used in ancient China, and they can be subclassified on the basis of their external form and unlocking mechanism as general locks, huaqi locks, or puzzle locks. The diversity of traditional Chinese locks reflects the ingenuity and exceptional craftsmanship of ancient Chinese artisans. The current study focused on Hunan locks, providing a concise overview of the characteristics and types of Hunan locks and analyzing the unlocking mechanism of Hunan puzzle locks.

1 INTRODUCTION

Locks have been used for millennia. However, no formal records have been discovered that document their development. Researchers have only been able to uncover traces of their evolution by analyzing scattered historical sources and unearthed artifacts. Wooden locks were among the earliest types of locks; the use of such locks has been traced back to the 20th century BCE (Pitt-Rivers A.H. 1883; Potts D.T. 1990). By the 2nd century BCE, simple metal locks appeared. These metal locks included springs that achieved locking through elastic force (Wagner D.B. 1996). Metal locks became widespread by the 2nd century CE, and these locks were primarily made of iron and bronze (Yan H.S. 2004). From approximately the 15th century CE onwards, puzzle locks, that is, those that must be unlocked using specific steps and methods, started to be manufactured and used. However, even with the correct key, these puzzle locks could not be quickly and easily opened.

Numerous modern scholars have studied ancient locks. For example, Homme analyzed several common Chinese wooden and metal locks, comparing them with wooden locks from rural regions in France, Germany, and Italy (Hommel R.P. 1937). In addition, Needham examined the historical development of Chinese and Western locks, discussed their mutual influences, and analyzed the internal structures of several representative locks. However, Needham noted that research on the development of Chinese locks is relatively scarce and expressed hope that such locks would be further discussed in future research (Needham J. 1965). Among the few studies that have investigated traditional Chinese locks, Yan and Huang systematically described the characteristics of such locks, including their historical evolution, the etymology of certain lock names, types, appearance, materials, and mechanical structures (Yan H.S. 2000; Yan H.S. and Huang H.H. 2004). In addition, Rasmussen *et al.* reported on the features of Chinese puzzle locks, stories of locksmiths in ancient China, different types of locks at the time, and manufacturing locations (Rasmussen P. et al. 2021). By employing mechanical structural analysis, Hsiao categorized Chinese spring locks as general locks or puzzle locks and provided a summary of numerous types of puzzle locks and the mechanisms for opening them (Hsiao K.H. 2022). Traditional Chinese locks serve as relics of the intricate craftsmanship of ancient Chinese artisans and represent an invaluable form of artistic, cultural, and folkloric heritage. However, these locks have received limited scholarly attention. In consideration of this, the current study investigated the historical development and mechanical structures of traditional Hunan locks. The current paper presents an overview of the types and characteristics of Hunan locks, an analysis of the mechanical structures of Hunan puzzle locks, and a final summary of its findings.

 DOI: 10.1201/9781003655534-4

2 TYPES AND CHARACTERISTICS OF HUNAN LOCKS

Hunan has a long-standing tradition of lock-making. The locksmiths of this region possess considerable technical skill and creativity. The locks they have created are aesthetically refined and diverse and are incredibly complex with respect to their unlocking mechanisms, achieving an impressive combination of beauty and functionality. Hunan locks can be broadly classified into four types: general locks, oxtail locks, huaqi (花旗, or floral-patterned flag) locks, and puzzle locks. Figure 1 presents a general lock from Hunan. It comprises a case, a bolt with a stem and a shackle, springs, and a key. When the correct key is inserted into the keyhole, the head of the key compresses the springs, causing them to separate from the inner wall. This enables the bolt to be removed from the case and achieves unlocking.

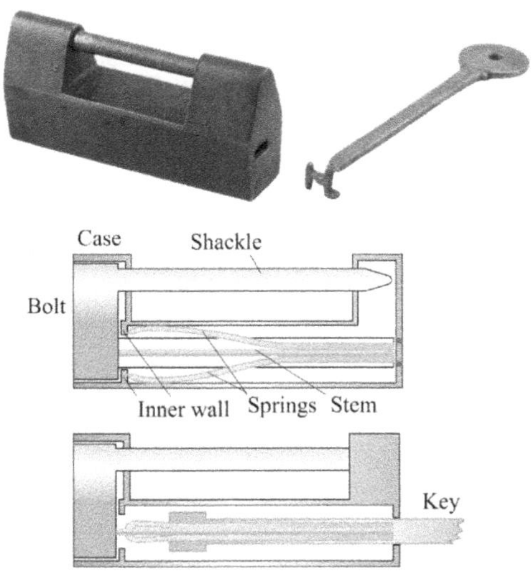

Figure 1. General lock.

The oxtail lock, so named for its resemblance to a curled oxtail, is a type of lock unique to Hunan. The lock body is fitted with anywhere from 3 to more than 10 copper rings, which improve the lock's appearance, durability, and slip-resistance. Oxtail locks can be categorized as spring locks or combination locks. Figure 2(a) presents a typical oxtail spring lock that features four springs of equal length mounted on the lock stem. The lock is opened by inserting a key, which compresses the springs. This type belongs to the category of open-keyhole locks without internal mechanisms. Figure 2(b) presents an oxtail combination lock, which comprises a lock body with a build-in shackle, numerous rotating wheels, and a bolt. When the rotating wheels on the case are turned to the correct combination, the notches on the wheels align and form a channel through which the raised lug on the bolt can pass. The bolt can then be slid out of the lock body. For such locks, no key is required to complete the unlocking process.

(a) Spring lock (b) Combination lock

Figure 2. Oxtail locks (Collection in C2P2).

An incredible variety of Hunan huaqi locks with exquisite designs have been discovered. For example, locks have been discovered in the shapes of musical instruments such as the guqin (an ancient zither) and in round, square, and vase shapes. Figure 3(a) and (b) respectively present an antique-style musical instrument–shaped lock and a box lock with a concealed keyhole. Researchers have also uncovered a wide variety of animal-shaped locks in the forms of, for example, cattle, turtles, crabs, fish, frogs, monkeys, and dogs. Animals often have symbolic meanings, and therefore, such locks have metaphorical significance and convey meaning regarding the owners' aspirations. Figure 3(c) presents a cupronickel cattle lock, the design of which is unique to the Hunan region. Cattle have historically symbolized diligence, loyalty, and strength, and ancient craftsmen often used the image of cattle on locks to represent steadfast protection of an owner's treasured possessions. Figure 3(d) presents a monkey lock. Monkeys are often considered clever, resourceful, courageous, and energetic and therefore often symbolize intelligence and energy. Figure 3(e) presents a fish lock. Fish symbolize wealth and prosperity, and because they have no eyelids and therefore do not close their eyes, even while sleeping, they also symbolize constant vigilance and protection. Notably, Hunan animal locks often have movable components, with movement of the heads, eyes, tongues, legs, and tails of the animals achieved through the use of mechanisms enabling rotation or sliding movements. These movements and the sophisticated carving craftsmanship lead to the animal designs appearing remarkably lifelike. Figure 3(f) presents a turtle lock with a movable head and four articulated legs, and Figure 3(g) provides an image of a lock with the design of a frog kissing a lotus flower.

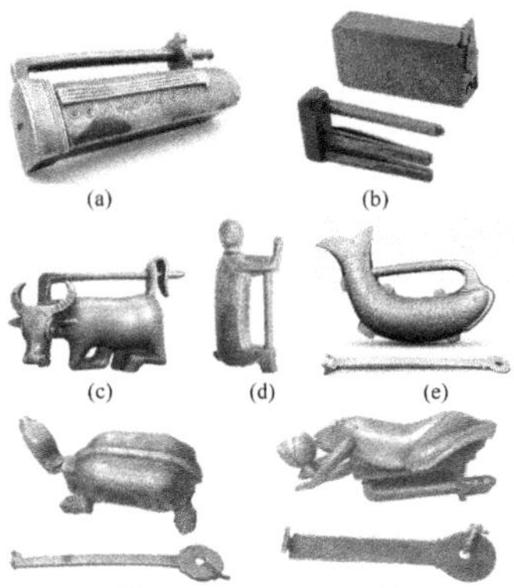

Figure 3. Huaqi locks. (a), (c), (e) Collection in Zhi-Jun Shen (沈志軍), Beijing, China. (b) Collection in C2P2. (d) Collection in Zhi-Ping Yuan (袁志平), Fuzhou, China. (f)-(g) Collection in Qi-Sheng Wu (吳啟勝), Changde, China.

3 MECHANICAL STRUCTURE ANALYSIS

An extensive variety of spring locks has been developed in Hunan. In addition to the previously mentioned general, oxtail spring, and huaqi locks, skilled artisans in the region have devised intricate, creative concepts, integrating various mechanisms to produce a multitude of mechanical lock designs. These locks achieved enhanced security and were often used as puzzle-like playthings by the literati and the wealthy (Shi K. et al. 2022). Hunan puzzle locks often featured finely engraved characters or illustrations on the lock case, as well as decorative elements such as buttons or miniature swords engraved or affixed to the lock body. In addition to being aesthetically pleasing, these adornments often provided hints at how the locks could be opened. The following describes two noteworthy examples of puzzle locks in ancient Hunan.

3.1 *Pushing down end-button-spring lock*

The pushing down end-button-spring lock was made using an ancient design common in many regions of China. Although its external appearance often slightly varied, the unlocking mechanism was generally the same across regions. Figure 4(a) provides an image of a Hunan spring lock whose front and back surfaces are respectively engraved with the Chinese phrase 壽比南山 (wishing for longevity as enduring as the southern mountains) and auspicious cloud patterns. Each end of the case has a decorative button, one movable and the other fixed. At the center of the bottom plate is a decorative sword, each end of which features a four-leaf ornamental element. This lock contains a total of four springs. One long spring positioned above the lock stem is connected to a movable button. The other three springs are short and of equal length, and they are distributed along the top, bottom-left, and bottom-right sides of the stem. When the lock is in the closed position, the long spring comes into contact with the inner wall of the case, which secures the bolt in place. The mechanism comprises seven main components: the case, the bolt, the movable button with long spring, the short springs, the end plate, the bottom plate, and the key.

In unlocking this type of spring lock, the movable button must be slid along the negative y-axis direction to its lowest position, which causes the long spring to lose contact with the inner wall of the case. The bolt must then be moved partway along the positive x-axis direction until the short springs come into contact with the inner wall. Because part of the bolt has been withdrawn, the end plate—which had hitherto be penetrated by a shackle—is able to be rotated. The end plate must then be rotated 90° in the negative x-axis direction to expose part of the keyhole. After, the bottom plate must be slid along the positive x-axis direction to its outermost position to reveal the entire keyhole. The key must be horizontally aligned with the keyhole and slid along the positive y-axis direction until it is fully inserted. Finally, the key must be moved along the positive x-axis direction, which compresses the short springs, and the entire bolt can be withdrawn. Figure 4(b) illustrates these steps in sequence.

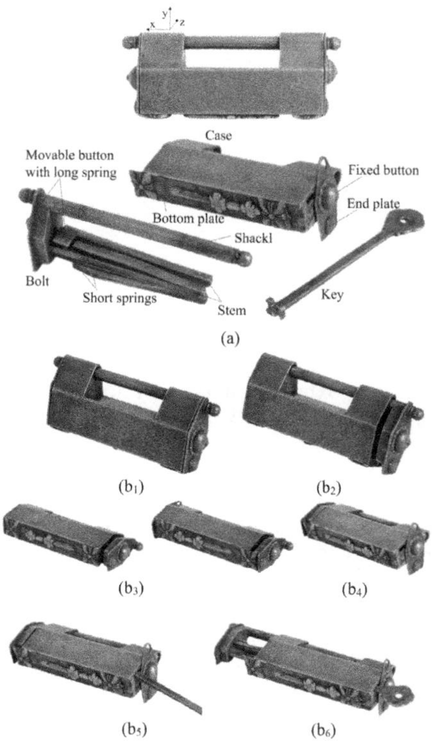

Figure 4. Pushing down end-button-spring lock.

3.2 *Sliding ornament lock*

In puzzle locks in ancient Hunan, the unlocking mechanism was often initiated by sliding or rotating a decorative element. These elements were often used in conjunction with mortise-and-tenon-based locking mechanisms, leading to highly intricate unlocking processes. Figure 5(a) presents a rare lock from Hunan that includes decorative sliding buttons positioned on either side on the bottom. The Chinese phrase 狀元及第 (achieving top honors in the imperial examination) is inscribed on the front of the case, whereas the back of the case has animal motifs, including frogs and crabs. This lock is unique in that both its left and right end plates are movable and secured to both sides of the bottom plate with mortise-and-tenon joints. At the center of the bottom plate is a fixed decorative sword, with each end featuring a four-leaf decorative button that is able to slide and rotate. These two decorative buttons conceal the mortise-and-tenon joints. In total, the lock has six springs—one long and five short. When in the locked state, the long spring comes into contact with the inner wall of the case, thus securing the bolt. The mechanism comprises 10 components: the case, the bolt, the long spring, the short springs, 2 end plates, 2 decorative buttons, and 2 keys.

To unlock the device, one must slide the movable decorative button on the left side of the bottom plate along the negative x-axis direction and subsequently rotate it in the negative y-axis direction. This exposes the mortise-and-tenon joint connecting the left end plate and bottom plate. Subsequently, the left end plate must be slid along the negative y-axis direction, removed from the mortise-and-tenon joint, and rotated 90° in the negative x-axis direction to reveal keyhole 1. When key 1 is inserted into keyhole 1, the long spring is depressed, and part of the bolt is moved outward along the positive x-axis direction. Figure 5(b_1) to (b_7) presents 3D simulations of these steps. Subsequently, one must slide the movable decorative button on the right side of the bottom plate along the positive x-axis direction and rotate it in the positive y-axis direction. This reveals the mortise-and-tenon joint connecting the right end plate and bottom plate. The right end plate must then be slid downward out of the mortise-and-tenon joint and rotated 90° along the positive x-axis direction to expose keyhole 2. Before key 2 can be fully inserted into keyhole 2, it must be sequentially rotated along the negative z-axis and negative y-axis directions. Finally, key 2 must be moved along the positive x-axis direction to compress the short springs and enable the bolt to be withdrawn. Figure 5(b_8) to (b_{14}) presents 3D simulations of these steps.

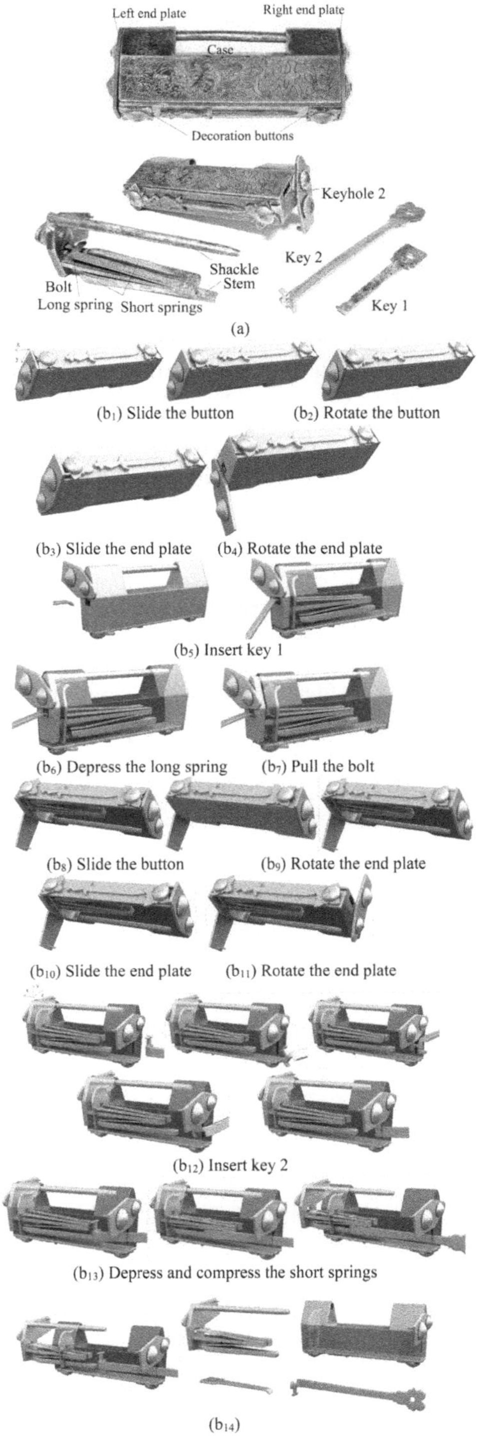

Figure 5. Sliding ornament lock.

4 CONCLUSION

Locks emerged with the development of the concept of private property. The earliest known locks were wooden locks developed in ancient Egypt in the 12th century BCE. By the 2nd century BCE, portable metal locks began to be used. Ancient locksmiths gradually accumulated experience and introduced innovative designs, which resulted in the development of a wide variety of locks with distinct characteristics. For example, huaqi locks were designed with a focus on both security and ornamentation, with the ornamentation often having symbolic meaning. Puzzle locks were developed to achieve greater security through the introduction of multiple unlocking steps, sometimes more than 10. Such locks often challenged the opener's patience and were used as puzzle-like toys for amusement or as an exhibition of ingenuity. This study investigated and summarized the distinctive features and categories of Hunan locks, including an oxtail combination lock, a general lock, an oxtail spring lock, and seven huaqi locks. It also described two noteworthy Hunan puzzle locks in detail. This research may lead to greater interest and attention with respect to traditional locks, which embody ingenious mechanical designs and unique aesthetic value.

REFERENCES

Hommel R.P., (1937). China at work: an illustrated record of the primitive industries of China's masses, whose life is toil, and thus an account of Chinese civilization, John Day Company, New York.

Hsiao K.H., (2022). *Traditional Chinese Puzzle Locks*, Shandong Education Press, Jinan, China.

Needham J., (1965). *Science and civilization in China*. vol. 4, Cambridge University Press, Cambridge.

Pitt-Rivers A.H., 1883. *On the Development and Distribution of Primitive locks and keys*, Chatto & Windus, London.

Potts D.T., (1990). *Lock and Key in Ancient Mesopotamia*, Mesopotamia, Università Di Torino, Torino.

Rasmussen P., Zhang W. and Liu N., (2021). *Traditional Chinese Puzzles II*, SDX Joint Publishing Company, Beijing

Shi K., Zhang Y., Lin J.L. and Hsiao K.H., (2022). Structural analysis of traditional chinese complex locks, *Scientific Reports*, 12:11237.

Wagner D.B., (1996). *Iron and Steel in Ancient China*, E.J. Brill Leiden, The Netherlands.

Yan H.S. and Huang H.H., (2000). On the spring configurations of ancient Chinese locks, *Proceedings of 2000 HMM International Symposium on History of Machines and Mechanisms*, pp. 87–92. Kluwer Academic Publishers, Casino, Italy.

Yan H.S. and Huang H.H., (2004). Design consideration of ancient Chinese padlocks with spring mechanisms, *Mech. Mach. Theory*, 39, pp. 797–810.

Yan H.S., (2004). *The beauty of ancient Chinese locks*, Ancient Chinese Machinery Cultural Foundation, Tainan, Taiwan.

System Innovation for a Global Economy – Lam et al. (Eds)
© 2026 The Author(s), ISBN 978-1-041-10520-6

The application and reflection of the FTC model in typography design courses

Tzu-Han Hung & Chang-Franw Lee
Department of Design, National Yunlin University of Science and Technology, Yunlin, Taiwan

ABSTRACT: Typography design courses are fundamental in visual communication design, where typography not only conveys messages but also serves as a crucial visual element. This study applies the FTC model—Form, Technique, and Content—as a pedagogical framework to explore the differences in student performance between hand-drawn and computer-based typography design, aiming to identify effective teaching strategies for modern design education. Using a qualitative approach, this study integrates FTC into curriculum planning and teaching activities, dividing the course into hand-drawing and digital design phases. Data was collected through classroom observation, student work analysis, learning journals, and interviews to investigate students' creative development and technical application. Results indicate that students performed notably well in the hand-drawing phase, showcasing creativity and structural form sensitivity. However, some students faced challenges translating their ideas into digital formats, resulting in reduced visual impact. In contrast, when students were allowed to define their own design themes, they exhibited stronger consistency in design logic and personal style from sketches to final outputs. Overall, the FTC model offers a structured framework that guides students through the complete learning process—from visual form analysis and technical execution to conceptual expression. It is recommended that future courses adopt semi-open thematic guidance to enhance students' motivation and creative diversity, while also expanding curriculum development into multilingual typography to further strengthen visual communication skills.

1 INTRODUCTION

Over the past few years, computer-assisted learning has become an indispensable component of education and has gradually emerged as a primary approach for enhancing learning efficiency and promoting autonomous learning. The development of graphic design has become a vital medium for modern communication, effectively conveying visual information while fostering deep connections among culture, commerce, and technology, and extending widely into various educational fields.

Typography courses are fundamental in visual communication design. Typography is not only a tool for conveying ideas and messages, but also a core element of visual expression. Within the context of design education, students' creativity and practical skills are tested concurrently, especially in the field of "typographic design," where observation of form and the visual execution of work are crucial. The creation and evolution of type is essentially a form-making activity, and a significant portion of the design process is spent shaping form (Lin Han-Yu *et al.* 2009). Typography can be shaped according to different themes and objectives to express content and meaning through various visual forms. Thus, typography becomes a medium through which emotion and expressive power can be visually communicated (Itatsu Chiyo 2008), making it a major challenge for creators in the field of design.

In the current trajectory of design education, cultivating both "creative thinking" and "technical operation" skills has become two of the most essential goals. This study focuses on the foundation courses in design departments at universities in Taiwan, guiding students to find a balance between creativity and technical skills, and further exploring effective teaching methods and instructional practices. Students will engage in practical exercises using both "hand-drawn typography" and "computer-based design." By analyzing the details of students' understanding and application of typographic form, technique, and content value, this study aims to examine how different design media influence students' thinking patterns and creative output. The findings will serve as important references for optimizing instructional strategies and refining course design.

2 LITERATURE REVIEW

2.1 *The nature and development of typography design education*

The invention of written characters is a crucial medium for conveying messages. Therefore, the

DOI: 10.1201/9781003655534-5

primary goal of typography design is to ensure that the intended meaning is clearly understood by viewers (Lin 1990). In Taiwan, across various stages of visual design education, typographic creation and layout design have long been regarded as essential components of foundational design courses. Typography-related subjects occupy a significant portion of required coursework in basic design education (Tseng 2003).

In recent years, many students tend to experiment with a variety of typographic styles; however, their understanding of the structure and characteristics of typefaces remains relatively limited. As a result, they often struggle to fully explore the creative potential of typography. In fact, typography holds infinite possibilities for creative expression. In practical applications such as poster and packaging design, hand-drawn typography is often used in titles or product names to enhance emotional appeal and establish a distinct and approachable visual identity.

Therefore, incorporating calligraphy training into the curriculum can further develop students' abilities in typographic form and handwritten expression, as well as refine their aesthetic sensitivity (Kang and Lee 2011).

2.2 *The concept of the FTC model*

The FTC model was proposed by American art education scholars Sandell (2009) and Sandell and Zimmerman (2017). It outlines the balanced compositional elements that constitute the visual language of art. FTC stands for Form, Theme, and Context. This model is not only applicable for analyzing and interpreting visual art, but also serves as a framework for artistic creation and design development.

When applied to practical research in university-level design education, the FTC model effectively integrates theoretical inquiry with creative practice. It guides students in embedding their creative inspirations into the design process through analytical planning, logical thinking, and reflective feedback, ultimately fostering the development of their own stylistic identity in their creative work (Ho and Yen 2011).

Based on this theoretical framework, the FTC model can be used as a reference point for both learning and critiquing design works.

3 RESEARCH DESIGN AND IMPLEMENTATION

This study adopts a qualitative research approach, utilizing curriculum design implementation and learning process documentation to analyze the performance differences of university students between hand-drawn and computer-based typography design. The FTC model (Form, Technique, Content) is employed as the analytical framework to understand students' level of engagement and the degree to which they internalize their learning during the course.

Through in-depth discussions and observations, the study aims to explore how learners adopt different strategies and learning styles, and evaluate the effectiveness of their learning outcomes upon completing the course. Additionally, the study focuses on students' experiences and engagement throughout the course implementation, assessing the effectiveness of the curriculum design and the applicability of the teaching strategies.

The FTC model is applied to the instruction of typography design, with the three core dimensions guiding the planning of students' learning processes and formative assessments. The teaching objectives and implementation steps are outlined in Table 1.

Table 1. Application of the FTC model in typography design curriculum.

Dimension	Teaching Description	Teaching Objectives
Form	Emphasizes the analysis of typeface shapes and visual structure	Develop students' observation skills of type design and practice basic contour and structural sketching
Technique	Focuses on practicing hand-drawing and digital design tools	Learn the rhythm of font strokes and software operation.
Content	Focuses on the meaning, theme, and style expression of typography	Develop appropriate typographic styles based on thematic expression

During the instructional process, the teacher adopted a proactive guiding approach to help students delve deeper into their creative themes and emphasized the importance of documenting the entire concept development process.

4 LEARNING ANALYSIS AND TEACHING INSIGHTS

This study was conducted based on the implementation and observation of a single class assignment, focusing primarily on English typography design as a preliminary teaching experiment. Further course planning and extended research will be developed depending on the teaching outcomes.

The results of students' learning performance indicate outstanding achievements in hand-drawn typography design. Students were able to skillfully express details through brushwork and demonstrate creative variations in letterform design. As shown in Figure 1, some students' hand-drawn English typography works revealed a strong sense of structure and aesthetic appeal, highlighting their progress and potential in mastering techniques and creative expression.

Figure 1. Variations of student hand-drawn English typography designs.

At the stage of computer-based design operation, students began by sketching out the form of the typography and then proceeded to finalize their designs using digital software. As shown in Figure 2, one student selected "Butterfly" as the design theme, attempting to incorporate the imagery of butterfly wings into the letter "B" to convey a sense of freedom and delight. However, after transitioning from the initial sketch to the digital composition, the overall visual impact and the creative flow demonstrated during the hand-drawn phase appeared diminished, falling short of fully retaining the refinement and originality of the original concept.

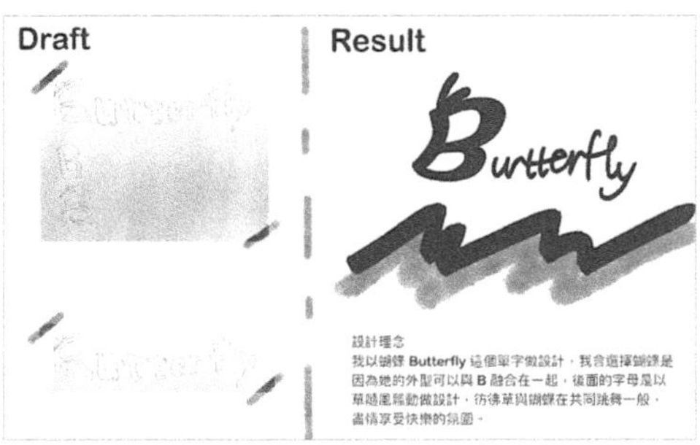

Figure 2. Student's digital typography design created with computer software.

In another phase of the course, students were required to independently conceptualize their design themes. As shown in Figure 3, their ideas were developed from initial sketches to finalized digital works. These outcomes demonstrated a high level of formal control and creative expression, effectively conveying the intended themes and stylistic direction. The results reflect students' growing maturity in thematic ideation, self-driven creation, and execution of design projects.

Figure 3. Student's thematic english typography design.

The overall learning outcomes indicate that the hand-drawn phase effectively cultivates students' sensitivity to typeform structures and stroke expression, fostering both observational skills and creativity. In contrast, while students demonstrated technical proficiency during the digital design phase, some were unable to fully carry over the design intentions from their initial sketches. Comparatively, when students were given autonomy in theme development and design, they were better able to articulate comprehensive conceptual thinking and translate it into a coherent visual language.

5 CONCLUSION AND RECOMMENDATIONS

Through the observation of course planning and implementation, it was found that when the design theme was predetermined by the instructor and students developed their sketches based on the given topic, most were able to demonstrate rich creativity and diverse stylistic forms through hand-drawing. These works exhibited a certain level of visual aesthetics and structural control. However, once students transitioned into the digital design phase, the overall quality and visual impact of some works declined, as they failed to fully carry over the creative energy and design quality from the hand-drawing phase.

On the other hand, when students were allowed to independently define their design themes and develop their work from hand-drawn sketches to finalized digital outputs, their performance in design logic, structural translation, and overall stylistic expression was significantly more coherent. These works showed greater consistency and a clearer articulation of design intentions. This suggests that when students are involved in theme development and encouraged to pursue personal interests, they are more likely to exhibit creative autonomy and individual style. Conversely, overly rigid or specific themes may constrain students' creative expression.

As such, future instructional strategies may consider adopting a "semi-open theme guidance" approach—providing direction and conceptual inspiration while preserving space for students to freely explore and express—thereby enhancing both their motivation and the depth and diversity of design outcomes.

This study applies the FTC model (Form, Technique, Content) to explore the effectiveness of a typography design course, integrating observations from instructional implementation and student learning processes to present the following teaching reflections and recommendations.

From an overall learning perspective, students demonstrated strong creativity and control over form during the hand-drawing stage, accurately depicting typographic contours and visual characteristics. This indicates that the **Form** component of the FTC model effectively cultivates students' sensitivity to type design and observational skills. At the **Technique** level, however, some students were unable to successfully transfer their hand-drawn concepts into the digital domain, resulting in final outputs that lacked the visual impact and expressive power of their initial sketches. This highlights a need for more scaffolded guidance and practice to bridge the gap between creative ideation and digital execution. In terms of **Content**, the study found that when students were given the freedom to define their own themes, the transition from sketch to digital product was more coherent and conceptually rich. These students were able to clearly interpret thematic content and shape distinctive typographic styles and narrative expressions, showing a growing maturity in their design storytelling and conceptual articulation.

The FTC model proves useful in structuring typography instruction, providing students with a comprehensive learning experience across form analysis, technical application, and content interpretation. Looking ahead, this course model can be further refined to enhance teaching quality and better meet learners' needs. Moreover, future research may extend this approach to multilingual typography instruction, aiming to build a more complete and effective teaching framework that helps students firmly acquire foundational skills and expressive capabilities in visual communication design.

REFERENCES

Chiyo Ida and Takahiko Uchifuji, (2008). *Rules of Typography*. Yuezhi Publishing.

Han-Yu Lin, Rong-Tai Lin and Hui-Yueh Hsueh, (2009). A feasibility study on transforming chinese characters into product forms. *Journal of Design 10*(2).

Min-Lan Kang and Meng-Ying Lee, (2011). A study on typography and layout courses in visual communication design programs of vocational education. *Journal of Business Design* 5, 159–178.

Pei-Yu Tseng, (2003). Exploring cultural cognition in western typography education through glyph design applications: A case study of course and assignment planning. *8th Conference on Design Academic Research Achievements*, Taiwan.

Pin-Chang Lin, (1990). *Commercial Design*. Artist Publishing.

Sandell R., (2009). Using Form + Theme + Context (FTC) for Rebalancing 21st-Century Art Education. *Studies in Art Education 50*(*3*), 287–299.

Sandell R. and Zimmerman E., (2017). Evaluating a museum-based professional learning community as a model for art education leadership development. *Studies in Art Education 58*(4), 292–311.

Wen-Ling Ho and Chen Yan, (2011). A study of art and design practice research applied to college students' art creation. *Journal of Art Education Research 21*, 85–110.

System Innovation for a Global Economy – Lam et al. (Eds)
 ISBN 978-1-041-10520-6

Exploring the roles of teachers in co-institutional social responsibility courses from a social design perspective

Chia-Wei Wang & Shyh-Huei Hwang
Graduate School of Design, National Yunlin University of Science and Technology, Douliu, Yunlin, Taiwan

ABSTRACT: Brigitte (2013) defines Social Responsibility as an ideological concept that requires organizations to proactively consider the well-being of the society or community in which they operate. Given the essential differences among institutional subjects, the scope of social responsibility varies accordingly. The field of this study is a local museum operated by a university, possessing dual institutional identities. As such, its social responsibility expands into what is termed Co-Institutional Social Responsibility (CISR). Under this context, the study focuses on a university-museum collaborative course that adopts design thinking as a pedagogical method. Utilizing qualitative research methods and guided by social design theory, this study analyzes and interprets the role of educators in this context. The results identify five key roles undertaken by social responsibility educators in CISR: (1) flexible curriculum designer, (2) organizer and coordinator, (3) co-discoverer of field issues, (4) moral gatekeeper, and (5) objective researcher. This framework clarifies the complex and multifaceted tasks of educators in social responsibility courses and offers practical guidance for future course design and teacher development.

1 INTRODUCTION

In pursuit of sustainable development for human society and the environment, assuming social responsibility has become a global initiative. However, existing research on social responsibility tends to adopt a single-subject perspective. For instance, Corporate Social Responsibility (CSR) and University Social Responsibility (USR) are conceptualized with corporations and universities as their respective core agents. These distinct paradigms reflect the intrinsic differences among institutional entities, resulting in varying scopes of responsibility, forms of practice, and mechanisms.

This study focuses on a local museum operated by a university, which possesses dual institutional identities. This duality implies an expansion of its social responsibility scope and necessitates integrated and innovative mechanisms of implementation. Such a practice model can no longer be fully interpreted through the lens of either USR or cultural institution responsibility alone. Instead, it represents a form of Co-Institutional Social Responsibility (CISR). Taken together, these differences in responsible agents constitute the contextual foundation of this study.

Under the framework of CISR, this study examines a collaborative social responsibility course co-developed by the university and the local museum. The course was designed using design thinking as a pedagogical method. Students were divided into four groups, each partnered with a university-operated local museum, and engaged in action projects based on issues raised by the partnered local museums. This research focuses on the roles and positions assumed by teachers within CISR-based practices. Given the close conceptual relationship between socially engaged design and social design theory, this study also draws on perspectives from social design as an analytical lens. In sum, this study aims to explore the roles and positions of social responsibility educators within CISR contexts, through the lens of social design.

2 LITERATURE REVIEW

2.1 *Co-institutional social responsibility of universities and local museums*

Brigitte (2013) defines social responsibility as an ideological notion, suggesting that organizations should proactively consider the well-being of the society or community in which they operate as part of their core functions. To clarify the concept of co-institutional social responsibility between universities and local museums, this section first discusses their respective interpretations of social responsibility.

Regarding University Social Responsibility (USR), Reiser (2008) defines it as “a moral and quality policy through which university communities (including students, faculty, and staff) responsibly manage the university’s impact in educational, cognitive, labor, and environmental domains, while engaging in interactive dialogue

DOI: 10.1201/9781003655534-6

with society to promote sustainable human development." Similarly, Larrán Jorge and Andrades Peña (2017) emphasize that USR urges universities to embed ethical, social, and environmental principles and values into their core functions, and to do so based on the needs and expectations of stakeholders. In summary, USR is a moral ideology centered on the university as the primary agent, focusing on the welfare of society and its stakeholders, and is realized through specific initiatives within the university's educational and research functions.

In contrast, the concept of social responsibility in local museums reflects characteristics derived from both museum practice and community development. In terms of museum-related features, Shih (2012) points out that many local museums in Taiwan have adopted the concept of the ecomuseum as a guiding principle for their operational practices. The ecomuseum, as a branch of New Museology, offers a practical foundation for applying its theoretical framework. This approach includes: (1) community participation, emphasizing active engagement of local residents; (2) bottom-up development, led by individuals or groups with a strong local commitment; and (3) open heritage management, in which the local area is treated as a "museum without walls" focused on both tangible and intangible cultural resources (Canavese *et al.* 2018).

Furthermore, in terms of its ideological foundation, the development of local museums in Taiwan has drawn on the spirit of the Community Empowerment Program (1994–2001) (Ministry of Culture 2015). In response to a policy shift from nationalism to local empowerment, Taiwan began promoting multiculturalism, encouraging the expression of community identity, and emphasizing the preservation of cultural assets—all of which became the cornerstone of local museum policies. Taken together, New Museology has shaped their vision, while the Community Empowerment Program has led them to prioritize the transformation of social capital into cultural capital, which further evolves into cultural services. As instruments of state policy for cultural localization and social synergy, the very existence of local museums can be seen as a manifestation of institutional social responsibility.

To summarize, in the research context, the university—as a higher education institution—implements USR through education and research as means to address social issues and enhance community well-being (Ali *et al.* 2021). Meanwhile, local museums emphasize the co-creation of cultural identity and social interaction within their communities, contributing to public good through cultural equity, multicultural representation, identity formation, and social cohesion (Rosenberg 2011; Ministry of Culture 2015; Lin 2013; Shih 2012). The social responsibilities of both institutions converge and expand within the research site, potentially giving rise to new forms and mechanisms of social responsibility practice. This theoretical framework forms the foundation of the present study.

2.2 *Conceptual framework of social design*

The Industrial Revolution of the 18th century marked a shift in production from handcrafting to mechanization, giving rise to the industrial design industry and catalyzing the emergence of consumerism and the middle class. Since then, the design industry has experienced four distinct developmental phases. The first three—Modernist Design, Postmodernist Design, and High Design—were grounded in capitalist values, which have, over time, contributed to irreversible harm to both society and the global environment. This has driven the field into a fourth phase that centers on social responsibility as its core value (Lin 2018; Lin and Huang 2022). It is in this context that social design has emerged as one of the key theoretical developments within the trend.

In other words, social design theory emerged from a paradigm shift in design practice—moving away from serving capitalist commodification and toward engaging with social issues (Liao 2022). Whiteley (1993/2020) observed that 50% to 75% of the world's population still lack access to basic living needs. Design driven by consumerism has long excluded the needs of marginalized groups, and thus the field must reexamine its foundational ideology. Victor Papanek (1971/2022), a leading advocate of social design, argued that design should be a tool capable of responding to real human needs—innovative, creative, and interdisciplinary in nature. He also emphasized the importance of research orientation and the moral and social responsibilities of designers (Papanek 1971/2022; translated by Yang 2013).

Based on the literature reviewed, this study categorizes the conceptual framework of social design into four dimensions:

1. **Social design as a historical stage of design:** In response to energy crises, environmental disasters, and moral critiques of social injustice, social design reveals the long-standing flaws embedded in capitalism-driven systems. A shift has begun from the pursuit of private wealth toward social responsibility. In other words, empathy-driven design trends are now emerging (Whiteley 1993/2020).
2. **Social design as a cognitive paradigm:** It redefines what constitutes "good" design—shifting from market-oriented and consumerist values to those centered on social welfare and the fulfillment of fundamental human needs.

3. **Social design as a methodology:** It offers design strategies, processes, and tools that emphasize research in the early stages. It also restructures team composition, advocating for interdisciplinary collaboration and the inclusion of both users and producers as members of the design team, with designers serving as facilitators bridging knowledge across domains. (Papanek 1971/2022; Yang 2013).
4. **Social design as an outcome or product:** Design and society exist in a mutually constitutive relationship—design arises from society and, in turn, shapes it (Liao 2022). Social design, as a product of social development, not only originates from social issues but also plays an active role in shaping society's future development.

3 RESEARCH METHODS

3.1 *Course pedagogy and planning*

According to Liao (2022), the concept of "designing for users" in design thinking involves two types of users: commercial clients and the general public. The former serves business interests, focusing on markets and product sales, while the latter views 'people in social contexts' as users, thus clarifying that design thinking can also serve as a method of social design. In other words, social design must be grounded in the real needs of the public, providing a value system, goals, and ethical foundations for design practice. De-sign thinking, with its emphasis on empathy, offers a concrete process or method to realize these goals. In this study, the course followed the design thinking process proposed by Stanford d.school (n.d.): Empathize, Define, Ideate, Prototype, and Test. Additionally, this study draws on the work of Bertão, Jung, Chung, and Joo (2023), who suggest adding a sixth step, Assess, to evaluate implementation outcomes in educational contexts. However, given that social responsibility courses often stress field impact and student engagement, this study adapted the model by incorporating Practice as a necessary step. The resulting framework—Empathize, Define, Ideate, Prototype, Practice, and Assess—formed the basis of the course's 18-week design.

3.2 *Research method and process*

This study adopted qualitative research methods, with the following research procedures:

1. **Research Design:** Establishing the theoretical framework through literature review.
2. **Data Collection:** Gathering data from (1) LINE group chats created during the course by each team, (2) semi-structured interviews (with student teams and curators), and (3) supplementary materials, including course video recordings, transcripts or recordings of group discussions, end-of-semester peer evaluations, and each team's project outputs.
3. **Reconstruction of Project Process:** Using open coding from grounded theory methodology to process a large volume of qualitative data, this study employed MAXQDA qualitative analysis software to support the contextual reconstruction of the four project cases. Objectivity was maintained throughout the process to accurately reflect real conditions and trace the actual development of each project.
4. **Research Analysis:** Interaction among the three key groups—students, curators, and the teacher—was first analyzed. Then, the findings were interpreted through the lens of social design theory to derive conclusions.

3.3 *Research cases and coding*

The field site for this course comprised four local museums in Yunlin County, all operated by the university offering the course. The participants were divided into three categories: students, the teacher, and curators. Student participants included 24 individuals from the teacher's class, with a gender ratio of 1:2 and an average age of 19. Students formed four self-selected groups of six. The teacher was one of the researchers and also served as the curator of one local museum. In addition to the researcher, there were three other curators, with a gender ratio of 2:1 and an average age of 31. Prior to the study, the research purpose was explained, and consent was obtained from all participants. See Table 1 for coding details.

Table 1. Coding details.

Student Team	Curator	Teacher
A	Acu	A-te
B	Bcu	B-te
C	Ccu	C-te
B	Dcu	D-te

Note: The same teacher instructed all groups. The case codes are used to distinguish the interaction contexts. (Source: Compiled by the researcher.)

4 RESEARCH INVESTIGATION AND ANALYSIS

4.1 *Summary of field-based action projects*

The outcomes of each group's action project during the course are summarized in Table 2.

Table 2. Summary of field-based action projects.

Group	A	Project	Ink Painting Brooch Craft Workshop
Description: Group A organized a brooch-making workshop as an ancillary session to the lecture event that accompanied the local museum's ink painting exhibition. Approximately 14 participants attended. The project added a dynamic element to the originally static lecture, bringing small-scale positive effects to the local museum.			
Group	B	Project	"Movie Passbook" Marketing Design
Description: Group B planned a marketing design campaign for the local museum, producing deliverables including a stamp card, a notebook, and marketing copy. However, the final outputs were not adopted by the local museum, resulting in limited practical impact.			
Group	C	Project	Local Bilingual Comic Series
Description: Group C created a four-part local bilingual comic series aligned with an existing program at the local museum. Their work was ultimately published as part of the local museum's publications, generating concrete contributions to the institution.			
Group	D	Project	Upcycled Book Labels from Discarded Picture Books
Description: Group D repurposed discarded picture books from the local museum to redesign old shelf labels, developing a lesson plan and conducting two family-oriented craft workshops with approximately 60 participants. Their project offered a new solution for discarded books, inspired the curator to implement a similar activity the following year, and the revised shelf labels remain in use at the local museum—producing sustained, mid- to long-term impact. Overall, Group D's project brought substantial benefits to the institution.			

(Source: Compiled by the researcher.)

4.2 *Interaction patterns among the three key stakeholders*

4.2.1 *Student team operation types*

The analysis revealed differences in how student teams operated. These differences can be categorized into three distinct types, as summarized in Table 3.

Table 3. Student team operation types.

Group	A, C	Type	Leader-led Model
Description: In both Groups A and C, the team leader played a central role in advancing the action project, including initiating discussions, planning tasks, organizing the division of labor, and setting schedules.			
Group	B	Type	Individually Executed Model
Description: The team leader of Group B played a relatively weak role. After tasks were assigned on a "first come, first served" basis, members proceeded to complete them individually. Due to the lack of internal coordination and discussion, most members approached the curator separately for guidance, which in turn led the curator to effectively take on the role of team coordinator.			
Group	D	Type	Collaborative Model
Description: Group D operated through collaborative decision-making, with the leader playing a less dominant role. Planning and task assignments were *mostly* carried out through group-wide discussion and collective decision-making. Unlike Group B, Group D maintained frequent communication, which contributed to more effective team organization and operation.			

(Continued)

(Source: Compiled by the researcher.)

4.2.2 *Curator interaction styles*

This section explores the interaction patterns of the curators, as presented in Table 4.

Table 4. Curator interaction styles.

Curator	Acu, Bcu	Interaction	Directive Type
Description: Curator Acu, who also served as the course teacher, exhibited a strong guiding presence in group interactions. Curator Bcu adopted a similar role due to the absence of internal coordination in Group B, which required them to lead and integrate group efforts directly.			
Curator	Ccu	Interaction	Managerial Type
Description: Group C's project was integrated into an existing initiative at the local museum. To ensure project alignment, Curator Ccu focused on project management tasks and was not directly involved in ideation, content creation, or the production process.			
Curator	Dcu	Interaction	Collaborative Type
Description: Curator Dcu showed an active and collaborative interaction style throughout the project, and fostered a positive atmosphere of cooperation, thereby enhancing the students' sense of autonomy in learning.			

(Source: Compiled by the researcher.)

4.2.3 *Teacher's differentiated guiding roles*

The roles adopted by the teacher across the different groups are outlined in Table 5.

Table 5. Teacher's guiding roles by group.

Group	A-te	Focus of Guidance	Quality Control
Description: In Group A, the teacher was also serving as the curator of the partnering museum and the organizer of the lecture event. As a result, the teacher's guidance in this group focused on ensuring overall quality and reflected a higher level of involvement.			
Group	B-te	Focus of Guidance	Conflict Resolution
Description: Group B experienced internal coordination difficulties. The teacher intervened to help resolve collaboration issues, such as imbalanced task distribution and procedural errors.			
Group	C-te	Focus of Guidance	Content Accuracy
Description: Since Group C operated smoothly overall, the teacher primarily provided guidance on factual or knowledge-related issues within the comic content.			
Group	D-te	Focus of Guidance	Implementation Readiness
Description: While Group D performed well in ideation, teamwork, and coordination with the curator, the innovative nature of their project required the teacher to monitor critical implementation details and offer targeted reminders.			

(Source: Compiled by the researcher.)

Table 6. Findings on the functions of design thinking in a social responsibility course.

Stage	Findings
Empathize	Fosters a space for dialogue and interaction between students and field partners, creating mutual understanding and trust.
Define	Beyond the conventional goal of clarifying core problems, this stage helps students reflect on key insights gathered during the empathize phase, linking those insights to their motivations for action and uncovering the value and meaning behind their initiatives.
Ideate	This stage represents a co-creative process between students and field partners. To support this process, the teacher facilitates creative thinking exercises that help expand students' capacities for generating solutions.
Prototype & Practice	Through hands-on implementation, this stage responds to the needs of both primary users—field partners and students—producing tangible outcomes and impact for both parties.
Assess	Teachers conduct integrated evaluations of both teaching and field activities. This includes assessing student learning and the effectiveness of problem-solving efforts, which then serve as a foundation for future course iterations.

(Source: Compiled by the researcher.)

4.3 *The role of social design as a method in social responsibility courses*

In this study, the teacher developed a semester-long course on social responsibility based on design thinking theory. The course was designed around the central theme of social responsibility, and was developed as a process that integrates both learning and practice, aiming to achieve two primary objectives: (1) to cultivate students' awareness and practical ability in social responsibility, and (2) to respond to the needs of local museums. In other words, the course functioned as a design process centered on learning and practicing social responsibility, addressing the dual "users" of students and field institutions.

Design thinking played the role of a practical methodology of social design in this study. Based on empirical investigation in authentic field settings, this study summarizes how design thinking functions as a social design method in the context of Co-Institutional Social Responsibility (CISR). The findings are presented in Table 6.

4.4 *How social designer competencies facilitate teachers' cognitive transition in social responsibility education*

The analysis revealed that, beyond the initial course design, teachers needed to embed diagnostic moments throughout the learning process to assess students' progress and adjust teaching strategies accordingly. These real-time calibrations enable the teacher not only to provide appropriate guidance but also to coordinate interactions between students, or between students and field partners. As a result, different groups may receive different types of support and course content based on their unique conditions and field issues. Thus, even within the same course, the knowledge and skills acquired by each student may differ to varying degrees.

Furthermore, as "social responsibility"—the core theme of the course—is itself a value-driven ideology, such courses differ fundamentally from conventional skill-based ones that follow structured knowledge systems, defined competencies, and linear learning progressions. From the perspective of social constructivism, knowledge in social responsibility courses is co-constructed through the interactions and feedback of all participants within the learning context. Accordingly, the role of a teacher in such a course diverges from the traditional function of delivering knowledge. Rather, the teacher functions more as a facilitator, organizer, and coordinator.

Taken together, this study views the concept of the social designer as a meaningful analogy for understanding and facilitating the teacher's cognitive and positional transition in social responsibility education. The fundamental competencies of a social designer can support teachers in transitioning away from the authoritative role of knowledge transmitter, helping them reshape their positioning and mindset in the course, attend to cross-sector user needs, and mediate the dual institutional demands of social responsibility. The corresponding competencies and roles are outlined below:

1. **Research-Oriented Thinking in Design:** Social design emphasizes research-driven design practices. As higher education professionals, university teachers can leverage their academic training to embed research into course planning and contextual analysis. This enables a stronger knowledge base for teaching and action while enhancing understanding of the course's impact on society and various stakeholders.
2. **Moral Responsibility Awareness:** Social designers are expected to act with strong ethical responsibility. Teachers, as course designers, must consider the impact of their curriculum on multiple stakeholders (e.g., students, institutional partners, communities, society), and take responsibility for ensuring the value and appropriateness of the outcomes.
3. **Bridging Across Domains:** Social designers are positioned as bridges between disciplines. Teachers, as mediators between pedagogy and practice, should exercise discourse authority and professional judgment to facilitate integration across perspectives. They must actively coordinate dialogue, validate needs, allocate resources, and guide actions between students and partners, as well as between student peers.
4. **Responsiveness to Real Needs:** Design in social design must originate from and respond to real human needs. As a form of design, the course must likewise address authentic needs from society or users. Teachers must possess the sensitivity to perceive both explicit and latent needs of students and field partners, and keep building their ability to sense and respond to needs through ongoing interaction with field partners and students.
5. **Co-Design with Users:** Social design emphasizes cross-disciplinary integration and advocates for users and producers to be part of the design team. Teachers should relinquish their authoritative role as sole knowledge providers and instead co-design the course with its users—students and field partners. In other words, teachers should embrace the spirit of "co-design," opening the course structure to allow participant involvement in shaping content and goals, thereby fostering a multi-stakeholder collaborative learning experience.

5 CONCLUSION

Through empirical investigation and analysis, this study first identified three types of student team operations, three modes of interaction among curators, and four guiding strategies adopted by the teacher. Drawing on the perspectives of social design, this study focused on the pedagogical approaches and functional roles of the teacher in social responsibility education. Furthermore, this study applied the core competencies of social designers to interpret and expand the understanding of the teacher's function within this context.

Based on the above, the study concludes by proposing five key roles that teachers play in the implementation of Co-Institutional Social Responsibility (CISR). These roles help clarify the multifaceted responsibilities and strategies required of social responsibility educators and may serve as practical references for future course design and teacher training.

5.1 *Flexible curriculum designer*

As the primary designer of the course, the teacher develops the instructional framework (e.g., design thinking) to address diverse and complex social issues. Since social responsibility courses lack standardized content, the actual learning materials emerge through the interaction between students and field partners. Therefore, teachers should maintain a flexible and open mindset, adapting the curriculum design according to different user combinations and interactions. In essence, teachers are expected to co-design the curriculum with users through participatory processes.

5.2 *Organizer and coordinator*

The teacher plays a central role in organizing and coordinating the design teams, including both the internal student teams and the cross-institutional teams formed between students and field-based partner institutions. This role entails addressing various operational challenges such as bridging the gap between student and field expectations, integrating resources, enhancing communication, and fostering effective collaboration.

5.3 *Co-discoverer of field issues*

Field-specific issues are the tangible expressions of social responsibility. In other words, they reflect the presence and value of social responsibility. Without engaging with real field problems, it is difficult to genuinely understand or address them. Thus, in addition to coordinating and organizing course participants, the teacher also serves as a co-discoverer of field problems. Leveraging their academic expertise, teachers can offer deeper insights and interpretations to support field engagement.

5.4 *Moral gatekeeper*

Teachers bear ethical responsibility for the potential impact of the course on both users and society. Although the curriculum is co-created with users, rather than solely led by the teacher, the teacher is responsible for safeguarding the quality and appropriateness of the course content and its outcomes. It is their responsibility to ensure that, even as the course is continuously adapted, it continues to address real societal needs and generate positive social impact.

5.5 *Objective researcher*

To comprehensively understand the course's impact on users and society, teachers should draw upon their research training and assume the role of an objective investigator throughout the course's planning, implementation, and reflection stages. This approach facilitates iterative course development and contributes to generating long-term, socially beneficial outcomes. Moreover, teachers may become key advisors in shaping policy for the institutions involved, playing a pivotal role in shaping their future directions.

REFERENCES

Ali, M., Mustapha, I., Osman, S., and Hassan, U. (2021). University social responsibility: A review of conceptual evolution and its thematic analysis. *Journal of Cleaner Production*, *286*, 124931.

Amineh, R. J., and Asl, H. D. (2015). Review of constructivism and social constructivism. *Journal of Social Sciences, Literature and Languages*, 1(1), 9–16.

Bertão, R. A., Jung, C. H., Chung, J., and Joo, J. (2023). Design thinking: A customized blueprint to train R and D personnel in creative problem-solving. *Thinking Skills and Creativity*, *48*, 101253.

Brigitte, P. (2013). Definitions of social responsibility. In S. O. Idowu, N. Capaldi, L. Zu, and A. D. Gupta (Eds.), *Encyclopedia of corporate social responsibility* (Vol. 21, pp. 768–772). Berlin: Springer.

Canavese, G., Gianotti, F., and De Varine, H. (2018). Ecomuseums and geosites community and project building. *International Journal of Geoheritage and Parks*, *6*(1), 43–62.

d.school (n.d.). *Design thinking bootleg*. Retrieved from https://reurl.cc/paW6Db.

Larrán Jorge, M., and Andrades Peña, F. J. (2017). Analysing the literature on university social responsibility: A review of selected higher education journals. *Higher Education Quarterly*, *71*(4), 302–319.

Liao, S.-C. (2022). Social design: Theory and method. Wu-Nan.

Lin, C.-H. (2013). *How does the Cultural Policy Weaken the Local Cultural Museums in Taiwan: the Community Construction as an Alternative Program. Museum and Culture*, (6), 3–34.

Lin, C.-H., and Huang, Y.-F. (2022). *Introduction to design: Reflections and analysis of new design concepts*. Chuan Hwa Book Co.

Lin, M.-H. (2018). *Design history and design movements*. Chuan Hwa Book Co.

Maybin, J., Mercer, N., and Stierer, B. (1992). Scaffolding learning in the classroom. *Thinking voices: The Work of the National Oracy Project*, 186, 195.

Ministry of Culture. (2015). *Development plan for museums and local museums promoted by the Ministry of Culture*. Retrieved from https://reurl.cc/9DO4zn<errortag-red153-green0blue255>.</errortag-red153green0blue255>

Nicholas, M., Veresov, N., and Clark, J. C. (2021). Guided reading–Working within a child's zone of proximal development. *Learning, Culture and Social Interaction*, *30*, 100530.

Papanek, V. (2022). Design for the real world: Human ecology and social change (Yang, L., Trans.). Wu-Nan. (Original work published 1971).

Puntambekar, S., and Hubscher, R. (2005). Tools for scaffolding students in a complex learning environment: What have we gained and what have we missed? *Educational Psychologist*, *40*(1), 1–12.

Reiser, J. (2008). University social responsibility definition. Retrieved from: http://www. usralliance. org/ resources/Aurilla_Presentation_Session6. pdf.

Rosenberg, T. J. (2011). History museums and social cohesion: building identity, bridging communities, and addressing difficult issues. *Peabody Journal of Education*, *86*(2), 115–128.

Shih, C.-I. (2012). *How Can Museums Make Communities Work? A Case Study of the Jinguashi Area. Museum Quarterly*, 26(4), 29–39.

Whiteley, N. (2020). Design for society (You, W.-L., Yang, M.-Y., and Li, Y.-Y., Trans., 2nd ed.). Linking. (Original work published 1993)

System Innovation for a Global Economy – Lam et al. (Eds)

A heart failure prediction model based on Fuzzy logic, Monarch butterfly optimization, and transfer learning

Li-Jia Yeah
Department of Mechanical Engineering, National Chung Cheng University, Chiayi, Taiwan

Chen-Wen Chang & Po-Hsun Feng
Department of Electrical Engineering, National Cheng Kung University, Tainan, Taiwan

Ting-Chun Yao
School of Medicine, College of Medicine, Taipei Medical University, Taipei City, Taiwan

Ping-Huan Kuo
Department of Mechanical Engineering, National Chung Cheng University, Chiayi, Taiwan
Advanced Institute of Manufacturing with High-Tech Innovations (AIM-HI), National Chung Cheng University, Chiayi, Taiwan

ABSTRACT: In clinical practice, cardiovascular disease (CVD) is associated with unnoticeable or unpainful symptoms. Therefore, patients with CVD tend to not go for regular checkups, resulting in an estimate of more than 400 000 sudden cardiac deaths each year. Therefore, quick heart failure diagnosis is a very important issue. In this study, body data obtained from patients with CVD were used to estimate their mortality rate. Pearson's product-moment correlation was used to remove irrelevant body data features. The remaining six parameters were then used as training data. Subsequently, a neural network, a k-nearest neighbor classifier, a voting classifier, a random forest classifier, logistic regression, and a support vector classifier were trained, and k-fold cross-validation was conducted to compare the quality of the models. The results of a random forest classifier, adaptive boosting classifier, and XGBClassifier were used as the input for multilayer perceptron, producing an accuracy, precision, recall, and F1 score of 0.86%, 0.755%, 0.833%, and 0.792%, respectively. This approach can not only help physicians make more appropriate treatment decisions but can also make patients more vigilant and visit hospitals to receive follow-up treatment more frequently.

1 INTRODUCTION

Artificial intelligence (AI) has been used in medicine, specifically in machine learning models to interpret medical data and help patients and physician (Abdalrahman *et al.* 2023; Feng *et al.* 2024; Nadimi-Shahraki *et al.* 2024; Tian *et al.* 2022). With the development of computer science and informatics, AI has become an indispensable part of modern health care. AI algorithms and other AI-powered applications greatly help healthcare personnel engage in clinical practice or in ongoing research. Currently, the most common roles of AI in the medical field are clinical decision support and imaging analysis. Clinical decision support tools facilitate quick interviews, patient data collection, and research, and they help healthcare providers make decisions regarding treatment, medication, mental health, and other patient needs. In the context of medical imaging, AI tools are used to analyze computed tomography (CT) images, radiographs, magnetic resonance images, and other images to identify lesions or other symptoms that radiologists may have missed. Cardiovascular disease (CVD) is a general term that refers to heart and vascular diseases. CVD results from the blockage of blood vessels and poor blood flow due to atherosclerosis, and shows symptoms including palpitations, dyspnea, cyanosis, vertigo, and syncope. The most common types of CVD are coronary artery disease, heart failure, and arrhythmia. According to statistics compiled by the World Health Organization (Cardiovascular diseases), a staggering 16.5 million people worldwide die from CVD every year, accounting for 31% of all deaths worldwide. One in every 19 people aged under 15 has heart disease, and one in every five older adults aged 65 and above has heart disease, indicating the immense threat of heart disease to human health. (Lee *et al.*

DOI: 10.1201/9781003655534-7

2022) indicated that people can avoid heart disease by drinking less alcohol, having a balanced diet, exercising more, and going for regular health checkups. In clinical practice, physicians typically use body data to estimate the mortality rate of patients with CVD. In the present study, artificial neural networks and the body data of patients with CVD were used to estimate their treatment duration and mortality rate. This method is expected to help physicians make more appropriate decisions regarding the treatment of their patients and thereby increase their survival rate.This method greatly increased the speed of judgment in diagnostic imaging and reduced healthcare costs. Images were then classified using the automatic image analysis characteristic of deep learning. The results indicated that this method exhibited not only favorable performance but also a robust discrimination ability. Therefore, a stacked denoising autoencoder was used to extract features through multilayer training, reduce noise in ultrasonic images, and analyze backscattered signals. Such a procedure allowed for establishing a classifier. Subsequently, four sets of images, namely, original images (with unevenness), original images after uneven intensity correction (without unevenness), Nakagami images converted from the original images (with unevenness), and Nakagami images converted from the original images after uneven intensity correction (without unevenness), were compared. The results revealed that the application of deep learning in the correction of the uneven grayscale intensity in ultrasound and Nakagami images increased the tumor discrimination rate. The system successfully differentiated between three cry patterns of newborns, namely, hunger, pain, and sleepiness, at different ages in a shorter execution time compared with other neural networks. (Hsu *et al.* 2017) introduced a deep-learning-based, real-time heart rate measurement technique, which was conducted in four steps. Step 1 was to use the constrained local neural field algorithm to detect the faces and landmarks in front of a camera. Step 2 was to select different face areas according to the landmarks, obtain the average value of the color information, and extract the signals by using three preprocessing methods. Step 3 was to use short-time Fourier transform to transform the one-dimensional signals that were previously extracted into a two-dimensional spectrogram. Step 4 was to input the spectrogram into a visual geometry group trained using heart rate databases to perform heart rate prediction. Compared with the latest noncontact, heart rate measurement methods based on image analysis, this method was more competitive. (Ibrahim *et al.* 2021) proposed a multiclassification deep-learning model that helped classify COVID-19, pneumonia, lung cancer, and normal images. Chest radiography and CT images of the four types of diseases were then used as datasets for classification, and the results indicated that the VGG19 + CNN model had an accuracy of 98.05%. (Arora *et al.* 2021) detected COVID-19 by inspecting lung CT scan data through transfer learning. A residual dense neural network was used for super-resolution CT imaging to improve the model accuracy. The results indicated that, in the COVID-19 CT scan and SARS-CoV-2 CT scan datasets, the MobileNet model had an accuracy of 94.12% and 100%, respectively. Concerning whether cesarean sections are to be performed, a stable prediction model is necessary. Accordingly, (Islam *et al.* 2022) introduced a random forest algorithm based on Henry's gas solubility optimization, which effectively predicted whether a cesarean section was required. (Chen *et al.* 2022) predicted and classified ventricular arrhythmia by using phase space reconstruction and fuzzy c-means clustering, obtaining an average accuracy of 98.4%, a sensitivity of 97.5%, and a specificity of 99.1%. (Hathaway *et al.* 2021) used a deep neural survival network for cardiovascular risk predictions and performed an analysis using only conventional risk factors. The results were less satisfactory than those of conventional neural network models.

In this study, heart failure clinical records were collected from the UCI Machine Learning Repository (Heart failure clinical records Data Set). As shown in Table 1, 299 data points, each containing 12 features, were retrieved. Among these features, anemia, high blood pressure, diabetes, sex, smoking, and death event were regarded as two-dimensional data and represented as 0 or 1. Generally, patients with a hematocrit level below 36% are considered to have anemia. Creatinine phosphokinase (CPK) refers to the concentration of CPK enzyme in the blood. When muscle tissue is damaged, CPK flows into the bloodstream. Therefore, patients with excessively high CPK levels are suspected to have heart failure or injury. Ejection fraction is the percentage of blood pumped out of the left ventricle with each contraction. Serum creatinine is the waste produced when muscles decompose. Physicians refer to the levels of serum creatinine in the blood to examine the kidney function of their patients. Patients with increased serum creatinine levels may have renal insufficiency. Sodium is a mineral that helps muscles and nerves function properly. Thus, serum sodium tests are routine blood tests that indicate whether patients have normal blood sodium levels. Heart failure may lead to abnormally low sodium levels in blood. In this binary classification study, time was used to indicate whether a patient died or survived before the end of the follow-up period. The average time was 130 days. Before the end of the follow-up period, 203 patients survived (death event = 0) and 96 patients died (death event = 1). Statistically, 32.11% of the patients died, and 67.89% survived.

Table 1. Meanings, measurement units, and intervals of each feature (heart failure clinical records data set).

Feature	Explanation	Measurement	Range
Age	Age of the patient	Years	[40 ,95]
Anaemia	Decrease of red blood cells or hemoglobin	Boolean	0, 1
High blood pressure	If a patient has hypertension	Boolean	0, 1
Creatinine phosphokinase	Level of the CPK enzyme in the blood	mcg/L	[23,7861]
Diabetes	If the patient has diabetes	Boolean	0, 1
Ejection fraction	Percentage of blood leaving	Percentage	[14, 80]
Sex	Woman or man	Binary	0, 1
Platelets	Platelets in the blood	kiloplatelets/mL	[25, 850]
Serum creatinine	Level of creatinine in the blood	mg/dL	[0.50,9.40]
Serum sodium	Level of sodium in the blood	mEq/L	[114,148]
Smoking	If the patient smokes	Boolean	0, 1
Time	Follow-up period	Days	[4,285]
(target) death event	If the patient died during the	Boolean	0, 1

The data applied contained 12 features and were used to predict the mortality rate of patients with heart failure. Among these features, the six that were more relevant to death (i.e., age, ejection fraction, high blood pressure, serum creatinine, serum sodium, and time) were extracted from the heat map shown in Figure 1 for model training.

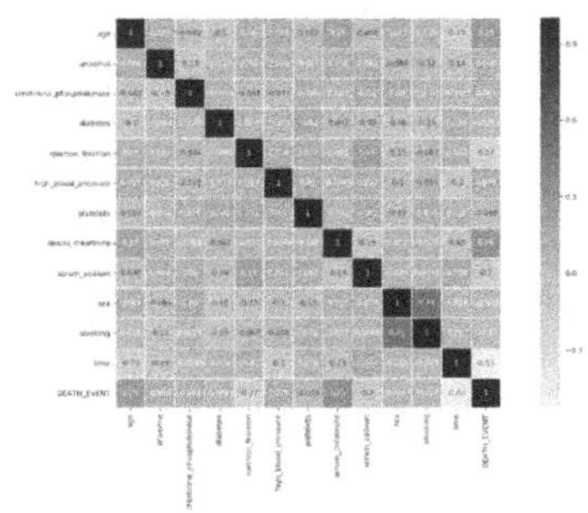

Figure 1. Pearson's product-moment correlation coefficient heat map.

2 EXPERIMENTAL

The data used in this study were retrieved from the UCI Machine Learning Repository (Heart failure clinical records Data Set). The 12 body data points of the 299 patients with CVD were age, anemia, CPK, diabetes, ejection fraction, high blood pressure, platelets, serum creatinine, serum sodium, sex, smoking, and time. Before the experimental model was built, Pearson's product-moment correlation coefficient was used for feature extraction, which revealed whether a linear relationship existed between the features. The value of the coefficient ranged between -1 and $+1$, where a coefficient value of 0 indicated no correlation, whereas a coefficient value of -1 or $+1$ indicated a strong linear relationship.

To avoid potential controversies regarding the data cutting process, the data were divided into training data and testing data by using k-fold cross-validation ($k = 10$). In the k-fold loop, the training data were processed using fuzzy logic (Júnior S. S. *et al.* 2023; Wang *et al.* 2023), which allowed for converting the Boolean truth value into a real interval because most of the results were nonbinary or inexact. Fuzzy logic was also used to convert binary results (i.e., 0 or 1) into an interval. Several optimization algorithms were used to obtain the optimal parameters of different models and the interval (a, b, c) of the membership function in the fuzzy set. These optimization algorithms, also called search algorithms, define a problem and an effective solution set or space, provide an objective function to determine the quality of the solution, and find a solution that meets the requirements of the solution set.

In this study, before the optimization algorithms were run, 30% of the training data were converted into validation data to ensure that the testing data would not enter the models all at once. All validation data were taken as random intervals. Subsequently, the following model was established to predict the patients' mortality rate.

The k-nearest neighbor (kNN) (Guo *et al.* 2004) is a nonparametric, supervised learning classifier that helps classify or predict a group of individual data points through proximity. Although kNN can be used for both regression and classification, it is most commonly used as a classification algorithm to assume that similarities can be found in proximity.

RanPdom forest classification (Breiman 2001) is a supervised learning algorithm used with classification and regression problems. It is also considered the most flexible and easy-to-use algorithm. Forests are composed of trees. A random forest creates decision trees with randomly selected data samples, obtains the prediction of each tree, and votes for the optimal solution.

Logistic regression (Peng *et al.* 2002) is a type of regression analysi. It is the process of modeling the probability of the discrete outcome of the input variables. In this study, because the outcome was divided into two categories, binary logistic regression was used.

XGBClassifier is a boosting algorithm (Figure 2). A boosting algorithm is an algorithm that combines multiple weak classifiers to form a strong classifier. XGBoost gathers several classification and regression trees (CART) to form a strong classifier. In this study, several optimization algorithms were used to obtain the optimal solutions of the maximum depth, number of estimators, and learning rate.

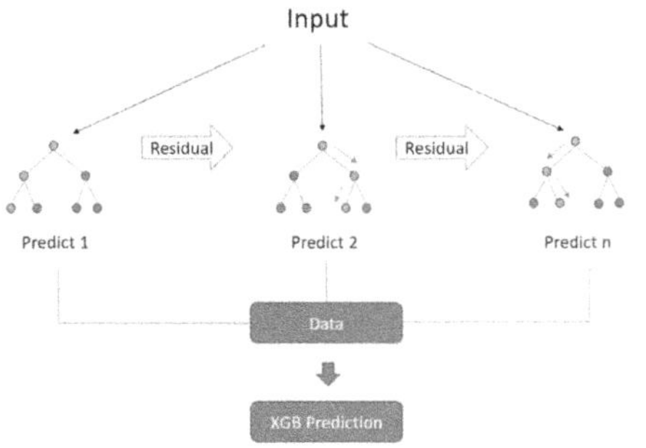

Figure 2. XGBClassifier.

3 RESULTS AND DISCUSSION

In this study, six different models were established, and k-fold cross-validation was applied. Each time, 10% of the total data were used as testing data, and predictions were made ten times. The sum was then presented using a confusion matrix. As shown in Figure 3, the accuracies of the (a) AdaBoost classifier, (b) logistic regression classifier, (c) k-neighbor classifier, (d) support vector classifier, (e) random forest classifier, and (f) XGBClassifier before fuzzification were only 80.9%, 80.9%, 74.6%, 79.9%, 81.9%, and 81.6%, respectively.

The results of all models are listed in Table 2, of which the three models with the most favorable results were selected and processed using fuzzy logic. MBO was then used to determine the optimal parameter. As shown in Figure 4, the results indicated that the accuracies of the XGBClassifier, AdaBoost classifier, and random forest classifier increased from 81.6%, 80.9%, and 81.9% to 84.9%, 83.6%, and 82.9%, respectively. These results indicated that the fuzzification process and optimization algorithm were effective.

The system flowchart of this study is presented in Figure 5. As shown in the figure, the standard deviation of the training data was taken to establish a k-fold loop. MBO was then used to determine the fuzzy attribution function and the optimal solutions of the parameters for each model. Next, validation data were used for verification to ensure that the testing data do not enter the models all at once. Subsequently, the coefficients were input into the AdaBoost classifier, XGBClassifier, and random forest classifier for predictions, and the prediction results were inserted into an Multilayer Perceptron (MLP) classifier for repredictions. The final prediction results are presented in Figure 6.

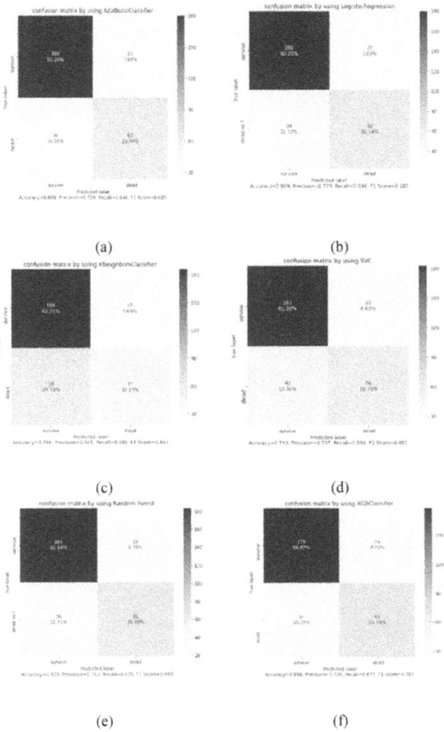

Figure 3. Confusion matrix with an (a) AdaBoost classifier, (b) logistic regression classifier, (c) k-neighbor classifier, (d) support vector classifier, (e) random forest classifier, and (f) XGBClassifier.

Table 2. Model performance without Fuzzy or optimization algorithms.

Model	Accuracy	Precision	Recall	F1-score
Adaboost	80.9%	72.9%	64.6%	68.5%
Logistic	80.9%	72.9%	64.6%	68.5%
KNN	74.6%	68.5%	38.5%	49.3%
SVC	79.9%	73.7%	58.3%	65.1%
RF	81.9%	76.2%	63.5%	69.3%
XGB	81.6%	73%	67.7%	70.3%
MBO-Fuzzy-XGB	84.9%	76.8%	76.0%	76.4%
MBO-Fuzzy-Adaboost	83.6%	73.7%	76.0%	74.9%
MBO-Fuzzy-RF	82.9%	71.8%	77.1%	74.4%
Stacked MLP Classifier	86.0%	75.5%	83.3%	79.2%

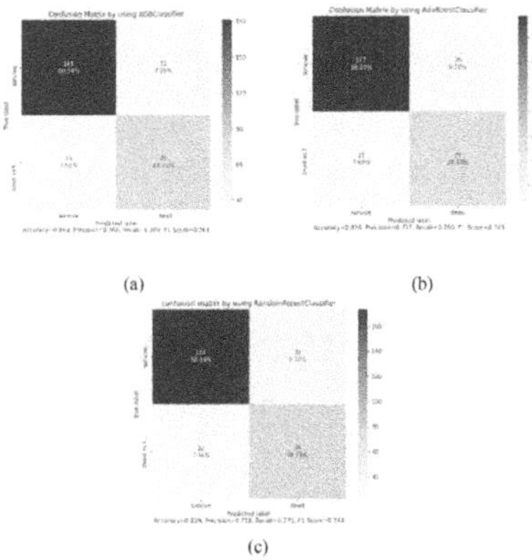

Figure 4. Results of the fuzzification process and optimization algorithm: (a) XGBClassifier, (b) AdaBoost classifier, and (c) random forest classifier.

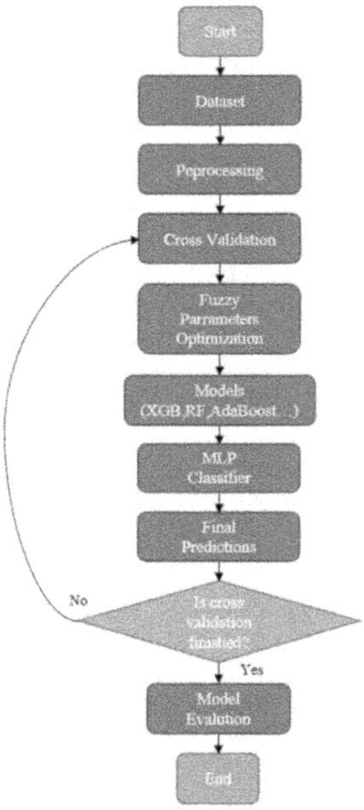

Figure 5. System flowchart.

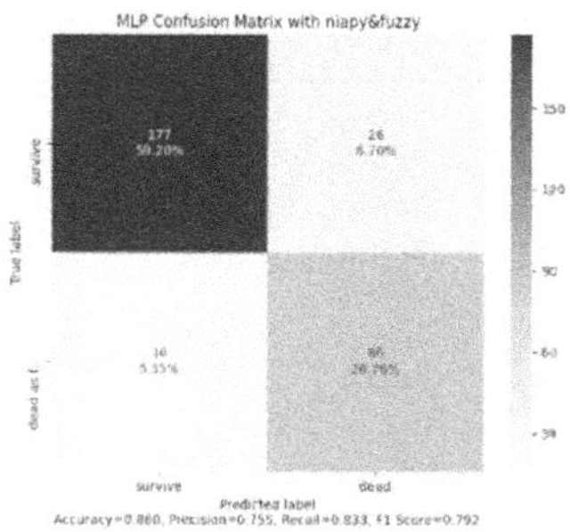

Figure 6. Confusion matrix created using a stacked MLP classifier with an optimization algorithm and fuzzy logic.

The prediction results of the AdaBoost classifier, XGBClassifier, and random forest classifier were used as input in the MLP classifier for repredictions. The architecture of the MLP classifier is presented in Figure 7.

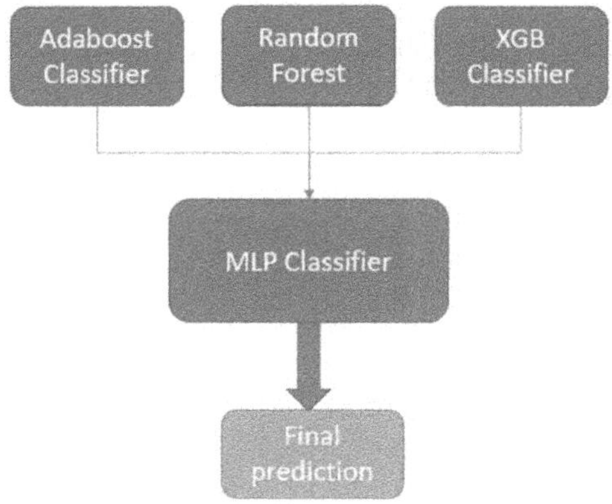

Figure 7. Architecture of the stacked MLP classifier.

As shown in Figure 8, the accuracy was 86%. Here, glowworm swarm optimization, gray wolf optimization, MBO, and particle swarm optimization were used as optimization algorithms. In addition, the prediction abilities of the algorithms were compared, and the learning curves are presented in Figure 8. As shown in the figure, when the iteration number was 260, the accuracy of MBO was the highest among the four optimization algorithms.

4 CONCLUSION

In this study, Pearson's product-moment correlation was used to compile the body data of patients with CVD and identify the features of these data. Subsequently, the standard deviation of the training data was used to establish a k-fold loop, MBO was used to determine the fuzzy attribution function and the optimal solutions of the parameters for each model, and validation data were used for verification. Next, the coefficients were input into an AdaBoost classifier, XGBClassifier, and KNN for predictions, and the results were inserted into an MLP classifier for repredictions. According to the final prediction results, the accuracy, precision, recall, and F1 score were 86%, 75.5%, 83.3%, and 79.2%, respectively. In conclusion, this algorithm can help frontline healthcare workers more accurately estimate the treatment duration and mortality rate of their patients, which may in turn help physicians make more appropriate treatment decisions and increase the survival rate of their patients.

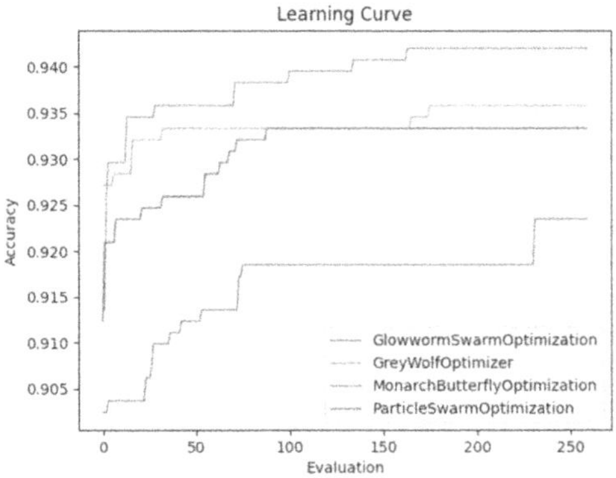

Figure 8. Learning curves of different optimization algorithms

FUNDING

This work is supported by the National Science and Technology Council, Taiwan, under Grants NSTC 113-2221-E-194-031 and NSTC 113-2224-E-006-003. This work was financially partially supported by the Advanced Institute of Manufacturing with High-tech Innovations (AIM-HI) from The Featured Areas Research Center Program within the framework of the Higher Education Sprout Project by the Ministry of Education (MOE) in Taiwan.

REFERENCES

Abdalrahman AO, Pilevarzadeh D, Ghafouri S and Ghaffari A. (2023). The application of hybrid krill herd artificial hummingbird algorithm for scientific workflow scheduling in fog computing. *J Bionic Eng.* 20(5):2443–2464. https://doi.org/10.1007/s42235-023-00389-z

Arora V, Ng EY-K, Leekha RS, Darshan M and Singh A. (2021). Transfer learning-based approach for detecting COVID-19 ailment in lung CT scan. *Comput Biol Med.* 135:104575. https://doi.org/https://doi.org/10.1016/j.compbiomed.2021.104575

Breiman L. (2001). *Random Forests. Mach Learn.* 45 (1):5–32. https://doi.org/10.1023/A:1010933404324

Cardiovascular diseases. https://www.who.int/health-topics/cardiovascular-diseases#tab=tab_1

Chen H, Das S, Morgan JM and Maharatna K. (2022). Prediction and classification of ventricular arrhythmia based on phase-space reconstruction and fuzzy c-means clustering. *Comput Biol Med.* 142:105180. https://doi.org/https://doi.org/10.1016/j.compbiomed.2021.105180

Feng L, Zhou Y and Luo Q. (2024). Binary hybrid artificial hummingbird with flower pollination algorithm for feature selection in Parkinson's disease diagnosis. *J Bionic Eng.* 21(2):1003–1021. https://doi.org/10.1007/s42235-023-00478-z

Guo G, Wang H, Bell D and Bi Y. (2004). *KNN Model-Based Approach in Classification.*

Hathaway QA, Yanamala N, Budoff MJ, Sengupta PP and Zeb I. (2021). Deep neural survival networks for cardiovascular risk prediction: The multi-ethnic study of atherosclerosis (MESA). *Comput Biol Med.* 139:104983. https://doi.org/https://doi.org/10.1016/j.compbiomed.2021.104983

Heart failure clinical records Data Set.https://archive.ics.uci.edu/ml/datasets/Heart+failure+clinical+records

Heart failure clinical records Data Set.https://archive.ics.uci.edu/ml/datasets/Heart+failure+clinical+records

Hsu G-S, Ambikapathi A and Chen M-S. (2017). Deep learning with time-frequency representation for pulse estimation from facial videos. *In: 2017 IEEE International Joint Conference on Biometrics (IJCB).* [place unknown]; p. 383–389. https://doi.org/10.1109/BTAS.2017.8272721

Ibrahim DM, Elshennawy NM and Sarhan AM. (2021). Deep-chest: Multi-classification deep learning model for diagnosing COVID-19, pneumonia, and lung cancer chest diseases. *Comput Biol Med.* 132:104348. https://doi.org/https://doi.org/10.1016/j.compbiomed.2021.104348

Islam MS, Awal MdA, Laboni JN, Pinki FT, Karmokar S, Mumenin KM, Al-Ahmadi S, Rahman MdA, Hossain MdS and Mirjalili S. (2022). HGSORF: Henry Gas Solubility Optimization-based Random Forest for C-Section prediction and XAI-based cause analysis. *Comput Biol Med.* 147:105671. https://doi.org/https://doi.org/10.1016/j.compbiomed.2022.105671

Lee C, Rosenqvist M and Mandrola J. (2022). Screening for atrial fibrillation in asymptomatic older adults. *N Engl J Med.* 387(6):565–567. https://doi.org/10.1056/NEJMclde2203726

Nadimi-Shahraki MH, Farhanginasab H, Taghian S, Sadiq AS and Mirjalili S. (2024). Multi-trial vector-based whale optimization algorithm. *J Bionic Eng.* 21 (3):1465–1495. https://doi.org/10.1007/s42235-024-00493-8

Peng J, Lee K and Ingersoll G. (2002). An Introduction to Logistic Regression Analysis and Reporting. *Journal of Educational Research - J EDUC RES.* 96:3–14. https://doi.org/10.1080/00220670209598786

Júnior J.S. S., Mendes J, Souza F and Premebida C. (2023). Survey on Deep Fuzzy Systems in Regression Applications: A View on Interpretability. *International Journal of Fuzzy Systems.* 25(7):2568–2589. https://doi.org/10.1007/s40815-023-01544-8

Tian S, Zhang J, Shu X, Chen L, Niu X and Wang Y. (2022). A novel evaluation strategy to artificial neural network model based on bionics. *J Bionic Eng.* 19 (1):224–239. https://doi.org/10.1007/s42235-021-00136-2

Wang H, Saad M, Karamti H, Garg H and Rafiq A. (2023). An approach toward pattern recognition and decision-making using the concept of bipolar T-spherical Fuzzy sets. *International Journal of Fuzzy Systems.* 25(7):2649–2664. https://doi.org/10.1007/s40815-023-01545-7

System Innovation for a Global Economy – Lam et al. (Eds)

Implicit high-dimensional union and intersection blends with outer and inner bound [0, 1] for soft object modeling

Pi-Chung Hsu
Department of Information Management Shu-Te University, Kaohsiung City, Taiwan, ROC

ABSTRACT: In soft object modeling, existing high-dimensional union and intersection operators B_U and B_I map $[0, 1]^k$ to $[0, L]$, $L \neq 1$. The range $[0, L]$ of B_U and B_I causes some problems, such as (a) generating unwanted distortion and discontinuity on union blending surfaces and (b) causing computational errors when union and intersection blends are used as subtracted primitives by compliments 1-B_U and 1-B_I in a difference blend. To solve these problems, this paper develops new high-dimensional union and intersection operators $B_s(x_{1,\ldots,}x_k)$ and $B_a(x_{1,\ldots,}x_k)$ that are able to map $[0, 1]^k$ to [0, 1], that is, they have outer and inner bound [0, 1]. Furthermore, their dual forms give two new families of set blends with inner and outer bounds [0, 1] by: (a) union $B_s(x_{1,\ldots,}x_k)$, intersection 1-B_s(1-$x_{1,\ldots,}$1-x_k) and difference 1-B_s(1-x_1, $x_{2,\ldots,}$ x_k); (b) Intersection $B_a(x_{1,\ldots,}x_k)$, union 1-B_a(1-$x_{1,\ldots,}$1-x_k) and difference B_a(x_1,1-$x_{2,\ldots,}$1-x_k).

1 INTRODUCTION

In soft object modeling, a soft object is defined as a level surface of a defining function $f_i(x,y,z)$ by $f_i(x,y,z)$=0.5. In fact, f_i is called field function, which is decreasing and also required to map R^3 to [0, 1] and so have outer and inner bounds [0, 1]. More precisely, a field function is composed of a potential function $P(d)$ and a distance function $d(x,y,z)$ by $f_i=P(d(x,y,z))$; $d(x,y,z)$ determines the shape of a soft object $f_i(x,y,z)$=0.5 and $P(d)$ enables f_i to be decreasing to zero. In the literature, potential functions can be found in (Blanc C. *et al.* 1995) and distance functions can be found in (Barr A. 1981, Crespin B. *et al.* 1996, Wyvill G. *et al.* 1989), including super-ellipsioids, super-quadrics and sweep objects.

Furthermore, based on set blending operator $B_*(x_1,\ldots,x_k)$, a complex surface is constructed from other soft objects f_i=0.5, i=1,...,k, and written by an implicit blend $B_*(f_1,\ldots,f_k)$=0.5. Set blend B_* smooths out sharp edges, corners and fillets through: (a) Union $B_U(f_1,\ldots,f_k)$, (b) Intersection $B_I(f_1,\ldots,f_k)$, and (c) Difference $B_D(f_1, f_2,\ldots, f_k)$. Besides, sequential blends also work (Hsu P.-C. *et al.* 2023).

In literature, the most important property of soft object modeling is that it have lower computing complexity of union blends such as Soft blend (Wyvill G. *et al.* 1989) and Perlin's set blends (Perlin K. 1989) due to the following requirements for field functions $f_i(x,y,z)$ are met: (a). Gradient $\nabla f_i(x,y,z)$ are zeros on surface $f_i(x,y,z)$=0. (b). Gradient $\nabla f_i(x,y,z)$ are zeros on $f_i(x,y,z)$=1.

In addition, other set blends for soft object modeling include:

1. Ricci's super-ellipsoidal union (Ricci A. 1973), offering curvature parameters to adjust the size of the transition of the blend;
2. Binary union (Barthe L. *et al.* 2004) and high-dimensional scale union and intersection (Hsu P.-C. 2003), offering blend range parameters to generate local blend. Besides, variable range method was developed in (Hsu P.-C. 2003) for bulge elimination on binary unions of intersecting cylinders.
3. Blends with special functions were also developed such as (a). blends with topology control (Zanni C. *et al.* 2015), (b). blends revisited (Bernhardt A. *et al.* 2010) which generate transitions only when primitives really contact each other, and (c). sketch-based blending (Angles B. *et al.* 2017) and Implicit Skinning (Hachette O. *et al.* 2011)

As for difference blends in soft object modeling,

1. Since each field function f_i has outer and inner [0, 1], the complement of soft object f_i=0.5 is obtained easily by $f_c(x,y,z)$=0.5 and f_c=1-f_i.
2. Since ∇f_i are zeros on $f_i(x,y,z)$=0 and $f_i(x,y,z)$ =1, it follows that ∇f_c of the compliment f_c=0.5 of f_i=0.5 are also zeros on $f_c(x,y,z)$=0 and on $f_c(x,y,z)$=1.

This means that based on compliments f_c=1-f_i, a new difference blend $B_D(f_1, f_2,\ldots,f_k)$ can be easily deducted from the dual form of an intersection $B_I(f_1, f_2,\ldots,f_k)$ by B_D=B_I(f_1,1-f_2 … ,1-f_k).

DOI: 10.1201/9781003655534-8

However, most existing union and intersection operators B_U and B_I have outer and inner bound [0, L], $L \neq 1$, but not [0, 1]. They are described below:

1. $B_U(f_1, \ldots, f_k)$, such as soft blend and high-dimensional scale union, has outer and inner bounds [0, L], i.e. $B_U(1, \ldots, 1)=L$, $L>1$. As a result, the complement $1-B_U(f_1, \ldots, f_k)$ has outer and inner bounds [$1-L$, 1] with outer bound ($1-L$) less than 0.
2. $B_I(f_1, \ldots, f_k)$, such as high-dimensional scale intersection, has outer and inner bounds [0, L], i.e. $B_I(1, \ldots, 1)=L$, $L<1$. It follows that complement $1-B_I(f_1, \ldots, f_k)$ has outer and inner bounds [$1-L$, 1], with outer bound ($1-L$) greater than 0.
3. Gradient $\nabla B_U(f_1, \ldots, f_k)$ are zeros on $B_U(f_1, \ldots, f_k)=0$, but not zeros on $B_U(f_1, \ldots, f_k)=1$. This causes that $\nabla(1-B_U(f_1, \ldots, f_k))$ of the compliment $1-B_U$ of $B_U(f_1, \ldots, f_k)$ are also not zeros on $1-B_U(f_1, \ldots, f_k)=0$.

Due to the reasons above, when existing B_U and B_I are used to define subtracting primitives $f_2, \ldots$ and f_k in difference $B_D=B_I(f_1, 1-f_2, \ldots, 1-f_k)$, some problems could occur as described below:

1. Problem 1: Unexpected computational errors might occur in difference $B_I(f_1, 1-B_U, \ldots, f_k)$ because $B_c=1-B_U$ might be negative in the region around $(1, \ldots, 1)$ and B_I is defined on non-negative spaces.
2. Problem 2: When $B_D=B_I(f_1, 1-B_U, \ldots, 1-f_k)$ or $B_D=B_I(f_1, 1-B_I \ldots, 1-f_k)$ is used as a primitive in soft union $f_1+B_D+ \ldots +fk$, the other primitives f_i might be deformed and distorted. For example: (a). f_i might be shrunk by $B_c=1-B_U$ because B_c might be negative somewhere and so surface $f_i=l$, $l>0.5$, is created; (b). f_i might be enlarged by $B_c=1-B_I$ because B_c could be positive somewhere and so surface $f_i=l$, $l<0.5$, is created.

To solve these problems, this paper proposes high-dimensional union and intersection operators $B_U(x_1,\ldots,x_k)$ and $B_I(x_1,\ldots,x_k)$ that have outer and inner bound [0, 1]. Especially, they satisfy the following requirements so that Problems 1-3 above can all be solved:

1. B_U and B_I map into [0, 1] with outer and inner bound [0, 1], that is, $B_U(0, \ldots, 0)=0$, $B_I(0, \ldots, 0)=1$, $B_U(1, \ldots, 1)=1$ and $B_I(1, \ldots, 1)=1$.
2. Gradients $\nabla B_U(f_1, \ldots, f_k)$ and $\nabla B_I(f_1, \ldots, f_k)$ both are zeros on surfaces $B_U(f_1, \ldots, f_k)=1$ and $B_I(f_1, \ldots, f_k)=1$.

Furthermore, dual forms of the proposed $B_U(x_1, \ldots, x_k)$ and $B_I(x_1, \ldots, x_k)$ also offer two new families of Boolean set operators by: (a). Union $B_U(x_1, \ldots, x_k)$, intersection $1-B_U(1-x_1, \ldots, 1-x_k)$ and difference by $1-B_U(1-x_1, x_2, \ldots, x_k)$; (b). Union $1-B_I(1-x_1, \ldots, 1-x_k)$, intersection $B_I(x_1, \ldots, x_k)$, and difference by $B_I(x_1, 1-x_2, \ldots, 1-x_k)$.

The remainder of this project is organized as follows: Section 2 reviews soft object modeling. Section 3 describes the problems caused by the outer and inner bounds of existing set blends. Section 4 presents union and intersection blends with outer and inner bound [0, 1]. Section 5 gives conclusion.

2 RELATED WORKS OF SOFT OBJECTS

2.1 *Feld function for soft object modeling*

In soft object modeling, a primitive soft object is defined by

$$f_i(x, y, z) = 0.5$$

$f_i(x,y,z)$ is a primitive field function required to map R^3 to [0, 1] and be decreasing from 1 to 0. Function f_i is usually defined as a composition of a potential function $P(d)$ and a distance function $d_i(x,y,z)$ by

$$f_i(x, y, z) = (P_o \; d_i)(x, y, z) = P(d_i(x, y, z)) \quad (1)$$

In Equation (1), $d(x,y,z){:}R^3 \to R_+$ determines the shape of soft object $P(d(x,y,z))=0.5$. $P(d)$ enables $P(d_i(x, y,z))$ to decrease from 1 to 0 as the value of $d_i(x,y,z)$ increases (Blanc C. *et al.* 1995). As shown in Figure 1, P(d) must satisfy the following requirements: (a) $P(0.5)=0.5$; (b) $P(d)$ decreases from 1 to 0 as d increases from 0 to 1; (c) $P'(0)=0$ and $P'(1)=0$ so that $\nabla f_i(x,y,z)$ can be zeros on $f_i(x,y,z)=0$ and $f_i(x,y,z)=1$. As result, soft and Perlin's set blends in Eqs. (2)-(3) can generate smooth blending surfaces.

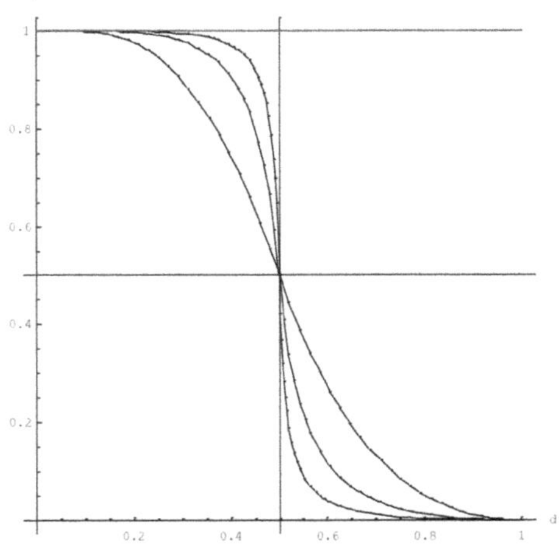

Figure 1. The shapes of Blanc's $p=P(d)$, which vary according to the value of parameter s.

2.2 *Outer and Inner bound of a field function*

The meaning of outer and inner bound [0, 1] of f_i (x,y,z) means that (a). the smallest value of $f_i(x,y,z)$ is 0 and a union blend is generated withing $f_i(x,y,z)$ = 0.5 and $f_i(x,y,z)$=outer bound=0, and (b). the largest value of $f_i(x,y,z)$ is 1 and an intersection blend is generated within $f_i(x,y,z)$=inner bound=1 and $f_i(x,y,z)$ =0.5.

2.3 *Boolean set blends for Soft object modeling*

2.3.1 *Soft blend*
Soft blend (Wyvill G. *et al.* 1989) performs a union of soft objects f_i=0.5, i=1 to k, through the operator below:

$$B_U(x_1,\ldots,x_k) = x_1 + \cdots + x_k, \qquad (2)$$

which maps $R_+{}^k$ to [0, k], where $R_+ \equiv [0, \infty]$.

2.3.2 *Perlin's Boolean set blends*
Perlin (Perlin K. 1989) offers set operators:

- Union : $B_U(x_1,\ldots,x_k)$
$$= 1-(1-x_1)*(1-x_2)*(1-x_k) \qquad (3)$$
- Intersection : $B_I(x_1,\ldots,x_k) = x_1 * x_2 * \ldots * x_k$ (4)
- Difference : $B_D(x_1,\ldots,x_k)$
$$= x_1 * (1-x_2) * \ldots * (1-x_k). \qquad (5)$$

2.3.3 *Ricci's union blend*
Ricci (Ricci A. 1973) offered pure union and intersection $Max(x_1, \ldots ,x_k)$ and $Min(x_1, \ldots ,x_k)$. Since they have C^0 continuity only, so super-ellipsoidal union operator with C^n continuous, n>1, was also proposed by:

$$B_U(x_1,\ldots,x_k) = \left(x_1^n + \ldots + x_k^n\right)^{1/n}, \qquad (6)$$

which maps $R_+{}^k$ to [0, L], L>1, and offer parameter n for adjusting the continuity of the blend.

2.3.4 *Scale union and intersection*
As shown in Figure 2(a), Ricci's union always deform primitives totally. To allow blended primitives to deform locally after blending, the scale method (Hsu P.-C. *et al.* 2003) developed set blends with blend range parameters r_i through an union operator $H(x_1,,\ldots, x_k)$=0. Thus, given by

$$H(x_1,,\ldots,x_k) = \sum_{i=1}^{k} [(r_1 - x_i)/r_i]_+^{pi} = 0,$$

scale union B_{SU} and intersection B_{SI} are created by:

$$(1).\ \text{Scale Union} : B_{SU}(x_1,\ldots,x_k) = p \qquad (7)$$

where p is the root of $H(1\text{-}x_1/p,,\ldots,1\text{-}x_k/p)$=0.

$$(2).\ \text{Scale Intersection} : B_{SI}(x_1,\ldots,x_k) = p \qquad (8)$$

where p is the root of $H(x_1/p\text{-}1,,\ldots,x_k/p\text{-}1)$=0.

$B_{SU}(f_1, \ldots ,f_k)$ and $B_{SI}(f_1, \ldots ,f_k)$ both map $R_+{}^k$ to [0, L], L>1, and provide each primitive f_i an individual range parameter r_i for adjusting the size of the blending region of f_i so that all primitives can be deformed locally after blending as shown in Figure 2(b).

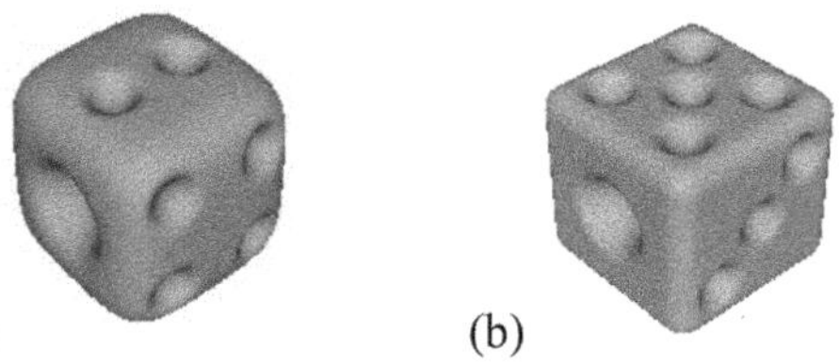

Figure 2. (a)-(b). Dices with faces deformed totally and locally.

3 PROBLEMS OF OUTER AND INNER BOUND OF EXISING SET BLENDS

3.1 *Dual forms of a union or an intersection*

The complement of soft object $f_i(x,y,z)$=0.5 is obtained directly from a compliment $f_{ci}=1\text{-}f_i(x,y,z)$ by

$$f_{ci} = (1-f_i(x,y,z)) \geq 0.5 \equiv f_i(x,y,z) \leq 0.5.$$

In terms of complements f_{ci}, dual forms of union B_U and intersection B_I operators in Eqs. (2)-(8) directly offer two families of set blends by

- Family $\boldsymbol{F_U}$ derived from $B_U(x_1, \ldots ,x_k)$: Union $B_U(x_1, \ldots ,x_k)$, intersection B_I=1-B_U(1-x_1, ... ,1-x_k) and difference B_D=1-B_U(1-x_1, ... , x_k).
- Family $\boldsymbol{F_I}$ derived from $B_I(x_1, \ldots ,x_k)$: Union B_U=1-B_I(1-x_1, ... ,1-x_k), intersection: B_I $(x_1, \ldots ,x_k)$, and difference $B_D=B_I(x_1$, 1-x_2, ... ,1-x_k).

3.2 *Problems of existing set blends about outer and inner bound*

However, when used as a new primitive in the blends of Family $\boldsymbol{F_U}$ and $\boldsymbol{F_I}$ to define a compliment f_{ci} by 1-B_U or 1-B_I, most of the existing union and intersection blends $B_U(f_1, \ldots ,f_k)$ and $B_I(f_1, \ldots , f_k)$, in Eqs. (2) and (6)-(8), cannot satisfy the conditions stated in Section 3.2. This incurs some problems due to the shortcomings below:

- Union $B_U(x_1, \ldots, x_k)$ in Eqs. (2) and (6)-(7) has outer and inner bound [0, L], $L>1$, because $B_U(0, \ldots, 0)$ is 0 and $B_U(1, \ldots, 1)$ is greater than 1, as shown in Figure 3(a)-(c);
- Intersection $B_I(x_1, \ldots, x_k)$ in Equation (8) has outer and inner bound [0, L], $L<1$, because of $B_I(0, \ldots, 0)$ is 0 and $B_I(1, \ldots, 1)$ is less than 1, as in Figure 3(d).

The shortcomings of existing B_U and B_I stated above further cause the following problems:

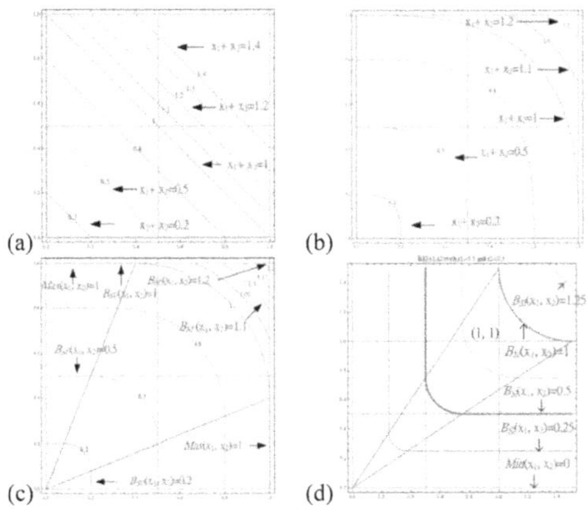

Figure 3. (a). Level curves of soft blend $x_1+x_2=p$ in Equation (2), (b). super-ellipsoidal union $(x_1^3+x_2^3)^{1/3}=p$ in Equation (5), (c). scale union $B_{SU}(x_1,x_2)=p$ with $r_1=r_2=0.6$ and (d). scale intersection $B_{SI}(x_1, x_2)=p$ with $r_1=r_2=0.5$ in Eqs. (6)-(7).

1. Problem 1: Unexpected computational errors might occur in $B_D=B_I(1-B_U, f_2 \ldots f_k)$ of family $\boldsymbol{F_U}$ and $B_D=B_I(f_1, 1-B_U, \ldots, 1-f_k)$ of family $\boldsymbol{F_I}$ because $1-B_U$ might be negative, not lying in the domain R_+^k of existing B_I and B_U.

   For example, in difference $B_D=B_{I2}(B_{I1}(f_1,f_2,, f_3), 1-B_U(f_4, f_5))=0.5$ as in Figure 4(d), $1-B_U(f_4, f_5)$ might be negative and out of the domain of B_{I2} and so computational errors occur in computing B_{I2}. This is solved by replacing a new $B_U(f_4, f_5)$ with outer and inner bound [0, 1].

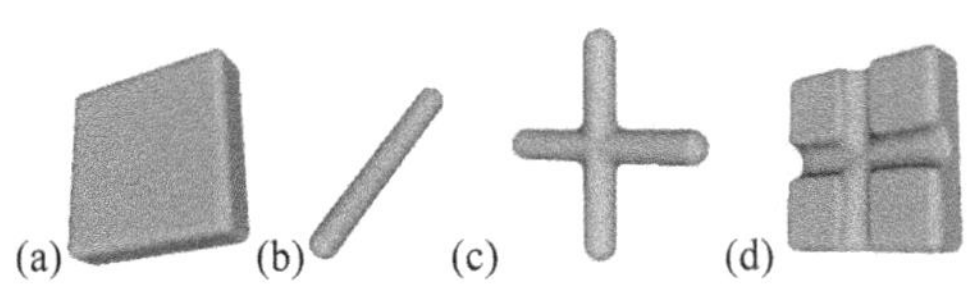

Figure 4. (a). Intersection B_{I1} of six planes. (b). Cylinder. (c). Union $B_U(f_4, f_5)$ of crossing cylinders in (b). (d). Difference $B_D=B_{I2}(B_{I1}(f_1,f_2,f_3), 1-B_U(f_4,f_5))$, which is the cube in (a) subtracted by (c).

2. Problem 2: In a soft blend $f_1+B_D+ \ldots +fk$ with $B_D=B_I(f_1, 1-B_U \ldots, 1-f_k)$ of $\boldsymbol{F_I}$, other f_i might deform totally and shrunk by $1-B_U$ of B_D because $1-B_U$ is negative and surface $f_i=l$, $l>0.5$, is created.
3. Problem 3: In soft blend $f_1+B_D+ \ldots +f_k$ with $B_D=B_I(f_1, 1-B_I \ldots, 1-f_k)$ of $\boldsymbol{F_I}$, other f_i might deform totally and enlarged by $1-B_I$ of B_D because $B_c=1-B_I$ is positive somewhere and surface $f_i=l$, $l<0.5$, is created.

As shown in Figure 5(d) where a difference $B_D=B_I(f_4, 1-B_{SI}(f_1,f_2,f_3))$ of $\boldsymbol{F_I}$ performs a union with intersecting cylinders $f_5=B_U(f_6,f_7)$ by soft blend $B_I(f_4, 1-B_{SI}(f_1,f_2,f_3))+f_5$. It is found that intersecting cylinders $f_5=B_U(f_6,f_7)$ is enlarged by B_D because $1-B_{SI}$ of B_D is positive somewhere. However, as in Figure 5(e), f_5 is deformed locally by replacing B_{SI} with outer and inner bound [0, 1] in Section 4.

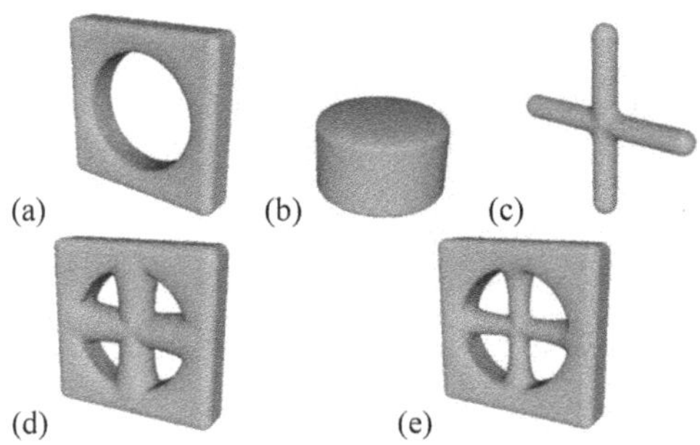

Figure 5. (a). An difference $B_D=B_I(f_4, 1-B_{SI})$ of a cube f_4 subtracted by B_{SI} in (b). (b). Scale intersection $B_{SI}(f_1, f_2, f_3)$ of three parallel planes by Equation (8). (c). Intersecting cylinders f_5 with bulge elimination. (d). Soft blend $B_I(f_4, 1-B_{SI})+f_5$ of (a) and (c), where B_{SI} enlarges f_5. (e). f_5 deforms locally because intersection with outer and inner bound [0, 1] is used instead of Equation (8).

3.3 *Requirements for union and intersection blends to be used to define complements*

To solve the problems of B_U and B_I in Eqs. (2) and (6)-(8) stated in Subsection 3.2, they must be extended to satisfy the following requirements:

- Requirement 1: $B_U(f_1, \ldots f_k)$ and $B_I(f_1, \ldots f_k)$ map $[0, 1]^k$ to [0, 1].
- Requirement 2: Union operator $B_U(x_1, \ldots, x_k)$ has outer and inner bounds [0, 1], i.e. $B_U(0, \ldots, 0)=0$ and $B_U(1, \ldots, 1)=1$.
- Requirement 3: Intersection operator $B_I(x_1, \ldots, x_k)$ has outer and inner bound [0, 1], i.e. $B_I(0, \ldots, 0)=0$ and $B_I(1, \ldots, 1)=1$.
- Requirement 4: Gradient $\nabla B_U(f_1, \ldots, f_k)$ are zeros on surfaces $B_U(f_1, \ldots f_k)=0$ and on $B_U(f_1, \ldots f_k)=1$; Gradient $\nabla B_I(f_1, \ldots, f_k)$ are zeros on $B_I(f_1, \ldots f_k)=0$ and on $B_I(f_1, \ldots f_k)=1$, too.

4 DEVELOPING NEW SCALE UNION AND INTERSECTION WITH OUTER AND INNER BOUND [0, 1]

This section extends scale union and scale intersection in Eqs. (7)-(8) and develop new scale union $B_s(x_1, \ldots, x_k)$ and scale intersection $B_a(x_1, \ldots, x_k)$ that have outer and inner bound [0, 1] and also satisfy the requirements stated in Section 3.3.

4.1 *Surface range function $b_i(p)$ for B_s and B_a*

Let $b_i(p)$ denote a surface range function to express the blending range's value of f_i in level surface $B(x_1, \ldots, x_k)=p$, $p\in[0,1]$. For example, $b_i(p)$ of $B_{SU}(x_1, \ldots, x_k)=p$ and $B_{SI}(x_1, \ldots, x_k)=p$ in Equations (7) and (8) is

$$b_i(p) = p * r_i$$

for each primitive f_i in $B_{SU}(f_1, \ldots, f_k)$ and $B_{SI}(f_1, \ldots, f_k)$.

In terms of $b_i(p)$, new scale union $B_s(x_1, \ldots, x_k)$ and intersection $B_a(x_1, \ldots, x_k)$ that can satisfy Requirements 1-4 in Section 3.3 are defined by

$$B_s = B_{SU}(x_1, \ldots, x_k) \text{ and } B_a = B_{SI}(x_1, \ldots, x_k), \quad (9)$$

and $b_i(p)$ of B_s and B_a fulfill the following:

- **Condition 1**: $b_i(0)=0$, $b_i(0.5)=0.5r_i$, and $b_i(1)=0$,
- **Condition 2**: $b_i(p)$ increases in interval $0 \leq p \leq 0.5$ but decreases in interval $0.5 \leq p \leq 1$.
- **Condition 3**: $b_i(p)$ is continuous in [0,1].

These conditions are shown in Figure 6.

(a)

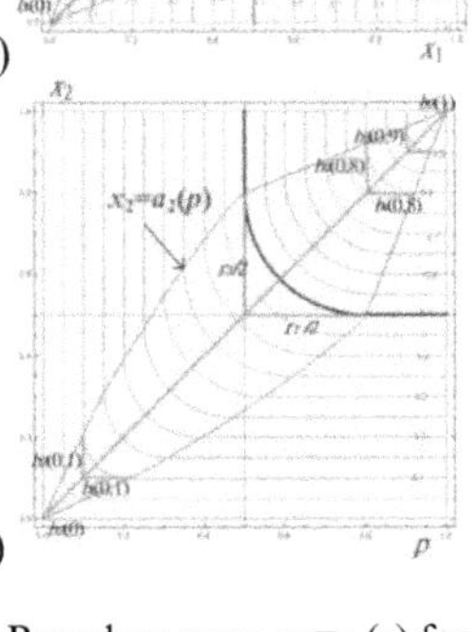

(b)

Figure 6. (a). Boundary curve $x_1=s_1(p)$ for $b_1(p)$ of $B_s(x_1, x_2)=p$. (b). Boundary curve $x_2=a_2(p)$ for $b_2(p)$ of $B_a(x_1,x_2)=p$.

4.2 *Blending range functions $f_{ri}(p)$ for B_s and B_a*

To make $B_{SU}(x_1, \ldots, x_k)=p$ and $B_{SI}(x_1, \ldots, x_k)=p$ have $b_i(p)$ satisfying the conditions in Section 4.1, values of range parameters r_i for level surfaces $B_{SU}(x_1, \ldots, x_k)=p$ and $B_{SI}(x_1, \ldots, x_k)=p$, $p\in[0,1]$, are varied as in Figure 6. That is, r_i are redefined with blending range function $f_{ri}(p)$ of variable p and new scale union $B_s(x_1, \ldots, x_k)$ and intersection $B_a(x_1, \ldots, x_k)$ are extended from Equations (7) and (8) and written by:

$$B_s = B_{SU}(x_1, \ldots, x_k) \text{ and } B_a = B_{SI}(x_1, \ldots, x_k),$$

but parameters r_i of Equations (7) and (8) are replaced with functions $f_{ri}(p)$. More precisely,

1. Union $B_s(x_1, \ldots, x_k)$ maps $[0,1]^k$ to[0,1], given by

$$B_s = \begin{cases} 0 & Max(x_0, \ldots, x_k) = 0 \\ h_p & Max(x_0, \ldots, x_k) > 0 \end{cases}, \quad (10)$$

where $0<r_i \leq 1$ and $n_i>1$ for $i=1, \ldots, k$, and h_p is the root p of the equation $T_s(p)=0$,

$$T_s(p) = \sum_{i=1}^{k} [(f_{ri}(p) + x_1/p - 1)/f_{ri}(p)]_+^{n_i} - 1 = 0.$$

2. Intersection $B_a(x_1, \ldots, x_k)$ maps $[0, 1]^k$ to [0, 1], written by

$$B_a = \begin{cases} 0 & Min(x_0, \ldots, x_k) = 0 \\ h_p & Min(x_0, \ldots, x_k) > 0 \end{cases}, \quad (11)$$

where $0<r_i \leq 1$ and $n_i>1$ for $i=1, \ldots, k$ and h_p is the root p of the equation $T_a(p)=0$,

$$T_a(p) = \sum_{i=1}^{k} [(f_{ri}(p) - x_1/p + 1)/f_{ri}(p)]_+^{n_i} - 1 = 0.$$

Moreover, dual forms of $B_s(x_1, \ldots, x_k)$ in Equation (10) give new intersection B_I and difference B_D by:

$$B_I(x_1, \ldots, x_k) = 1 - B_s(1 - x_1, \ldots, 1 - x_k) \text{ and } B_D(x_1, \ldots, x_k) = 1 - B_s(1 - x_1, \ldots, x_k). \quad (12)$$

Similarly, dual forms of $B_a(x_1, \ldots, x_k)$ in Equation (11) offer new union B_U and difference B_D by

$$B_U(x_1, \ldots, x_k) = 1 - B_a(1 - x_1, \ldots, 1 - x_k) \text{ and } B_D(f_1, \ldots, f_k) = B_a(x_1, 1 - x_2, \ldots, 1 - x_k). \quad (13)$$

4.3 *Blending range functions $f_{ri}(p)$ for B_s and B_a*

This section presents $f_{ri}(p)$ such that $b_i(p)$ of B_s and B_a in Equations (10) and (11) can vary like the level curves sketched in Figure 6 and satisfy the conditions in Section 4.1. To fulfill this, the following two steps are required:

- Step 1: Find a boundary curve $x_i=s_i(p)$ for B_s with a shape like $x_1=s_1(p)$ shown in Figure 6 (a); Find a boundary curve $x_i=a_i(p)$ for B_a with a shape like $x_2=a_2(p)$ shown in Figure 6 (b).
- Using boundary curves to derive $b_i(p)$ and $f_{ri}(p)$.

4.3.1 *Boundary curves $x_i=s_i(p)$ and $x_i=a_i(p)$*
As shown from $x_1=s_1(p)$ and $x_2=a_2(p)$ in Figure 6, C^0 continuous boundary curves $x_i=s_i(p)$ and $x_i=a_i(p)$ for defining $f_{ri}(p)$ in B_s and B_a with exactly linearly increasing and then decreasing $b_i(p)$ is presented by:

$$s_i(p) = \begin{cases} p(1-r_i) & p \le 0.5 \\ p(1+r_i) - r_i & p > 0.5 \end{cases} \tag{14}$$

$$a_i(p) = \begin{cases} p(1+r_i) & p \le 0.5 \\ p(1-r_i) + r_i & p > 0.5 \end{cases} \tag{15}$$

4.3.2 *Deriving $f_{ri}(p)$ from $x_i=s_i(p)$ and $x_i=a_i(p)$*
It follows that:

1. Bsased on $x_i=s_i(p)$, $f_{ri}(p)$ for $B_s(x_1, \ldots, x_k)$ in Equation (10) is written by:

$$f_{ri}(p) = (p - s_i(p))/p, \tag{16}$$

2. Bsased on $x_i=a_i(p)$, $f_{ri}(p)$ for $B_a(x_1, \ldots, x_k)$ in Equation (11) is written by:

$$f_{ri}(p) = (a_i(p) - p)/p, \tag{17}$$

When Equation (16) is used to define $f_{ri}(p)$ for $B_s(x_1, \ldots, x_k)$ in Equation (10), level surfaces of set blends $B_U=B_s(x_1,x_2, \ldots, x_k)=p$, $B_I=1\text{-}B_s(1\text{-}x_1,1\text{-}x_2 \ldots, 1\text{-}x_k)=p$ and $B_D=1\text{-}B_s(1\text{-}x_1,x_2 \ldots, x_k)=p$ with $p>0$ from Equation (12) have increasing and then decreasing $b_i(p)$, as shown in Figure 7(a)-(c). Similarly, when Equation (17) is used to defines $B_a(x_1, \ldots, x_k)$, set blends from Equation (13) also have linearly increasing and then decreasing $b_i(p)$.

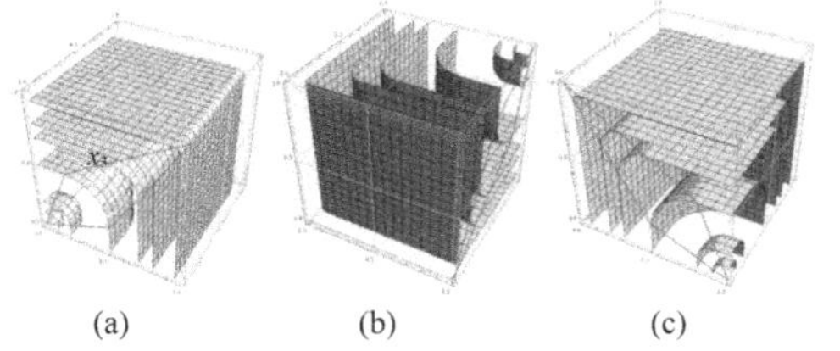

(a) (b) (c)

Figure 7. 3D level surfaces of (a) $B_s(x_1,x_2,x_3)=p$, (b) $1\text{-}B_s(1\text{-}x_1, 1\text{-}x_2,1\text{-}x_3)=p$ and (a) $1\text{-}B_s(x_1,1\text{-}x_2,1\text{-}x_3)=p$ for $p>0$, which have linearly increasing and then decreasing $b_i(p)$.

5 CONCLUSION

In soft object modeling, exist union and intersection blends $B(f_1, \ldots f_k)$, such as soft blend and scale union and intersection have outer and inner bound [0, L], $L>1$ or $L<1$. Hence, when they are reused to define a compliment $1\text{-}B(f_1, \ldots, f_k)$ in a union or a difference blend, a lot of problems, such as computational errors and unexpected surface distortion or deformation might occur. So, this paper has developed new high-dimensional union and intersection operators with outer and inner bound [0, 1] and successfully solved these problems.

ACKNOWLEDGEMENT

The author would like to thank NTSC of Taiwan for the support of Project No. NSTC 113-2221-E-366-001.

REFERENCES

Angles B., Tarini M., Wyvill B., Barthe L., and Tagliasacchi A., (2017), Sketch-based implicit blending, ACM Trans. on Graphics, *Proceeding of Siggraph Asia* 2017, 36(6).

Barr A., (1981), Superquadrics, *IEEE Computer Graphics and Applications*, 1(1), 11–23.

Barthe L., Wyvill B., Groot ED., (2004), Controllable binary CSG operators for soft objects, *International Journal of Shape Modeling*, 10(2), 135–154.

Bernhardt A., Barthe C., Cani M.-O., Wyvill Brian B., (2010), Implicit blending revisited, *Computer Graphics Forum*, 29(2), 367–375.

Blanc C. and Schlick C., (1995), Extended field functions for soft objects, *Implicit Surfaces 5*, 21–32.

Crespin B., Blanc C., and Schlick C., (1996), Implicit sweep objects, *EUROGRAPHICS'96* 15(3), 165–175.

Hachette O., Canezin F., Vaillant R., Mellado N. and Barthe L., (2021), Automatic shape adjustment at joints for the Implicit Skinning, *Proc. of SMI 2021.*

Hsu P.-C. and Jen Jiun Hu, (2023), The Design of an Object-Oriented Constructive Solid Geometry Tree for Representing Sequential Set blends in Constructive Geometry, Soft Object, Function Representation and Zero Implicit Surface. *Proceedings of ACM ICGSP 2023.*

Hsu P.-C. and Lee C., (2003), The scale method for blending operations in functionally based constructive geometry, *Computer Graphics Forum*, 22(2), 143–156.

Perlin K., (1989), Hypertexture, In *SIGGRAPH Computer Graphics*, 23(3):253–262.

Ricci A., (1973), A constructive geometry for computer graphics, *The Computer Journal*, 16(2),157–160.

Wyvill G. and Wyvill B., (1989), Field functions for implicit surfaces, *The Visual Computer*, *5*, 78–52.

Zanni C., Gleicher M. and Cani M., (2015), N-ary implicit blends with topology control. *Computers & Graphics 46*, 1–13.

System Innovation for a Global Economy – Lam et al. (Eds)
© 2026 The Author(s), ISBN 978-1-041-10520-6

Development and user acceptance study of a dysphagia rehabilitation training device integrating CTAR technology and interactive game design

Kuang-Chieh Hsu, Chih-Fu Wu, Chi-Hsueh Yeh & Jing-Yan Wang
The Graduate Institute of Design Science, Tatung University; Department of Industrial Design, Tatung University, Taipei, Taiwan

ABSTRACT: Dysphagia in aging populations causes severe complications like malnutrition and pneumonia. Early intervention reduces risks. Chin Tuck Against Resistance (CTAR) exercises outperform traditional methods, especially when paired with gamified training to improve engagement. However, current CTAR devices are often complicated and lack enjoyment, limiting patient use. This study used the UTAUT2 framework to identify key adoption factors for adults aged 60+. Social influence, personal motivation, and cost-value perceptions strongly impacted willingness to use devices. Based on these insights, we designed an interactive CTAR device combining gamification with real-time health monitoring, prioritizing ease of use and affordability. This system supports home rehabilitation and increases accessibility. Findings revealed low awareness of swallowing decline in older adults, reducing external motivation. Surprisingly, device performance expectations did not significantly influence adoption. Future work should focus on raising health awareness to encourage early intervention. Our results guide practical, low-cost rehabilitation tools while highlighting the need for education to drive proactive elderly care.

Keywords: Dysphagia, CTAR, UTAUT2, Interactive device, Rehabilitation training

1 INTRODUCTION

Dysphagia has become a critical health challenge in aging populations, primarily caused by age-related physiological decline in swallowing function (Sura *et al.* 2012). Epidemiological data indicate substantial disease burden, with 300,000-600,000 annual cases in the U.S. (U.S. Department of Health and Human Services 1999) and 15% prevalence among older adults (Barczi *et al.* 2000). Extrapolating from 2010 Census data, over 6 million seniors face risks of life-threatening complications including aspiration pneumonia and malnutrition (Zeng and Zhao 2011), underscoring the urgency of early intervention strategies (Jiao *et al.* 2021). Research confirms accelerated tongue muscle weakening in adults aged ≥ 60 (Arakawa *et al.* 2021), establishing this demographic as the study's priority group. Current clinical interventions exhibit dual limitations: compensatory approaches like dietary modification and tube feeding incur choking risks and social stigma (Meng 2020), while traditional rehabilitative tools (e.g., rehabilitation balls, electrotherapy) suffer from unproven efficacy and poor patient engagement (Carnaby-Mann and Crary 2019). Emerging evidence highlights the superiority of Chin Tuck Against Resistance (CTAR) exercises over conventional methods, particularly when integrated with game-based training paradigms. However, existing CTAR devices remain underutilized due to operational complexity and insufficient entertainment value. The evolution of technology adoption theories, particularly the Unified Theory of Acceptance and Use of Technology 2 (UTAUT2), provides a validated framework for analyzing healthcare technology acceptance (Venkatesh *et al.* 2012). This study applies UTAUT2 through multidisciplinary investigations involving user testing, product evaluations, and interviews with occupational/speech therapists, aiming to address three gaps: first, identifying rehabilitation standards through expert consultations with therapists and target users (healthy/at-risk adults ≥ 60); second, establishing design guidelines for interactive swallowing rehabilitation devices that overcome traditional tools' limitations; third, exploring 3D printing applications in medical assistive devices to enhance affordability and industry-academia collaboration. Key findings reveal social influence, intrinsic motivation, and cost-value perceptions as dominant adoption drivers, informing the development of a novel CTAR device integrating gamified training with real-time physiological monitoring. The research acknowledges two limitations: its preventive focus on healthy/at-risk seniors excludes clinically diagnosed patients, while applicability remains restricted to CTAR-compatible cases

DOI: 10.1201/9781003655534-9

without medical contraindications. These constraints highlight the need for complementary studies on advanced dysphagia cases while validating the prototype's effectiveness in early-stage intervention.

2 LITERATURE REVIEW

2.1 *Current status of dysphagia treatment*

Neuromuscular Electrical Stimulation (NMES) induces muscle contractions by electrically stimulating intact neural pathways. While widely used in dysphagia rehabilitation, its clinical efficacy remains debated. The FDA-approved VitalStim Therapy (2002) stimulates atrophied muscles without significant side effects, yet its high cost limits accessibility. Traditional muscle-strengthening devices like rehabilitation balls show effectiveness but suffer from monotonous operation and poor adaptability. Pharyngeal muscle assessment trainers with gamified feedback face limitations such as inconsistent force application due to hand displacement.

2.2 *Swallowing physiology and CTAR*

Insufficient laryngeal elevation is a core mechanism of dysphagia, making suprahyoid muscle training critical. Chin Tuck Against Resistance (CTAR), proposed in 2014, demonstrates comparable or superior efficacy to traditional Shaker exercises with higher patient compliance. However, existing CTAR devices lack parameter adjustability and data tracking, limiting training outcomes.

2.3 *Dysphagia screening tools*

The Water Swallow Test serves as a common preliminary screening tool but has subjective limitations. The Eating Assessment(EAT-10), a standardized 10-item 5-point scale, quantifies dysphagia severity. This study adopts EAT-10 to screen healthy/at-risk older adults aged 60+ (score ≤ 3) as the target cohort.

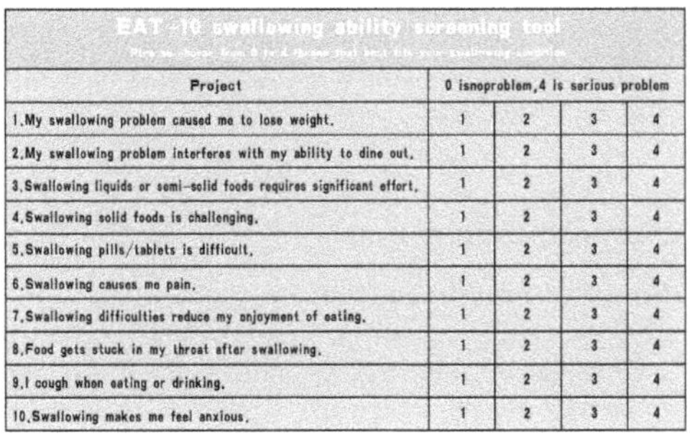

EAT-10 swallowing ability screening tool

Project	0 isnoproblem,4 is serious problem			
1.My swallowing problem caused me to lose weight.	1	2	3	4
2.My swallowing problem interferes with my ability to dine out.	1	2	3	4
3.Swallowing liquids or semi-solid foods requires significant effort.	1	2	3	4
4.Swallowing solid foods is challenging.	1	2	3	4
5.Swallowing pills/tablets is difficult.	1	2	3	4
6.Swallowing causes me pain.	1	2	3	4
7.Swallowing difficulties reduce my enjoyment of eating.	1	2	3	4
8.Food gets stuck in my throat after swallowing.	1	2	3	4
9.I cough when eating or drinking.	1	2	3	4
10.Swallowing makes me feel anxious.	1	2	3	4

Figure 1. EAT-10 swallowing screening tool. Image source: National Health Foundation (adapted for academic use).

2.4 *Serious games*

Serious games achieve educational/therapeutic goals through entertainment design. Their interactivity enhances rehabilitation motivation, reducing monotony and improving engagement compared to traditional methods.

2.5 *Extended unified theory of acceptance and use of technology (UTAUT2)*

Building on UTAUT, UTAUT2 adds hedonic motivation, price value, and habit constructs, increasing explanatory power to 74% (behavioral intention) and 52% (actual usage). This study adapts UTAUT2 for swallowing rehabilitation devices by incorporating physiological mechanisms and training objectives as moderators.

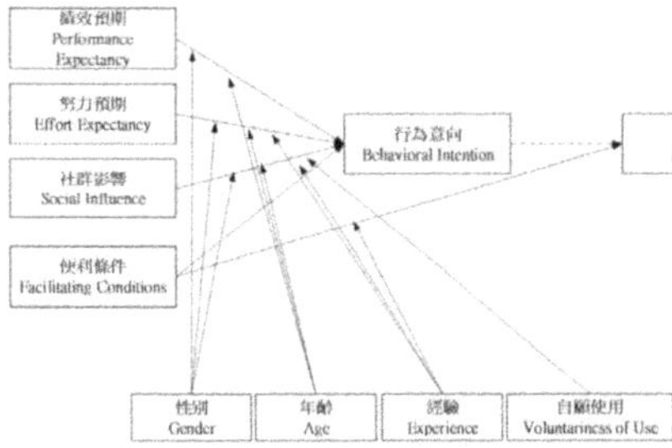

Figure 2. Unified theory of acceptance and use of technology (UTAUT).

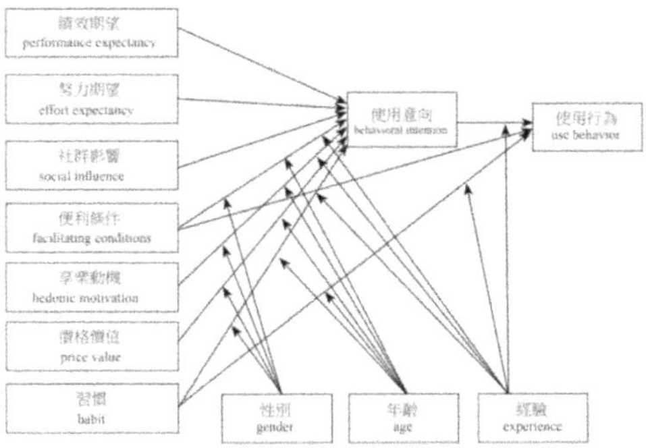

Figure 3. Extended UTAUT2 model.

2.6 *Summary*

Focusing on healthy/at-risk older adults (screened via EAT-10), this study employs UTAUT2 to analyze acceptance factors for CTAR-based gamified devices. Addressing limitations of current equipment (e.g., poor interactivity, lack of data tracking), it proposes a novel design integrating gamification with physiological monitoring to enhance adherence and rehabilitation outcomes.

3 METHODOLOGY

3.1 *Preliminary investigation and analysis*

Status Survey of Swallowing Rehabilitation Aids: Through literature review, we systematically analyzed the development and outcomes of swallowing rehabilitation aids to establish their design principles, functional mechanisms, and theoretical foundations. Market analysis was conducted to evaluate existing products, identifying their features, strengths, and limitations. Interviews with occupational therapists and speech-language pathologists were held to explore practical challenges in traditional devices, such as monotonous training protocols, lack of interactivity, and poor adjustability. These insights provided clinical perspectives and professional recommendations for novel device design.

Table 1. Therapist interview participants.

Institution	Experience	Title
Adile Physical Therapy Clinic	4–5 years	Occupational Therapist
NTUH Rehabilitation Department	4–5 years	Speech Therapist
Xiangxiang Speech Therapy Clinic	9 months	Intern Speech Therapist

User Profile Analysis: Participants aged 60+ (healthy individuals or those at risk of dysphagia) were screened using the EAT-10 Swallowing Screening Tool. This 10-item scale assesses swallowing function across dimensions including eating, drinking, and swallowing comfort to identify individuals with dysphagia risks. Participants scoring ≤ 3 were selected as the target cohort.

Identification of Influencing Factors: By synthesizing survey data and expert opinions, we identified key factors affecting user acceptance of swallowing rehabilitation technology. A hypothesis-driven "Technology Acceptance Model for Interactive Swallowing Rehabilitation Devices" was developed, systematically theorizing these factors to guide subsequent experiments and device design.

3.2 *Experiment*

3.2.1 *Product introduction videos*

Three demonstration videos (1280×720 pixel resolution, 30 fps frame rate) were produced to illustrate:

1. Device specifications: 360° rotating visualization of dimensions ($18\times12\times6$ cm^3) and adjustable neck strap (elastic modulus 2.1 MPa)
2. Functional demonstration: Animated overlay showing swallowing muscle trajectory monitoring (±0.3 mm spatial resolution)
3. Interactive scenarios: Gamified interface with adaptive difficulty algorithms (Fitts' Law-based) and real-time biofeedback (latency <50 ms)

3.2.2 *Technology acceptance assessment*

A mixed-methods study was conducted with 32 participants (age 68.5±5.2 years, 1:1 gender ratio):

1. Pre-screening phase:
   - Eating Assessment Tool-10 (EAT-10) screening excluded severe dysphagia patients (total score ≥ 15)
   - Informed consent obtained from eligible participants
2. Quantitative analysis:
   - 25-item UTAUT questionnaire using 7-point Likert scale (Cronbach's α=0.89)
   - Key scores: Performance Expectancy 4.32±0.61, Effort Expectancy 3.87±0.53
3. Qualitative investigation:
   - Semi-structured interviews transcribed and coded via Nvivo 12
   - Frequent feedback: adjustable vibration intensity (85% preference), diversified game levels (72% demand)

3.3 *Development of Novel Device*

3.3.1 *Data-driven optimization: Pareto analysis identified critical parameters:*

1. Ergonomic requirements: Device weight $\leq$ 300 g (meets 92% elderly grip strength thresholds)
2. Biomechanical constraints: Resistance range 5-35 N (covers 80% clinical training demands)
3. HCI standards: Touchscreen response time <0.2 s (ISO 9241-411 compliant)

3.3.2 *Cross-disciplinary collaboration*

Development integrated:

1. Clinical validation: Biweekly safety evaluations by therapist panel (n=6, IRB ethical review approved)
2. Industrial design: 12 housing prototypes via 3D printing, finalized with TPU/PC composite (Shore hardness 75D)
3. Software development: Unity-engine games with machine learning integration (CNN classification accuracy 96.4%)

3.3.3 *Iterative prototyping*

Final system components:

1. Smart terminal hardware:
   - 6-axis IMU sensor (LSM6DSO, ±16 g range)
   - Programmable linear actuator (0-30 mm stroke, 5 μm precision)
2. Interactive platform:
   - Adaptive difficulty system (Bayesian optimization-based)

- Data dashboard with SDK export (HL7 FHIR standard compatible)
- Emergency stop function (dual redundant physical buttons)

4 RESEARCH FINDINGS

4.1 *Participant characteristics*

The study included 30 participants aged 50 and above (8 males [27%], 22 females [73%]), with a mean age of 70 years (range: 50–91). Participants were recruited from the Senior University of Tatung University and surrounding communities.

4.2 *Technology acceptance questionnaire results*

Structural equation modeling via smartPLS revealed:

H1 (Effort Expectancy → Performance Expectancy) supported ($p<0.05$)
H2 (Performance Expectancy → Usage Intention) not supported ($p>0.05$)
H3 (Social Influence → Usage Intention) supported ($p<0.01$)
H4 (Hedonic Motivation → Price-Value) supported ($p<0.05$)
H5 (Price-Value → Usage Intention) supported ($p<0.01$)
H6 (Usage Intention → Usage Behavior) not validated

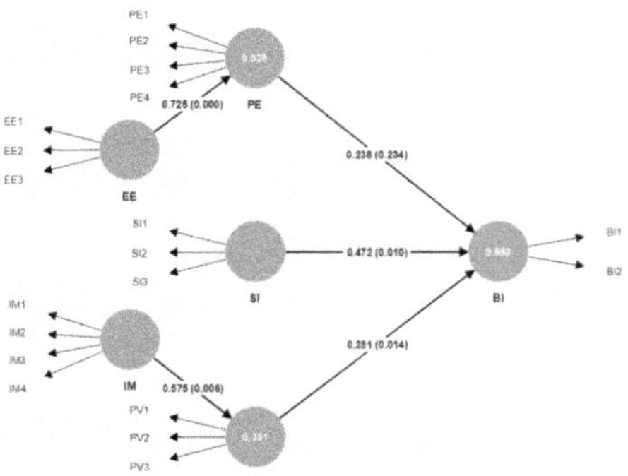

Figure 4. Technology acceptance analysis SmartPLS results.

5 CONCLUSIONS AND RECOMMENDATIONS

5.1 *Key conclusions*

Social recommendation (e.g., peer/family endorsements) significantly increased adoption intention.

Usage satisfaction enhanced perceived price value, driving sustained engagement.

Device ease of use positively influenced perceived usefulness, though most users lacked awareness of swallowing function changes, weakening the impact of performance expectancy.

5.2 *Recommendations*

Device design: Prioritize simplicity and affordability to broaden accessibility.

Game enhancements: Introduce multiplayer connectivity to leverage community-based promotion.

5.3 *Future research*

Compare outcomes with dysphagia patients to refine game difficulty levels.

Conduct mechanical analyses of chin-tuck angles, training gradients, and swallowing severity classifications to optimize rehabilitation protocols.

REFERENCES

Arakawa, I., Igarashi, K., Imamura, Y., *et al.* (2021), 'Variability in tongue pressure among elderly and young healthy cohorts: a systematic review and meta-analysis', *J. Oral Rehabil.*, 48, (4), pp. 430–448

Barcszi, S. R., Sullivan, P. A., Robbins, J. A. (2000). 'How should dysphagia care of older adults differ? Establishing optimal practice patterns', *Proc. Semin. Speech Lang.*, 21, (4), pp. 347–364

Blaxter, M.: 'The causes of disease: Women talking', *Soc. Sci. Med.*, 1983, 17, (2), pp. 59–69

Carnaby-Mann, G. D. and Crary, M. A., 2007). Examining the evidence on neuromuscular electrical stimulation for swallowing: a meta-analysis, *Arch. Otolaryngol. Head Neck Surg.*, 133, (6), pp. 564–571

Center for universal design: The Principles of Universal Design Version 2.0 (North Carolina State University, Raleigh, 1997)

Gaia: The laboratory for Games and Intelligent Animation (GAIA), George Mason University' (George Mason University Press, Fairfax, 2010)

Jiao, H., Mei, L., Liang, C., *et al.*, (2018), Upper esophageal sphincter augmentation reduces pharyngeal reflux in nasogastric tube-fed patients, *Laryngoscope*, 128, (6), pp. 1310–1315

Ji, J-Y. (2013). *Exploring factors influencing teachers' adoption of interactive whiteboards: An extended UTAUT model*, Master's thesis, Vanung University, Taoyuan (in Chinese)

Jiao, Y., Li, G. and Dai, Y. (2022), Clinical effect of repetitive transcranial magnetic stimulation on dysphagia due to stroke, *Neurol. Sci.*, 43, (5), pp. 3139–3144

Karsten, R. T., Ter beek, L. C., Jasperse, B., *et al.* (2021), MRI assessment of swallow muscle activation with the swallow exercise aid and with conventional exercises in healthy volunteers: an explorative biomechanical study, *Dysphagia*, 36, (1), pp. 41–53

Kilinç, H. E., Arslan, S. Demir, N., *et al.* (2020), The effects of different exercise trainings on suprahyoid muscle activation, tongue pressure force and dysphagia limit in healthy subjects, *Dysphagia*, 35, (4), pp. 717–724

Li, C. M., Wang, T. G., Lee, H. Y., *et al.* (2016), Swallowing training combined with game-based biofeedback in poststroke dysphagia, *PM&R*, 8, (8), pp. 773–779

Lin, K.-C. and Wu, C.-F. (2015), Practicing universal design to actual hand tool design process, *Appl. Ergon.*, 50, (1), pp. 8–18

Meng, N-X. (2020). Assessment and treatment of dysphagia, Special Lecture, Medical Ethics Committee of Fu Jen Catholic University Hospital, New Taipei City (in Chinese)

Park, J.-S., Lee, G. and Jung, Y.-J. (2019), Effects of game-based chin tuck against resistance exercise vs head-lift exercise in patients with dysphagia after stroke: an assessor-blind, randomized controlled trial, *J. Rehabil. Med.*, 51, (10), pp. 749–754

Pauloski, B. R. and Yahnke, K. M. (2022). Using ultrasound to document the effects of expiratory muscle strength training (EMST) on the geniohyoid muscle, *Dysphagia*, 37, (4), pp. 788–799

Pollard, K. A., Smith, A. R., Johnson, L. M., *et al.* (2020). Level of immersion affects spatial learning in virtual environments: results of a three-condition within-subjects study with long intersession intervals, *Virtual Real.*, 24, (3), pp. 1–14

Ren, J., Lv, D. and Liu, S., (2020), Progress in evaluation of swallowing function after treatment of head and neck malignant tumors, *J. Clin. Otorhinolaryngol. Head Neck Surg.*, 34, (9), pp. 861–864 (in Chinese)

Sura, L., Madhavan, A., Carnaby, G., *et al.* (2012), Dysphagia in the elderly: management and nutritional considerations, *Clin. Interv. Aging*, 7, (1), pp. 287–298

Venkatesh, V., Thong, J.Y., Xu, X. (2012), Consumer acceptance and use of information technology: Extending the unified theory of acceptance and use of technology, *MIS Q.*, 36, (1), pp. 157–178

Wang, J-M., Wu, Y-R. and Wang, T-G., (2021), Recent advances in dysphagia rehabilitation for Parkinson's disease: evidence-based treatment recommendations, *Taiwan J. Phys. Med. Rehabil.*, 49, (1), pp. 1–10 (in Chinese)

Yoon, W. L., Khoo, J. K. P., Liow, S. J. R. (2014). Chin tuck against resistance (CTAR): new method for enhancing suprahyoid muscle activity using a Shaker-type exercise, *Dysphagia*, 29, (2), pp. 243–248

Zyda, M., (2005), From visual simulation to virtual reality to games, *Computer*, 38, (9), pp. 25–32

System Innovation for a Global Economy – Lam et al. (Eds)

Study on hot water temperature control using remote control

Jui-Chang Lin
Department of Mechanical Design Engineering, National Formosa University, Yunlin, Taiwan

Cheng-Jen Lin
Institute of Mechanical and Electro-Mechanical Engineering, National Formosa University, Yunlin, Taiwan

ABSTRACT: This study uses IoT chips in conjunction with sensors and temperature control systems to build a remote water temperature monitoring system. This system can monitor water temperature through the mobile APP program, and upload and record the water temperature to the cloud server. This system includes: (1)Heating system: liquid heating rod, temperature display, relay, etc.; (2) Remote monitoring system: including server, mobile phone monitoring program, network line monitoring system, Bluetooth or WIFI module; (3) Hot water system: including inner and outer barrels and insulation device; (4) Internet of Things chip: including Arduino chip control card and other communication protocols. This system can be used in large-scale corporate hot water heating control systems or household hot water system, and can be remotely controlled and accessed via a mobile phone. Monitoring via a mobile phone APP has the following advantages: (1) Remote access to system heating status, record and query usage status. The data stored in the cloud can be used to analyze energy efficiency and provide policy decisions on energy consumption for the company. (2) Remote monitoring via mobile APP can help you detect heating system damage in advance and make repairs in advance. (3) Through statistical data, the heating temperature status can be adjusted, and the system can be optimized according to time and temperature changes to save energy. This study applies the APP for network monitoring management, temperature sensing and control, and data access control. The experimental statistical analysis shows that the average control temperature error is 3%. The data access time error is 3 seconds. Data access stability is over 99%.

Keywords: Remote Monitoring System, Hot Water System, IoT Chips, Statistical Data

1 INTRODUCTION

The core of the development trend of high-end water heaters lies in "customer experience meets demand". Any viable product is to continuously meet customer needs: (1) Smart interconnection: Smart interconnection technology has become the development trend of high-end water heaters. The rapid development of Internet of Things technology and smart APP has rapidly heated up smart home appliances and improved customer remote needs. Its customers can use their mobile phones to remotely control the hot water system, and can use it intelligently, log in and other functions. (2) Instantaneous heating circulation: One of the trends in high-end water heaters is instantaneous machines with hot water circulation function. (3) Higher safety configuration: The safety configuration of water heaters has always been one of the highest requirements. They are equipped with leakage protection, combustion detection, overheating protection, wide voltage safety protection, waterproof design, anti-burn protection, low water pressure start-up, intelligent antifreeze device, CO/NOx safety protection, etc. Higher safety configuration of products is always the development trend of high-end products [1–6].

2 EXPERIMENTAL METHODS AND DESIGN

The sensing system developed for electric water heaters for big data collection uses the physical structure of the electric heater to connect, and uses the existing temperature sensor and flow sensor installed inside the electric water heater. The electric water heater switch is activated to drive the potentiometer to measure the voltage size. The digital signal is then transmitted to the computer using the instruNet signal capturer. The program written by the compiled software is combined with the micro switch signal captured by the Arduino hardware platform to convert it into the corresponding hot water data. It can also be directly exported as an Excel file to facilitate the subsequent establishment of a database and data storage. The specifications are shown in Table 1.

DOI: 10.1201/9781003655534-10

Arduino Uno is suitable for developing various sensors or IoT applications.

Table 1. Arduino Uno specifications.

Mico-Switch	ATmega328P	Analog Iput Pins	6 Sets
Operating Voltage	5V	Each pin DC current	20 mA
Recommended Input Voltage	7-12V	3.3V Pin DC Current	50 mA
Maximum Input Voltage	6-20V	Memory	32 KB
Digital I/O Pins	14 Sets	PWM digital I/O Pins	6 Sets

The data acquisition device is temporarily used as instruNet Model 100, a product of GW Instruments, USA, or other data acquisition devices such as 8050, which has 8 channels and its specifications are shown in Table 2.

Table 2. Specifications of instruNet Model 100.

A / D Conversion Time	4μs min
Voltage Input Range	±5V, ±.6V, ± 78mV max (80 typ), ± 8mV max (10 typ)
Number of Channels	8di
Input Resistance	10Mohm±1%

3 EXPERIMENTAL DESIGN

The design of the sensing system proposed in this study includes: cloud monitoring, APP software design, security protection detection and intelligent software design, etc., and is mainly constructed based on the Internet of Things system architecture. The water volume sensor and water temperature sensor installed in the perception layer of the client water heater regularly transmit data to the host server APP of wireless communication. The host server APP also schedules to actively upload data to the cloud server. The cloud big data is the basis for building a smart energy-saving hot water reconnection system, a smart cloud APP system, and a smart monitoring system. The overall system hardware and software operation architecture is shown in Figures 1 and 2.

Figure 1. Sensing system design diagram.

Figure 2. Sensing system installation and setting.

4 RESULTS AND DISCUSSION

From Table 3, we know that the temperature control points for temperature measurement are 35°C, 40°C, 45°C, 50°C, 55°C, and 60°C. The temperature is measured 10 times at each control point as the average value, and the standard deviation is calculated.

Table 3. 6 Temperature control experiment data sheets.

Exp. NO.	Set Temperature	Measurement times	Measurement data	Average Error
1	35°C	10	36.2°C	3.18%
2	40°C	10	41.2°C	
3	45°C	10	46.4°C	
4	50°C	10	51.7°C	
5	55°C	10	56.8°C	
6	60°C	10	62.1°C	

Server data acquisition experiment: This experiment uses temperature heating at 35°C, 40°C, 45°C, 55°C, and 60°C to measure the accuracy of the controlled temperature and the correctness of the uploaded cloud data. A piece of data is uploaded every 3 seconds, and the experiment lasts for 3 minutes to capture data for analysis. The experimental results are shown in.

Table 4. Server data acquisition experiment.

EXP. NO.	Measurement Data Set Temperature	Storage Data Volume/3 MIN	Error Value	Average Error
1	35°C	59 DATA	1.67%	2.22%
2	40°C	59 DATA	1.67%	
3	45°C	58 DATA	3.33%	
4	50°C	59 DATA	1.67%	
5	55°C	58 DATA	3.37%	
6	60°C	59 DATA	1.67%	

5 CONCLUSION

This research is applied to remote control heating systems, which can save energy, electricity and manpower under intelligent management. The conclusions are as follows:

(1) Using the concept of the Internet of Things to remotely monitor the hot water system can save manpower and optimize processing to achieve power-saving control.
(2) The heating part can be directly managed by the sensing system and recorded by the cloud. The temperature error is within 5%.
(3) The number of cloud data storage records is less than 1%, and data can be calculated and saved. After the big data is collected in the future, it can be used to optimize the heating parameters of the system.

REFERENCES

[1] Vera T. L. J. T., and Siren K., (May 2014), Multi-objective optimization of hybrid photovoltaic-thermal collectors integrated in a DHW heating system, *Energy and Buildings.*

[2] Genjo S. T. K., Matsumoto S., Hasegawa K., and Yoshino H., (Mar 2005), Relationship between possession of electric appliances and electricity for lighting and others in Japanese households, *Energy and Buildings.*

[3] Chen Y.-C. C. C.-L., and Chan T.-S., (Jan 2014), Applying smart models for energy saving in optimal chiller loading, *Energy and Buildings.*

[4] Dominguez J. J. F. M., Alonso S., Prada M. A., Moran A., and Barrientos P., (Apr 2013), Power monitoring system for university buildings: Architecture and advanced analysis tools, *Energy and Buildings.*

[5] Android SDK, http://developer.android.com/.

[6] LeJOS, "Java for LEGO Mindstorms", http://lejos.sourceforge.net/, 2009.

System Innovation for a Global Economy – Lam et al. (Eds)
© 2026 The Author(s), ISBN 978-1-041-10520-6

Action research on integrating innovative constructivist teaching methods into the basic design practice in the multimedia design program

You-Shan Zhou
Graduate School of Design, National Yunlin University of Science and Technology, Yunlin, Taiwan

Chang-Franw Lee
Professor, Graduate School of Design, National Yunlin University of Science and Technology, Yunlin, Taiwan

ABSTRACT: This study aims to apply the action research model to explore the integration of innovative constructivist teaching methods into the "Basic Design Practice" course within the design group, with the goal of enhancing students' practical skills in Composition Techniques in Graphic Design. It also investigates the students' learning process and outcomes in the course. The participants were first-year students from the Multimedia Design Program at National Houbi High School in Tainan, Taiwan. The course consisted of one sessions per week over 18 weeks, totaling 54 sessions, with 30 participants and 270 learning sheets collected. The study was conducted from September 2024 to January 2025. Research methods included participatory observation, questionnaire surveys, interviews, and artwork content analysis. The results showed that: The innovative constructivist teaching method effectively enhanced students' learning interest and outcomes. Through a structured framework, group activities, and systematic review steps, students were able to achieve learning goals efficiently. Pre- and post-tests confirmed significant improvement. This approach offers valuable insights for designing the Basic Design Practice course and supports instructors in applying constructivist strategies, echoing the Bauhaus spirit of collaborative creativity.

1 RESEARCH BACKGROUND AND MOTIVES

Throughout global art history, the relationship between fine arts and design has always been closely intertwined. Before the Industrial Revolution, art and craft were often inseparable. Afterward, design gradually emerged as an independent discipline, focusing on functionality and practicality, while fine arts leaned more toward expression and aesthetics (Heskett 1980; Pevsner 1936). This division is also reflected in education systems, professional fields, and societal roles (Gropius 1965).In Taiwan, the development of design can be traced back to the Japanese colonial period, during which design concepts from Japan were introduced. In 1968, Shih Tsui-Feng published The Current Status of Design Education in Taiwan, noting that the foreign term "デザイン" (design) was translated into Chinese as "設計." This indicates that Taiwan began adopting the concept of "design" in the early 1950s. According to Professor Lai Chien-Tu (2001), design-related courses in Taiwan first appeared in the 1950s. At that time, the Department of Fine Arts at the National Academy of Arts already offered subjects such as Basic Design and Pattern Techniques (Lin 2009).

Over the decades, the main objective of Basic Design has remained consistent: to help students understand fundamental design knowledge and principles, and apply them in various design practices (Lee 2019). Since the Industrial Revolution, disciplines within the arts have become increasingly specialized. Courses in art and drawing typically focus on painting, design, printmaking, and ceramics, while craft and practical courses may include handicrafts, home economics, horticulture, and life-related content (Wang and Cheng 2011).Today, Taiwan's art and design education system includes not only formal fine arts programs, but also departments such as Commercial Design, Advertising Design, Multimedia Design, and Interior Design. All of these are rooted in the concept of Basic Design from the Bauhaus School, which has evolved into what is now known in Taiwan as Fundamental Design, officially titled Fundamental Design Practice under the 2019 Curriculum Guidelines (commonly referred to as the 108 Curriculum). Since 2001, Taiwan's Ministry of Education has required vocational students to take the Unified Entrance

DOI: 10.1201/9781003655534-11

Examination for Four-Year Technical Colleges and Two-Year Junior Colleges. In addition to core academic subjects such as Chinese, English, and Mathematics, the professional subjects are divided into a written section—Professional Subject (I), which includes Color Principle, Principle of Form, and Introduction to Design—and a practical section—Professional Subject (II), which includes Basic Design Practice, Basic Painting and Drawing, and Basic Drawing Practice (UEC-TVE 2024).

An analysis of Taiwan's current 2019 Curriculum Guidelines (commonly referred to as the "108 Curriculum") reveals that students in the Design Cluster are generally required to take a mandated core course titled Fundamental Design Practice. Moreover, Basic Design has become one of the most critical subjects in the national entrance examination for higher education. However, for many students, the theoretical content of this subject is typically taught by high school teachers following the textbook materials outlined by the 108 Curriculum. Based on teacher interviews, it was found that most instructors tend to adopt a "follow-the-syllabus" teaching approach.As a result, without effective guidance from design teachers, students—who are growing up in a technology-saturated, 3C (computer, communication, and consumer electronics) environment—may find it difficult to construct a complete and meaningful learning framework on their own. In the AI era, it becomes increasingly essential for design educators to develop innovative teaching systems that help students achieve tangible learning outcomes within a limited timeframe.This study therefore conducts an in-depth analysis of the curriculum focus and assessment content of Fundamental Design Practice. A summary of the findings is presented in Table 1 (Ministry of Education 2024).

Table 1. Key Learning Focuses of Design Cluster Subjects in Southern Taiwan High Schools for the 2024 Academic Year (Compiled by the Author) (Ministry of Education 2024).

Curriculum Objectives and Key Concepts (as defined by the 2019 Curriculum Guidelines by the Ministry of Education	
A. Basic concept of fundamental design	E. Formal principle of beauty
B. Elements of fundamental design	F. Visual effect presentation
C. Plane composition method	G. Graphic aided design
D. Principle and implementation of visual illusion	H. Graphic and text visual composition

The author, with over 30 years of experience in art and design, has observed through practical experience, design theory, and analysis of past examination questions that there exists a logical structure in the creative problem-solving process of design. To support students in both Fine Arts Classes and the Design Cluster in comprehensively mastering the core content of Basic Design Practice, and to help them cope more efficiently with examination pressure within a limited timeframe, the author has developed a specialized set of teaching materials and an innovative constructivist teaching strategy tailored for this subject. However, such innovation in curriculum and pedagogy cannot be achieved overnight. In reality, curriculum development is a cyclical process of exploration and accumulation of experience between teachers and students. Ralph W. Tyler (1902–1994), a pioneer in curriculum development, proposed a goal-oriented approach, viewing curriculum as a means to achieve educational objectives (Tsai 2015). In this traditional model, teachers implement the curriculum faithfully based on expert-designed plans and evaluate students' achievement of learning goals. Teachers were seen merely as implementers, lacking control over the curriculum, which led to concerns over de-skilling (Apple 1982).

Reviewing the historical evolution of curriculum development, this study summarizes several stages: (1) pre-1960s, teacher-dominated instruction; (2) post-1960s, emphasis on teacher-student collaboration; (3) post-1980s, focus on individual learning experiences (Tsai 2014). According to literature, postmodernist approaches to teaching consider the teacher not only as a designer and active researcher of the curriculum but also as a facilitator of student potential (Jao 1999). Grounded in the principles of postmodern curriculum development, this study applies a researcher-designed set of innovative constructivist teaching materials and methods to evaluate the efficiency and effectiveness of stude nt learning outcomes. The research focuses on integrating theoretical knowledge and practical skills in Basic Design Practice, aiming to enable students to quickly acquire design techniques through hands-on experience, deepen their subject knowledge, and enhance their professional competence and application ability.

2 RESEARCH PURPOSE

This study aims to develop an innovative constructivist teaching model for the Basic Design Practice course and to achieve the following specific objectives:

1. To construct an innovative constructivist teaching model that enables students to rapidly grasp theoretical knowledge of academic subjects and enhance their ability to apply such knowledge in practical skill assessments.
2. To apply action research methodology in developing effective teaching and learning

strategies suitable for students in the Design Cluster, and to conduct an in-depth analysis of changes in students' understanding of design techniques and their practical performance before and after instruction.

3 LITERATURE REVIEW

3.1 *Overview of the development of art and design education in Taiwan*

In early Taiwan, the distinctions among "art," "fine arts," and "design" were rather ambiguous. The term design originally evolved from the concepts of fine arts or patterns. According to Lin Pin-Chang (2009), the earliest subject related to design was known as "Drawing and Handicraft," established during the reign of Emperor Guangxu of the Qing Dynasty (1875–1910). The curriculum primarily focused on Chinese painting, Western painting, and pattern education. It was not until around 1952, in the mid-20th century, that the term design was formally established in Taiwan. Regarding art education, Tseng Hui-Yun (2020) pointed out that the Japanese colonial period marked the beginning of art education in Taiwan (Wu Kuo-Chun 1997; Chen Mu-Tzu 1998; Yang Meng-Che 2011). This historical process began in 1902, when drawing education was introduced at normal schools. The curriculum included areas such as decorative design and pattern drawing (Tsung Liang-Huan 1930). During this era, "drawing courses" emerged for the first time under Japanese rule, and within these courses, the "pattern drawing" component already hinted at the early forms and models of design (Tseng Hui-Yun 2020).

3.2 *Overview of the Development of Basic Design Curriculum in the West*

The history of foundational design education can be traced back to the Bauhaus. Its director, Walter Gropius, emphasized a pedagogical philosophy that integrated making and thinking through hands-on workshops. Students created visual compositions or forms based on aesthetic principles such as repetition, balance, unity, symmetry, rhythm, proportion, order, contrast, and harmony (Anandasivam 2005; Chu 1999; Lin 1990). Gropius believed that establishing a foundational curriculum was the key to institutionalizing this educational approach (Lupton and Miller 2019).

As a result, many schools, both in Taiwan and internationally, continue to follow this modernist educational model (Yang 2007). In Taiwan, the course title has evolved from Design Foundation or Basic Design to the officially approved term Fundamental Design Practice, as designated by the Ministry of Education. Based on a comparison with the Ministry's authorized Fundamental Design textbooks, the structure and content of the curriculum have shown little change since the founding of the Bauhaus. According to the Curriculum Guidelines for the Technical High School Design Cluster under the 12-Year Basic Education Program (Ministry of Education 2024), the Fundamental Design Practice course consists of eight core areas, which are outlined in Table 1.The Fundamental Design Practice curriculum encompasses a wide range of diverse learning content. This study focuses specifically on Unit H: Visual Composition of Images and Text (H. Graphic and Textual Composition). According to two key instructional guidelines outlined by the Ministry of Education: (1) group-based instruction must be implemented, and (2) students' fundamental design skills must be strengthened. These requirements not only align with the Bauhaus philosophy of collective creation, but also provide a crucial theoretical foundation for this action research. Therefore, group-based teaching will serve as a central element in this study. In response to the practical needs of the design cluster, this research will develop relevant lesson plans and teaching materials aimed at more effectively integrating them into course implementation.

3.3 *Action Research in Teaching*

Action research is regarded as an effective approach for educational practitioners to clarify and resolve issues arising from practice (Chen 1998). This methodology allows educators to conduct research within educational practice, taking innovative actions during the process to solve existing problems. At the same time, action research facilitates professional development and promotes bottom-up educational reform, leading to comprehensive progress and advancement (Tsai 2000b). During the course implementation and design process, teachers must take students' life experiences into account in order to help them integrate knowledge with personal experience and thereby develop appropriate curricula (Tsai 2015). In today's educational system, action research has become a widely adopted area of inquiry, and related studies are frequently published.

Yang (2001) noted that action research is highly appealing to practitioners and is considered a key strategy for enhancing professionalization. Yet, in the field of design education, few teachers employ action research for classroom observation, and the development of innovative, independent instructional systems for design education still requires further exploration.Accordingly, this study adopts an action research framework to explore the teaching process of the Fundamental Design Practice course. By integrating student feedback and teacher reflection, the study aims to support students in efficiently producing high-quality visual compositions that combine images and text.

3.4 *Constructivist Teaching Model*

The theoretical foundation of Constructivist Teaching is primarily rooted in the works of early 20th-century psychologists such as Jean Piaget (1896–1980) and Lev Vygotsky (1896–1934). However, it was the American educator Jerome Bruner (1915–2016) who truly applied constructivist theory to the field of education. In the 1960s, Bruner proposed the concept of discovery learning, emphasizing that students construct knowledge through exploration and problem-solving, rather than passively receiving information from teachers.For over sixty years, constructivist teaching has been widely practiced in Europe and the United States. In recent years, Taiwan's education system has increasingly valued the cultivation of students' independent thinking skills. Efforts have been made to introduce constructivist approaches from the U.S. into Taiwanese classrooms, thereby shifting the focus of education back to a learner-centered model (Cheng and Lee 2015).

Chou (2003) pointed out that learning must originate from intrinsic motivation in order to effectively construct knowledge. In this action research, the scaffolding method, a key constructivist strategy, is adopted to develop the instructional model. This theory of scaffolding is derived from Vygotsky's concept of assisted learning. Constructivist teaching also frequently incorporates cooperative learning, as posing problems to stimulate student thinking is central to the approach (Cheng and Lee 2015).If certain students are unable to complete a task independently, they may receive assistance from more capable peers within their zone of proximal development (ZPD). In such cases, the more advanced learners not only help others but also reinforce and internalize their own knowledge through the process of teaching. Therefore, this study argues that constructivist teaching methods are especially well-suited for contemporary secondary school students, who are often heavily influenced by digital devices and tend to have shorter attention spans.

4 RESEARCH METHOD

4.1 *Action research process*

This study adopts the participatory action research model proposed by Kemmis and McTaggart (1988) as its framework, aiming to address the challenges faced by teachers in real classroom settings. In postmodern pedagogy, teachers take on multiple roles as researchers, curriculum designers, and implementers (Stenhouse 1975). The research methods employed include: (1) participant observation, (2) pre- and post-test design, (3) field experiments, (4) analysis of student works. The research then progresses to the development of an innovative constructivist curriculum, instructional planning, and classroom implementation. Subsequently, student learning processes and outcomes are assessed through questionnaires, post-class interviews, and the analysis of completed learning worksheets. The action research strategy consists of five instructional steps: (1) building prior knowledge before class, (2) conducting pre-tests, (3) practicing with scaffolded worksheets during class, (4) group presentations, and (5) conducting post-tests. Throughout the action research cycles, continuous reflection and instructional adjustments are made to evaluate the effectiveness of teaching practices. The research framework and process are illustrated in Figure 1 (Research Framework).

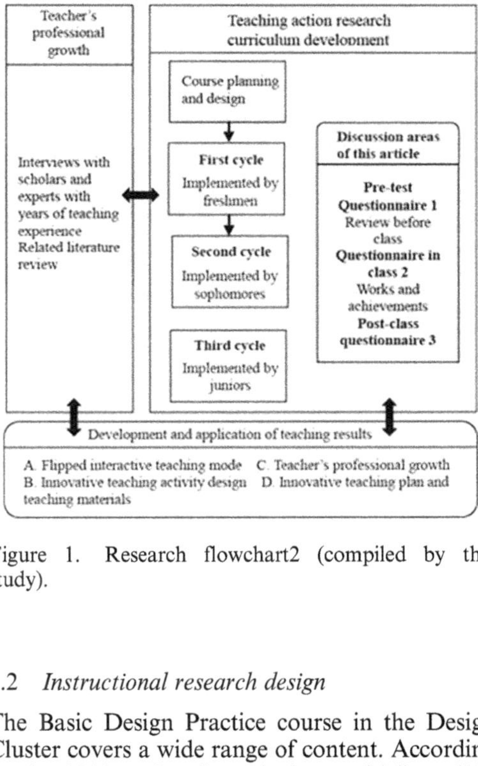

Figure 1. Research flowchart2 (compiled by this study).

4.2 *Instructional research design*

The Basic Design Practice course in the Design Cluster covers a wide range of content. According to the 2019 national curriculum guidelines (108 Curriculum), the course consists of two volumes with eight chapters (Chapters A to G; see Table 9). The topic Visual Composition of Text and Image is introduced only in the final chapter. Therefore, this study focuses specifically on Chapter H: Visual Composition of Text and Image, including (a) the process of integrating text and image design and (b) hands-on practice in visual composition. This study combines theoretical content from the course with insights from expert focus group interviews to build and apply a new teaching approach. Since assessment in the course "Basic Design Practice (Professional Subject II)" is usually based on the subjective judgment of the lead instructor, this study emphasizes the action research process of implementing the new teaching model, rather than evaluating students solely based on their final works. Finally, this research is inspired by the Bauhaus ideal of collective creativity, which serves as a guiding concept in the design and implementation of the curriculum.

5 RESEARCH FINDINGS AND DISCUSSION

Due to limitations in length, this section focuses directly on the presentation and interpretation of the key research findings.

5.1 *Literature review and analysis results*

Based on the results of the literature review, this study identifies and summarizes the key elements and definitions of basic design techniques in graphic and visual composition. Please refer to Table 2 for details:

Table 2 "Visual Elements of Graphic and Visual Composition" (Compiled in this study).

Core element group of the second subject of the unified test "Basic Design Practice"	
Image	Text
Concrete shape, abstract shape Course Outline: B. Basic Design Elements Figures, animals and other concrete pictograms often appear; followed by abstract shapes, such as: elements which composed of dots, lines and planes. Various composition methods are employed to position elements, arranged according to their visual importance.	Heading, middle heading, subheading, body text Course Outline: H. Text and Image Composition Arrange the position according to the visual focus and importance, and choose the font and bold according to the importance. Arrange the groups of characters using composition methods, organize their sequence and positioning according to their importance.
Literature source: C. Plane composition method, E. Principle of aesthetic form	Literature source: C. Plane composition method, E. Principle of aesthetic form
In the current curriculum, most teachers tend to follow the materials provided by the 108 Curriculum and implement a linear teaching approach, strictly adhering to the syllabus. This approach makes it difficult for students with lower attention spans to fully integrate and apply the concepts. To address this issue, this study draws on the theoretical framework of the Basic Design Practice course, employing the concept of a "layered hierarchical structure" to systematically summarize and analyze the above-mentioned elements.	

This study utilizes literature analysis and, through the "layered structure" strategy, groups design elements in a structured manner. For example, elements such as text, primary images, and supporting objects are categorized into different groups. These groups are further layered (e.g., Layer 1, Layer 2, Layer 3), with similar or related visual elements placed within the same conceptual layer to enhance their visual connectivity and overall consistency. The specific structure of group layering is illustrated in the figure below:

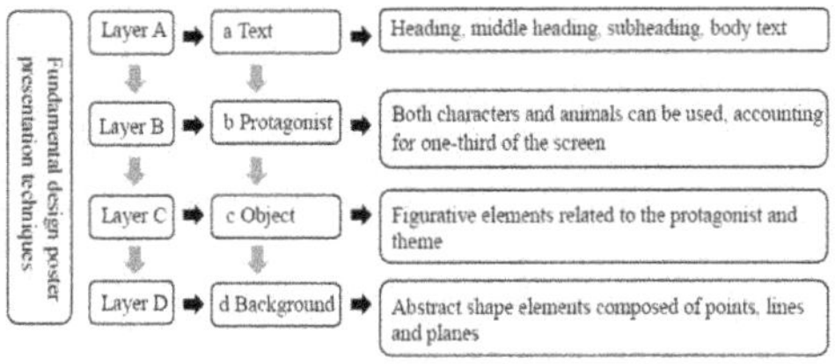

Figure 2. Standard process of graphic and text visual composition design group layering (designed by the author).

Table 3. Display of Students' after-class Works (Compiled in this study).

Achievements and analysis of students' after-class works	
Layer A: Main Subject (Group) → Layer B: Text (Group) → Layer C: Objects (Group) → Layer D: Background (Group)	

Work ID: NS2023-1-S007	Work ID: NS2023-1-S025

5.2 *Teaching field record*

Table 4. Teaching Demonstration Record of "Graphic and Text Visual Composition".

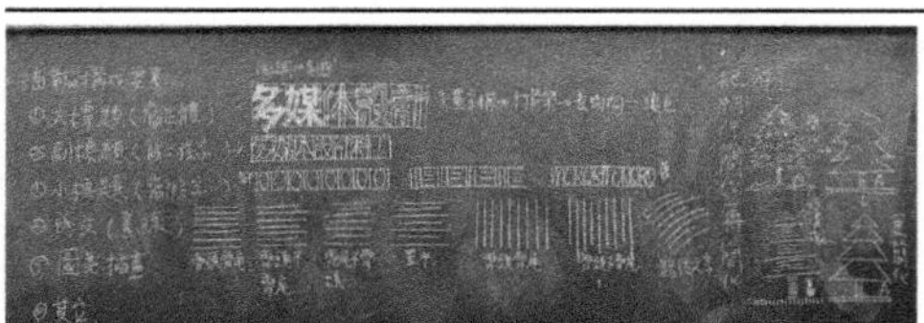

(*continued*)

Table 4. Continued

Instruction Description: Teacher Demonstration of "Basic Design Practice" 4-4 Layout Planning – Demonstration of Graphic and Text Visual Composition Elements

Lesson Description: Teacher Demonstration of "Basic Design Practice" 4-4 Layout Planning – Demonstration of Main Title Lettering Techniques

Lesson Description: Teacher Demonstration of "Basic Design Practice" 4-5 Graphic and Text Design and Drawing, and 4-6 Graphic-Text Integration and Composition Techniques

Lesson Description: Team Presentation Practice Record – Exercise on Elements of Graphic and Text Visual Composition

5.3 *Student worksheet record*

Table 5. Records of Student Worksheets from Pre- and Post-Instruction in Week 1 and Week 18.

NS2023-1-S001-Week1	NS2023-1-S001-Week18

Instructor's Rating: 65	Instructor's Rating: 95

The test results of this study show that through the teacher-designed curriculum and effective guidance of the constructivist teaching system, the same group of students made significant progress in both the pre-test and post-test of the innovative constructivist teaching course.

5.4 *Conclusion and Suggestions*

After this action research, the following conclusions were drawn:

1. The "Basic Design Practice" course has a strong practical nature. To enhance learning efficiency, this study developed a Constructivist Teaching Standard Operating Procedure (SOP) to help students gradually understand and master the design process.
2. The constructivist teaching model emphasizes a student-centered approach and incorporates a multi-stage, progressive teaching strategy. This method enables students to more easily construct knowledge structures during the learning process and apply what they have learned to their practical works, leading to deeper learning retention.
3. The course design of the innovative constructivist teaching model integrates theoretical instruction, worksheet exercises, and practical demonstrations. After the course, students showed significant improvement in their practical skills and enhanced their academic abilities in problem-solving processes.
4. Before the course, the instructor organized the scattered design theory knowledge in the "Basic Design Practice" syllabus and transformed it into systematic instructional content. Through the constructivist teaching method, students were able to absorb classroom knowledge and cultivate practical and integrative skills.
5. The constructivist learning method provided students with a clear and actionable design framework, further improving learning outcomes.
6. In group presentations and post-class worksheet tests, students were able to quickly recall and apply the steps taught by the instructor, successfully completing their test works. This demonstrates that the teaching model is not only practical but also helps students effectively cope with high-pressure exam situations.

REFERENCES

Anandasivam, K. (2005). Thinking with hands: Intuitive structural design. *In The 2005 IDSA National Education Conference [CD-ROM]*. IDSA.

Apple, M. W. (1982). *Education and Power*. Routledge & Kegan Paul.

Chen, H. (1998). *Educational Action Research*. Taipei: Shida Bookstore.

Chen, M. (1998). *History of Art Education in Taiwan*. Taipei: Huan Yu Publishing.

Chen, M., Li, M., and Lin, H. (2019). Basic design practice (Part 2). *New Taipei City: National Taiwan University of Science and Technology Publishing.*

Design Group Center (2024). *Design Group Center - Curriculum Guidelines.* Retrieved from https://vtedu.k12ea.gov.tw/nss/s/design/p/4
Gropius, W. (1965). *The New Architecture and the Bauhaus.* MIT Press.
Heskett, J. (1980). *Industrial Design.* Thames & Hudson.
Kemmis, S., and McTaggart, R. (1988). *The Action Research Planner (3rd ed.).* Geelong, Australia: Deakin University Press.
Li, M. (2019). *Basic Design Practice (Part 1).* Taipei: National Taiwan University of Science and Technology.
Lin, P. (1990). *Basic Design Education.* Taipei: Artist Publishing.
Lin, P. (2009). *Overview of Taiwan Design History Research.* Retrieved from https://www.nstc.gov.tw/nstc/attachments/f6202a40-ef4f-49fb-84fb-e1d9e1e633e6
Lupton, E., and Miller, J. A. (1991). The ABCs of Bauhaus: The Bauhaus and design theory. *Princeton Architectural Press.*
Ministry of Education and National Preschool Education Department (2019). *Curriculum guidelines for design courses in 12-year national education technical high schools.* Retrieved from https://vtedu.k12ea.gov.tw/uploads/16086947174643H4c9KRe.pdf
Mo, J., Sun, S., and Weng, Z. (2023). *Basic design practice (Part 2).* New Taipei City: Quanhua Publishing.
National Education Research Institute (2014). *General guidelines for the 12-year national education curriculum.* Retrieved from https://www.naer.edu.tw/PageSyllabus?fid=52
National Science and Technology Commission (2009). *Overview of Taiwan Design History Research.* Retrieved from https://www.nstc.gov.tw/nstc/attachments/f6202a40-ef4f-49fb-84fb-e1d9e1e633e6
Pevsner, N. (1936). *Pioneers of modern design: From William Morris to Walter Gropius.* Penguin Books.
Rao, J. (1999). The implementation strategy of the nine-year integrated curriculum and teacher professional development. *In Proceedings of the 9-Year Integrated Curriculum Conference - Towards a New Era of Curriculum* (pp. 305–323).
Shi, C. (1968). *Current situation of design education in Taiwan. IDEA Magazine*, January issue, p. 38.
Stenhouse, L. (1975). *An introduction to curriculum research and development.* Heinemann.
Tsai, Q. (2000). *Educational action research.* Taipei: Wu Nan Publishing.
Tsai, R. (2014). The meaning and critical issues of flipped classrooms in the digital age. *Educational Research and Development Journal*, 10(2), 115–138.
Tsai, R. (2015). Flipped classroom: Past, present, and future. *National Education Research Institute Educational Pulse Electronic Journal.* Retrieved from https://epaper.naer.edu.tw/edm.php?grp_no=2&edm_no=111&content_no=2510
Wang, L., and Zheng, M. (2011). Transformation and growth in Taiwan's visual education over a century. *Journal of Aesthetic Education*, 180, 11.
Wu, G. (1997). *Post-war Taiwan's art education in elementary and secondary schools (Doctoral dissertation).* National Taiwan Normal University, Taipei City, Taiwan.
Yang, M. (2007). Design basics: Teaching concepts and practices of basic design courses in universities. *Aesthetic Education*, 158, 14–21.
Yang, M. (2011). *Art classes under the sun: The process of Taiwan's Japanese colonial art textbooks.* Taipei: Nantian Publishing.
Yang, R., Chen, M., and Huang, L. (2001). The concept of action research and its application in nursing. *Journal of Medical and Health Science*, 3(3), 244–254.
Zeng, H. (2020). Post-WWII Taiwan's elementary school art education curriculum and teacher training research (Master's thesis). *National Changhua University of Education*, Department of Art Education, Changhua City, Taiwan.
Zheng, N., and Li, D. (2015). *Constructivist teaching with visual learning integration in pictographs course: A case study of Xing'an Elementary School's third-grade Chinese course.* Retrieved from https://aictw.wordpress.com/author/aictw/

System Innovation for a Global Economy – Lam et al. (Eds)

Analyzing the multisensory experience journey: When food culture meets the technology of immersive performance

Hsin-Ying Li & Li-Shu Lu
Department of Digital Media Design, National Yunlin University of Science and Technology, Dou-Liu, Yunlin, Taiwan

ABSTRACT: As an essential carrier of cultural memory, culinary culture has evolved with technological advancements, presenting new modes of interpretation. Multisensory technology has increasingly become a key tool of enhancing affective experiences and fostering cultural identity. This study utilizes technologies such as projection, sound, and lighting effects as sensory experience media, aiming to examine restaurants that create immersive dining experiences as research cases. The research focuses on five immersive restaurants: Ultraviolet by Paul Pairet, Sublimotion, MoonFlower Sagaya Ginza, The Alchemist, and Krasota, analyzing the current state and distinctive characteristics of technology applications and summarizing their operational models. This study primarily employs the comparative research method, exploring the operational model of integrating technology and culinary culture from three perspectives: Technology, food, and synesthetic design. It examines the application of multisensory technologies, the cultural representation and significance of ingredients and cooking techniques, as well as the integration and interaction of multisensory experiences, including sensory elements such as scent, lighting, and sound. The findings of this study are expected to serve as a reference for the development of immersive dining experiences and digital transformation applications.

Keywords: Multisensory Technology, Immersive Restaurant, Integration of Technology and Food Culture, Comparative Research Method, Synesthetic Design

1 INTRODUCTION

Digital technology and interactive media in the 21st century have provided new platforms for cultural expression. As a fusion of digital art and cultural innovation, immersive exhibitions are gradually becoming a vital form of cultural storytelling. Through multisensory interactions, immersive restaurants can reshape the imagery of food culture using visuals, sound, touch, and even smell and taste. This approach allows audiences to deeply engage with historical cultural contexts, transforming static culinary symbols into vivid, tangible sensory experiences. A prime example of a fully immersive dining experience that integrates technology and multisensory design is Ultraviolet by Paul Pairet (2012). As one of the earliest pioneers in this field, Ultraviolet's innovative model marked the beginning of a new era in the fusion of technology and food culture, setting a new standard for immersive dining experiences. With advancements in technology and the growing consumer demand for multisensory experiences, an increasing number of restaurants are incorporating similar interactive technologies to deliver unforgettable, immersive dining experiences.

1.1 *Multisensory dining*

As technology advances and sensory experiences deepen, dining is no longer merely a matter of taste; instead, it integrates light, sound, scent, and touch to create immersive culinary experiences. Therefore, this study aims to explore how immersive restaurants utilize technology to represent food culture. The research focuses on the following objectives: 1. Examining the operational model of integrating technology and food culture – Understanding the current status and operational models of immersive restaurants, including the application of multisensory technologies and the cultural representation of ingredients and cooking techniques. 2. Integration and interaction of multisensory experiences – Investigating how synesthetic design in immersive restaurants expresses the core essence of food culture.

The analytical framework of this study is structured around three key aspects: technology (multisensory technologies), food (ingredients and cooking techniques), and synesthetic design (the integration and interaction of multisensory experiences). These aspects will be examined to analyze how immersive restaurants shape unique dining experiences through these elements.

DOI: 10.1201/9781003655534-12

Technology serves as the core driving force behind immersive restaurant experiences, with multisensory technologies playing a particularly crucial role. This study will explore how different technologies impact diners' sense of immersion and analyze the role of technology in enhancing the food culture experience.

Food is the central component of the dining experience, not only as a vehicle for taste but also as a bearer of cultural significance. Immersive restaurants incorporate carefully selected ingredients and innovative cooking techniques to make food an integral part of the multisensory experience. This study will examine how these restaurants use ingredients and culinary techniques to present food culture and analyze the role of food in multisensory experiences.

Synesthetic design emphasizes the connection and interaction between different senses, allowing diners to develop deeper engagement and emotional resonance during their meals. This study will analyze how synesthetic design is applied in immersive restaurants and investigate its impact on customer experience and cultural identity.

By exploring these three aspects, this study will establish an analytical framework to evaluate how immersive restaurants utilize technology, food, and synesthetic design to create unique culinary experiences. It will also examine how these elements interact to enhance the overall sense of immersion.

This research focuses on immersive restaurants that use projection technology, sound, and lighting effects as sensory media to create immersive dining experiences. Five immersive restaurants have been selected for analysis: Ultraviolet by Paul Pairet, Sublimotion, MoonFlower Sagaya Ginza, The Alchemist, and Krasota.

The study will examine the application of multisensory technologies in these restaurants, with particular emphasis on how lighting and sound contribute to spatial design. It will also explore their roles in creating immersive experiences, evoking emotional resonance, and presenting the characteristics of food culture.

This study adopts a comparative research method as its primary approach to explore the application and impact of lighting and sound as sensory media in immersive restaurants. First, by collecting and organizing literature related to multisensory design and immersive experiences, this study establishes a theoretical foundation to support case analysis. Next, selected immersive restaurants serve as the research subjects for in-depth examination. During the comparative analysis, this study conducts a cross-sectional comparison of various elements, including lighting and sound technologies, ingredients and cooking techniques, pricing, thematic design, spatial planning, and experience processes. Through this comparison, the study identifies shared characteristics and differences, summarizing key factors and design models of contemporary immersive restaurants. Additionally, this research integrates theoretical discussions on immersive experiences to examine how these technologies interact with multisensory experiences, enhancing food culture innovation. By employing this research method, the study systematically analyzes the practical implementation of lighting and sound technologies in immersive restaurants, providing design recommendations and areas for improvement. The findings aim to offer both theoretical insights and practical guidance for the future development of immersive dining experiences.

2 LITERATURE REVIEW

Food culture, as an essential part of human daily life, reveals its potential in multisensory engagement and cultural representation when combined with immersive experiences. By integrating lighting, sound, scent, and tactile technologies, immersive experiences evoke strong emotional and sensory participation, allowing consumers to go beyond mere taste enjoyment and deeply perceive the cultural significance embedded in food (Pine and Gilmore 1999). As Bitner (1992) pointed out in his research, sensory stimuli in physical environments significantly impact customer emotions and behavioral responses, suggesting that sensory design in immersive experiences can effectively foster connections between culture and emotions.

Immersive experiences refer to multisensory design and interactive technologies that enable participants to immerse themselves in blended virtual and real environments, achieving a high sense of presence and engagement. Studies indicate that sensory immersion can be achieved through the integration of visual, auditory, and sometimes tactile elements (Dede 2009). Pine and Gilmore (1999) introduced the concept of the experience economy, emphasizing the importance of contextual design in creating emotional resonance. The growing trend of crafting unforgettable experiences is particularly prevalent in the tourism and dining industries, where many service providers strive to fulfill modern consumers' demand for unique and memorable experiences, rather than merely offering functional products and services (Han *et al.* 2022). Additionally, Gutiérrez *et al.* (2008) analyzed the development and challenges of immersive experiences from both interactive storytelling and technological application perspectives, providing a multidimensional reference for immersive experience theories and practices. Jinsop Lee's Five Senses Design Theory (2013) suggests that sensory-integrated design enhances audience engagement and immersion. A successful immersive exhibition may evoke surprise and delight through well-crafted spaces, but what remains unforgettable is often the "indescribable" holistic experience (Lee 2013). When conveying a specific experience, sensory design should be structured according to sensory attributes, which can be used to sequentially deliver experience content tailored to each sensory modality (Silvennoinen and Monone 2023).

In terms of technological applications in immersive experiences, projection mapping technology involves accurately mapping projected images onto irregular three-dimensional surfaces, creating unique visual effects and immersive experiences (Bimber 2005). 360-degree panoramic projection environments can enhance immersive dining experiences by dynamically adapting projection scenes to match menu changes, simulating various cultural atmospheres or natural environments, and offering diners a dual sensory experience of visuals and ambiance (Yemsi-Paillissé 2020). Regarding olfactory sensory engagement, numerous companies have developed aroma-diffusing tableware and systems to further enhance the dining experience (Spence and Youssef 2015). Specific scents can also influence the duration of a customer's stay in a restaurant, where operators might use fragrances like lavender to promote relaxation and increase consumer spending (Guéguen and Petr 2006). Moreover, olfactory elements contribute to extending the temporal engagement of diners in multisensory dining experiences (Spence 2022).

In the contemporary immersive dining industry, digital technology applications have not only transformed the presentation of food but have also elevated food culture into a new dimension. Restaurants are no longer merely places to consume meals; they have become multisensory convergence points, where visual, auditory, and tactile experiences intertwine with culinary elements to create unique dining atmospheres. The following restaurants illustrate the integration of digital technology with food culture in immersive dining practices.

Ultraviolet by Paul Pairet combines digital art with gastronomy, using visual and auditory effects to alter diners' perceptions of the dishes (Yemsi-Paillissé 2023). Similarly, Sublimotion integrates video mapping and projection technologies, along with the use of VR, merging the presentation of each dish with digital artistry (Hahn 2021). Compared to other restaurants, Le Petit Chef focuses primarily on projection mapping onto the dining table (Batat 2021). At The Alchemist, lighting, sound effects, projections, and theatrical elements are combined to make each dish feel like a carefully curated work of art (Yemsi-Paillissé 2023). The immersive experience designed by teamLab for MoonFlower Sagaya Ginza employs interactive projection technology and artificial intelligence (Salim 2022). TREE by NAKED yoyogi park creates an interactive space that blends trees with digital projections, enhanced by VR headsets and installation art (NAKED INC., n.d.). Krasota offers two different show experiences—one presenting a futuristic vision of human development and another reviving classical paintings—with table projections and 3D animations that reimagine iconic art styles (WRF Group, n.d.). Ephemera creates themed immersive dining scenes using projection mapping and scenographic elements (Ephemera Group, n.d.). Other examples include Cafe.bot, which combines robotics and artificial intelligence, using robot servers to deliver drinks and meals to guests (d'strict, n.d.).

Across immersive restaurants worldwide, digital technologies not only diversify the dining experience but also offer new interpretations and representations of food culture. These restaurants break the boundaries of traditional dining through a fusion of virtual reality, interactive technologies, and visual art.

This study selects immersive restaurants as the subjects of analysis primarily because these establishments redefine traditional dining experiences through the integration of digital technology and art. They demonstrate how food culture can be extended and innovatively interpreted in a contemporary, multisensory technological context. Rather than including all immersive restaurants that employ relevant technologies, this research focuses on five specific cases: Ultraviolet by Paul Pairet, Sublimotion, MoonFlower Sagaya Ginza, The Alchemist, and Krasota. These restaurants were chosen due to their clear and consistent use of multisensory technologies. Their similar technological foundations provide a coherent basis for examining how such technologies collectively shape the dining cultural experience.

3 IMMERSIVE CASE STUDY

This study adopts a comparative research method as its primary approach, selecting immersive restaurants that utilize projection technology, lighting, and sound effects as research subjects. The aim is to explore how multisensory technologies are applied in the representation and innovation of food culture. The selected case studies include five immersive restaurants: Ultraviolet by Paul Pairet, Sublimotion, MoonFlower Sagaya Ginza, The Alchemist, and Krasota. Through the collection and analysis of relevant literature, official sources, and media reports, this study examines how these restaurants employ multisensory interactive technologies—such as lighting, sound, and scent—to create powerful immersive experiences. The basic information of each case study is presented in Table 1.

Table 1. Basic Information of Immersive restaurant case studies.

Case Number	01	02	03	04	05
Case Name	Ultraviolet by Paul Pairet	Sublimotion	MoonFlower Sagaya Ginza	The Alchemist	Krasota
Location	China, Shanghai	Spain, Ibiza	Japan, Tokyo	Denmark, Copenhagen	UAE, Dubai
Using Technologies	Projection mapping, Sound System, Fragrance System	Projection mapping, Sound System, VR	Projection mapping, Sound System, AI,Motion Interaction	Projection mapping, Sound System	Projection mapping, Sound System, AI, Motion Interaction
Ingredients and Cooking Techniques	French haute cuisine techniques and ingredients, Chinese-French fusion cuisine	French haute cuisine techniques and ingredients, Spanish-style molecular gastronomy	Premium wagyu and seasonal Japanese ingredients, Japanese culinary techniques	Seasonal Nordic ingredients, Minimalist style	French haute cuisine techniques and ingredients, Traditional Middle Eastern ingredients and cooking methods
Experience	20 courses in 4 acts/ 6 hrs	20 courses/ 3 hrs	9 courses/ 3 hrs	50 shows&courses/ 6 hrs	8 courses/ 2 hrs

4 ANALYSIS AND DISCUSSIONS

4.1 *Applications of multisensory technologies*

These five immersive restaurants share a core concept in their use of multisensory technologies: enhancing immersion through advanced technology. However, each restaurant differs in its approach and purpose of technological application. Ultraviolet uses full-scale projections, lighting, surround sound, and scent diffusion systems to fully immerse diners in scenarios corresponding to each dish. Sublimotion takes dramatic immersive technology further by combining projection with real-world transformations, creating highly theatrical dining experiences with a strong sense of narrative and surprise. MoonFlower Sagaya Ginza and Krasota employ interactive digital art technologies; their AI and sensing systems allow the dining environment to respond to diners' movements in real time, enabling immediate interaction with the space. The Alchemist emphasizes a fusion of science and art, guiding diners' sensory perceptions through light and sound changes, molecular gastronomy, and specific audio frequencies to explore the relationship between food and biological responses.

Overall, while all five restaurants utilize multisensory technologies to enhance immersion, each emphasizes different technical aspects. These range from environmental control, interactive technologies, and theatrical storytelling to sensory experiences, projection design, and digital art—each showcasing a unique conceptual direction in immersive dining.

4.2 *Cultural representation and significance of ingredients and cooking techniques*

Ultraviolet uses French haute cuisine to support its immersive storytelling. Each dish is meticulously crafted to emphasize layers and textures through taste, temperature, and presentation, strengthening the narrative behind each course. Sublimotion focuses on Spanish molecular gastronomy, combining science and art with techniques like liquid nitrogen, foaming, and sous-vide to challenge traditional culinary practices and highlight Spain's innovative culinary culture. Krasota, while also based on French fine dining, incorporates international fusion cuisine. Each dish draws inspiration from global art styles and integrates ingredients and techniques from various cultures, with projection art emphasizing their cultural contexts. MoonFlower Sagaya Ginza centers on Japanese kaiseki, highlighting seasonal ingredients and aesthetic presentation, while combining interactive digital art to reflect Japan's reverence for nature, seasons, and aesthetics. The Alchemist underscores food philosophy and environmental awareness, applying New Nordic cuisine principles, using sustainable local ingredients, and addressing social and ecological issues.

Overall, the five restaurants present diverse cultural expressions through food and culinary techniques. Ultraviolet is rooted in French fine dining but incorporates Chinese culinary methods; MoonFlower Sagaya Ginza and The Alchemist both emphasize the relationship between ingredients and the environment—SAGAYA leans toward Japanese aesthetics, while The Alchemist is more experimental and critical. Sublimotion and Krasota use multicultural and technological approaches: the former dramatizes food transformation, while the latter interprets the cultural context of ingredients through artistic styles. These similarities and differences reflect each restaurant's cultural foundation and technological direction, demonstrating the global diversity in immersive dining development.

4.3 *Integration and interaction of multisensory experiences*

In terms of visual and spatial immersion, Ultraviolet matches each dish with a specific scene—such as desert, ocean, or Paris streets—combining visuals with culinary storytelling to immerse diners in the narrative. Sublimotion centers its visual design on theatrical storytelling, swiftly transitioning scenes from ancient palaces to futuristic cities with lighting and holographic projections that dynamically transform the dining table. MoonFlower Sagaya Ginza uses dynamic digital projections to allow real-time interaction between diners and their surroundings. The Alchemist emphasizes atmospheric and contemplative visual design, using dome projections, video art, and lighting changes to connect food with global issues like sustainability and social justice. Here, visual effects act not only as ambience tools but as catalysts for reflection. Krasota adopts artistic immersive projections, pairing each dish with a specific art style—such as Impressionism or Surrealism—turning the dining table into a canvas and immersing guests in an art exhibition.

In sound and musical atmosphere, Ultraviolet employs surround sound to synchronize music, ambient sounds, and voice narratives. For example, seafood may be accompanied by ocean waves, enhancing taste and sight through sound. SAGAYA uses traditional Japanese instruments and nature sounds to create a tranquil, flowing atmosphere. Sublimotion enhances dramatic tension with cinematic music and sound effects—surprising elements are often accentuated with sudden sound changes. The Alchemist uses calm or provocative soundscapes, sometimes immersing diners in silence to highlight food details, or intensifying impact through electronic music to emphasize political or environmental themes. Krasota synchronizes sound design with visual art styles—Impressionist dishes may feature soft classical music, while Cubist ones may be accompanied by experimental modern compositions, deepening the artistic experience.

In summary, all five immersive restaurants integrate multisensory design to elevate the dining experience, though their conceptual approaches and technical implementations differ. Common elements include projection, lighting, and sound to shape visual and auditory immersion. Ultraviolet incorporates scent, MoonFlower Sagaya Ginza and Krasota use interactive sensors, and The Alchemist adds theatrical elements to intensify the experience. The differences lie in each restaurant's stylistic and purposeful application: Ultraviolet, MoonFlower Sagaya Ginza, and Sublimotion emphasize immersive storytelling that draws diners into a narrative world. The Alchemist focuses on environmental and social topics, making multisensory design a tool for critical thought. Krasota transforms dining into a visual and gustatory art exhibition through themed art styles. These variations reveal that while multisensory technology is central to immersive dining, its application remains highly flexible and creative.

5 CONCLUSIONS

This study compares and analyzes five immersive restaurants to explore how immersive dining combines technology and multisensory design. It summarizes operational models of immersive restaurants and aims to offer insights for future developments in experiential dining and digital transformation.

5.1 *Multisensory design and technological applications in immersive dining models*

By analyzing these five cases, the study identifies a clear operational pattern centered on multisensory design, including visual projection, sound design, scent diffusion, interactive technologies, and tactile experiences. These sensory stimuli are not randomly presented but carefully arranged following a ritual-like structure: Preparation – Transformation – Climax – Conclusion, guiding diners through emotional and sensory transitions.

Technology plays a crucial role by enabling precise control over the dining atmosphere through projection, virtual reality, AI-generated environments, and lighting and sound systems. Multisensory design is tightly synchronized with the pacing of each dish, transforming food into a medium for storytelling and cultural expression.

Overall, immersive restaurants construct experiences through multisensory and digital technologies, enhancing the entertainment and sensory richness of dining while shaping a ritualistic culinary environment.

5.2 *Reference for experiential dining and digital transformation*

This study reveals how immersive dining redefines the culinary experience through technological innovation and cultural integration, potentially influencing the future direction of the food and beverage industry. Focusing on the application of immersive exhibitions and digital technologies in the representation of food culture, this study achieves the following:

1. Explores the operational model of integrating technology and food culture.
2. Investigates how multisensory design (such as scent, light and shadow, and sound) is used in immersive dining to recreate the core essence of food culture.

REFERENCES

Almerico, G. M. (2014). Food and identity: Food studies, cultural, and personal identity. *Journal of International Business and Cultural Studies*, 8, 1. https://citeseerx.ist.psu.edu/document?repid=rep1&type=pdf&doi=d18391873c365730a1e31e1b0583971396e6083d

Anne-Claire Yemsi-Paillissé. (2020, July 10). Multisensory restaurants, Art and Tourism - Case study on Ultraviolet by Paul Pairet. *Contemporary Asian Artistic Expressions and Tourism*. 271–288. https://link.springer.com/chapter/10.1007/978-981-15-4335-7_13

Anne-Claire Yemsi-Paillissé. (2023). Fine dining multi-sensory restaurants and intermediality: an exploratory case study on Ultraviolet and The Alchemist. *International Journal of Gastronomy and Food Science*, *35*, https://doi.org/10.1016/j.ijgfs.2024.100882

Batat, W. (2021). How augmented reality (AR) is transforming the restaurant sector: Investigating the impact of "Le Petit Chef" on customers' dining experiences. *Technological Forecasting and Social Change*, 172, 121013. https://doi.org/10.1016/j.techfore.2021.121013

Bimber, O. (2005). *Spatial augmented reality: merging real and virtual worlds*. AK Peters.

Bitner, M. J. (1992). Servicescapes: The impact of physical surroundings on customers and employees. *Journal of Marketing*, *56*(2), 57–71. https://doi.org/10.1177/002224299205600205

d'strict. (n.d.) café.bot. https://www.dstrict.com/COMMERCIAL/?bmode=view&idx=7999668

Dede, C. (2009). Immersive interfaces for engagement and learning. *science*, *323*(5910), 66–69. https://www.science.org/doi/10.1126/science.1167311

Ephemera Group. (n.d.) Ephemera. https://en.ephemera-group.com/

Guéguen, N. and Petr, C., (2006). Odors and consumer behavior in a restaurant, *International Journal of Hospitality Management*, Volume 25, Issue 2, 335–339. https://doi.org/10.1016/j.ijhm.2005.04.007

Gutiérrez, M., Vexo, F., and Thalmann, D. (2008). *Stepping into Virtual Reality*.

Hahn, K. (2021). *Augmented and Reduced Realities*. In: Social Digitalisation. Palgrave Macmillan, Cham. https://doi.org/10.1007/978-3-030-79867-3_6

Hall, S. (1997). *Representation: Cultural Representations and Signifying Practices*. https://www.semanticscholar.org/paper/Representation%3A-Cultural-representations-and-Hall/4ad02a43ad5923ead74b7a37914e4d617d460d8f

Han, D.-I. D., Boerwinkel, M., Haggis-Burridge, M., and Melissen, F. (2022). Deconstructing immersion in the experience economy framework for immersive dining experiences through mixed reality. *Foods*, *11* (23), 3780. https://doi.org/10.3390/foods11233780

Jinsop Lee. (2013, February). *Design for all 5 senses*. https://www.ted.com/talks/jinsop_lee_design_for_all_5_senses

Le petit chef. (2025). https://www.lepetitchef.com/

NAKED, INC. (n.d.). TREE by NAKED Yoyogi park. https://tree.naked.works/

Pine, B. J., and Gilmore, J. H. (2011). *The experience economy*. Harvard Business Press.

Reddy, G. and van Dam, R., Food, culture, and identity in multicultural societies: Insights from Singapore, *Appetite*, Volume 149, 2020, 104633, ISSN 0195-6663, https://doi.org/10.1016/j.appet.2020.104633

Salim, P. (2022). *Immersive Technology Study As A Science Innovation to Enhance Modern Dining Experience*. [Conference presentation]. *3rd Asia Pacific International Conference on Industrial Engineering and Operations Management*. https://doi.org/10.46254/AP03.20220505

Silvennoinen, J., Mononen, L. (2023). Multisensory MAYA – A Design Thinking Method to Enhance Predictability of Experience Design. In: Marcus, A., Rosenzweig, E., Soares, M.M. (eds) Design, User Experience, and Usability. HCII 2023. *Lecture Notes in Computer Science*, vol 14030. Springer, Cham. https://doi.org/10.1007/978-3-031-35699-5_23

Spence, C. (2022). On the use of ambient odours to influence the multisensory experience of dining. *International Journal of Gastronomy and Food Science*, *27*, 100444. https://doi.org/10.1016/j.ijgfs.2021.100444

Spence, C. and Youssef, J. (2015). Olfactory dining: designing for the dominant sense. *Flavour* 4, 32. https://doi.org/10.1186/s13411-015-0042-0

Sublimotion. (n.d.). https://sublimotionibiza.com/

teamLab. (n.d.). MoonFlower Sagaya Ginza by teamLab. https://moonflower-sagaya.com/en/

The Alchemist. (n.d.) https://www.alchemist.dk/

Ultraviolet by Paul Pairet. (n.d.). https://uvbypp.cc/

WRF Group. (n.d.) Krasota. https://krasota.art/

Yu, Y., and Sen, Z. (2023, March). Research on Immersive Dining Space Design Based on New Media Digital Technology. *In Proceedings of the 2nd International Conference on Information, Control and Automation, ICICA 2022, December 2-4, 2022, Chongqing, China*. http://dx.doi.org/10.4108/eai.2-12-2022.2327948

System Innovation for a Global Economy – Lam et al. (Eds)
© 2026 The Author(s), ISBN 978-1-041-10520-6

How different signage designs influence public perceived effectiveness

Pei-Yu Liu & Meng-Cong Zheng
Department of Industrial Design, National Taipei University of Technology, Taipei, Taiwan (R.O.C.)

ABSTRACT: With increasing consumer demand leading to a significant rise in waste generation, the prevalence of littering has also escalated. To mitigate this issue, public spaces frequently install signage with communicative functions; however, noncompliance remains a persistent problem. This study examines the perceived effectiveness of existing no littering signages and proposes design optimizations. A quantitative analysis was conducted using 167 survey responses to understand public perceptions of waste disposal. Additionally, 18 pieces of signage content were analyzed to explore the impact of emotional responses on compliance with instructions. Finally, semi-structured interviews were conducted to gain deeper insights into participants' perceptions. The findings indicate that public consensus on waste disposal reaches 72.4%. However, the perceived effectiveness of signage varies across different age groups. Only two signage contents elicited consistent perceptions across all age groups: fear and compliance with instructions. The signage content "Technological Enforcement in Progress" had the highest compliance with instructions rate, as it not only evoked fear but was also positively associated with feelings of shame. Interviews revealed that participants felt afraid due to their uncertainty about the specific "technology" being implemented. While previous research suggests that higher message clarity enhances the perceived effectiveness of sign, this study found that ambiguous wording can still lead to high perceived effectiveness. The signage content "Littering in Secret, but the Deities See It" elicited interested among participants. Based on these findings, this study recommends that signage design should incorporate regional cultural considerations to align with public perceptions and effectively reduce littering behavior.

1 INTRODUCTION

When waste is not properly disposed of in trash bins, it becomes a source of environmental pollution (Reno 2015). Recent studies have also discovered the presence of microplastics in tropospheric air (Paris 2021), posing potential health risks to humans. Furthermore, increasing consumer demand has led to a significant rise in waste generation in recent years (Barles 2014) , accompanied by a steady rise in littering cases in Taiwan (Wu 2021). However, waste management has historically been a moral and political issue, often constrained by financial barriers (Pollans 2017; Reno 2015). To address this issue, public spaces frequently install signage, which serves as a cost-effective maintenance tool with communicative functions (McDougall *et al.* 1999). Nevertheless, noncompliance remains a persistent problem (Wu 2021).

Through a synthesis of factors influencing littering behavior, this study identifies human cognition as the fundamental starting point. The Focus Theory of Normative Conduct suggests that activating social norms can effectively reduce littering behavior (Cialdini *et al.* 1990). This activation process involves the interplay between cognitive and emotional factors (Han *et al.* 2017). Previous research has confirmed that emotions can directly motivate pro-environmental and pro-social behaviors (Han *et al.* 2017; Rees *et al.* 2014). For instance, emotions such as pride, guilt, and shame play significant roles, with negative emotions demonstrating a stronger effect—especially when targeting audiences engaged in preventing socially undesirable behaviors. In particular, the use of threat appeals has been shown to be highly effective (Flechsenhar *et al.* 2022). From a communication perspective, witty posters are preferred over authoritarian ones and are perceived as more effective (Hansmann and Steimer 2015). Craig and Leland Jr. (1983) further demonstrated through experiments that aesthetically appealing waste disposal posters promote higher compliance with waste management behaviors. According to Meis and Kashima (2017), the transition from "understanding" a sign's message to making a "decision" to act upon it is influenced by how clearly the behavior is represented. Thus, the clearer the intended purpose of a sign, the more predictable its impact, and the higher its perceived effectiveness.

This study examines the perceived effectiveness of existing no littering signage and proposes design optimizations. A quantitative survey was conducted to understand the public's perceptions

DOI: 10.1201/9781003655534-13

and awareness of legal regulations and waste disposal attitudes. Additionally, statistical analysis and sample interviews were employed to assess the perceived effectiveness of current signage, serving as a foundation for signage optimization.

2 EXPERIMENTAL

This study conducted a quantitative analysis through an online survey titled *"Survey on the Perceived Effectiveness of Existing No Littering Signage."* The objective was to understand the public's perceptions and awareness of legal regulations and waste disposal attitudes while assessing the perceived effectiveness of existing no littering signages. A statistical analysis was performed to explore the impact of emotional responses on compliance with instructions. Additionally, semi-structured interviews were conducted to gain deeper insights into participants' perceptions. These findings collectively serve as a foundation for evaluating the perceived effectiveness of current signages and informing recommendations for signage optimization.

The questionnaire was designed specifically for this study. The emotional agreement scale utilized a five-point Likert scale, and an indirect questioning techniques was applied by referring to the general public as "citizens." The questionnaire comprised three main sections.

The first section gathered demographic information and assessed legal awareness. This was conducted anonymously and included demographic variables such as gender, age, and highest educational attainment. Considering regional cultural factors, including religious beliefs (six specified religions, other religious beliefs, and non-religious), the survey also included questions on legal awareness, perceptions of legal penalties (fines) and reward incentives for reporting.

The second section focused on the perceived effectiveness of existing no littering signages. As shown in Table 1, current signages exhibit considerable diversity in presentation and content complexity. Therefore, this study deconstructed and categorized signage messages into six major types, as presented in Table 2. To ensure objective evaluation, participants were not informed of these categories, and the 18 signages were presented in randomized order within the questionnaire. The measurement items were adapted from previous studies that identified five emotions influencing littering behavior reduction: afraid, ashamed, guilty, proud, and interested. Additionally, this study incorporated compliance with instructions as an indicator of perceived effectiveness, referencing Meis and Kashima (2017).

Table 1. Collection of existing no littering signage.

Example	Content Translate
	Technological Enforcement in Progress. Don't put the garbage outside the trash can. Violators may be fined up to NT$6,000. Keelung City Environmental Protection Bureau.
	Littering in Secret, but the Deities See It. Hukou Cleaning Team Rminds You – Advertisement.
	Littering is Forbidden. Show Public Morality, We Can All Do It! Maximum Fine of NT$6,000 for Violators. This area is under surveillance. New Taipei City Environmental Protection Bureau & Xinzhuang District Cleaning Team. Report Hotline 2201-9811.
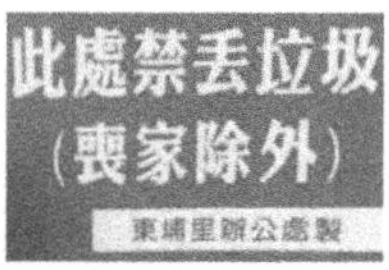	No Littering Here. (Except for Bereaved Families). Produced by Dongpu Village Office.
	Beautiful mountains, clean water, and fresh air—please help protect them. Restore the mountains to their natural state by taking your trash with you. Produced by Taichung County Transportation and Tourism Bureau & Daxueshan Community Development Association.
	Notice. On October 20, 2021, the Environmental Protection Bureau and the Police Department conducted an on-site crackdown on individuals illegally dumping household waste in this area. Joint inspections will continue to be carried out irregularly. Please do not violate the law. We urge everyone to uphold public morality and refrain from disposing of household waste, which causes environmental pollution. This area is under surveillance and enforcement. Unauthorized disposal of household

(continued)

Table 1. Continued

Example	Content Translate
	waste and other refuse is strictly prohibited. Violators will be prosecuted under the Waste Disposal Act and may be fined up to NT$6,000.

Table 2. Compilation and classification of existing no littering signage content.

Code	Existing Signage Content
A. Thematic Keywords	
A1	Strictly Prohibited from Disposing of Waste
A2	Do Not Litter
A3	Littering is Forbidden
B. Legal Warnings	
B1	Violators Will Be Prosecuted by Law
B2	Violators Will Be Fined According to the Waste Disposal Act
B3	Maximum Fine of NT$6,000 for Violators
C. Social and Emotional Constraints	
C1	Show Public Morality, We Can All Do It
C2	Littering is Prohibited, Except for Mourning Families
C3	Littering in Secret, but the Deities See It
C4	Children Are Learning – Accumulate Virtue for Future Generations and the Environment
D. Environmental Protection	
D1	Protecting Our Homeland Requires Collective Effort
D2	Littering Causes: Degradation of City Aesthetics, Blockage of Drains and Sewers, Pollution of Rivers and Oceans, Disruption of Natural Ecosystems
E. Surveillance Warnings	
E1	Technological Enforcement in Progress
E2	Under Surveillance
F. Institutional Announcement	
F1	Report Hotline: 1999
F2	Issued by the Environmental Protection Bureau of XX City
F3	Issued by the XX District Cleaning Team
F4	Joint Enforcement by the Environmental Protection Bureau and Police Department

The third section examined public attitudes toward waste disposal. The questionnaire items on personal norm (2 items) were adapted from Godin *et al.* (2005), while items related to self-managing behavior (3 items) and other-managing behavior (2 items) were referenced from Rosenthal and Ho (2020).

A total of 187 questionnaire responses were collected. After filtering out inconsistent responses, 167 valid samples were retained. Participants were categorized into three age groups: 18–40 years old (n = 74), 41–64 years old (n = 50), and 65 years and older (n = 43). First, a reliability analysis was conducted on the emotional agreement scale, yielding a Cronbach's Alpha of .981, indicating high internal consistency. As a result, no items were removed, and subsequent statistical analyses proceeded directly. To assess public perceptions of legal awareness and waste disposal attitudes, descriptive statistics were applied to the first and third sections of the questionnaire. Further subgroup analyses were conducted (excluding n=1) and included age, highest educational attainment, and religious beliefs. To evaluate the perceived effectiveness of existing no littering signages, descriptive statistics were first applied to the second section, followed by an age-based subgroup analysis. The relationship between emotional responses and compliance with instructions was examined using Pearson correlation analysis, while regression analysis was employed to predict potential causal relationships. This approach assessed both the influence of signage messages and their perceived effectiveness.Finally, to ensure that the quantitative findings accurately reflected participants' real-world perspectives, five participants (aged 25–62 years) were selected for semi-structured interviews. These findings collectively inform recommendations for optimizing no littering signage design.

3 RESULTS AND DISCUSSION

Through statistical analysis, this study has identified public perceptions of legal awareness and waste disposal attitudes. Regarding legal awareness, respondents rated the perceived effectiveness of fines at an average score of 3.87, slightly higher than the reward incentives for reporting littering violations at 3.75. Across both items, the proportion of respondents selecting 4 or 5 points averaged 62.6%. Regarding waste disposal attitudes, the *"personal norm"* category had an average score of 4.81. *"Self-managing behavior"* varied by location, averaging above 4.17, while *"other-managing behavior"* averaged above 3.37. Across all seven items, the proportion of respondents selecting 4 or 5 points averaged 72.4%, indicating a 70% consensus level on waste disposal attitudes. Further subgroup analysis based on individual differences (age, highest educational attainment, and religious beliefs) revealed that the average score for legal awareness was at least 3.52, while the average score for waste disposal attitudes was at least 3.41. This suggests that, overall, public awareness of legal regulations is relatively strong.

Regarding the perceived effectiveness of signage, a reliability analysis examining the correlation between item scores and total scores revealed that Signage content A1 ("Strictly Prohibited from Disposing of Waste") and Signage content E1 ("Technological Enforcement in Progress") showed differences in compliance with instructions compared to other signages. To determine general public perception of signage perceived effectiveness, descriptive statistics were applied. The results indicated that, based on average compliance with instructions scores, the highest-ranked was E1 ("Technological Enforcement in Progress") with a score of 3.95, followed by B3 ("Maximum Fine of NT$6,000 for Violators") at 3.90, and F4 ("Joint Enforcement by the Environmental Protection Bureau and Police Department") at 3.80. The three highest-ranked signage contents elicited fear as the dominant emotional response, with a maximum fear rating of 3.41.

However, when conducting subgroup analysis based on age, a detailed examination of the six types of signage content revealed variations within each type. Different signage content categories triggered distinct dominant emotional responses and levels of compliance with instructions. This indicates that perceived effectiveness of signage varies across different age groups. As shown in Table 3, only E1 ("Technological Enforcement in Progress") and F4 ("Joint Enforcement by the Environmental Protection Bureau and Police Department") consistently elicited consistent perceptions across all age groups:

elicited consistent perceptions across all age groups: fear and compliance with instructions.

Further Pearson correlation and regression analyses demonstrated a significant positive correlation between emotional responses and compliance with instructions for all 18 pieces of signage content, with F-values reaching statistical significance, confirming predictive validity and indicating that all signage contents possessed perceived effectiveness. As shown in Table 4, the signage contents with the strongest predictive influence (β) was A2 ("Do Not Litter"). Controlling for other emotional variables, pride had a significant relationship with compliance with instructions ($\beta = .50$, $p < .001$), suggesting that higher pride scores correlated with better

Table 3. Descriptive statistics summary table of uniform perceptions across all age groups for existing "no littering" signage contents.

	18–40 years old (n = 74)		41–64 years old (n = 50)		65 years and older (n = 43)		Total participants (N = 167)		
	Emotion *M*	CI *M*	Emotion *M*	CI *M*	Emotion *M*	CI *M*	Emotion *M*	CI *M*	Total Participants Ranking
E1	AF 3.15	4.01	AF 3.50	3.94	AF 3.74	3.84	AF 3.41	3.95	1
F4	AF 3.05	3.85	AF 3.32	3.70	AF 3.67	3.84	AF 3.29	3.80	3

*AF = Afraid. CI = Compliance with Instructions.

Table 4. Summary table of pearson correlation and regression analysis on emotional responses and compliance with instructions for existing "no littering" signage contents.

	Pearson correlation		Regression analysis				
	Emotion & CI r	Explained Variance(r^2)	Emotion & CI β	Model explanatory power(R^2)	r^2 Ranking	β Ranking	R^2 Ranking
A2	PR & CI .433***	variance 18.7% .1874	PR & CI .50***	Total variance 21% .205	6	1	8
F2	GT & CI .427***	variance 18.2% .1823	GT & CI .42*	Total variance 24% .242	7	2	5
C1	PR & CI .446***	variance 19.9% .1989	PR & CI .38***	Total variance 22% .221	5	3	7
C3	IT & CI .541***	variance 29.3% .2926	IT & CI .38***	Total variance 36% .363	1	3	1

Significance is for the following levels:$p<.05$;** $p<.01$;*** $p<.001$.

*GT = Guilty. PR = Proud. IT = Interested. CI = Compliance with Instructions.

compliance. In terms of emotional prediction, it elicited pride. The model with the highest explanatory power (R2) was C3 ("Littering in Secret, but the Deities See It"), with R2 = .363, accounting for 36% of total variance, which is considered a large effect size. Controlling for other emotional variables, the relationship between interest and compliance with instructions was significant (β = .38, $p < .001$), indicating that the more interest the signage was perceived to be, the higher the compliance with in perceived to be, the higher the compliance with instructions. In terms of emotional prediction, it elicited interest.

Table 5. Summary table of the ranking of emotional responses and compliance with instructions for the perceived effectiveness of existing "no littering" signage contents.

	Emotion (*M*)	CI (*M*)	Emotion & CP (β)	CI(*M*) Ranking	β Ranking
A1	AF (2.46)	3.49	PR (.29*)	8	13
A2	AF (2.25)	3.34	PR (.50***)	13	**1**
A3	AF (2.37)	3.11	AF (.36**)	16	6
B1	AF (3.23)	3.72	AF (.35***)	6	7
B2	AF (3.30)	3.79	GT (.33*)	4	10
B3	AF (3.31)	3.90	AF (.33***)	**2**	10
C1	PR (2.58)	3.38	PR (.38***)	11	**3**
C2	AS (2.20)	3.03	PR (.25*)	18	15
C3	IT (2.78)	3.29	IT (.38***)	14	**3**
C4	GT (2.58)	3.36	GT (.37*)	12	5
D1	PR (2.87)	3.44	PR (.34**)	10	9
D2	GT (2.68)	3.51	GT (.25*)	7	15
E1	AF (3.41)	3.95	-	**1**	-
E2	AF (3.22)	3.76	AF (.23*)	5	17
F1	AF (2.74)	3.44	PR (.35*)	9	7
F2	AF (2.17)	3.07	GT (.42*)	17	**2**
F3	PR (2.14)	3.23	GT (.27*)	15	14
F4	AF (3.29)	3.80	AF (.31**)	**3**	12

*Significance is for the following levels: *$p<.05$; ** $p<.01$; *** $p<.001$.

*AF = Afraid. AS = shamed. GT = Guilty. PR = Proud. IT = interested. CI = Compliance with Instructions.

*Emotion: Only the most prominent emotion is displayed.

Additionally, as shown in Table 5, E1 ("Technological Enforcement in Progress") had the highest fear rating. Pearson correlation analysis showed that shame was significantly positively correlated with compliance with instructions. However, regression analysis indicated that none of the emotional variables had a significant predictive effect on compliance with instructions. This suggests that a single emotional factor may not be strong enough to influence compliance with instructions. Semi-structured interviews revealed that respondents felt afraid because they were uncertain about what specific "technological" enforcement measures were being used. Although Meis and Kashima (2017) suggested that greater clarity in sign messaging enhances perceived effectiveness, this study found that ambiguous wording can still lead to high perceived effectiveness.

In summary, rankings based on descriptive statistics and regression analysis differed, and the emotions elicited by signage contents varied. As shown in Table 5, the results indicate that signage contents where subjective emotional responses aligned with actual behavioral influence included A3, B1, B3, C1, C3, C4, D1, D2, E2, and F4, totaling ten signage contents. For signage design, if the goal is to elicited fear, the content of A1, B3, E1, and F4 should be utilized. If the goal is to prompt participants to change their behavior, A2, C1, C3, and F2 should be prioritized. This study recommends that signage design consider regional cultural factors to ensure alignment with public perceptions and enhance effectiveness.

4 CONCLUSION

This study employed a statistical analysis of a current survey to investigate public perceptions of legal awareness and waste disposal attitudes, as well as to assess the perceived effectiveness of existing anti-littering signage and propose optimization recommendations. The findings indicate that, regarding legal awareness, the proportion of respondents selecting 4 or 5 points averaged 62.6%. For waste disposal attitudes, public consensus reached 72.4%. In terms of signage perception, all 18 existing signage contents demonstrated predictive validity, confirming their perceived effectiveness. However, subgroup analysis by age revealed that perceived effectiveness varied across different age groups. Only two signage contents, E1 ("Technological Enforcement in Progress") and F4 ("Joint Enforcement by the Environmental Protection Bureau and Police Department"), elicited consistent perceptions across all age groups, specifically fear and compliance with instructions.

Among the respondents, E1 ("Technological Enforcement in Progress") received the highest compliance with instructions score, with an average of 3.95. This signage content not only evoked fear but was also positively associated with feelings of shame. However, regression analysis suggested that the influence of a single emotional factor on compliance with instructions was not sufficiently strong. Semi-structured interviews further revealed that participants experienced fear due to their uncertainty about the specific "technological" enforcement measures being implemented. Although previous research by Meis and Kashima (2017) suggested that higher message clarity enhances perceived effectiveness, this study found that ambiguous wording can also result in high perceived effectiveness. Additionally, in terms of predictive influence, A2 ("Do Not Litter") ranked the highest, primarily eliciting pride as an emotional response. The model with the highest explanatory power was C3 ("Littering in Secret, but the Deities See It"), where interest was the dominant emotional response.

Overall, rankings based on descriptive statistics and regression analysis differed, and the emotions elicited by signage content varied accordingly. For signage design, if the objective is to evoke fear, the content of A1, B3, E1, and F4 should be utilized. If the goal is to prompt participants to change their behavior, A2, C1, C3, and F2 should be prioritized. Existing research has confirmed that imagery of eyes effectively reduces littering behavior by creating a sense of being watched (Vaish *et al.* 2017). Therefore, integrating eye imagery into signage design could further enhance the perception of surveillance, increasing the signage's perceived effectiveness.

This study recommends that signage design should incorporate regional cultural considerations to align with public perceptions and enhance effectiveness. By doing so, littering behavior can be mitigated, preventing waste from becoming a source of pollution and reducing its negative impact on the environment.

REFERENCES

Barles, S. (2014). History of waste management and the social and cultural representations of waste. *The Basic Environmental History (P199–226)*. Springer. https://doi.org/10.1007/978-3-319-09180-8

Cialdini, R. B., Reno, R. R. and Kallgren, C. A. (1990). A focus theory of normative conduct: Recycling the concept of norms to reduce littering in public places. *Journal of Personality and Social Psychology*, 58 (6), 1015–1026. https://doi.org/10.1037/0022-3514.58.6.1015

Craig, H. B. and Leland Jr, L. S. (1983). Improving cafeteria patrons' waste disposal. *Journal of Organizational Behavior Management*, 5 (2), 79–88.

Flechsenhar, A., Levine, S. and Bertsch, K. (2022). Threat induction biases processing of emotional expressions. *Front Psychol*, 13, 967800. https://doi.org/10.3389/fpsyg.2022.967800

Godin, G., Conner, M. and Sheeran, P. (2005). Bridging the intention-behaviour 'gap': The role of moral norm. *Br J Soc Psychol*, 44 (Pt 4), 497–512. https://doi.org/10.1348/014466604X17452

Han, H., Hwang, J. and Lee, S. (2017). Cognitive, affective, normative, and moral triggers of sustainable intentions among convention-goers. *Journal of Environmental Psychology*, 51, 1–13. https://doi.org/10.1016/j.jenvp.2017.03.003

Hansmann, R. and Steimer, N. (2015). Linking an integrative behavior model to elements of environmental campaigns: An analysis of face-to-face communication and posters against littering. *Sustainability*, 7 (6), 6937–6956. https://doi.org/10.3390/su7066937

McDougall, S. J., Curry, M. B. and de Bruijn, O. (1999). Measuring symbol and icon characteristics: Norms for concreteness, complexity, meaningfulness, familiarity, and semantic distance for 239 symbols. *Behav Res Methods Instrum Comput*, 31 (3), 487–519. https://doi.org/10.3758/bf03200730

Meis, J. and Kashima, Y. (2017). Signage as a tool for behavioral change: Direct and indirect routes to understanding the meaning of a sign. *PLoS One*, 12 (8), e0182975. https://doi.org/10.1371/journal.pone.0182975

Paris, A. i. (2021). *No mountain high enough: Study finds plastic in 'clean' air. The Guardian.* . https://www.theguardian.com/environment/2021/dec/21/no-mountain-high-enough-study-finds-plastic-in-clean-air

Pollans, L. B. (2017). Trapped in trash:'Modes of governing'and barriers to transitioning to sustainable waste management. *Environment and Planning A*, 49 (10), 2300–2323. https://doi.org/https://doi.org/10.1177/0308518X17719461

Rees, J. H., Klug, S. and Bamberg, S. (2014). Guilty conscience: Motivating pro-environmental behavior by inducing negative moral emotions. *Climatic Change*, 130 (3), 439–452. https://doi.org/10.1007/s10584-014-1278-x

Reno, J. (2015). Waste and waste management. *Annual Review of Anthropology*, 44, 557–572. https://doi.org/https://doi.org/10.1146/annurev-anthro-102214-014146

Vaish, A., Kelsey, C. M., Tripathi, A. and Grossmann, T. (2017). Attentiveness to eyes predicts generosity in a reputation-relevant context. *Evolution and Human Behavior*, 38 (6), 729–733. https://doi.org/10.1016/j.evolhumbehav.2017.07.004

Wu Qiuquan (2021). *A study on people's littering behavior: A policy compliance perspective* [Master's thesis, Department of Political Science, School of Social Sciences, National Taiwan University].

System Innovation for a Global Economy – Lam et al. (Eds)

Design of a mobile health intervention system for preschool feeding based on grounded theory and user-centered design

Yu-Wei Lin
School of Design, Fujian University of Technology, Fuzhou, China

Jeng-Chung Woo
School of Design, Fujian University of Technology, Fuzhou, China
Design Innovation Research Center of Humanities and Social Sciences Research Base of Colleges and Universities in Fujian Province, Fuzhou, China

Ruo-Xi Li
School of Design, Fujian University of Technology, Fuzhou, China

ABSTRACT: Preschool children are increasingly exposed to nutrition-related health risks, largely shaped by parental feeding behaviors. Many first-time parents lack systematic feeding knowledge. This study combines grounded theory (GT) and User-Centered Design (UCD) methodologies with usability evaluations, employing both qualitative and quantitative approaches to develop the "BaoBao," a mobile application providing structured feeding strategies for parents of preschool-aged children (2-6 years). The research consists of two phases: Phase 1 involved in-depth interviews with 15 experts. The resulting 104,258-word transcripts were analyzed using GT, generating 596 concepts, 106 open codes, 24 axial codes, and 6 selective codes. These informed a comprehensive framework addressing developmental needs, feeding strategies, dietary environment, nutritional education, food literacy, and collaborative parenting. In Phase 2, an initial prototype was developed and tested by 6 parents, yielding a usability score of 64.58. After optimization, a second round of testing with 8 parents produced an improved usability score of 82.50, indicating enhanced user acceptance. The app was finalized following iterative refinement based on this feedback. This study demonstrates a successful translation of theoretical insights into practical design, offering evidence-based feeding guidance. Future work will further examine the app's impact on parental feeding practices and intervention effectiveness.

Keywords: Grounded Theory, User-Centered Design, Preschool Children, Feeding, Mobile Health

1 INTRODUCTION

Malnutrition and overweight remain pressing global health challenges, affecting more than one-third of children under the age of five (UNICFF 2019). According to the World Health Organization (WHO), in 2020, approximately 149 million children were stunted, 45 million were wasted, and 38.9 million were overweight or obese (WHO 2021). Malnutrition is a leading cause of mortality in children under five and has long-term implications for health, cognitive development, and socioeconomic outcomes (WHO 2021). A healthy diet is not only essential for preventing childhood malnutrition but also for reducing the risk of chronic conditions such as diabetes, cardiovascular diseases, stroke, and certain cancers in adulthood (WHO 2018). The preschool years (ages 2-6) represent a formative stage in the development of lifelong eating habits, as children begin to acquire autonomy, cognitive skills, and basic self-care abilities. Interventions during this stage are particularly valuable for fostering sustainable healthy eating behaviors.

The home food environment, particularly the role of parents as primary feeding agents, plays a key role in shaping children's eating behaviors (Birch L. L. *et al.* 2001, Campbell K. J. *et al.* 2006, Mahmood L. *et al.* 2021). Parents influence eating behaviors by managing food variety, portion sizes, and meal timing (Nishtar S. *et al.* 2016). Supportive practices, such as repeated exposure to a variety of foods, can increase food acceptance, whereas controlling practices—such as pressuring children to eat or restricting certain foods—may contribute to food aversions and disordered eating (Moore S. N. *et al.* 2007). Despite their critical role, many first-time parents face barriers such as

DOI: 10.1201/9781003655534-14

limited feeding knowledge, low confidence, and insufficient strategies(Branco D. *et al.* 2021), leading to problematic behaviors in children, including picky eating, food neophobia, and poor mealtime engagement(Fraser K. *et al.* 2004). Educating caregivers about effective feeding strategies is essential for promoting healthy dietary behaviors in children. However, traditional health education methods—typically involving in-person sessions at community centers or preschools, followed by phone or email follow-ups—are often constrained by low participation, limited personalization, and poor continuity of care(ChaoHua Peng *et al.* 2018).

These limitations highlight the urgent need for scalable, accessible, and effective intervention strategies. In recent years, mobile health (mHealth) technologies have emerged as a promising solution, offering parents flexible, evidence-informed, and cost-effective tools to support children's nutrition and reinforce healthy habits within the home environment(Haycraft E. *et al.* 2020).

2 LITERATURE REVIEW

With the rapid development of information technologies, increasing health awareness, and the widespread adoption of mobile devices, mHealth has become a vital tool in public health promotion (Marcolino M. S. *et al.* 2018). The WHO defines mHealth as the delivery of medical or health-related services through mobile devices, including smartphones, PDAs, and wearable monitoring tools (Istepanian R. S. H. *et al.* 2004). Owing to its high accessibility and affordability, mHealth offers distinct advantages in health management by enabling users to access services anytime and anywhere, and by reducing the time and financial costs associated with traditional, location-dependent care (Luxton D. D. *et al.* 2011).

The application of mHealth in the context of children's nutrition and health management has grown steadily in both scope and relevance. Blakeslee *et al.* conducted a systematic review of child health apps published between 2017 and 2023, identifying 39 studies across eight thematic areas: parental feeding and nutrition, physical activity, maternal and child health, parent–child relationships, healthy environments, dental care, mental health, and sleep (Blakeslee S. B. *et al.* 2023). Among these, parental feeding and nutrition emerged as the most frequently explored theme, underscoring its increasing academic and practical significance.

Globally, mHealth applications targeting children are becoming increasingly diverse (Schoffman D. E. *et al.* 2013). A growing number of parenting and nutrition-related apps are now available on platforms such as the Google Play Store (Srivastava R. *et al.* 2022), enabling parents to access timely guidance on nutrition and reduce unhealthy feeding practices. Nevertheless, concerns persist regarding the scientific rigor and effectiveness of these tools (WenJie Duan *et al.* 2018). Most commercial apps lack validated theoretical foundations, and many have not undergone systematic evaluation (Yasini M. *et al.* 2016). In addition, the absence of well-integrated design features limits their practicality and continuity of use (Wan T. T. H. *et al.* 2017).

Current research tends to prioritize evaluating the outcomes of mHealth interventions, while paying limited attention to their design methodologies. For example, Haycraft *et al.* evaluated the "Child Feeding Guide" website through a four-week intervention with 25 mothers of children aged 6 months to 4 years, finding reduced controlling feeding behaviors and lower parental anxiety (Haycraft E. *et al.* 2020). Similarly, Nystrom *et al.* developed the "MINISTOP" app and reported decreased sugary beverage consumption among 4-year-olds in Sweden, with potential benefits for adiposity control (Delisle C. *et al.* 2015). Rageliene *et al.* introduced the "Food Boss" app targeting children aged 9–13 and observed improved dietary knowledge, fruit and vegetable intake, and self-efficacy (Ragelienė T. *et al.* 2022). However, many of these interventions are built on existing commercial platforms or websites and lack comprehensive, reproducible design frameworks, limiting their utility for informing future mHealth development.

Some studies have begun incorporating user-centered design (UCD) methodologies into mHealth development (Gabrielli S. *et al.* 2017, Vázquez-Paz A. M. *et al.* 2022). However, there remains a lack of clarity on how specific design content is identified, structured, and integrated. For instance, the "PersuHabit" app was evaluated with only six parents, raising concerns about generalizability. The "KhunLook" app, though based on early user interviews and showing high acceptability in a small sample (Areemit R. *et al.* 2020), relied exclusively on qualitative data, potentially limiting objectivity and failing to yield behavioral insights at scale. These examples reveal a critical research gap: there is an urgent need for scientifically grounded, systematically developed mHealth tools that integrate empirical user needs and theoretical principles—particularly in the context of promoting healthy eating among preschool-aged children.

Despite evidence that mHealth interventions can improve nutrition-related knowledge and behaviors, current efforts often lack comprehensive design guidance, target limited age groups (typically infants or school-aged children), and address only isolated components of the feeding process.

To address these limitations, the present study proposes a theoretical framework that combines Grounded Theory (GT) and UCD to systematically identify and integrate key design elements influencing parental feeding practices. Based on this framework, we aim to develop an mHealth app "BaoBao" tailored for families with preschool-aged children. The specific objectives are as follows:

- To design and develop the "BaoBao" app to assist parents in adopting supportive feeding practices.
- To apply GT to construct a comprehensive, evidence-based content framework for mHealth app development.
- To evaluate the usability and preliminary effectiveness of the app using the System Usability Scale (SUS) and validated feeding behavior measures.

This study will detail how GT and UCD are integrated into the app's development process and assess the usability and intervention outcomes of the "BaoBao" app. GT enables the extraction of empirical insights from real-world data (Strauss A. *et al.* 1990) and has been effectively employed in mHealth research targeting mental health conditions such as anxiety and depression (Price M. *et al.* 2014). This study adopts a similar approach, applying it to the design of a child feeding guidance system, with the goal of creating evidence-based design content.

For usability evaluation, we adopt the SUS developed by John Brooke (Brooke J. 1996), which has demonstrated high reliability even in small-sample studies (Tullis T. S. *et al.* 2004). According to Borsci *et al.*, a minimum of five participants is sufficient for usability testing (Borsci S. *et al.* 2013), while Bastien reports that 80-85% of usability issues can be identified with just 4-5 users (Bastien J. M. C. 2008).

3 MATERIAL AND METHODS

This study was conducted in three phases. In Phase 1, grounded theory was used to identify user needs and inform the content and functional design of the "BaoBao" app. In Phase 2, based on these findings, the app's functional architecture and prototype were developed following UCD approach, with iterative refinement through qualitative interviews and quantitative usability testing. In Phase 3, a pilot intervention was conducted to evaluate the effectiveness of "BaoBao" among parents.

3.1 *Phase 1: Defining the content and functions of "BaoBao"*

3.1.1 *Study design*

To comprehensively explore the factors influencing preschoolers' dietary behaviors and parental feeding practices, a literature review was first conducted to construct a semi-structured interview guide. In-depth interviews with experts were then performed. With informed consent, all interviews were audio-recorded, transcribed verbatim, and analyzed using GT methodology, including open, axial, and selective coding procedures. A theoretical saturation test was also conducted (Figure 1).

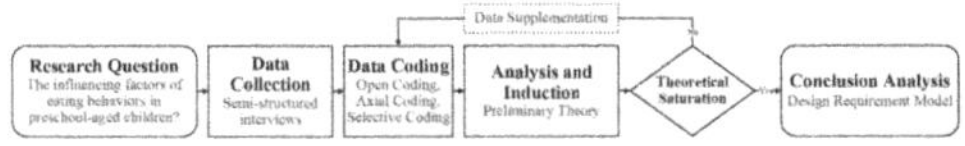

Figure 1. GT procedure applied in this study.

3.1.2 *Participants*

Three expert groups were included:

Parents (n = 8): All had raised at least two preschool-aged children.
Preschool teachers (n = 5): With an average of 9 years of teaching experience.
Psychologists (n = 2): Each had an average of 8 years of clinical experience and were parents of preschool-aged children.

3.1.3 *Data collection*

Data were collected between August and September 2023. Each interview lasted approximately 30–60 minutes. The total transcript corpus amounted to approximately 104,258 words.

3.1.4 *Data analysis*

Data were analyzed using NVivo software. A three-level coding process was applied, following GT procedures. The final codes and themes informed the content and functional requirements for the mHealth application "BaoBao," targeting improvements in parental feeding behaviors for preschool children.

3.2 *Phase 2: Design and development of "BaoBao"*

3.2.1 *Study design*

Building upon the findings from Phase 1, the app's architecture was developed using a UCD approach (IOS 2019). A stepwise prototype testing and refinement strategy was employed to enhance usability and user experience. Two rounds of iterative design evaluation were completed to produce the final version of "BaoBao."

3.2.2 *Participants*

Parents of preschool-aged children were recruited for user testing. Six parents participated in the first round, and eight in the second round, to ensure diversity of feedback and sufficient data for usability assessment.

3.2.3 *Data collection*

Participants were asked to complete specific tasks using the "BaoBao" app. Afterward, they were interviewed to report difficulties, suggestions, and overall impressions. Feedback focused on interface design, interaction logic, and task flow. The SUS was used for quantitative assessment. Additionally, a structured usability interview adapted from Peischl *et al.* (2015) was conducted to examine user comprehension and operational fluency under realistic usage scenarios.

3.2.4 *Data analysis*

Qualitative data were analyzed to extract key themes, usability problems, and improvement suggestions. Quantitative SUS scores were calculated and compared across iterations. The combined findings informed iterative modifications to improve app functionality, user interaction, and visual experience.

4 RESULTS AND DISCUSSION

4.1 *Phase 1: Defining the content and functions of "BaoBao"*

Using GT, a three-stage coding analysis was conducted. A total of 596 concepts, 106 open codes, 24 axial codes, and 6 selective codes were generated. Theoretical saturation was reached when no new themes emerged from subsequent interviews, ensuring the comprehensiveness and validity of the data. Detailed results are presented in Tables 1 and 2.

Table 1. Example of open coding categorization.

Sub-category	Concept	Label	Original Representative Quotes
Mindful Eating	M59 Enjoying food in the moment	m73 Teaching children to enjoy food in the present moment	"We teach children to enjoy their food in the present moment, eat quietly, and finish their meal without waste."
	N14 Joyful Eating	n14 Eating should be a joyful experience	"We hope eating brings joy to the child. Ideally, mealtime should be a happy moment. If you want them to eat more, it has to be an enjoyable experience."
		n31 Avoid treating eating as a task	"If they rush through eating just to finish, it becomes a problem. They might only eat the rice and skip the vegetables—it's like a task, not a real meal."

Table 2. Summary of GT coding results.

Selective Coding	Axial Coding (Opening Coding Counts)	Total Open Codes
Developmental Needs	Physical Indicators (3), Nutritional Assessment (4), Health Management (5), Nutrition Management (3)	15
Feeding Strategies	Eating Behavior (5), Feeding Philosophy (4), Feeding Practices (9), Behavioral Guidance (9), Parenting Style (5)	32
Food Literacy	Meal Planning (6), Food Selection (6), Food Preparation (5), Nutritional Knowledge (1)	18
Dietary Environment	Mealtime Setting (6), Mealtime Atmosphere (3), Table Manners (7), Food Hygiene and Safety (4), Mealtime Emotions (3)	23
Nutritional Education	Food Education (6), Behavioral Practice (2), Self-feeding Skills (5), Social Eating Interactions (1)	14
Collaborative Parenting	Parent-child Relationship (2), Parent-School Collaboration (2)	4

Based on the coding results, a design requirement framework was established, comprising six core domains: Developmental Needs, Feeding Strategies, Dietary Environment, Nutritional Education, Food Literacy, and Collaborative Parenting (Figure 2).

- Developmental Needs serve as the foundation of the system, guiding feeding strategies through the tracking of physical indicators and health data.
- Feeding Strategies encompass evidence-based practices, feeding philosophy, and behavioral guidance to promote responsive and developmentally appropriate feeding.
- Dietary Environment emphasizes the importance of structured and emotionally supportive mealtime settings for healthy habit formation.
- Nutritional Education involves interactive and experiential content that facilitates knowledge transmission and habit-building in children.
- Food Literacy provides theoretical support by equipping parents with fundamental knowledge about nutrition, food preparation, and meal planning.
- Collaborative Parenting: This emphasizes collaboration between families and kindergartens in delivering consistent and complementary dietary education, forming a supportive and unified feeding environment.

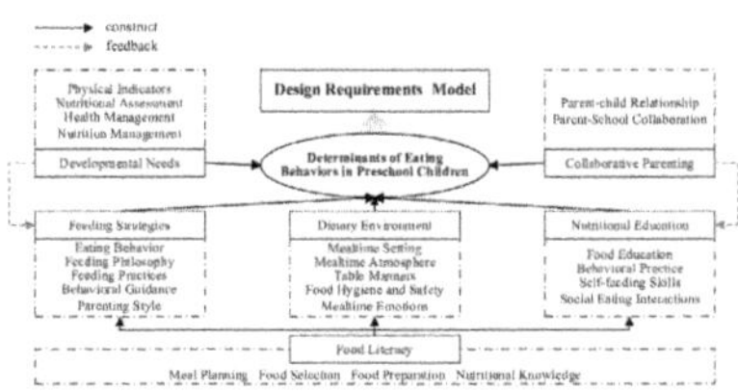

Figure 2. Design requirement model for a preschool feeding-focused mHealth application.

4.2 *Phase 2: Design and development of "BaoBao"*

Based on the six thematic domains identified in Phase 1, the "BaoBao" was developed as a WeChat mini-program, following the design logic of "knowledge–action" linkage. Five core modules were implemented, each addressing specific parental feeding needs, as shown in Figure 3.

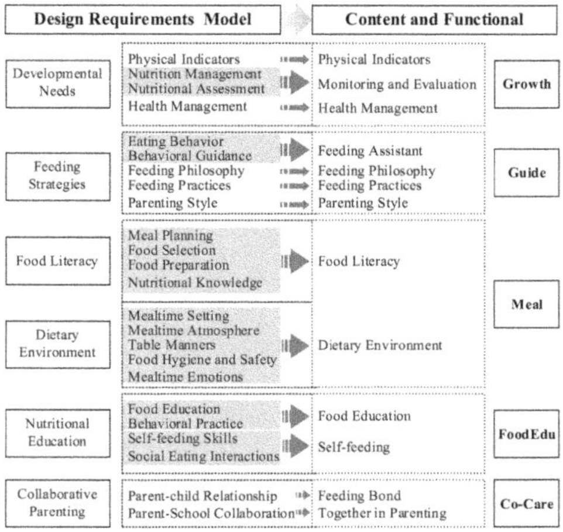

Figure 3. Mapping of design elements to functional modules.

4.2.1 *The "BaoBao" functional modules are as follows*

a) Growth Module (Developmental Needs): Tracks physical development indicators such as body weight (using WHO growth standards), sleep behavior, oral hygiene, and bowel movements (via the Bristol Stool Chart). All data are visualized through charts to enhance parental awareness.

b) Guide Module (Feeding Strategies): Enhances parental feeding capacity through
- Knowledge Popularization integrates feeding practices, philosophies, and parenting styles to establish a structured knowledge base.
- Smart Search for fast information retrieval.
- Feeding Assistant provides real-time guidance and reminders during meals.
- Knowledge Carousel for pushe-based tip delivery.

c) Meal Module (A composite unit integrating Dietary Environment and Food Literacy):
- Food Facts offers comprehensive information on food selection and nutritional matching to improve parental nutrition literacy.
- Meal Planning allows parents to generate menus based on dietary guidelines recommended by the system, with one-click sharing to family members to promote collaborative feeding.

d) FoodEdu Module (Nutritional Education):
- Promotion of Food Education Concepts, which provides popular science content on children's eating behaviors and habit formation to foster scientific awareness among parents.
- Training of Independent Eating Skills, which introduces relevant knowledge and practical guidance. Personalized recommendations are offered based on users' thematic preferences to enhance relevance and practicality.

e) Co-Care Module (Collaborative Parenting)
- Parent-School Collaboration Guidelines on item preparation, life skills development, and psychological transition strategies.
- Together in Parenting, allowing users to share questions or experiences and engage in mutual support focused on child nutrition.
- Feeding Bond (Parent-child Relationship), which offers accessible guidance on interaction, attachment, and feeding communication.

4.2.2 *Iterative design stages of the "BaoBao"*

To enhance usability, two rounds of iterative user testing were conducted. In the first round, the prototype achieved a SUS score of 64.58, reflecting moderate usability. Participants pointed out several key issues, such as interface complexity, unclear interaction flows, and ambiguous functional labels. In response, targeted improvements were made, leading to a marked increase in system performance. The second iteration focused on refining interaction logic and adjusting specific interface elements, which further improved operational fluency and user satisfaction. The Meal interface serves as a representative example:

- "Diet Diary" was renamed "Meal Plan" to clarify its forward-planning function rather than a record of past intake.
- A sliding interaction format was adopted to reduce visual clutter and improve layout clarity.
- An "Add Menu" guide text was added to enhance hierarchical cues.
- Introduced a menu sharing feature for family collaboration.

Following these changes, the SUS score rose to 82.50 in the second round, achieving Grade A usability according to Sauro's scale (Sauro J. *et al.* 2014). As the primary users are Chinese parents, the prototype was originally developed in Chinese. Translated screenshots are shown in Figure 4, and all 61 interface screens are available via the following link:https://www.figma.com/design/0uvxIFnRAwRvPa496TaQni/Untitled?node-id=1297-4116&t=7M2I9YlFXshoj0gG-1.

4.2.3 *Deployment via WeChat mini program*

The system was deployed as a WeChat mini-program to maximize accessibility and parental engagement. With over one billion monthly active users, WeChat provides an ideal platform for recruiting participants and collecting data

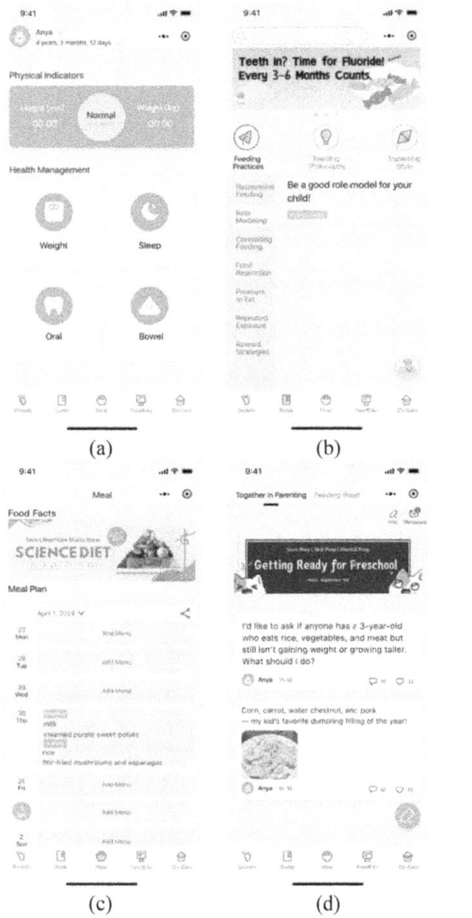

Figure 4. Screenshots of the "BaoBao" interface (a) Growth, (b) Guide, (c) Meal, (d) Co-Care.

efficiently. Its lightweight architecture eliminates installation barriers and ensures compatibility across iOS and Android systems (Dandan Chen *et al.* 2023). The implementation process included: needs analysis, system architecture design, feature development, service integration, testing, and platform deployment, as illustrated in Figure 5. This marks the completion of the "BaoBao" development.

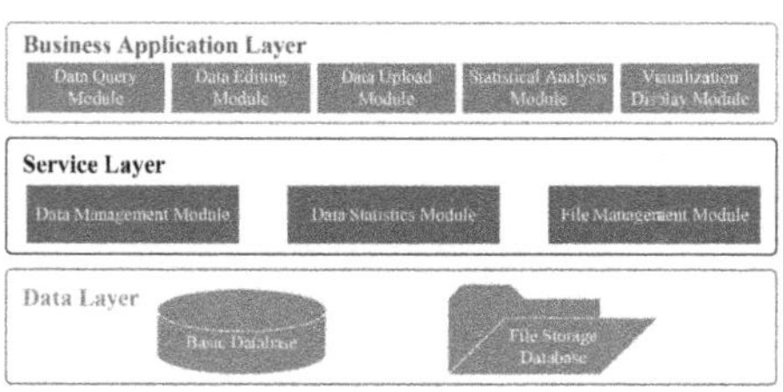

Figure 5. Mapping of design elements to functional modules.

5 CONCLUSION

Adequate nutrition is essential for children's physical growth and cognitive development, with parental influence playing a pivotal role in shaping children's dietary behaviors. However, parents often require structured guidance to implement effective feeding practices. mHealth applications present a promising approach to support such efforts. The "BaoBao" mHealth application, developed in this study, demonstrates strong feasibility and potential in supporting parents to improve their children's feeding behaviors. This application provides a structured method to help parents guide and improve feeding practices.

- Based on GT and UCD, this study successfully designed and developed the "BaoBao" mHealth app. The theoretical framework and design process used in this study can serve as a model for the development of similar applications in the field.
- After two rounds of interviews and usability testing, the app achieved an "A" grade on the SUS, indicating high usability and positive parental acceptance.

Future research should focus on evaluating the intervention efficacy of the "BaoBao" in improving parental feeding practices and promoting healthier dietary behaviors among young children.

ACKNOWLEDGEMENTS

This work was supported by Fujian University of Technology [grant numbers GY-S21081 2021], and Design Innovation Research Center of Humanities and Social Sciences Research Base of Colleges and Universities in Fujian Province.

REFERENCES

Areemit R., Lumbiganon P., Suphakunpinyo C., Jetsrisuparb A., Sutra S. and Sripanidkulchai K., (2020), *JMIR mHealth and uHealth*, 810, e15116.

Bastien J. M. C., (2008), *International Journal of Medical Informatics*, 794, e18–e23.

Birch L. L. and Davison K. K., *Pediatr. Clin. North Am.*, 48, 4, 893–907.

Blakeslee S. B., Vieler K., Horak I., Stritter W., Seifert 和G., (2023), *JMIR Mhealth Uhealth*, 11, e39929.

Borsci S., Macredie R. D., Barnett J., Martin J., Kuljis J., Young T., *ACM Trans. Comput. Hum. Interact.*, 205, 1–23.

Branco D., Pires A. C., Siñao H., Gomes A., Pereira A., Sousa J., Barros L., and Guerreiro T., (2021), *Human-Computer Interaction-INTERACT 2021*, 12935, 211–220.

Brooke J., (1996), *Usability evaluation in industry*, 189194, 4–7.

Campbell K. J., Crawford D. A., Ball K., *Int. J. Obes.*, 30, 8, 1272–1280.

ChaoHua Peng, ShanShu Du, YuLing Zhang, YinTong Liu and YongMei Lu, (2018), *J. Nurs. Sci.*, 335, 9–11. (In Chinese)

Dandan Chen, Jing Shao, Hui Zhang, Jingjie Wu, Erxu Xue, Pingping Guo, Leiwen Tang, Nianqi Cui, Xiyi Wang, Liying Chen and Zhihong Ye, (2023), *Ann. Med.*, 552, 2267587.

Delisle C., Sandin S., Forsum E., Henriksson H., Trolle-Lagerros Y., Larsson C., Maddison R., Ortega F. B, Ruiz J. R, Silfvernagel K., Timpka T. and Löf M., (2015), *BMC Public Health*, 151, 95.

Fraser K., Wallis M. and John W. S., (2004), *Health Education Journal*, 633, 229–241.

Gabrielli S., Dianti M., Maimone R., Betta M., Filippi L., Ghezzi M., Forti S., (2017), *JMIR Mhealth Uhealth*, 54, e48.

Haycraft E., Witcomb G. L. and Farrow C., (2020), *Nutrition Bulletin*, 454, 474–482.

ISO, 2019, Ergonomics of human-system interaction—Part 210, ISO 9241-210:2019.

Istepanian R. S. H., Jovanov E., Zhang Y. T., (2004), *IEEE Transactions on Information Technology in Biomedicine*, 84, 405–414.

Luxton D. D., McCann R. A., Bush N. E., Mishkind M. C. and Reger G. M., (2011), *Professional Psychology: Research and Practice*, 426, 505–512.

Mahmood L., Flores-Barrantes P., Moreno L. A., Manios Y., Gonzalez-Gil E. M., *Nutrients*, 13, 4, 1138.

Marcolino M.S., Oliveira J. A. Q., D'Agostino M., Ribeiro A. L., Alkmim M. B. M., Novillo-Ortiz D., (2018), *JMIR mHealth and uHealth*, 61, e23.

Moore S. N., Tapper K., Murphy S., (2007), *Appetite*, 493, 704–707.

Nishtar S., Gluckman P.和T. Armstrong, (2016), *The Lancet*, 387, 10021, 825–827.

Peischl B., Ferk M. and Holzinger A., (2015), *Software Qual J*, 233, 509–536.

Price M., Yuen E. K., Goetter E. M., Herbert J. D., Forman E. M., Acierno R. and Ruggiero K. J., (2014), *Clin Psychology and Psychoth*, 215, 427–436.

Rageliené T., Aschemann-Witzel J. and Grønhøj A., (2022), *Health Promot. Int.*, 371, daab081.

Sauro J. and Lewis J. R., (2014), *Quantifying the User Experience*. China Machine Press. (In Chinese)

Schoffman D. E., Turner-McGrievy G., Jones S. J. and Wilcox S., (2013), *Translational Behavioral Medicine*, 33, 320–325.

Srivastava R., Kushwaha S., Khanna P., Gupta M., Bharti B. and Jain R., (2022), *Nutrition*, 103–104, 111773.

Strauss A. and Corbin J., (1990), *Basics of Qualitative Research*. Sage.

Tullis T. S. and Stetson J. N., (2004), *A comparison of questionnaires for assessing website usability*.

UNICEF, (2019). [Online]. Available: https://www.unicef.cn/reports/sowc-2019-executive-summary.

Vázquez-Paz A. M., Michel-Nava R. M., Delgado-Pérez E. E., Lares-Michel M., Espinosa-Curiel I. E., (2022), *J. Med. Syst.*, 4611, 70.

Wan T. T. H., Gurupur V. P., Tanik M. M., (2017), *JID*, 213, 1–5.

WenJie Duan, JieWen Zhang and Lei He, (2018), *Adv. Psychol. Sci.*, 267, 1232–1243 (In Chinese)

WHO, (2020). [Online]. Available: https://www.who.int/zh/news-room/fact-sheets/detail/healthy-diet.

WHO, (2021). [Online]. Available: https://www.who.int/zh/news-room/fact-sheets/detail/malnutrition.

Yasini M., Beranger J., Desmarais P., Perez L. and Marchand G., (2016), *Studies in health technology and informatics*, 228, 205–209.

System Innovation for a Global Economy – Lam et al. (Eds)
© 2026 The Author(s), ISBN 978-1-041-10520-6

Imperceptible color image steganography based on magic cube

Ching-Ting Chen & Jason Lin
Department of Computer Science and Engineering, National Chung Hsing University, South Dist., Taichung, Taiwan

Chun-Wei Yang
Master Program for Digital Health Innovation, College of Humanities and Sciences, China Medical University, Beitun Dist., Taichung, Taiwan

ABSTRACT: Steganography is the art of concealing secret messages within multimedia information such as images, videos, sounds, and text to protect their transmission. Regarding image steganography, the objective is to improve the visual imperceptibility of camouflage to thwart eavesdroppers and safeguard the secrecy of the message. However, the visual quality decreases as the embedding capacity increases. Thus, this study introduces an efficient color image steganographic scheme that utilizes the properties of a magic cube, aiming to boost embedding capacity while maintaining high image visual quality. The magic cube extends with varying side lengths into a 256×256×256 reference space and utilizes it as an index for embedding secret messages. The experimental results demonstrate significant improvements achieved by applying the proposed method to both embedding capacity and visual quality for color images. Compared to the method proposed by Ashraf AbdelRaouf (2021) at similar embedding rates, there is a maximum increase in PSNR of 23.6%. Additionally, the embedding capacity can be controlled by adjusting the size of the magic cube, which increases its number of combinations and enhances the security level.

Keywords: Steganography, Color image, Magic cube, Visual imperceptibility, Security

1 INTRODUCTION

With new network technologies, sending messages through the internet has become faster and more convenient. However, protecting classified information has also emerged as a crucial topic for discussion. Unlike cryptography, which aims for intractability, steganography ensures that a third party remains unaware that important information is being transmitted. By hiding the secret within the carrier, steganography quietly transmits the information without drawing attention. If hackers are unaware of the existence of confidential information, they cannot steal it. Additionally, suppose the embedded message body is combined with the ciphertext. In that case, it not only provides an additional layer of protection but also offers additional information to aid in embedding, significantly reducing the likelihood of theft and decryption. Thus, it enhances the security of information transmission.

Steganography using images as the carrier has three parts worth improving. The first is the visual imperceptibility. The lower the value, the more likely to gain interest of the eavesdropper. The second is the embedding capacity. If the amount of embedding is too small, it will require many carriers to conceal the transmission of the secret message, increasing the likelihood of detection accordingly. Obviously, it does not meet the desired convenience and security. Therefore, it is hoped that the amount of embedding can be increased. The higher, the better. The earliest information hiding is to embed the message body into the carrier directly. If statistical attack, visual attack, and other methods are used, there is still a chance of finding hidden confidential information, which the hiding algorithm can deduce. As a result, there is another security worth considering. The approach that increases the difficulty of deciphering by adding information to improve security without reducing the quality of the above two parts.

In this paper, with the premise of not sacrificing visual quality and storage capacity, the objective is to enhance security by utilizing steganography to embed confidential information. The proposed method is then compared with other existing methods to demonstrate its advantages and reliability in safeguarding data security in practice.

DOI: 10.1201/9781003655534-15

2 RELATED WORK

Image steganographic techniques can be broadly categorized into the transform and spatial domains. Pixel values are transformed into frequency coefficients before embedding confidential messages in the transform domain. Common mathematical transformations include discrete cosine transform [1], discrete Fourier transform [2], and discrete wavelet transform [3,4]. The proposed method in this study focuses on research in the spatial domain, where data embedding is achieved by directly modifying the pixel values of an image. This type of method is relatively simple and can embed high-capacity confidential messages while preserving the quality of the original image. Common methodologies in the spatial domain include least significant bit (LSB) replacement [5], exploiting modification direction (EMD) [6], pixel value difference [7], difference expansion [8], and histogram shifting [9] methods. As research in color image processing gains more attention, numerous methods based on the LSB technique and utilizing color images as carriers have been proposed [10–15]. Among these, a number of studies [10–12] have utilized the lower sensitivity of the blue channel, according to color sensitivity theory, for data hiding. This enhancement of imperceptibility over traditional LSB substitution methods is evident. The proposed method also based on this visual characteristic to design the embedding algorithm. The following paragraphs briefly review relevant prior work to contextualize our approach.

In 2006, Zhang *et al.* [6] proposed the EMD method to embed data into the cover image, using every n pixels to embed a secret number d in base $(2n+1)$, where n is a non-negative integer, d is an integer in the range of 0 to $2n$. Given an example of their method, in the case of $n=2$, consider the process of hiding the secret message $(01)_2$ into the pixel pair $(1,3)$. First of all, convert the secret message into a base number, that is $(1)_5$. Next, check whether its value is consistent with confidential information $(1)_5$ at the embedded position $(1,3)$. If they are different, find the same value at the position adjacent to the embedding position. Since the values in Figure 1 is different, the corresponding number of the secret number is searched at the adjacent position, we replace $(1,3)$ with $(0,3)$ as the position for recording the secret number.

In 2009, Lin *et al.* [16] improved the Sudoku method proposed by Chang *et al.* [17], utilizing a 3×3 grid to construct a 256×256 secret reference matrix (SRM) for embedding and extracting confidential messages. Unlike Sudoku matrices, SRM is created using a 3×3 grid with different numbers ranging from 0 to 8. The embedding process of this method is similar to that of Sudoku reference matrices. Since the numbers in the table are generated using a random seed, the SRM has a total of 9! $(= 362,880)$ possible configurations in experiments. Compared to the Sudoku method, it offers better visual quality and enhances the security.

In 2021, Ashraf AbdelRaouf [10] proposed a color image steganography method based on visual color sensitivity. The technique builds upon the traditional LSB method and incorporates two embedding rules. First, it considers the human visual system's sensitivity to different color channels and applies the rule of thirds. The secret message is embedded by modifying the LSB of each pixel sequentially, following a spiral path from the outer edge to the center. The blue channel is modified first, followed by the red and green channels.

In the same year, another method was proposed that also operates in the RGB color space, using a color image as the carrier. The adjacent mean method, introduced by Chuang *et al.* [18], applies the average value of adjacent image pixels combined with confidential data. Figure 2 illustrates the detailed process of this method.

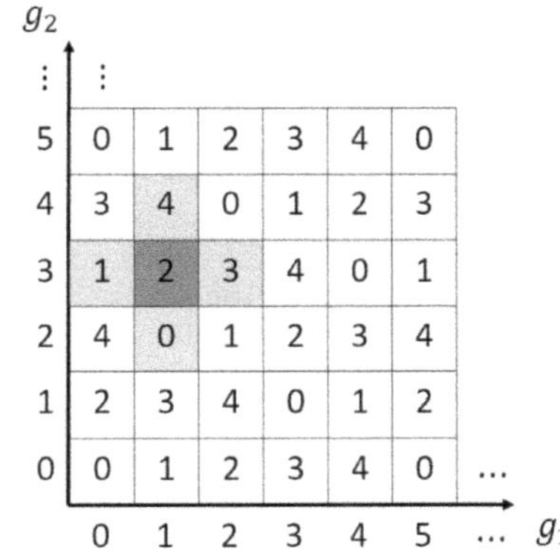

Figure 1. Two-dimensional hypercube reference table.

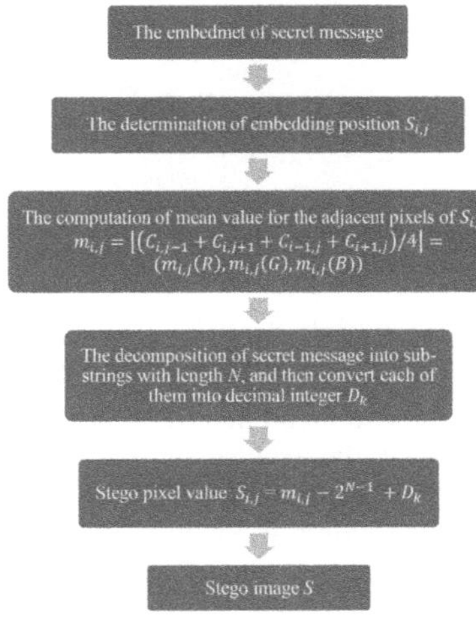

Figure 2. The embedding process of Chuang et al.'s method [18].

3 PROPOSED METHOD

Most of the existing color image data hiding techniques commonly apply grayscale image approaches within the RGB color space. Unlike grayscale image approaches, in this study, we employ a three-dimensional magic cube-generated reference space for embedding. Within the existing framework, we realize the proposed method using color images as carriers. The RGB channel of each pixel are considered as XYZ coordinates in the reference space. Furthermore, the proposed method is optimized based on the characteristics of the human visual system.

For the proposed method, we will first introduce the magic cube and the generation of reference space. Then, we will further illustrate the core concepts of embedding the secret messages using the reference space consists of a magic cube with side length M. The magic cube proposed in this paper is a three-dimensional matrix filled with unrepeated digits in base $\left(M^3 - 1\right)$, where $M \in \mathbb{Z}^+$ within the range of 2 to 256, which controls the maximum pixel modification. For example, if $M = 2$, then the construct of the magic cube will become $3 \times 3 \times 3$ and filled in with non-repeated digits 0 to 26, as shown in Figure 3. After creating a magic cube of length M, it is used as a unit to expand to a three-dimensional matrix of $256 \times 256 \times 256$. This expanded matrix serves as the magic cube reference space named RS for embedding, as shown in Figure 4. The values corresponding to the reference space are given by $\text{RS} = (x, y, z) = \text{RS}(x \pm aM, y \pm bM, z \pm cM)$, where (x, y, z) represents any coordinate within the reference space, and $a, b, c \in N$. The values satisfy the conditions $0 \leq x \pm aM \leq 255$, $0 \leq y \pm bM \leq 255$, and $0 \leq y \pm bM \leq 255$.

Figure 3. The example of $3 \times 3 \times 3$ magic cube.

With the above preliminary knowledge, we can further illustrate the detailed steps of the steganographic method proposed in this study. The following is a description of the proposed steps:

Step 1: Convert the embedded confidential information into a numerical sequence $S = \{d_1, d_2, \ldots, d_{H \times W}\}_{M^3}$ based on the M^3.

Step 2: Construct a $256 \times 256 \times 256$ reference space based on the magic cube.

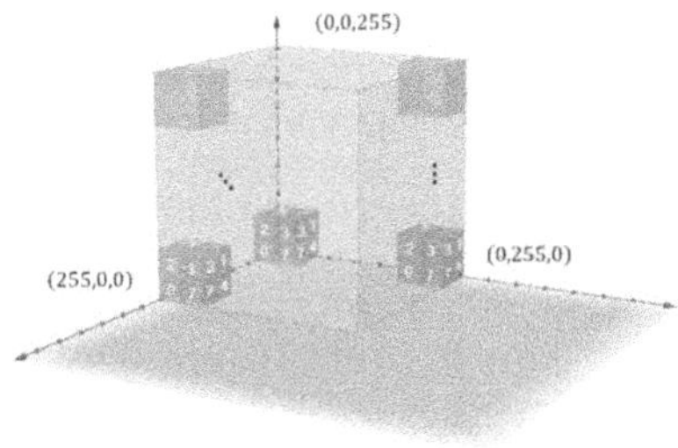

Figure 4. The example of $256 \times 256 \times 256$ reference space.

Step 3: Establish an index table of the same size as the cover image, recording which corresponding combination is used to embed secret messages. The corresponding combinations are as shown in Step 4.

Step 4: Formulate three corresponding combinations between RGB pixel values and reference space XYZ coordinates. We select the three combinations: (R, G, B), (R, B, G), and (G, R, B), in which the encoding of the three combinations is 0, 1, and 2, respectively. Due to the sensitivity of human vision to green light, when modifying pixels, the combinations with the least variation in green pixel values are chosen and recoded in the index table. Taking the RGB pixel values $\left(P_{i,j}^R, P_{i,j}^G, P_{i,j}^B\right) = (99, 103, 204)$ of color pixel $P_{i,j}$ as an example, the corresponding XYZ coordinates are $(99, 103, 204)$, $(99, 204, 103)$, and $(103, 99, 204)$, as shown in Figure 5 and Table 1.

Figure 5. RGB pixels value of color image.

Table 1. The corresponding RGB pixel values of coordinates.

	The corresponding combination	*The corresponding RGB pixel values of XYZ coordinates*	
(X, Y, Z)	0	$\left(P_{i,j}^R, P_{i,j}^G, P_{i,j}^B\right)$	$(99, 103, 204)$
	1	$\left(P_{i,j}^R, P_{i,j}^B, P_{i,j}^G\right)$	$(99, 204, 103)$
	2	$\left(P_{i,j}^G, P_{i,j}^R, P_{i,j}^B\right)$	$(103, 99, 204)$

Step 5: For the embedment of secret message, we first scan the cover image from left-to-right and then top-to-bottom. If the secret messages s_i equals the values of RGB pixels and (X, Y, Z) corresponding to the magic cube reference space, then the pixel value remains unchanged. If the secret messages s_i differs from the values in the reference space, then take (X, Y, Z) as the center point, search in the vicinity within a range of $\pm\left\lfloor\frac{M}{2}\right\rfloor$, denoted as (X^*, Y^*, Z^*). However, to prevent candidate pixels from exceeding the boundaries of the reference space, the search range for candidate pixels is defined according to the rule outlined in Equation (1) below.

$$(X^*, Y^*, Z^*) = \begin{cases} [0, M-1] & \text{if } (X,Y,Z) - \left\lfloor\frac{M}{2}\right\rfloor - 1 < 0 \\ [255-(M-1), 255] & \text{if } (X,Y,Z) + \left\lfloor\frac{M}{2}\right\rfloor > 255 \\ \left[(X,Y,Z) - \left\lfloor\frac{M}{2}\right\rfloor, (X,Y,Z) + \left\lfloor\frac{M}{2}\right\rfloor\right] & \text{if } 0 \le (X,Y,Z) \pm \left\lfloor\frac{M}{2}\right\rfloor \le 255 \end{cases} \quad (1)$$

Next, we calculate the corresponding combination with the smallest difference $\left|P_{i,j}^{G*} - P_{i,j}^{G}\right|$ between green pixel values in the three combinations. $P_{i,j}^{G*}$ represents the green channel pixel value of the candidate pixel, and $P_{i,j}^{G'}$ represents the best green channel pixel value obtained from the three combinations to embed the secret message s_i. Then, modify the pixel and add the code of the selected combination to the index table. Repeat this step until all secret digits are embedded.

Step 6: Output the stego image and the index table of the embedded combinations.

Given an example of the embedding process. As shown in Table 1, assuming the RGB pixel values of pixel $P_{i,j}$ are $(205, 108, 171)$ and the secret message is $(16)_{27}$. First, determine if the values in the reference space match the secret message $(16)_{27}$. If it does not match the embedded number, then apply Equation (1) to search for candidate pixels within the search range. The range is $(205 \pm 1, 108 \pm 1, 171 \pm 1)$, $(205 \pm 1, 171 \pm 1, 108 \pm 1)$, $(108 \pm 1, 205 \pm 1, 171 \pm 1)$. After finding the coordinates that match the secret message to be embedded, calculate the smallest difference in the green channel pixel values and replace it with the new pixel value $P'_{i,j}$. As shown in Table 2, in this example, the green channel difference for the first combination is 0, which is the smallest value among the three combinations. Therefore, the pixel $(206, 108, 172)$ from combination 0 is chosen as the value for the embedded pixel $P'_{i,j}$, replacing the original pixel value $P'_{i,j} = (205, 108, 171)$.

The extraction process of the proposed method is also very simple. Based on the index table recorded during embedding, the corresponding combinations

Table 2. Embedding example.

	(X, Y, Z)		
The corresponding combination	0	1	2
The correspond-ing RGB pixel values of XYZ coordinates	$(205, 108, 171)$	$(205, 171, 108)$	$(108, 205, 171)$
Candidate pixels within the search range	$(206, 108, 172)$	$(205, 170, 109)$	$(107, 204, 172)$
The difference of green channel pixel	0	1	1

of XYZ coordinates and RGB pixel values used during embedding can be obtained. By mapping the values to the reference space, we can obtain the secret messages. Continuing from the previous embedding example, during the extraction of secret messages, we extracting the RGB pixel values $(206, 108, 172)$ of the embedded position $P'_{i,j}$, and mapping it through the index table. From the example in Table 2, it can be inferred that the embedding of $P_{i,j}$ was performed using combination 0: $\left(P_{i,j}^{R}, P_{i,j}^{G}, P_{i,j}^{B}\right)$ to embed the secret message. Next, the pixel value $(206, 108, 172)$ is mapped back to the XYZ coordinates in the reference space, resulting in the extraction of the secret message $(16)_{27}$.

The structure of the magic cube is influenced by the value of M. In the proposed method, the length of the magic cube M can be used to control the embedding capacity and security of the embedding process. The embedding capacity EC can be evaluated by M using $log_2 M$. For example, the EC is 1 bit-per-pixel (bpp) when $M = 2$, and EC is 2 bpp when $M = 4$. It can be observed that the embedding capacity increases with the increase of M.

Additionally, Table 3 presents the experimental data obtained in the proposed method for different lengths of M values. The embedding capacity of the proposed method can be freely adjusted from 1 to 8 bpp. The table displays the number of combinations and the embedding capacity corresponding to the value of M from 2 to 10.

Table 3. The corresponding number of combinations and bpp.

M	Combinations	bpp
2	8!	1
3	27!	1.58
4	64!	2
5	125!	2.32
6	216!	2.58
7	343!	2.81
8	512!	3
9	729!	3.17
10	1000!	3.32

4 EXPERIMENTAL RESULTS AND DISCUSSIONS

In this study, we utilize four 512 × 512 color images: Baboon, Peppers, Airplane, and Splash, as shown in Figure 6, to test the performance of the proposed method. The remainder of this section will first introduce the evaluation method used to assess performance. Subsequently, we will discuss the experimental results in comparison with existing state-of-the-art research.

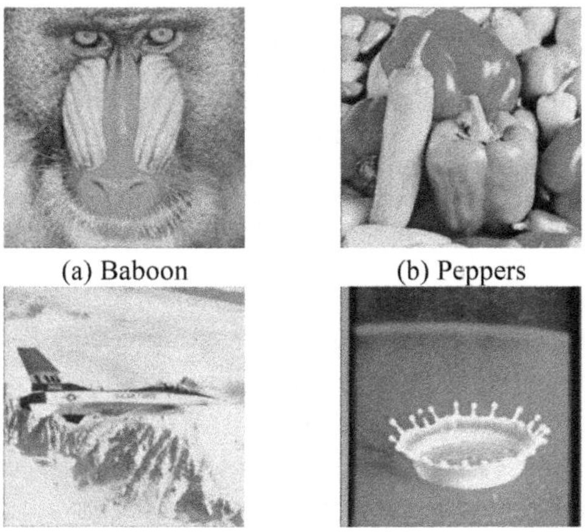

(a) Baboon (b) Peppers (c) Airplane (d) Splash

Figure 6. Four 512 × 512 color images.

4.1 *Performance metrics*

This research employs two metrics to evaluate the algorithm's performance: visual quality and embedding capacity. First, we apply the peak signal-to-noise ratio (PSNR) to assess the visual quality of the stego images and compare them with their corresponding cover images. A higher PSNR value indicates better visual imperceptibility, and the calculation of PSNR is defined as follows:

$$PSNR = 10\, log_{10} \frac{255^2}{MSE}\ (dB), \qquad (2)$$

where the mean square error (MSE) between the stego image and the cover image can be calculated by the following equation:

$$MSE = \frac{1}{H \times W} \sum\nolimits_{i=1}^{H} \sum\nolimits_{j=1}^{W} [I'(i,j) - I(i,j)]^2, \qquad (3)$$

where H and W are the height and width of the cover image, respectively. A lower MSE indicates less distortion in the stego image. Since this study employs color images as carriers for embedding, the calculation is performed using Equation (4) shown below. It calculates the MSE separately for the three RGB channels and takes their average, resulting in the PSNR value for the entire color image.

$$PSNR = 10\, log_{10} \frac{255^2}{\frac{1}{3}[MSE(R) + MSE(G) + MSE(B)]} (\mathrm{dB}) \qquad (4)$$

The embedding capacity EC is measured as bpp, which can be calculated as follows:

$$\mathrm{EC} = \frac{S}{H \times W}\ (\mathrm{bpp}), \qquad (5)$$

where s represents is the total number of bits of the secret messages embedded in the cover image, and H and W are the height and width of the cover image I, respectively. A higher value of B indicates that the cover image contains more confidential data, indicating better embedding capacity of the proposed method.

4.2 *Experimental results*

Table 4 shows the comparison of the experimental results before and after the improvement of the proposed method in this paper. The comparisons are made for three different mapping combinations used for embedding. Another method disregards the human visual system and employs a single mapping combination, where the RGB pixel values of the color image correspond solely to the XYZ coordinates in the reference space. From the experimental results, it can be seen that under the same embedding capacity, the PSNR values of the embedding methods utilizing three mapping combinations show improvement compared to the method using a single mapping combination.

From Table 5, the experimental results demonstrate the image visual quality at embedding rates ranging from 1 to 4 bpp between the proposed and AbdelRaouf's method [10]. It can be seen that

Table 4. Embedding example

	RGB pixel value maps to (X, Y, Z)		*Proposed Method*	
	Baboon	Airplane	Baboon	Airplane
bpp	*PSNR (dB)*			
1	51.144	51.145	52.394	52.400
1.58	49.891	49.890	50.773	50.785
2	46.371	46.374	47.501	47.490
2.32	45.117	45.110	46.174	46.136
2.58	43.128	43.120	44.267	44.272
2.81	42.108	42.105	43.207	43.296
3	40.729	40.722	41.872	42.025
3.17	39.888	39.886	41.017	41.193
3.32	38.827	38.823	39.978	40.179
3.46	38.122	38.124	39.254	39.441
3.58	37.270	37.276	38.424	38.590
3.7	36.657	36.663	37.797	37.913

Table 5. Comparison of the proposed method and AbdelRaouf's method

	Proposed Method		*AbdelRaouf [10]*	
Image	*bpp*	*PSNR*	*bpp*	*PSNR*
Baboon	1	52.39	1.01	50.97
	2	47.50	2.02	43.31
	3.17	41.02	3.19	35.46
	4	35.94	4.01	28.27
Peppers	1	52.39	1.01	50.98
	2	47.39	2.02	43.27
	3.17	40.77	3.19	35.40
	4	35.60	4.01	28.25
Airplane	1	52.40	1.01	50.97
	2	47.49	2.02	43.30
	3.17	41.19	3.19	35.42
	4	35.92	4.01	28.47
Splash	1	52.39	1.01	50.98
	2	47.46	2.02	43.29
	3.17	40.94	3.19	35.44
	4	35.90	4.01	27.99

under the similar embedding rates, our method has higher visual imperceptibility with an average increase of 4.68% in PSNR values.

Table 6 shows a comparison between the proposed method and Chuang *et al.*'s method [18]. As Chuang *et al.*'s method is based on embedding messages using pixel averages, the quality of the stego image is dependent on the characteristics of the original image. We observed from Table 6 that when the embedding rate does not exceed 4 and when the testing images are not suitable for averaging (i.e., meaning the images themselves are not sufficiently smooth), the proposed method achieves better visual imperceptibility compared to Chuang *et al.*'s [18] method. From Figure 7, it can be observed that the PSNR of the proposed method outperforms Chuang *et al.*'s method with embedding capacity of 1.58 bpp and 3 bpp. However, when the embedding capacities are around 3.5 to 4.5, a crossover occurs. The proposed method experiences a stable decline in values, while Chuang *et al.*'s [18] method maintains a steady curve, staying within the range of 30 to 40, indicating its relative insensitivity to changes in embedding rate. However, since the proposed method allows for the adjustment of the M value during data embedment, the embedding rate can be flexibly controlled. Thus, compared to Chuang *et al.*'s [18] method, the proposed method offers higher flexibility and security.

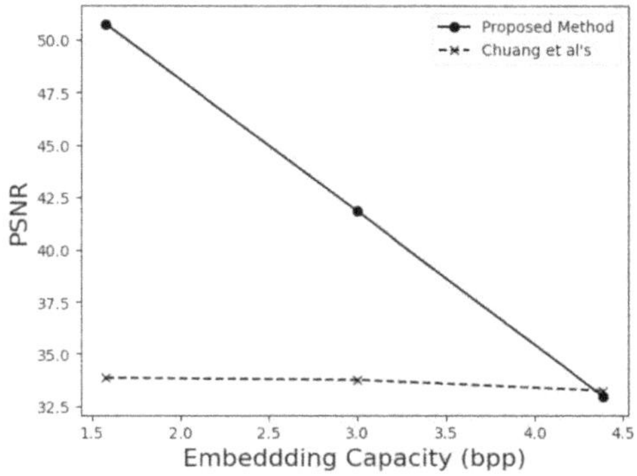

Figure 7. Trend chart of average PSNR between the proposed method and Chuang et al.'s method.

Table 6. Comparison of the proposed method and Chuang et al's method

	Proposed Method		*Chuang et al's [18]*	
Image	*bpp*	*PSNR*	*bpp*	*PSNR*
Baboon	1.58	50.773	1.476	26.08
	3	41.872	2.959	26.07
	4.39	32.656	4.439	26.01
Peppers	1.58	50.679	1.476	33.49
	3	41.654	2.959	33.42
	4.39	33.172	4.439	33.15
Airplane	1.58	50.785	1.476	36.74
	3	42.025	2.959	36.59
	4.39	33.365	4.439	36.02
Splash	1.58	50.756	1.476	39.09
	3	41.798	2.959	38.94
	4.39	32.650	4.439	37.77

5 CONCLUSION

This paper is inspired by the concept of Lin *et al.*'s SRM method (2009) to propose a novel color image steganography based on a magic cube. The proposed method maps the RGB channel values of each pixel in a color image to the XYZ coordinate space (X, Y, Z) of the magic cube reference space, and uses it as the embedding foundation. The core of the embedding method in this study lies in combining the magic cube reference space and calculating the least difference in pixel values of the green channel among three corresponding combinations. This method significantly enhances the quality of the stego image. Furthermore, the embedding capacity and the number of magic cube combinations can be increased by adjusting the M value. Therefore, the use of magic cube possesses advantages of adaptability and scalability. Given that the carrier is the color image, this study further optimizes the embedding algorithm by incorporating the characteristics of the human visual system. Experimental results demonstrate that the method proposed in this paper achieves good visual quality in embeddings on various carriers. With an embedding capacity of 1 bpp, the highest PSNR value can reach 52.394 dB. Balancing embedding capacity and security, this method effectively estimates the rates between the two as the smoothness of the original cover image does not significantly affect visual quality during the embedding of confidential messages. However, image visual quality may be compromised at high embedding rates. Thus, future work can aim to explore and identify more efficient embedding criteria that maintain visual imperceptibility while minimizing computational complexity.

ACKNOWLEDGMENTS

This work was partially supported by the National Science and Technology Council, Taiwan, R.O.C. (Grant Nos. NSTC 113-2221-E-039-020, NSTC 113-2221-E-005-086, NSTC 111-2221-E-005-048, and NSTC 113-2634-F-005-001-MBK) and China Medical University, Taiwan (Grant No. CMU113-MF-121).

REFERENCES

[1] Chang C.-C., Chen T.-S., and Chung L.-Z., (2002), A steganographic method based upon JPEG and quantization table modification, *Information Sciences*, vol. 141, no. 1–2, pp. 123–138.

[2] Alturki F. and Mersereau R., (2001), Secure blind image steganographic technique using discrete Fourier transformation, *in Proceedings 2001 International Conference on Image Processing (Cat. No. 01CH37205)*, vol. 2: IEEE, pp. 542–545.

[3] Hsieh M.-S., Tseng D.-C., and Huang Y.-H., (2001), Hiding digital watermarks using multiresolution wavelet transform, *IEEE Transactions on Industrial Electronics*, vol. 48, no. 5, pp. 875–882.

[4] Abdelwahab A. A. and Hassaan L. A., (2008), A discrete wavelet transform based technique for image data hiding, in *2008 National Radio Science Conference*: IEEE, pp. 1–9.

[5] Bender W., Gruhl D., Morimoto N., and Lu A., (1996), Techniques for data hiding, *IBM Systems Journal*, vol. 35, no. 3.4, pp. 313–336.

[6] Zhang X. and Wang S., (2006), Efficient steganographic embedding by exploiting modification direction, *IEEE Communications Letters*, vol. 10, no. 11, pp. 781–783.

[7] Wu D.-C. and Tsai W.-H., (2003), A steganographic method for images by pixel-value differencing, *Pattern Recognition Letters*, vol. 24, no. 9–10, pp. 1613–1626.

[8] Tian J., (2003), Reversible data embedding using a difference expansion, *IEEE Transactions on Circuits and Systems for Video Technology*, vol. 13, no. 8, pp. 890–896.

[9] Ni Z., Shi Y.-Q., Ansari N., and Su W., (2006), Reversible data hiding, *IEEE Transactions on Circuits and Systems for Video Technology*, vol. 16, no. 3, pp. 354–362.

[10] AbdelRaouf A., (2021), A new data hiding approach for image steganography based on visual color sensitivity, *Multimedia Tools and Applications*, vol. 80, no. 15, pp. 23393–23417.

[11] Singh A. and Singh H., (2015), An improved LSB based image steganography technique for RGB images, in *2015 IEEE International Conference on Electrical, Computer and Communication Technologies (ICECCT)*: IEEE, pp. 1–4.

[12] Rawat D. and Bhandari V., (2013), A steganography technique for hiding image in an image using LSB method for 24 bit color image, *International Journal of Computer Applications*, vol. 64, no. 20, pp. 15–19.

[13] Islam A. U. et al., (2016), An improved image steganography technique based on MSB using bit differencing, in *2016 Sixth International Conference on Innovative Computing Technology (INTECH)*: IEEE, pp. 265–269.

[14] Dumre R. and Dave A., (2021), Exploring LSB Steganography Possibilities in RGB Images, in *2021 12th International Conference on Computing Communication and Networking Technologies (ICCCNT)*: IEEE, pp. 1–7.

[15] Emam M. M., Aly A. A., and Omara F. A., (2016), An improved image steganography method based on LSB technique with random pixel selection, *International Journal of Advanced Computer Science and Applications*, vol. 7, no. 3.

[16] Lin C.-N., Chang C.-C., Lee W.-B., and Lin J., (2009), A novel secure data hiding scheme using a secret reference matrix, in *2009 Fifth International Conference on Intelligent Information Hiding and Multimedia Signal Processing*: IEEE, pp. 369–373.

[17] Chang C.-C., Chou Y.-C., and Kieu T. D., (2008), An information hiding scheme using Sudoku, in *2008 3rd International Conference on Innovative Computing Information and Control*: IEEE, pp. 17–17.

[18] Chuang Y.-H., Lin B.-S., Chen Y.-X., and Shiu H.-J., (2021), Steganography in RGB images using adjacent mean, *IEEE Access*, vol. 9, pp. 164256–164274.

System Innovation for a Global Economy – Lam et al. (Eds)
© 2026 The Author(s), ISBN 978-1-041-10520-6

Integrating grounded theory with the MDA framework: A game design approach for visual fatigue alleviation

Ruo-Xi Li
School of Design Institute, Fujian University of Technology, Fuzhou, China

Jeng-Chung Woo
School of Design Institute, Fujian University of Technology, Fuzhou, China
Design Innovation Research Center of Humanities and Social Sciences Research Base of Colleges and Universities in Fujian Province, Fuzhou, China

Yu-Wei Lin
School of Design Institute, Fujian University of Technology, Fuzhou, China

ABSTRACT: As digitalization accelerates, visual health issues, especially eye fatigue, are becoming more prominent, yet their seriousness is often underestimated. Gamified design offers a novel solution for eye exercises. This study, aiming to relieve eye fatigue, combines the MDA framework (Mechanics, Dynamics, Aesthetics) and Grounded Theory to build a dual-dimensional design strategy. Literature review confirms the scientific basis and practical value of eye-tracking relief games. Semi-structured interviews were conducted with 15 cross-disciplinary experts, including ophthalmologists, game developers, interaction designers, and design educators. Grounded Theory was applied to perform three levels of coding, extracting 44 open codes, 11 axial codes, and 3 selective codes, leading to the identification of three core categories: User Motivation, Interaction Guidance, and Visual Relaxation. The Mechanics layer incorporates ocular yoga principles with quantitative duration protocols, while Dynamics enhance sustained engagement through adaptive challenges, educational elements, and gameplay diversification. Aesthetics leverage minimalist interfaces, chromatic optimization, and iconographic innovation to reduce cognitive load. Two prototype iterations of the eye-tracking game demonstrated significant usability improvements (SUS score: 70 up to 80.71). This research establishes an evidence-based design paradigm for visual health technologies, with future work focusing on clinical validation of fatigue reduction efficacy.

Keywords: Digital Eye Strain, Grounded Theory, MDA Framework, Eye Tracking Technology, Gratification Design

1 INTRODUCTION

The increasing use of digital devices has raised concerns about the prevalence of eye health conditions such as myopia, digital eye strain, and dry eye disease. The World Health Organization (WHO) and the International Telecommunication Union (ITU) are collaborating to develop a global standard for safe viewing devices and systems. This standard aims to guide manufacturers and software developers in integrating features that promote healthy viewing habits (WHO 2025). The standard highlights the potential impact of digital devices on eye health, including digital eye strain and dry eye disease. Studies indicate that digital eye strain (or Computer Vision Syndrome, CVS) is widespread among digital device users, with an incidence rate potentially reaching 50% or higher (Charpe N.A. and Kaushik V. 2009; Ranasinghe P. *et al.* 2016; Sen A. and Richardson S. 2007). A study in Sri Lanka found that among 2,500 computer users, the incidence of CVS was approximately 64% to 90% (Ranasinghe P. *et al.* 2016). Another study identified factors associated with CVS, including personal factors (gender, age, poor posture, improper viewing distance, underlying medical conditions, use of optical correction, rest frequency, and computer usage time) and environmental factors (inadequate workstations, low screen brightness, imbalance between screen and environmental brightness, and low contrast) (Blehm C. *et al.* 2005). Prolonged Visual Display Terminal (VDT) work often results in prolonged staring at screens, leading to visual fatigue (Shall

M.S. and Goldberg S.J. 1992). Tension in the extraocular muscles (EOMs) caused by prolonged contraction can increase intraocular pressure, thereby increasing the risk of strabismus and glaucoma (Krishna N. and Botelho S.Y. 1963).

Relieving visual fatigue has become an urgent issue. Ophthalmologists recommend eye exercises to prevent vision problems and eye diseases such as myopia and hyperopia, and to reduce eye fatigue and improve vision. Compared to traditional drug or device-based treatments, eye yoga aligns with the "prevention-first" health concept and is particularly suitable for groups with prolonged eye use, such as students, office workers, and designers. If practiced daily, eye exercises can improve accuracy and letter recognition, potentially delaying the need for glasses in some individuals. In recent years, physical interventions for visual fatigue have gained popularity. Eye yoga, which involves specific eye movements, focusing adjustments, and relaxation exercises for the eye muscles, is believed to improve ocular blood circulation and relieve ciliary muscle tension (Singh J. *et al.* 2023). Eye yoga typically includes exercises such as eye movements, blinking, gazing (e.g., Tratak gazing), and rotational movements, practiced for several minutes to hours daily over several weeks. Some studies have combined specific breathing exercises or relaxation techniques to enhance intervention effectiveness. Eye yoga consists of eight steps: palming, blinking, lateral gaze, forward-backward gaze, vertical gaze, rotational gaze, nose-tip gazing, and distance-near viewing. The entire routine lasts 15 minutes. Palming relaxes the periocular muscles and stimulates aqueous humor circulation, which helps correct vision defects (Rizanti A. P. 2021). Blinking exercises encourage spontaneous blinking reflexes and induce relaxation of the eye muscles (Bang J.W. *et al.* 2014). Lateral gaze relieves tension in the medial and lateral rectus muscles caused by near work, preventing and correcting strabismus while improving muscle coordination (Di Stasi L.L. *et al.* 2014). Rotational viewing restores overall balance to the eye muscles, exercising the two oblique muscles and improving coordination between the two eyes. Vertical viewing balances the superior and inferior rectus muscles. Nasal gazing improves the focusing and accommodation ability of the eye muscles, while distance viewing expands the accommodation range and enhances the sensitivity of the accommodation system, thereby reducing the occurrence of visual fatigue (Vienne C. *et al.* 2012). A study on eye yoga for college students showed that the intervention group had significantly lower visual fatigue scores, with an increased proportion of asymptomatic individuals. The study highlighted the standardized nature of systematic yoga eye movement routines, which are easy to promote and can be combined with technologies such as Virtual Reality (VR) to develop dynamic eye movement training adapted to digital eye-use scenarios (Marandi R.Z. *et al.* 2018).

However, people often do not perform eye health exercises regularly or at all, as these exercises are perceived as boring. Another well-known reason is that individuals do not know how to perform eye yoga correctly. Existing solutions often passively remind users to rest or provide general eye care advice, which have obvious limitations. First, they lack real-time biometric feedback mechanisms to adjust interventions based on the user's eye condition. Second, these solutions often ignore the individualized needs and behavioral habits of users during digital device use, leading to limited intervention effectiveness. Additionally, traditional methods fail to fully utilize modern technological tools such as eye-tracking and gamification to enhance user engagement and compliance. Serious games are considered an attractive way to engage people in beneficial activities such as learning and rehabilitation through task completion.

Salen and Zimmerman defined the core of game design as "constructing rules and structures to shape player experiences." (Tekinbas K.S. and Zimmerman E. 2003) Their research further proposed that successful game design aims to create meaningful play, where players establish value connections between decision sequences and outcome feedback. Therefore, gamification, as a behavioral incentive framework, can effectively enhance participation in rehabilitation training and compliance with diagnostic processes, encouraging self-health management. Achtman's team found that users prefer game-based training materials over conventional rehabilitation programs, indicating that patients are more inclined toward gamified rehabilitation processes (Achtman R.L. *et al.* 2008). From a medical management perspective, gamification can promote autonomy and guidance in the training process. Studies have shown that active eye-tracking exercises are more effective than static visual display exercises. However, existing research primarily focuses on optimizing eye-tracking control interface element recognition technologies and has not yet systematically constructed a comprehensive framework for eye-movement-based gamified visual fatigue relief.

Since the iOS 18 update introduced eye-tracking functionality, the App Store has launched two applications leveraging eye-tracking for vision exercises: "Eyeye Vision Training" and "iBright-Eye Relaxation." These applications are very similar to the game mechanisms proposed in this study, guiding users through specific eye movements to relieve visual fatigue. Both applications include similar actions, guiding users to move their gaze across the screen to exercise the eye muscles. However, due to limitations in screen size and distance, the amplitude and frequency of these movements may not be natural, affecting exercise effectiveness. In terms of cross-gaze, the applications guide users through specific graphics or text, but users may struggle to grasp the rhythm and amplitude of the movements accurately, leading to operational errors. The relaxation of distant viewing is limited by device screen size and usage environment, failing to provide sufficient distance for relaxation. Both applications include a rest segment with closed eyes, but the rest time settings are inflexible and do not meet the needs of different users. Neither application includes rotational viewing or distant relaxation, which this study aims to address.

In game design and development, usability testing is a crucial phase. It ensures that the game is acceptable and satisfactory to users, thereby guaranteeing usability, efficiency, and interaction performance. In 1986, John Brooke developed the System Usability Scale (SUS), a ten-item questionnaire where odd items are positive statements and even items are negative statements. The SUS is more reliable than custom questionnaires or other commercial questionnaires, even in studies with small sample sizes.

The innovation of this study lies in the first integration of Grounded Theory and the MDA (Mechanics, Dynamics, Aesthetics) game design framework, proposing a gamified design solution for eye-movement yoga. This approach provides users with biofeedback on their eye fatigue status through game scores and offers personalized relief strategies. Additionally, gamification elements enhance user engagement and long-term interest, effectively alleviating digital eye strain. This innovative GT-MDA dual-loop design model not only breaks the limitations of traditional game design theories reliant on experience but also provides a reusable methodological tool for health game design, promising to drive a paradigm shift in gamified visual fatigue relief.

2 METHODOLOGY

2.1 *Grounded theory implementation*

Grounded Theory, proposed by Glaser and Strauss in 1967, resonates methodologically with the iterative development logic of game design. In commercial games, improving designs to encourage player spending is a common strategy (Glaser B. and Strauss A. 2017). Elena P. *et al.* found that designing for specific groups (e.g., limited-time rewards) can sustain player spending impulses, driven by social pressures to avoid team failure (Petrovskaya E. and Zendle D. 2022). In this study, literature reviews and semi-structured questionnaires were conducted with 15 cross-disciplinary experts (2 ophthalmologists, 2 game programmers, 9 industrial designers, and 2 design educators) to address gamified interventions for visual fatigue, eye-tracking technology adaptation, and visual comfort design. Interviews were conducted face-to-face, recorded with consent, and transcribed. NVivo software assisted in the three-tier coding process (open, axial, and selective) of Grounded Theory.

2.2 *MDA framework mapping*

The MDA framework, proposed by Hunicke *et al.* in 2004, decomposes games into Mechanics, Dynamics, and Aesthetics (Hunicke R. *et al.* 2004). Mechanics refers to the rules and algorithms governing game behavior; Dynamics describes the runtime behavior of Mechanics; and Aesthetics represents the user's emotional response. This framework helps diagnose and optimize game design issues by structuring problems into three dimensions: mechanical imbalance, dynamic instability, and aesthetic deviation (Ouriques L. *et al.* 2021). The MDA framework has been applied to therapeutic video games (TVGs) to improve patient rehabilitation experiences. Yang *et al.* used the MDA framework to develop a TVG for preschool children with acute lymphoblastic leukemia, showing reduced anxiety levels in the experimental group compared to the control group (Yang D.J. *et al.* 2022).

3 RESULTS

3.1 *Grounded theory*

Through systematic text deconstruction and conceptual aggregation, 135 concepts, 44 open codes, 11 axial codes, and 3 selective codes were identified, forming a three-level indicator system for visual fatigue relief game design. Open coding extracted key information from interview transcripts, creating foundational labels. For example, the concept "C3 Simple Interface Guides Well" was derived from statements like "A simple interface better guides users and reduces confusion." These labels were further categorized into open codes, which were then into axial codes. Finally, three selective codes were identified: User Motivation, Interaction Guidance, and Visual Relaxation. These core categories formed the design element model for visual fatigue relief eye-movement games.

Table 1. Conceptualization of interview data (Example).

Interview Data	Labeling	Conceptualization
I think simplicity better guides users and reduces confusion.	c3 Simple Interface Guides Well	C3 Strong Guidance of Simple Interface

(*continued*)

Table 1. Continued

Interview Data	Labeling	Conceptualization
I believe users make more deliberate choices in simple layouts, leading to more precise relief.	c4 Simple Interface Aids User Selection	

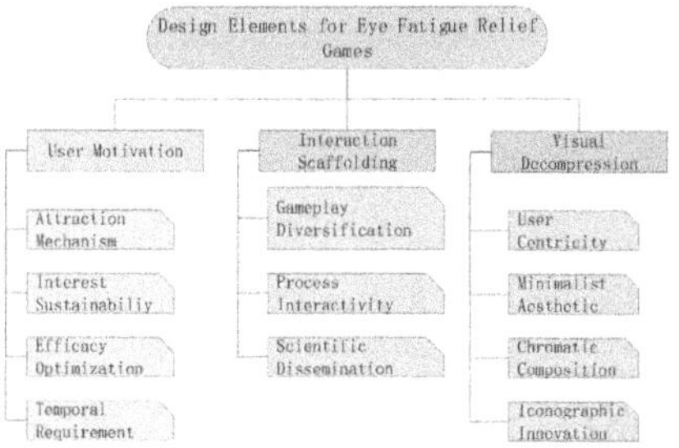

Figure 1. Design element model for visual fatigue alleviation in games.

3.2 *GT-MDA framework*

By integrating these design elements into the MDA framework, we have established a design logic that balances scientific rigor with user experience (see Figure 2). The Mechanics Layer is built on the principles of eye yoga, incorporating duration requirements and relief rules to ensure the game's scientific validity and quantifiability. The Dynamics Layer sustains user engagement by maintaining long-term interest, attracting users, providing professional education, offering diverse gameplay, and ensuring smooth interaction. This layer ensures a positive user experience and enhances participation and sustained usage motivation. The Aesthetics Layer, guided by user-centered principles, minimalist design, color schemes, and creative icons, resonates emotionally with users and optimizes their visual and cognitive experiences, all within the architecture of the Mechanics and Dynamics Layers.

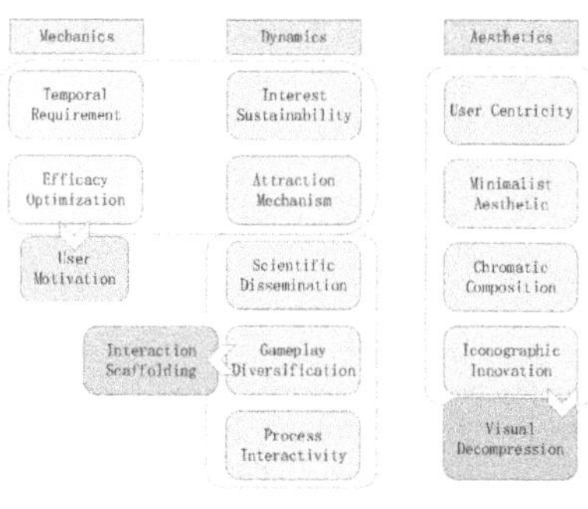

Figure 2. Construction of the GT-MDA theoretical framework.

In summary, this framework translates core user needs, extracted via Grounded Theory, into design elements. Combined with the MDA framework's structured approach, it ensures scientific rigor, experience-driven design, and behavior change mechanisms for eye-tracking games (see Figure 3 and Table 3). Eye movement data capture and visual ergonomics ensure quantifiable relief effects, while smooth interaction and minimalist aesthetics reduce users' cognitive load. Gamification elements transform short-term relief behaviors into long-term eye-care habits. The design meets VDT users' immediate relief needs and, through knowledge embedding and cultural integration, enhances their eye-care awareness, forming a closed-loop eye health management system from "relief" to "prevention."

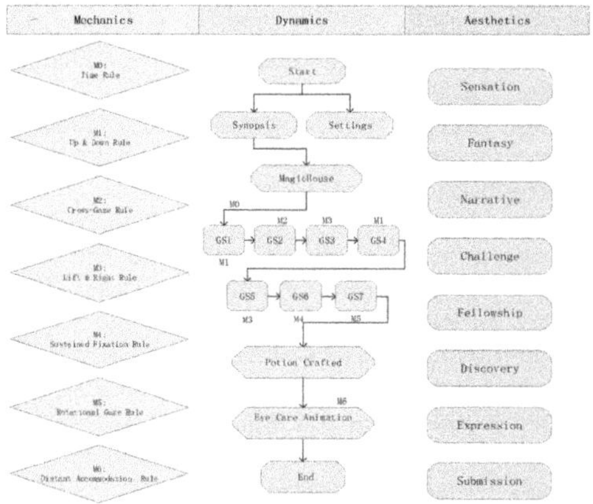

Figure 3. MDA design framework for visual fatigue-alleviating games.

Table 3. Game rules description.

	Description of Rules
M0	Time Rule: Completes prompted actions within designated time intervals; non-completion incurs penalty points
M1	Up & Down Rule: Executes vertical ocular movements (superior/inferior directional shifts) following interface prompts
M2	Cross-Gaze Rule: Achieves diagonal gaze patterns intersecting horizontal and vertical axes
M3	Lift & Right Rule: Performs lateral eye movements along the horizontal plane
M4	Sustained Fixation Rule: Maintains ocular focus on interface elements meeting predefined duration thresholds
M5	Rotational Gaze Rule: Executes clockwise/counterclockwise eye movement trajectories
M6	Distant Accommodation Rule: Performs visual system adjustments for far-plane focal accommodation

3.3 *Game design*

The game design, based on eye-yoga movements, includes specific eye exercises to improve ocular blood circulation and relieve ciliary muscle tension. Eye-tracking technology monitors user movements in real-time, ensuring accurate exercise execution. Forest therapy elements are incorporated to reduce psychological stress during game loading, providing users with knowledge snippets on visual fatigue (Mohamad Yahaya N.A. *et al.* 2023). Game tasks increase in difficulty, starting with basic eye movements and progressing to complex challenges. The game uses Tobii Eye Tracker 5, with APIs compatible with multiple programming languages, to integrate eye-tracking data into the game for real-time feedback.

Figure 4. Page display of visual fatigue relief game.

3.4 *SUS score improvement*

The initial test involved 9 VDT workers, yielding an average SUS score of 70 (C rating) (Sauro J. and Lewis J.R. 2014). After iterative modifications based on user feedback, a second test with 7 participants resulted in an average SUS score of 80.71 (A-rating). The improvement was statistically significant ($t(13) = 2.98$, $p = 0.011$), with a large effect size (Cohen's $d = 1.62$).

Table 4. Comparison of SUS scores between two tests.

Test Phase	Sample Size (n)	Mean (M)	Standard Deviation (SD)	95%CI	Jeff's Rating
Initial Test	8	70.00	8.15	[63.75, 76.25]	C
Iterative Test	7	80.71	5.43	[75.84, 85.58]	A-

4 CONCLUSION

This study combines Grounded Theory and the MDA framework to provide a systematic theoretical foundation for visual fatigue relief game design. The GT-MDA dual-loop design model enhances scientific rigor and operability, offering methodological support for gamified interventions. The developed game demonstrates good usability, with potential applications in related fields. Future research will expand the GT-MDA model to multi-scenario applications, conduct long-term follow-up experiments, and perform cost-benefit analyses.

ACKNOWLEDGMENT

This work was supported by Fujian University of Technology [grant numbers GY-S21081, 2021], and Design Innovation Research Center of Humanities and Social Sciences Research Base of Colleges and Universities in Fujian Province.

REFERENCES

Achtman R. L., Green C. S. and Bavelier D., (2008), *Restorative Neurology and Neuroscience*. 26(4–5) 435–446.

Antona B., Barrio A. R., Gascó A., et al., *Applied Ergonomics*, 2018.68 12–17.

Bando T., Iijima A. and Tano T., (2012), *Journal of Vision*.12(6) 1–12.

Bang J. W., Heo H., Choi J. S., et al., (2014), *Sensors*.14 (9) 16467–16485.

Blehm C., Vishnu S., Khattak A., et al., (2005), *Survey of Ophthalmology*.50(3) 253–262.

Cantó-Sancho N, Ronda E, Cabrero-García J, et al., (2022), *International Journal of Environmental Research and Public Health*. 19(8) 4506.

Cantó-Sancho N, Seguí-Crespo M, Zhao G, et al., (2023), *BMC Ophthalmology*. 23(1) 298.

Charpe N. A. and Kaushik V., (2009), *Journal of Human Ecology*.28(1) 67–69.

Dabrowiecki A, Villalobos A and Krupinski E A., (2020), *Journal of Medical Imaging*. 7(2) 022402.

Di Stasi L. L., McCamy M. B., M. L. Macknik, et al., (2014), *Annals of Surgery*. 259(4) 824–829.

Glaser B, Strauss A., (2017), *Discovery of Grounded Theory: Strategies for Qualitative Research*, Routledge.

Gupta S. K. and Aparna S., (2020), *International Journal of Yoga*.13(1) 76–79.

Hunicke R., LeBlanc M. and Zubek R., (2004), *Proceedings of the AAAI Workshop on Challenges in Game AI*, 1722.

Krishna N. and Botelho S. Y., (1963), *Experimental Eye Research*.2(2) 173–IN33.

Lin Y. H., Chen C. Y., Lu S. Y., et al., (2008), *Displays*.29(5) 487–492.

Lovell-Patel R, Ajiboye A and Manfrin A., (2023), *Contemporary Clinical Trials*. 125 107046.

Mar Seguí M, Cabrero-García J, Crespo A, et al., (2015), *Journal of Clinical Epidemiology*. 68(6) 662–673.

Marandi R. Z., Madeleine P., Omland Ø., et al., (2018), *Scientific Reports*. 8(1) 13148.

Mazloum A., Kumashiro M. Izumi H., et al., (2008), *Industrial Health*. 46(3) 269–280.

Menozzi M., Näpflin U. and Krueger H., (1999), *Displays*. 20(1) 3–10.

Niu Y., Tian J., Han Z., et al., (2022), *International Journal of Environmental Research and Public Health.* 19(17) 10737.

Ouriques L., Xexéo G., Barbosa C. E., (2021), *Brazilian Symposium on Games and Digital Entertainment (SBGames).*

Petrovskaya E. and Zendle D., (2022), *Human Behavior and Emerging Technologies.* 2022(1) 1260174.

Price D. J. D. S., (1963), *Little Science, Big Science,* Columbia University Press.

Ranasinghe P. and Wathurapatha W. S., 2016, Perera Y. S., *et al.*, BMC Research Notes.9 1–9.

Rizanti A. P., (2021), *Jurnal Berita Ilmu Keperawatan.*14 (1) 1–9.

Rosenfield M., (2011), *Ophthalmic and Physiological Optics.* 31(5) 502–515.

Rossi G C M, Bettio F, González-Pérez M, et al., (2022), *International Journal of Environmental Research and Public Health.* 19(5) 2517.

Sánchez-Brau M, Domenech-Amigot B, Brocal-Fernández F, et al. (2020), *International Journal of Environmental Research and Public Health.* 17(3) 1003.

Sauro J. and Lewis J. R., (2014), *User Experience Metrics: Statistical Methods for Quantifying User Experience*, Beijing: China Machine Press.

Seguí-Crespo M, Cantó-Sancho N, Sánchez-Brau M, et al., (2022), *Gaceta Sanitaria.* 37 102264.

Sen A. and Richardson S., (2007), *Journal of Human Ergology.* 36(2) 45–50.

Shall M. S. and Goldberg S. J., (1992), *Brain Research.*587(2) 291–300.

Singh J., Katiyar V. K., Singh D. S., et al., (2023), *Journal of Applied Consciousness Studies.*11(2) 85–90.

Tekinbas K. S. and Zimmerman E., (2003), *Rules of Play: Game Design Fundamentals,* MIT Press.

Vienne C., Blondé L. and Doyen D., (2012), *Stereoscopic Displays and Applications XXIII (SPIE).* 8288 361–371.

WHO, WHO Newsroom, (2025).

Yang D. J., Lu M. Y., Chen C. W., et al., (2022), *JMIR Serious Games.*10(3) e37079.

System Innovation for a Global Economy – Lam et al. (Eds)

Development of damage scale mapping technology for collapsed houses using generative AI

Haruhiro Shiraishi & Yuichiro Usuda
University of Tsukuba, Graduate School of Science and Technology Degree Programs in Systems and Information Engineering, Tsukuba, Japan
National Research Institute for Earth Science and Disaster Resilience, Tsukuba, Japan

ABSTRACT: In recent years, the increasing frequency of natural disasters has highlighted the need for rapid and accurate damage assessment. This study develops a technology that utilizes generative AI to automatically map the scale of damage to collapsed houses. Traditional methods using aerial and satellite imagery are time-consuming and subject to weather conditions. Our approach leverages street view images and AI-based image analysis to assess damage more accurately. By analyzing images obtained via the Ma-pillary API, our AI model categorizes building damage into four levels: "No Damage," "Mild Damage," "Moderate Damage," and "Severe Damage," enabling the automatic generation of damage maps. This advancement facilitates prompt rescue efforts and recovery planning. Furthermore, to implement this technology effectively in society, enhancing AI transparency and establishing data-sharing frameworks are essential. The results of this study are expected to contribute to improving damage assessment accuracy.

1 INTRODUCTION

As the frequency and severity of natural disasters increase, researchers have been exploring machine learning and deep learning techniques to develop rapid and accurate damage assessment methods (Linardos *et al.* 2022). Recent studies have attempted real-time damage assessment using satellite imagery, social media data, and IoT sensor data. By incorporating generative AI, such as the GPT-4o API, it becomes possible to analyze vast amounts of image data and immediately verbalize post-disaster conditions (Estêvão *et al.* 2024). This system could significantly enhance rescue operations and damage investigations. Additionally, integrating real-time data provided by citizens could enable a more comprehensive understanding of disaster impacts.

To maximize the effectiveness of AI in disaster response, it is crucial to increase public awareness and acceptance of AI technologies. Successful implementation of AI in disaster management requires collaboration among local governments, disaster response agencies, and private organizations. Many machine learning and deep learning models have been proposed to assess post-disaster damage at an infrastructure level. However, most research has focused on qualitative identification of building damage rather than precise quantification and classification based on standardized damage scales. Furthermore, many studies rely on individual images (typically from satellite imagery), which provide an overall view of damage but do not necessarily reflect the precise condition of individual buildings. To address this issue, researchers have proposed various methods. For example, studies utilizing ground-level video footage from dashboard cameras have made significant progress (Shiraishi *et al.* 2025). These studies calculate the area of the footage displaying damage to standardize damage assessments.

Additionally, researchers have explored crowdsourcing techniques to analyze large datasets rapidly and accurately. For instance, distributed networks involving citizen participation have been introduced, proving effective in disaster response efforts such as the 2010 Haiti earthquake and the 2011 Christchurch earthquake (Heinzelman *et al.* 2010). In conclusion, integrating machine learning and deep learning into disaster damage assessment has revolutionized the field. Leveraging remote sensing and AI advancements enables the extraction of meaningful features from satellite imagery, rapid damage assessment, and large-scale data analysis through crowdsourcing. These techniques hold the potential to enhance disaster response, save lives, and reduce economic losses. Moreover, street view imagery is increasingly used for disaster mapping, often in combination with user-generated content from platforms like Mapillary (Ma Dawei 2019). Mapillary, a crowdsourced street view platform, has been employed in various studies to analyze street-level data. This study aims to combine generative AI APIs (GPT-4o) with

DOI: 10.1201/9781003655534-17

Mapillary's street view database to develop a rapid and accurate damage assessment technique. Additionally, by comparing our approach with an image analysis method with remote sensing index [6], we conduct research in stages, considering the social background of each approach. The positioning of this research is shown in Figure 1.

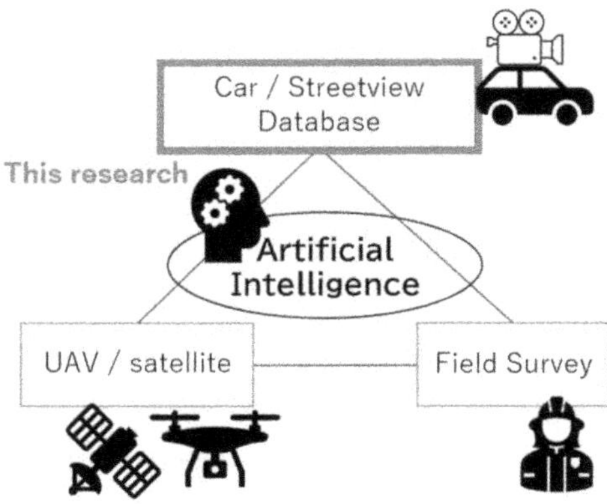

Figure 1. The positioning of this research.

The SIGMA D-Sorbitol (98%) doped the Clevios PH 500 PEDOT: PSS was used as solution for preparation of thin films by a spin-coating method. The Sorbitol was added to the PEDOT: PSS directly, and then the doped PEDOT: PSS was stirred for 30 min at room temperature. The mixed solution was doped again by adding different molar concentrations of H_2SO_4. At last, the mixed PEDOT: PSS solution is the so-called the double doped PEDOT: PSS solution. The double doped PEDOT: PSS solution was coated by spinner on 2 × 2 cm^2 glass substrates and formed the double doped PEDOT: PSS film. The glass substrates were pre-cleaned with acetone, methanol and de-ionized (DI) water in an ultrasonic bath, sequentially. The spin-coating was performed at a rotation rate of 3500 rpm for 20 sec. The double doped PEDOT: PSS film was heated at 150 °C for 20 min on a hotplate in ambient lab conditions.

The sheet resistance was measured with four point sheet resistivity meter (SRM103). The transmittance and surface roughness of the thin films were characterized using the spectrophotometer (HITACHI U-3900) and atomic force microscope (AFM) (XE-70).

2 MATERIALS AND METHODS RESULTS AND DISCUSSION

For this study, we selected Suzu City in Ishikawa Prefecture, one of the most affected areas by the 2024 Noto Peninsula Earthquake, as our case study. Our goal was to assess the damage by utilizing Mapillary's API to analyze post-disaster street view images and extract geographic data such as latitude, longitude, and azimuth to estimate the damage scale. Flowchart for map generation process is shown in Figure 2.

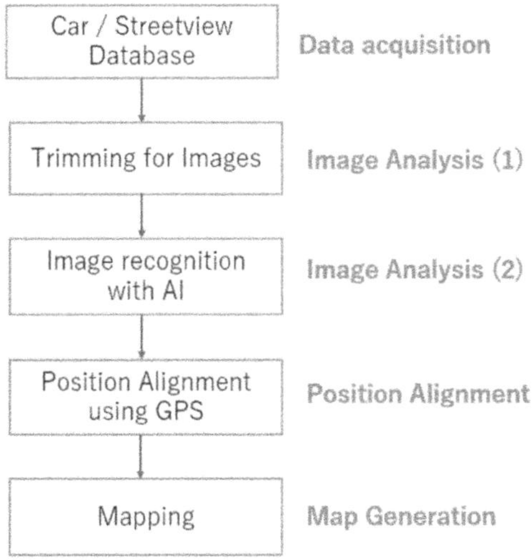

Figure 2. Flowchart for map generation process.

Traditional methods relying on aerial and satellite imagery are susceptible to weather conditions and require significant time for analysis. In contrast, by utilizing ground-level street view images, our method aims to capture detailed damage conditions more accurately and facilitate rapid damage assessments.

This methodology enables the identification of localized building damage and environmental changes that traditional image analysis techniques may overlook. Additionally, collaboration between local governments and residents in providing street view images can enhance the accuracy of damage assessments. By integrating past disaster data, we aim to estimate disaster scale and impact range more precisely. In our study, we conducted damage assessments using two approaches: remote sensing indicators and generative AI. The remote sensing-based approach used post-disaster street view images to log geographic data (latitude, longitude, azimuth) and estimate damage scales efficiently. Conventional aerial and satellite-based methods often suffer from accuracy issues due to weather and timing constraints. Our study emphasized direct observation of damage from a ground-level perspective.

Conversely, our generative AI-based approach utilized images obtained via the Mapillary API, feeding them into an AI model to classify and estimate building damage. By training the AI model on visual damage features, we achieved higher accuracy in damage assessments. Comparing the strengths of remote sensing indicators and generative AI, we examined the criteria for selecting the optimal approach. Using the Mapillary API, we extracted positional and azimuth information from vehicle-mounted cameras to estimate the locations of buildings along both sides of the road. Applying spherical trigonometry, we calculated the new positions based on azimuth adjustments. For instance, in Suzu City, we used parameters x = 70 and y = 2 to estimate new location data. This process enabled us to determine precise building locations, forming the basis for damage estimation. Next, we processed 360-degree images to trim the field of view to the front-facing section of vehicles as shown in Figure 3. Subsequently, we applied generative AI to classify damage levels into four categories. The calculations assigned damage levels to sections A (left front) and B (right front), generating a damage map displaying affected areas as radius-based zones.

Figure 3. Trimming method for 360-degree images to focus on front-facing sections.

3 RESULTS

Our study successfully developed a technology that utilizes generative AI to automatically map the scale of house collapse damage. Traditional damage assessment methods using aerial and satellite imagery face challenges such as long processing times, weather dependence, and difficulty in identifying localized damage. Our approach, leveraging street view images and AI-based image analysis, provided a more rapid and accurate method for evaluating damage conditions. By analyzing street view images obtained via the Mapillary API, our AI model categorized building damage into four levels—"No Damage," "Mild Damage," "Moderate Damage," and "Severe Damage"—to automatically generate visual damage maps as shown in Figure 4.

3.1 *Implementation of damage scale analysis using generative AI*

To efficiently analyze damage, we developed a system that automatically classifies building

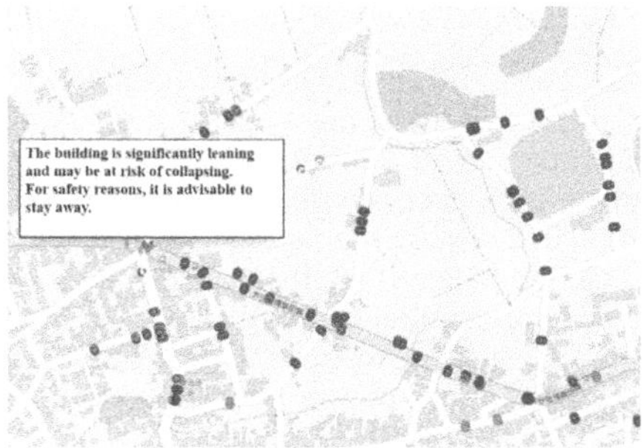

Figure 4. Damage status map automatically generated using generative AI image recognition.

collapse conditions using generative AI. The AI model was trained on street view images obtained via the Mapillary API, evaluating building appearance changes and degrees of collapse. This classification was based on four levels of damage, allowing for objective quantification. Additionally, we created damage maps by processing analysis results into geographical visualizations. Severely damaged areas were highlighted in red, moderately damaged areas in yellow, mildly damaged areas in green, and undamaged areas in blue. This structured visualization supports swift decision-making in disaster response efforts.

3.2 *Comparison with remote sensing (Satellite and drone)*

A comparison between our method and conventional damage assessment techniques using remote sensing revealed that leveraging generative AI enables higher accuracy in damage analysis. Our study demonstrated that the proposed method offers several advantages:

1. Improved Speed
   Traditional remote sensing techniques require time to acquire aerial and satellite images, making real-time damage assessment difficult. In contrast, our method allows for real-time analysis of street view images, facilitating rapid damage evaluation.
2. Detailed Damage Identification
   While aerial and satellite images provide a broad overview of the affected area, they struggle to capture detailed damage information for individual buildings. By utilizing street view images, our approach enables a more precise and localized damage assessment.
3. Enhanced Accuracy
   Generative AI allows for more accurate classification of building damage. The AI model learns damage features and automatically detects collapsed houses, enabling an objective evaluation without relying on human visual inspection.

3.3 *Generation of damage status map*

In this study, we visualized the results of street view image analysis on a map and created a damage status map. This map displays the damage status of each location using color coding, and when clicked, it shows images of the corresponding buildings and details of the damage assessment. This system enables municipalities and disaster prevention agencies to quickly grasp the damage situation and take appropriate actions.

3.4 *Challenges of generative AI technology and future prospects*

The technology developed in this study has proven effective for rapid assessment of damage situations. However, several challenges have also been identified.

1. Ensuring Transparency of AI Technology
   Although generative AI can achieve high accuracy in damage analysis, its decision-making criteria tend to be opaque. To present AI judgment criteria in an explainable manner, the introduction of Explainable AI (XAI) is necessary.
2. Establishing a Framework for Data Sharing
   To apply this method to actual disaster prevention activities, it is essential to establish a data-sharing framework with municipalities and disaster prevention agencies. Special attention must be paid to privacy protection when utilizing SNS data and street view images.
3. Integration with Autonomous Driving Technology
   Further development of this method can be achieved by integrating it with autonomous driving technology. For example, deploying unmanned vehicles to disaster-stricken areas to collect real-time street view images would enable even faster damage assessment. Additionally, combining this approach with drones would facilitate a system capable of assessing damage from both aerial and ground perspectives. This study developed a method to rapidly and accurately evaluate the extent of building collapse damage by analyzing street view images with generative AI. Compared to traditional remote sensing methods, this approach offers superior accuracy and localized damage assessment. Moreover, visualizing the damage status on a map allows disaster prevention agencies and municipalities to take more appropriate actions.

4 DISCUSSION

Previous studies have developed methods for real-time estimation of damage extent using remote sensing indices. However, recent advancements in machine learning and deep learning suggest that integrating generative AI can enable more precise damage recognition. This study compares the characteristics of RI indices and generative AI technologies, clarifies their respective advantages and challenges, and discusses their trade-offs from a societal significance perspective.

4.1 *Development of explainable generative AI*

Although this study employed a simplified method using generative AI for mapping, the application of AI technology presents several challenges. First, the computational resource burden is high, requiring advanced infrastructure for large-scale data processing. Particularly in disaster scenarios, where communication infrastructure is often damaged, real-time data collection and analysis can be difficult.

Second, the opacity of AI decision-making remains an issue. Deep learning models often function as "black boxes," making it unclear how damage severity is determined. Therefore, when utilizing AI as a basis for rescue operations and administrative decisions, the adoption of Explainable AI (XAI) is crucial. Considering these challenges, a hybrid approach is desirable, where simple image analysis is used for rapid response, while AI is leveraged for detailed accuracy. For instance, in the immediate aftermath of a disaster, rough damage estimates can be made using simple indices to allocate resources efficiently. Subsequently, AI technology can be employed to conduct a more detailed damage assessment and optimize recovery and reconstruction plans. This hybrid approach balances both speed and accuracy, enhancing overall disaster response effectiveness. To further enhance AI risk management, developing a "disaster-specific AI" that minimizes data accumulation and optimizing models for emergency response is necessary. Additionally, reviewing how simple image analysis is integrated with AI could improve both speed and accuracy in damage assessment.

4.2 *Integration with autonomous driving technology*

Future advancements in autonomous driving technology could enable the automated collection of damage data. Deploying unmanned vehicles to disaster-affected areas to gather and analyze real-time damage information would enhance both safety and speed in assessing the situation. Autonomous vehicles could be deployed to hazardous zones where human entry is difficult, ensuring the safety of rescue teams while efficiently collecting crucial information. In disaster scenarios such as earthquakes, tsunamis, or volcanic eruptions, where secondary hazards pose significant risks, autonomous vehicles could rapidly reach affected areas and analyze the extent of structural damage and road conditions using digital cameras. By integrating AI, the collected video data could be instantly analyzed to determine damage severity and identify priority rescue areas. This would enable optimal allocation of human resources and the efficient routing of relief supplies.

In the future, a system combining autonomous vehicles and drones could be developed to assess damage from both aerial and ground perspectives. For example, autonomous vehicles could navigate disaster areas while deploying drones to provide an aerial view, thus collecting extensive damage information. This integrated system would not only improve accuracy in damage assessment but also significantly enhance disaster response speed. The evolution of autonomous driving technology has the potential to revolutionize disaster response strategies fundamentally. Along with technological advancements, conducting verification experiments and establishing legal frameworks will be essential for societal adoption.

4.3 *Integration with other damage assessment systems*

This method should also consider integration with existing damage assessment systems. In disaster situations, ensuring the accuracy and speed of information collection is a fundamental aspect of disaster prevention and mitigation. While AI technology has significantly improved damage recognition accuracy, its true value lies in practical application for disaster response rather than remaining as an academic concept. To maximize its benefits, these technologies must be incorporated into real-world disaster response systems to directly contribute to public safety.

AI technology enables rapid damage assessment but may face challenges in societal acceptance and regulatory frameworks. Thus, integrating AI with existing disaster recognition systems and leveraging their strengths to build a comprehensive disaster response system is crucial. Specifically, AI-driven damage analysis could be combined with meteorological satellites, drones, and field survey results to enhance real-time information provision (Table 1). This approach could facilitate swift evacuation decisions and improve rescue operations.

By combining AI with simple image analysis, optimal decision-making can be achieved for both immediate disaster response and long-term recovery planning. AI excels in large-scale data analysis, accurately grasping the overall damage situation. Using its results, simple image analysis could be applied to devise concrete disaster countermeasures, making disaster response more practical. Consequently, integrating these technologies could become the new standard in disaster prevention. To achieve this, not only technological advancements but also increased societal acceptance, proactive government involvement, and public awareness improvements are essential. By considering these elements comprehensively and incorporating them into actual disaster response strategies, the effectiveness of disaster management can be maximized.

Table 1. Comparison of speed, accuracy, and practicality across different damage assessment methods.

		Car/ Street-view (AI)	Field survey	UAV	Satellite	Car (Simple Analysis)
Speed	Temporal resolution	△	×	△	△	○
Accuracy	Prediction Accuracy	○	○	○	△	△
Practicality	Navigability	○	○	△	○	○
	Weather Resistance	○	○	×	△	○
	Spatial Resolution	○	○	○	×	○
	Wide Area Coverage	○	×	×	○	○

4.4 *Societal significance and future prospects of rapid damage assessment using ground-based video*

The technology developed in this study—rapid damage assessment using ground-based video—has significant potential for enhancing disaster information collection, especially when combined with municipal disaster response departments and community-based data collection efforts. Traditional disaster response has relied on aerial and satellite imagery to estimate damage, but these methods are time-consuming and lack immediacy. By utilizing ground-based video, it is possible to quickly assess the specific damage conditions in affected areas and optimize rescue operations. By leveraging cloud-based systems, massive video data can be automatically analyzed, enabling municipalities and disaster agencies to make swift decisions. Future research should focus on accelerating societal implementation through collaboration with relevant agencies and conducting pilot tests to refine operational models. The widespread adoption of this technology among municipalities could significantly enhance disaster response speed and improve the accuracy of damage assessments.

Furthermore, if this technology is widely adopted by municipalities across the country, it is expected to significantly contribute to the rapid assessment of damage during earthquakes and the advancement of disaster prevention planning. Currently, many municipalities rely on officials conducting on-site inspections to visually assess damage after a disaster. However, by implementing this technology, that process can be greatly streamlined. For example, immediately after a disaster, drones and vehicle-mounted cameras can be used to capture footage, which can then be analyzed by AI in real time. This would enable the identification of severely affected areas, allowing rescue teams to be dispatched with priority. Additionally, the use of 3D building models for visualizing damaged structures is also being considered. This approach could support Digital Twin and DX (Digital Transformation) initiatives, further enhancing disaster response capabilities as shown in Figure 5.

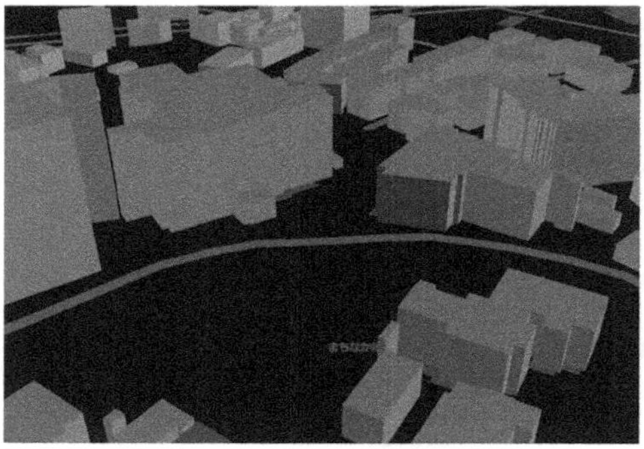

Figure 5. 3D building damage assessment map. (Scenario in Kashiwa City, Chiba, Japan – **Red:** Damaged, **Blue:** Not Damaged).

Authors should discuss the results and how they can be interpreted from the per-spective of previous studies and of the working hypotheses. The findings and their im-plications should be discussed in the broadest context possible. Future research direc-tions may also be highlighted.

5 CONCLUSIONS

In this study, we clarified the advantages of utilizing generative AI and examined ways to improve the transparency and social acceptance of AI technology. We developed a damage mapping technology using generative AI, with a particular focus on improving the accuracy of damage recognition. Traditional damage recognition methods have typically relied on analyzing aerial and satellite images. However, these methods are susceptible to weather conditions and shooting timing, making real-time assessment challenging. On the other hand, by leveraging generative AI, it is possible to rapidly analyze on-site footage immediately after a disaster and instantly map the extent of the damage.

For instance, in this study, we developed a method to automatically recognize collapsed buildings by analyzing street view images using AI. This method involves processing street view images captured by 360-degree cameras, trimming the images, and utilizing generative AI to evaluate damage levels, thereby enabling high-precision damage analysis. Based on these results, we generated a visualized damage map, creating a system that allows intuitive understanding of the scale of the damage.

AI technology can analyze vast amounts of image data, enabling immediate linguistic and quantitative assessments of post-disaster situations. However, deep learning models tend to become "black boxes," making it difficult to understand the criteria by which damage severity is determined. Therefore, this study highlights the need for the introduction of Explainable AI (XAI) to ensure transparency in AI decision-making.

To implement the technology developed in this study in real-world disaster response, collaboration with national research institutes and municipal disaster prevention departments is essential, and pilot studies should be conducted for practical application. In the future, if this technology is widely adopted by municipalities across the country, it will enable faster disaster response and improve the accuracy of damage recognition. Furthermore, as AI technology continues to evolve, improvements in image analysis accuracy and processing speed are expected, necessitating ongoing research and development. By widespread adoption of this technology in society, it has the potential to save more lives and revolutionize disaster response efforts, making significant contributions to disaster management innovation.

REFERENCES

Estêvão, João MC. (2024). Effectiveness of generative ai for post-earthquake damage assessment. *Buildings* 14.10: 3255.

Heinzelman, Jessica, and Carol Waters, (2010). *Crowdsourcing crisis information in disaster-affected Haiti.* Washington, DC: US Institute of Peace.

Linardos, Vasileios, et al. (2022). Machine learning in disaster management: recent developments in methods and applications. *Machine Learning and Knowledge Extraction* 4.2.

Ma, Dawei, et al. (2019). *ISPRS International Journal of Geo-Information, The state of mapillary: An exploratory analysis.* 9.1: 10.

Shiraishi, H., and Usuda, Y. (2025). Real-time building-damage-extraction technology from ground-based video footage using normalized difference red/green redness index. *Geomatics and Environmental Engineering*, 19(1), 143–159.

System Innovation for a Global Economy – Lam et al. (Eds)
© 2026 The Author(s), ISBN 978-1-041-10520-6

Segmentation of decorative texture from Jomon pottery with image processing and statistical clustering methods

Hsiang-En Chou, Yung-Hsiang Ma, Tung-Chin Liu & Che-Chern Lin
National Kaohsiung Normal University, Kaohsiung, Taiwan

Kouichi Konno
Iwate University, Morioka, Iwate, Japan

Tsutomu Kinoshita
Tohoku Gakuin University, Sendai, Miyagi, Japan

Mengbo You
Iwate University, Morioka, Iwate, Japan

ABSTRACT: The Jomon pottery is a kind of ancient pottery used in the Jomon period of Japan. The characteristic of Jomon pottery is the rope-patterned decorative texture on its surface. The decorative texture of the Jomon pottery varies depending on different eras and locations. The amount of excavated Jomon pottery could be limited for some certain eras and locations. Therefore, if we use machine learning algorithms to segment the decorative texture, the training sets might be small. Accordingly, in this study we utilize image processing and statistical clustering methods to segment decorative texture from the images of seven Jomon potteries originally from the Ruins Learning Center in Morioka city. In this study, two edge detection methods, the Sobel filter and the Canny algorithm, have been used to detect the decorative texture from the pottery images. Furthermore, we used closing operations to make the decorative texture more continuous and smoother. Meanwhile, two statistical clustering methods, the K-means algorithm and the Otsu method, were utilized to segment decorative texture from theses pottery images. Intersection of Union (IOU) is used to evaluate the performance of the segmentation of decorative texture. Experimental results have suggested that 1) in the image processing methods, the use of closing operation can increase IOU; 2) in the statistical clustering methods, if the number of clusters decreases, the IOU increases.

Keywords: Jomon pottery, Texture segmentation, Closing operation, Edge detection, K-means, Otsu method

1 INTRODUCTION

The Jomon pottery is the oldest pottery in Japan, which has been dated as early as 14,500 BCE (Wiki[a]). The Jomon pottery is so-named because it is featured by rope-patterned decorative texture on its surface. People are interested in automatically extracting the decorative texture from the images of Jomon pottery. The decorative patterns of Jomon pottery varied depending on different eras and locations. In reality, the amount of excavated Jomon pottery for certain eras and locations might be limited. It is sometimes difficult to use machine learning methods to segment the decorative texture from Jomon pottery images due to small-sized datasets. To overcome this problem, Chen (2024) has utilized meta-learning methods which used similar datasets to pre-train the machine learning models in order to get better initial parameters. In general, the use of machine learning methods could spend a lot of computation time during their training stage, and sometime would cause over-fitting problems due to small-sized training sets. In this study, instead of using machine learning method, we utilize traditional image processing and statistical clustering methods to segment decorative texture from Jomon pottery images. The image processing methods include edge detection with the Sobel filter and the Canny algorithm. After using these edge detection methods, a closing operation was then employed to get better segmentation results. In statistical clustering methods, the K-means algorithm and the Otsu Method were used to cluster the pottery images into two groups: the decorative texture and the background. Severn Jomon pottery images, originally from the Ruins

DOI: 10.1201/9781003655534-18

Learning Center in Morioka, Iwate, Japan, were used as samples. We conducted experiments to segment the decorative texture from these pottery images with the image processing and statistical clustering methods. In the experiments, Intersection of Union (IOU) was used to evaluate the segmentation performance. Experimental results have shown that in the image processing methods, use of closing operation can increase IOUs. Meanwhile, in the statistical clustering methods, if the number of segmented groups decreases, the IOU increases; the best number of segmented groups is 2.

2 RELATED WORK

The Sobel filter is named after Irwin Sobel and Gary M. Feldman for their talk at the Stanford Artificial Intelligence Laboratory (Sobel and Feldman 1968). It is widely used in image processing, especially in edge detection based on the gradient of values of neighboring pixels. However, the detection capability of the Sobel filter is limited to two directions (the horizontal and vertical directions). Therefore, some studies have applied more directions to improve the original Sobel filter. For example, Tang *et al.* (2020) have added two directions (45 degrees and 135 degrees) to improve the detection capability of the original Sobel filter. Tang *et al.* (2020) have furthermore conducted experiments to validate their improved filter, where two human face images were used as samples. Experimental results have shown that their improved filter outperformed the original Sobel filter (Tang *et al.* 2020). Meanwhile, Gayathri and Remya Ajai (2021) have presented an eight-direction Sobel filter to detect more edge directions in images. To do this, the original Sobel filter has been extended to a 5×5 masking matrix for convolution operations (Gayathri and Remya Ajai 2021). Experimental results have shown that the eight-direction Sobel filter had better performance than the original Sobel filter in term of MSE (Mean Squared Error), RMSE (Root Mean Squared Erros), entropy, SNR (Signal-to-Noise Ratio), and PSNR (Peak Signal-to-Noise Ratio) (Gayathri and Remya Ajai 2021).

Canny (1986) has proposed a multi-stage computational method, called Canny algorithm, to determine several kinds of edges in images, where functional criteria were utilized to determine edges based on a numerical optimization procedure. The Canny algorithm uses optimal operators to efficiently detect different kinds of edges such as step, ridge-like, and roof-like edges. Wang *et al.* (2018) have proposed a hybrid edge detection algorithm combining the fractional differential algorithm and the Canny algorithm, where more detailed texture can be efficiently detected. In this hybrid method, the Canny algorithm serves to detect strong edges, and the fractional differential algorithm preserves texture details (Wag *et al.* 2018). The experimental results have shown that this hybrid method performed better than using the Canny algorithm and the fractional differential algorithm individually. In addition, Ji *et al.* (2022) have presented an improved Canny algorithm for image edge detection. In this improved algorithm, instead of utilizing the Gaussian function, the MeanShift algorithm was used to retain edge information when performing denoising process (Ji *et al.* 2022). Meanwhile, the improved algorithm also employed the maximum inter-variance to get a better threshold in order to enhance the adaptability of edge detection. Experimental results have also shown that this improved algorithm outperformed the original Canny algorithm.

Sezgin *et al.* (2004) have presented a survey about image thresholding methods according to six types of techniques: histogram-based, clustering-based, entropy-based, attribute-based, spatial, and local methods. The Otsu method is an efficiently automatic threshold selection method based on the histogram in gray-scale images (Otsu 1979). It can be extended to solve unsupervised classification problems. In the Otsu method, distinct peaks in histogram can be used to classify different objects. The K-means algorithm is a well-known and widely-used clustering algorithm, which assigns samples to clusters according to the Euclidean distances between the samples and cluster centers by an iterative procedure (Tou and Gonzalez 1974). It is simple and straightforward but limited to numeric datasets. In addition, in the K-means algorithm the number of cluster centers is pre-specified. Liu and Yu (2009) have compared the Otsu method and the K-means algorithm, and proved that in multi-level thresholding problems, both methods used the same criterion to minimize the within-class variance. The work by Liu and Yu (2009) has also proved that the computational time of the K-means algorithm was more efficient than that of the Otsu method. This is because the Otsu method is an exhaustive approach to find the global solution, while the K-mean algorithm performs local searching.

3 METHODS

3.1 *Image processing methods*

3.1.1 *Soble filter*

For an image, the Soble Filter basically takes gradient operations on two directions: the x-direction and the y-direction, which performs a convolution manipulation on a 3× 3 window for each pixel in the image. The x-direction and y-direction Soble

Filters are indicated as follows (Sobel and Feldman 1968; Wiki[b]).

$$\nabla_x f = G_x = \begin{bmatrix} -1 & 0 & 1 \\ -2 & 0 & 2 \\ -1 & 0 & 1 \end{bmatrix}$$

$$\nabla_y f = G_y = \begin{bmatrix} -1 & -2 & -1 \\ 0 & 0 & 0 \\ 1 & 2 & 1 \end{bmatrix}$$

The overall gradient G for both x-direction and y-direction is simply calculated by the following formula.

$$\text{G} = \sqrt{G_x^2 + G_y^2}$$

One can set a threshold h to determine whether a pixel p is an edge pixel by the following criterion.
p is an edge pixel, if $G_p \geq h$
p is not an edge pixel, if $G_p < h$
where G_p is the overall gradient of p.

3.1.2 *Canny algorithm*

The Canny algorithm is a method to further determine weak edges using the Sobel filters. The procedure of the Canny algorithm is demonstrated as follows (Canny 1986; Wiki[c] 2025).

Step 1: Covert an RGB image to a gray-scale image with the following formula.

$$\text{Gray Scale} = 0.2126 \times \text{r} + 0.7152 \times \text{g} + 0.0722 \times \text{b}$$

where r, g, and b are the red, green, and blue components of an RGB pixel, respectively.
Step 2: Perform normalization according to the following Gaussian normalization equation.

$$\text{Gaussian}(x, y) = \frac{1}{2\pi\sigma^2} e^{-\frac{x^2+y^2}{2\sigma^2}}$$

where $\sigma = 1.5$
Step 3: Use the Sobel Filters
Step 4: Determine weak edges. In the Canny algorithm, we utilize two thresholds, a high threshold and a low threshold, to determine edges. The criteria to determine edges are illustrated below.

- If the value is greater than the high threshold, it is considered as a strong edged-pixel.
- If the value is less than the low threshold, it is not considered as an edged-pixel.
- If the value is between the two thresholds and if there are any strong edges next to it, we consider it as an edged-pixel.

3.1.3 *Closing operation*

The closing operation is a kind of image morphology operation. Consider a pixel x in a binary image with its eight neighboring pixels (x_0 to x_7) as shown in Figure 1.

X 3	X 2	X1
X 4	X	X 0
X 5	X 6	X 7

Figure 1. Pixel x and its eight neighboring pixels.

An eight-neighboring dilating operation on x is defined as follows.

$$\text{Dilate}(x) = x \cup (x_0 \cup x_1 \cup x_2 \cup x_3 \cup x_4 \cup x_5 \cup x_6 \cup x_7)$$

In addition, an eight-neighboring eroding operation on x is defined as follows

$$\text{Erode}(x) = x \cap (x_0 \cap x_1 \cap x_2 \cap x_3 \cap x_4 \cap x_5 \cap x_6 \cap x_7)$$

A closing operation is basically performed by taking dilating operations followed by eroding operations, where the number of the dilating operations is equal to the number of the eroding operations.

3.2 *Statistical clustering methods*

3.2.1 *K-means algorithm*

The K-means algorithm is an early method to cluster data into different groups. Although it is simple and straightforward, the K-means algorithm is widely utilized to cluster numerical data, and works perfectly with equal-size clustering. The pre-assumption of the K-means algorithm is that K must be pre-assigned in advance. The drawback of the K-mean algorithm is that it cannot explain the importance of individual attributes. The procedure of the K-means algorithm is briefly described as follows (Tou and Gonzalez 1974).

Pre-condition: Given a set of instances to be grouped into K clusters.

Step 1: From the instance set, randomly select K instances as the initial cluster centers.
Step 2: For each instance, assign this instance to the cluster having the shortest distance from its center to this instance.
Step 3: Calculate the new centers for the K clusters obtained in Step 2, respectively. If the new centers do not change, stop the algorithm; otherwise, go to Step 2.

3.2.2 *Otsu method*

The Otsu's method basically performs automatic image thresholding that separates pixels into two classes, the foreground and background classes, by the following criteria (Otsu 1979; Wiki[d]).

- Minimizing within-class variance
- Maximizing between-class variance

In the Otsu method, the between-class variance is defined as follows (Otsu 1979; Wiki[d]).

$$\sigma_B = \omega_1(\mu_1 - u_T)^2 + \omega_2(\mu_2 - \mu_T)^2$$

where

ω_1 = the sum of the probability in Class 1,
ω_2 = the sum of the probability in Class 2,
μ_1 = the mean of Class 1,
μ_2 = the mean of Class 2, and
μ_T = the threshold mean.

The required criteria for this equation are
$\omega_1 + \omega_2 = 1$, and

$$\omega_1\mu_1 + \omega_2\mu_2 = \mu_T$$

4 EXPERIMENTS AND RESULTS

In the experiments, 7 Jomon potteries from the Ruins Learning Center in Morioka were used as samples. The gray-scale images of these potteries are shown in Figure 2. In this study, three experiments were conducted to segment decorative texture from these images.

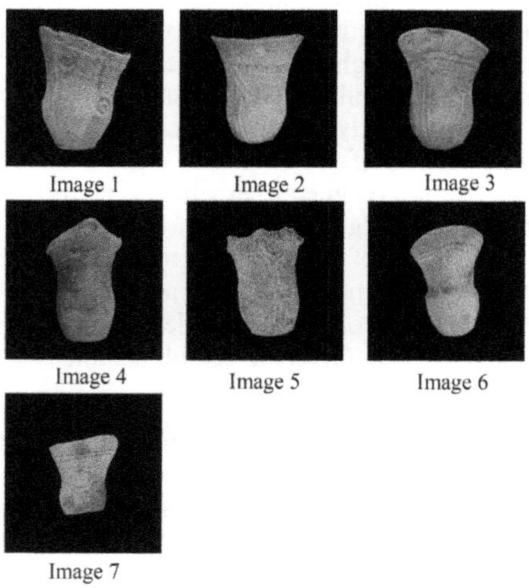

Figure 2. Gray-scale images of the 7 Jomon potteries.

To measure IOU, the decorative texture of each image is manually marked as a targeted texture image. Figure 3 shows a selected gray-scale mage and its targeted texture image.

The performance measurement of these experiments is Intersection of Union (IOU), which is

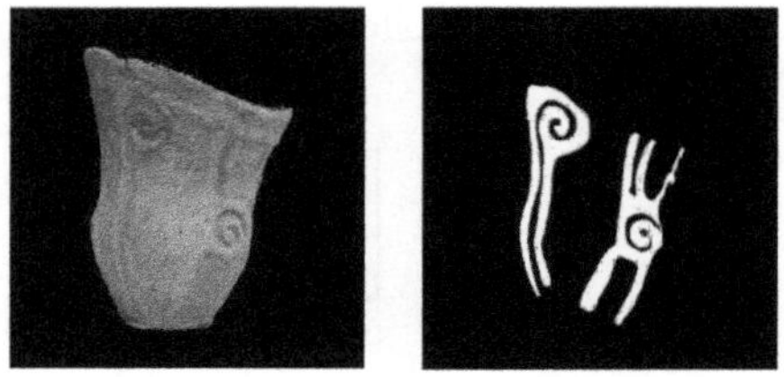

(a) Gray-scale image (b) Targeted texture

Figure 3. Image 1 and its targeted texture image.

defined as follows.

$$\text{IOU} = \frac{\text{Number of pixels in } A \cap B}{\text{Number of pixels in } A \cup B}$$

Figure 4. Shows an illustrate figure of IOU.

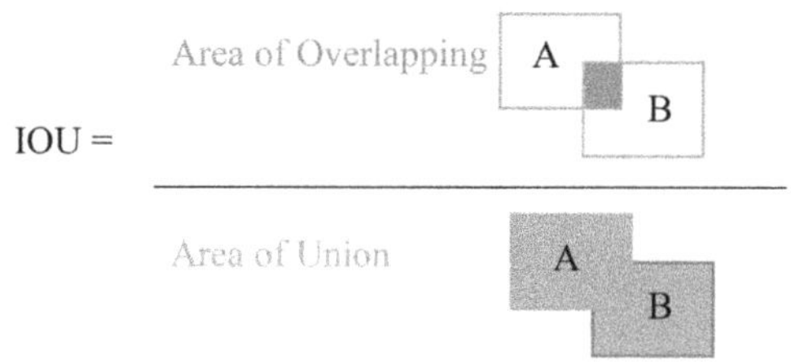

Figure 4. Illustrative figure of IOU.

In this study, A is the area of the targeted decorative texture in a pottery image, and B is the area of the decorative texture segmented by the image processing and the statistical methods used in this study. Obviously, a higher IOU means a better segmentation result.

4.1 *Experiment 1: Edge detection methods*

In this experiment, we utilized two edge detection methods: the Sobel filter and the Canny algorithm. Furthermore, we utilized closing operations after using the Sobel filter and the Canny algorithm, respectively. The summarized results of Experiment 1 are shown in Table 1.

Table 1. Results of experiment 1.

	IOU			
	Without any closing operation		With one closing operation	
Image No.	Sobel Filter	Canny Alg.	Sobel Filter	Canny Alg.
1	0.0973	0.0862	0.1145	0.1054
2	0.1338	0.1279	0.1488	0.1696

(continued)

Table 1. Continued

	IOU			
	Without any closing operation		With one closing operation	
Image No.	Sobel Filter	Canny Alg.	Sobel Filter	Canny Alg.
3	0.1317	0.1178	0.1620	0.1498
4	0.0913	0.1148	0.1099	0.1486
5	0.1517	0.1412	0.1637	0.1875
6	0.1440	0.1290	0.1748	0.1695
7	0.1653	0.1618	0.1902	0.2441
Average	0.1307	0.1255	0.1520	0.1678

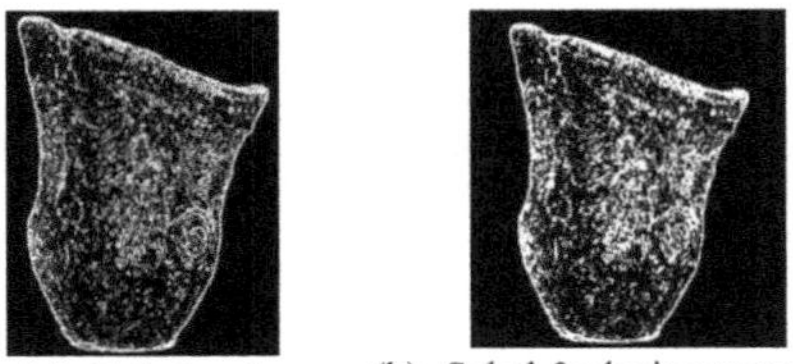

(a) Sobel only (b) Sobel & closin goperation

Figure 5. Image 1 with Sobel and closing operation.

From Table 1, one can find that use of closing operation can improve IOUs by approximately 2% (Sobel) and 4% (Canny). The best IOU is to use the Canny algorithm together with one closing operation. Figure 5 shows selected segmentation results of using the Sobel filter solely, and using the Sobel filter together with a closing operation.

4.2 *Experiment 2: K-mean algorithm*

In this experiment, we used the K-means algorithm to cluster the pixels in a gray-scale image into different groups (clusters), and then to assign these groups to either the decorative texture or the background. The experimental parameters are k = 2, 3, 4, and 5 (i.e., 2, 3, 4, and 5 means, respectively). The results of Experiment 2 are illustrated in Table 2.

Table 2. Results of experiment 2.

	IOU			
Image No.	K= 2	K= 3	K= 4	K= 5
1	0.1565	0.1489	0.1132	0.1021
2	0.2864	0.1416	0.0306	0.0306
3	0.1220	0.1247	0.0820	0.0412
4	0.1585	0.1508	0.1373	0.1075
5	0.1488	0.1507	0.1260	0.0559
6	0.2872	0.0582	0.0324	0.0181
7	0.1128	0.1980	0.0690	0.0160
Average	0.1817	0.1390	0.0844	0.0531

From Table 2, One can conclude that IOU decreases when K increases. The best K is 2, followed by 3, 4, 5, respectively. Selected segmented results are shown in Figure 6.

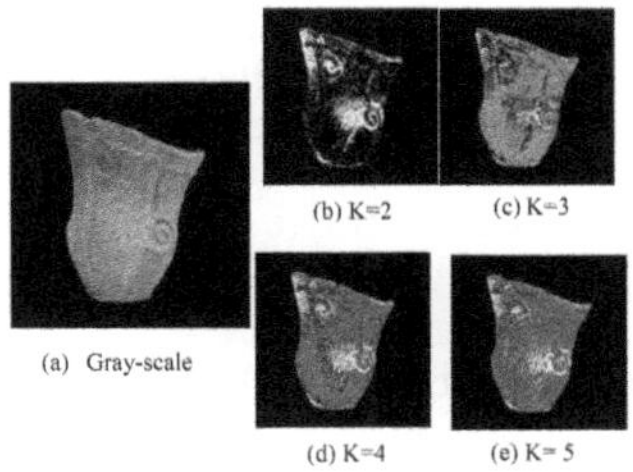

Figure 6. Segmentation results of Image 1 after using the K-means algorithm with K=2, 3, 4, and 5.

4.3 *Experiment 3: Otsu method*

In this experiment, we employed the Otsu method to divide the pixels in an image into 2, 3, 4, and 5 levels, respectively, and then to merge these levels into two groups: decorative texture and background. The results of this experiment are shown in Table 3. From Table 3, one can find that IOU decreases when number of levels increases. The best number of levels for the Otsu method is 2, followed by 3, 4, 5, respectively. Selected segmented results in Experiment 3 are shown in Figure 7.

Table 3. Results of experiment 3.

	IOU			
Image No.	2 levels	3 levels	4 levels	5 levels
1	0.2308	0.1194	0.0896	0.0680
2	0.2729	0.0958	0.0700	0.0518
3	0.2639	0.1045	0.0642	0.0426
4	0.2576	0.0909	0.0777	0.0728
5	0.2160	0.1049	0.0644	0.0482
6	0.3033	0.0391	0.0204	0.0121
7	0.3885	0.0919	0.0605	0.0364
Average	0.2761	0.0924	0.0638	0.0474

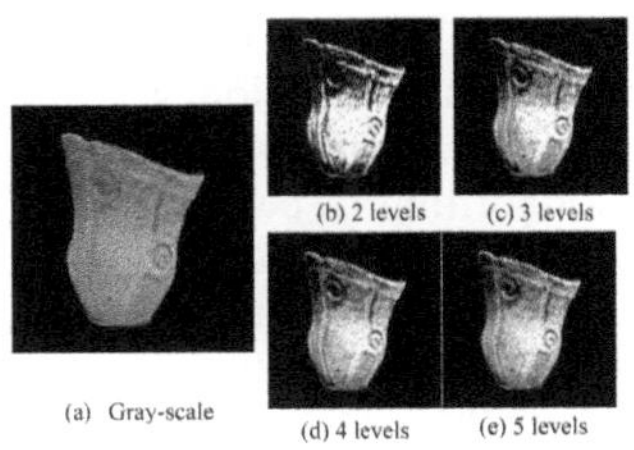

Figure 7. Segmentation results of Image 1 after using the Otsu Method with 2, 3, 4, and 5 levels.

From Tables 2 and 3, one can observe that the results of Experiments 2 and 3 are similar. Therefore, we can conclude the increment of clusters in the K-means algorithm or the increment of levels in the Otsu method will decrease IOU. The best number of clusters in the K-means algorithm is 2. Similarly, the best number of levels in the Otsu method is also 2.

4.4 *Concluding remarks*

From Tables 1 to 3, the concluding remarks for the experiments are stated as follows.

(1) In image processing methods, use of closing operations can improve the IOU by approximately 2% for the Sobel filter, and 4% for the Canny algorithm.
(2) In clustering methods, IOU increases when the segmented groups (i.e., number of clusters in the K-means algorithm or number of levels in the Otsu method) decreases. The best number of segmented groups is 2 for the K-means algorithm and the Otsu method.
(3) Overall, the best result is to use the Otsu method wilt 2 levels.

5 CONCLUSIONS

The Jomon pottery is an import cultural heritage of humanity in Japan. During the Jomon period, people used cords to make decorative patterns (texture) on pottery. However, the decorative patterns of Jomon pottery varied depending on different ears and locations. The amount of unearthed Jomon pottery might be limited for a certain era and location. It is an interesting research topic of using image segmentation methods to automatically extract (segment) these decorative texture from Jomon pottery images. However, using machine learning methods needs a relatively large amount of samples. In reality, it is sometimes difficult to obtain more Jomon pottery for a certain era and location. In this study, we used 7 Jomon pottery images from the Ruins Learning Center as samples. Since the amount of image samples is few, instead of using machine learning methods, this study utilized traditional image processing and statistical clustering methods to segment the decorative texture from the 7 pottery images.

The image processing method used in this study include the Sobel filter and the Canny algorithm. In addition, closing operation was employed to improve the performance of the Sobel filter and the Canny algorithm. The statistical clustering methods utilized in this study are the K-means algorithm and the Otsu method.

We conducted three experiments to validate the performance of these method used in this study. The findings of these experiments can be highlighted as follows.

- In the image processing methods, use of closing operation can increase IOU.
- In the clustering methods, if the number of segmented groups decreases, the IOU increases; the best number of segmented groups is 2.

As about possible directions for future studies, one may use more statistical or image processing methods to improve the segmentation performance. The Watershed method might be a possible approach. Besides, the use of image features together with appropriate neural networks might be another possible approach to segment decorative texture from Jomon pottery images.

ACKNOWLEDGMENT

We would like to thank the Ruins Learning Center in Morioka-city for providing the Jomon pottery data.

REFERENCES

Canny J., (1986). A computational approach to edge detection, *IEEE Transaction on Pattern Analysis and Machine Intelligence*, PAMI-8(6).

Chen T.-L., (2024). *Texture segmentation of pottery images with fully convolutional neural networks and meta-learning algorithms.* Master Thesis, National Kaohsiung Normal University, Taiwan, June, 2024.

Gayathri A.G. and Remya Ajai A.S., (2021). VLSI imple mentation of improved Sobel edge detection algorithm. *2021 International Conference on Communication, Control and Information Sciences (ICCISc)*.

Ji D., Liu Y. and Wang C., (2022). Research on image edge detection based on improved Canny operator, *the 3rd International Conference on Information Science, Parallel and Distribution Systems (ISPDS)*, 229–232.

Liu D. and Yu J., (2009). *Otsu method and K-means, the 9th International Conference on Hybrid Intelligent Systems.* 344–349.

Otsu N., (1979), A threshold selection method from gray-level histogram. *IEEE Transaction on Systems, Man, and Cybernetics*, 62–66.

Sezgin M., Kocaeli G. and Sankur B., (2004). Survey over image thresholding techniques and quantitative performance evaluation. *Journal of Electronic Imaging* 13(1), 146–165.

Sobel I. and Feldman G. (1968), *A 3x3 isotropic gradient operator for image processing, presented at the Stanford Artificial Intelligence Project (SAIL).* Available on https://www.researchgate.net/publication/239398674_An_Isotropic_3x3_Image_Gradient_Operator. (Accessed on 2025/01/15).

Tang X., Wang X., Hou J., Wu H. and Liu D., (2020). An Improved Sobel face gray image edge detection algorithm. *Proceeding of the 39th Chinese Control Conference*, 6639–6643.

Tou J.T. and Gonzalez R.C., (1974). *Pattern Recognition Principle*, 94–97.

Wang L., Ma X. and Wang H., (2018). Hybrid image edge detection based on fractional differential and Canny algorithm. *The 11th International Symposium on Computational Intelligence and Design*, 210–213.

Wiki[a]. Jomon pottery. Available on https://en.wikipe dia. org/wiki/J%C5%8Dmon_pottery, (Accessed on 2025/01/15).

Wiki[b]. Sobel operator. Available on https://en.wikipe dia. org/wiki/Sobel_operator. (Accessed on 2025/01/15).

Wiki[c]. Canny edge detector, Available on https://en. wikipedia.org/wiki/Canny_edge_detector. (Accessed on 2025/01/16).

Wiki[d]. Otsu's method. Available on https://en.wikipedia. org/wiki/Otsu%27s_method#:~:text=In%20computer %20vision%20and%20image,two%20classes%2C% 20foreground%20and%20background. (Accessed on 2025/01/16)

System Innovation for a Global Economy – Lam et al. (Eds)

Research on constructing a novel interactive music perceptual environment for interactive art exhibitions

Wen-Li Huang & Chao-Ming Wang
Department of Digital Media Design, Nation Yunlin University of Science and Technology, Yunlin, Taiwan

ABSTRACT: With the advancement of technology, interactive art has manifested increasingly diverse forms and possibilities. This research proposes a novel interactive music perception environment that utilizes sensors and computer vision to detect individuals' positions and movement trajectories in real time, transforming this data into musical parameters and visual feedback. Each participant is assigned a unique instrumental timbre, and when individuals approach or pass by one another, brief harmonies are generated, brief harmonies are generated, symbolizing transient human connections. If the duration of interaction extends, these melodies gradually merge into a more complete composition, fostering deeper levels of engagement. A prototype was developed through case analysis to explore the phenomenon of social alienation in contemporary urban settings. The installation aims to encourage spontaneous interaction and communication among strangers through sound and visuals. This research offers a new perspective on social connection within the fields of human-computer interaction and interactive music, and serves as a reference for the future design of socially interactive installations.

A prototype was developed through case analysis to explore the phenomenon of social alienation in contemporary urban settings. The installation aims to encourage spontaneous interaction and communication among strangers through sound and visuals. This research offers a new perspective on social connection within the fields of human-computer interaction and interactive music, and serves as a reference for the future design of socially interactive installations.

1 INTRODUCTION

In traditional art exhibitions, audiences have often played a passive role, maintaining a static and distanced relationship with the artwork. However, with the continuous development of interactive technologies, this mode of viewing is gradually transforming. As Stern (2011) notes, interactive art is no longer merely something to be observed—it is an invitation to participate and act. The audience is no longer a bystander, but becomes an integral part of the work, shaping its content and meaning through their actions and interactions with the environment. This type of participation not only enriches the artistic experience but also opens up new possibilities for social connection and collective creation.

According to Seth (2023), the prevalence of digital media in modern society has intensified feelings of interpersonal alienation. While we are globally connected via the internet, face-to-face interactions in physical spaces have been steadily decreasing. In response to this condition, Brignull and Rogers (2003) found that artistic installations capable of encouraging interaction among strangers in physical spaces can help alleviate this growing sense of social disconnection.

In everyday life, music is frequently used to regulate emotions, create atmospheres, and even serve as a catalyst for social interaction. As DeNora (2000) points out, with the maturation of interactive music technologies, sound—as a vital medium of emotional communication—has increasingly been adopted in interactive art practices.

Therefore, this study conducts a case analysis to summarize interaction patterns and emotional engagement strategies in related interactive art installa tions. Based on these insights, a prototype of an interactive music environment is proposed—one that can perceive the positions and interactions of people within a space. Through sound and visual feedback, this installation aims to draw attention to urban loneliness and promote brief yet meaningful encounters among strangers.

2 LITERATURE REVIEW

2.1 *Urban loneliness and social disconnection*

In modern urban environments, despite high population density, genuine interpersonal interactions are becoming increasingly scarce. This paradox—physical proximity yet psychological

DOI: 10.1201/9781003655534-19

distance—has gradually given rise to what is now referred to as "urban loneliness." As cities continue to grow rapidly and life accelerates, the rise of digital media has significantly altered the way people communicate and form relationships. Horan (2024) points out that although social media has enhanced the efficiency of information exchange, it has also led to an overreliance on virtual interactions, reducing face-to-face encounters and deepening individual psychological isolation and social disconnection.

In the context of digital technology and urbanization, reigniting authentic human connection has become a critical challenge for contemporary design and art. Zohny (2025) argues that installation art, through its site-specific nature, interactivity, and multisensory experiences, can create engaging spaces for communication in public settings. These environments encourage participation and interaction, offering new possibilities for addressing social isolation.

Interactive installations are increasingly seen as vital artistic practices that foster social connection. Brignull and Rogers (2003), in their study on large-scale interactive installations in public spaces, found that well-designed interactions can effectively lower the social barriers and awkwardness between strangers, prompting brief yet meaningful exchanges. Such installations not only enhance public engagement but also offer sensory feedback, real-time responses, and spatial cues that create opportunities for non-verbal connection—addressing the growing emotional detachment prevalent in urban life.

2.2 *Interactive music and imagery*

Interactive art has become increasingly diverse in its forms of expression. Installation artworks that integrate sensors, computer vision, and generative music technologies have emerged as a significant trend in contemporary media art. One representative example is the interactive dance performance system designed by James *et al.* (2006), in which dancers' movements directly influence both sound and visual output in real time, making performances more accessible and impactful for the audience. In such systems, music is no longer merely a background element; it becomes an integral part of the creative process, even directly reflecting the users' physical gestures and emotional states.

Tanaka (2009) also emphasizes the inseparable relationship between music and bodily movement. In his research, gestures, swaying motions, and changes in posture are not only methods of system control but can also be considered as dynamic input interfaces for music. This real-time, sensory feedback-based interaction profoundly shapes participants' perception and experience of music, transforming sound into a responsive and tactile medium.

On an emotional level, music has long been recognized for its deep connection to human emotions. DeNora (2000) points out that music functions as a tool for emotional regulation in everyday life. People actively select different musical styles and rhythms to adjust, support, or even amplify their emotional states. This behavior indicates that music is not merely passively consumed but serves as an active medium for emotional modulation.

In terms of how music conveys emotion, Juslin and Laukka (2004) provide a detailed analysis of how various acoustic features can evoke specific emotional impressions. For instance, major keys are often associated with happiness and positive emotions, whereas minor keys tend to elicit feelings of sadness or melancholy. Similarly, fast tempo and high volume are linked to excitement, energy, and dynamism, while slow tempo and soft timbres tend to create a calm and introspective atmosphere. These musical characteristics give rise to intuitive musical imagery—a kind of emotional signaling system that transcends language and can be understood across cultures.

3 RESULTS AND DISCUSSION

This study aims to explore how interactive art can evoke emotional connections among strangers through sound and visual interfaces, in response to issues such as urban loneliness and social disconnection. A case study methodology is adopted to extract key interaction and emotional design elements, which are then translated into the foundation of a prototype design.

Three representative interactive installation works were selected for analysis: Pulse Room, Resonating Microcosms, and Subtitled Public. Table 1 summarizes these works and highlights

Table 1. Basic content of the case.

Case Name	Pulse Room	Resonating Microcosms	Subtitled Public
Years	2006	2022	2005
Location	Puebla, México,	Kuala	Mexico City,
Technological Elements	Heart rate sensor sphere, lighting control	Internal sensor, sound device	Infrared sensors, projectors, and a body tracking system.
Interaction	A body-contact sensor that reads the user's heartbeat and represents it through rhythmic light pulses.	When pushed, the light sphere triggers audiovisual changes and interacts with surrounding spheres.	Each individual is randomly assigned a text label that follows them and changes when they come into contact with others.

(*continued*)

Table 1. Continued

Case Name	Pulse Room	Resonating Microcosms	Subtitled Public
Emotional Communication	Visualizes individual life rhythms to evoke collective resonance	Creating connections between people and their environment through 'resonance.	Labels serve to prompt contemplation of human relationships and elicit social interactions.

their core interaction processes and emotional communication strategies identified through a review of relevant documentation and project analysis.

3.1 *Case analysis*

Pulse Room uses heartbeat sensors to capture the viewer's heart rhythm, which is then visualized through the pulsing of light bulbs. As participants observe the heartbeats of others, their own rhythms are incorporated into the overall spatial resonance. In this non-verbal, non-direct form of interaction, participants are prompted to reflect on their sense of social connection.

Resonating Microcosms features light spheres that, when pushed, emit sound and light, influencing nearby spheres and triggering a chain reaction. This dynamic interaction environment invites other viewers to become co-creators of the audio-visual experience.

Subtitled Public randomly assigns participants a set of text labels that are projected onto their bodies for others to read. These labels only change upon contact with another person. Through the gaze and reaction of others, spontaneous social interactions are initiated.

Overall, although these three works differ in terms of interaction forms and technical approaches, they share a common core: using the human body as the medium for interaction, creating non-verbal and real-time sensory feedback systems, and fostering moments of social connection or identity construction.

3.2 *Prototype and interaction flow*

This study further proposes a prototype concept. The device is designed to facilitate non-verbal interaction by providing real-time visual and musical feedback in response to participants' movements within a spatial environment. The goal is to guide participants to perceive and respond to others, thereby fostering interpersonal interaction.

The interaction flow is as follows: when a participant enters the camera's field of view and steps into the sensing area of the device, the system randomly assigns them a unique instrumental timbre. Their movements are then translated into musical parameters such as melody, tempo, and pitch. As individuals walk, they generate independent melodic lines, symbolizing their personal presence. When participants approach or pass by each other, the music temporarily merges, creating harmonies or rhythmic interactions. The longer the overlap, the deeper the musical fusion, eventually forming a complete melodic segment that symbolizes a deeper emotional connection. If no attention or interaction occurs between participants, the music quickly reverts to an individual state. The interaction flow is illustrated in Figure 1.

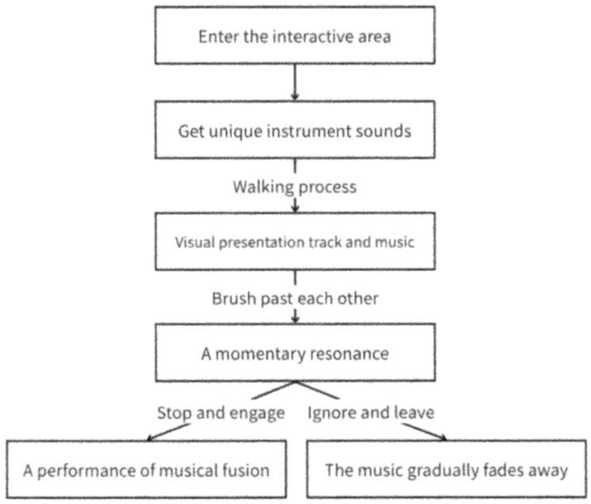

Figure 1. Interaction flowchart.

3.3 *Prototype exhibition space design*

The prototype is designed to be installed in an indoor exhibition space. The interactive environment consists of a camera, a projection wall, a computer vision module, and a sound generation system. At the core of the setup is a camera mounted above the space, which tracks participants' positions and movement trajectories. Using computer vision, the system analyzes users' behavior in real time and translates it into corresponding musical and visual feedback, creating a responsive and interactive environment (Figure 2).

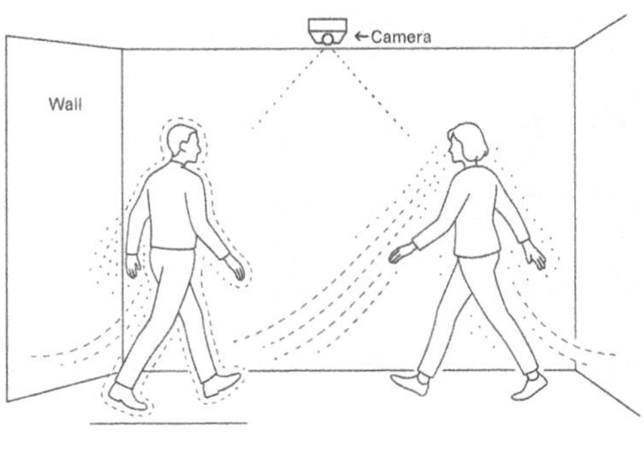

Figure 2. Spatial design layout.

The spatial layout is deliberately arranged to allow participants to enter from the left and right sides, encouraging encounters or near-passes at the center of the space. This simulates spontaneous meetings often seen in urban environments. The design emphasizes spatial relationships and musical interactions between individuals, allowing "moments of intersection" to be expressed through sound and visuals. This setup further explores the connection between interactive behavior and emotional resonance.

4 CONCLUSION

This study addresses urban loneliness and social disconnection by analyzing case studies to extract key design elements—such as the body as a medium for interaction, non-verbal perception, and real-time feedback. Based on these elements, we propose a prototype of an interactive installation that integrates sensing technology and computer vision, with real-time musical and visual feedback at its core. Through participants' movements and intersecting paths, the system transforms spatial relationships among individuals into musical and visual changes, endowing fleeting encounters with emotional resonance and symbolic meaning. In a non-verbal context, simple bodily movements allow participants to perceive and approach one another, fostering brief yet meaningful social connections.

In the future, we aim to further develop the prototype for real-world exhibitions and participant observation, in order to evaluate its effectiveness in enhancing interpersonal interaction and emotional resonance in actual environments. Ultimately, this research seeks to provide a feasible reference and an innovative approach for applying interactive art and interactive music in social installations.

REFERENCES

Brignull, H., and Rogers, Y. (2003). Enticing people to interact with large public displays in public spaces. *Proceedings of INTERACT*, *3*, 17–24.

DeNora, T. (2000). *Music in everyday life.* Cambridge University Press.

Horan, T. (2024). *The Effects of Urbanization and Social Media Use on Individuals' Perceived Social Isolation. Online Journal of Communication and Media Technologies*, 14(1), e202411.

James, J., Ingalls, T., Qian, G., Olsen, L., Whiteley, D., Wong, S., and Rikakis, T. (2006). Movement-based interactive dance performance. *In Proceedings of the 14th Annual ACM International Conference on Multimedia* (pp. 470–480). ACM. https://doi.org/10.1145/1180639.1180733

Juslin, P. N., and Laukka, P. (2004). Expression, perception, and induction of musical emotions: A review and a questionnaire study of everyday listening. *Journal of New Music Research*, *33*(3), 217–238. https://doi.org/10.1080/0929821042000317813

Seth, S. (2023). *The impact of social media on societal dynamics. International Journal of Scientific Research in Engineering and Management (IJSREM)*, 7(10), 1–6. https://doi.org/10.55041/IJSREM25906

Stern, N. (2011). The implicit body as performance: Analyzing interactive art. *Leonardo*, 44(3), 233–238.

Tanaka, A. (2009). Gesture. In R. T. Dean (Ed.), *The Oxford handbook of computer music* (pp. 218–233). Oxford University Press.

Zohny, H. T. (2025). *Installation art as a visual art that supports the presence of the viewer to confront social isolation. International Design Journal*, *15*(1), 447–454. DOI:10.21608/idj.2025.395721

WEBSITES

'Rafael Lozano-Hemmer: Pulse', https://hirshhorn.si.edu/exhibitions/rafael-lozano-hemmer-pulse/, accessed 10 April 2025.

'Play of light, colour and sound at Lalaport', https://malaysia.news.yahoo.com/play-light-colour-sound-lalaport-033251056.html, accessed 10 April 2025.

'teamLab: Resonating Microcosms', https://www.teamlab.art/e/lalaport_kualalumpur/, accessed 10 April 2025.

'Pulse Room', https://www.lozano-hemmer.com/pulse_room.php, accessed 10 April 2025.

'Subtitled Public', https://www.lozano-hemmer.com/subtitled_public.php, accessed 10 April 2025.

'Subtitled Public – Rafael Lozano-Hemmer – Tate', https://www.tate.org.uk/art/artworks/lozano-hemmer-subtitled-public-t12565, accessed 10 April 2025.

System Innovation for a Global Economy – Lam et al. (Eds)

Using generative pre-trained transformers for predictive modeling of traffic accidents in Taiwan

An-Syu Li, Hao-Quan Liu, Yi-Chung Chen & Yu-Ling Zhong
Department of Computer Science & Engineering, National Chung Hsing University, Taichung, Taiwan

Yu-Hao Chen
Department of Computer Science & Information Engineering, Ming Chuan University, Taoyuan, Taiwan

Cheng-An Tsai
College of Electrical Engineering and Computer Science, National Chung Hsing University, Taichung, Taiwan

ABSTRACT: Road safety is significantly threatened by Taiwan's increasing traffic accident rate, and we believe that developing a system to forecast future trends would assist government organizations in taking appropriate action. Previously, researchers utilized machine learning models, such as Boosting and Bagging, to create this system. Despite their strengths in various fields, several challenges still persist due to the nature of the dataset. For instance, frequent occurrences of certain values may lead the models to produce identical predictions. Furthermore, the accumulation of errors when these models are used for autoregressive predictions affects their overall performance. Therefore, Generative Pre-trained Transformers (GPTs) were employed to address the aforementioned issues, leveraging their proven proficiency in predicting long-term sequences and understanding complex input contexts. After testing the comparative methods and the GPT model on Taiwan's traffic accident dataset, the experimental results and sample analysis indicate that the GPT model predicts a more accurate trajectory and outperforms the models on datasets with recurring values, which supports our hypotheses.

1 INTRODUCTION

Traffic accidents continue to pose a significant challenge in Taiwan, with 2023 recording the highest number of traffic-related deaths since 2013 (Charlier 2023). According to Taiwan's Ministry of Transport and Communications, in 2020, the data from the last ten years showed no signs of decreasing or leveling off, highlighting the pressing need for action. Inspired by these alarming figures, we propose developing a forecasting system to predict traffic accident patterns. Specifically, we aim to predict injury counts over a defined period by leveraging historical data to forecast future trends. For example, as shown in Figure 1, a dataset of injury counts in Xin Bei Shi could be used to train a model on past records (indicated in blue). Such a model could accurately predict future injuries or yield insights to guide preventive measures. By identifying high-risk areas, this approach would enable policymakers and agencies to implement targeted interventions, ultimately reducing traffic-related injuries.

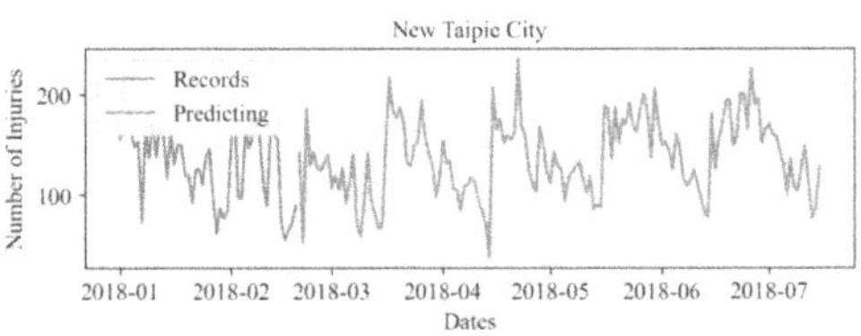

Figure 1. Traffic injury count in New Taipie City.

We address this issue by framing it as a time-series prediction challenge, an area in which researchers have made significant strides through the application of machine-learning techniques. Among these, ensemble learning has emerged as one of the most widely adopted approaches due to its ability to combine multiple models for improved predictive performance. Notably, XGBoost has been successfully applied to time-series forecasting for energy consumption, demonstrating superior accuracy (RS *et al.* 2024). Similarly, AdaBoost, another boosting-based method, has been employed to develop a wave height forecasting system. While its performance in the study was found to be lower than that of XGBoost (Anggraeni *et al.* 2021), it still yielded highly effective results, showcasing its potential for handling complex predictive tasks. Despite these advancements, ensemble learning models, particularly those used in an autoregressive manner,

DOI: 10.1201/9781003655534-20

still encounter certain challenges. Bagging and boosting, while widely used in ensemble learning, can lead to distorted results when applied to time-series forecasting problems such as predicting the number of people injured in traffic accidents, due to their treatment of temporal structure. Imagine daily traffic injury counts steadily rising: Day 1 has 100 injuries, Day 2 has 110, Day 3 has 120, and Day 4 reaches 130. Bagging trains models on bootstrapped subsets like {Day 1, Day 3}, {Day 2, Day 1}, or {Day 3, Day 2}, disrupting the temporal sequence essential for modeling trends. As a result, each model misses the progression and may predict Day 4 as 105, 108, and 115, averaging to 109.3—significantly underestimating the true value. Boosting, in contrast, overemphasizes local fluctuations. Consider weekly injury data: Week 1 has 400 cases, Week 2 has 420, Week 3 has 430, then Week 4 spikes to 500 due to a holiday, before returning to 440 in Week 5. A boosting model may start with a baseline prediction of 435 for Week 5, but after being penalized for underpredicting Week 4 (e.g., predicting 435 instead of 500), it aggressively adjusts, predicting 480 or higher in the next iteration. The final prediction might land around 470, overshooting the actual value because the model overfits to the short-term anomaly. In both cases, these ensemble methods introduce structural mismatches: bagging breaks continuity, while boosting magnifies outliers—both of which undermine accurate forecasting in time-sensitive domains like traffic injury prediction. Additionally, one of the primary limitations of autoregressive models is the accumulation of errors over time, where minor inaccuracies in early predictions can compound, leading to significant deviations from actual values. Another issue is the zero-inflation problem, which arises when time-stamped count data contain an unusually high frequency of a particular value, such as zero. This skewed distribution can mislead models into classifying most instances as the dominant value rather than identifying meaningful underlying trends, ultimately affecting forecasting reliability.

Given these challenges, we explore alternative modeling approaches to improve the accuracy and robustness of time-series forecasting. Specifically, we adopt a technique inspired by (T. B. Brown *et al.* 2020), leveraging the decoder component of the transformer model to construct Generative Pre-trained Transformers (GPTs). While GPTs are primarily designed for natural language processing (NLP), their versatility enables adaptation to other domains, including time-series prediction. Unlike ensemble methods, which face issues like bagging's disruption of temporal dependencies or boosting's over-sensitivity to local fluctuations, GPTs treat time-series values as tokens and use their attention mechanism to automatically identify closely related patterns within a sequence. For example, consider predicting daily traffic injury numbers in a city, where injuries peak every Friday at 5 PM (e.g., 10 injuries) due to rush hour congestion at the start of the weekend, then drop to 3 injuries by midnight—a recurring cycle. If we encode these values as tokens in a sequence (e.g., [3, 5, 10, 7, 3] for a day), GPT's attention mechanism learns that the token representing 10 injuries at the 5 PM position consistently correlates with similar peaks in prior and future Fridays, forecasting 10 injuries for the next Friday's 5 PM accurately. Similarly, in a suburban area, where every Monday morning sees a 30% spike in traffic injuries (e.g., 6 injuries vs. 4 on other days) due to commuters returning to work, GPT recognizes the positional pattern across weeks, predicting 6 injuries for the next Monday morning without overfitting to a single instance or losing sequence context. This ability to holistically capture recurring trends and dependencies gives GPT an edge over ensemble approaches. By leveraging the model's ability to recognize underlying temporal trends and contextual information, we aim to develop a more reliable traffic injury number forecasting system. Our implementation is publicly available (Li and Liu 2025).

2 METHODS

The workflow includes two major processes: (1) online process and (2) offline process, as shown in Figure 2.

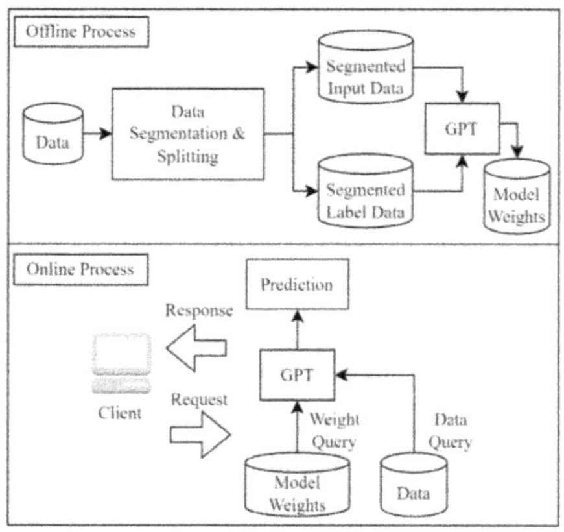

Figure 2. Workflow of the construction of the traffic injury forecasting system.

2.1 *Offline process*

The upper part of Figure 2 exhibits the workflow of the offline process, where the models are trained and data is pre-processed. It consists of two steps: (1) Data segmentation and splitting (2) Model training and storage.

1. **Data segmentation and Splitting.** Since we are dealing with data by city, the data is first segmented based on its corresponding city to ensure that patterns unique to each region are preserved. This allows the model to account for city-specific variations in traffic accidents. Additionally, due to the nature of the decoder-only transformer that GPT relies on, the input and output data need to be formatted as sequences, even though the data is fundamentally different from text. To achieve this, we format the data such that each sequence represents a time window of traffic accident statistics, and the corresponding output represents the subsequent period. For example, if the input sequence is defined as $\boldsymbol{x} = [i, i + 1, \ldots, i + n]$, the output sequence is defined as $\boldsymbol{y} = [i + 1, i + 2, \ldots, i + n + 1]$, where:

- i represents the starting time step of the sequence (e.g., a specific month or day).
- n is the length of the input sequence (e.g., the number of months or days in the window).
- $\boldsymbol{x}$ represents the input features, such as the number of fatalities and injuries for each time step in the sequence.
- $\boldsymbol{y}$ represents the output features, i.e., the number of fatalities and injuries predicted for the subsequent time steps.

For instance, if $\boldsymbol{x} = [10, 15, 12]$ represents the number of fatalities in three consecutive months, the model learns to predict $\boldsymbol{y} = [15, 12, 18]$, where 18 represents the forecasted number of fatalities in the month following the input sequence. This approach ensures that the data is appropriately formatted for the autoregressive nature of the transformer model, allowing it to effectively learn temporal dependencies in traffic accident trends.

(2) **Model Training and Storage.** To facilitate quick access while conserving storage space, only parameters—weights and biases—are stored in the hash table for the models trained on the dataset for each city.

2.2 *Online process*

The lower section of Figure 2 illustrates the system's workflow, which consists of the following operations:

1. **User Access:** Users send a request to the server to access a model trained for the desired city.
2. **Weight Query:** The system retrieves the corresponding model weights from the hash table and loads the model.
3. **Data Query:** To generate predictions, the system fetches data from the designated city to create a prompt suitable for the GPT model.
4. **Prediction and Response:** The GPT model processes the input and produces the predicted results, which are then returned to the client.

This workflow ensures the efficient handling of user requests by dynamically loading model parameters and leveraging city-specific data for accurate predictions. The flowchart visually represents these steps for better comprehension.

3 EXPERIMENT

3.1 *Dataset description*

The dataset utilized in this study was obtained from the Taiwan Government Open Data Platform (National Police Agency, Ministry of the Interior. 2015). This open-access dataset provides detailed records of traffic accidents, categorized as A1 (fatal accidents involving deaths within 24 hours) and A2 (accidents resulting in injuries or deaths beyond 24 hours). The data spans multiple years and is available in semi-annual CSV files, allowing researchers to analyze traffic trends across time and regions in Taiwan. Due to a lack of information and incomplete features over certain periods, for this study, we specifically focus on the number of injuries aggregated across all available cities in Taiwan between January 2018 and January 2020. This subset of the dataset captures the temporal trends in accident severity during this period. Each record consists of the following key attributes:

- **Time of occurrence:** The specific date and time when the traffic accident occurred.
- **Location of occurrence:** The geographical location or administrative region where the accident occurred.
- **Number of fatalities and injuries:** The aggregated count of people who were injured or died as a result of the accident during the selected timeframe.
- **Vehicle types:** The types of vehicles involved in the accident, such as motorcycles, cars, or trucks.
- **Environmental factors:** Additional details such as weather conditions, road type, and presence of traffic signals at the accident site.

In this study, the dataset will be segmented by the city where the accidents occurred, with separate models trained and evaluated on each city's data. Additionally, because injuries occur more frequently than fatalities, the models will focus on forecasting the number of injuries.

3.2 *Experiment setup*

The absolute distance between sequences fails to account for temporal differences, rendering mean squared error (MSE) an unsuitable metric for evaluating model performance in this context. To illustrate, consider a scenario where the predicted sequence and target sequence contain nearly identical tokens, but the predicted sequence is offset by one timestamp relative to the target sequence. In such a case, despite the high similarity in content, the absolute difference between the sequences would yield an inaccurate assessment of alignment due to the temporal shift.

Therefore, to account for both temporal and spatial distances between sequences, dynamic time warping (DTW) is employed instead of relying on Euclidean distance to evaluate model accuracy. DTW minimizes discrepancies across timestamps (Chu *et al.* 2002).

According to Equation 1, function D(***X***, ***Y***) takes the minimum values from the designated cost function, which is typically Euclidean distance, that measures the difference or similarity between sequence ***X*** and ***Y***.

$$D(\boldsymbol{X}, \boldsymbol{Y}) = \min_{\pi} \sum_{(i,j)\in\pi} \text{cost}(x_i, y_j) \tag{1}$$

$$\text{cost}(x_i, y_j) = (x_i - y_j)^2 \tag{2}$$

The cumulative cost d(*i*, *j*), which incorporates both the current alignment cost and the minimum accumulated cost from previous alignments, is computed using Equation 3.

$$\text{d}(i,j) = \text{cost}(x_i, y_j) + \min\begin{cases} d(i, j-1) \\ d(i-1, j) \\ d(i-1, j-1) \end{cases} \tag{3}$$

With the boundary conditions: d(0, 0) = 0, d(*i*, 0) = ∞, d(0, *j*) = ∞ for $i > 0, j > 0$.

The final DTW distance between sequences $\boldsymbol{X} = [x_1, x_2, \ldots, x_n]$ and $\boldsymbol{Y} = [y_1, y_2, \ldots, y_m]$ is described in Equation 4:

$$D(\boldsymbol{X}, \boldsymbol{Y}) = d(n, m) \tag{4}$$

where n and m are the lengths of ***X*** and ***Y***, respectively.

3.3 *Performance assessment*

To fairly evaluate the performance of the GPT model, baseline models such as Gradient Boost, Random Forest, and AdaBoost are used.

As shown in Table 1, the GPT model achieves the best performance among the models based on the DTW metric. However, it is important to note that the high DTW scores across all models are due to the long sequence lengths. Since DTW aggregates the distances over the entire sequence, longer sequences naturally result in higher scores. This highlights the challenges posed by the autoregressive task, where predicting extended sequences amplifies the cumulative differences.

Table 1. Average DTW scores of GPT and baseline models across all available Taiwan cities.

Model	DTW
Gradient Boost	135.49
AdaBoost	134.14
Random Forest	139.74
GPT Model	**121.44**

To better understand the differences in model performance across individual cities, we refer to Figure 3. This figure presents the DTW (Dynamic Time Warping) scores for various models and reveals that the GPT's DTW scores are generally lower than baseline models in many cities' datasets.

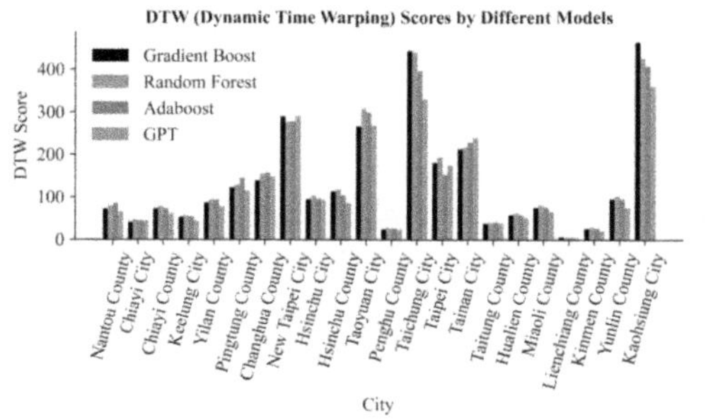

Figure 3. Models' DTW scores from all available cities.

3.4 *Case study*

Figure 4a and 4 b illustrate that the Lienchaing County's dataset contains a high frequency of zeros. For simplicity, we selected the Random Forest method to represent ensemble learning techniques due to its common use in ensemble methods. As seen in Figure 4a, Random Forest's later predictions tend to converge to zero. In contrast, although the GPT model's predictions are not entirely precise, they successfully maintain the spikes and seasonal trends, indicating that the GPT model is less sensitive to datasets with frequent zeros.

4 CONCLUSION

The persistent rise in traffic-related injuries and fatalities in Taiwan underscores the urgent need for effective predictive systems to inform proactive safety measures. Traditional time-series forecasting methods, such as ensemble techniques like Random Forest and AdaBoost, often face

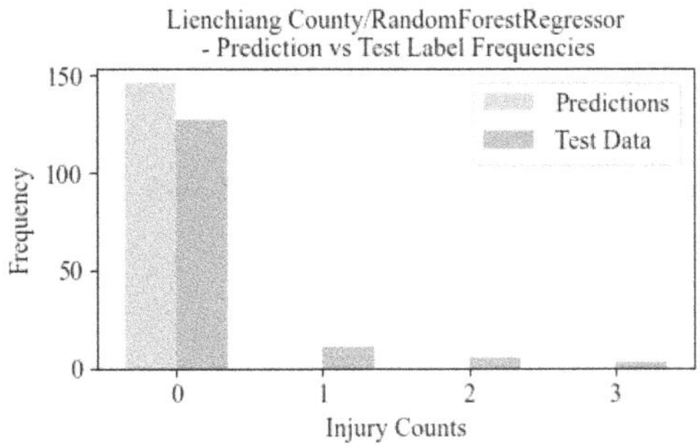

(a)

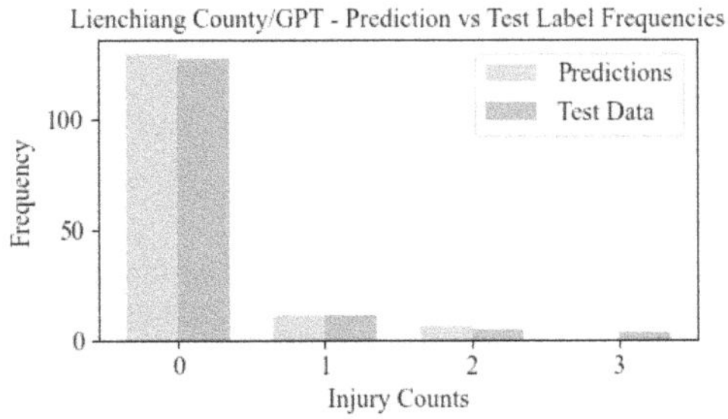

(b)

Figure 4. Injury counts for Lienchiang Country's testing data versus predictions: (a) Random Forest model and (b) GPT model.

challenges in capturing complex temporal dependencies and handling datasets with recurring values or zero-inflation issues. These limitations can lead to less accurate predictions, hindering timely interventions.

In this study, we introduced a forecasting framework employing Generative Pre-trained Transformers (GPTs) to model temporal patterns in traffic injury data. By leveraging GPTs' capacity to capture intricate temporal dependencies, our approach demonstrated superior performance over traditional ensemble methods. The GPT model consistently achieved lower Dynamic Time Warping (DTW) scores across various city-level datasets, indicating more accurate and reliable forecasts.

These findings highlight the potential of transformer-based models in enhancing traffic injury prediction, offering valuable insights for policymakers and urban planners aiming to implement targeted interventions. Future research could explore integrating additional contextual factors, such as weather conditions and traffic volume, to further refine predictive accuracy. Moreover, extending this framework to real-time data streams may facilitate the development of dynamic, responsive traffic safety systems.

REFERENCES

Anggraeni, F., Adytia, D., and Ramadhan, A. W. (2021). Forecasting of wave height time series using adaboost and xgboost, case study in pangandaran, indonesia. *2021 International Conference on Data Science and Its Applications (ICoDSA)*, 97–101. https://doi.org/10.1109/ICoDSA53588.2021.9617524

Brown T. B., Mann B., Ryder N., Subbiah M., Kaplan J. D., Dhariwal P., Neelakantan A., Shyam P., Sastry G., Askell A., Agarwal S., Herbert-Voss A., Kruegerc G., Henighan T., Child R., Ramesh A., Ziegler D. M., Wu J., Winter C., Hesse C., Chen M., Sigler E., Litwin M., Gray S., Chess B., Clark J., Berner C., McCandlish S., Radford A., Sutskever I., and Amodei D., (2020). *Language Models Are Few-Shot Learners.* arXiv, vol. 4, May 2020.

Charlier P., (2023). *Taiwan traffic deaths in 2022 up year on year and highest since 2013.* Taiwan English News. Retrieved January 2025. [Online]. Available: https://taiwanenglishnews.com/taiwan-traffic-deaths-in-2022-up-year-on-year-and-highest-since-2013/

Chu S., Keogh E., Hart D., and Pazzani M., (Apr. 2002), Iterative deepening dynamic time warping for time series, *Proceedings of the 2002 SIAM International Conference on Data Mining*, doi: https://doi.org/10.1137/1.9781611972726.12

Li, A.-S., and Liu, H.-Q. (2025). *GitHub - nchu-machine-learning/Taiwan-Traffic-Safety-Forecast-System.* GitHub. https://github.com/nchu-machine-learning/Taiwan-Traffic-Safety-Forecast-System

National Police Agency, Ministry of the Interior (Taiwan), 2015. Historical traffic accident data. Retrieved December 14, 2024. [Online]. Available: https://data.gov.tw/dataset/12197

RS, R., K, Y. P., P, S. D. R., D, Y., and D'Souza, S. M. (2024). Time series forecasting for energy consumption using xgboost and lstm. *2024 Asia Pacific Conference on Innovation in Technology (APCIT)*, 1–8. https://doi.org/10.1109/APCIT62007.2024.10673558

System Innovation for a Global Economy – Lam et al. (Eds)
© 2026 The Author(s), ISBN 978-1-041-10520-6

Using social media itineraries and spatial discretization methods to implement the personalized travel recommender systems

An-Syu Li, Yu-Ling Zhong & Yi-Chung Chen
Department of Computer Science & Engineering, National Chung Hsing University, Taichung, Taiwan

Yu-Hao Chen
Department of Computer Science & Information Engineering, Ming Chuan University, Taoyuan, Taiwan

Ya-Chuan Hsu
College of Electrical Engineering and Computer Science, National Chung Hsing University, Taichung, Taiwan

ABSTRACT: This research paper presents a novel personalized recommendation system that combines social media travel itineraries with spatial discretization to address the limitations inherent in traditional approaches like K-Nearest Neighbors (KNN). In our methodology, travel data is scraped from the Ptt forum, where Taiwan LLM, an advanced language model, is utilized to extract locations from narrative articles, later transforming these into coordinates to capture both the sequence and specific order of visited destinations. After extraction, a grid-based technique is employed to discretize these coordinates, simplifying data management for computational models while preserving essential spatial proximity details. Utilizing this refined dataset, we introduce an adapted n-grams algorithm that translates the extracted sequential patterns into practical travel recommendations. This innovative technique provides a robust and computationally efficient alternative to conventional machine learning methods, which often incur high processing costs. Our experimental evaluations, conducted using Dynamic Time Warping (DTW) across varied regions including Hokkaido, Kanto, Okinawa, Tohoku, and Taiwan, demonstrate that our approach reduces computational overhead while delivering more precise and contextually relevant travel recommendations.

1 INTRODUCTION

Travel has become a prominent topic of discussion among contemporary individuals, particularly since the onset of the COVID-19 pandemic. This period has seen a marked rise in interest and discourse surrounding travel, driven by a dual motivation: the longing to explore new destinations and the necessity to reimagine travel experiences in a post-pandemic context. Both travel agencies, which aim to craft innovative packages to captivate prospective clients, and independent travelers, who value the autonomy to design their own itineraries, grapple with the perennial question of destination selection—an issue that remains fluid and multifaceted. Many travelers begin planning with a handful of well-known attractions in mind, such as iconic landmarks, cultural centers, or picturesque natural sites. However, these initial choices often represent only a starting point. Transforming a conventional trip into a memorable adventure typically requires additional recommendations, including lesser-known destinations or complementary sites that enrich the journey. Such suggestions play a critical role in creating itineraries that are not only distinctive but also aligned with individual preferences.

Recognizing the demand for comprehensive and personalized travel planning, the development of an effective recommender system offers a promising solution. This system is designed to generate a curated list of attractions that complements the traveler's preliminary selections while introducing novel options that might otherwise be overlooked. By integrating user preferences with a diverse array of potential destinations, the recommender system bridges the gap between traditional travel planning and the pursuit of a tailored travel experience. Specifically, this study proposes a model that accepts a small set of user-selected attractions as input and generates additional recommendations to enhance the itinerary. Through an iterative process—where outputs are reintroduced into the system—users can construct a complete, customized travel plan that meets their unique desires and expectations.

Previous research has explored machine learning techniques, such as k-nearest neighbors (KNN), one of the most popular and classic methods in recommender systems, to develop recommender systems. For instance, Anamisa, Jauhari, and Mufarroha (2023) applied KNN to a tourism recommender system in Bangkalan, noting that the choice of k significantly influences prediction accuracy. Similarly, Weng (2024) demonstrated KNN's effectiveness in a book recommendation system, highlighting its superiority over Random Forest in terms of Mean Squared Error (MSE), though computational efficiency diminishes as dataset size grows. Despite these applications, KNN exhibits notable limitations that

 DOI: 10.1201/9781003655534-21

undermine its suitability for advanced recommender systems, particularly in the context of travel planning. One critical drawback of KNN is its computational inefficiency with large datasets. As the volume of data increases, the algorithm's reliance on distance calculations for each query results in prohibitively slow prediction times, rendering it impractical for real-time or scalable applications. Furthermore, KNN struggles to address the cold start problem, a persistent challenge in recommender systems (Yuan and Hernandez 2023). This issue manifests in two forms: item cold start, where rare or newly introduced items lack sufficient interaction data, and user cold start, where insufficient user history hampers personalized recommendations. Both scenarios lead to reduced accuracy and reliability in KNN-based systems. Beyond these well-documented issues, KNN's fundamental mechanics present additional shortcomings for travel recommender systems. The algorithm's reliance on selecting a fixed *k* value and aggregating the "votes" of nearest neighbors oversimplifies the recommendation process. This voting mechanism assumes that proximity in feature space—typically based on user preferences or historical interactions—sufficiently captures the complexity of travel planning. However, this approach lacks robustness, as the arbitrary selection of *k* may not consistently reflect meaningful patterns or relationships in the data. Moreover, KNN predominantly focuses on user-based similarities, identifying neighbors based on shared preferences while neglecting critical spatial or contextual relationships, such as the geographic proximity or thematic coherence of attractions. For example, consider a traveler planning a trip to Paris with an initial interest in visiting the Eiffel Tower. A KNN-based system might identify *k* nearest neighbors—other users who also favored the Eiffel Tower—and recommend additional attractions based on their preferences, such as the Louvre Museum, a popular choice among similar users. While this suggestion aligns with user similarity, it overlooks the spatial and experiential context: the Louvre, though nearby, is an indoor cultural site, whereas the traveler might prefer a complementary outdoor landmark, like the Champ de Mars, to enhance their itinerary's variety. Furthermore, if a less-visited but thematically related site, such as the Musée de la Sculpture en Plein Air, lies slightly farther away, KNN's user-centric focus might exclude it entirely, as it prioritizes neighbor preferences over location-based coherence. This example underscores how KNN's neglect of geographic relationships and reliance on simplistic voting limits its ability to generate cohesive, contextually relevant travel itineraries.

Nonetheless, contemporary scholars propose the concept of discretizing human mobility trajectories to address the previously mentioned bottlenecks. For example, the original coordinates were mapped onto a 500-meter grid cell (Yabe *et al.* 2024). This operation reduces the complexity of the problem, as certain unique coordinates are counted as one due to their proximity. However, we must acknowledge that the technology for discretizing human mobility trajectories has not yet been widely implemented in the field of travel recommendations. Therefore, new methods should be proposed to address this issue.

This paper proposes a modified n-gram approach (Peng and Schuurmans 2003). for recommending travel itineraries using discretized human flow trajectories. We derived this idea from the observation that discrete human flow trajectories resemble text sentences. The scenic spots that users frequently visit can be viewed as commonly used words, while the unique scenic spots that users occasionally visit can be seen as more specialized vocabulary. Additionally, when traveling, people typically visit scenic spots in a specific order. For instance, outdoor attractions are generally visited in the morning, while shopping excursions are often made in the evening. We contend that these characteristics can also be likened to human language sentences, making it reasonable to design algorithms based on n-grams. Furthermore, to test the validity of our proposed approach and draw comparisons with existing methods, we scraped the itinerary dataset from the PTT forum, which is a platform for Taiwanese discussions on various topics. We used Taiwan LLM to process the data.(Chen *et al.* 2024; Lin and Chen 2023)

2 DATASET

Our data processing procedure is divided into two major steps: (1) data scraping and (2) data processing, as shown in Figure 1.

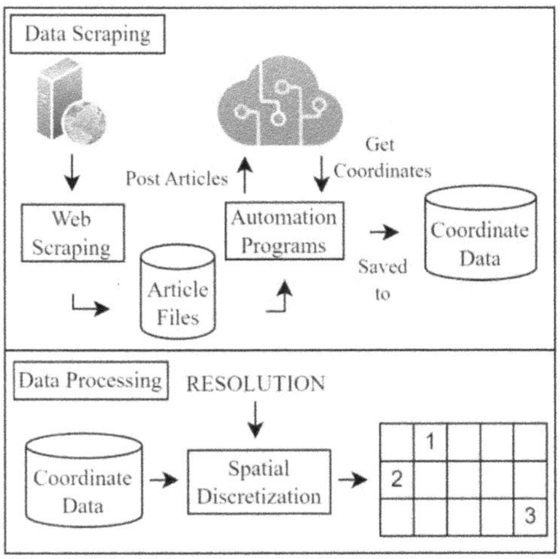

Figure 1. Workflow for scraping travel itineraries from the PTT forum and processing them into discretized coordinates.

2.1 *Data scraping*

During the data collection phase, our program systematically scans the PTT forum—a popular platform where travelers share detailed accounts of their journeys—to identify posts by individuals who have visited specific countries and documented their travel experiences. The focus is primarily on renowned destinations in Japan, including regions such as Hokkaido, Kanto, Okinawa, and Tohoku, as well as Taiwan, which are widely recognized as popular tourist spots.

To ensure relevance, the web scraping tool is designed to detect special identifiers embedded in the post titles. These identifiers act as markers indicating that the article is related to travel experiences. The program filters and collects only those articles that contain these unique tags, thereby narrowing down the dataset to the most pertinent content.

Once an article is identified and collected, it is immediately stored in a local repository for further processing. Given the volume of data retrieved from the forum, managing and extracting useful information from these posts presents a significant challenge. To address this, we utilize Taiwan LLM, an advanced language model, to analyze each article. The process entails submitting the article to Taiwan LLM, which then parses the text to extract the sequence of visits mentioned by the traveler.

The automation program patiently awaits the response from Taiwan LLM, ensuring that the extracted sequence of visits is accurate and complete. Once the language model returns the sequence data, the automation system consolidates the information by saving it alongside the associated coordinate details. This meticulous process of data collection, filtering, and extraction guarantees that the final dataset is comprehensive and structured, providing a robust foundation for subsequent analysis and recommendation tasks.

2.2 *Data processing*

We utilize a grid-based spatial discretization to convert continuous coordinates (x, y) into discrete cell indices (i, j) Let $x_{\min}$, $x_{\max}$, $y_{\min}$, and $y_{\max}$ be the minimum and maximum values of the x- and y-coordinates in the dataset, respectively. Then, choosing a resolution parameter determines the size of each grid cell. We compute the number of cells along each axis as:

$$M = \lceil \frac{x_{\max} - x_{\min}}{r} \rceil, \quad N = \lceil \frac{y_{\max} - y_{\min}}{r} \rceil \tag{1}$$

For each data point (x, y), its corresponding discrete grid cell (i, j) is given by:

$$i = \lceil \frac{x - x_{\min}}{r} \rceil, \quad j = \lceil \frac{y - y_{\min}}{r} \rceil \tag{2}$$

where $0 \leq i < M$ and $0 \leq j < N$. Each cell index thus represents one spatial bin at the chosen resolution r.

3 METHODS

The algorithm flow of this paper will be divided into two parts: (1) the offline process and (2) the online process, as illustrated in Figure 2.

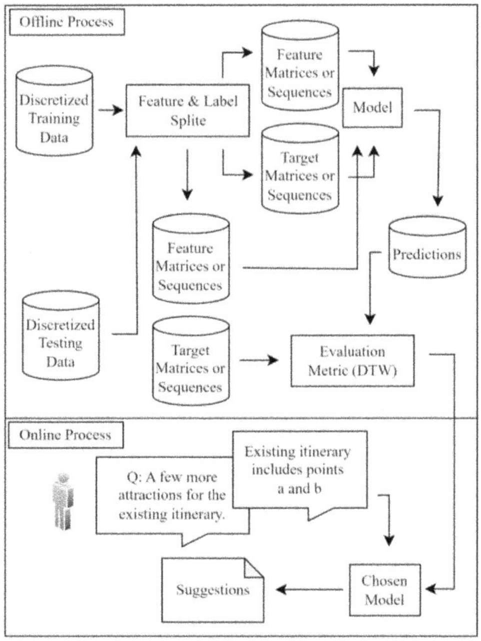

Figure 2. Offline process for model training and online process for generating recommendations.

3.1 *Offline process*

In this section, the discretized dataset is first split into training and testing subsets. Then, a feature-label splitter separates the data into feature sequences (or matrices) and target sequences. The feature sequences are used as inputs for sequence-based models, while the target sequences serve as inputs for vector-based models.

In the sequence-based approach, each 2D coordinate (i_n, j_n) is mapped to a single integer label y_n. Formally, define a label mapping function ϕ: $\mathbb{R}^2 \rightarrow \mathbb{R}$ such that: $y_n = \phi(i_n, j_n)$, $n = 1, 2, \ldots, T$. For example, $\phi(1, 1) = 1$, $\phi(1, 2) = 2$, etc. Hence, the entire dataset in a sequence-based format becomes $\{y_1, y_2, \ldots, y_n\}$.

In the matrix-based approach, we keep the 2D structure and use a matrix M to record the visit order. For a grid of size $M \times N$, define: $M[i_n, j_n] = n$, $n = 1, 2, \ldots, T$, where $M[i_n, j_n]$ stores an integer indicating that the (i_n, j_n)-th location was visited at the n-th step.

Concretely, if the first visited coordinate is (1,1), we set $M[1,1] = 1$, if the second visited coordinate is (1,2), then $M[1,2] = 2$, and so on for all visited coordinates.

3.2 *KNN offline setup*

For the attraction recommendation task, we adopt classification-based models since we view them as the most effective means to suggest optimal subsequent attractions for users. In our KNN configuration, we employ cosine similarity as the distance metric and set $k = 1$.

3.3 *N-grams offline setup*

Our n-grams model is constructed using a method that diverges from the standard vanilla approach. For model training, Let

$$\mathcal{D} = \left\{ \left(x^{(i)}, y^{(i)} \right) \right\}_{i=1}^{N} \quad (3)$$

be the training dataset, where each $x^{(i)}$ is an input sequence (with padding removed) and $y^{(i)}$ is the corresponding output sequence.

For each training pair, the model collects frequency counts of output sequences given their associated contexts. Specifically, for each context c and output sequence y, define the count:

$$N(c, y) = \sum_{i=1}^{N} 1\{c = \text{context extracted from } x^{(i)} \text{ and } y^{(i)} = y\},$$

where $1\{\cdot\}$ is the indicator function. The total count for context c is then given by

$$N(c) = \sum_{y} N(c, y) \quad (5)$$

For the prediction, the context can be either the entire input sequence or, for a given n-gram size n, any sliding window within the sequence. That is, for an input sequence $x = (x_1, x_2, \ldots, x_t)$
we consider:

- The full context: $c_{\text{full}} = (x_1, x_2, \ldots, x_t)$
- And for each $k = 1, \ldots, T - n + 1$ the n-gram context: $c_k = (x_k, x_{(k+1)}, \ldots, x_{(k+n-1)})$.

Given a new input sequence x, the model predicts an output sequence $\hat{y}$ by first attempting to match the full context:

$$\hat{y} = \arg\max_{y} N(x, y). \quad (6)$$

If no prediction is available for the full context, the model progressively considers shorter contexts by removing the earliest tokens. For example, for $k = 2, \ldots, T$:

$$\hat{y} = \arg\max_{y} N((x_k, x_{k+1}, \ldots, x_T), y), \quad (7)$$

until a matching context is found. If no match is found in any context, the model defaults to the globally most common output:

$$y^{*} = \arg\max_{y} \sum_{c} N(c, y). \quad (8)$$

Finally, the predicted output sequence is post-processed to have a fixed length max_len by padding with zeros or truncating as necessary.

3.4 *Evaluation step*

After fitting the models on the feature sequences or matrices along with their corresponding target sequences from the training set, the next phase involves inputting the features from the testing set into the trained models to generate predictions. This step is critical as it allows us to assess the models' ability to generalize to unseen data. The predictions generated by the models are then rigorously compared to the ground truth sequences using Dynamic Time Warping (DTW) as the evaluation metric (Bringmann *et al.* 2023).

DTW is selected because of its unique capability to measure the similarity between temporal sequences while simultaneously accounting for spatial differences. Unlike conventional distance metrics, DTW is particularly adept at handling sequences that may be misaligned in time, making it ideal for our application where both the order and the spatial arrangement of events are crucial. This method of evaluation provides a nuanced assessment by effectively aligning the predicted and actual sequences, thereby capturing the inherent temporal shifts and spatial deviations that occur in real-world travel itineraries.

Once the DTW scores are computed for each model, the one with the lowest DTW score—which signifies the closest match between the predicted sequences and the target sequences—is deemed the best performer. This model is then earmarked for deployment in the online process, where it will be used to generate real-time recommendations. The rigorous evaluation using DTW not only ensures the model's accuracy and reliability but also confirms its suitability for handling the complexities of both temporal and spatial data in a dynamic, real-world setting.

3.5 *Online process*

In the online process, the user might have an existing itinerary and want to visit different places. The model that performs the best in the offline process will then utilize the given few attractions to generate additional recommendations.

4 EXPERIMENT

4.1 *Models' DTW scores*

The experimental design involved the implementation of N-grams and KNN models across five distinct regions: Hokkaido, Kanto, Okinawa, Tohoku, and Taiwan. K-fold cross-validation was employed to evaluate model efficacy. As shown in Figure 3, the N-grams model consistently exhibited the lowest average Dynamic Time Warping (DTW) scores across all regions. Notably, the variant 'N-grams No Look Down,' which omits Equation 6, resulted in similar performance. Among the KNN models, the DTW distance metric achieved the lowest DTW score, followed by TF-IDF inputs. Conversely, the flattened grid representation as input yielded the highest DTW score, albeit with results closer to the TF-IDF model.

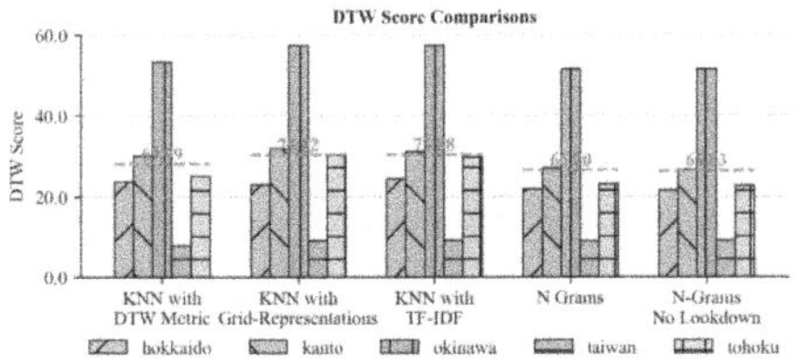

Figure 3. Regional performance comparison of models: DTW score analysis across Hokkaido, Kanto, Okinawa, Tohoku, and Taiwan.

4.2 *Case study*

In order to examine the models‘ performance under challenging conditions, specifically those exhibiting maximum divergence from target sequences, we analyzed a sample characterized by the top-performing model's peak Dynamic Time Warping (DTW) distance. Figure 4 presents the input, target, and predicted sequences, denoted by black, red, and blue markers, respectively. Across the Japanese regions of Hokkaido, Kanto, Okinawa, and Tohoku, the models demonstrated a consistent pattern, despite the N-grams model's comparatively poor performance. Conversely, the DTW distance observed in Taiwan was notably reduced, likely due to the geographical proximity of attractions. The observed similarity in predicted sequences across models suggests a potential influence of the classification methodology and the limited dataset size, leading to convergent classification outcomes.

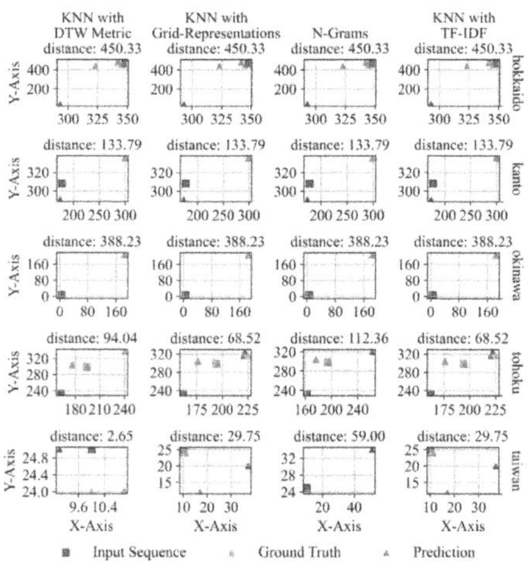

Figure 4. Input Feature Sequences, Target Sequences, and Model Predictions Across Different Cities.

5 CONCLUSION

Driven by the growing demand for travel, users are increasingly searching for recommendation systems that can suggest additional attractions to complement their initial plans. Traditionally, such systems were implemented using machine learning algorithms like K-Nearest Neighbors; however, the substantial computational overhead of this method proved to be a critical limitation. With the advent of NLP-based techniques—most notably, the application of N-grams in other domains—we propose a novel approach that goes beyond traditional N-grams and delivers superior performance across various regions.

REFERENCES

Anamisa, D., Jauhari, A., and Mufarroha, F. (2023, 05). K-nearest neighbors method for recommendation system in bangkalan's tourism. *ComTech: Computer, Mathematics and Engineering Applications*, 14, 33–44. doi: 10.21512/comtech.v14i1.7993.

Bringmann, K., Fischer, N., van der Hoog, I., Kipouridis, E., Kociumaka, T., and Rotenberg, E. (2023). *Dynamic dynamic time warping*. Retrieved from https://arxiv.org/abs/2310.18128.

Chen, P., Cheng, S., Chen, W., Lin, Y., and Chen, Y. (2024). *Measuring taiwanese mandarin language understanding. CoRR, abs/2403.20180*. Retrieved from https://doi.org/10.48550/arXiv.2403.20180 doi: 10.48550/ARXIV.2403.20180.

Lin, Y., and Chen, Y. (2023). Taiwan LLM: bridging the linguistic di vide with a culturally aligned language model. *CoRR, abs/2311.17487*. Retrieved from https://doi.org/10.48550/arXiv.2311.17487 doi: 10.48550/ARXIV.2311.17487.

Peng, F., and Schuurmans, D. (2003). Combining naive bayes and n-gram language models for text classification. In F. Sebastiani (Ed.), *Advances in information retrieval* (pp. 335–350). Berlin, Heidelberg: Springer Berlin Heidelberg.

Weng, J. (2024). Comparison of machine learning-based book comments sentiment analysis for constructing recommendation system. *Applied and Computational Engineering*, 47, 120–124.

Yabe, T., Tsubouchi, K., Shimizu, T., *et al.* (2024). YJMob100K: City-scale and longitudinal dataset of anonymized human mobility trajectories. *Scientific Data*, 11, 397. Retrieved from https://doi.org/10.1038/s41597-024-03237-9 doi: 10.1038/s41597 024-03237-9.

Yuan, H., and Hernandez, A. (2023, 12). User cold start problem in recommendation systems: A systematic review. *IEEE Access*. doi: 10.1109/AC CESS.2023.3338705.

System Innovation for a Global Economy – Lam et al. (Eds)
© 2026 The Author(s), ISBN 978-1-041-10520-6

A study on the design strategy of Guizhou batik cultural and creative products based on grounded theory

Bo-Jun Chen
School of Design, Fujian University of Technology, Fuzhou, China

Jeng-Chung Woo
School of Design, Fujian University of Technology, Fuzhou, China
Design Innovation Research Center of Humanities and Social Sciences Research Base of Colleges and Universities in Fujian Province, Fuzhou, China

Long-Yi Yin
School of Design, Fujian University of Technology, Fuzhou, China

ABSTRACT: In the new consumer era, cultural and creative products play a crucial role in intangible cultural heritage preservation.Guizhou batik, as an intangible cultural heritage, faces challenges in integrating traditional craftsmanship with modern market demands and lacks a systematic design strategy. This study uses grounded theory to explore design strategies for Guizhou batik products, aiming to innovate traditional techniques' dynamic transmission.Firstly, CiteSpace visualization tool was used to sort out research literature on batik cultural and creative product design in Guizhou. And then through literature review,a semi-structured interview questionnaire was developed, and in-depth interviews were conducted with 9 batik experts with over ten years of experience, resulting in 82,995 words of transcribed data.Through this process, 225 initial concepts, 97 open codes, 39 axial codes, and 6 selective coding categories were identified. From this analysis, a design strategy model for Guizhou batik cultural and creative products was constructed, encompassing six core categories: "Composition strategies," "Design requirements," "Development potential," "Pattern applications," "Development status," "Market demands" This model provides theoretical and practical guidance for batik product design, innovation, branding, and market implementation.

Keywords: grounded theory, batik, Guizhou, cultural and creative products, citespace

1 INTRODUCTION

As vital carriers of ethnic culture, the inheritance and innovation of Intangible Cultural Heritage (ICH) have emerged as critical priorities for safeguarding cultural diversity in globalization, particularly in the new consumer era. China's Guiding Opinions on Cultural-Creative Product Development (2016), jointly issued by the Ministry of Culture and the National Cultural Heritage Administration, explicitly positions cultural-creative development as a strategic pathway for revitalizing traditional culture, emphasizing design-driven integration of heritage with modern markets to rejuvenate its relevance. Guizhou batik, among China's first nationally recognized ICH items, encapsulates ethnic historical narratives and aesthetic philosophy through its distinctive patterns and artisanal techniques. however, include a structural disconnect between traditional craftsmanship and market dynamics, underdeveloped systematic design frameworks, and limited alignment with contemporary aesthetic expectations. (Yang D.N. *et al.* 2020) This has created a notable theory-practice gap in the field. To address this issue, this study employs the CiteSpace visualization tool to systematically review literature on Guizhou batik cultural and creative product design, revealing its evolutionary patterns and research hotspots. Through a comprehensive literature analysis, we developed a semi-structured interview questionnaire and conducted in-depth interviews with nine batik experts, each possessing over ten years of experience. By applying grounded theory, the study explores design strategies to provide actionable guidance for batik's sustainable development.

2 LITERATURE REVIEW

Guizhou batik, as a representative of the southwestern ethnic minority culture, carries the history and aesthetics of the Miao people. It reached its

DOI: 10.1201/9781003655534-22

peak during the Sui and Tang dynasties due to the influence of the Silk Road and was hailed as the "First Dye of the East." (Quan H. *et al.* 2024) In recent years, Guizhou batik cultural and creative products have gained increasing market recognition for their cultural symbolism and distinctive characteristics, particularly among young consumers. These products have diversified into various categories, including tourism souvenirs, home decor, and apparel. However, under the influence of modernization, intangible cultural heritage has experienced audience attrition, while traditional products often fail to meet the public's growing demand for innovation and uniqueness. (Zheng X. *et al.* 2024) Existing Guizhou batik cultural and creative products have a limited range of design elements, lack a systematic strategy, and suffer from insufficient innovation and attention to detail. (Ding W.Y. *et al.* 2024) Moreover, most research relies on subjective judgment, lacking objective design basis.

CiteSpace, as a visual knowledge analysis tool, unveils complex data structures and trends intuitively. (Li X. *et al.* 2018) This tool pinpoints research themes, reveals trends, and provides intuitive data support for studies, (Liu H. *et al.* 2021) such as Chinese scholar Han Chaoyan explored the integration of traditional culture in product design through CiteSpace-based visual analysis of CNKI literature, mapping domestic cultural-creative design research landscapes, core themes, and developmental trajectories. (Han C.Y. *et al.* 2025).

Grounded theory employs progressive coding of user data and interviews to extract core concepts, constructing design models and theoretical frameworks. (Wei Y. *et al.* 2025) This theory is applicable to exploratory research, systematically revealing ICH-inspired cultural-creative design strategies and latent influencing factors. For instance, Chinese scholar Sun interviewed 32 members at City University of Macau using grounded theory, developing a three-tiered demand model (functional, experiential, innovative) to address campus cultural-creative homogenization through theoretical and practical pathways. (Sun Y. *et al.* 2024).

In summary, To address the research gaps concerning Guizhou batik cultural and creative products, this study employs CiteSpace to analyze scholarly hotspots and evolutionary trends in batik design, thereby establishing conceptual guidance and theoretical anchoring for subsequent research. Furthermore, through the integration of grounded theory with in-depth expert interviews, the study synthesizes design praxis and strategic insights to formulate evidence-based theoretical propositions, ultimately constructing a systematic design strategy framework for Guizhou batik cultural innovation. This approach fills research gaps and supports Guizhou batik's innovation and sustainable heritage.

3 METHODOLOGY

3.1 *Data collection*

To ensure research comprehensiveness, this study retrieved literature from CNKI and Web of Science. On CNKI, keywords including "batik," "Guizhou batik," and "batik cultural-creative" were searched within academic journals and doctoral and master's theses. Web of Science queries combined "Batik," "Batik patterns," and "Miao Batik," with a search period ending January 2025. After excluding irrelevant and duplicate records, 536 articles were retained, with 210 selected as valid references and exported in Refworks format.

Semi-structured interviews, balancing guided flexibility and exploratory depth, enable nuanced insights into participants' perspectives. This study developed a semi-structured protocol through literature analysis, structured around four domains: pattern symbolism, expressive forms, user characteristics, and product typologies, comprising nine questions. Nine experts with over a decade of Guizhou batik expertise participated in one-on-one offline interviews. Sessions were audio-recorded with consent and transcribed verbatim (82,995 words total). Data were coded using NVivo14 qualitative analysis software to systematically extract core concepts.

3.2 *Quantitative trend analysis of research*

Analysis of publication quantity dynamics reveals phased development intensity and research attention, aiding in understanding overall trends. (Cao X. *et al.* 2023) Based on this, data from the CNKI and Web of Science databases were used, and CiteSpace was employed for bibliometric analysis to create a trend chart of the annual publication volume in Guizhou batik cultural research (see Figure 1). As shown in the figure, research in this field has exhibited continuous growth from 2010 to 2024, divided into three main developmental stages.

From 2010 to 2016, research remained in its initial phase. Spurred by the 2009 *Cultural Industry Revitalization Plan* Guizhou batik gradually gained academic attention, though studies were primarily characterized by descriptive analyses focusing on its integration with tourism, home decor, and related sectors, while systematic design frameworks remained underdeveloped.

From 2017 to 2020, research entered a steady development phase. Supported by the 2018 *Several Policy* Opinions *on Encouraging and Promoting Tourism Commodity Industry Development* issued by the General Office of the State Council of China, Guizhou batik cultural-creative research progressively shifted focus toward product lifestyle integration and pattern innovation, establishing preliminary design methodology frameworks.

Since 2021, research has entered a rapid development phase. Policy frameworks such as the *20th National Congress Report of the Communist Party of China and Guizhou Provincial Government's Implementation Opinions on Building the "Gui Series" Brand with Ethnic-Cultural Distinctiveness (2023)* have amplified institutional support, driving substantial growth in annual publications. Research themes have matured, demonstrating interdisciplinary and diversified trends.

Notably, Guizhou batik cultural-creative research has garnered international scholarly attention. For instance, Yang proposed that metaverse technology facilitates digital preservation and innovative dissemination of batik, expanding ICH's developmental pathways in modern society. (Yang T. and Hu Z. 2024) Fujita Xiang comprehensively examined Miao batik's conservation and sustainable development, emphasizing the pivotal roles of cross-sector collaborations and "bridge individuals" in engaging youth and advancing cultural continuity. (Fujita K. 2021).

In summary, this research is transitioning from a regional discourse to an internationalized paradigm, enhancing global perspectives on ICH safeguarding while opening broader research trajectories.

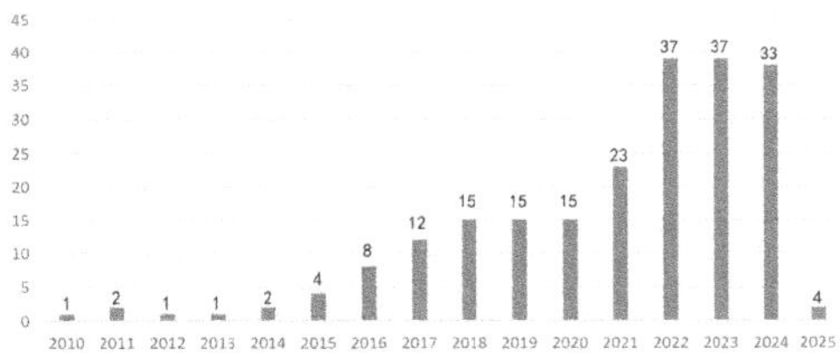

Figure 1. Annual publication volume in guizhou batik cultural-creative research.

3.3 *Keyword timezone map analysis*

Keyword time-zone maps visually represent temporal evolution trends of research themes, (Chen J. *et al.* 2024) with color intensity gradients (early to recent periods) indicating temporal progression. Leveraging the CiteSpace-generated time-zone map for Guizhou batik cultural-creative research (Figure 2), this study analyzes dynamic developmental trajectories of research hotspots in the field.

The timeline analysis (2018–2023) reveals heightened focus on Guizhou batik's modern applications, marked by the introduction of novel design technologies and concepts. From 2018 onward, clusters #1 ("Batik"), #2 ("Design Practice Application"), #6 ("Ethnic Culture"), and #9 ("Abstraction") indicate scholars' growing emphasis on integrating heritage preservation with modernization. During 2020–2023, Research entered a rapid development phase, prioritizing innovation-driven design, market demands, and sustainable development, as evidenced by clusters #3 ("Innovative Design"), #4 ("Applied Research"), and #8 ("Guizhou Batik Culture"). It reflects scholars' attention to the diversified application and sustainability of batik culture. Emerging clusters—#0 ("Innovation"), #5 ("Batik Product Design"), #7 ("Apparel Design"), and #10 ("Artisanal Exploration"), appear in light-yellow hues, signifying recent thematic expansions.

The change in keyword color indicates that from 2018 to 2020, research in the field of batik cultural and creative products gradually diversified, with the research topics expanding from traditional craftsmanship preservation to design innovation, market application, and other dimensions. This marks the rise of batik cultural and creative products in the field of modern design. Keywords such as "digitalization" and "packaging design" frequently appeared, with colors shifting from deep purple to light yellow. During 2021–2024, the research entered a deeper stage, with keyword colors becoming lighter yellow and even approaching bright yellow, indicating the academic community's heightened attention to the modernization and diversification of batik applications. Keywords such as "New Chinese style," "cultural and creative design," and "pattern research" gradually became hot topics. Similarly, high-frequency keywords such as "fashion design," "innovative applications," and "product design" have consistently maintained an important position over the past decade, highlighting their core role in the field of Guizhou batik cultural and creative products.

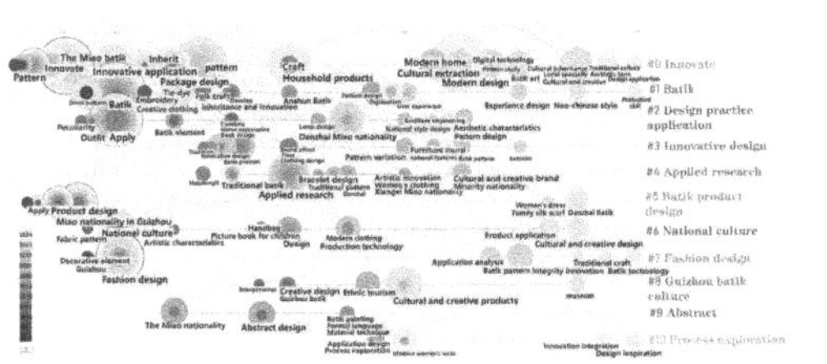

Figure 2. Keyword co-occurrence time-zone map.

3.4 *Citespace summary*

Since 2010, Guizhou batik cultural-creative design has gradually evolved, exhibiting diversified development trajectories particularly through the integration of digital technologies. Keyword time-zone maps demonstrate sustained growth in academic attention to batik's roles in modern design and cultural continuity. These visualization results not only provide valuable reference for cultural and creative product designers but also clarify key research directions and anchor points for this study. They lay the foundation for the subsequent systematic and comprehensive inductive analysis of expert interviews using grounded theory, ultimately leading to the development of a design strategy framework for Guizhou batik cultural and creative products.

3.5 *Open coding*

Open coding, as the initial phase of qualitative analysis, strictly derives codes from raw interview transcripts. (Aemmi S.Z. *et al.* 2022) Through iterative comparison and refinement, similar or redundant labels were consolidated into "concepts," yielding 225 initial concepts subsequently categorized into 97 open codes (see Table 1 for exemplar process).

Table 1. Categorization of open codes (exemplar).

Open coding	Concept	Label	Original material
Designers favor playful designs	H22: Designers tend to design for fun	h27:Wax-dyeing designers prioritize playfulness	"The New batik designers tend to focus more on playfulness in their creations."
Designers should explore motif origins	H16: Designers need to look at the roots of patterns	h21: Designers must investigate pattern origins	"you have to know where this pattern comes from, you have to feel this thing clearly"
	G19: Designers need to know the pattern story	g27: Designers should grasp motifs objectively	"if you want to study the design of batik, please be sure to first understand the story behind it"
......	......	......	......

3.6 *Axial coding*

Axial coding, building upon open coding, systematically analyzes data interrelationships and categorizes conceptual linkages. (Chien M.K. *et al.* 2012) This study cross-referenced the 97 open codes with original transcripts to discern intrinsic connections and logical hierarchies. Through iterative synthesis, 39 axial codes with heightened abstraction and representational capacity were derived, forming a structured theoretical framework (see Figure 3).

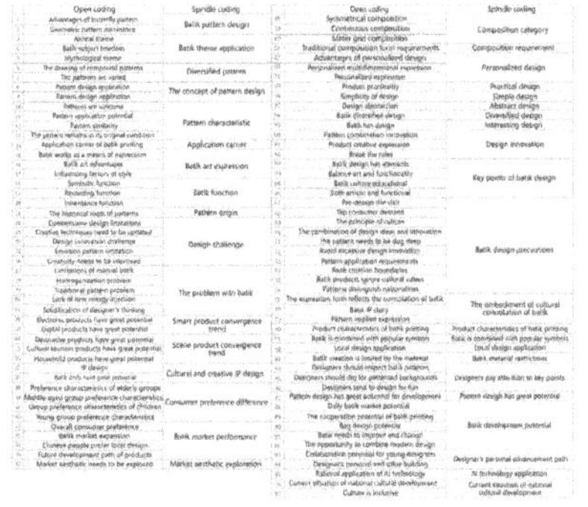

Figure 3. Axial coding process.

3.7 *Selective coding*

Selective coding is the key stage in refining the core categories and constructing the logical relationships among the main categories, with the resulting core categories representing the macro-factors influencing the design demands of Guizhou batik cultural and creative products. Therefore, on the basis of integrating axial coding, it is essential to further clarify their intrinsic connections and abstract a core category capable of encompassing the overall research framework. This study ultimately identified six core categories: "Composition Strategies," "Design Requirements," "Development Potential," "Pattern Applications," "Development Status," and "Market Demands." These core categories subsume other subcategories, and thus, through a re-examination of interview data and coding analysis, a design strategy model for Guizhou batik cultural and creative products was derived (as illustrated in Figure 4).

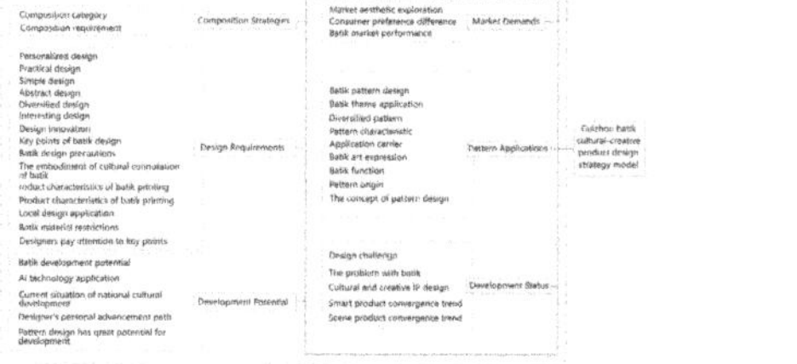

Figure 4. Guizhou batik cultural-creative product design strategy model.

3.8 *Theory saturation test*

Theoretical saturation, a critical grounded theory benchmark, determines whether core categories are sufficiently refined with no emergent concepts. This study employed single-cycle interview data collection with continuous comparative analysis during coding. The absence of emergent concepts in later stages confirmed saturation, thus validating the Guizhou Batik Cultural-Creative Product Design Strategy Model as demonstrating robust completeness and theoretical validity.

3.9 *Design strategy elaboration*

Guided by grounded theory, this study constructed a Guizhou batik cultural-creative product design strategy model comprising 6 selective codes, 39 axial codes, and 97 open codes. The following section explicates core categories and their interrelationships, proposing corresponding design strategies.

(i) Composition strategies

This approach integrates pattern layout, morphological design, and cultural symbolism, balancing aesthetic value with traditional-modern equilibrium. For multi-scenario applications, designs should innovatively reinterpret traditional compositions while enhancing visual impact, thereby amplifying batik's cultural symbolism and natural philosophy to strengthen cultural depth and market adaptability. As Experts A and I mentioned: "Visually creating a sense of ambiance, and making it feel comfortable and beautiful is sufficient." "The original composition had this meaning, but if you excessively destroy its inherent unique charm, the cultural significance embedded in the pattern will be lost." Therefore, future batik composition design should strike a balance between innovation and tradition, enhancing its cultural symbolism and natural philosophy expression through modernized and artistic pattern structures and color layouts.

(ii) Design requirements

Designers should ground their work in traditional symbolism while gaining an in-depth understanding of contemporary demands, balancing individuality, functionality, innovation, and aesthetics. Furthermore, they should emphasize pattern innovation and minimalist abstraction in their designs to enhance modernity and facilitate cultural dissemination and market integration. As Expert G stated: "If designers want to study batik design, they must first understand the story behind it. Once you've completed this important step, you can combine it with your own interests and hobbies, which I think is excellent."

(iii) Pattern applications

As a crucial medium for Guizhou batik cultural and creative products, batik patterns demonstrate strong adaptability across diverse themes, styles, and applications due to their ethnic symbolism. Among them, classic motifs such as animal and geometric patterns remain highly favored and retain significant potential for reinterpretation. Coding analysis reveals that integrating mythological themes, composite patterns, and abstract elements can expand the boundaries of batik design, propelling it toward premium, artistic, and cross-disciplinary development. As Experts F, I, and B pointed out: "In ancient China, any subject matter was actually free, with no restrictions, but due to reverence for nature, there was a particular focus on animal and plant motifs." "I believe every subject matter has great potential; it's hard to say that a specific animal or flower or bird has more potential, I think all of them have great potential." "When the artistic value is elevated, it has a huge space for value, and its subsidiary value can then be realized." Therefore, future applications of batik patterns should emphasize enhancing artistic expression and innovative design while preserving traditional cultural connotations, ensuring their distinctive appeal in a diversified market. Meanwhile, the redesign of composite patterns and the diversification of thematic choices can further broaden the scope of batik product applications, thereby strengthening market competitiveness and fostering cross-industry integration and global dissemination of batik culture.

(iv) Development potential

Against the backdrop of rising enthusiasm for intangible cultural heritage innovation, batik culture is demonstrating promising development momentum. Coding analysis reveals that pattern redesign not only enhances product appeal but also exhibits particularly broad potential in everyday consumer goods. Brand cross-over collaborations have shown significant advantages, with the integration of luxury and popular brands serving to elevate batik's cultural value. The participation of young designers is injecting new vitality into batik, facilitating its convergence with contemporary design paradigms. Concurrently, experts note that the incorporation of AI technology could assist in batik design processes and improve innovation efficiency. Regarding batik's future developmental potential, strategic focus should be directed toward: optimizing everyday product design, strengthening cross-brand collaborations, promoting technological empowerment, and cultivating new-generation design talent. These initiatives will ensure batik's sustained growth in modern markets and its enduring cultural influence.

(v) Development status

This reflects the challenges of design innovation, market adaptability, and industry constraints facing Guizhou batik cultural and creative products. Coding analysis indicates that current batik design is constrained by factors such as intricate craftsmanship, high production costs, pattern homogenization, and rigid design thinking, which limit its modern applications and result in insufficient market competitiveness.However, experts unanimously agree that emerging markets—including electronic products, home decor, and IP-based cultural creations—present significant development opportunities for batik. Consequently, to address these challenges, there should be a focused exploration of digital batik applications across diverse products and scenarios, thereby enhancing its cultural value and market competitiveness. As Experts E and D pointed out: "Personally, I believe IP design has great potential. It can easily be incorporated into various fields, such as home decor products, fashion, and tourist souvenirs, all of which have their own place and can integrate well." "IP design and the cultural decorative products I create can be innovative. It is essentially a medium, and it also serves as an effective way to promote the craftsmanship of batik. Therefore, I am particularly inclined towards these two directions. Given the current challenging situation, I believe this is a very good solution."

(vi) Market demands

Understanding consumer demand not only influences design quality and market acceptance but also bears significance for the dissemination and preservation of cultural heritage. Expert interviews reveal that Guizhou batik currently holds substantial potential for national market expansion, with consumers showing preference for localized designs. The high-end market exhibits lower price sensitivity while demonstrating untapped aesthetic demands.Coding analysis indicates distinct consumer preferences across demographics: older generations favor nostalgic and practical designs, middle-aged consumers prioritize functionality and cultural significance, children are drawn to playful and colorful patterns, while younger consumers pursue individuality and fashion. Expert H pointed out: "There are differences in the selection of pattern products among different age groups. With so many pattern products available, there are also diverse consumer groups. Therefore, it is essential to understand the preferences of different age groups, so that my design will not go astray."

4 CONCLUSION

This study first employs CiteSpace's visual analysis to identify research hotspots, developmental trends, and evolutionary trajectories in Guizhou batik cultural and creative products, elucidating their directional evolution across modern design paradigms, innovative applications, and cultural heritage preservation. This analysis establishes foundational research orientations and theoretical anchors for the study. Subsequently, building upon systematic literature analysis, we developed a semi-structured questionnaire and conducted expert interviews. Applying grounded theory methodology, we constructed a comprehensive design strategy model comprising six core categories (Figure 3) for Guizhou batik cultural products. The findings indicate that the innovative development of Guizhou batik must balance the preservation of traditional cultural elements with modern market demands, optimizing composition design, enhancing product functionality, promoting cross-brand collaboration, strengthening technological empowerment, and expanding diverse application scenarios to enhance market competitiveness and cultural influence. Additionally, accurately targeting different consumer groups and developing corresponding design strategies will contribute to the sustainable inheritance and global dissemination of batik culture.

ACKNOWLEDGMENT

This research was funded by Fujian University of Technology [grant numbers GY-S21081], and Design Innovation Research Center of Humanities and Social Sciences Research Base of Colleges and Universities in Fujian Province.

REFERENCES

Aemmi S.Z., Mohammadi E., Fereidooni-Moghadam M., Zarea K., Boostani H., (2022). *Collegian* 29 493–499.

Cao X., Furuoka F. and Rasiah R., (2023). *Sustainability* 15 16547.

Chen J., Zhang X., Xu L. and Xu J., (2024). *Ocean Coast. Manage.* 255 107206.

Chien M.K., Chang T.M., Kuo W.C., (2012). *Int. Technol. Manage. Conf.*

Ding W.Y., (2024). *Cult. Ind.* 12 115–117.(in Chinese)

Fujita K., (2021). *J. Int. Dev. Stud. 30 41-58. (in Japanese).*

Han C.Y., Sun S. and Wei Y.X., (2025). *Packag. Eng.* 46 336–344.(in Chinese)

Li X. and Li H., (2018). *IEEE Access* 6 63243–63257.

Liu H., Luo Y., Geng J. and Yao P., (2021). *Appl. Sci.* 11 6759.

Quan H., Li Y., Liu D. and Zhou Y., (2024). *Herit. Sci.* 12 202.

Sun Y., (2024). *Highl. Art Des.* 5 31–35.

Wei Y. and Chen J., (2025). *Sustainability* 17 42.

Yang D.N., Wu M.J. and Han S.H., (2020). *Design* 33 137–139.(in Chinese)

Yang T. and Hu Z., (2024). *Art Perform. Lett.* 5 102–109.

Zheng X., Lyu J. and Pan W.J., (2024). *Ind. Des.* 10 113–118. (in Chinese).

System Innovation for a Global Economy – Lam et al. (Eds)

Design of a lower-limb strength training game for older adults based on self-determination theory

Long-Yi Yin
School of Design, Fujian University of Technology, Fuzhou, China

Jeng-Chung Woo
School of Design, Fujian University of Technology, Fuzhou, China
Design Innovation Research Center of Humanities and Social Sciences Research Base of Colleges and Universities in Fujian Province, Fuzhou, China

Bo-Jun Chen
School of Design, Fujian University of Technology, Fuzhou, China

ABSTRACT: Sarcopenia, an age-related condition marked by muscle mass and strength loss, increases the risk of falls, fractures, and disabilities in older adults. Due to low adherence to traditional exercise, gamified training has emerged as a promising alternative. However, research on gamified lower-limb strength training for the elderly remains limited, and a systematic framework is lacking. This study combines Self-Determination Theory and the Game Motivation Scale to develop a gamified lower-limb strength training system, "The Tortoise and the Hare Race." Through literature analysis, 18 key design elements were identified and integrated into the game. After feedback from 16 elderly participants, 16 elements were retained. Further testing with 17 more participants finalized the game content. The system uses wearable sensors to track movements, providing accurate feedback while engaging users. A social module enhances participation by promoting social support. The game includes three training modes—warm-up, strength enhancement, and balance improvement—targeting ankle, knee, and hip joints. Preliminary tests showed improved user engagement and satisfaction. Future research will evaluate its effectiveness.

Keywords: Self-determination Theory, Older Adults, Lower-limb Strength Training, Game Design, Sarcopenia

1 INTRODUCTION

The trend of global population aging has made improving the health and well-being of the elderly a key issue of scholarly concern. After age 50, muscle strength declines by 12%-15% per decade (Macaluso and Vito 2004). Leg muscle mass decreases by 1-2% per year, and strength loss increases by 1.5-5% annually (Keller and Engelhardt 2019). Sarcopenia is linked to various chronic diseases, increasing the risk of depression (Li *et al.* 2022) and diabetes due to sarcopenia-induced obesity (Lim *et al.* 2018). The loss of lower limb muscle mass increases the risk of falls in older adults and may heighten fear of falling, limiting daily activities. Physical exercise is an effective intervention, improving muscle strength, endurance, and balance in frail older adults (Delbaere *et al.* 2010). Effective interventions, such as balance and endurance training, can enhance the physical function of frail older adults (Li *et al.* 2023). Exercise can be categorized into active and passive training. While neuromuscular electrical stimulation prevents muscle atrophy by inducing muscle contractions with minimal effort, its effectiveness is lower than that of voluntary resistance training (Rahmati *et al.* 2021). Recent studies show that active training, including aerobic and resistance exercises, provides health benefits for older adults. These benefits include improvements in cardiovascular health, muscle strength, cognitive function, and overall quality of life (Bouaziz *et al.* 2017).

The Otago Exercise Program (OEP) is a physical activity regimen designed for older adults, combining both aerobic and resistance training (Nicholson *et al.* 1997). As a home-based intervention, OEP has proven effective in reducing fall incidence among older adults with a history of falls (Dadgari *et al.* 2016). Due to degeneration of physical and cognitive functions, older adults

DOI: 10.1201/9781003655534-23

experience slower information reception, processing, and feedback, impairing control and motor responses (Tsai *et al.* 2022). Different populations need tailored training approaches. This highlights the importance of personalized programs that consider both physical and psychological factors (Jiménez-Morcillo *et al.* 2024). Exercise enjoyment is crucial, and training should be engaging (Tarakci *et al.* 2013). Research on lower limb games for older adults is limited, with a lack of systematic theoretical support. Knee exercises strengthen quadriceps in individuals with arthritis (Weng *et al.* 2009). Hip abduction exercises alleviate pain, improve function, and increase muscle strength (Bennell *et al.* 2010). Heel-raising exercises are used to diagnose lower limb arterial insufficiency (Amirhamzeh *et al.* 1997). Knee flexion exercises target hamstrings, enhancing performance (Yanagisawa and Fukutani 2020). Single-leg stance training, common in ankle sprain rehabilitation, is effective for reducing postural sway (Verhagen *et al.* 2005). Pre-training warm-up exercises (ankle dorsiflexion and plantarflexion) improve activity levels in older adults (Lloyd 2013).

2 LITERATURE REVIEW

The Wii Fit, launched by Nintendo Japan in 2007, was one of the first gamified lower limb training devices. Silver Fit Mile, created by the Dutch company Silver Fit, uses virtual reality and interactive games to assist in lower limb training. It also provides real-time monitoring of progress. These games offer functional training in a simulated environment. They increase enjoyment and motivation during rehabilitation. While commercial games can provide effective results, the games mentioned were not designed for older adults. A study on Nintendo Wii Exergames showed age-related barriers and their impact on frail elderly individuals. Designing these games requires addressing specific needs and challenges to ensure safety and effectiveness for older adults (Gerling *et al.* 2010).

Self-Determination Theory (SDT) is a macro theory of human motivation, focusing on the role of volition or self-determination in behavior (Ryan and Deci 2000). It includes two types of motivation: intrinsic and extrinsic. The theory examines the energy and direction of behavior, as well as the forces that promote, transfer, or hinder natural energy (Tang *et al.* 2020). Research on SDT has shown that video games that meet SDT needs provide more enjoyable experiences for players (Oliver *et al.* 2016).

The Gaming Motivation Scale (GAMS), developed on the basis of SDT, is a 7-point Likert scale with six motivational factors: Intrinsic Motivation, Integrated Regulation, Identified Regulation, Introjected Regulation, External Regulation, and Amotivation (Lafrenière *et al.* 2012). GAMS has been used in previous studies to measure players' gaming motivation (Peracchia *et al.* 2019) and to assess the risk of gaming addiction (Beard 2016).

A systematic literature search and review of the six topics mentioned above will be conducted on the Google Scholar and Web of Science platforms. Based on the analysis of GAMS items, game design elements will be extracted. These elements will be applied in game development to improve user experience and motivation. This will identify 18 key game design elements (Hamari *et al.* 2014; Seaborn *et al.*2015): points, voice encouragement, leaderboards, meaningful storylines; personalized avatars, social interaction, customizable training; long-term goals, reward systems, progression systems; time-limited challenges, daily tasks, social pressure; achievement points, badge system; goal setting, encouraging hints, guided tasks.

A shortened version of the Guess, Guess-18 has appeared in multiple studies (cite relevant references). This scale retains the 9 original subscales but reduces the number of items to 18, with two items corresponding to each subscale. The complete Guess typically takes 10-15 minutes to complete, while the Guess-18 requires approximately 3-5 minutes. Considering the cognitive load and response burden of older adults, the Guess-18 is suitable for this study.

This study uses the System Usability Scale (SUS) and the Guess-18. SUS measures the usability of the system for older adults. The GUESS-18 evaluates their enjoyment of the game, assessing their emotional experience across 9 dimensions.

3 DESIGN

3.1 *Interaction design*

After adding SDT game elements, the interface includes simple controls, button sounds, system prompts, large icons, and high-contrast colors for older adults. It avoids complex operations that could confuse older users and reduces cognitive load. The game offers three difficulty modes: easy, intermediate, and advanced, to suit different levels of ability. Users select the mode that suits their abilities (Figure 1). If users feel discomfort, they can press the Esc button to stop the game. Upon re-entering, users will be asked if they want to continue from their last session. The game records users' training data, allowing them to review progress at any time. After the design is complete, its effectiveness will be assessed, and updates will be made based on results.

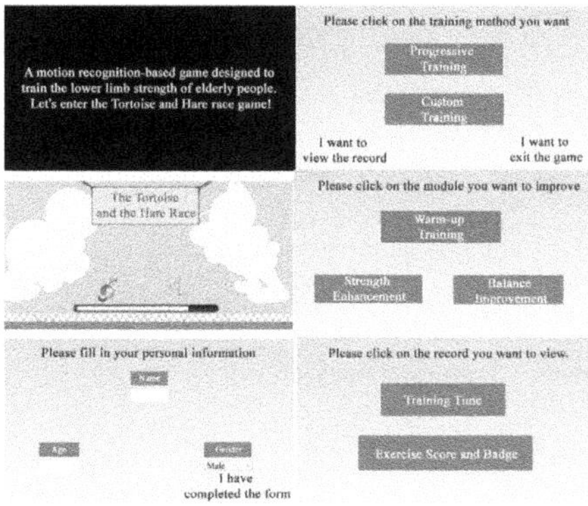

Figure 1. Game interaction.

3.2 *Programs and games*

After four rounds of brainstorming, the research team chose the theme "The Tortoise and the Hare Race." Older adults play as the tortoise, racing against the hare and earning badges by winning all six competitions. The game includes six mini-games: balloon popping, sandbag kicking, tight-rope walking, ice climbing, star collecting, and ninja balance. A coach in the game demonstrates the correct movements for each exercise. Evidence suggests multi-level training in video games improves the physical and cognitive functions of older adults. This informed the multi-level design strategy in the game (Adcock *et al.* 2020. The game includes natural background sounds to enhance comfort for older adults. The game's primary color is green, considered a health determinant in environmental design (Rojas-Rueda 2019). Practical training tips provide older adults with information on exercise benefits and targeted muscles.

The game's lower limb training includes six exercises, grouped into three programs: warm-up, strength, and balance. Game screen elements are designed with Adobe Photoshop. Data communication between the game and sensors is handled by Visual Studio 2022 (Figure 2), and the game is developed with Unity 2022.

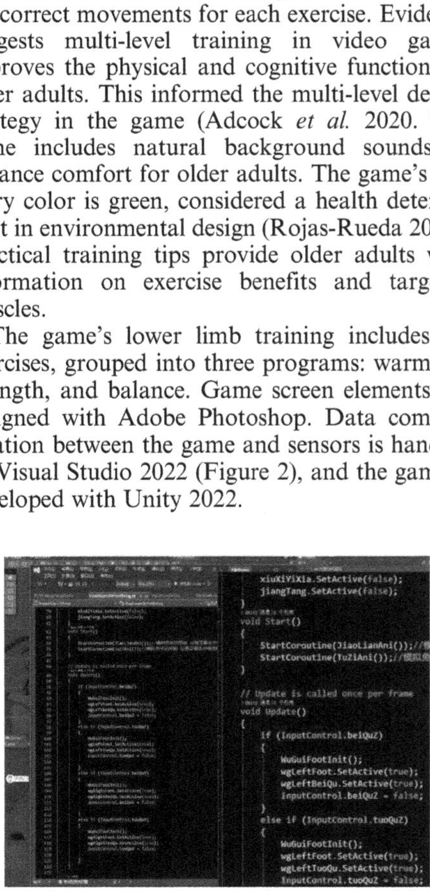

Figure 2. Game code (section).

This study uses the WT9011DCL-BT50 Bluetooth 5.0 posture sensor from VITE Intelligent Technology Co., Ltd. (Shenzhen, Guangdong, China). It monitors user movements in real-time within a 50-meter range, converts the data into control signals, and transmits it to the PC for system interaction and feedback.

4 RESULT

This study employs two key measurement tools to assess the usability and satisfaction of the game system: SUS and the GUESS-18. The SUS is widely used for evaluating the overall usability of systems, while the GUESS-18 is specifically designed to measure gamers' satisfaction of the gaming experience. Both scales utilize a 7-point Likert scale, which allows participants to provide detailed feedback on various aspects of the game, such as ease of use, enjoyment, and motivational factors. This feedback is invaluable for guiding modifications to the game design, ensuring that the final product is more user-friendly and engaging.

The GUESS-18 scale, a short version of the original GUESS scale, was validated in this study to allow for quicker evaluation of video games, especially in contexts where time constraints make it impractical to use longer assessment tools. The Cronbach's alpha values for the two scales—GUESS-18 (Keebler *et al.* 2020) and SUS (Bangor *et al.* 2008) were found to be 0.785 and 0.91, respectively. These values indicate that both scales possess good internal consistency and reliability, ensuring that the results obtained from the evaluations are robust and trustworthy. This high reliability further supports the validity of the data used to inform the game design modifications, providing strong evidence for the efficacy of these scales in assessing video game usability and satisfaction.

The researchers recruited 33 elderly participants aged 55 and above from the community (15 males, 18 females; average age 64.93±9.73) and obtained informed consent before starting. During the trial, the researchers did not intervene in the participants' game progress but observed and recorded the process. After a 30-minute gameplay session, participants filled out the system usability and user satisfaction experience scales, and interviews were conducted to collect feedback (Figure 3) and further understand their specific feelings about the game elements. The interviews covered 18 aspects of the game design, and participants suggested removing "achievement points," believing that this would make the game design more flexible and focus on intrinsic motivation (Figure 4). They also pointed out that the fixed structure of "daily tasks" could limit their autonomy, and removing this feature would allow users to arrange their training plans more freely. Through literature review and interviews, 16 effective game design elements that meet the expectations of the elderly were identified. Based on this feedback, the final game interface (Figure 5) and training tips (Figure 6) were optimized, and elderly participants were invited to play the game again and provide data (Figure 7).

Figure 3. First-round image collection during gameplay testing.

a

b

Figure 4. The achievement points (a) before modification, (b) after modification.

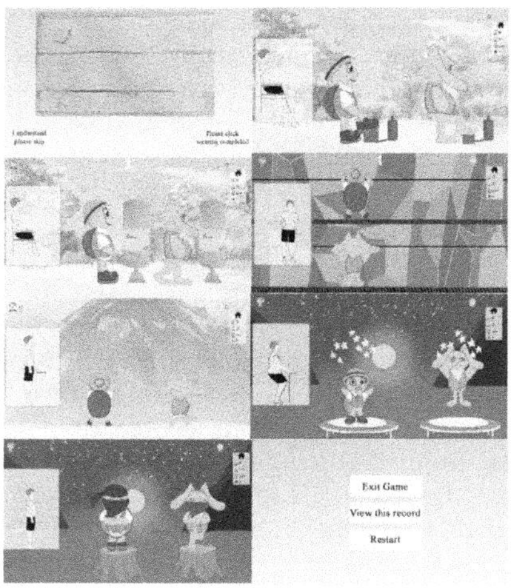

Figure 5. Game content.

Figure 6. Training tips (section).

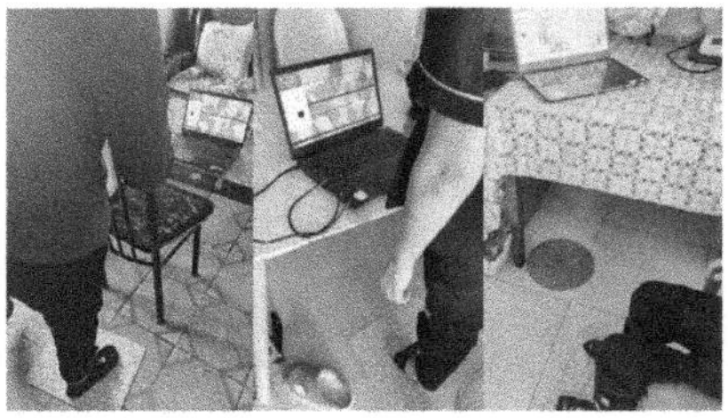

Figure 7. Second-round image collection during gameplay testing.

After the data was collected, IBM SPSS Statistics 26 was employed for analyzing the results. The first SUS score was 73.28 ± 6.99, which was rated as A- and categorized as "Good." This first evaluation provided insight into the initial usability of the game. Based on the feedback from participants and the first SUS evaluation, modifications were made to improve the game's design and functionality. After implementing these changes, the second SUS score was calculated to be 87.79 ± 4.99, which was rated as A+ and categorized as "Excellent" (Bangor *et al.* 2009). This improvement in the score reflects a more favorable perception of the game's usability after the adjustments.

To verify the effectiveness of the modifications, an independent samples t-test was conducted. The results of this test showed a statistically significant difference ($p < 0.01$), indicating that the second SUS score was significantly higher than the first. Specifically, the second score improved by an average of 14.51 points compared to the first. The evaluations from each sample group remained relatively stable, which suggests that the improvements were consistent and led to a positive overall enhancement in the system's usability. The findings are further illustrated in Table 1, highlighting the impact of the modifications on user experience.

Table 1. Independent samples t-test.

	N	M	SD	Rating	F	*p*
Pre-test	16	73.281	6.9952	A-	2.587	0.000**
Post-test	17	87.794	4.9908	A+		

*p<0.05 **p<0.01

Therefore, the game mechanics corresponding to this scale can serve as a reference standard for the design of future games for older adults. Although the GAMS scale was originally developed for younger players, its core motivational dimensions are also applicable in the game experiences of older adults. This provides theoretical support for the design and optimization of lower limb games for older adults.

The GUESS-18 evaluation results are as follows: usability 89%, story 76%, appeal 67%, enjoyment 89%, creative freedom 78%, auditory aesthetics 86%, personal fulfillment 94%, social interaction 74%, and visual aesthetics 88% (Figure 8). Usability (M=6.24, SD=0.69), enjoyment (M=6.21, SD=0.54), and personal fulfillment (M=6.57, SD=0.57) had the highest scores. This shows the game met users' expectations for usability and entertainment, providing a positive and rewarding experience. While the scores for game appeal (M=4.71, SD=1.69) and social interaction (M=5.19, SD=0.97) were relatively lower, the game still exhibited a certain level of appeal and interactivity for participants.

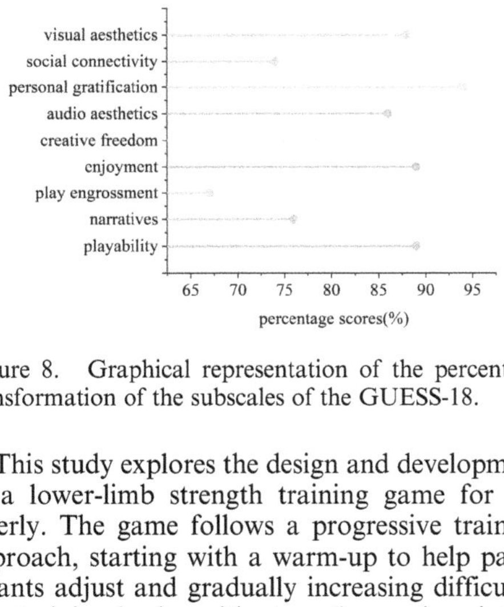

Figure 8. Graphical representation of the percentage transformation of the subscales of the GUESS-18.

This study explores the design and development of a lower-limb strength training game for the elderly. The game follows a progressive training approach, starting with a warm-up to help participants adjust and gradually increasing difficulty. The training begins with strength exercises, intensifying to promote muscle growth and heart rate management. The final phase includes balance training to enhance stability while maintaining a steady heart rate to prevent fatigue or injury. The design ensures elderly users can improve fitness safely at a comfortable pace.

Most older adults expressed high satisfaction and strong interest in the system during the experiment. Many felt curious and pleased while using the system and were willing to engage in long-term training to improve their physical health. Research shows that older adults are highly interested in the feedback mechanism, supporting the system's promotion and long-term use. Positive feedback suggests that the game's interactive and progressive design motivated participants and helped them overcome exercise difficulties due to aging. The evaluation results of usability (87.79 ± 4.99) and game satisfaction (Figure 7) show a positive reception. Participants found the system easy to operate. The training content was challenging and effectively met their exercise needs, especially in balance and strength. They considered the combination of entertainment and functionality in training highly promising.

ACKNOWLEDGEMENTS

This research was funded by Fujian University of Technology [grant numbers GY-S21081], and Design Innovation Research Center of Humanities and Social Sciences Research Base of Colleges and Universities in Fujian Province.

REFERENCES

Adcock, M., Sonder, F., Schättin, A., Gennaro, F., and de Bruin, E. D. (2020). *European Review of Aging and Physical Activity*, 17, 3.

Amirhamzeh, M. M. R., Chant, H. J., Rees, J. L., Hands, L. J., Powell, R. J., and Campbell, W. B. (1997). *European Journal of Vascular and Endovascular Surgery*, 13 (3), 301–305.

Bangor, A., Kortum, P. T., and Miller, J. T. (2008). *Intl. Journal of Human–Computer Interaction*, 24 (6), 574–594.

Bangor, A., Kortum, P., and Miller, J. (2009). *Journal of Usability Studies*, 4 (3), 114–123.

Beard, C. L., and Wickham, R. E. (2016). *Computers in Human Behavior*, 61, 507–515.

Bennell, K. L., Hunt, M. A., Wrigley, T. V., Hunter, D. J., McManus, F. J., Hodges, P. W., Li, L., and Hinman, R. S. (2010). *Osteoarthritis and Cartilage*, 18 (5), 621–628.

Bouaziz, W., Vogel, T., Schmitt, E., Kaltenbach, G., Geny, B., and Lang, P. O. (2017). *Archives of Gerontology and Geriatrics*, 69, 110–127.

Dadgari, A., Hamid, T. A., Hakim, M. N., Chaman, R., Mousavi, S. A., Hin, L. P., and Dadvar, L. (2016). *Iranian Red Crescent Medical Journal*, 18 (5), e26340.

Delbaere, K., Close, J. C., Brodaty, H., Sachdev, P., and Lord, S. R. (2010). *BMJ*, 341, c4165.

Gerling, K. M., Schild, J., and Masuch, M. (2010). *In Proceedings of the 7th International Conference on Advances in Computer Entertainment Technology*. 66–69.

Hamari, J., Koivisto, J., and Sarsa, H. (2014). In 2014 47th Hawaii international conference on system sciences. ***IEEE***. 3025–3034.

Jiménez-Morcillo, J., Rodriguez-Besteiro, S., and Clemente-Suárez, V. J. (2024). *Behavioral Sciences*, 14 (4), 267.

Keebler, J. R., Shelstad, W. J., Smith, D. C., Chaparro, B. S., and Phan, M. H. (2020). *Journal of Usability Studies*, 16 (1), 49–62.

Keller, K., and Engelhardt, M. (2014). *Muscles, Ligaments and Tendons Journal*, 3 (4), 346–350.

Lafrenière, M. A. K., Verner-Filion, J., and Vallerand, R. J. (2012). *Personality and Individual Differences*, 53 (7), 827–831.
Li, Y., Gao, Y., Hu, S., Chen, H., Zhang, M., Yang, Y., and Liu, Y. (2023). *Journal of Clinical Nursing*, 32 (9–10), 1795–1805.
Li, Z., Tong, X., Ma, Y., Bao, T., and Yue, J. (2022). ***Journal of Cachexia***, *Sarcopenia and Muscle*, 13 (1), 128–144.
Lim, H. S., Park, Y. H., Suh, K., Yoo, M. H., Park, H. K., Kim, H. J., Lee, J. H., and Byun, D. W. (2018). *Journal of Bone Metabolism*, 25 (3), 187–193.
Long, L., Jackson, K., and Laubach, L. L. (2013). *International Journal of Physical Medicine and Rehabilitation*, 1 (3), 1–6.
Macaluso, A., and De Vito, G. (2004). *European Journal of Applied Physiology*, 91, 450–472.
Nicholson, K. G., Kent, J., Hammersley, V., and Cancio, E. (1997). *BMJ*, 315 (7115), 1060–1064.
Oliver, M. B., Bowman, N. D., Woolley, J. K., Rogers, R., Sherrick, B. I., and Chung, M. Y. (2016). *Psychology of Popular Media Culture*, 5 (4), 390–405.
Peracchia, S., Presaghi, F., and Curcio, G. (2019). *International Journal of Environmental Research and Public Health*, 16 (6), 1008.
Rahmati, M., Gondin, J., and Malakoutinia, F. (2021). ***Physical Therapy***, 101 (9), *pzab144*.
Rojas-Rueda, D., Nieuwenhuijsen, M. J., Gascon, M., Perez-Leon, D., and Mudu, P. (2019). *The Lancet Planetary Health*, 3 (11), e469–e477.
Ryan, R. M., and Deci, E. L. (2000). *American Psychologist*, 55 (1), 68–78.
Seaborn, K., and Fels, D. I. (2015). *International Journal of Human-Computer Studies*, 74, 14–31.
Tang, M., Wang, D., and Guerrien, A. (2020). *Psych Journal*, 9 (1), 5–33.
Tarakci, D., Ozdincler, A. R., Tarakci, E., Tutuncuoglu, F., and Ozmen, M. (2013). *Journal of Physical Therapy Science*, 25 (9), 1123–1127.
Tsai, S. Y., and Hong, S. Y. (2019). *Sensors and Materials*, 31 (5), 1739–1749.
Verhagen, E., Bobbert, M., Inklaar, M., van Kalken, M., van der Beek, A., Bouter, L., and van Mechelen, W. (2005). *Clinical Biomechanics*, 20 (10), 1094–1100.
Weng, M. C., Lee, C. L., Chen, C. H., Hsu, J. J., Lee, W. D., Huang, M. H., and Chen, T. W. (2009). *The Kaohsiung Journal of Medical Sciences*, 25 (6), 306–315.
Yanagisawa, O., and Fukutani, A. (2020). *Journal of Human Kinetics*, 72, 51–59.

System Innovation for a Global Economy – Lam et al. (Eds)

Research on the applicability of virtual exhibition design using VR eye-tracking technology

Hung-Ying Lee
Graduate School of Design, Yunlin University of Science and Technology, Yunlin, Taiwan
Department of Multimedia and Game Development, Minghsin University of Science and Technology, Hsinchu, Taiwan

Chao-Ming Wang
Department of Digital Media Design, Yunlin University of Science and Technology, Yunlin, Taiwan

ABSTRACT: Eye-tracking technology has been widely applied in fields such as medical training, educational simulations, and psychological experiments. This study focuses on exploring its potential in the field of design by constructing a VR virtual gallery featuring a digital exhibition of Tan Teng-Pho's painting "*Tamsui after the Rain*". A VR eye-tracking device will be used to record viewers' visual behavior. Based on gaze duration, three types of heatmaps—green, orange, and red—will be generated to trigger corresponding visual effects: green areas will produce a liquefying animation effect, orange areas will cause objects to sway slightly and emit sound, and red areas will display a brief dynamic narrative. The study adopts prototype development, expert interviews, and questionnaire surveys as its research methodologies. In the prototype development phase, the VR virtual gallery will be created. Expert interviews will evaluate the aesthetics and usability of the design, followed by an experiment that analyzes viewers' gaze patterns while they observe the artwork. The study ultimately aims to examine whether the viewers' eye movements align with the experts' expected viewing patterns of the painting.

Keywords: VR Eye-Tracking Device, Human-Computer Interaction, Exhibition Design

1 INTRODUCTION

In the current climate, contemporary art exhibitions increasingly prioritize multi-sensory interaction, transforming the traditional static viewing process. Exhibitions often culminate in immersive segments designed to enhance the audience's perception and emotional connection to the artworks. These segments utilize technology to promote greater viewer involvement and a deeper interaction with the art.

As an example, in 2023, the Musée d'Orsay's 2023 Van Gogh in Auvers-sur-Oise: "*The Final Months*" exhibition included "*La Palette de Van Gogh*", a special VR immersive experience. This allowed visitors to immerse themselves in Van Gogh's creative process through virtual reality, effectively re-experiencing his artistic journey.

In this study, a new immersive approach is applied to a traditional painting by taiwanese artist tan teng-pho's titled "*tamsui after the rain*", using a vr headset combined with eye-tracking technology. The vr setup presents a virtual single-person gallery space to build a more engaging and personalized interaction. The viewer's gaze on different parts of the painting will trigger dynamic animations, allowing them to immerse more deeply into the virtual experience. This research will explore and analyze various aspects of "*tamsui after the rain*" through the application of vr eye-tracking interaction. The study is guided by the following research questions:

1) Focus Patterns & Traditional Art: Does viewing traditional paintings elicit consistent visual focus patterns, and do these align with compositional/aesthetic principles?
2) VR Eye-Tracking Impact: How does VR eye-tracking interaction affect viewer participation, immersion, and understanding of the painting?
3) Interactive Guidance & Exhibition Strategy: Can interactive guidance foster deeper emotional connection and serve as an effective new exhibition design strategy for enhancing the viewing experience?

1.1 *VR eye-tracking*

VR, as a medium in contemporary exhibition design, uses dynamic images and interactive installations to strengthen the connection with the audience and enhance the sense of immersion within the artwork. This study applies eye-tracking technology in the VR space to analyze gaze movements, combining them with heatmaps based

DOI: 10.1201/9781003655534-24

on viewing duration. The focus of this research is on the gaze trajectory and the distribution of attention in the virtual environment. Audience behavior patterns and attention distribution in the VR space also become one of the key concerns in the study. By observing users' fixation points and their participation methods, it was found that audience behavior in virtual environments is not only about free exploration, but often follows a more structured pattern, which provides concrete references for future exhibition design.

1.2 *Case analysis*

1.2.1 *User attention and behaviour in virtual reality art encounter*

This study takes Blortasia, a VR game by Kevin Mack available on the Steam platform, as a case study. The work constructs a virtual world composed of abstract images and sculptural forms, emphasizing the user's experience of free modeling and coloring. During the experience, participants' visual focus and movement directions were influenced by visual stimuli within the VR environment, which further triggered interactive behaviors between the viewer and the artwork (Figure 1 & 2).

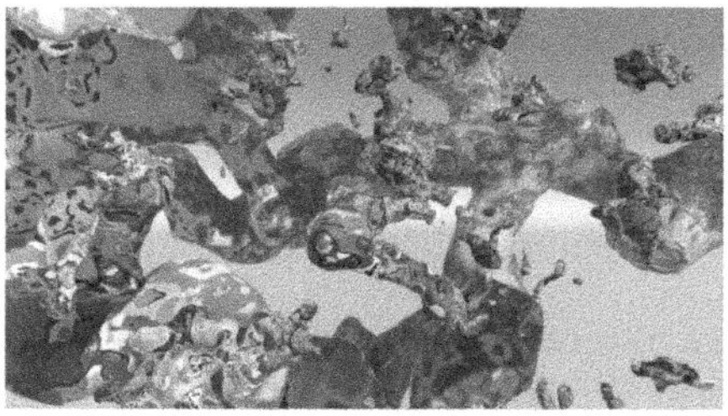

Figure 1. The screenshot in VR game *Blortasia*.

Figure 2. Audience is using VR to play *Blortasia*.

The research team also developed another abstract VR piece, *Caverna Coelo*. In this work, it was observed that some participants, when approaching the artwork, moved their heads and eyes in different directions, which indicates that not only the eyes were moving individually. When attention shifted from point A to point B, the eyes often scanned other visual objects along the environmental path. Moreover, participants demonstrated significantly different behavioral patterns. Overall, those who were more active tended to exhibit a multi-directional visual exploration style. In general, active participants were more likely to look in various directions. While some individuals shared similar viewing preferences, no consistent eye movement pattern was found across the participant group.

Figure 3. The screenshot in VR artwork Caverna Coelo.

The paper concludes:

"Alternate realities are becoming the new pathways for content creation, distribution and audience engagement in the creative communities. Understanding how audiences explore and interact in new forms of media is essential to realise the full potential of alternate realities." (Mu *et al.* 2022).

This study suggests that the application of VR eye-tracking as an interaction interface serves as a medium for audience-artwork interaction. It not only enables real-time responses to the viewer's gaze behavior but also allows the design of virtual exhibitions to become more targeted and personalized, thereby enhancing the overall immersive experience.

1.2.2 *Survey on the impact of historical museum exhibition forms on visitors' perceptions based on eye-tracking*

Historical art museums currently face the dual challenges of attracting considerable audiences and enabling visitors to effectively absorb the overwhelming amount of information presented in exhibitions. To address these issues, this study combined eye-tracking technology with value evaluation to explore the impact of different exhibition display formats (including standalone exhibits, graphic-assisted displays, and 3D models combined with visual displays) on audience cognition.

Figure 4. Displays 3 types of ancient objects sample.

Figure 5. The Gaze-movement is with the 3 types sample.

Through image analysis and eye-movement data analysis (for example, the viewing duration and number of fixations on different exhibits), the study found that different display methods significantly affect the audience's visual perception and emotional experience, revealing a certain correlation between these aspects. As shown in Figure 4, standalone and isolated sculptures were generally less popular and received the lowest impression scores. Hu *et al.* (2024) point out in the article: "The use of the standalone display form can highlight the exhibits and satisfy visitors' need for in-depth exploration." These findings suggest that future art exhibition planning should focus on the development of immersive spatial design to improve the viewing experience and deepen memory retention. This study systematically analyzed the impact of different exhibition formats on audience perception by integrating eye-movement data with pre-evaluation, providing a corresponding reference for museum exhibition experience design.

1.2.3 *Gaze-based human–computer interaction for museums and exhibitions: technologies, applications and future perspectives*

In recent years, the application of eye-tracking technology in art museums and exhibition spaces has gradually increased, becoming an important tool for enhancing interaction and immersion during art viewing. According to Dondi and Porta (2023), traditional exhibition modes can lead to cognitive overload due to excessive amount of content, poorly designed layouts, or too rigid routes. This can reduce visitors' engagement and compromise the retention of information. Based on this issue, the introduction of real-time eye-tracking may allow exhibitions to respond to audience gaze in a timely manner, offering more personalized and targeted feedback.

Figure 6. The Gaze-tracking is in the paintings.

With the increasing use of Virtual Reality (VR) and Augmented Reality (AR) in exhibitions, the integration of eye-tracking shows new potential. Through wearable eye-tracking devices, systems can monitor viewers' gaze in real time. When the audience looks at a certain exhibit, interactive effects may be triggered automatically, such as zooming in the image, playing audio explanations, or displaying layered content based on the duration of gaze. This kind of "eye-controlled" interaction does not require a mouse or handheld controller. Users only need to look in order to interact, making the experience more natural and engaging.

From an exhibition design perspective, eye-tracking is not only an auxiliary tool, but also a part of curatorial strategy. By analyzing viewers' gaze points and movement paths, curators can better understand which exhibits are most attractive and adjust spatial routes and interactive designs accordingly. Although there are still some challenges, such as the need for device calibration, hygiene concerns in shared use, and user privacy, the progress of AI and sensing technologies suggests that eye-tracking interaction will become increasingly common in the future and serve as a key component of immersive exhibition experiences.

1.3 *Summary*

This study explores the application of eye-tracking across virtual reality interaction, artwork perception, and exhibition design. Leveraging eye-tracking data enables real-time interactive triggers for enhanced immersion and provides insights into visitor visual behavior, informing improvements to exhibition content and spatial layout. Building on the understanding that audience exploration in new media is crucial (Mu *et al.* 2022), this section outlines three related research directions and their associated keywords:

Table 1. Related research directions and keywords.

A	Virtual Reality, User Behavior, Interaction Design
B	Eye-Tracking, Exhibition Design, Visitor Perception
C	Gaze-Based Interaction, Human–Computer Interaction, Future Applications

Chapter A emphasizes VR's potential to enhance art experiences by using eye-tracking to understand viewing patterns and propose immersive design strategies. Chapter B investigates three art display methods (standalone, with background, and with 3D enhancement), combining eye-tracking with subjective feedback for practical design insights. Chapter C highlights eye-tracking as a growing trend in exhibition evaluation, anticipating increased adoption of AI and advanced technologies in art spaces. In summary, these chapters collectively demonstrate the significant potential of VR and eye-tracking in revolutionizing art experiences and exhibition design by focusing on immersion (A), evidence-based display strategies (B), and future technological integration (C), ultimately underscoring a user-centered approach to create more engaging and impactful art exhibitions.

2 RESEARCH METHODS

2.1 *VR eye-tracking interactive prototype*

After putting on the VR headset, the audience first goes through the eye-tracking calibration process, which allows the system to confirm the accuracy of the user's eye position and movements. Once completed, the participant enters a pre-designed virtual gallery space. In this virtual scene, only the painting After the Rain, Tamsui is displayed, while the rest of the space remains dark, with the purpose of naturally directing the viewer's attention to the artwork.

When the audience begins to gaze at the painting, the eye-tracking system starts recording and classifies the gaze into three levels based on the duration and intensity of fixation: light, medium, and deep. Each level corresponds to a specific interactive effect, including: (1)the subtle liquefaction of the image, (2)the gentle swinging of the painting with sound effects, (3)a short narrative animation sequence.

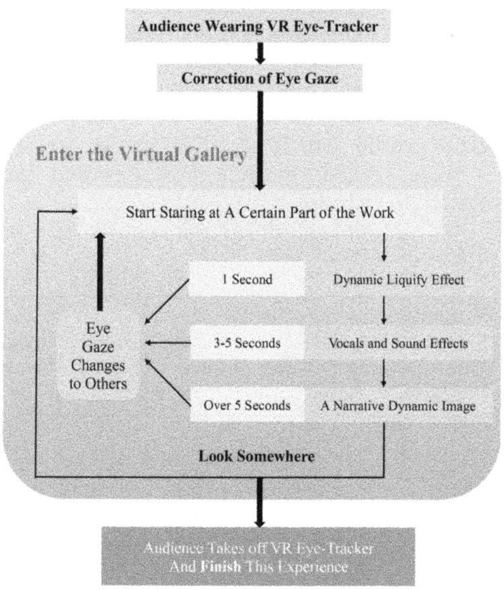

Figure 7. The eye-tracking flow is in VR gallery.

These interactions are triggered by the position and time of the gaze, allowing the audience to create emotional connections with the artwork during the viewing process, and further understand the intention of the artist. The overall design aims to enhance viewer focus and engagement through interaction and motion images, and to evoke new perceptions and interpretations of the artwork, leading to a deeper immersive experience.

Figure 8. The audience is in the single VR gallery.

2.2 *Methods*

This study aims to construct a VR Eye-Tracking System. At first, the theoretical foundations of Gaze-based Interaction Design and Emotional Design will be reviewed through literature analysis, and preliminary design principles will be summarized accordingly.

2.2.1 *Gaze-based interaction design*

Gaze-based Interaction Design is a kind of interactive method that uses the user's gaze as a natural input. Through the duration and position of eye fixation, it can trigger operations, which enhances user participation and interaction efficiency in immersive experiences. Menges *et al.* (2021) point out that understanding and effectively utilizing interface semantics can significantly reduce users' cognitive and operational load during gaze-based interactions, thereby enhancing the overall user experience.

2.2.2 *Emotional design*

In his book Emotional Design, Donald Norman (2003) mentions that pleasure can be influenced not only by products, but also by physiological and psychological factors. Physiology may include taste, touch, smell, or even higher-level perception. Emotional Design is often used as a strategy to change people's behaviors. In this context, perception design refers to the use of visual responses to increase the user's emotional satisfaction.

2.3 *Expert interview*

This research will first adopt the expert interview method to rigorously discuss the logical relationships and assess the rationality of the proposed design principles. Experts from different professional backgrounds will help verify and optimize the principles, and ultimately integrate various perspectives to establish the core design framework of this study. Once the design principles are confirmed, the study will proceed with the prototype development. After the system development is completed, a public exhibition will be held, during which users will be invited to experience the system in practice.

As part of this research, three experts in the relevant field will be interviewed to provide professional input on the questionnaire, experiment methodology, and final data interpretation.

The interview method is a qualitative research technique that collects information through dialogue between the interviewer and the interviewee, aiming to gain a deeper understanding of the interviewee's perspectives, motivations, and attitudes (Yuan 2002). This method is useful not only for exploring specific topics but also for uncovering rich, in-depth experiences and viewpoints of participants.

This study adopts a semi-structured interview approach. During the interviews, participants will respond to questions based on a pre-designed outline. However, the researcher will also adjust the order and content of questions flexibly, depending on the interviewee's responses, in order to obtain more detailed opinions and insights (Kuan *et al.* 2018).

The main purpose of these interviews is to enhance the completeness and relevance of the questionnaire. The initial draft of the questionnaire items was developed based on the researcher's own observations and perspectives. However, from a research design point of view, only through discussions with domain experts can the appropriateness of the items be reviewed, deficiencies filled, and redundancies removed. This process helps ensure the questionnaire's content validity and academic value.

In summary, expert interviews not only improve the quality of the questionnaire but also help confirm its relevance and applicability within the research context.

According to the research topic, a total of three experts will be invited for interviews, specializing in the fields of interaction design, affective computing technologies, and technological art. Each interview is expected to last approximately 30 to 45 minutes, as shown in Table 2.

Table 2. List of interview experts.

Respondent code	Areas of Expertise
A1	Expertise in Human-Computer Interaction and Interactive Design
A2	Specialist in Emotion Perception and Recognition Technologies
A3	Cross-disciplinary Artist specializing in Technology Art

2.3.1 *Interview content*

The expert interviews were mainly based on four aspects: device design, device operation, interface design and other suggestions, as shown in Table 3.

Table 3. Expert interview outline.

Interview Aspect	Question Outline
Device Design	Regarding device design, do you have any suggestions for mitigating "false triggers" caused by unintended glances?
Device Operation	How can the system effectively convey the user's eye-tracking status (e.g., current viewpoint, gaze area) and provide clear interactive feedback to enhance user understanding?
Interface Design	What guidance or prompting mechanisms should be integrated into the system interface upon initial user interaction?

2.4 *Questionnaire survey*

The questionnaire survey in this study will invite 60 university students aged 18 to 22 to participate as experimental subjects. The questionnaire and interview content will focus on at least three main aspects: human-computer interaction, device usability, and emotional perception through dynamic images. After the experiment, data will be collected through the questionnaire. When each participant enters the system or device, they will complete specific tasks or freely explore the content. At the same time, the system will record their eye-tracking data for later analysis.

Table 4. Questionnaire content outline outline.

Interview Aspect	Question Outline
Human Computer Interaction	To analyze whether the collected gaze data reflects the intended design effects.
Device and Exhibition	To solicit recommendations for enhancing exhibition and system design.
Dynamic Image and Emotional Perception	To compare the differential impact of design on audience emotion and attention.

3 RESULTS AND ANALYSIS

3.1 *Results*

This experiment aims to explore whether gaze-based interaction, designed through the integration of virtual reality (VR) and eye-tracking technology, can effectively guide viewers to develop deeper emotional perception and artistic understanding. Traditional art exhibitions are often limited to static viewing and text-based guides, making it difficult for audiences to fully grasp the meaning behind artworks, and attention is usually hard to maintain for a longer time.

Through this study, it is expected that viewers can interact with the painting naturally by simply "gazing." The image will change dynamically according to the length of the viewer's gaze, gradually presenting different layers of visual feedback, auditory stimulation, and narrative animations. These transitions aim to bring out the emotions and historical background behind the artwork, reflecting the artist's context and state during the creation process.

In addition, the eye tracker can detect the viewer's gaze point in real time. Compared to traditional interaction methods such as mouse clicking or hand gestures, this approach is more intuitive and personalized. It may help trigger emotional responses and psychological projection from the audience. Wang *et al.* (2023) point out: Understanding how audiences explore and interact in new forms of media is essential to realize the full potential of alternate realities. This study emphasizes that the interaction between dynamic visuals and audience emotions plays a key role in deepening viewer experiences.

Therefore, this research attempts to investigate whether the integration of VR and eye-tracking can make gaze-based interaction a new approach in future exhibition design for enhancing emotional engagement and artistic understanding. It is also hoped that the findings can provide useful references for immersive art interaction design.

3.2 *Analysis*

This research uses an interactive system that combines eye-tracking and VR, not simply using VR to display artworks. By using real-time gaze tracking as an interactive trigger, viewers can shift from being passive observers to active participants. The goal of this study is to achieve a more natural and intuitive gaze-driven interactive interface, where viewers interact with the artwork through layered visual engagement (light – moderate – deep levels), allowing a progressive and deeper experience beyond just looking.

This kind of dynamic interaction design helps maintain viewers' attention and stimulates their curiosity to explore further. The emotional connection between the viewer and the artwork is built through the gaze duration and visual feedback. This mechanism imitates how emotional resonance is often created during mutual gaze between humans. (Cotter *et al.* 2025) This study provides the first evidence that reflection during art viewing can enhance well-being, especially when combined with social connection. Such findings also open new perceptual pathways for immersive art experiences.

Furthermore, this interactive method reflects the current trend in museum technology applications, which is shifting toward more personalized, emotionally-driven, and immersive exhibition formats.

4 CONCLUSION AND FUTURE RESEARCH

4.1 *Conclusion*

This research presents a practical case integrating eye-tracking, virtual reality, and exhibition design, demonstrating the potential of technological intervention in art presentation. It also acknowledges that observed gaze patterns may not perfectly align with human focal points, especially for untrained viewers whose visual attention might not consistently adhere to aesthetic principles. Nevertheless, the study suggests that VR can enhance immersion for this demographic. Furthermore, it proposes an interactive framework utilizing gaze as a trigger, emotion as a mediator, and dynamic visuals as feedback. This model offers a valuable reference for future immersive exhibitions and emotion-driven interaction design. Looking ahead, eye-tracking can assist exhibition organizers in designing visitor flow that aligns more closely with human cognitive logic and provides insights into deeper dynamic emotional engagement.

4.2 *Future research*

While this study highlights the potential of innovative integrations, key challenges remain. Firstly, simplifying eye gaze as a direct emotion indicator requires further validation, as gaze can reflect confusion, pressure, or fatigue, potentially oversimplifying affective states.

Furthermore, high interactivity in art exhibitions risks overshadowing the artwork's aesthetic intent, demanding careful deliberation.

Consequently, future design should prioritize a nuanced balance between technology and artistic integrity, avoiding excessive interactivity that detracts from the core experience. Further research is also needed to clarify the applicability and limitations of such interactions across diverse cultures and art forms.

REFERENCES

Cotter, K. N., Mahlobo, C. T., Smith, B., Niepold, S., Rizzo, A., and Pawelski, J. O. (2024). Examining the ability of digital visual art engagement to cultivate empathy and social connection. *Empirical Studies of the Arts*, 02762374241309878.

Dondi, P., and Porta, M. (2023). Gaze-based human–computer interaction for museums and exhibitions: technologies, applications and future perspectives. *Electronics*, 12(14), 3064.

https://www.eslite.com/product/1001116711307992?srsltid=AfmBOoqHZPpy-yL8o_CFP5ydw2c0CS2hduvLFCI5g-UW6wObPvZhajgg

Hu, L., Shan, Q., Chen, L., Liao, S., Li, J., and Ren, G. (2024). Survey on the impact of historical museum exhibition forms on visitors' perceptions based on eye-tracking. *Buildings*, 14(11), 3538.

Kuan, H.-S., *et al.* (2018). *Design Research Methods* (Vol. 4). *Chuan Hwa Book Co.*https://www.books.com.tw/products/0010803970

Menges, R., Kumar, C., and Staab, S. (2019). Improving user experience of eye tracking-based interaction: Introspecting and adapting interfaces. *ACM Transactions on Computer-Human Interaction (TOCHI)*, *26*(6), 1–46.

Mu, M., Dohan, M., Goodyear, A., Hill, G., Johns, C., and Mauthe, A. (2024). User attention and behaviour in virtual reality art encounter. *Multimedia Tools and Applications*, 83(15), 46595–46624.

Norman, D. A. (2004). *Emotional design: Why we love (or hate) everyday things.* Basic Books.

Wang, J. Z., Zhao, S., Wu, C., Adams, R. B., Newman, M. G., Shafir, T., and Tsachor, R. (2023). Unlocking the emotional world of visual media: An overview of the science, research, and impact of understanding emotion. *Proceedings of the IEEE*, 111(10), 1236–1286.

Yuan, F. (2002). *Social Research Methods. Wu-Nan Book Inc.*

Constructing the consensus map for imageries of pervasive games of children

Min-Chieh Shih & Iwen Huang
Department of Information and Learning Technology, National University of Tainan, Tainan, Taiwan

ABSTRACT: High-quality gamified digital learning environments inherently reflect user needs. Designing games to accommodate these needs and fulfill intrinsic values is a critical issue, particularly among children. This study examines pervasive games as a case study and employs the Zaltman Metaphor Elicitation Technique (ZMET) in conjunction with Means-End Chain (MEC) theory to explore children's experiences and perspectives. Analysis identified twenty common constructs, including six attributes, eight consequences, six values, and three overarching expectation dimensions—namely, "physical and mental health," "enjoyment motivation," and "self-actualization." Additionally, an Attribute-Consequence-Value (ACV) consensus map model was developed. These findings provide valuable insights for research in gamified digital learning and serve as a reference for improving both learning outcomes and user experience associated with pervasive games.

1 INTRODUCTION

In digital learning, creating effective educational experiences for children is a significant challenge (Kasapakis and Gavalas 2015; Kai *et al.* 2023). Digital games, with their interactive and immersive features, have emerged as powerful learning media (Costa *et al.* 2021). Pervasive games—which merge real-world contexts with virtual environments—offer new opportunities for situated learning, but their success depends on effectively aligning design objectives with children's cognitive and emotional needs (Kai *et al.* 2023). When misaligned, gaps between design intentions and actual user experiences can lead to suboptimal outcomes (Schmitz *et al.* 2014).

Situated learning theory suggests that embedding educational content in meaningful, real-life contexts enhances learning through active participation (Lave and Wenger 1991; Zender *et al.* 2014). However, the complexity of game design often results in a gap between assumed and actual user needs (Kasapakis and Gavalas 2015). To address this, methods such as the Zaltman Metaphor Elicitation Technique (ZMET) and the Means-End Chain (MEC) offer valuable tools for uncovering deep-seated metaphors, cognitive constructs, and the relationships among attributes, consequences, and values (Gutman 1982; Lin and Lin 2014; Meng *et al.* 2020).

This study investigates the cognitive structures and emotional experiences of children in pervasive games using ZMET and MEC. It identifies key design attributes, user outcomes, and intrinsic values, and develops a consensus mapping model that illustrates children's cognitive frameworks. The findings provide recommendations for optimizing digital game design in line with situated learning principles and inform future design initiatives.

2 RESEARCH METHOD

2.1 *Research process*

Understanding user needs is fundamental to designing effective learning content and objectives. From a design perspective, exploring users' perceptions of pervasive games is essential for aligning learning content with user needs. Accordingly, this study employs the Zaltman Metaphor Elicitation Technique (ZMET) and the Means–End Chain (MEC) approach to investigate children's underlying thoughts and experiences regarding pervasive games. This combined approach provides guidance for digital learning research and development and improves consistency between user experience and design. Specifically, ZMET is used to extract relationships among the conceptual constructs of children's perceptions. The associated attributes, consequences, and values are then categorized and mapped into a consensus model using MEC. Figure 1 illustrates the overall research process.

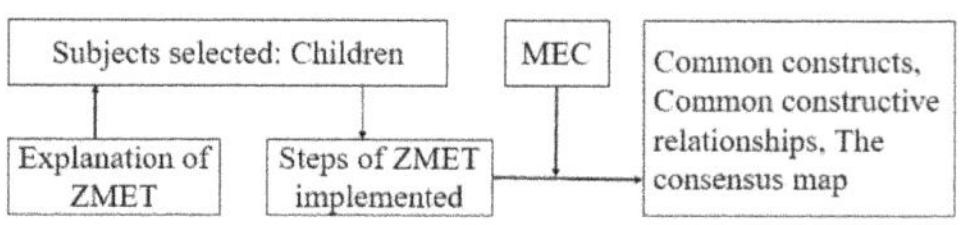

Figure 1. Research process.

DOI: 10.1201/9781003655534-25

2.2 *Research subjects*

ZMET is a qualitative research method. Previous studies have shown that a sample of just 4 to 5 participants can capture over 90% of the relevant concepts in a ZMET study (Coulter *et al.* 2001); however, it is common practice to recruit 10 to 15 participants in practical ZMET studies (Christensen 2002; Shin *et al.* 2014). Accordingly, this study employed purposive sampling. Based on criteria related to learning performance and cognitive abilities in design, we selected the top 10 high-achieving upper-grade elementary school students who had prior experience with pervasive games through a digital design course as representative participants.

2.3 *Steps of ZMET implemented*

One week prior to the interviews, participants were asked to collect 8 to 10 images that they felt represented their expectations regarding the design or emotional experience of pervasive games. This preparatory task helped participants clarify their understanding of the concepts and objectives associated with pervasive games. The interviews were then conducted using these images as stimuli, following the ZMET interview protocol as outlined by Zaltman (1997). The procedure included the following steps:

(1) Storytelling: Participants described the thoughts and emotions associated with each image.
(2) Missing Images: Participants identified and discussed ideas for which no suitable images could be found.
(3) Sorting and Labeling: Participants categorized the images and assigned descriptive labels to each group.
(4) Construct Elicitation: Through triadic comparisons, participants' underlying cognitive constructs regarding pervasive games were identified. Using the Kelly Grid and laddering techniques, relationships among constructs were further developed until saturation was reached.
(5) Most and Least Representative Images: Participants selected and explained the images that most and least reflected their perceptions.
(6) Sensory Metaphors: Participants described pervasive games using sensory-based metaphors and imagery.
(7) Summary Collage: Participants compiled the 8 to 10 images into a cohesive collage that visually summarized their perceptions.
(8) Short Essay: Finally, participants reaffirmed and articulated their reflections in a brief written essay.

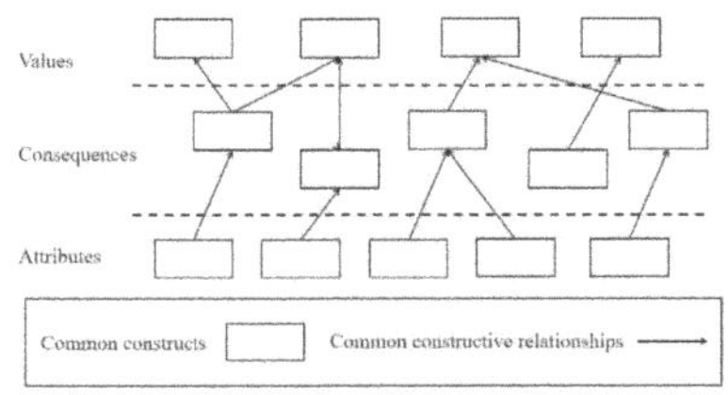

Figure 2. The consensus map.

2.4 *Data coding*

Interview data from 10 participants were analyzed and coded using the MEC methodology by three coders: the lead researcher and two digital learning experts. The process involved identifying common constructs, mapping common constructive relationships, and developing a consensus map (Figure 2). Common constructive relationships represent causal links between common constructs. Following academic guidelines, the map includes constructs mentioned by at least one-third of participants and relationships cited by at least one-quarter (Zaltman and Coulter 1995). In this study, a minimum of three participants was required to reference a construct or relationship for inclusion. The validity of the findings was supported by strong inter-coder agreement, and the data were collected using the ZMET method.

3 RESULTS AND DISCUSSION

3.1 *Common constructs extracted*

Personal constructs are built to be used as a basis for common constructs. 52 personal constructs were extracted from the interview data. According to the ZMET framework, a construct is considered "common" if it is confirmed by at least three participants. Therefore, 20 common constructs are extracted as shown in Table 1, including 6 attributes (A), 8 consequences (C), and 6 values (V).

Children's understanding of pervasive game attributes includes the integration of gameplay with real-world contexts, social interaction, mission-based tasks, game routes, offline (synchronized) app access, and augmented reality (AR) technology. The perceived outcomes of participating in pervasive games include physical exercise, exploration and adventure, outdoor activity, reaction enhancement, teamwork, improved problem-solving skills, real-time interaction, and the fusion of physical and virtual environments. The values associated with pervasive games, as perceived by children, encompass health, emotional support, enjoyment, excitement, a sense of achievement, and immersion.

Table 1. Common constructs extracted form students.

No	MEC	Common construction	Ch1	Ch2	Ch3	Ch4	Ch5	Ch6	Ch7	Ch8	Ch9	Ch10	Frquency
			Research subjects										
1	Attributes	Integration of Gameplay with Real-World Contexts	•	•	•	•		•	•		•	•	8
2		Games Routes	•		•						•	•	4
3		Social Interaction	•					•		•			3
4		Mission -Base Play				•	•	•	•			•	5
5		AR Technology	•		•	•							3
6		Offline App Access		•	•	•	•	•	•		•		7
7	Consequences	Reaction Enhancement	•	•							•		3
8		Outdoor Activity	•					•	•				3
9		Exploration & Advanture	•	•				•	•	•	•	•	7
10		Physical -Virtual Fusion	•		•	•			•		•		5
11		Problem Solving	•				•	•	•	•			5
12		Physical Exercise	•	•	•	•						•	5
13		Team Work	•	•	•	•	•	•		•	•	•	9
14		Game Interaction	•	•	•	•	•	•	•	•	•	•	10
15	Values	Excitement		•	•	•			•		•	•	6
16		Health		•	•	•					•	•	5
17		Immersion						•	•	•		•	4
18		Enjoyment	•	•	•	•	•	•	•	•	•	•	10
19		Achievement	•		•			•	•	•	•	•	7
20		Emotional Support	•				•	•		•	•		5

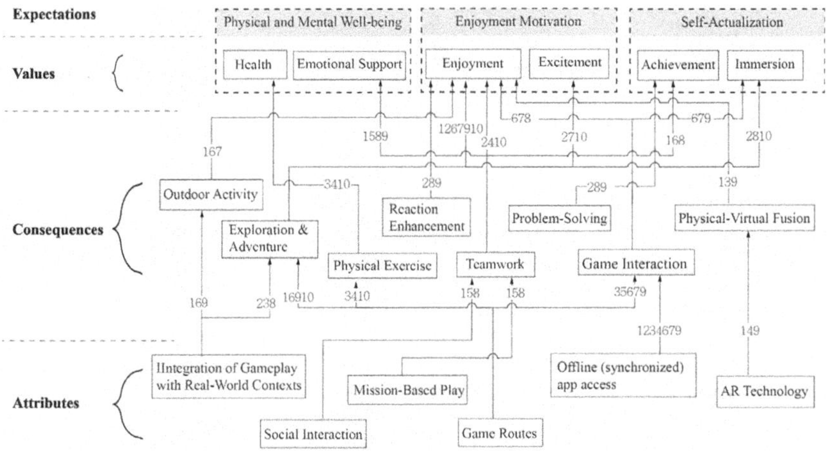

Figure 3. The consensus map for imageries of pervasive games of children. Note : "→" indicates common constructive relationships, and the number on the line indicates the children number.

Expectation Dimension 2: Enjoyment Motivation, comprises six attributes—integration with real-world contexts, social interaction, game missions, game routes, offline (synchronized) app access, and augmented reality (AR) technology; six consequences—outdoor engagement, exploration and adventure, enhanced reaction time, teamwork, fusion of physical and virtual environments, and real-time interaction; and two values—enjoyment and excitement. Children

3.2 *The consensus map*

The consensus map was developed based on common constructs and common constructive relationships, providing a comprehensive representation of children's cognitive perceptions of pervasive games. From the six identified values, three overarching expectation dimensions were inductively derived: Physical and Mental Well-being, Enjoyment Motivation, and Self-Actualization. Figure 3 presents the consensus map constructed from the responses of ten student participants, organized by attributes, consequences, and values.

Expectation Dimension 1: Physical and Mental Well-being, includes three attributes—social interaction, game missions, and game routes; two consequences—physical exercise and teamwork; and two values—health and emotional support. The findings suggest that children view pervasive games as facilitating both physical engagement and emotional connection, particularly through outdoor activity and collaborative play. Emotional support was perceived to emerge from peer interaction enabled by social features and cooperative mission design.

reported that the immersive contexts and technical features of pervasive games contributed to high levels of fun and stimulation. The thrill of exploration and real-time play, driven by the challenge and unpredictability of game missions and routes, was particularly emphasized.

Expectation Dimension 3: Self-Actualization, consists of five attributes—integration with real-world contexts, game missions, game routes, offline (synchronized) app access, and social interaction; four consequences—real-time interaction, exploration and adventure, enhanced problem-solving, and teamwork; and two values—sense of achievement and immersion. Children noted that the combination of real-world exploration and dynamic route design required real-time decision-making and problem-solving, fostering a sense of adventure and cognitive growth. Additionally, collaborative play and social interaction reinforced teamwork and contributed to a strong sense of accomplishment upon completing challenges.

4 CONCLUSION

Understanding children's underlying thoughts and experiences is critical to the effective design of pervasive games. However, children often struggle to articulate their needs and gameplay expectations, which can lead designers and educators to overlook their actual requirements. To address this challenge, pervasive game design should adopt a user-centered approach that integrates educational and entertainment value through technological innovation, content refinement, and emotional engagement. Based on the findings of this study, the following recommendations are proposed to enhance children's learning motivation and outcomes:

(1) Employ mixed-method approaches to evaluate behavioral patterns and long-term learning effects.
(2) Incorporate greater exploratory and challenging elements into task and scenario design.
(3) Establish bidirectional communication channels between designers and users.
(4) Optimize design features that foster engagement and enjoyment.

These recommendations aim to promote the meaningful integration of pervasive games into educational practice and provide a more systematic, evidence-based foundation for the future development of digital learning tools.

REFERENCES

Christensen G.L. and Olson J.C., (2002), Mapping consumers' mental models with ZMET. *Psychology & Marketing*, 19(6), 477–501.

Coelho A., Rodrigues R., Nóbrega R., Jacob J., Morgado L., Cardoso P., Sousa A.A., (2020), Serious pervasive games. *Frontiers in Computer Science*, 2, 30.

Coulter R.A., Zaltman G. and Coulter K.S., (2001), Interpreting consumer perceptions of advertising: An application of the Zaltman Metaphor Elicitation Technique. *Journal of Advertising*, 30(4), 1–21.

Costa M.C., Santos P., Patrício J.M. and Manso A., (2021), An interactive information system that supports an augmented reality game in the context of game-based learning. *Multimodal Technologies and Interaction*, 5(12), 82.

Gutman J., (1982), A means-end chain model based on consumer categorization processes. *Journal of Marketing*, 46(2), 60–72.

Kai L., Tan W.H. and Saari E.M., (2023), Dimensions of interactive pervasive game design: Systematic review. *JMIR Serious Games*, 11, e42878.

Kasapakis V. and Gavalas D., Pervasive gaming: Status, trends and design principles. *Journal of Network and Computer Applications*, 2015, 55, 213–236.

Lave J. and Wenger E., (1991), *Situated Learning: Legitimate Peripheral Participation*. Cambridge University Press.

Lin H.W. and Lin Y.L., (2014), Digital educational game value hierarchy from a learners' perspective. *Computers in Human Behavior*, 30, 1–12.

Meng X., Liu Y. and Chen H., (2020), Investigating students' attitudes towards digital learning platforms using ZMET. *Computers & Education*, 145, 103712.

Schmitz B., Klemke R. and Specht M., (2014), The impact of coupled games on the learning experience of learners at-risk: An empirical study. *Pervasive and Mobile Computing*, 14, 57–65.

Shin L., Ya C.T. and Lu C.L., (2014), The relation of imagination and learning performance of the advertising design students toward project study courses in vocational high school. *J. CAGST*, 468–482.

Zaltman G., (1997), Rethinking market research: Putting people back in. *Journal of Marketing Research*, 34(4), 424–437.

Zaltman G. and Coulter R.H., (1995), Seeing the voice of the customer: Metaphor-based advertising research. *Journal of Advertising Research*, 35(4), 35–51.

Zender R., Metzler R. and Lucke U., (2014), FreshUP—A pervasive educational game for freshmen. *Pervasive and Mobile Computing*, 14, 47–56.

System Innovation for a Global Economy – Lam et al. (Eds)
© 2026 The Author(s), ISBN 978-1-041-10520-6

Case study analysis of AI applications in cultural value enhancement

Kuan-Yu Chen & Li-Shu Lu
Department of Digital Media Design, National Yunlin University of Science and Technology, Douliu, Yunlin, Taiwan

ABSTRACT: With the rapid advancement of artificial intelligence (AI) technologies, AI has not only transformed traditional content creation models—such as generative art, music, and imagery through AIGC (AI-Generated Content)—but has also gradually integrated into cultural industries, resulting in a range of innovative applications. These applications have significantly impacted cultural preservation, dissemination, and experience, while also being utilized in tasks such as historical image restoration and the automatic generation of multilingual subtitles. Such uses of AI not only enhance the value of cultural content and the efficiency of its production, but also reshape the interactions between creators, audiences, and markets, offering new opportunities and challenges.

This study aims to organize and analyze representative cases of AI applications in cultural value-added contexts in Taiwan. It begins with a review of the historical development of AI, including its origins, technological foundations, and recent innovations. The research then focuses on the application value of AI in the cultural sector, providing an in-depth case analysis of AI-driven cultural enhancement practices. Grounded in Bourdieu's theory of cultural capital (1979), the study selects five cases for analysis: *Chronicles of the Planet ASOMROF,* the Preservation project of the Sanyi Wood Sculpture Museum collection, the Taroko and Mandarin bidirectional translation AI model, the Restoration of traditional metal movable type culture, A cross-disciplinary 5G-based museum-grade art and technology integration project.

These cases collectively demonstrate the diverse applications and values of AI in Taiwan's cultural sector. The study also offers strategic insights for practical implementation in related industries.The research concludes that AI development should continue with a focus on the integration of technological innovation and industrial upgrading, in order to support cultural preservation. The findings provide critical references for the cultural applications of AI in Taiwan, aiming to contribute to future industrial innovation and social development.

Keywords: Artificial Intelligence, Cultural Value-Added Applications, Case Study, Cultural Preservation

1 INTRODUCTION

With the continuous advancement of technology, artificial intelligence (AI) was first conceptualized by John McCarthy in 1956 during the "Dartmouth Conference," laying the foundation for AI research. The 1980s saw the emergence and development of machine learning, which gained significant momentum in the following decades. In the 2010s, the rise of deep learning brought about revolutionary breakthroughs and rapid progress in the field of AI.

AI is transforming the way we live, work, and think, and is expected to profoundly impact various domains of human society—including education, economy, politics, and social structures (Lee and Wang 2017). Moreover, generative AI provides a practical tool and platform for beginners to acquire new skills. Through the effective use of software, users are able to simplify workflows and focus on innovation and strategic development (National Science and Technology Council 2024; Institute for Information Industry 2023).

AI has been applied across a wide range of fields. One notable example is the emergence of generative AI in 2022. In domains such as text composition, image generation, music creation, and the film and television industry, generative AI has demonstrated versatile capabilities. These include translation and question answering, artistic creation and character design, music composition, video editing, animation production, and content generation. Users can simply input keywords via a keyboard to generate content instantly. This not only enhances content production efficiency for individuals and businesses, but also introduces a wealth of creative possibilities.

DOI: 10.1201/9781003655534-26

In addition, recent advancements in AI-generated virtual characters—such as AI news anchors and AI vocalists—have become an emerging trend, signaling a new direction in AI-driven media and cultural applications.

Building upon this context, the present study aims to systematically review Taiwan's research achievements and current policy landscape related to artificial intelligence (AI), and to further explore the potential applications of AI in the cultural and creative industries. As Lin Rong-Tai (2009) pointed out, the transformation of raw cultural artifacts into creative knowledge through the value-added processes of information and knowledge, followed by creative enhancement, can ultimately result in the generation of intellectual property. This research aspires to propose development strategies tailored to Taiwan's context for AI applications in cultural value-added domains, offering practical contributions to both academic research and policy planning.

The study focuses on the following key aspects:

1. Integrating literature on the historical development of AI and its relevance to cultural value enhancement;
2. Analyzing the applications and value of AI within the cultural industry.

It is hoped that this research will serve as a foundational reference for the continued advancement of AI in Taiwan, fostering greater innovation across both society and industry.

2 HISTORY OF AI DEVELOPMENT

2.1 *Artificial intelligence*

Artificial Intelligence (AI), also referred to as "machine intelligence," broadly denotes intelligence exhibited by non-human entities (Kuo 2023). According to Yang Li-Teng (2023), in his report on AI developments in Switzerland, the Swiss Federal Council's 2022 publication *Artificial Intelligence and International Norms* defines AI as the ability of computers to perform tasks that typically require human or biological intelligence. These tasks include image recognition, speech recognition, translation, and rule-based gameplay. Kai-Fu Lee (2017), in his book *AI Superpowers*, described AI as computer programs that simulate human thinking—a definition that was especially prevalent during the early stages of AI development.

In 1950, John McCarthy proposed the concept of artificial intelligence at the Dartmouth Conference, laying the foundation for AI research. Machine learning and deep learning—two core components of AI—were introduced in the 1980s and 2010s, respectively (Chiang 2023). AI technology encompasses a broad spectrum of applications, which can generally be categorized into three major domains: (1) computer vision, (2) natural language processing, and (3) data science. These domains are respectively applied to image recognition, language understanding, and data analysis and prediction (Chiang 2023).

2.2 *Historical development of AI*

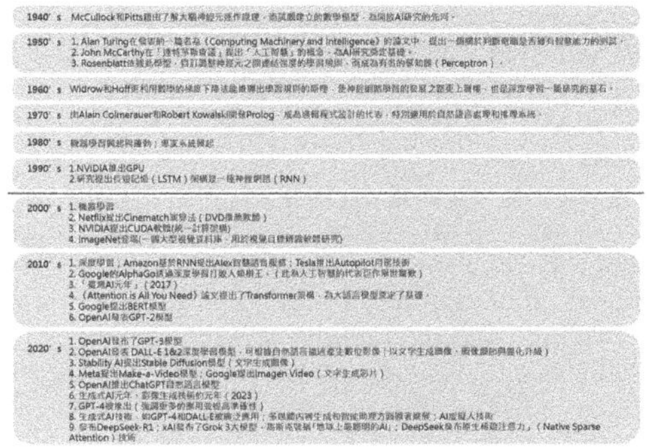

Figure 1. Historical development of AI. (Synthesis by This Study).

Based on Figure 1, machine learning and deep learning constitute two core components of modern AI technologies. Machine learning, introduced in the 1980s, refers to algorithms that infer decision-making functions from large datasets—such as Support Vector Machines (SVM) and Decision Trees (Chiang 2023). These algorithms are primarily applied in basic pattern recognition tasks and have laid the foundation for data analysis in the cultural domain, such as language identification in corpus linguistics. Deep learning, which emerged in the 2010s, utilizes neural network architectures by extending the depth of network nodes to achieve more advanced levels of intelligent decision-making (Chiang 2023). This has led to significant breakthroughs in image recognition and speech processing technologies. Such advancements have further enabled cultural value-added applications—for instance, image restoration (e.g., cultural artifacts) and speech synthesis (e.g., language preservation).

2.3 *AI in cultural value-added applications*

As times evolve rapidly, the discourse surrounding cultural and creative value-added design continues to shift accordingly. According to Yang Dong-Han (2009), cultural value-added design refers to the transformation of digital archive content into products that embody cultural identity and meaning. This process of transformation is defined as cultural value-added design. Once a product is developed, its embedded cultural meaning can be strategically employed to capture public attention and generate discourse, thereby raising awareness of related cultural issues and promoting the cultural essence conveyed by the product. Through value-adding processes, archived cultural content can be liberated from its traditionally rigid or unfamiliar presentation and reintroduced to the public in innovative, diverse, and approachable forms. This not only enhances accessibility but also significantly increases the perceived value of cultural artifacts (Yang 2009).

Cultural value-added applications are rooted in cultural resources and aim to enhance cultural value across various domains through innovative technologies or strategies. These applications contribute to the preservation, revitalization, and innovation of culture. In particular, the integration of cutting-edge technologies such as Artificial Intelligence (AI), Generative AI, Augmented Reality (AR), and Virtual Reality (VR) has become a major driving force behind contemporary cultural value-added practices. In 2023, Chi Po-Hao highlighted an interdisciplinary project led by Professor Shih Kuo-Chen and a research team composed of experts from diverse fields such as traditional music, visual arts, and engineering. The project, titled "Erhu Performance Behavior and Musical Style Analysis through Artificial Intelligence," demonstrated how AI can be employed to preserve and popularize the erhu—a traditional Chinese musical instrument with a long-standing history—by analyzing performance behaviors and stylistic nuances (Chi 2023). In the public sphere, common examples of AI-driven cultural value-added applications include AI-guided tour systems in museums and ecological centers. Unlike traditional unidirectional guidance, AI enables dynamic and interactive experiences. Through AI-enhanced narration and responsive interaction, visitors are offered engaging and personalized ways to explore exhibition content, ultimately enriching their cultural understanding.

3 APPLICATUIONS OF AI IN THE CULTURAL INDUSTRY

This study employs a combination of literature review and case data analysis to explore the application of artificial intelligence (AI) in cultural value-added practices. The research first examines the historical development of AI to establish a foundational understanding of its technological evolution. Based on this historical context, the study seeks to investigate how contemporary AI technologies can be integrated into cultural domains. To this end, five representative cases of AI-assisted cultural value-added applications were selected for in-depth analysis.

The findings indicate that AI plays a supporting role in enhancing the cultural value of heritage and creative content. This study aims to synthesize and conceptualize the process through which original cultural artifacts are transformed into intellectual property via information and knowledge value-added processes, followed by creative augmentation (see Figure 2). In the first phase, the historical trajectory of AI technologies is reviewed to provide a basis for subsequent case analysis. In the second phase, the five cases are examined to identify specific pathways through which AI contributes to cultural value creation.

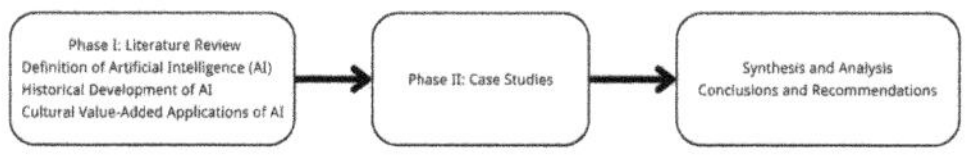

Figure 2. Research process.

4 ANALYSIS AND DISCUSSION

4.1 *Case description*

Hsu Hung-Ju (2004) referenced Bourdieu's theory of cultural capital, which outlines three distinct states. Among them, the *embodied state* holds particular significance, as it suggests that cultural capital, when transmitted across generations, carries deeper meaning than economic capital. This is because it conveys cultural references rooted in specific spatial and temporal contexts. Through the presence of cultural goods, this form of capital serves an educational function, and its accumulation is what enables tangible cultural artifacts to acquire rich cultural and educational value. Based on this theoretical foundation, the present study collected and analyzed five distinct cases in which artificial intelligence (AI) technologies have been employed to enhance cultural value. Each case demonstrates a unique approach to AI-driven cultural value creation. The basic information for each case—including project title, year of presentation, exhibition location, design team, and sources—is summarized in Table 1.

Table 1. Basic information of AI technology case studies(Synthesis by This Study).

No	Case Study Title	Years	Technological Approach	Location	Research Team	Data Sources	Schematic Diagram
01	ASOMROF:A Transmedia Project of Sci-Fi Content Inspeied by the Local Ethnic History for Technology Art Works	2023-2024	Dance Movement Datebase, Text Sentiment Analysis System and 5G Remote Co Performance	Metaverse	Yen-Jung Chang Hsin-Chien Huang, Yu-ting Hsueh	AVANCA| CINEMA	
02	Sanyi Woodcarving Museum Collection Preservation and Maintenance Plan	2024	AI Intelligent Voice Recognition Technology and AI Intelligent Image Recognition Technology	Sanyi Woodcarving Museum	Intelligent Recognition Industry Service Research Center (IRIS), National Yunlin University of Science and Technology	Youtube	
03	Taroko Language and Mandarin Bidirectional Translation AI Model	2024	Natural Language Model, Speech Recognition and Text Translation Technology	Department of Humanities and Social Sciences, NSTC	NCHC, NARLabs, Department of Humanities and Social Sciences, NSTC	Inclusive Technology Program, Department of Humanities and Social Sciences, NSTC	
04	Traditional Type Foundry Cultural Restoration	2020	AI Engineering Techonology	Jixing Type Foundry	Arphic Technology Co.,Ltd., MukauS Co., Ltd.	Business Today Magazine	
05	Museum and Art 5G Technology Cross-Domain Application Plan	2024	5G+AI+8K 3D Metaverse OMO	National Taiwan Museum	National Taiwan Museum, Rays Information Co., Ltd.	National Taiwan Museum	

Table 2. Content of AI technology case studies. (Synthesis by This Study). (AVANCA | CINEMA 2024; Intelligent Recognition Industry Service Research Center, National Yunlin University of Science and Technology 2024; NCHC, NARLabs 2024; Arphic Technology Co., Ltd. 2020; National Taiwan Museum & Rays Information Co., Ltd. 2024).

	AI Technology	Application Levels	Impacts of Cultural Enhancement
ASOMROF:A Transmedia Project of Sci-Fi Content Inspied by the Local Ethnic History for Technology Art Works	Dance Movement Database, Text Sentiment Analysis System and 5G Remote Co-Performance	Hakka Culture Preservation	Improving the Preservation of Hakka Cultural Values to Enhance Public Understanding of Hakka Culture
Sanyi Woodcarving Museum Collection Preservation and Maintenance Plan	AI Intelligent Voice Recognition Technology and AI Intelligent Image Recognition Technology	Cultural Relic Preservation	Using AI Woodcarving Insert Sound Detection Technology, Intelligent Insert Borehole Monitering, and Automated Low-Oxygen Insect Elimination Technology to Preserve the Historical and Cultural legacy of Woodcarving Artifacts Forever
Taroko Language and Mandarin Bidirectional Translation AI Model	Natural Language Model, Speech Synthesis, Speech Recognition and Text Translation Technology	Ethnic Language and Culture Preservation	Bridging the Gap Between Different Linguistic and Cultural Ethnic Groups While Preserving and Passing Down Ethnic, Language and Culture
Traditional Type Foundry Cultural Restoration	AI Engineering Technology	Preservation of Traditional Culture and Technology	Long-term Preservation of Taiwan's Letterpress Printing Technology
Museum and Art 5G Technology Cross-Domain Application Plan	AI+8K Digital Twin Technology, Combined with AI Computing to Overcome Material Limitations	Preservation of Cultural Artifact Collections	Enhancing the Visual Accuracy and Integrity of Cultural Artifacts

4.2 *Comprehensive analysis and discussion*

After synthesizing the case analyses of AI cultural value-added applications, the following conclusions can be drawn:

1. AI Technology: AI technologies provide more precise analytical and processing capabilities, making cultural heritage preservation more scientific. In terms of natural language processing, AI also aids in the digitization and educational application of minority languages, promoting the equal development of language cultures. Additionally, the integration of AI with VR and AR enhances interactivity, thereby increasing user engagement.
2. Application Domains: The majority of applications focus on the preservation of traditional culture and cultural artifacts.
3. Impact of Cultural Value-Addition: The integration of interdisciplinary collaborations has demonstrated the practical benefits of combining cultural preservation with technological development. Through AI, cultural value can be enhanced, leading to the creation of new cultural products. This not only elevates cultural influence but also transforms into commercial value, offering new business models for traditional cultural industries.

5 CONCLUSION

The purpose of AI and cultural value-added applications is to further integrate and deepen AI technologies with culture, creating more innovative applications. With the development of AI, experts have dedicated significant time to exploring new possibilities for cultural heritage preservation and innovative applications. These efforts have had a profound impact, both in academic research and practical applications, allowing the general public to connect with culture and the world through AI. The boundless potential of AI has prompted many people to notice, understand, and value cultural issues, thus facilitating the sustainable transmission and development of culture.

Furthermore, in this study, AI plays an auxiliary role. As such, the application of AI in cultural value addition raises important future challenges, such as technological ethics, data governance, and cultural sensitivity. These issues need to be further explored and addressed. Therefore, finding a balance between technology and culture will be a critical issue in the future development of cultural technology.

REFERENCES

ADMIN (May 22, 2024). Museum Tours with Integrated Technology and Multimedia: Explore a New Exhibition Experience. *BLOCKSY NEWS.* https://blog2.qshop.net.tw/

AI HUB Editorial Team (July 30, 2020). [2020 Application Case] Arphic x Woodcut Thinking: Creating an AI Font Assistant to Revive Traditional Type Foundry Culture. *AI HUB.* https://aihub.org.tw/post/149

Botpress (September 23, 2023). The Ultimate Guide to Artificial Intelligence (AI) and Augmented Reality (AR). *Botpress.* https://botpress.com/tw/blog/ultimate-guide-to-artificial-intelligence-ai-and-augmented-reality-ar

Bourdieu, P. (1979). The Three States of Cultural Capital. *Actes de la Recherche en Sciences Sociales*, (30), 3–6.

China Times (November 28, 2024). New Technology for Cultural Relic Preservation: AI Precision Pest Control Technology Introduced at Sanyi Woodcarving Museum. National Yunlin University of Science and Technology. https://www.yuntech.edu.tw/index.php/2019-04-10-08-06-20/item/11442-ai

CNYES News Center (February 19, 2025). DeepSeek Unveils NSA Technology to Further Reduce Costs and Enhance AI Model Efficiency. *CNYES.* https://news.cnyes.com/news/id/5866075

Chang, Y.-J., Huang, H.-C., and Hsueh, Y. (January 2024).ASOMROF: A Transmedia Project of Sci-Fi Content Inspired by Local Ethnic History for Technology Art Works. *AVANCA | CINEMA,* 576–582. DOI:10.37390/avancacinema.2023.a547

Gao, J.-T. (December 10, 2024). AI-Powered Real-Time Translation: Breaking Down Language Barriers. *Tech Addiction.* https://www.charmingscitech.nat.gov.tw/post/ai-translation

He, P.-S. (2025). Deep Analysis of the DeepSeek Effect. *Business Weekly*, (1943), 62–68. https://www.businessweekly.com.tw/Archive/Article?StrId=7011785

Hong, W.-B. (2020). A Brief History of Artificial Intelligence Development. *China-Taiwan Monthly*, (246), 44–51. https://www.ctworld.org.tw/monthly-ebook/246ebook/index.html

Hong, Q.-H., and Huang, S.-Z. (October 2024). Trends and Strategies for Generative AI Applications. Taiwan Institute of Economic Research, Division of Taiwan Economy.

Institute for Information Industry (2023). *Taiwan Digital Content Industry Report.* Digital Industry Agency, Ministry of Digital Affairs.

Jiang, W.-D. (2023). *100 Charts to Understand the AI Industry Chain: A Comprehensive Guide to AI Technology and Applications for Investment and Career Success.* Financial News Agency.

Ji, B.-H. (2023). The Harmonious Resonance of Erhu and Artificial Intelligence: The Modernization Journey of Traditional Music. *Interdisciplinary Research Project on Technology and Art Integration and Innovation.* https://nstc-artstech.net/observation-report-zh/226693.html

Lee, K.-F., and Wang, Y.-G. (2017*). Artificial Intelligence Is Here.* Commonwealth Publishing.

Lin, R.-T. (2009). Cultural and Creative Product Design: From Affective Technology, Human Centered Design, and Cultural Creativity. *Newsletter for Humanities and Social Sciences*, 11(1), 32–42.

Lynn (October 7, 2024). From Artificial Intelligence and Machine Learning to Deep Learning: A Must-Know Brief History of AI. INSIDE. https://www.inside.com.tw/feature/ai/9854-ai-history

Ministry of Economic Affairs, Industrial Development Bureau (November 30, 2019). AI Boosts the Information Service Industry: Arphic Reinvigorates Font Design. *Business Today*. https://www.businesstoday.com.tw/article/category/80393/post/201912030011/
National Science and Technology Council (June 5, 2023). Special Report on "Current Status and Future Directions of Artificial Intelligence (AI) Promotion". *Education and Culture Committee, 11th Term, 1st Session, Legislative Election.*
National Taiwan Museum (October 30, 2024). Integrating Cultural Heritage and Innovative Technology: National Taiwan Museum Partners with Raytheon to Build a 5G, AI, 8K 3D VR Smart Museum Benchmark. https://www.ntm.gov.tw/News_Content.aspx?n=5651&s=226411
Trend Micro (February 4, 2025). AI Breakthrough: A Review of AI Developments in 2024 and Future Outlook. *Trend Micro*. https://www.trendmicro.com/zh_tw/research/25/a/top-ai-trends-from-2024-review.html
Wu, J.-R. (July 26, 2023). [Infographic] 80 Years of AI Development: Ten Milestones Driving Today's AI! What Are the Three Pillars of Future Development? *Business Next*. https://www.bnext.com.tw/article/76138/computing-algorithm-big-data-artificial-intelligence-bedrock?
Xu, H.-R. (2004). Bourdieu's Concept of "Cultural Capital"and Its Explanation of Equal Educational Opportunities. *Educational Research Information*, 12 (3), 75–102.
Yang, D.-H. (2010). Research on the Value-Added Application of Teng Yu-Hsien's Digital Archive: A Case Study on Cultural Product Design. *Journal of Library and Information Studies*, 8(2), 95–123.
Yang, L.-T. (2023). *Special Report on Swiss Artificial Intelligence*. International Trade Administration, Ministry of Economic Affairs.
Yuquan (October 7, 2024). Understanding the Major Milestones in AI History. iThome. https://ithelp.ithome.com.tw/articles/10364464?sc=rss.qu

System Innovation for a Global Economy – Lam et al. (Eds)
© 2026 The Author(s), ISBN 978-1-041-10520-6

Analysis of immersive performance cases in Taiwanese indigenous culture

Feng-Chien Wu & Li-Shu Lu
Department of Digital Media Design, National Yunlin University, Douliu, Taiwan

ABSTRACT: With the rapid advancement of digital technology, immersive performances have become an essential tool in modern cultural exhibitions, breaking through the spatial and temporal limitations of traditional displays and creating a new way of viewing. They are widely applied in cultural exhibitions, education, and entertainment. In the dissemination of Indigenous culture, the use of technological tools (such as virtual reality, projection technology, and augmented reality) has introduced new possibilities for cultural exhibitions, enabling audiences to more deeply experience Indigenous history, art, and culture. Therefore, this study aims to further explore the application forms and effects of Indigenous cultural elements in immersive performances through case analysis, focusing on five Indigenous immersive performance cases in Taiwan. The study examines these cases from multiple dimensions, including presentation forms, technological applications, interactivity, narrative, and spatial design, to explore their similarities and differences. The research findings include: (1) analyzing the presentation forms and characteristics of Indigenous cultural elements in immersive performances; (2) exploring the relationship between immersive experiences and exhibition spaces as well as cultural contexts; (3) understanding how digital technology can enhance the interactivity and multi-sensory experiences of cultural exhibitions, and discussing the potential and challenges of immersive technology in the dissemination of Indigenous culture. This study recommends that future cultural exhibitions incorporating immersive performances should place greater emphasis on balancing cultural authenticity with technological innovation, ensuring that the depth and essence of the culture are preserved while enhancing audience engagement and cultural understanding.

Keywords: Immersive Performances, Performance Forms, Case Analysis, Taiwanese Indigenous Culture

1 RESEARCH BACKGROUND AND MOTIVATION

With the rapid development of global digital technology, immersive performance technology has gradually become a core tool in modern cultural exhibitions, widely applied in education, entertainment, and cultural dissemination. These technologies break through the temporal and spatial limitations of traditional displays, creating a new way of viewing, allowing the audience to engage more deeply with cultural content. For example, the Louvre uses VR technology to bring the character of the "Mona Lisa" out of the frame and allow the audience to step into Van Gogh's paintings (Doreen Carvajal 2019), providing an unprecedented immersive experience. Many museums and galleries are reorganizing their exhibition spaces to accommodate immersive experiences. In Australia, museums are increasingly focusing on using immersive experiences to showcase Indigenous art. This trend demonstrates that immersive exhibitions have become an important tool for cultural institutions in disseminating Indigenous culture (Zhang and Peng 2024). Through carefully designed scenarios, visitors can feel as though they are immersed in the history and culture of Indigenous people, fostering deeper emotional connections and understanding. Moreover, the application of digital technology not only attracts the visual and auditory senses but also stimulates other senses, further enhancing the audience's understanding of Indigenous culture. Visitors are eager to see how museums use technological means to present Indigenous culture. To meet these expectations, curators and designers are continuously exploring new creative approaches, from concept design to storytelling and sensory design, striving to communicate the essence and cultural value of Indigenous art more effectively (Taiwan Creative Content Agency 2024; Zhang and Peng 2024).

In recent years, immersive exhibition spaces have also rapidly emerged in Taiwan, with many cultural institutions and newly built venues utilizing XR technology to provide diverse performance experiences, meeting the public's demand for culture and entertainment. For example, the "Island Culture Pavilion" in Nantou's Ban Mountain

 DOI: 10.1201/9781003655534-27

Dream Factory (Taiwan Creative Content Agency 2024; Zhang Xie-sheng 2023), as Taiwan's first immersive exhibition space dedicated to Indigenous culture, has used advanced projection technology and sound equipment to combine Indigenous cultural elements, creating a unique artistic and educational experience.

Based on this background, this study will explore the following questions: In five different Indigenous immersive exhibition cases: (1) Analyze the presentation forms and characteristics of Indigenous immersive cases, (2) Understand the relationship between Indigenous immersive experiences, exhibition spaces, and cultural contexts. Based on the above, this study will compare the similarities and differences between these cases and discuss the interpretation of Indigenous culture in these designs and their future development directions, providing reference material for future research on Indigenous immersive performances.

2 LITERATURE REVIEW

2.1 *Definition of immersive performances*

Immersive performance is a type of display that creates a highly interactive and multi-sensory experience through digital technology, aiming to immerse the audience in the exhibition's context (Pine and Gilmore 1998). According to Slater and Sanchez-Vives (2016), the core of immersive performance is "immersion," meaning that through technological means, the audience is temporarily removed from reality and enters a world made of virtual or augmented environments. This form of performance not only relies on visual and auditory stimulation but also includes multi-sensory experiences such as touch, smell, and even taste, further enhancing the audience's sense of immersion (Slater and Sanchez-Vives 2016). In short, the characteristics of immersive performance include contextualization, interactivity, and multi-sensory experience. Contextualization refers to the creation of a complete scenario through technological means that allows the audience to escape reality and enter the exhibition world (Grau 2003). Interactivity emphasizes that the audience is no longer a passive viewer but an active participant in the exhibition (Roussou 2004). Multi-sensory experiences involve stimulating various senses such as vision, hearing, and touch, to further enhance the audience's immersion (Zhang and Peng 2024). For example, many museums now use virtual reality technology to allow the audience to interact with artworks, even entering the world inside the paintings. This innovative display method not only breaks through the spatial and temporal limitations of traditional exhibitions but also offers the audience an unprecedented immersive experience.

2.2 *Development of immersive performances*

The concept of immersive performances can be traced back to the early 20th century in theater and performance arts, where stage design, lighting effects, and sound were used to make the audience temporarily leave reality and enter the story's context (Pine and Gilmore 1998). This "escape from reality" experience was considered an early form of immersive experience. With technological advancements, immersive experiences gradually expanded from traditional performance arts to digital realms, particularly with the development of virtual reality (VR), augmented reality (AR), and mixed reality (MR), opening up more possibilities for immersive performances (Grau 2003). By the 21st century, the rapid development of digital technology brought about revolutionary changes in immersive performances. The maturation of virtual reality (VR) technology enabled the audience to enter a fully virtual environment through headsets (Slater and Sanchez-Vives 2016). For instance, in the early 2010s, VR technology began to be applied in museums and galleries, allowing the audience to interact with artworks (Freeman *et al.* 2019). This technology not only broke the temporal and spatial limitations of traditional exhibitions but also created more immersive visual effects, further enhancing the audience's sense of immersion.

Recently, immersive performances have become increasingly popular internationally, particularly in the fields of cultural exhibitions and education. For example, the National Museum of the American Indian uses augmented reality (AR) technology to transform Indigenous art into dynamic interactive exhibits, where visitors can view traditional ceremonial scenes and interact with 3D models (National Museum of the American Indian 2023). In addition, the Canadian Museum of History in Gatineau uses virtual reality (VR) technology to recreate traditional Indigenous villages and hunting scenes, allowing the audience to experience oral stories and ecological knowledge (Canadian Museum of History 2021). These examples show that immersive performances have become an important tool for showcasing Indigenous cultures internationally.

In Taiwan, immersive exhibition spaces have quickly emerged in recent years, with many cultural institutions and newly built venues utilizing extended reality (XR) technology to provide diverse performance experiences. For example, the Kaohsiung Indigenous Story Museum uses VR technology to showcase traditional Indigenous architecture and life scenes, allowing the audience to experience Indigenous culture and history firsthand. Additionally, augmented reality (AR) technology is used to transform traditional Indigenous clothing into an interactive experience, where visitors can try on traditional costumes and role-play different Indigenous groups (Hot Dot Imaging Co., Ltd. 2020). These examples show that immersive performances have become an important tool for cultural exhibitions in Taiwan. Although immersive performances have already been applied in cultural displays, many challenges remain in their future development. For instance, how to accurately present the core values of culture through immersive technology and how to strike a balance between technological applications and cultural authenticity, are issues that still need thorough exploration. As technology continues to advance, the application fields of immersive performances will expand further, including education, healthcare, and business (Slater and Sanchez-Vives 2016).

3 RESEARCH METHOD

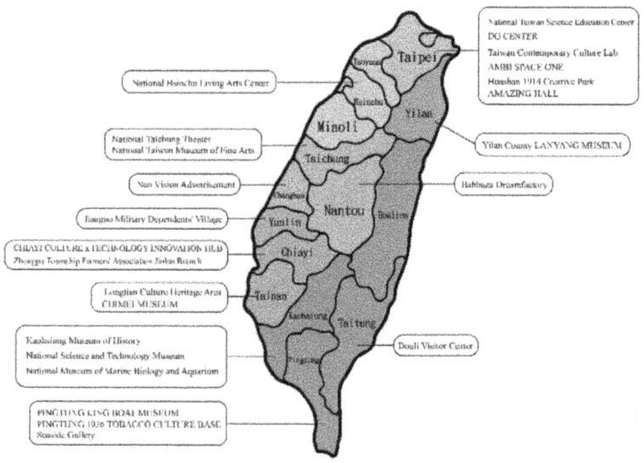

Figure 1. Distribution map of immersive performances in Taiwan.

This study uses case analysis to explore and analyze data, comparing and analyzing the application of immersive performance technology in Indigenous cultural exhibitions. The application of immersive performance technology involves multiple technical elements and can create a more interactive and immersive experience in cultural displays. Therefore, the study selects several Indigenous cultural exhibition cases that have applied immersive technology for in-depth exploration, comparing their presentation forms and characteristics, and analyzing how immersive technology is used to present Indigenous history, culture, and art. The research process (Figure 2) is divided into two major parts: "Data Collection" and "Inductive Analysis." Data collection includes literature review (definitions of immersive performance, development of immersive performances, cultural applications of immersive performances) and case analysis (presentation forms, technological applications, interactivity, storytelling, educational capabilities, spatial and cultural relationships, related ethnic groups, exhibition locations and ethnic associations, user control). Inductive analysis includes conclusions and recommendations.

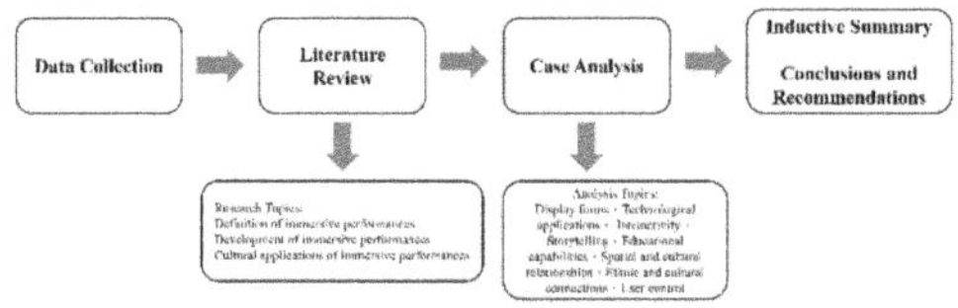

Figure 2. Research process.

Table 1. Basic information of immersive performance cases.

Case Number	Case Name	Technology Used	Year	Exhibition Location	Designers/ Teams
01	Kacalisian on the Slopes	Projection + Interaction	2023	Pingyan 1936 Cultural Base	Lao Pai Bo Fen, Yi Tan. Ba Wa Wa Long
02	The Kamalan Adventure	Projection + Interaction	2024	National Taiwan Literature Museum	Huang Nianjue, Chen Lixuan, Lin Zhao
03	The Fish on the Tree "Lokot Bird Nest Fern"	Projection + Animation	2024	National Taiwan Literature Museum	Gui Chun•Miya
04	Courageous Roots	Projection + Animation	2023	Shuter Babbuza Dreamfactory	Babbuza Dreamfactory
05	Alpha Sound Forest	Projection + Audio-visual	2025	National Taiwan Museum of Fine Arts	Xie Jing-ying, Timothy Wood, Qiu Wei-hao

4 ANALYSIS AND DISCUSSION

4.1 *Case description*

This study collected cases, considering the variety of immersive technologies used. Five selected cases, all utilizing projection technology within the last two years, were chosen for comparison and analysis. These case studies include: "Kacalisian on the Slopes," "The Kamalan Adventure," "The Fish on the Tree," "Courageous Roots," and "Alpha Sound Forest." These will be analyzed using the nine immersive criteria outlined in Table 2.

Table 2. Content of immersive performance case analysis.

Case	Kacalisian on the Slopes	Kamalan Adventure	The Fish on the Tree 'Lokot Bird Nest Fern'	The Origin of Courage	Alpha Sound Forest
Display Form	Combination of animation and projection, recreating Indigenous life scenes where the audience can search for cultural elements.	Interactive game combined with projection, where the audience assembles Kamalan cultural stories and experiences tribal history.	Combination of animation and projection, telling Indigenous mythological stories where the audience follows the plot's development.	Combination of animation and projection, where the audience participates in an adventure task to experience Indigenous culture.	Combination of sound and projection, where the audience experiences the fusion of Indigenous music and the natural environment.
Technology Used	Projection + Animation	Projection + Game	Projection + Animation	Projection + Animation	Projection + Sound
Interactivity	Medium (audience passively experiences through animation)	High (audience assembles the story through interactive devices)	Medium (audience passively experiences through animation)	Medium (audience participates in tasks through animation)	Low (audience experiences the environment through sound and image)
Storytelling	Entrance → View projection animation→ Experience Indigenous life scenes → End	Entrance → Play to assemble the story → Experience Kamalan history → End	Entrance → View animation and projection → Experience Indigenous mythology → End	Entrance → Participate in adventure tasks → Experience Indigenous culture \rightarrow*End*	Entrance → Experience sound and projection → Experience music and nature → End
Educational Ability	Learn about tribal history and culture	Learn about Kamalan culture	Understand mythological stories	Learn about the spirit of adventure	Experience music and nature
Relationship with Venue and Culture	The industrial style of the Pingyan 1936 Cultural Base contrasts with Indigenous culture, enhancing cultural immersion.	The cultural atmosphere of the National Taiwan Museum of Literature complements the Kamalan story, enhancing cultural understanding.	he literary atmosphere of the National Taiwan Museum of Literature complements the mythological stories, increasing the story's immersion.	The modern venue at Shude Ban Mountain Dream Factory contrasts with Indigenous stories, creating a unique experience.	The artistic atmosphere of the National Taiwan Museum of Fine Arts complements the music culture, enhancing music immersion.
Related Ethnic Group	Paiwan, Rukai	Kamalan	Amis	Bunun	Atayal
Exhibition Location and Ethnic Relationship	The Pingyan 1936 Cultural Base in Pingtung corresponds with the cultural background of the Paiwan and Rukai, enhancing cultural immersion.	The National Taiwan Museum of Literature in Tainan corresponds with the history and migration background of the Kamalan tribe, enhancing cultural understanding.	The National Taiwan Museum of Literature in Tainan complements the Amis mythological stories, enhancing story immersion.	The Shude Ban Mountain Dream Factory in Nantou contrasts with the Bunun tribe's adventurous spirit, creating a unique experience.	The National Taiwan Museum of Fine Arts in Taichung complements the Atayal tribe's music culture, enhancing music immersion.
Control over Experience	Medium (audience can watch the animation but cannot directly control the storyline)	High (audience can control the interactive device, affecting the exhibition's content presentation)	Medium (audience can watch the animation but cannot directly control the storyline)	Medium (audience can watch the animation but cannot directly control the storyline)	Low (audience experiences sound and image but cannot directly control the music changes)

Figure 3. "Kacalisian on the Slopes" projection screen.

Figure 4. "Kacalisian on the Slopes" Life Scene.

Figure 5. “Kamalan Adventure” Game Screen.

Figure 6. “Kamalan Adventure” Gameplay Screen.

Figure 7. “The Fish on the Tree ‘Lokot Bird Nest Fern’” Viewing Screen.

Figure 8. “The Fish on the Tree ‘Lokot Bird Nest Fern’” Animation Scene.

Figure 9. “The Origin of Courage” Viewing Screen.

Figure 10. “The Origin of Courage” Exhibition Entrance.

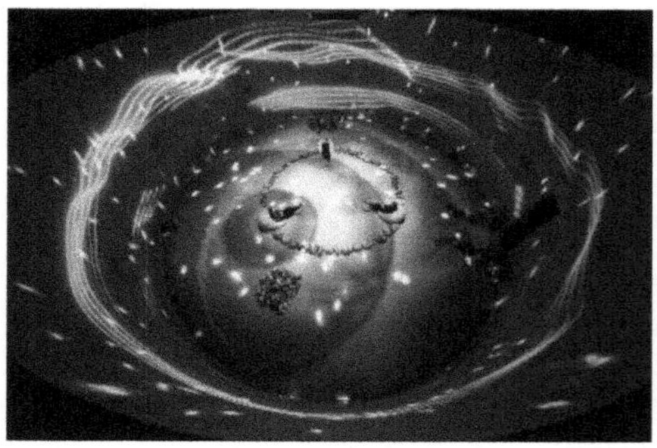

Figure 11. “Alpha Sound Forest” Experience Screen.

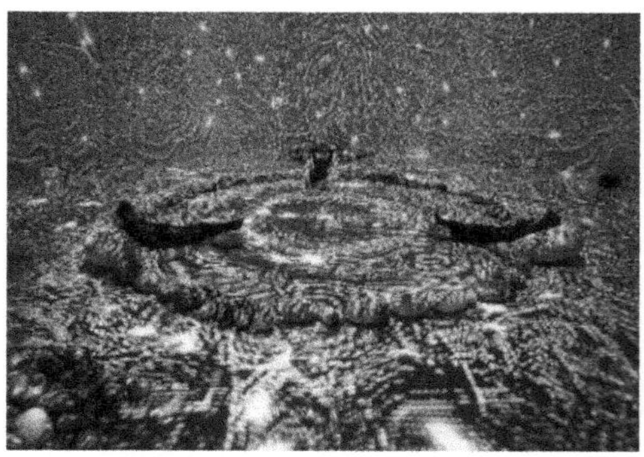

Figure 12. “Alpha Soun d Forest” Experience Screen.

4.2 *Comprehensive analysis and discussion*

This study analyzes five Taiwanese Indigenous immersive performance cases to explore the application of Indigenous cultural elements in immersive exhibitions and their effects. The main findings and discussions are as follows:

(1) Diversity in Display Forms Each case demonstrates diversity in display forms, such as using projection technology, interactive devices, animation, and audiovisual elements. These digital technologies transform Indigenous cultural elements like traditional totems, rituals, music, and stories into immersive experiences. These technologies not only enhance visual and auditory effects but also further engage the audience through multi-sensory stimulation. For example, "Kacalisian on the Slopes" combines projections with exhibition design to recreate Indigenous life scenes, allowing the audience to feel immersed in history and culture.

(2) Interactivity and Storytelling Interactivity and storytelling are key to immersive performances, effectively enhancing audience engagement and cultural understanding. For example, "Kamalan Adventure" allows the audience to assemble cultural stories through interactive devices, strengthening cultural identity. In contrast, "The Fish on the Tree 'Lokot Bird Nest Fern'" uses animation and projection technology to tell Indigenous mythological stories, enhancing the immersion of the narrative.

(3) Integration of Exhibition Space and Cultural Background The design of the exhibition space combined with cultural background can enhance immersion and create a unique cultural experience. For example, the industrial style of the Pingyan 1936 Cultural Base echoes the cultural background of the Paiwan and Rukai tribes, strengthening the cultural immersion. The artistic atmosphere of the National Taiwan Museum of Fine Arts complements the Atayal tribe's music culture, enhancing the music immersion experience.

(4) Educational Value Cases with strong educational capabilities are more effective in conveying Indigenous cultural knowledge and have educational value. For instance, "The Origin of Courage" uses animation and projection to teach the audience about the Bunun tribe's adventurous spirit. "Alpha Sound Forest," using sound and projection technology, enables the audience to experience the Atayal tribe's music and the natural environment.

(5) Balancing Technology and Cultural Content Technology applications should be balanced with cultural content to avoid overly relying on technology, which could dilute cultural meaning. For example, "Kacalisian on the Slopes" and "Kamalan Adventure" use interactive devices and projection technology to preserve cultural authenticity while creating a modern viewing experience.

(6) Higher Control Enhances Engagement Cases with higher control can enhance audience participation and immersion. For example, in "Kamalan Adventure," the audience interacts with the work, while in "Alpha Sound Forest," the audience can only passively experience the sound and images, leading to lower control.

5 CONCLUSION

This study analyzed five Taiwanese Indigenous immersive performance cases, exploring the use of digital technology in the presentation and dissemination of Indigenous culture. The findings suggest that immersive performance technology can significantly enhance audience understanding and recognition of culture by providing a multi-sensory experience. Interactivity and storytelling are key to engaging audiences, while the integration of exhibition space design and cultural context can strengthen the immersive experience. However, the application of immersive technologies must balance cultural authenticity to avoid diluting cultural values. Future developments should focus on achieving this balance and exploring how immersive technologies can more accurately represent core cultural values while avoiding oversimplification.

I would like to express my sincere gratitude to the National Science and Technology Council (NSTC) for providing the financial support of this research, which made this study possible. I am truly thankful for their support in advancing research on immersive performances and Taiwanese Indigenous culture.

REFERENCES

Canadian Museum of History. (2021). *Indigenous Perspectives Virtual Reality Experience*. https://www.historymuseum.ca

Doreen Carvajal. (2019). *Meeting the 'Mona Lisa' for an Intimate (Virtual) Rendezvous*. Retrieved December 7 from https://www.nytimes.com/2019/10/15/arts/design/mona-lisa-vr-louvre.html

Grau, O. (2003). *Virtual Art: From Illusion to Immersion*. MIT Press. https://mitpress.mit.edu/9780262572231/virtual-art/

Hot Dot Imaging Co., Ltd. (2020). Kaohsiung Indigenous Story *Museum: AR/VR Interactive Multimedia Equipment*. Retrieved February 14 from https://www.hot-dot.url.tw/works/%E9%AB%98%E9%9B%84-%E5%8E%9F%E4%BD%8F%E6%B0%91%E6%95%85%E4%BA%8B%E9%A4%A8-ar-vr%E5%A4%9A%E5%AA%92%E9%AB%94%E4%BA%92%E5%8B%95%E8%A8%AD%E5%82%99/

National Museum of the American Indian. (2023). *Native Knowledge 360°. Smithsonian Institution.* https://americanindian.si.edu/nk360

Pine, J. B. II, and Gilmore, J. H. (1998). Welcome to the Experience Economy. *Harvard Business Review*, 76 (6), 97–105. https://hbr.org/1998/07/welcome-to-the-experience-economy

Roussou, M. (2004). Learning by doing and learning through Play: An exploration of interactivity in virtual environments for children. *Computers in Entertainment*, 2(1), 10. https://doi.org/10.1145/973801.973818

Slater, M., and Sanchez-Vives, M. V. (2016). Enhancing our lives with immersive virtual reality. *Frontiers in Robotics and AI*, 3, 74. https://doi.org/10.3389/frobt.2016.00074

Taiwan Creative Content Agency. (2024). *The Fusion of Technology and Art: A Study on the Business Models of Immersive Performance Venues.* Retrieved November 12 from https://culturetech.taicca.tw/resources/business-models-for-immersive-2024

Zhang Xie-sheng. (2023). *Combining "Tree of Life" with Adventure Experiences: Nantou Ban Mountain Dream Factory Breaks Visitor Records.* Retrieved July 12 from https://news.ltn.com.tw/news/Nantou/breakingnews/3989221

Zhang, R., and Peng, F. (2024). Connection: Digitally representing australian aboriginal art through the immersive virtual museum exhibition. *Arts*, 13(1), 9. https://doi.org/10.3390/arts13010009

System Innovation for a Global Economy – Lam et al. (Eds)
© 2026 The Author(s), ISBN 978-1-041-10520-6

Research on interaction design of E-Books based on mediapipe hand gesture recognition

Cheng-Hao Shao
Graduate School of Design, Nation Yunlin University of Science and Technology, Yunlin, Taiwan
Department of Information Management, Chaoyang University of Technology, Taichung, Taiwan

Chao-Ming Wang
Department of Digital Media Design, Nation Yunlin University of Science and Technology, Yunlin, Taiwan

Rong-San Lin
Department of Information Management, Chaoyang University of Technology, Taichung, Taiwan

ABSTRACT: In recent years, the rapid development of digital technology has promoted the advancement of computer software, hardware and sensing technology, especially in the design of human-machine interfaces. This research will use MediaPipe gesture recognition technology for human-computer interaction to design an innovative application of gesture-interactive human-computer interface in e-books. Previous related research has mostly focused on game design and the application of limbs, gestures and faces of virtual characters. In the field of e-books, gesture interaction is mostly limited to page turning operations, and there is less in-depth discussion of richer gesture applications.This study uses MediaPipe gesture recognition technology to conduct two research experiments on e-books: (1) gesture recognition experiment, and (2) spatial interaction between gestures and physical elements. The research findings indicate that (1) MediaPipe performs well in gesture recognition and can accurately recognize gestures, (2) the movement trajectory of gestures can be utilized for task triggering and interactive operations, and (3) the accuracy and complexity of gesture recognition are superior to those of the LEAP Motion and Kinect approaches. Based on these research findings, we can provide a reference for future research and applications of gesture recognition technology, and subsequently design a gesture-based interactive interface that is user-friendly and systemically stable.

1 INTRODUCTION

1.1 *Research background and motivation*

With the advancement of digital reading technologies, e-books have become an essential tool for learning and reading. However, their interactive mechanisms remain largely limited to mouse clicks, keyboard inputs, and touchscreen operations, which offer only basic functionality and lack naturalness and immersion (Lin and Chen 2020). To enhance the user experience, Natural User Interfaces (NUI) have gained increasing attention—particularly gesture recognition technologies, which provide intuitive and contactless interaction. These technologies have been widely applied in fields such as gaming, virtual reality, and educational technology (Karam and Schraefel 2005; Wigdor and Wixon 2011).Despite this progress, the application of gesture control in e-books is still primarily confined to page-turning, with limited exploration of more advanced functions such as annotation or object selection (Huang *et al.* 2022). Traditional gesture recognition methods often rely on external hardware such as LEAP Motion or Kinect. While these devices offer high precision, they are constrained by cost, bulk, and environmental limitations, making them less suitable for mainstream consumer products (Ren *et al.* 2013).

In contrast, MediaPipe—a framework developed by Google—enables real-time hand landmark detection using a standard camera. Its high portability and cross-platform compatibility reveal strong potential for application in e-book interaction design (Lugaresi *et al.* 2019; Zhang *et al.* 2021).

1.2 *Research questions and objectives*

With the growing application of natural gesture control in multimedia and educational technology, effectively integrating gesture recognition into e-book interaction design has become a research issue of increasing importance. This study focuses

DOI: 10.1201/9781003655534-28

on the potential of the MediaPipe gesture recognition framework for enhancing e-book operations. Through system development and empirical analysis, the following research questions are explored:

1. Can MediaPipe reliably and accurately recognize specific gestures for use in e-book interactions?
2. Can the dynamic trajectories of gestures serve as effective input for advanced interactive functions such as selection, annotation, and bookmarking?
3. Compared to traditional gesture recognition technologies (e.g., LEAP Motion and Kinect), what are MediaPipe's advantages and limitations in terms of recognition accuracy and system integration?

Based on these questions, the study sets out the following research objectives:

1. To develop an interactive e-book prototype system that integrates MediaPipe gesture recognition, utilizing TouchDesigner as the development platform to enable contactless interaction.
2. To evaluate the accuracy and stability of MediaPipe in recognizing both static and dynamic gestures, and to conduct a comparative analysis with existing recognition technologies.
3. To explore the feasibility and usability of gesture-based interactions across various e-book functions, including page navigation, paragraph selection, text annotation, and function triggering.

Ultimately, this study aims to provide new perspectives and practical models for e-book interface design, and to validate the potential of MediaPipe as a human-computer interaction input method, promoting diverse applications of natural gesture control in interactive systems.

2 LITERATURE REVIEW

2.1 *Development of gesture recognition technologies*

Gesture recognition is a key component of Natural User Interfaces (NUI) and is widely applied in human-computer interaction systems. Current mainstream technologies include MediaPipe, LEAP Motion, and Microsoft Kinect, each with distinct characteristics. Developed by Google, MediaPipe supports real-time hand landmark detection without requiring additional hardware, offering high-performance gesture recognition particularly suited for mobile and web-based applications (Lugaresi *et al.* 2019). LEAP Motion utilizes infrared sensors to achieve high recognition accuracy but is limited in operational space, making it more suitable for fixed desktop scenarios (Weichert *et al.* 2013). Kinect, on the other hand, combines RGB and depth-sensing technologies to track full-body skeletons and is commonly used in gaming and educational contexts. However, its physical size and operational constraints reduce its flexibility (Zhang 2012). Overall, MediaPipe's real-time capabilities, deployment flexibility, and low resource demands position it as a promising solution for next-generation gesture recognition applications.

2.2 *The role of gestures in human-computer interaction design*

Due to their high level of naturalness and intuitiveness, gesture-based controls have become an effective means of enhancing human-computer interaction (HCI). Wigdor and Wixon (2011) highlight that gestures lower the learning curve and enhance user immersion. Applications have extended to multimedia presentations, menu navigation, and virtual object manipulation (Karam and Schraefel 2005). In augmented reality (AR) and virtual reality (VR), gesture recognition serves as a central interaction medium, significantly enhancing system immersion and interaction flexibility (Billinghurst *et al.* 2015). Additionally, gesture control has found applications in educational technology, telemedicine, and robotic operations, showcasing its cross-disciplinary potential (Turan *et al.* 2021).

2.3 *Related research on e-book interaction design*

E-books initially focused on content presentation and basic page-turning functionality. With the rise of mobile devices, touch-based interaction became the standard. However, touch interaction can lead to discomfort and fatigue over extended use, reducing convenience (Lin and Chen 2020). Recent research has begun integrating innovative input methods—such as voice control, eye tracking, and gesture interaction—to enhance usability and efficiency (Huang *et al.* 2022). Among these, gesture control stands out for its contactless and intuitive nature, making it particularly suitable for educational, exhibition, and accessibility-related applications (Tsai *et al.* 2021).

Despite such advancements, gesture applications in e-books remain limited to basic operations like page-turning and zooming, lacking in interaction depth and functional diversity (Cheng *et al.* 2019). Research into more advanced functionalities—such as content selection, annotation, object manipulation, and multimodal switching—remains insufficient, constraining the pedagogical and practical potential of e-books.

2.4 *The contributes of this study*

This study aims to overcome the current limitations of gesture-based operations in e-books by constructing a gesture-controlled system with multi-functional interaction capabilities. Utilizing MediaPipe technology, both static and dynamic gesture tracking is implemented to enable complex interactions such as selection, annotation, and dragging, thereby enriching the interactive depth of digital reading. Furthermore, the study compares MediaPipe with LEAP Motion and Kinect in terms of recognition accuracy, usability, and system stability, offering empirical insights for future e-book interaction design. This research contributes to the evolution of e-book interfaces from single-mode operations toward immersive and diversified interaction experiences.

3 METHODOLOGY

This study explores the feasibility of applying MediaPipe gesture recognition technology to e-book interaction design. The research includes two main parts: system architecture and experimental design, aiming to evaluate both technical accuracy and user experience.

3.1 *System architecture*

3.1.1 *MediaPipe framework and gesture definitions*

MediaPipe was selected as the core gesture recognition engine due to its real-time image processing, high accuracy, and cross-platform compatibility (e.g., PC, Android, Web). It uses computer vision to track 21 hand landmarks and analyzes their vectors to recognize gestures.

The system defines six static gestures—open palm, fist, pointing index finger, pinch, victory sign, and OK sign—and three dynamic gestures—swipe, circle, and drag. Each gesture is linked to specific e-book functions, such as page turning, text selection, and adding annotations.

3.1.2 *E-book platform and gesture interface integration*

A custom e-book platform was developed, supporting text, images, and interactive annotations. MediaPipe is integrated as the input module. Users interact via a standard webcam, and the system recognizes gestures in real time to trigger functions.

To improve stability and reduce errors, the system includes a delay setting and tolerance mechanism to prevent accidental triggers. The interface also offers clear visual feedback, such as showing the current recognized gesture, its linked function, and a visual trail of hand movements.

3.2 *Experimental design*

Two main experiments were designed to evaluate the system's performance and user interaction quality:

Table 1. Experimental design and content planning.

Item	Experiment 1: Gesture Recognition Accuracy Test	Experiment 2: Gesture Interaction with Interface and Virtual Objects
Objective	To assess the accuracy and stability of MediaPipe in recognizing static and dynamic gestures.	To explore the feasibility and user experience of applying dynamic gestures (e.g., drag, select) in an e-book interface.
Procedure	Participants were asked to perform nine predefined gestures, each repeated 10 times. The number of successfully recognized gestures was recorded.	Participants completed five interaction tasks, such as selecting a paragraph with a gesture, dragging annotation icons, turning pages, and highlighting text. Success rate and interaction smoothness were observed.
Evaluation	Comparison: LEAP Motion and Kinect were used simultaneously for gesture recognition to compare the accuracy and latency of all three systems.	Data Collection: Video recordings, task completion time, and error count were documented. Questionnaires and semi-structured interviews were conducted to assess user experience.
Platform and Tools	MediaPipe + TouchDesigner development environment	MediaPipe + Custom e-book interface (developed with TouchDesigner)
Metrics	Recognition accuracy, false recognition rate, response latency, system stability	Task completion rate, interaction accuracy, user satisfaction (including questionnaire and interview feedback)

Participants and Sampling Design

A total of 30 participants took part in this study, including students from computer science-related departments and general users. Participants were aged between 18 and 35 and had basic experience using computers and e-books. They were randomly assigned to different gesture interaction tasks and completed a post-test satisfaction questionnaire based on a 5-point Likert scale.

4 SYSTEM IMPLEMENTATION

The development of the interactive e-book system in this study includes the use of software tools, gesture-function design, interaction flow, and integration with the e-book platform. The system was built using TouchDesigner as the main development environment, combined with MediaPipe for gesture recognition, enabling real-time gesture control and visual interaction.

4.1 *Development environment and tools*

The system was developed using the following tools and libraries:

1. TouchDesigner: A real-time visual programming platform developed by Derivative, offering robust image processing and interactive interface design capabilities. It supports Python scripting and integration with various input sources.
2. MediaPipe: An open-source, cross-platform machine learning framework by Google, focused on high-performance real-time hand gesture recognition. It transmits hand landmark coordinates to TouchDesigner via Python.
3. Python: Acts as a bridge between MediaPipe and TouchDesigner, responsible for transmitting and formatting gesture data.
4. OpenCV: Used for capturing camera input and preprocessing images to improve the stability of gesture recognition by MediaPipe.
5. OSC/WebSocket: Communication protocols used to transmit gesture data in real time between Python scripts and the TouchDesigner interface.

4.2 *Gesture Types and Function Mapping*

The system defines a total of nine gestures, categorized into two types:

Table 2. Gesture types and function definitions.

Gesture Type	Gesture Action	Function Description
Static Gesture	Open Palm	Open Menu / Initial State
	Fist	Go Back to Previous Page
	Pointing with Index Finger	Highlight Cursor Target Area
	Victory Gesture (V)	Insert Bookmark or Annotation
	OK Gesture	Confirm or Select
Dynamic Gesture	Swipe Left	Next Page
	Swipe Right	Previous Page
	Drag	Select Paragraph Text
	Circle	Customize Annotation Area

TouchDesigner receives gesture recognition results from Python via OSC (Open Sound Control) and executes corresponding e-book interaction functions, such as page turning, annotation insertion, or text selection. Visual prompts and audio feedback are also implemented to enhance user clarity and interaction awareness.

4.3 *Gesture recognition data flow*

The overall system architecture is illustrated in the figure below:

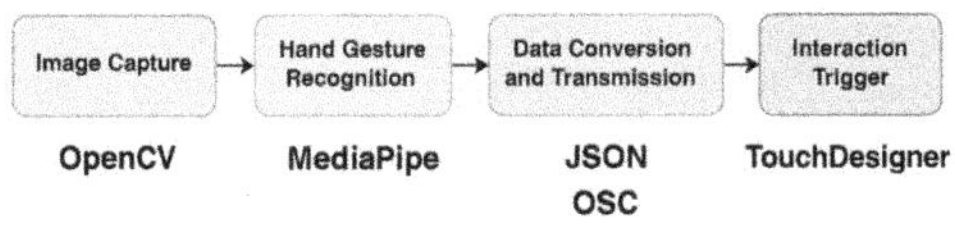

Figure 1. System architecture diagram.

Process Steps:

1. Image Capture: Real-time video input is captured using OpenCV and fed into the MediaPipe model.
2. Gesture Recognition: The MediaPipe module detects 21 hand landmarks and performs vector analysis to recognize the user's hand movements.
3. Data Conversion and Transmission: The recognition results are converted into JSON format and transmitted to TouchDesigner via the OSC (Open Sound Control) protocol.
4. Interaction Triggering: TouchDesigner receives the data and triggers the corresponding e-book interactions and visual effects, such as page-turn animations or cursor highlights.

4.4 *User interface design and interaction flow*

The user interface is divided into three main areas:

1. Reading Area: Displays the e-book content (text and images), supporting gesture-based page turning and annotations.
2. Interaction Prompt Area: Provides visual feedback, including the currently recognized gesture, operational hints, and detection stability indicators.
3. Bookmark and Annotation Area: Allows users to insert bookmarks or notes using specific gestures and quickly return to marked sections.

Interaction Flow:

1. The user activates the system and performs gestures in front of the camera.
2. The system recognizes the gesture and displays the corresponding icon and function in the prompt area.
3. When the gesture is held steadily for a specific duration (e.g., 1 second), the corresponding function is triggered.

Users can perform multiple operations in sequence for example, turning a page and immediately annotating a paragraph, or selecting a section and dragging it to save.

4.5 *System integration and stability testing*

To ensure system stability and cross-platform compatibility, the following integration tests were conducted:

1. System Performance Monitoring: Touch Designer's Frame Rate Monitor was used to observe real-time processing performance, maintaining a stable operation above 30 FPS during interactions.
2. False Trigger Detection and Error Tolerance: A gesture recognition threshold and multi-pass verification mechanism were implemented to minimize accidental activations caused by brief or unintended movements.
3. Platform Testing: The system was tested on different platforms, including Windows 10 and macOS, to confirm that all modules can be deployed smoothly across various hardware environments.

5 EXPERIMENTAL RESULTS AND DISCUSSION

To verify the feasibility and practicality of the MediaPipe-based gesture-controlled e-book system developed in this study, two core experiments were conducted: (1) Gesture recognition accuracy testing, and (2) User experience evaluation in interactive tasks.Additionally, the performance and user feedback of MediaPipe were compared with LEAP Motion and Kinect.

5.1 *Gesture recognition accuracy test*

A total of 15 participants performed recognition tests for nine predefined gestures (both static and dynamic) in a controlled environment. Each participant repeated each gesture 10 times, resulting in 1,350 total samples.

Table 3. Gesture recognition results.

Gesture Type	MediaPipe Accuracy	LEAP Motion Accuracy	Kinect Accuracy
Open palm	98.7%	93.2%	90.5%
Fist	97.4%	91.6%	88.8%
Pointing finger	95.1%	87.5%	84.3%
Victory sign (V)	96.8%	89.1%	86.0%
OK sign	94.6%	85.7%	81.2%
Swipe left	92.3%	83.0%	78.5%
Swipe right	91.8%	82.7%	79.1%
Drag	89.5%	76.2%	74.4%
Circle	90.1%	78.6%	72.0%

MediaPipe achieved over 95% accuracy in static gestures and maintained over 89% accuracy for dynamic gestures, which are generally more complex. Overall, it outperformed both LEAP Motion and Kinect. Participants also noted that MediaPipe offered more natural and responsive interaction.

5.2 *User experience in interactive tasks*

Three scenario-based tasks were designed to evaluate interaction performance and usability:

Task 1: Quick page navigation (Next/Previous)

Task 2: Paragraph selection and dragging

Task 3: Inserting bookmarks and annotations via gesture

Participants completed each task in sequence. Task completion time and success rate were recorded, and the System Usability Scale (SUS) questionnaire was used to assess user experience.

Table 4. Task operation records

Task	Avg. Completion Time (sec)	Success Rate	User Rating (1–5)
Page navigation	5.3	100%	4.6
Paragraph drag	8.7	92%	4.2
Insert annotation	6.1	95%	4.5

Most users were able to complete the tasks quickly and easily, with nearly perfect results in page-turning. Dragging and circle gestures required more precise control, suggesting that future improvements could include enhanced visual cues or auto-correction support.

5.3 *User feedback from questionnaire and interviews*

A total of 15 valid SUS questionnaires were collected, with an average score of 86.2 out of 100, placing the system in the "Excellent" usability category.

Positive feedback:

1. Natural and intuitive interaction without the need for external controllers.
2. Real-time system response with clear animations and prompts.
3. Bookmarking and annotation functions added value beyond traditional page-turning.

Suggested improvements:

1. Recognition accuracy decreased under bright lighting or cluttered backgrounds.

2. Some gestures required repetition; users suggested adding audio cues or haptic feedback.
3. Desire for more interactive tools, such as voice commands or eye-tracking integration.

5.4 *Comparative analysis: MediaPipe vs. LEAP motion and kinect*

Based on development and testing experiences, the following comparative summary was compiled:

Table 5. Comparative analysis of each tool.

Evaluation Criteria	MediaPipe	LEAP Motion	Kinect
Hardware Requirements	None (standard webcam)	Dedicated device	Dedicated device
Real-Time Responsiveness	High	Medium	Medium
Platform Support	Cross-platform	Windows/ Mac only	Mostly Windows
Development Flexibility	High (open-source)	Medium	Low
Recognition Accuracy	High	Medium	Lower-medium
Cost	Low	High	High

MediaPipe stands out as a cost-effective, flexible, and scalable solution. It works with standard cameras, is fully open-source, and is backed by Google's development support—making it especially suitable for educational and interactive system applications.

In summary, MediaPipe has proven to be a stable, responsive, and versatile gesture recognition solution, effectively applied to an interactive e-book scenario. It enhances usability while demonstrating strong potential for future development in multi-functional gesture-based interfaces.

6 RESULTS AND DISCUSSION

6.1 *Research findings*

This study focused on the application of MediaPipe gesture recognition technology within interactive e-book interfaces. By integrating it with the TouchDesigner platform, a contactless interaction system was developed and tested for technical feasibility and user acceptance. The key findings are as follows:

1. High Recognition Performance: MediaPipe reliably recognized various static and dynamic gestures, with overall accuracy surpassing that of LEAP Motion and Kinect, indicating strong potential for use in natural human-computer interaction scenarios.
2. Enhanced Interaction Features: The system extended traditional e-book functions beyond page-turning to include paragraph selection, text annotation, and bookmark insertion, increasing the flexibility and depth of user interaction.
3. Positive User Feedback: Based on surveys and observational data, most users found the gesture interaction intuitive and smooth, contributing to higher engagement and learning motivation.

6.2 *Merits of gesture-based interaction*

The study confirms that gesture control not only supports basic navigation but also enables more complex interactive behaviors. This opens new possibilities for e-book interface design. As a form of Natural User Interface (NUI), gesture interaction is especially suitable for applications in education, exhibitions, and visual learning materials, where immersive and context-rich experiences are critical.

6.3 *Limitations and areas for improvement*

Despite the promising results, several limitations remain:

1. Environmental Sensitivity: Recognition accuracy can be affected by lighting conditions and background complexity. Incorporating auto-calibration or image preprocessing mechanisms is recommended.
2. Gesture Misrecognition: Fast or unclear gestures may trigger incorrect responses. Future systems could integrate auxiliary inputs such as voice commands or eye-tracking to improve accuracy.
3. Limited Device Compatibility: The system was only tested on PC and webcam setups; support for mobile platforms and AR/VR devices remains underdeveloped.

6.4 *Future development directions*

Future work may explore the following directions:

1. Cross-Platform Deployment: Enhance support for smartphones, tablets, and AR devices using platforms like Unity or WebGL.
2. Multimodal Integration: Combine gesture control with voice input, gaze tracking, and environmental sensing to better interpret user intent.
3. Personalized Interaction Design: Incorporate AI-driven models to dynamically adjust gesture sensitivity and function mapping based on user behavior.

4. Expanded Application Scenarios: Extend usage to interactive learning environments such as digital textbooks, museum guides, and smart classrooms.

In summary, the prototype system developed in this study demonstrates the practical potential of gesture-based interaction in digital reading contexts. It offers a concrete reference for future research and design of more natural and immersive human-computer interfaces.

REFERENCES

Billinghurst, M., Clark, A., and Lee, G. (2015). A survey of augmented reality. *Foundations and Trends in Human–Computer Interaction*, 8(2–3), 73–272.

Cheng, C. Y., Lin, P. J., and Hsu, T. H. (2019). *Gesture-based control in digital textbooks: Limitations and future opportunities. Journal of Interactive Media*, 15 (1), 33–48.

Huang, M., Lee, Y., and Chang, H. (2022). *Gesture-based interaction in digital reading environments: A comparative study of user experience. International Journal of Human-Computer Studies*, 158, 102738.

Huang, M., Lee, Y., and Chang, H. (2022). *Gesture-based interaction in digital reading environments: A comparative study of user experience. International Journal of Human-Computer Studies*, 158, 102738.

Karam, M., and Schraefel, M. C. (2005). *A Taxonomy of Gestures in Human Computer Interactions. Technical Report.*

Karam, M., and Schraefel, M. C. (2005). *A Taxonomy of Gestures in Human Computer Interactions. Technical Report.*

Lin, C. H., and Chen, W. J. (2020). Designing natural interaction in e-learning platforms: a gesture-based approach. *Computers & Education*, 148, 103807.

Lin, C. H., and Chen, W. J. (2020). Designing natural interaction in e-learning platforms: A gesture-based approach. *Computers & Education*, 148, 103807.

Lugaresi, C., Tang, J., Nash, H., et al. (2019). *MediaPipe: A Framework for Building Perception Pipelines. arXiv preprint arXiv*:1906.08172.

Lugaresi, C., Tang, J., Nash, H., et al. (2019). *MediaPipe: A Framework for Building Perception Pipelines. arXiv preprint arXiv*:1906.08172.

Ren, Z., Yuan, J., Meng, J., and Zhang, Z. (2013). Robust part-based hand gesture recognition using Kinect sensor. *IEEE Transactions on Multimedia*, 15 (5), 1110–1120.

Tsai, J. R., Huang, Y. C., and Wu, S. C. (2021). A study on the accessibility of touchless interaction in digital reading systems. *Universal Access in the Information Society*, 20(3), 601–613.

Turan, M., Zeppelzauer, M., and Gürpinar, F. (2021). *Deep learning-based hand gesture recognition: A review. Pattern Recognition Letters*, 145, 106–118.

Weichert, F., Bachmann, D., Rudak, B., and Fisseler, D. (2013). *Analysis of the accuracy and robustness of the Leap Motion controller. Sensors*, 13(5), 6380–6393.

Wigdor, D., and Wixon, D. (2011). *Brave NUI World: Designing Natural User Interfaces for Touch and Gesture.* Elsevier.

Wigdor, D., and Wixon, D. (2011). *Brave NUI World: Designing Natural User Interfaces for Touch and Gesture.* Elsevier.

Zhang, X., Liu, S., and Wu, H. (2021). Lightweight real-time hand gesture recognition using MediaPipe and convolutional networks. *Journal of Ambient Intelligence and Humanized Computing*, 12, 8853–8863.

Zhang, Z. (2012). *Microsoft Kinect sensor and its effect. IEEE Multimedia*, 19(2), 4–10.

System Innovation for a Global Economy – Lam et al. (Eds)
© 2026 The Author(s), ISBN 978-1-041-10520-6

Exploring polychronicity, computing devices choices, and interface behaviors among generations in online learning

Ssu-Min Chang
Master Program of Innovation and Design, National Taipei University of Technology, Taipei, Taiwan

Meng-Cong Zheng
Department of Industrial Design, National Taipei University of Technology, Taipei, Taiwan

ABSTRACT: Multitasking is common in contemporary online learning environments. This study investigates generational differences (X, Y, Z) in online learning polychronicity, device selection, and interface operation habits. A questionnaire survey was conducted using convenience sampling, collecting responses from 115 participants. Data were analyzed using one-way ANOVA, Friedman Test, and Kruskal-Wallis test. Results showed that Generation X scored significantly lower than Generations Y and Z in the "Involvement with people" dimension, and lower than Generation Z in "Scheduling preference." In daily life, Generations X and Y preferred "Single Device - Window Switching," while Generation Z favored "Single Device - Split Screen," used at a significantly higher frequency. For static learning materials, Generation X preferred "Multi-Device (with Monitor) - Extended Desktop," while Generations Y and Z showed a clear preference for "Single Device - Split Screen." In contrast, all generations preferred "Multi-Device (with Monitor) - Extended Desktop" when engaging with dynamic learning materials. Overall, Generation X prefers linear tasks and screen-switching on larger, full-screen devices. Generation Y also leans toward linear tasks but selects devices and interfaces based on task context. Generation Z demonstrates a strong preference for dynamic, multi-screen interfaces that support fast task switching. These findings underscore the importance of recognizing generational differences to optimize online learning environments and enhance learning experiences across age groups.

1 INTRODUCTION

Online learning has become the most prevalent application in educational institutions (Younas *et al.* 2021), gradually superseding traditional face-to-face teaching as the preferred choice for most learners due to its accessibility and cost-effectiveness (McCarthy 2015).

However, in terms of digital usage, Lissitsa and Laor (2021) posit that the differing personality traits of different generations contribute to their divergent motivations for playing online video and audio. With regard to the phenomenon of information overload in modern society, Generation Z is reported to be more inclined to consume brief messages and visual content due to their long-term immersion in digital platforms (Hampton and Keys 2017). They also express a preference for blended learning methods that combine technology and multimedia content, such as learning through images, videos, and audio (Seemiller & Grace 2017). These differences may have implications for their selection of devices and the manner in which they engage with online learning environments.

Furthermore, multitasking is a common occurrence in online learning environments, such as when watching an instructional video and operating software concurrently. Indeed, the human cognitive system is not well equipped to absorb and process multitasking information (Wannagat *et al.* 2024), and rapid and repetitive switching between tasks may lead to resource allocation and reduced learning performance (Salvucci and Taatgen 2008). Polychronicity is generally considered to be a preference for multitasking (Howard *et al.* 2023). Polychronicity can be divided into three dimensions: "scheduling preference, involvement with people and time tangibility" (Capdeferro *et al.* 2014). This is a concept and measure that can help to understand behaviors during online learning.

Drawing upon the extant literature, this study aspires to achieve a more profound comprehension of multitasking behavior during online learning by investigating the disparities in multitasking, and computing devices selection and interface operation preferences across diverse generations. The following research hypotheses are thus proposed:

H1: There is a significant difference in the tendency of multitasking when learning online among different generations.

H2: Generations differ in their usual computing devices choices and interface operation habits.

H3: Generational differences affect the choice of computing devices and interface preferences in online learning.

2 METHODOLOGY

2.1 *Participants and sampling procedure*

This study's participants were drawn from Generation X (Uçar *et al.* 2024), Generation Y (Scheling and Richter

DOI: 10.1201/9781003655534-29

2021), and Generation Z (Fu *et al.* 2024). However, due to the presence of overlapping years between each generation, this study referenced the work of Carrier *et al.* (2009) for the classification of generations. The categorization of generations was conducted based on the year of birth, with the interval of Generation X, Y, and Z divided into those born in 1965-1979, 1980-1994, and 1995-2010. The recruitment of subjects was limited to individuals aged 18-65 years (adult but not yet retired).

devices and interface operation methods (see Figure 1). A 5-point Likert scale was adopted to investigate the frequency of typical use (never, seldom, sometimes, often, and always), and a ranking question was used to investigate the preference of computing devices and interface operation when using static or dynamic teaching materials for online learning.

Table 1. Four types of screen interaction modes categorized by the number of devices and interface operation method.

Illustration	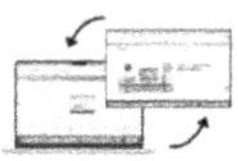			
Device Configuration	Single Device	Single Device	Multi-Device (with Monitor)	Multi-Device (with Monitor/Tablet/Phone)
Screen Interaction Mode	Window Switching	Split Screen	Extended Desktop	Independent Screen (No Desktop Extension)

Convenience sampling was adopted, with recruitment conducted through an online platform. Prior to commencing the questionnaire, written informed consent was obtained from each participant. The final number of valid questionnaires received was 115. The mean age of the respondents was 39.50 years (SD = 9.76), with 29 respondents belonging to Generation X, 63 to Generation Y, and 23 to Generation Z. The demographic composition of the study sample is summarized as follows: 77% female, 37% male, and 1% non-binary. With respect to educational attainment, the sample included five respondents from junior high schools (including those below junior high school level), 42 from high schools, 35 from universities, and 33 from graduate schools (including those with master's degrees and doctorates)

2.2 *Instruments*

2.2.1 *Multitasking behavior during online learning*

The present study used the multidimensional polychronicity scale for information technology learning, as proposed by Luo *et al.* (2021), which comprises three components. These components are time tangibility (TT), involvement with people (IP), and scheduling preference (SP). The study used a 5-point Likert scale to assess the responses, where 1 represented "completely disagree" and 5 represented "strongly agree".

2.2.2 *A survey of computing devices, selection and interface operation*

The different screen interaction modes were classified into four categories according to the number of

2.3 *Data analysis methods*

The present study used Python for the execution of the statistical analyses, adopting the following methodologies:

2.3.1 *One-Way ANOVA*

This study used one-way ANOVA to test whether there were significant differences between generations X, Y and Z in terms of multitasking behavior during online learning, computing device habits and interface operation. Where the results of the ANOVA indicated a significant level, the Tukey HSD post hoc test was used.

2.3.2 *Friedman test*

The Friedman Test was adopted in this study to examine the ranking of preferences for computing devices selection and interface operation in online learning contexts of different learning materials (static learning materials/dynamic learning materials) within the same generation. In instances where the Friedman test attained a significant level, the Nemenyi test was conducted.

2.3.3 *Kruskal-Wallis test*

The Kruskal-Wallis H test was used in this study to compare the differences in the ranking of preferences for computing devices selection and interface operation in online learning contexts with different types of learning materials (static learning materials/dynamic learning materials) across generations. In cases where the test results indicated significant differences, the Dunn-Bonferroni test was used.

3 RESULTS

3.1 *Polychronicity differences across generations in online learning contexts*

The findings of the one-way analysis of variance (ANOVA) revealed that there was no significant difference in "time tangibility" between the different generations. However, a significant divergence was observed between generations with regard to "interpersonal communication" and "scheduling preference" (F = 8.8627, p = 0.0003; F = 4.7262, p = 0.0107). The Tukey HSD post-hoc test revealed that there were significant differences in "involvement with people" between Generation X and Generation Y (p = 0.0061), and between Generation X and Generation Z (p = 0.0003), with Generation X being significantly higher than Generation Y and Generation Z. In terms of "scheduling preference", a significant difference was observed between Generation X and Generation Z (p = 0.0075), with Generation X being significantly higher than Generation Z (see Table 2 for descriptive statistics of multidimensional polychronicity for online learning across generations).

Table 2. The descriptive statistics on the frequency of computing devices and interface operations used in disparate generations.

	Time tangibility		Involvement with people		Scheduling preference	
	M	SD	M	SD	M	SD
Generation X	4.02	0.64	3.97	0.68	3.79	0.76
Generation Y	3.87	0.54	3.49	0.70	3.45	0.86
Generation Z	3.97	0.69	3.20	0.63	3.07	0.91

* *The background color of the table is indicated by yellow to denote significant differences between groups.* * *The fonts are marked in red for scores that are significantly higher than average, and in blue for scores that are significantly lower than average.*

3.2 *Generational differences in device selection and interface operation in daily life*

In terms of mean frequency, Generations X and Y most frequently use the practice of "Single Device - Window Switching", while Generation Z most frequently adopts "Single Device - Split Screen". The least frequently used practice by these three generations is "Multi-Device (with Monitor) - Extended Desktop".

The results of one-way analysis of variance (ANOVA) demonstrated a statistically significant difference in the use of "Single Device - Split Screen" across different generations (F = 5.5397, p = 0.0051). A Tukey HSD post-hoc test revealed that the differences between Generation X and Z (p = 0.0124) and Generation Y and Z (p = 0.0066) were significant, with Generation Z demonstrating a higher level of use compared to Generation X and Y.

3.3 *Generational preferences for device use and interface operation in online learning (Static/ Dynamic Materials)*

In terms of mean ranking, Generation X demonstrates a preference for "Multi-Device (with Monitor)

Table 3. The descriptive statistics on frequency of screen interaction modes in disparate generations.

	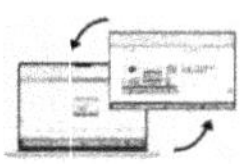							
Screen Interaction Modes	M	SD	M	SD	M	SD	M	SD
Generation X	4.17	1.31	3.66	1.14	3.24	1.15	3.41	0.95
Generation Y	4.27	1.49	3.73	1.67	3.22	1.78	3.52	1.75
Generation Z	4.70	1.22	4.83	1.07	3.26	2.09	4.04	1.61

* *The background color of the table is indicated by yellow to denote significant differences between groups.* * *The fonts are marked in red for scores that are significantly higher than average, and in blue for scores that are significantly lower than average.*

Table 4. The mean rankings of computing devices and interface preferences by generation when learning online (static/dynamic materials).

Computing Devices and Interface Operation Types		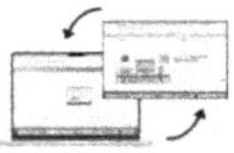			
Static teaching materials	**Generation X**	2.34	**2.62**	1.93	3.10
	Generation Y	2.44	2.41	2.49	2.65
	Generation Z	2.83	1.91	2.35	2.91
Dynamic teaching materials	**Generation X**	2.17	2.45	2.17	3.21
	Generation Y	2.71	2.44	2.16	2.68
	Generation Z	2.91	2.52	2.22	**2.35**

* It is evident that a lower average is indicative of a higher ranking. * The background color of the table is indicated by yellow to denote significant differences between groups. * The fonts are marked in red indicate significant differences within groups.

- Extended Desktop" when static teaching materials are adopted. In contrast, Generations Y and Z demonstrate a stronger preference for "Single Device - Split Screen". However, when dynamic teaching materials are adopted, a uniform prioritization of the "Multi-Device (with Monitor) - Extended Desktop" option emerges across all three generations, with the "Single Device - Window Switching" option being the most preferred choice among Generation X.

3.3.1 *Static learning materials*

Friedman's test demonstrated that Generation Y did not exhibit any significant differences across the four modes of operation, whereas Generation X and Generation Z each demonstrated significant differences ($\chi^2 = 12.64$, $p = 0.0055$; $\chi^2 = 8.90$, $p = 0.0307$). Nemenyi test further demonstrated a significant difference between Generation X's preference for the "Multi-Device (with Monitor) - Extended Desktop" option and the "Multi-Device (with Monitor/Tablet/Phone) - Independent Screen" ($p = 0.0031$), indicating a stronger inclination towards the "Multi-Device (with Monitor) - Extended Desktop" approach among Generation X. In contrast, a significant difference was identified ($p = 0.0428$) between the preferences for "Single Device - Split Screen" and "Multi-Device (with Monitor/Tablet/Phone) - Independent Screen" among Generation Z, indicating a propensity for the latter. It is evident that for both Generation X and Z, the "Multi-Device (with Monitor/Tablet/Phone) - Independent Screen" option is unequivocally the least preferred choice.

3.3.2 *Dynamic learning materials*

Friedman's test revealed a significant difference exclusively for Generation X ($\chi^2 = 12.48$, $p = 0.0059$). Further Nemenyi test revealed significant differences between Generation X for the categories of "Multi-Device (with Monitor/Tablet/Phone) - Independent Screen" and "Single Device - Window Switching" ($p = 0.0122$), and between "Multi-Device (with Monitor/Tablet/Phone) - Independent Screen" and "Multi-Device (with Monitor) - Extended Desktop" ($p = 0.0122$). The results of the study indicated a clear preference among Generation X for the "Single Device - Window Switching" and "Multi-Device (with Monitor) - Extended Desktop" categories, but a clear disinclination for "Multi-Device (with Monitor/Tablet/Phone) - Independent Screen".

3.4 *Comparison* of *Generational Preferences for Devices and Interfaces in Online Learning (Static/Dynamic Materials)*

3.4.1 *Static learning materials*

The Kruskal-Wallis test demonstrated that "Single Device - Split Screen" was statistically significant ($H = 6.5618$, $p = 0.0376$). Furthermore, Dunn-Bonferroni test post-test revealed that Generation Z exhibited significantly higher sorting choices compared to Generation X.

3.4.2 *Dynamic learning materials*

The Kruskal-Wallis test demonstrated that both "Single Device - Window Switching" and "Multi-Device (with Monitor/Tablet/Phone) - Independent Screen (No Desktop Extension)" met the significant standard ($H = 6.0256$, $p = 0.0492$; $H = 8.0373$, $p = 0.0180$). Dunn-Bonferroni test revealed that there was no significant difference between the groups for "Single Device - Window Switching". However, Generation Z was significantly higher than Generation X in the ranking of choices for "Multi-Device (with Monitor/Tablet/Phone) - Independent Screen (No Desktop Extension)".

4 DISCUSSION

4.1 *Interpretation of generational polychronicity in online learning*

The findings revealed no significant differences in "time tangibility" among generations; yet distinct variations emerged in "involvement with people" and "scheduling preference." Generation X demonstrated higher scores in "interpersonal communication," indicating a stronger propensity for interactive features and collaborative learning modes. In contrast, Generations Y and Z exhibited a preference for independent learning. Prior studies (Elshami *et al.* 2021) indicate that Generation Z students may experience anxiety in online discussions, potentially due to concerns about misinterpretation, which could explain their lower interpersonal scores. Furthermore, Generation X demonstrated a marked preference for multitasking and frequent task-switching, as evidenced by their significantly higher scores in the "scheduling preference" domain compared to Generation Z. A further finding suggests that, within the paradigm of media multitasking, Generation X has been observed engaging in paper-based tasks concurrently with media consumption (Voorveld and Van der Goot 2013), which may be the reason why this generation has a higher multitasking score.

4.2 *Implications of device and interface preferences across generations*

The device usage habits of different generations are shaped by environmental exposure and technological familiarity. A comparative analysis of device usage habits across generations reveals a distinct trend. A comparative analysis of device usage habits across generations reveals a distinct trend: Generation X and Y predominantly adopt a "Single Device - Window Switching" mode, while Generation Z exhibits a preference for "Single Device - Split Screen". ANOVA results confirmed that Generation Z's use of split-screen mode is significantly higher than that of the other groups. Research supports the notion that Generation Y frequently switches between media (Brasel and Gips 2011) and is generally more adaptive to emerging platforms (Voorveld and Van der Goot 2013). However, Generation Z, who have been raised in a digital-native context (Prasanna and Priyanka 2024), has been observed to demonstrate a marked preference for visual content in the online environment that is easily comprehensible and which saves time (Rajapakse 2018). This proclivity for visual engagement may have influenced Generation Z's propensity to adopt the technique of dividing the screen into multiple frames, a strategy that is theorized to assist in the management of their limited attention span while ensuring the autonomy in the selection of the learning input they receive.

4.3 *Optimizing the learning experience based on generational interface needs*

The selection of device varies depending on the format of the learning material. While all generations tend to use a single device in everyday scenarios, learning contexts reveal different behaviors. For static materials, Generation X demonstrates a preference for "multi-device/extended desktop" configurations, while Generations Y and Z exhibit a propensity for "single-device/picture split" approaches. In dynamic content scenarios, a preference for "multi-device/extended desktop" is exhibited by all generations, potentially attributable to the elevated screen demand characteristic of animated or video-based content.

The study revealed that single devices are more frequently used in everyday life. However, in circumstances where online learning is necessary, the preference is for Split Screen or multiple devices. This phenomenon underscores the multitasking nature of online learning. The consistent preference of Generation X for multiple screens indicates a need for larger screens and full-screen displays. In contrast, Generations Y and Z exhibit a predilection for learning on a single screen when engaging with less visually demanding static materials. This finding aligns with the observations of increased appeal of mobile learning among younger generations, although larger screens continue to offer superior usability (Nurhudatiana *et al.* 2018).

4.4 *Design considerations for inclusive online learning tools*

As posited by Chang (2015), generational differences have been demonstrated to exert a substantial influence on the adoption and use of digital devices and interfaces. The results of this study demonstrate that Generation X may prefer linear tasks and switch back and forth between tasks, and that interface operation is characterized by switching screens and requires a larger screen, with a preference for full-screen mode. Generation Y still has a certain tendency towards linear tasks, but does not have a specific computing device preference. They may choose computing devices and interface operation modes according to the context of the task. Generation Z, meanwhile, prefers a dynamic, multiplexed interface, which uses multiple screens for operation, such as splitting the screen or multiple screens to quickly switch attention between tasks.

The configuration that received the lowest ranking across all generations was "Multi-Device (with Monitor/Tablet/Phone) - Independent Screen", suggesting a preference for screen continuity and contextual coherence. Generation Z in particular show a high level of fluency in multitasking, often adapting their use of the screen according to the type of content. However, visualized information can cause varying degrees of additional cognitive load (Zheng and Chen 2022). Cognitive load and the user's learning experience need to be considered in the design of instructional materials and interfaces.

5 CONCLUSION

In the context of the increasing prevalence of digital learning environments, the capacity of learners to select from a range of computing devices and operating modes has become paramount. The increasing prevalence of electronic devices and the inundation of information have resulted in the accumulation of cognitive, emotional and physical burdens. The findings of this study can serve as a valuable reference point for the design of e-learning systems that are better tailored to the needs of diverse learners. It is hoped that in the future, suitable design principles for carriers and interfaces can be identified, with the aim of reducing cognitive loads and enhancing learning efficiency in e-learning contexts and according to the characteristics of different learners.

REFERENCES

Brasel, S. A., and Gips, J. (2011). Media multitasking behavior: Concurrent television and computer usage. *Cyberpsychology, Behavior, and Social Networking, 14* (9), 527–534. https://doi.org/10.1089/cyber.2010.0350

Capdeferro, N., Romero, M., and Barberà, E. (2014). Polychronicity: review of the literature and a new configuration for the study of this hidden dimension of online learning. *Distance Education, 35*(3), 294–310. https://doi.org/ 10.1080/01587919.2015.955249

Carrier, L. M., Cheever, N. A., Rosen, L. D., Benitez, S., and Chang, J. (2009). Multitasking across generations: Multitasking choices and difficulty ratings in three generations of Americans. *Computers in Human Behavior, 25*(2), 483–489. https://doi.org/10.1016/j.chb.2008.10.012

Chang, Y. M. (2015). Media multitasking across generations: Simultaneous mobile internet and television usage behaviors and motives. *Mass Communication Research, 124*, 83–116.

Elshami, W., Saravanan, C., Taha, M. H., Abdalla, M. E., Abuzaid, M., and Al Kawas, S. (2021). Bridging the gap in online learning anxiety among different generations in health professions education. *Sultan Qaboos University Medical Journal, 21*(4), 539. https://doi.org/10.18295/squmj.4.2021.040

Fu, M., Fraser, B., and Arcodia, C. (2024). Digital natives on the rise: A systematic literature review on generation Z's engagement with RAISA technologies in hospitality services. *International Journal of Hospitality Management, 122*, 103885. https://doi.org/10.1016/j.ijhm.2024.103885

Hampton, D. C., and Keys, Y. (2017). Generation Z students: Will they change our nursing classrooms. *Journal of Nursing Education and Practice, 7*(4), 111–115. https://doi.org/10.5430/jnep.v7n4p111

Howard, M. C., and Cogswell, J. E. (2023). A meta-analysis of polychronicity: Applying modern perspectives of multitasking and person-environment fit. *Organizational Psychology Review, 13*(3), 315–347. https://doi.org/10.1177/20413866221143370

Lissitsa, S., and Laor, T. (2021). Baby boomers, generation X and generation Y: Identifying generational differences in effects of personality traits in on-demand radio use. *Technology in society, 64*, 101526. https://doi.org/10.1016/j.techsoc.2021.101526

Luo, Y. F., Yang, S. C., and Lu, C. M. (2021). Development of a multidimensional polychronicity scale for information technology learning. *Journal of Computer Assisted Learning, 37*(2), 387–395. https://doi.org/10.1111/jcal.12496

McCarthy, J. (2015). Learning in the Café: Pilot testing the collaborative application for education in Facebook. *Australasian Journal of Educational Technology, 31*(1). https://doi.org/10.14742/ajet.1500

Nurhudatiana, A., Hiu, A. N., and Ce, W. (2018, September). *Should I use laptop or smartphone? A usability study on an online learning application.* In 2018 International Conference on Information Management and Technology (ICIMTech) (pp. 565–570). IEEE. https://doi.org/10.1109/ICIMTech.2018.8528134

Prasanna, M. P., and Priyanka, A. L. (2024). Marketing to Gen Z: Understanding the preferences and behaviors of next generation. *International Journal For Multidisciplinary Research*, 6. https://doi.org/10.36948/ijfmr.2024.v06i04.26612

Rajapakse, A. (2018, May). *Generation Y and Generation Z visual attention in the online environment: Evidence from eye tracking and laddering.* Paper presented at the 2018 NeuroPsychoEconomics Conference, Zürich, Switzerland.

Salvucci, D. D., and Taatgen, N. A. (2008). Threaded cognition: an integrated theory of concurrent multitasking. *Psychological review, 115*(1), 101. https://doi.org/10.1037/0033-295X.115.1.101

Scheling, L., and Richter, D. (2021). Generation Y: Do millennials need a partner to be happy? *Journal of Adolescence, 90*, 23–31. https://doi.org/10.1016/j.adolescent.2021.05.006

Seemiller, C., and Grace, M. (2017). Generation Z: Educating and engaging the next generation of students. *About Campus, 22*(3), 21–26. https://doi.org/10.1002/abc.21293

Uçar, Ö., Çelik, S., Karahan, E., Altıntaş, S., and Yücel, M. (2024). Exploring the relationship between spiritual care and patient advocacy of nurses from generations X, Y and Z working in intensive care clinics: A cross-sectional study. *Intensive and Critical Care Nursing, 84*, 103754. https://doi.org/10.1016/j.iccn.2024.103754

Voorveld, H. A., and Van der Goot, M. (2013). Age differences in media multitasking: A diary study. *Journal of broadcasting & electronic media, 57*(3), 392–408. https://doi.org/10.1080/08838151.2013.816709

Wannagat, W., Martin, T., Nieding, G., Rohleder, N., & Becker, L. (2024). Media Multitasking: Performance differences between younger and older adults and the role of working memory. *Computers in Human Behavior*, 108313. https://doi.org/10.1016/j.chb.2024.108313

Younas, A., Faisal, C. N., Habib, M. A., Ashraf, R., and Ahmad, M. (2021). Role of design attributes to determine the intention to use online learning via cognitive beliefs. *IEEE Access, 9*, 94181–94202.

Zheng, M. C., and Chen, C. Y. (2022). Types of major league baseball broadcast information and their impacts on audience experience. *Informatics 2022*, 9(4), 82; https://doi.org/10.3390/informatics9040082

System Innovation for a Global Economy – Lam et al. (Eds)
© 2026 The Author(s), ISBN 978-1-041-10520-6

The power of diversity: Board knowledge, social capital, and innovation success

Jung-Ho Lai
Department of Finance, National Taipei University of Business, Taipei, Taiwan

ABSTRACT: This study examines the strategic role of board diversity in fostering product innovation and enhancing firm performance within high-tech industries. Addressing the ongoing debate surrounding the benefits and limitations of board diversity, it highlights the shift from traditional measures of demographic diversity (e.g., gender, ethnicity, and age) to a focus on board knowledge and information diversity, which more comprehensively capture the directors' human and social capital. Using an event-study methodology, the research analyzes 395 new product introduction (NPI) announcements from publicly listed firms, evaluating their economic impact through cumulative abnormal returns. The findings reveal that board knowledge diversity significantly boosts market reactions, particularly for high-novelty NPIs. Conversely, board information diversity does not exhibit a measurable effect, potentially due to diminished oversight from directors holding multiple board memberships. The study further identifies moderating factors, demonstrating that the positive influence of board knowledge diversity is amplified in the case of highly novel products, while it diminishes as firm size increases. These results emphasize the contextual nature of board diversity's impact on innovation performance. This research provides valuable insights for corporate governance by illustrating how board capital can be strategically leveraged to drive innovation and value creation, especially in environments characterized by high risk and high reward, such as those involving NPIs.

1 INTRODUCTION

The strategic relevance of board diversity in shaping firm outcomes has long intrigued researchers, though the empirical findings remain inconsistent. While proponents suggest that diverse boards bring a wide array of perspectives that improve problem-solving, strategic direction, and resource allocation (Carter *et al.* 2003; Phan and Yu 2022), critics argue that such diversity may hinder consensus and communication, thereby impairing firm performance (Anderson *et al.* 2011; Nurrizkiana *et al.* 2024). Much of the existing literature has focused on demographic indicators of diversity such as gender, ethnicity, and age. However, these observable characteristics only partially capture the cognitive and social resources directors contribute to board deliberations. Consequently, this study advances the literature by examining board knowledge diversity (human capital) and board information diversity (social capital) and their specific influence on innovation performance, particularly during New Product Introduction (NPI) events. Innovation contexts—characterized by complexity and risk—are ideal for evaluating the strategic value of diverse board capital, as they demand both creative thinking and access to external knowledge and networks. While traditional proxies of innovation performance such as R&D expenditure and patent counts offer some insight (Frick *et al.* 2021; Morales *et al.* 2024), they often fail to directly capture market valuation or product success. To overcome these limitations, this research employs event-study methodology to examine stock market responses to NPI announcements. This approach is grounded in the efficient market hypothesis (Brown and Warner 1985), which asserts that financial markets respond immediately to new information. Thus, abnormal returns around NPI announcements reflect investors' assessment of the innovation's potential impact on firm value. Moreover, this study incorporates two contingency factors—product newness and firm size—to further understand when and how board diversity plays a more critical role in value creation.

2 HYPOTHESIS DEVELOPMENT

The literature suggests that the success of NPIs—of which failure rates often exceed 80% (Victory *et al.* 2021; Frick *et al.* 2021)—depends heavily on the firm's strategic decision-making infrastructure, of which the board is a crucial component. However, studies exploring the relationship between board diversity and innovation have

DOI: 10.1201/9781003655534-30

largely emphasized demographic traits, producing mixed and often contradictory results (Griffin *et al.* 2020; Schifilliti and La Rocca 2024). A more refined lens is needed—one that focuses on cognitive and relational capital embedded within the board. Board knowledge diversity, defined by the functional background and expertise of directors, equips the board with multifaceted problem-solving capacity crucial for navigating the complex phases of NPI development (Griffin *et al.* 2020). These capabilities are especially salient during early stages of innovation when technical and strategic challenges are greatest.

In parallel, board information diversity—rooted in directors' social networks and multiple board affiliations—provides the firm with timely access to critical market data, strategic partnerships, and funding opportunities (Burt 1992; Koskinen and Edling 2012). Such networks can facilitate faster recognition of trends and more effective responses to market shifts. Although theoretically compelling, empirical support for the influence of board information diversity remains limited, especially in high-stakes innovation settings.

Contextual factors also moderate the board diversity–performance relationship. High-newness NPIs introduce significant uncertainty but also higher potential returns. In such cases, the combination of diverse perspectives and expansive external networks becomes especially valuable (Jin *et al.* 2019; Mahsina and Agustia 2023). Conversely, large firms—despite possessing more resources—may dilute the influence of board capital due to organizational complexity and bureaucratic inertia (Sánchez *et al.* 2017; Kim 2022). Therefore, this study hypothesizes that board knowledge and information diversity will more strongly impact innovation outcomes in smaller firms and for more novel products.

3 SAMPLE AND METHODOLOGY

The study analyzes 395 NPI announcements from 248 U.S.-listed high-tech firms between the years covered in the dataset. Firms were included if they were listed on NYSE, AMEX, or NASDAQ, and their announcements met specific criteria: no confounding events within five days, availability of return data (CRSP), and full director biographies (SEC filings). NPIs were identified using keywords such as "launch" and "introduce" in Lexis/Nexis.

Innovation performance was measured using two-day cumulative abnormal returns (CAR [-1, 0]) to capture market reactions to NPIs. Expected returns were estimated via the market model, adjusted against the CRSP value-weighted index (Brown and Warner 1985). Board knowledge diversity was quantified using Blau's Index across ten professional categories (e.g., legal, finance, R&D), reflecting the variety of human capital on the board (Timmerman 2000). Board information diversity was assessed through "industry embeddedness," calculated as the number of external board seats in the same industry (Haynes and Hillman 2010).

Moderating variables included firm size (log of total assets) and product newness (binary-coded based on whether the product was radically new or incremental, following Wang *et al.* 2011). Control variables were added for R&D intensity, marketing capabilities, investment opportunities (Tobin's Q), debt ratio, board independence, and director age. Multicollinearity was mitigated using mean-centering and interaction terms were constructed accordingly.

4 EMPIRICAL RESULTS

Regression results confirm that board knowledge diversity significantly and positively influences market reactions to NPI announcements, supporting Hypothesis 1. The positive and statistically significant coefficient suggests that diverse functional expertise enhances decision quality and investor confidence during high-stakes innovation events. However, Hypothesis 2 is not supported; board information diversity was found to have no significant effect. One potential explanation is the phenomenon of board "busyness," where directors serving on multiple boards may lack the time or focus required for effective oversight (Falato *et al.* 2014).

Moderation analyses revealed further nuances. High-newness products benefit more from board knowledge diversity, confirming Hypothesis 3. These findings align with theoretical expectations that more novel products require greater creativity, foresight, and strategic guidance—all benefits conferred by a knowledgeable board (Griffin *et al.* 2020). Likewise, Hypothesis 4 is supported: firm size negatively moderates the effect of knowledge diversity. In smaller firms, board expertise plays a more central role in shaping innovation strategies, whereas in larger firms, internal complexity may limit the board's influence. Notably, these moderation effects were observed only for board knowledge diversity, not board information diversity.

Robustness checks validated these findings across alternative model specifications. Substituting a simplified Blau's Index and adjusting the event window (CAR [-1,1]) yielded consistent results. The significance of board knowledge diversity and its interaction with newness and firm size remained intact. Visual plots further confirmed that the impact of board diversity is strongest in smaller firms and for novel NPIs.

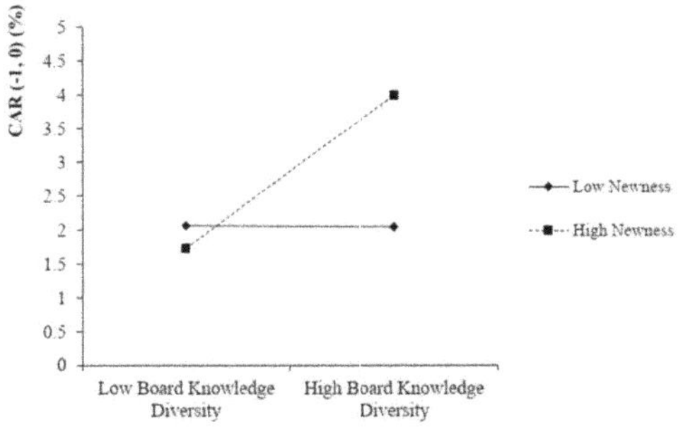

Figure 1: The Moderating Effect of the Degree of New Product Newness on the Relationship between Board Knowledge Diversity and Abnormal Returns of NPI Announcements.

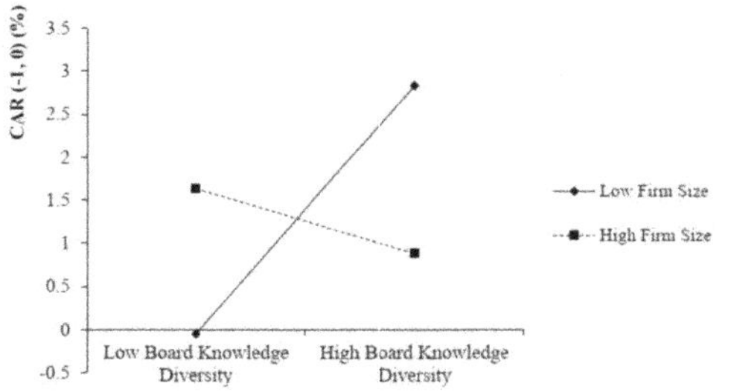

Figure 2: The Moderating Effect of Firm Size on the Relationship between Board Knowledge Diversity and Abnormal Returns of NPI Announcements.

Table 1. Cross-sectional Regression Analyses of Abnormal Returns of the NPI Announcements.

Independent variables	Model 1	Model 2	Model 3	Model 4	Model 5	Model 6 (Full sample)
Intercept	0.011	0.004	0.013	0.025	0.013	0.022
	(0.340)	(0.112)	(0.389)	(0.786)	(0.417)	(0.714)
	0.250	0.224	0.240	0.204	0.195	0.178
Marketing	(2.216)**	(1.990)**	(2 096)	(1.827)*	(1.768)*	(1.620)
Intensity	0.041	0.042	0.042	0.042	0.044	0.044
R&D	(3.981)***	(4.140)***	(4.019)***	(4.164)***	(4.373)***	(4.391)***
Intensity	−0.002	−0.002	−0.002	−0.002	−0.002	−0.002
Tobin's q	(−1.281)	(−1.457)	(−1.280)	(−1.553)	(−1.432)	(−1.524)
	−0.018	−0.018	−0.018	−0.019	−0.009	−0.010
Debt-to-asset	(−1.367)	(−1.329)	(−1.329)	(−1.403)	(−0.713)	(−0.796)
Ratio	−0.001	−0.001	<−0.001	−0.001	<−0.001	<−0.001
Log (Finu	(−0.445)	(−0.619)	(−0.340)	(−0.651)	(−0.296)	(−0.335)
Size)	0.009	0.009	0.009	0.009	0.009	0.009
Newness	(1.863)*	(1.815)*	(1.851)*	(1.939)*	(1.893)*	(2.008)**
	0.003	0.003	0.003	0.003	0.002	0.002
Multiple	(1.002)	(0.802)	(0.974)	(0.982)	(0.491)	(0.668)
	−0.005	−0.004	−0.005	−0.003	−0.005	−0.004
Board	(−0.351)	(−0.295)	(−0.353)	(−0.217)	(−0.361)	(−0.286)
Independence	<−0.001	<−0.001	<−0.001	<−0.001	<−0.001	<−0.001
Board Age	(−0.290)	(−0.384)	(−0.314)	(−0.501)	(−0.462)	(−0.570)
		0.025		0.024	0.023	0.023
Board Knowledge Diversity		(2.746)***	−0.002	(2 702)***	(2.603)***	(2.566)**
Board Information Diversity			(−0.601)			
Board Knowledge Diversity				0.056		0.051
X Newness				(2.721)***		(2 565)**
Board Knowledge Diversity					−0.018	−0.017
x Log (Firm Size)					(−4.204)***	(−4.098)***
Adjusted R^2	0.058	0.074	0.057	0.089	0.112	0.125
F value	3.70***	4.14***	3.36***	4.50***	5.53***	5.69***
N	395	395	395	395	395	395

(continued)

Table 1. Continued

T-values are in parentheses.
"***", "**",and "*" represent 1%, 5%, and 10% significance levels using a two-tailed test respectively.

5 CONCLUSIONS

This study refines the understanding of board diversity by focusing on knowledge and information diversity rather than demographics. Findings indicate that board knowledge diversity positively affects investor response to NPIs, especially for novel products and in smaller firms. In contrast, board information diversity does not yield significant effects, likely due to the diminishing returns from director overextension.

These insights have practical implications for firms seeking to enhance innovation outcomes through strategic board composition. Rather than relying solely on demographic diversity, firms should assess the human and social capital of their board members to better align governance structures with innovation goals. This research also broadens the scope of corporate governance literature by demonstrating how board capital affects value creation through the lens of product innovation.

REFERENCES

Anderson, R. C., Reeb, D. M., Upadhyay, A., and Zhao, W. (2011). The economics of director heterogeneity. *Financial Management*, 40(1), 5–38.

Burt, R.S. (1992) *Structural Holes: The Social Structures of Competition*, Harvard University Press, Cambridge, MA.

Brown, S. J., and Warner, J. B. (1985). Using daily stock returns: The case of event studies. *Journal of Financial Economics*, 14(1), 3–31.

Carter, D. A., Simkins, B. J., and Simpson, W. G. (2003). Corporate governance, board diversity, and firm value. *Financial Review*, 38(1), 33–53.

Falato, A., Kadyrzhanova, D., and Lel, U. (2014). Distracted directors: Does board busyness hurt shareholder value? *Journal of Financial Economics*, 113(3), 404–426.

Frick, F., Jantke, C., and Sauer, J. (2021). Firm-level innovation and efficiency in the food sector: Insights from a literature-based innovation output indicator. *Applied Economics*, 53(43), 5000–5017.

Griffin, D., Li, K., and Xu, T. (2020). Board gender diversity and corporate innovation: International

evidence. *Journal of Financial and Quantitative Analysis*, 56(1), 123–154.
Haynes, K. T., and Hillman, A. (2010). The effect of board capital and CEO power on strategic change. *Strategic Management Journal*, 31(11), 1145–1163.
Jin, J. L., Shu, C., and Zhou, K. Z. (2019). Product newness and product performance in new ventures: Contingent roles of market knowledge breadth and tacitness. *Industrial Marketing Management*, 76, 231–241.
Kim, J. (2022). Innovation failure and firm growth: dependence on firm size and age. *Technology Analysis & Strategic Management*, 34(2), 166–179.
Koskinen, J., and Edling, C. (2012). Modelling the evolution of a bipartite network—Peer referral in interlocking directorates. *Social Networks*, 34(3), 309–322.
Mahsina, M., and Agustia, D. (2023). Does green innovation have an important role in the effect of board gender diversity and firm performance? *Intangible Capital*, 19(2), 146–164.
Morales, P., Flikkema, M., Castaldi, C., and De Man, A. (2024). When do trademarks improve the measurement of innovation? *An analysis of innovations from Dutch SMEs. Science and Public Policy*, 51(5), 923–938.
Nurrizkiana, R., Adhariani, D., Setiawan, D., and Harymawan, I. (2024). Board Effectiveness and Firm Risk: The Moderating Role of ESG Performance. *Australasian Accounting, Business and Finance Journal*, 18(1), 108–129.
Phan, T. T., and Yu, H. C. (2022). Innovation, institutional ownerships and board diversity. *Review of Quantitative Finance and Accounting*, 59(4), 1647–1693.
Sánchez, L. P. C., Guerrero-Villegas, J., and Hurtado Gonzalez, J. M. (2017). The influence of organizational factors on board roles. *Management Decision*, 55(5), 842–871.
Schifilliti, V., and La Rocca, E. T. (2024). Board gender diversity in innovative SMEs: an investigation across industrial sectors. *European Journal of Innovation Management*, 27(9), 461–486.
Timmerman, T. A. (2000). Racial diversity, age diversity, interdependence, and team performance. *Small Group Research*, 31(5), 592–606.
Victory, K., Nenycz-Thiel, M., Dawes, J., Tanusondjaja, A., and Corsi, A. M. (2021). How common is new product failure and when does it vary? *Marketing Letters*, 32, 17–32.
Wang, C. F., Chen, L. Y., and Chang, S. C. (2011). International diversification and the market value of new product introduction. *Journal of International Management*, 17(4), 333–347.

System Innovation for a Global Economy – Lam et al. (Eds)
© 2026 The Author(s), ISBN 978-1-041-10520-6

Investigation of the impact of fuel temperature control on internal combustion engine performance and exhaust emissions in an EFI system

Wei-Ting Chen & Ming-Hsien Hsueh
Department of Industrial Engineering and Management, National Kaohsiung University of Science and Technology, Taiwan

Chia-Hsin Hsieh
Department of Mechanical Engineering, National Kaohsiung University of Science and Technology, Taiwan

Chao-Jung Lai
Department of Fashion Design and Management, National Pingtung University of Science and Technology, Pingtung, Taiwan

Chia-Chi Chang & Bing-Ru Zhan
Department of Industrial Engineering and Management, National Kaohsiung University of Science and Technology, Taiwan

ABSTRACT: The internal combustion engine (ICE) has long served as the primary power source for automobiles and various other applications, relying on fuel combustion to generate energy. Common fuel types include gasoline, diesel, and liquefied petroleum gas (LPG). Compared to gasoline, LPG can effectively reduce emissions and the formation of harmful pollutants. This study investigates the effects of a fuel temperature control system on the power performance and exhaust emissions of a spark-ignition internal combustion engine. The system employs thermoelectric chips for energy conversion and an aluminum oil-cooling head for heat exchange, thereby forming a closed-loop fuel temperature control cycle. Its objective is to raise the fuel temperature to enhance fuel atomization and promote more complete combustion. Experimental results are compared with those obtained from an engine using a conventional ambient-temperature fuel system to evaluate the impact of fuel temperature variation on engine performance and emissions. The findings indicate that increasing the fuel temperature enhances engine horsepower, although the improvement diminishes progressively at higher engine speeds. Moreover, elevated fuel temperatures significantly reduce hydrocarbon (HC) and carbon monoxide (CO) emissions, with the most notable reduction observed at the optimal air-fuel ratio (A/F = 13). However, as engine speed increases, the reduction in HC emissions becomes less pronounced. Under lean combustion conditions (high air-fuel ratio), increasing the fuel temperature contributes to a reduction in nitrogen oxide (NO_x) emissions, whereas under rich combustion conditions (low air-fuel ratio), it results in a rise in NO_x emissions.

1 INTRODUCTION

The ICE is extensively utilized in transportation, power generation, and industrial machinery. However, the environmental impact of exhaust emissions from ICEs has remained a major concern for decades. While fully electric and hybrid vehicles are gaining popularity, they still face significant challenges, including limited driving range, high costs, underdeveloped charging infrastructure, and complex system integration [1]. A primary way in which ICEs affect environmental sustainability is through their emissions, which include carbon monoxide (CO), nitrogen oxides (NO_x), and particulate matter (PM). These pollutants contribute to climate change, smog formation, and various respiratory illnesses. To mitigate these adverse effects, considerable efforts have been devoted to reducing ICE emissions by enhancing combustion efficiency and promoting the use of cleaner fuels. For example, the European Union has continuously implemented increasingly stringent emission standards for fuel-powered vehicles to reduce the environmental footprint of ICEs. Extensive research is currently underway to reduce exhaust emissions from ICEs. For instance, studies have investigated the effects of achieving superheated fuel conditions on flash-boiling spray behavior by adjusting fuel temperature. When high-pressure fuel is injected into the

DOI: 10.1201/9781003655534-31

combustion chamber, flash boiling may occur, resulting in rapid vapor expansion and enhanced vaporization, which improves atomization and boosts combustion performance. Maintaining the outlet temperature of the liquefied petroleum gas (LPG) regulator between 30°C and 40°C has been shown to increase brake power by approximately 1.85% while reducing nitrogen oxide (NO_x) emissions by around 2%. Stabilizing variations in LPG density and pressure also contributes to a more consistent air-fuel ratio (AFR) in LPG injection systems. As the LPG temperature increases from 20°C to 44°C, NO_x emissions rise from 1950 ppm to 2025 ppm, representing a 3.85% increase. Lower fuel temperatures can reduce consumption while maintaining equivalent power output. Substituting gasoline with LPG in motorcycle ICEs improves emissions performance due to better air-fuel mixing, leading to a 10% increase in thermal efficiency, a 61.9% reduction in carbon monoxide (CO), a 13.3% reduction in hydrocarbon (HC), and a 14.9% reduction in NO_x. Other studies confirm that replacing gasoline with LPG enhances thermal efficiency by 6.6%, lowers fuel consumption by 6%, and cuts NO_x by 14.33%. A comparative evaluation of spark-ignition (SI) engines using syngas, gasoline, and LPG has shown that LPG's gaseous state promotes homogeneous mixing in carbureted engines, improving combustion and reducing HC emissions. Real Driving Emissions (RDE) tests have demonstrated that as ambient temperature drops from 25°C to 8°C, emissions of all pollutants except NO_x increase, since NO_x is formed at higher combustion temperatures while colder conditions reduce the effectiveness of after-treatment systems. Once the three-way catalytic converter reaches its optimal operating temperature, CO and HC emissions significantly decrease ($CO < 0.01\%$, $HC = 15$ ppm), but cold-start conditions result in elevated CO and HC due to incomplete vaporization, with minimal effect on CO_2 concentrations. Excessive fuel temperature in gasoline direct injection (GDI) engines can lead to wall-wetting and a single large fuel film, causing increased soot production, emphasizing the importance of consistent initial fuel temperature. Investigations into five-hole GDI injectors under varied ambient pressure (0.5–10.0 bar) and fuel temperature (20°C–80°C) reveal that high-speed jet flows can induce near-field spray collapse under high pressure, while flash boiling can cause far-field collapse due to condensation and vapor cooling. High-pressure, multi-hole injectors used in direct-injection SI engines have shown that elevated fuel temperatures can induce nozzle cavitation, which enhances spray atomization and fuel-air mixing, improving combustion efficiency. Research on dual-spark lean-burn gasoline engines indicates that as λ (excess air coefficient) increases to 1.2, CO emissions decrease while NO_x remains relatively stable, suggesting that lean-burn expansion can improve emission outcomes without compromising engine output. In high-temperature port fuel injection (PFI) systems, variables such as injector targeting, injection timing, backflow, and impact location affect fuel evaporation. Increasing intake air temperature to 80°C and intake valve temperature to 120°C significantly improves vaporization, especially when fuel impingement occurs near the valve tip. A comparison of CO emissions between cold and hot starts in gasoline ICEs shows that coolant temperatures of 25°C during cold starts result in CO emissions that are 1.95 and 39.3 times higher than hot starts at 71°C and 87°C, respectively, due to higher fuel viscosity and lower volatility inhibiting vaporization. In biodiesel engines, raising fuel temperature lowers combustion pressure and delays heat release, increasing smoke output, while lower fuel temperatures can reduce NO_x emissions by 7.6–9.1%, indicating the sensitivity of biodiesel performance to fuel temperature control. Cold diesel exhibits longer ignition delay, narrower spray angles, and extended penetration lengths, which suppress peak pressure and flame luminosity under cold-start conditions. Partially premixed compression ignition (PPCI) strategies using variable injection pressure and exhaust gas recirculation (EGR) have proven effective for low-temperature combustion and NO_x reduction in diesel ICEs. In alternative fuel applications, blending diesel with Botryococcus braunii microalgae and titanium dioxide (TiO_2) nanoparticles increased exhaust gas temperature by 9% (up to 600°C), improved volumetric thermal efficiency by 5%, and reduced emissions of CO, HC, and CO_2. Testing biodiesel-diesel blends enhanced with nanoparticles found that a B60 blend (60% biodiesel) reached peak exhaust temperature of 371°C under full load, while B20 reduced NO_x by 3.7% compared to diesel. Adding TiO_2 nanoparticles to rapeseed biodiesel boosted engine performance with increases in power, torque, and thermal efficiency by 23%, 4%, and 6.55 kW, respectively, along with reductions in CO and unburned hydrocarbons (UHC) by 3.5% and 100 ppm. Finally, blending animal fat-based biodiesel with 10% and 20% ether decreased exhaust gas temperature by 1.35%, CO by 0.15%, UHC by 37.8%, and NO_x by 4.18%, highlighting improved combustion characteristics and thermal performance.

In this study, a thermoelectric module system is integrated into the fuel line between the fuel tank and the injector of a gasoline-powered internal combustion engine. By regulating the input voltage via a dedicated power supply, selected regions of the thermoelectric chip are actively heated to achieve a target fuel temperature. Preheating the fuel enhances atomization and promotes more efficient vaporization of the air-fuel mixture, resulting in more complete combustion within the engine cylinder. This process helps reduce secondary combustion phenomena and mitigates engine knock. Four distinct air-fuel ratios (AFRs) are configured by varying injection pulse widths. Engine performance is evaluated using a chassis dynamometer equipped with an eddy current load system, while emissions are measured with an exhaust gas analyzer. Tests are conducted under a constant-gear, fixed-ratio drivetrain setup on a test motorcycle. Emission outputs—including carbon monoxide (CO), nitrogen oxides (NO_x), hydrocarbons (HC), and carbon dioxide (CO_2)—are analyzed to assess the impact of fuel temperature on combustion efficiency and overall engine performance.

2 EXPERIMENTAL

2.1 *Experimental setup*

The experimental setup in this study consists of three primary systems: the test equipment, the fuel temperature control system, and the fuel temperature monitoring system. The test equipment includes the test motorcycle, electronic control unit (ECU), oxygen sensor, chassis dynamometer, and exhaust gas analyzer. The overall configuration is shown in Figure 1. The test vehicle is a KYMCO NIKITA 300i, a maxi-scooter manufactured in Taiwan. Engine speed is held constant at 3500, 4000, 4500, and 5000 rpm, representing typical mid-to-low range speeds under real-world riding conditions. The transmission is configured with a fixed-axis, fixed-gear ratio (1:1) to eliminate drivetrain variability. Key specifications and parameter settings for the test vehicle are listed in Table 1.

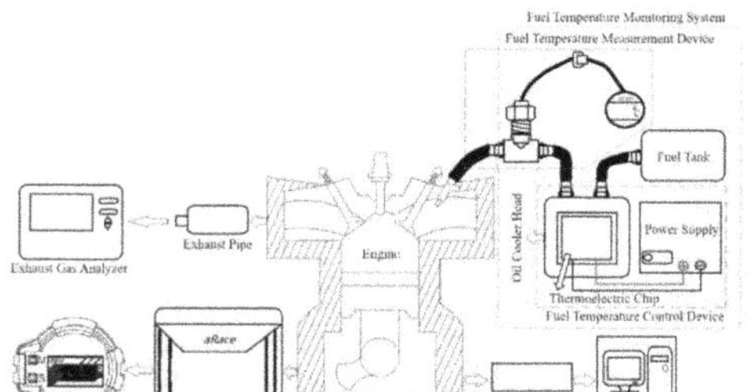

Figure 1. Schematic of the experiment and setup location.

The engine control unit (ECU) used in this study is the aRacer Supper2 Gold, a fully programmable fuel injection ECU developed by aRacer SpeedTek (Taiwan). It is paired with a Bosch wideband oxygen sensor for precise closed-loop control of key engine parameters. Engine performance data is collected using a Dynostar

Table 1. Specification of the engine.

Engine Specifications		Parameter Settings
Motorcycle Model	NIKITA 300i	-
Wheelbase (mm)	1545	-
Frame Type	Steel Tube Frame	-
Fuel Type	Unleaded Gasoline 92,95,98	92
Motorcycle Weight (kg)	189	-
Maximum Load Capacity (kg)	354	-
Displacement (c.c.)	298	-
Transmission Type	CVT Belt Drive	-
Engine Type	4-Stroke Single Cylinder SOHC-4V	-
Bore x Stroke (mm)	72.7x72	-
Compression Ratio	10.8:1	-
Maximum Cylinder Pressure (kg/cm^2)	16	-
Maximum Horsepower (PS/rpm)	29/8500	-
Maximum Torque (kg-m/rpm)	2.7/6500	-
Standard Idle Speed (rpm)	1600±100	-
Cooling System	Liquid Cooling	-
TPS Throttle Opening (%)	0-100	100
Engine Speed (rpm)	0-10000	3500,4000,4500,5000
Intake Air Temperature (°C)	25	25

D50ECB eddy current chassis dynamometer, with its specifications listed in Table 2. The dynamometer enables controlled engine speed testing at 3500, 4000, 4500, and 5000 rpm, with measurements taken at 500 rpm intervals. For each test condition, the system records maximum wheel horsepower (HP), peak torque (N·m), and actual engine speed (rpm). Data is transmitted to a connected computer, and the integrated eddy current brake dynamically adjusts roller resistance to simulate real-world riding loads. The system also calibrates the motorcycle's effective load on the rollers to ensure accurate replication of on-road performance.

The exhaust gas analyzer used in this study is the EF-306EN model manufactured by Exford. It measures key exhaust components, including hydrocarbons (HC), carbon monoxide (CO), carbon dioxide (CO_2), nitrogen oxides (NO_x), and oxygen content (O_2). The measurement ranges for each gas species are provided in Table 3.

Table 2. Specification of the chassis dynamometer.

Weight (kg)	400
Dimensions (m)	2.21 x 0.89 x 0.75
Roller Diameter (m)	0.39
Roller Width (m)	0.25
Max. speed (km/h)	300
Rated AC Voltage (V)	230
Calibration Weight (Nm)	233
Drive Motor Type	Eddy Current

Table 3. Measurement range of EF-306EN exhaust gas analyzer.

Measured Gas	Measurement Range	Error Margin
HC(ppm)	0~14000	±12
CO(%)	0~10	±0.06
CO_2(%)	0~20%	±0.5
NO_x(ppm)	0~5000	±25
O_2(%)	0~25	±0.1

The fuel temperature control system is installed in the fuel line upstream of the injector, with fuel supplied by the pump from the motorcycle's tank. The system comprises a thermoelectric module, an aluminum oil cooler head, and a regulated power supply. The layout of the system is illustrated in Figure 2. The thermoelectric device used is the TB-2-(127-127)-1.15 model from KRYOTHERM (Russia), while the power supply unit is the HJS-480-0-24, manufactured by Hangjia (China). System specifications are detailed in Table 4. In this study, the fuel temperature is regulated at 50°C and compared against ambient (uncontrolled) fuel temperature conditions to evaluate the impact of elevated fuel temperature on engine performance and exhaust emissions.

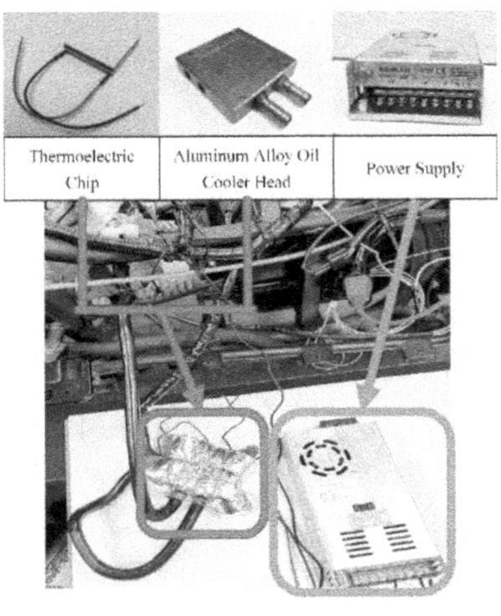

Figure 2. Fuel temperature control system equipment diagram.

Table 4. Specification of the fuel temperature control system.

Equipment Name	Model	Specification	
Thermoelectric Chip	TB-2-(127-127)-1.15	Maximum Voltage (V)	15.4
		Maximum Current (A)	5.8A
		Maximum Temperature Difference (°C)	84°C
		Dimensions (mm)	40*40*8.5
Power Supply	HJS-480-0-24	Input Voltage (AC/V/Hz)	110/60
		Output Voltage (V)	0~24
		Output Current (A)	20
		Dimensions (mm)	81*165*220
Aluminum Alloy Oil Cooler	-	Barb Fitting (mm)	8
		Dimensions (mm)	40*40*12
		Material	Aluminum

The fuel temperature monitoring system consists of a temperature sensor and an LCD digital display. The system layout is shown in Figure 3. The sensor used is the i-GEAR TEMP METER (Celsius) from Koso North America, installed upstream of the fuel injector to accurately measure the fuel temperature after thermal regulation by the thermoelectric module. The heated fuel is delivered directly into the combustion chamber to minimize temperature fluctuations prior to combustion. Sensor specifications are provided in Table 5.

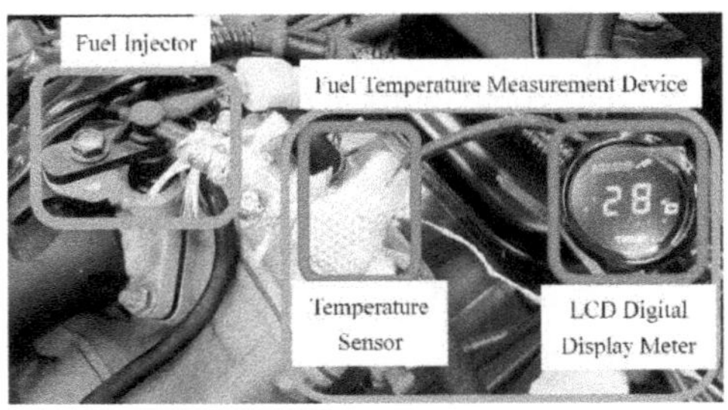

Figure 3. Schematic of the fuel temperature measurement device.

2.2 *Experimental procedure*

Prior to testing, routine maintenance was performed on the test motorcycle, including engine oil, oil filter, and gear oil replacement, fuel tank

Table 5. Specification of the temperature sensor.

Equipment Name	Model	Specification	
Temperature Sensor	i-GEAR TEMP METER (CELSIUS)	Power Supply Voltage (DC/V)	12
		Temperature Range (°C)	0~120
		Gauge Standard	JIS D D203 S2
		Gauge Dimensions (mm)	⌀40*11

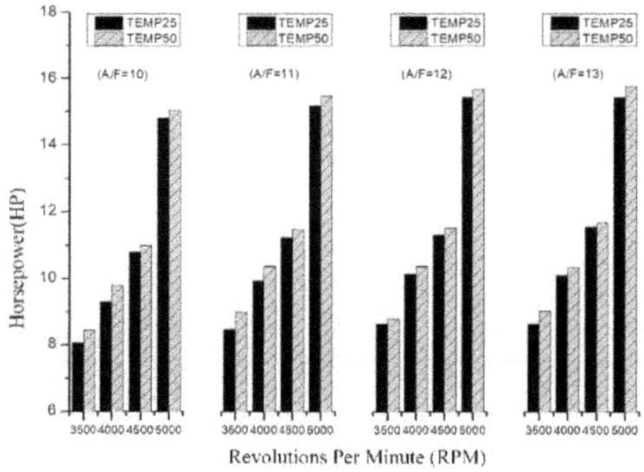

Figure 4. Horsepower comparison at different AFRs.

refueling, tire pressure adjustment, and coolant level inspection. The motorcycle was then mounted on the Dynostar D50EBC eddy current chassis dynamometer and secured using ratchet straps. The exhaust gas analyzer was powered on and preheated for 300 seconds before calibration. The motorcycle's ignition system was activated and connected to the aRacer standalone fuel injection ECU via software. Global fuel mapping and ignition timing values were configured, and system connectivity was confirmed. The engine was started and warmed up to an operating temperature between 90°C and 99°C, during which the cooling fan cycled twice, indicating the completion of the warm-up phase. The fuel temperature control and monitoring systems were then activated. Voltage was applied to the thermoelectric module, which heated the fuel until the injector-side temperature reached the preset value. During testing, the Dynostar D50EBC maintained a constant engine speed. The exhaust gas analyzer probe was inserted into the tailpipe, and exhaust gas measurements were recorded over a 120-second interval, with data from the final 20 seconds used for analysis.

This experimental study evaluates motorcycle performance and exhaust emissions to identify trends and correlations among key operating parameters. Tests were conducted at fixed engine speeds of 3500, 4000, 4500, and 5000 rpm, with air-fuel ratios (AFRs) set to 10, 11, 12, and 13. During all test conditions, the fuel temperature was maintained at 50°C using the fuel temperature control system.

3 RESULTS AND DISCUSSION

3.1 *Engine performance*

Figure 4 presents engine power output under four AFR settings—10, 11, 12, and 13—comparing fuel temperatures of 25°C and 50°C. The results show that preheating the fuel to 50°C consistently improves power output across all tested engine speeds. Figure 5 illustrates the percentage difference in power output (DP%) between the heated and unheated fuel conditions under each AFR. The calculation for DP% is provided in Equation (1).

$$\mathrm{DP\%} = \frac{W_{p50} - W_{p25}}{W_{P25}} \times 100\% \tag{1}$$

where W_{p50} represents the measured power output at a fuel temperature of 50°C, and W_{p25} represents the measured power output at room temperature.

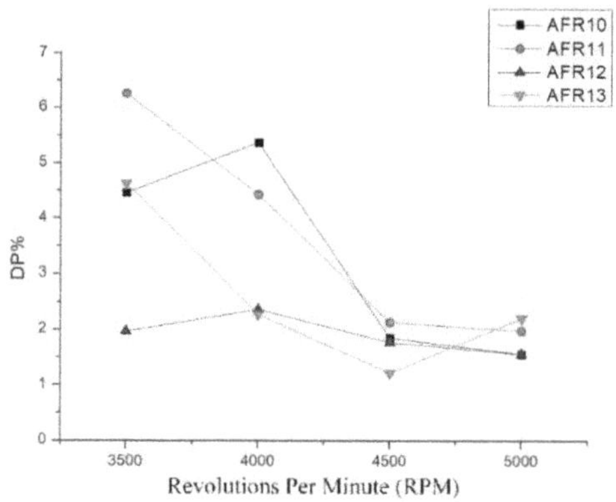

Figure 5. Horsepower increase Rate DP% at Different AFRs.

As shown in Figure 5, at an AFR of 10, the power output using heated fuel increased by 4.5% and 5.4% at 3500 rpm and 4000 rpm, respectively, compared to room-temperature fuel. At lower engine speeds, internal combustion engines typically operate under rich conditions (low AFR), where limited oxygen availability restricts combustion efficiency under low-load scenarios [41]. However, increasing fuel temperature improves spray atomization and vaporization, leading to more complete combustion [12]. As engine speed increases, the percentage difference in power output ($\Delta P\%$) gradually decreases. This trend is attributed to the higher air intake and oxygen availability at elevated engine speeds, which already support efficient combustion and conversion to mechanical energy. Although heating a rich fuel mixture enhances atomization, the associated endothermic effect during combustion absorbs thermal energy, potentially offsetting gains in combustion efficiency. Consequently, $\Delta P\%$ at higher speeds is lower than at lower speeds [42].

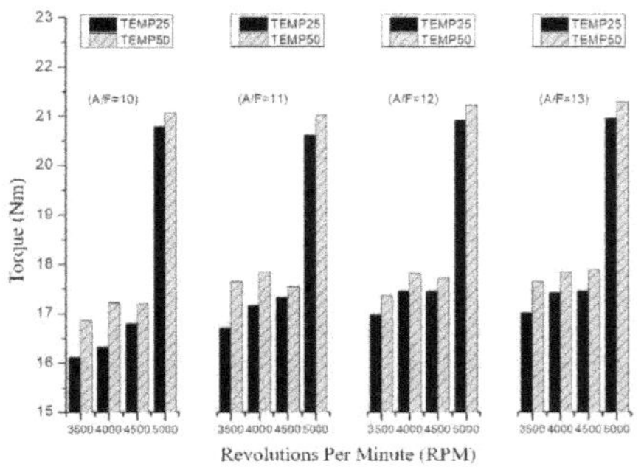

Figure 6. Torque comparison at different AFRs.

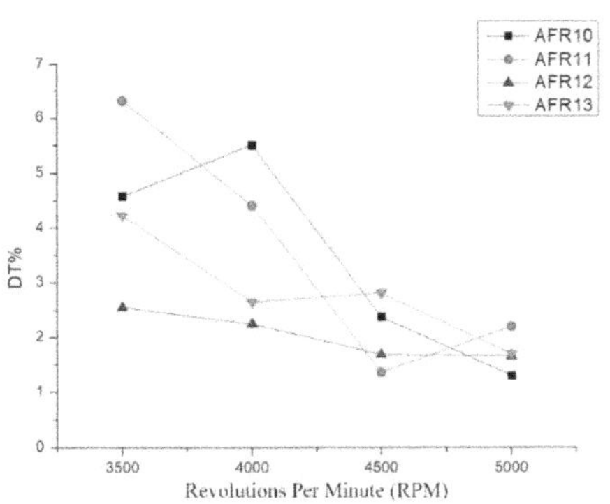

Figure 7. Torque increase rate DT% at different air-fuel ratios.

Figure 6 illustrates engine torque output under four AFR settings—10, 11, 12, and 13—comparing fuel temperatures of 25°C and 50°C. The results show that preheating the fuel to 50°C consistently yields higher torque across all tested engine speeds. Figure 7 presents the percentage difference in torque (DT%) between heated and unheated fuel conditions under each AFR. The calculation for DT% is provided in Equation (2).

$$DT\% = \frac{T_{p50} - T_{p25}}{T_{P25}} \times 100\% \qquad (2)$$

where T_{p50} represents the measured torque values at a fuel temperature of 50°C, and T_{p25} represents the measured torque values at room temperature.

As shown in Figure 7, at an AFR of 10, preheating the fuel resulted in torque gains of 4.6% at 3500 rpm and 5.5% at 4000 rpm. These improvements are attributed to the richer mixture at low AFRs, which increases injection pulse width and ensures adequate fuel delivery. Heated fuel undergoes earlier atomization, promoting more efficient combustion [41]. However, as engine speed increases, the percentage difference in torque (DT%) gradually decreases. At AFR = 11, torque improvements of 6.3% and 2.2% were observed at 3500 rpm and 5000 rpm, respectively, compared to unheated fuel. For AFR = 12, DT% remains relatively constant across the tested speeds, indicating minimal sensitivity to fuel temperature changes. Under AFR = 13, preheated fuel produced a 2.8% torque gain at 4500 rpm, which can be attributed to the leaner mixture; the higher air-to-fuel ratio enhances fuel atomization, resulting in improved torque output under these conditions.

The experimental results demonstrate that preheating the fuel improves atomization, significantly increasing torque at 3500–4000 rpm under an AFR of 10. However, DT% declines with increasing engine speed due to reduced sensitivity to fuel temperature at higher loads. At AFR = 11, DT% gradually decreases from 3500 to 4500 rpm but shows a slight rebound at 5000 rpm, indicating a non-linear torque response to fuel temperature at elevated speeds. Under AFR = 12, the torque difference between heated and unheated fuel remains minimal, likely because peak engine power typically occurs near an AFR of 12.6 [42], where combustion efficiency is already near optimal. For AFR = 13, DT% decreases between 3500 and 4000 rpm and rises slightly at 4500 rpm, reflecting the non-linear nature of engine torque characteristics, which fluctuate with changes in engine speed and load conditions.

3.2 *HC emission*

Figure 8 illustrates hydrocarbon (HC) emissions under four AFR settings—10, 11, 12, and 13—comparing fuel temperatures of 25°C and 50°C. The results show that increasing fuel temperature consistently reduces HC emissions across all tested engine speeds. However, as engine speed increases, the difference in HC emissions between heated and unheated fuel narrows. Figure 9 presents the percentage reduction in HC emissions (DHC%) under each AFR condition. The calculation for DHC% is provided in Equation (3).

$$DHC\% = \frac{W_{HC50} - W_{HC25}}{W_{HC25}} \times 100\% \qquad (3)$$

In this study, W_{HC50} and W_{HC25} represent hydrocarbon (HC) emissions measured at fuel temperatures of 50°C and ambient conditions, respectively. As shown in Figure 9, at AFR = 10, preheating the fuel reduced HC emissions by 31.6% at 3500–4000 rpm, but the reduction dropped to only 9.3% at 5000 rpm. Under AFR = 11, DHC% was 27.4% at 3500 rpm and 11.1% at 4000 rpm. For AFR = 12, the reduction was 24.5% at 3500 rpm and decreased to 4.6% at 4000 rpm. As engine speed increased, DHC% consistently approached zero, indicating diminishing impact of fuel preheating on HC emissions. This trend is primarily due to the catalytic converter reaching its optimal operating temperature at higher engine speeds, thereby effectively reducing HC emissions regardless of fuel temperature [9]. At AFR = 13, the most significant HC reduction of 17% occurred at 3500 rpm. This can be attributed to improved fuel atomization at elevated fuel temperatures, which facilitates faster catalyst light-off, enhancing HC conversion efficiency [5]. Overall, the results confirm that increasing fuel temperature reduces HC

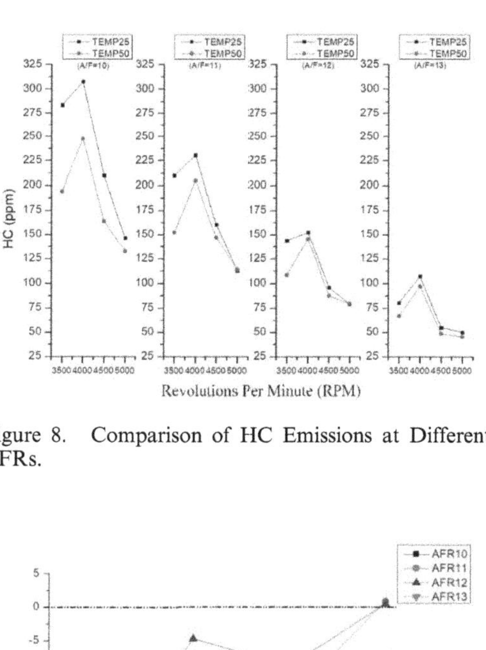

Figure 8. Comparison of HC Emissions at Different AFRs.

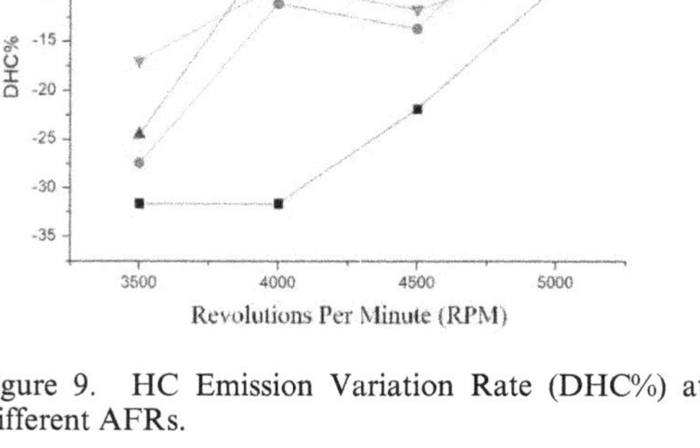

Figure 9. HC Emission Variation Rate (DHC%) at Different AFRs.

emissions, particularly at lower engine speeds and under leaner combustion conditions. However, as engine speed rises, the effect becomes less pronounced. Among all tested AFRs, AFR = 12 showed the smallest change in HC emissions, likely because it is close to the stoichiometric point (AFR ≈ 12.6), where combustion efficiency is already near optimal, and further fuel heating yields minimal additional benefit.

3.3 *CO emission*

Figure 10 illustrates carbon monoxide (CO) emissions measured at fuel temperatures of 25°C and 50°C under AFRs of 11, 12, and 13. The results show that preheating the fuel consistently reduces CO emissions across all tested engine speeds. However, under AFR = 10, the mixture becomes excessively rich, leading to incomplete combustion and elevated CO levels that exceeded the measurement range of the analyzer; therefore, data for this condition are not presented. Figure 11 presents the percentage reduction in CO emissions (DCO%) when fuel temperature is increased to 50°C, under various AFR settings. The calculation for DCO% is provided in Equation (4).

$$\text{DCO\%} = \frac{W_{CO50} - W_{CO25}}{W_{CO25}} \times 100\% \qquad (4)$$

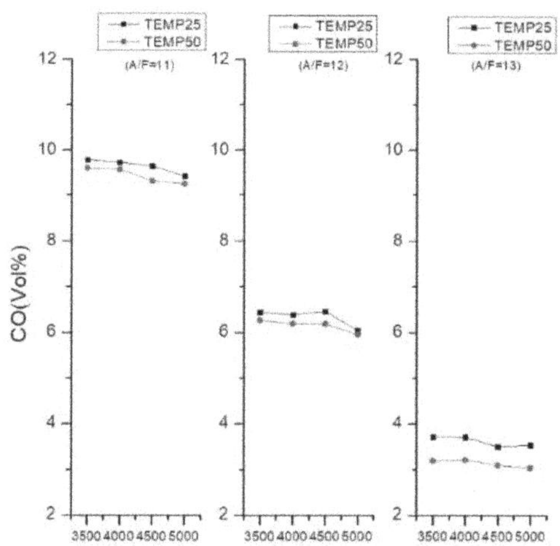

Figure 10. CO emission comparison at different air-fuel ratios.

where W_{CO50} and W_{CO25} represent CO emission measurements at fuel temperatures of 50°C and ambient conditions, respectively. As shown in Figure 11, under AFR = 11, preheating the fuel reduced CO emissions by 2.0% and 1.6% at 3500 rpm and 4000 rpm, respectively, with the largest reduction of 3.4% observed at 4500 rpm. For

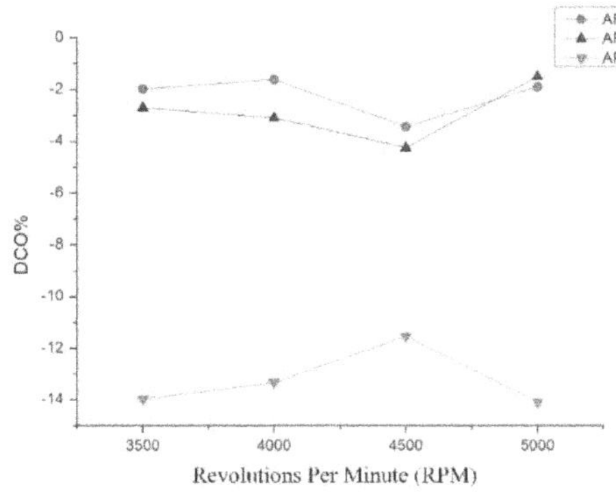

Figure 11. CO Emission variation rate (DCO%) at different AFRs.

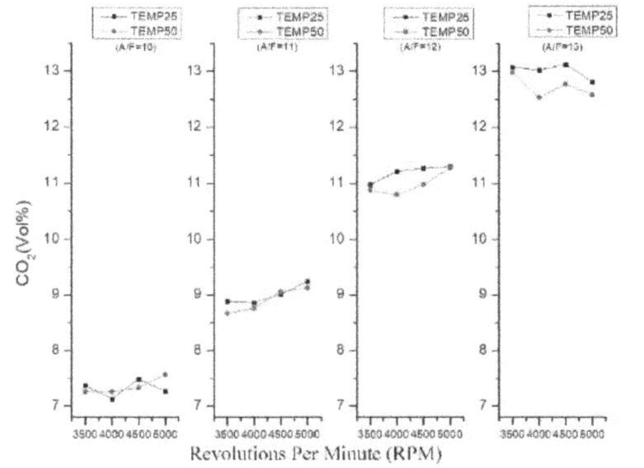

Figure 12. CO_2 comparison chart for different AFRs.

AFR = 12, DCO% exhibited a consistent downward trend across all engine speeds, reaching a maximum reduction of 4.2% at 4500 rpm. Under AFR = 13, CO emissions dropped significantly, with reductions of 14.0% at 3500 rpm, 13.3% at 4000 rpm, and a peak reduction of 14.1% at 5000 rpm. This substantial decrease is attributed to the shift from a richer mixture toward a leaner combustion regime as fuel temperature increases, which enhances combustion completeness and reduces CO formation [13].

The experimental results show that at AFR = 13, preheating the fuel produced the most pronounced reduction in CO emissions among all tested AFR conditions. This outcome is attributed to lean combustion characteristics: a higher air-fuel ratio reduces the injection pulse width and increases available oxygen for combustion, thereby enhancing combustion efficiency and significantly lowering CO formation.

3.4 *CO_2 emission*

Figure 12 illustrates carbon dioxide (CO_2) emissions at fuel temperatures of 25°C and 50°C under four air-fuel ratio (AFR) conditions: 10, 11, 12, and 13. The results indicate that preheating the fuel consistently reduces CO_2 emissions compared to ambient-temperature fuel, with reductions observed across all engine speeds. Figure 13 presents the percentage change in CO_2 emissions (DCO_2%) under each AFR condition. The calculation for DCO_2% is provided in Equation (5).

$$DCO_2\% = \frac{W_{CO_2 50} - W_{CO_2 25}}{W_{CO_2 25}} \times 100\% \quad (5)$$

where $W_{CO_2 50}$ represents the measured exhaust emissions at a fuel temperature of 50°C, and $W_{CO_2 25}$ represents the CO_2 emissions measured at room-temperature fuel. From Figure 13, it can be observed that under an A/F of 10, the CO_2 emission variation rate (DCO_2%) at an engine speed of

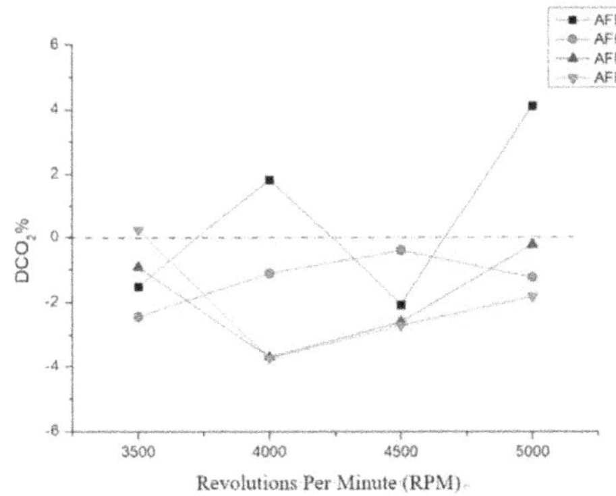

Figure 13. CO_2 emission variation rate (DCO_2%) for different AFRs.

3500 and 4500 rpm decreased by 1.52% and 2.1%, respectively. However, at 4000 and 5000 rpm, CO_2 emissions increased by 1.8% and 4.1%, respectively. This indicates that under a richer fuel mixture, CO_2 emission variations are less stable, possibly due to the combined effects of fuel atomization and fuel heat absorption on CO_2 emissions. For an air-fuel ratio of A/F = 11, the difference in CO_2 emission variation rate (DCO_2%) between heated and room-temperature fuel was not significant. Under an air-fuel ratio of A/F = 12, the CO_2 emission variation rate (DCO_2%) at an engine speed of 4000 and 4500 rpm decreased by 3.7% and 2.6%, respectively. Under an air-fuel ratio of A/F = 13, the CO_2 emission variation rate (DCO_2%) at engine speeds of 4000, 4500, and 5000 rpm decreased by 3.7%, 2.7%, and 1.8%, respectively.

3.5 *NO_x*

Figure 14 illustrates nitrogen oxides (NO_x) emissions measured at fuel temperatures of 25°C and 50°C under four AFRs conditions: 10, 11, 12, and

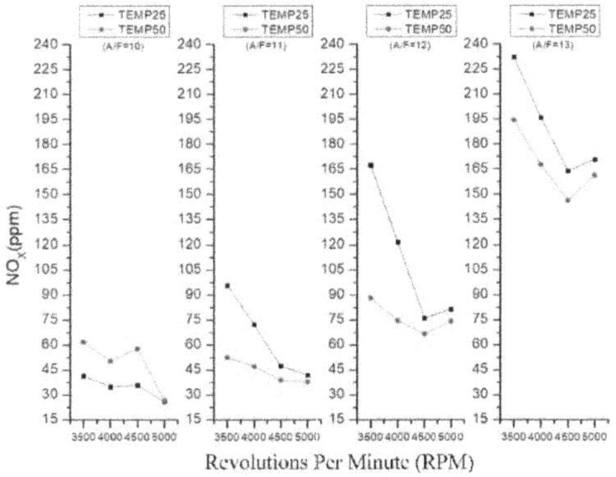

Figure 14. NO_x comparison at different AFRs.

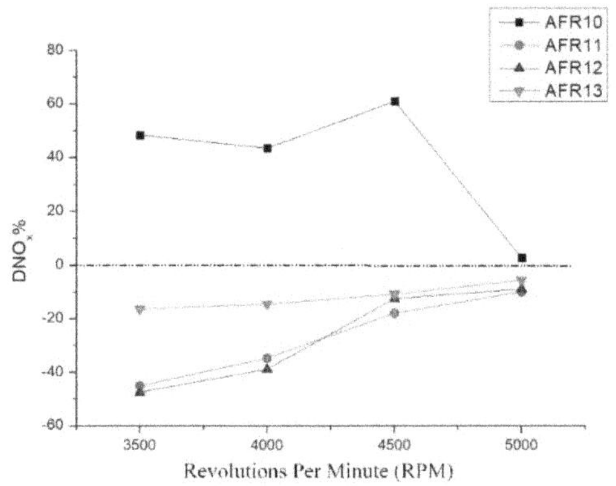

Figure 15. NOx Emission Variation Rate (DNO_x%) at Different AFRs.

13. The results show that preheating the fuel increases NO_x emissions at AFR = 10 but decreases NO_x emissions under AFR conditions of 11, 12, and 13. Figure 15 presents the percentage change in NO_x emissions (DNO_x%) between heated and unheated fuel conditions for each AFR. The calculation for DNO_x% is provided in Equation (6).

$$DNO_x\% = \frac{W_{NO_x50} - W_{NO_x25}}{W_{NO_x25}} \times 100\% \quad (6)$$

In this analysis, $W_{NO_x50}$and W_{NO_x25} represent NO_x emission measurements at fuel temperatures of 50°C and ambient conditions, respectively. As shown in Figure 15, under AFR = 10, NO_x emissions increased across all engine speeds following fuel preheating, with DNO_x% values of 48.4%, 43.4%, 61.0%, and 2.7% at 3500, 4000, 4500, and 5000 rpm, respectively. This increase is attributed to the richer fuel mixture at low AFR, which results in longer injection pulse widths [41], and to secondary combustion of residual exhaust gases triggered by elevated fuel temperature, which promotes NO_x formation due to incomplete high-temperature combustion. Under AFR = 11, the reduction in NO_x emissions was most notable at lower engine speeds, with DNO_x% decreasing by 45.1% at 3500 rpm and 34.6% at 4000 rpm. However, as engine speed increased, the difference between heated and unheated fuel conditions diminished, likely due to higher combustion temperatures enhancing NO_x generation. For AFR = 12, NO_x emissions were reduced by 47.4%, 38.8%, and 12.5% at 3500, 4000, and 4500 rpm, respectively. At 5000 rpm, the values converged, suggesting that elevated combustion efficiency raised the catalyst temperature, potentially increasing NO_x formation [4]. At AFR = 13, preheating consistently reduced NO_x emissions at all engine speeds. This outcome is consistent with lean combustion behavior, where excess air lowers peak combustion temperatures and suppresses NO_x formation [43].

The experimental results indicate that preheating the fuel increases NO_x emissions at AFR = 10 due to richer combustion and higher local flame temperatures. However, at higher AFRs, preheating generally leads to a reduction in NO_x emissions. This effect is attributed to increased fuel velocity and improved air-fuel mixing at elevated fuel temperatures, which result in a smaller flame front area and reduced peak combustion temperatures, thereby suppressing NO_x formation [44].

4 CONCLUSIONS

This study investigates the impact of a fuel temperature monitoring and control system on the performance and emissions of a spark-ignition engine. The system employs thermoelectric modules and an aluminum oil cooler head to regulate fuel temperature through a closed-loop energy exchange cycle, aiming to enhance combustion efficiency. Experimental results demonstrate that increasing fuel temperature improves both horsepower and torque, particularly under rich air-fuel ratios between 3500 and 4000 rpm. However, as engine speed increases and combustion becomes more efficient, the influence of fuel temperature on power output diminishes. Elevated fuel temperature also reduces HC emissions, confirming that improved atomization promotes more complete combustion. At AFR = 12, fuel temperature variation has negligible effects on engine performance and emissions, likely due to proximity to the stoichiometric point. Under lean-burn conditions, fuel preheating significantly reduces NO_x, CO, HC, and CO_2 emissions. In contrast, at lower AFRs, higher fuel temperatures lead to increased NO_x emissions, attributed to intensified local combustion temperatures and secondary combustion effects.

REFERENCES

[1] Serrano J. R., Novella R., and Piqueras P. (2019). Why the development of internal combustion engines is still necessary to fight against global climate change from the perspective of transportation, *Applied Sciences*, vol. 9, no. 21, doi: 10.3390/app9214597.

[2] Li T., Dong, D. L. S. Hung, X. Li, and M. Xu, Analysis of evaporation characteristics and heat transfer for flash-boiling sprays, *International Journal of Heat and Mass Transfer*, vol. 127, pp. 244–254, doi: 10.1016/j.ijheatmasstransfer.2018.07.023.

[3] Ceviz M. A., Kaleli A., and Güner E. (2015). Controlling LPG temperature for SI engine applications, *Applied Thermal Engineering*, vol. 82, pp. 298–305, doi: 10.1016/j.applthermaleng.2015.02.059.

[4] Ceiz M. A., Öner İ. V., Kaleli A. R., Mavi A., and Sen A. K. (2012). Fuel temperature control in LPG fuelled SI engines, in *2012 IEEE International Conference on Electro/Information Technology*, 2012: IEEE, pp. 1–4.

[5] Duc K. N. and Duy V. N. (2018). Study on performance enhancement and emission reduction of used fuel-injected motorcycles using bi-fuel gasoline-LPG, *Energy for Sustainable Development*, vol. 43, pp. 60–67, doi: 10.1016/j.esd.2017.12.005.

[6] Mohammed M. K., Balla H. H., Al-Dulaimi Z. M. H. and Mudhaffar S. A.-Z. (2020). The Effect of Using LPG in a SI engine instead of using Gasoline fuel, in *IOP Conference Series: Materials Science and Engineering*, vol. 928, no. 2: IOP Publishing, p. 022089.

[7] Ganesan N. *et al.* (2022). Experimental based comparative exergy analysis of a spark-ignition Honda GX270 Genset engine fueled with LPG and syngas, *Energy Science & Engineering*, vol. 10, no. 7, pp. 2191–2204, doi: 10.1002/ese3.1125.

[8] Kurtyka K. and Pielecha J. (2020). Cold start emissions from a gasoline engine in RDE tests at different ambient temperatures, *Combustion Engines*, vol. 181, no. 2, pp. 24–30, doi: 10.19206/ce-2020-204.

[9] Kuranc A. (2005). A continuous measurement of CO, CO_2, HC and NO_X at the work of a combustion engine fed with petrol in unstable thermal conditions, *Teka Komisji Motoryzacji i Energetyki Rolnictwa*, vol. 5, pp. 107–115.

[10] Schulz F. and Beyrau F. (2017). The influence of flash-boiling on spray-targeting and fuel film formation, *Fuel*, vol. 208, pp. 587–594, doi: 10.1016/j.fuel.2017.07.047.

[11] Guo H. *et al.*, (2017). Comparison of spray collapses at elevated ambient pressure and flash boiling conditions using multi-hole gasoline direct injector, *Fuel*, vol. 199, pp. 125–134, 10.1016/j.fuel.2017.02.071.

[12] Aleiferis P. G., Serras-Pereira J., Augoye A., Davies T. J., Cracknell R. F. and Richardson D. (2010). Effect of fuel temperature on in-nozzle cavitation and spray formation of liquid hydrocarbons and alcohols from a real-size optical injector for direct-injection spark-ignition engines, *International Journal of Heat and Mass Transfer*, vol. 53, no. 21–22, pp. 4588–4606, doi: 10.1016/j.ijheatmasstransfer.2010.06.033.

[13] Deng B. *et al.*, (2019). The effect of air/fuel ratio on the CO and NO_x emissions for a twin-spark motorcycle gasoline engine under wide range of operating conditions, *Energy*, vol. 169, pp. 1202–1213, doi: 10.1016/j.energy.2018.12.113.

[14] Z. Ma, P. Xu, and X. Wang, (2017). Analysis of fuel evaporation for PFI gasoline engine at high engine body temperature, *UPB Scientific Bulletin, Series D: Mechanical Engineering*, vol. 79, no. 1, pp. 107–118.

[15] Du B., Zhang L., Geng Y., Zhang Y., Xu, H. and Xiang G. (2020). Testing and evaluation of cold-start emissions in a real driving emissions test, *Transportation Research Part D: Transport and Environment*, vol. 86, doi: 10.1016/j.trd.2020.102447.

[16] Hwang J., Park Y., Bae C., Lee J., and Pyo S. (2015). Fuel temperature influence on spray and combustion characteristics in a constant volume combustion chamber (CVCC) under simulated engine operating conditions, *Fuel*, vol. 160, pp. 424–433, doi: 10.1016/j.fuel.2015.08.004.

[17] Chen H., Guo Q., Zhao X.-y., Xu M.-l, and Ma Y. (2016). Influence of fuel temperature on combustion and emission of biodiesel, *Journal of the Energy Institute*, vol. 89, no. 2, pp. 231–239, doi: 10.1016/j.joei.2015.01.024.

[18] Jain A., Singh A. P., and Agarwal A. K. (2017). Effect of split fuel injection and EGR on NO_x and PM emission reduction in a low temperature combustion (LTC) mode diesel engine, *Energy*, vol. 122, pp. 249–264, doi: 10.1016/j.energy.2017.01.050.

[19] Ge S. *et al.*, (2022). Performance, combustion and emission characteristics of the CI engine fueled with Botryococcus braunii microalgae with addition of TiO2 nanoparticle, *Fuel*, vol. 317, doi: 10.1016/j.fuel.2021.121898.

[20] Al-Kheraif A. A., Syed A., Elgorban A. M., Divakar D. D., Shanmuganathan R., and Brindhadevi K. (2021). Experimental assessment of performance, combustion and emission characteristics of diesel engine fuelled by combined non-edible blends with nanoparticles, *Fuel*, vol. 295, doi: 10.1016/j.fuel.2021.120590.

[21] Zhang X., Lan Chi N. T., Xia C., Khalifa A. S. and Brindhadevi K. (2022). Role of soluble nanocatalyst and blends for improved combustion performance and reduced greenhouse gas emissions in internal combustion engines, *Fuel*, vol. 312, doi: 10.1016/j.fuel.2021.122826.

[22] Ashfaque Ahmed S. *et al.* (2023). Investigation of ternary blends of animal fat biodiesel-diethyl ether-diesel fuel on CMFIS-CI engine characteristics, *Fuel*, vol. 332, doi:10.1016/j.fuel.2022.126200.

[23] Salah W. A. and Abuhelwa M. (2020). Review of thermoelectric cooling devices recent applications, *Journal of Engineering Science and Technology*, vol. 15, no. 1, pp. 455–476.

[24] Wang W.-W., Yang H.-F., Zhang H.-L., Xu T.-Y., Zhao F.-Y. and Wu S.-J. (2023). Pulsating heat pipe and thermo-electric generator jointly applied in renewable energy exploitation: Analytical and experimental investigations, *Energy*, vol. 263, p. 125573.

[25] Riffat S. B. (2003). Thermoelectrics: a review of present and potential applications, *Applied Thermal Engineering*, vol. 23, no. 8, pp. 913–935.

[26] Alkidas A. C. (2007). Combustion advancements in gasoline engines, *Energy Conversion and Management*, vol. 48, no. 11, pp. 2751–2761, 10.1016/j.enconman.2007.07.027.

[27] An Y.-z., Teng S.-p., Pei Y.-q., Qin J., Li X., and Zhao H. (2016). An experimental study of polycyclic aromatic hydrocarbons and soot emissions from a GDI engine fueled with commercial gasoline, *Fuel*, vol. 164, pp. 160–171, doi: 10.1016/j.fuel.2015.10.007.

[28] Sinigaglia T., Eduardo Santos Martins M., and Cezar Mairesse Siluk J. (2022). Technological evolution of internal combustion engine vehicle: A patent data analysis, *Applied Energy*, vol. 306, doi: 10.1016/j.apenergy.2021.118003.

[29] Wu C. (2003). *Thermodynamic Cycles: Computer-Aided Design and Optimization*, CRC Press.

[30] Moran M. J., Shapiro H. N., Boettner D. D. and Bailey M. B. (2010). *Fundamentals of engineering thermodynamics*, John Wiley & Sons.

[31] Reitz R. D. *et al.* (2019). IJER editorial: The future of the internal combustion engine, *International Journal of Engine Research*, vol. 21, no. 1, pp. 3–10, doi: 10.1177/1468087419877990.

[32] Shinjoh H. (2006). Rare earth metals for automotive exhaust catalysts, *Journal of Alloys and Compounds*, vol. 408–412, pp. 1061–1064, doi: 10.1016/j.jallcom.2004.12.151.

[33] Fayyazbakhsh A. *et al.* (2022). Engine emissions with air pollutants and greenhouse gases and their control technologies, *Journal of Cleaner Production*, vol. 376, doi: 10.1016/j.jclepro.2022.134260.

[34] Takahashi N. *et al.* (1996). The new concept 3-way catalyst for automotive lean-burn engine: NO_x storage and reduction catalyst, *Catalysis Today*, vol. 27, no. 1–2, pp. 63–69.

[35] Ogen Y. (2020). Assessing nitrogen dioxide (NO (2)) levels as a contributing factor to coronavirus (COVID-19) fatality, *Sci otal Environ*, vol. 726, p. 138605, Jul 15, doi: 10.1016/j.scitotenv.2020.138605.

[36] Zhao Z., Huang Y., Yu X., Guo Z., Li M., and Wang T. (2022). Effect of brown gas (HHO) addition on combustion and emission in gasoline engine with exhaust gas recirculation (EGR) and gasoline direct injection, *Journal of Cleaner Production*, vol. 360, doi: 10.1016/j.jclepro.2022.132078.

[37] Atarod P. *et al.* (2021). Soft computing-based modeling and emission control/reduction of a diesel engine fueled with carbon nanoparticle-dosed water/diesel emulsion fuel, *J Hazard Mater*, vol. 407, p. 124369, doi: 10.1016/j.jhazmat.2020.124369.

[38] Environmental protection administration, executive yuan notice is hereby given, to commence a period of public comments for the draft amendment of *Air Emission Standards of Mobile Source*, Available: https://join.gov.tw/policies/detail/b73ec892-56d0-4260-a1af-d0b3c5fd5427, Accessed on: 2023.

[39] Al-Arkawazi S. A. F. (2019). Analyzing and predicting the relation between air–fuel ratio (AFR), lambda (λ) and the exhaust emissions percentages and values of gasoline-fueled vehicles using versatile and portable emissions measurement system tool, *SN Applied Sciences*, vol. 1, no. 11 doi: 10.1007/s42452-019-1392-5.

[40] Lauber J., Guerra T. M. and Dambrine M. (2010). Air-fuel ratio control in a gasoline engine, *International Journal of Systems Science*, vol. 42, no. 2, pp. 277–286, doi: 10.1080/00207720902957236.

[41] Woo S., Lee J., and Lee K. (2021). Experimental study on the performance of a liquefied petroleum gas engine according to the air fuel ratio, *Fuel*, vol. 303, 2021, doi: 10.1016/j.fuel.2021.121330.

[42] Souder J. S. and Hedrick J. K. (2004). Adaptive sliding mode control of air–fuel ratio in internal combustion engines, *International Journal of Robust and Nonlinear Control*, vol. 14, no. 6, pp. 525–541, 2004, doi:10.1002/rnc.901.

[43] Odunlami O. A., Oderinde O. K., Akeredolu F. A., Sonibare J. A., Obanla O. R. and Ojewumi M. E. (2022). The effect of air-fuel ratio on tailpipe exhaust emission of motorcycles, *Fuel Communications*, vol. 11, 2022, doi: 10.1016/j.jfueco.2021.100040.

[44] Khoshhal A., Rahimi M., and Alsairafi A. A. (2011). CFD study on influence of fuel temperature on NOx emission in a HiTAC furnace, *International Communications in Heat and Mass Transfer*, vol. 38, no. 10, pp. 1421–1427, doi: 10.1016/j.icheatmasstransfer.2011.08.008.

System Innovation for a Global Economy – Lam et al. (Eds)
© 2026 The Author(s), ISBN 978-1-041-10520-6

The ENGAWA space in Japanese colonial architecture in Taiwan

Ying-Chu Chen & Chen-Yu Chen
Department of Architecture, National Cheng Kung University, Tainan

ABSTRACT: The *Engawa* space originates from traditional Japanese architecture as an intermediary corridor connecting indoor and outdoor areas. Through literature review and field investigation, this study examines the composition of *Engawa* spaces in Japanese colonial architecture in Taiwan and the relationship with Building morphology. The *Engawa* spaces in Taiwan have the following characteristics: 1. The installation of *Uchi-en* is more widespread and common than *Soto-en*. 2. In Taiwan, both *Soto-en* and *Uchi-en* types are evenly distributed across different regions. Additionally, cases of extended eaves (*Hisashi*) and pillars are consistently south-facing and more concentrated in the central and southern regions, suggesting a correlation with the hot climate. 3. Beyond the basic classification of *Soto-en* and *Uchi-en*, other categories have emerged based on factors such as the addition of architectural components or variations in width. Some *Engawa* spaces also exhibit characteristics of multiple categories at the same time. 4 The architectural appearance of a building also influences the characteristics and distribution of *Engawa*. According to the survey results, in single-family house (*Ikkodate*), *Hiro-en* types are more widespread, and arrangement of *Mawari-en* are more common, suggesting that in higher-class buildings, *Engawa* spaces tend to occupy a broader area.

1 INTRODUCTION

The *Engawa* (縁側, Japanese veranda) is typically installed along the edges of Japanese architecture and refers to a wooden corridor (or passage) that connects the *Washitsu* (和室, Japanese-style room) with the garden. The term originates from the combination of the words "縁" (Fuchi) and "側" (Soba), originally referring to the edge or side space of a building. The word "縁" (En) is also related to the concept of "ご縁" (Go-en), which signifies the fate of meeting between people (Kawakami Yukio 2014). Due to its spatial characteristic of blurring the boundary between indoors and outdoors, this type of space is often described as "In Between".

During the Japanese colonial period in Taiwan (1895–1945), Japanese settlers introduced their familiar living habits and residential styles, including the timber-framed construction method. These residences and dormitories became one of the architectural types of Japanese colonial buildings in Taiwan. Due to the influence of the officials‘ residential ranks, the buildings can be categorized by their exterior appearance into types such as Single bungalow house (*Ikkodate*), Single two-storey houses (*Ikkodate-nikaidate*), Twin house (*Nikodate*), Row house(Four or Multi-family), and other types. (Figure 2)

Figure 1. Engawa space.

Figure 2. Japanese colonial architecture in Taiwan, Building morphology.

Although numerous studies have been conducted on Japanese colonial architecture in Taiwan, there is still a lack of research specifically focusing on the *Engawa* space within these buildings. Therefore, this study aims to investigate the spatial composition and morphological characteristics, and regional distribution of *Engawa* spaces in Taiwan. (Figure 3)

DOI: 10.1201/9781003655534-32

The basic form of *Engawa* includes the *Soto-en* (外縁), which is installed outside the *Kawabashira* (側柱, the peripheral support pillars of a building.) Since this type of *Engawa* is directly exposed to the outdoors and gets wet when it rains, it is also called *Nure-en* (濡縁). To improve functionality, Amado (雨戸, rain shutters, wooden sliding doors) were installed on the *Kawabashira* side, while *Akarishoji* (明障子, translucent paper sliding doors) were placed on the *Irigawabashira* (入側柱, the support pillars set slightly inward), this structural form is known as *Uchi-en* (内縁) or *Kure-en* (榑縁) (Nokagawa Takeshi 2006).

Based on the literature review, *Engawa* can be classified into *Soto-en* (外縁, Outer *Engawa*) and *Uchi-en* (内縁, Inner *Engawa*) as a fundamental categorization for this investigation at first. Through further analysis, this study explores the differences in the composition of *Engawa* spaces and their relationship with the building morphology.

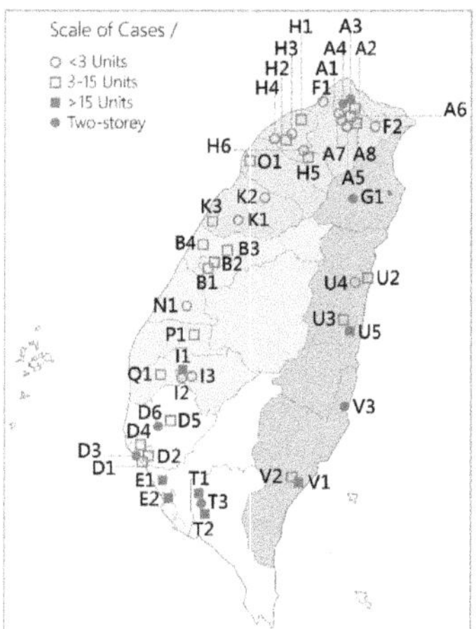

Figure 3. Case distribution map of this study's investigation in Taiwan.

2 EXPERIMENTAL

The subjects of this study are Japanese-style buildings with *Engawa* spaces constructed during the Japanese colonial period in Taiwan (1895–1945).

This study adopts field investigations to record the spatial composition categories, morphological characteristics, and regional distribution of *Engawa* spaces in Taiwan. Through measured drawings, the study records various types of *Engawa* and classifies them accordingly. The documentation process is divided into four methods (as shown in Figures 4 and 5 below, Case F2): 1. Indicating the location on floor plans. 2. Drawing sectional diagrams(views). to record spatial information. 3. Photographs record the current state of space. 4. Create a survey form, covering case information, building morphology (architectural appearance), and *Engawa* composition categories. (Refer to Table 1 below.)

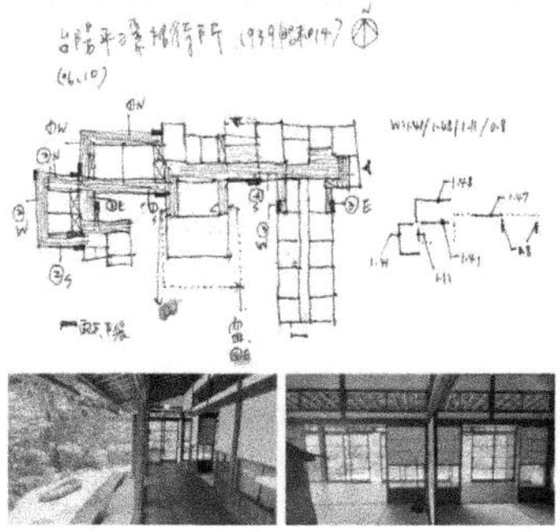

Figure 4. Marking position on plan drawing and Photo record.

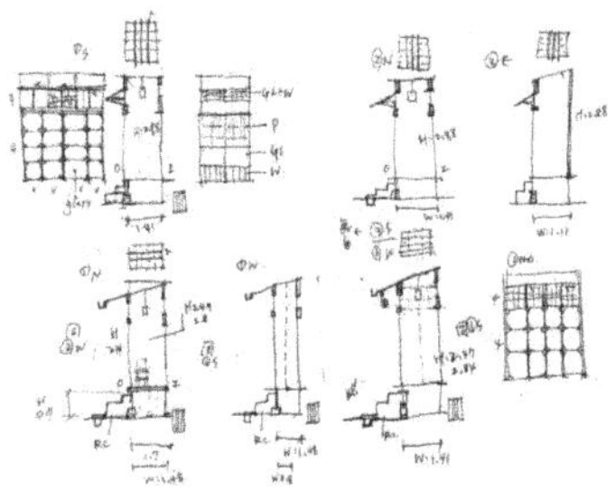

Figure 5. Recording the information through sectional diagram.

Table 1. Survey form.

Case NAME Research projects Building No.	 Research Date Case ID
Building morphology	□Single bungalow (*Ikkodate*) (S) □Single two-storey (S2) □Twin (*Nikodate*) (T) □Row house(Four or Multi-family) (F) □Others________
Engawa No.	Number of *Engawa*
Engawa categories, (Appearance form)	□*Soto-en* (Outer *Engawa*)(O) ________ □*Uchi-en* (Inner *Engawa*)(I) ________ □None(N) □Others________
Engawa characteristic	

3 RESULTS AND DISCUSSION

The field investigations(survey) recorded a total of 209 cases of *Engawa* spaces. Based on the investigation, the study observed the morphological characteristics and regional distribution of *Engawa* in Taiwan under the classification of *Soto-en* (Outer *Engawa*) and *Uchi-en* (Inner *Engawa*).

Soto-en (外縁, Outer *Engawa*) : The typical form of *Engawa* is installed on the exterior of a house. Based on the survey, it can be categorized into an outward-protruding type and a recessed type, as well as whether a *Kouran* (高欄, handrails) is installed.

In some cases, pillars are placed on the outer edge of the *En-ita* (縁板, *Engawa* board). This type is often found in Japanese-Western Eclectic (Japanese-Western hybrid) Architectural examples. It is also installed in ritual places, such as Shinto shrines, where it connects the main building (*Moya*) with the extended eaves (*Hisashi*). Additionally, some cases were observed where columns were positioned at a certain distance from the outer edge of the *Engawa*.

The wooden flooring of the *Engawa* appears in two primary patterns: *Kirime-en* (切目縁), where the planks are arranged perpendicularly to the building. *Kure-en* (榑縁), where the planks are arranged parallel to the building.

Among the *Soto-en* types, a form known as *Ochi-en* (落縁) was identified. This type of *Engawa* is installed slightly lower than the interior floor level. However, this form is not commonly found in Taiwan. (Figure 6)

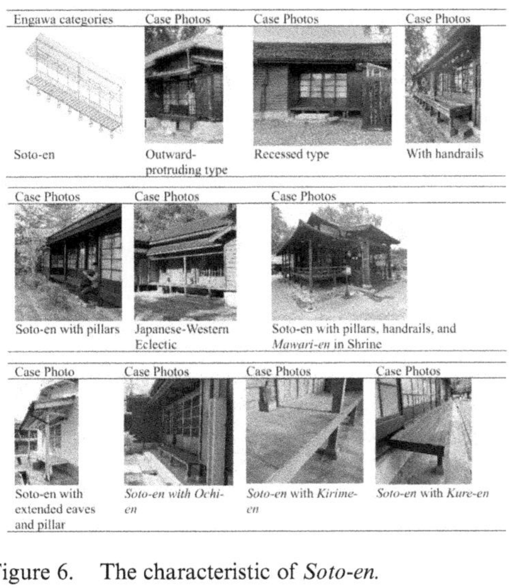

Figure 6. The characteristic of *Soto-en*.

Uchi-en (内縁, Inner *Engawa*) : The basic *Uchi-en* type refers to an *Engawa* with door and window frames on the outer side. This enclosed *Engawa* typically has a width of half a *Ken* (間, approximately 90 cm). Among the surveyed cases, it is the most common type, with the widest distribution and the highest number of *Engawa* categories.

It was also observed that in some cases, the width of *Uchi-en* exceeds half a *Ken*. This type is classified as *Hiro-en*, referring to an *Uchi-en* that is wider by an additional half a *Ken* compared to a standard *Engawa*. Since a typical *Engawa* is half a *Ken* width, many cases in this study fell between half and one *Ken* in width, so in this study, any *Engawa* exceeding 1.2 meters in width is categorized as *Hiro-en*. This type of *Engawa* is commonly found in Single bungalow houses, and Single two-storey houses of higher social status. Additionally, some second-floor *Engawa* spaces also adopt this form.

Within the *Uchi-en* type, cases were found where columns were placed at a certain distance from the edge of the *Engawa*. These spaces feature extended *Hisashi*(庇, eaves) covering an external *Doma* (土間, an earthen-floored space without wooden planks), referred to as *Sutebisashi* (捨庇) or *Tsuchibisashi* (土庇). In the survey, all cases of this form were oriented southward and were primarily distributed in the central and southern regions of Taiwan.

The wooden board installation method for the *Uchi-en* is primarily done with *Kure-en* (榑縁) style, which is arranged parallel with the building. Typically, a *Kutsunugi-ishi* (沓脱石, stepping stone) is placed outside the *Engawa*. The survey also found instances where platforms, stairs, or additional structures were added to the exterior. (Figure 7)

Figure 7. The characteristic of *Uchi-en*

In addition to the classification of the above appearance types, the investigation also observed other morphological characteristics present in *Engawa* spaces that combine multiple forms of characteristics at the same time.

Other Features : *Irigawa-en* (入側縁) features a double-layered *Engawa* space, with an additional corridor-style *Engawa* on the inner side of the main *Engawa*. This category had the fewest cases in the investigation and can be composed of a combination of *Soto-en* (外縁), *Uchi-en* (内縁), and *Hiro-en* (広縁).

In Single two-storey houses, the *Engawa* space on the second floor is often designed as either *Hiro-en* (広縁) or *Irigawa-en* (入側縁). When the *Engawa* extends outward from the exterior wall, supported by cantilevered beams or other structural methods, it is called *Hanedashi-en* (跳ね出し縁). Some cases with *Kouran* (高欄, handrails) on the outer side, while others include a balcony.

Additionally, the survey found the forms of *Mawari-en* (回縁), a type of *Engawa* that wraps around two or more sides of a room. This type is most commonly found in Single bungalow (*Ikkodate*) house or in ritual places. (Figure 8)

Figure 8. The characteristic of Other Features.

In Taiwan, Japanese architecture can be categorized into timber construction and brick construction. These two methods are often used in combination. In the *Engawa* space, cases of "composite construction" were observed. This form not only combines these two construction methods but also blends Japanese and Western architectural styles. (Figure 9)

Figure 9. The characteristic of Other Features.

4 CONCLUSION

Through this study, observations on the morphological characteristics and distribution of *Engawa* in Taiwanese architecture under the classification of *Soto-en* (outer *Engawa*) and *Uchi-en* (inner *Engawa)* reveal several key points:

1. The installation of *Uchi-en* is more widespread and common than *Soto-en*. (Table 2)
2. In Taiwan, both *Soto-en* and *Uchi-en* types are evenly distributed across different regions. Additionally, cases of extended eaves and pillars are consistently south-facing and more concentrated in the central and southern regions, suggesting a correlation with the hot climate. (Table 2)
3. Beyond the basic classification of *Soto-en* and *Uchi-en*, other categories have emerged based on factors such as the addition of architectural components or variations in width. Some *Engawa* spaces also exhibit characteristics of multiple categories at the same time. (Table 3)
4. The architectural appearance of a building also influences the characteristics and distribution of *Engawa*. According to the survey results, the exterior form of a building—often determined by social class—affects the style and composition of the engawa. In single-family house (*Ikkodate*), *Hiro-en* types are more widespread, and arrangement of *Mawari-en* are more common, suggesting that in higher-class buildings, *Engawa* spaces tend to occupy a broader area. (Table 3)

Table 2. Regional distribution.

Regional Disturibution	Southern	Central	Northern	Eastern	Subtotal
Soto-en (O)	4	7	4	8	23
Uchi-en (I)	56	44	59	27	186
Subtotal	60	51	63	35	209
Eaves Extension	6	6	0	2	14

Table 3. Building Appearance and *Engawa* Category Distribution.

Exterior Type	Features	Single bungalow (S)	Single two-storey (S2)	Twin house (T)	Row house (F)	Ritual places	Subtotal
Soto-en (O)	Basic Type	2	0	6	2	0	10
	With Pillars	4	0	2	2	1	9
	Ochi-en	0	0	1	0	0	1
	Eaves Extension	0	1	0	0	0	1
	Irigawa-en	0	1	1	0	0	2
	Subtotal	6	2	10	4	1	23
Uchi-en (I)	Basic Type	34	2	44	5	3	88
	Hiro-en (>1.2m)	36	22	18	2	2	80
	Eaves Extension	4	1	8	0	0	13
	Irigawa-en	2	4	1	0	0	5
	Subtotal	74	29	71	7	5	186
	Total	80	31	81	11	6	209
Mawari-en	12	9	1	0	4	26	

REFERENCES

Kenji Horikomi (2007). Japanese wooden dormitories – Restoration, reuse, and interpretation manual (日式木造宿舍-修復．再利用．解說手冊).

Masato Takagi, kazuto Ogawa, and Mitsuru Senda, (1998). The function of Ro –space in the house from the showa era, A study focused on the transition of children 's play in En –gawa and Rσka, J-*Archit .Plann. Environ. Eng.*, AIJ, No .507, 95 –101, May, 1998.

Miyatani Ai, (2021). Engawa in japanese traditional houses (日本の民家における縁側), https://sotsuten.nagaoka-id.ac.jp/artwork/11789/.

Nokagawa Takeshi, (2006). The Japanese house: In *Space, Memory, and Language* (日本の家:空間　記憶　言葉).

Tetsuro Yoshida, (2002). Das Japanische Wohnhaus (建築家　吉田鉄郎の「日本の住宅」), 2002.

Yukio Kawakami, (2015). Koto ~ 100 that I want to know in order to live in harmony with (old house demolition Shinsho) - old houses old houses ? (古民家解體新書(II) 古民家を未来に残すための１２４の知識) ', 2015.

System Innovation for a Global Economy – Lam et al. (Eds)
© 2026 The Author(s), ISBN 978-1-041-10520-6

Design workshop inspires exploration of community school establishment and learning: Taking brand packaging design course as an example

Huang Hsiao Chien & Hwang Shyh Huei
National Yunlin University of Science and Technology, Yunlin, Taiwan

ABSTRACT: This study explores the application of design workshops in the construction of community-based education and their impact on learning outcomes, with a particular focus on the integration of brand and packaging design courses into local industrial development. Drawing on seven workshops conducted between 2015 and 2021, the research adopts a participatory action research methodology combined with in-depth interviews to analyze pedagogical strategies and their effectiveness. The study proposes a five-stage instructional model incorporating paper-based exercises, case analysis, and creative facilitation techniques, which collectively enhance learners' design observation skills and problem-solving abilities. Findings indicate that although the one-off workshop format is time-constrained, it is nonetheless highly stimulating and effective in guiding participants, successfully triggering learning motivation and deepening local design awareness. This research confirms that design-based pedagogy can serve as a critical intervention strategy for community empowerment and local revitalization. It also offers valuable implications for future community design education and adult learning practices. Keywords: local industry, adult education, teaching construction.

1 INTRODUCTION

1.1 *Research background motivation*

In recent years, Taiwan's rural regions have been increasingly affected by pressing challenges such as the outmigration of young people, the over-concentration of populations in metropolitan areas, rapid demographic aging, and the hollowing out of local industries. In response to these issues, Taiwan's former Council for Cultural Affairs (now the Ministry of Culture) launched the Community Building Movement in 1994, promoting a bottom-up approach to local governance and encouraging civic participation in community affairs. This initiative laid the foundation for the emergence of grassroots autonomy, offering citizens opportunities for self-empowerment and collective capacity building. It also fostered a wave of locally grounded, participatory actions aimed at collaborative problem-solving and the revitalization of community life (Ministry of Culture, 2009). In 2016, Taiwan's National Development Council introduced the concept of "Design-Driven Local Revitalization," advocating for the strategic use of design thinking to enhance regional balance, strengthen local cultural identities, attract returning talent, and stimulate both economic development and cultural regeneration (National Development Council, 2017). This approach aligns with the philosophies of early 20th-century reformers such as James Yen, a global advocate of mass education, and Kiyoto Miyazaki, who promoted community-based development in both Japan and Taiwan. Both emphasized the principle of "learning from the people in the field" and the notion that local residents should be the protagonists of place-making, thereby valuing local resources, indigenous knowledge, and bottom-up, endogenous development models. As academia increasingly engages with real-world social contexts, it is confronted with deeper epistemological reflections—raising questions not only about the nature of knowledge but also about its societal role. This includes challenges such as how academic expertise can be mobilized to address urgent social issues and how scholarship can meaningfully serve and transform society (Huang, 2004).

1.2 *Research purpose*

This study investigates the role of design workshops in enhancing community-based educational frameworks and learning outcomes, using a brand and packaging design course as a practical case. The research aims to achieve the following three core objectives:

1.2.1 To explore the instructional design and pedagogical strategies employed in design workshops.
1.2.2 To examine the learning outcomes and skill development of participants engaged in the workshops.

DOI: 10.1201/9781003655534-33

1.2.3 To reflect on the implications of design workshops for community-based teaching practices.

2 LITERATURE DISCUSSION

2.1 *Definition of local specialty industries*

The term local industry in the context of community-based specialty industries typically refers to economic activities rooted within a specific administrative scope, such as a township, district, or municipality. A specialty industry is characterized by its reliance on unique local conditions, including climate, geographic resources, historical narratives, traditional craftsmanship, and ethnic or cultural customs. These industries are often distinguished by their uniqueness, cultural depth, historical relevance, and local identity. The emergence of such specialty industries is largely driven by the presence of distinctive humanistic elements or natural resources that enable the formation of industry clusters with clear regional characteristics. Several key features define local specialty industries: they are usually concentrated within a specific geographic area (such as a town, village, or neighborhood); they operate based on the use of local raw materials and labor; and they often belong to traditional or labor-intensive sectors. These features align with definitions provided in the White Paper on Small and Medium Enterprises (SMEA, 2005).

2.2 *Adult education*

The framework of adult education includes the planning stages, steps, main work items and participants. The planning process is shown in Figure 1. This model is divided into five stages: 1. Planning stage, the responsible department of the institution drafts a preliminary work plan based on relevant academic and legal basis and past experience; 2. Design stage, design curriculum and implementable plans; 3. Development stage, develop teaching content and activities; 4. Implementation stage, the main task is to carry out teaching activities; 5. Evaluation stage, the focus is on summative evaluation, etc. Through these stages, the quality of adult education courses and adult education activities can be provided (Huang Zhengjie 1995), as shown in Figure 1:

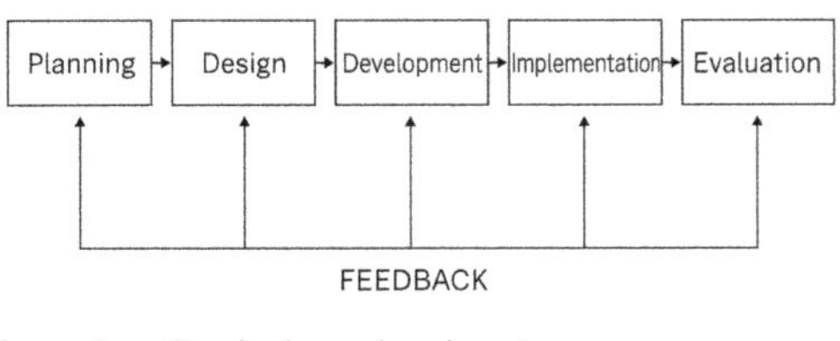

Figure 1. Curriculum planning stages.

2.3 *Teaching construction*

According to the experiential learning theory of American educational theorist David Kolb, the learning process is divided into four stages, including concrete experience, reflective observation, abstract concepts and active verification. The four stages form a cyclical learning process and are repeated continuously. Experiential learning provides a dynamic learning model that describes the learning and development model between individuals, groups and organizational environments through a four-stage interactive cycle. It is also possible to discover learners' behavioral performance in the four learning stages of concrete experience, reflective observation, abstract concepts, and active verification. As shown in Figure 2:

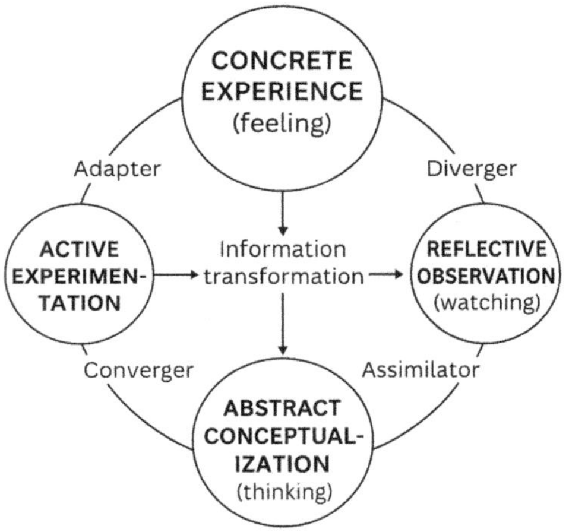

Figure 2. David Kolb's experiential learning circle.

3 RESEARCH METHODS

3.1 *Research scope and objects*

This study selected 7 workshops from brand and packaging design teaching workshops from 2015 to 2021 for research and analysis. The teaching time was approximately 3-6 hours. It explored the integration of brand and packaging design into local design workshops, how to use teaching to inspire community local design brands and packaging in the industry, as well as the roles and task execution directions of participating members and the design practice empowerment model, and made adjustments through feedback given in and after class. Teaching workshops are commissioned by public departments and the counseling units are invited to teach in different places to share brand and packaging design courses. The participants are divided into three categories: 1. Active and developmental communities selected by the counseling units or organizers, and community decision makers (chairmen, general secretaries, village heads, etc.) 2. Owners or second-generation operators of self-operated and self-created brands 3. Community residents who have not yet developed brands and products. The number of students in each class is about 10-40, and each class lasts about 3-6 hours. The design workshops mainly target existing brands and packaging visual images, and inspire the community to discover industrial design problems and think about the direction of subsequent adjustments in the workshop.

3.2 *Research methods*

This research adopts a qualitative approach, using participatory research and in-depth interviews as research methods. It solves and discusses problems encountered by participating residents during actual class teaching discussions, and focuses on how to stimulate residents to participate in the teaching discussion brought about by the brand and packaging design workshop process during the entire workshop discussion. Through teaching courses with different exercises, we transform professional abstract theoretical thinking into approachable sharing, and conduct design thinking with the community to complete the activities of different exercises. During the entire workshop process, we formulate questions and introduce relevant cases, and constantly observe and think to see the current problems and subsequent creative directions.

4 FINDINGS AND DISCUSSION

The biggest feature of the workshop is that through the design workshop, a group of community laymen who have not learned design can learn and discuss design teaching practice and presentation. Participatory action research is a cycle of proposing analysis and countermeasures for the problems to be solved, then implementing them in real situations, reviewing and analyzing the implementation status, and then re-drafting new countermeasures. By connecting past experience and future actions, this process is continuously repeated. Among them, for problems that occur in real situations, these problems are verified in the research process, which can solve the problems and improve the feasibility of the theory. It is a "problem-solving-oriented" research method that emphasizes periodic critical reflection, problem changes, and improvement processes, which means going through the "problem-reflection-summary-plan-action-discovery of new problems-reflection" cycle (McTaggart, 1991; Walter, 2009).

4.1 *Brand and packaging design workshop teaching operation mode*

The brand and packaging design teaching workshop is mainly to enable participants to quickly think about the problem points and find places where the design can be adjusted through the course content. In terms of teaching construction, 5 aspects and 10 stages are organized into a teaching framework. The 5 aspects include specific experience, observation and reflection, practical application, creative thinking, and summary of experience. The content of each activity is shown in Figure 6. First, in the specific experience, we first establish relationships through mutual introductions and exchanges, and share design theories to convey professional design concepts; secondly, in the observation and reflection stage, we focus on the community sharing the cultural characteristics and knowledge of the local industry, and through paper exercises, each community can collect and summarize information; in practical applications, a large number of shared design cases are used to inspire the community's observation ability, and then discover design problems; when it comes to the creative ideation stage, the discovered problems are used to guide the design problems through design strategies, and inspire the community's thinking and ideation; in the final experience summary stage, strategies are formulated and feedback is given for the subsequent improvement of the design direction, so that the community can improve the aesthetics and design capabilities of decision makers through a one-time workshop, and then explore areas for subsequent design improvements, as shown in Figure 3:

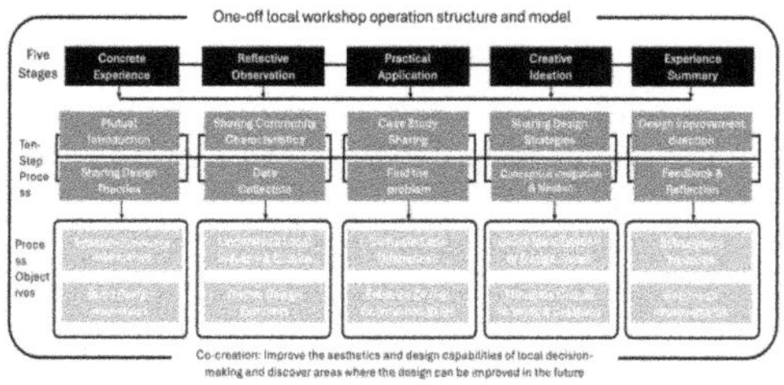

Figure 3. Stages and steps of one-time design teaching workshop (Source: drawn by this study).

4.2 *Learning outcomes of participants in the brand and packaging design workshop*

4.2.1 *Teacher's action qualities*

One-time design teaching workshop: advance planning and preparation, using high-speed stimulation to enable community decision makers to think and act quickly through the course, and establishing groups to extend subsequent communication and cooperation.

(1) Collecting student data and understanding background information: Most of the participants in the one-time design teaching workshop are major decision-makers in the community and most of them have already designed related

products. Therefore, in order to quickly understand the characteristics and industries of the community units in just a few hours, we will ask for a list of the members who will attend the class before the course, and use the list to search for fan groups or websites and other information online, so that the instructor can be prepared when entering the course.

(2) Requiring students to bring design products to facilitate rapid learning: Usually, design-related items are already available in one-time design teaching workshops. In order to allow the community to learn in a short period of time and then apply what they have learned immediately, students are encouraged to bring their own specialties and other design items.

(3) Use paper exercises to quickly understand theoretical knowledge and obtain first-hand information: Transform rigid theoretical knowledge into interesting paper exercises, so that each community can quickly understand the design theory indirectly through the fun of paper experience. Through exercises, each party can also have a clearer understanding of local characteristics and elements, so that the next stage of the course can be quickly connected to direct dialogue with decision makers and obtain first-hand local information. "When I was thinking of the brand name, I didn't think too much about it. I saw that the door of my house was Lane 341, so I just picked the fruits from Lane 341..." (Interviewee D1, 2020/11/09).

(4) Highly stimulating use of multiple cases to enable students to think quickly: By finding product examples close to the community industry in which the class is being taught in advance, and sharing a large number of different design cases to stimulate learners to quickly discover the current product design of the community, find out what the problems are, and immediately know how to make subsequent adjustments. This period of time is the highest point of learning in the entire class and the moment when students feel the most fulfilled.

(5) Diversified communication through the establishment of groups: In the past few years, social networks have become widely popular. Therefore, in recent years, we have made good use of the establishment of groups in the classroom so that during each mutual practice, we can directly open an album in the group and upload the results of each community. This is conducive to directly viewing the situation of each group on the projector during the class, so that everyone in the community can learn from each other, and can also communicate with each other after class if there are any problems.

(6) Teaching style generates subsequent cooperation: indirectly let the community understand the teaching style and direction of the researcher, and let them know that the researcher can lead them through the process of applying for a design plan, and is one of the teachers who can accompany the community to produce local designs. Many subsequent design cases are extended from the one-time teaching reputation. "Teacher, I really like today's class. I can apply for a plan next year, so I want to ask you to come to the community to give lectures and do design ... " (Interviewee D2, 2018/09/25).

4.2.2 *Movement restrictions for educators*

One-off design teaching workshop: time constraints, shallow design involvement, funding issues and seeking support

(1) Due to time constraints, the design intervention is shallow: With a time limit of 3-6 hours, only a more conceptual design solution process can be absorbed, and it is difficult to deeply explore how to modify the design details. Also, because there is only a one-time design teaching workshop, there is no subsequent extension course after the teaching, and it is difficult to take into account the subsequent development of community design products. Therefore, the scope of design intervention will be relatively shallow.

(2) Funding issues and requests for support: After completing the one-time design workshop, many communities observed problems and wanted to solve them with design solutions, but were unable to continue adjusting their designs because they could not obtain government subsidies. Some even hoped that the teachers could directly serve the community and provide free design services. For example, when a unit in Youkouhu discovered that the lack of overall design led to the inability to present the highlights of the design brand, they directly explained, "Teacher, our previous designs were all done by teachers from other schools who saw our hard work and brought their students to help us design for free. But now they see that our things are done piecemeal and lack integrity. I hope you can also help us..." (Interviewee D6, 2020/11/12).

4.2.3 *Community student action characteristics*

One-time design teaching workshop: high learning attitude and positive expression, open up design horizons, discover problems, solve problems, and plant the seeds for subsequent cooperation

(1) High learning attitude and active expression: Almost all participants in the one-time design teaching workshop are community decision makers, who are also the main operators representing the community. Therefore, in terms of participation, they will actively showcase their products and recommend their product features.

(2) Quickly organize local characteristics and interpretations: During the workshop practice, local characteristics and elements can be quickly organized through paper exercises. In

addition to making it easier for the community to organize, through the sharing of each community, we can quickly understand the industries and characteristics of other communities. The benefit of paper practice and sharing is that it can avoid being too excited and starting to talk about stories and not being able to stop, which will affect the time of other sharers.

(3) Design perspectives constantly stimulate and expand design horizons: In the workshop, many design cases are shared, and through the guidance part, students are no longer limited to their own perspectives, but extend more design direction possibilities. For example, there will be different presentation styles and color combinations in graphics, and the performances designed will be different depending on the stories and directions you want to interpret. "We sell candied fruit, and we put it directly on the packaging without thinking too much. After seeing the case you did, I realized that we can also use local cultural stories to add it (elements)..." (Interviewee D7, 2020/11/8).

(4) Identify problems and find solutions: By the end of the course, most of the community participants have improved their design skills, aesthetics and problem-solving abilities through the guidance of the course, and can quickly understand how to improve the product through design methods. "During the Japanese colonial era, Japanese experts saw that our place (Lugao Community) was a good place to grow black tea, so they built the Chimu Tea Factory here. This is the characteristic of our place (Yuchi Black Tea), but we don't see this (the black building) on the packaging. We can see how to add it (to the design) later..." (Interviewee D8, 2021/04/30).

(5) Planting the seeds for subsequent cooperation: In the workshop, although the community can only discover problems and how to improve them through the course, there is no way to truly provide them with follow-up practice. However, in the course, we can see that the teachers have rich experience and are locals. Therefore, in the subsequent application for design brand or packaging projects, they will usually become one of the community's main candidates so that the design can continue to be implemented. For example, all short-term teaching workshops are recommended by the community or the counseling unit through word of mouth.

4.2.4 *Movement restrictions for community students*

One-time design teaching workshop: follow-up design issues and seeking grant funding

1. Subsequent design cannot solve the problem: When the workshop knows the product solution direction, it is limited to one-time teaching, so the subsequent design is mostly stagnant because they don't know how to do the subsequent design.
2. Seeking sources of subsidies: After taking the course, many communities come forward to seek whether there are any sources of subsidies for subsequent design. It is rare to encounter a community that wants to pay for it out of their own pockets.

5 IN CONCLUSION

This study is based on the theme of "Exploration of Design Workshops to Inspire Community Teaching Construction and Learning Effectiveness", focusing on the application of brand packaging design courses in local communities. It uses seven local design workshops from 2015 to 2021 as an empirical basis, attempting to respond to three core research objectives: (1) strategies and methods for design teaching construction; (2) students‘ learning outcomes and action feedback; and (3) the role and reflection of teachers in community practice. Through participatory action research and in-depth interviews, this study not only presents the evolution and structure of teaching methods, but also proposes a specific practical model for designing teaching interventions in the community.

5.1 *One-time workshop to build an efficient teaching model with "five aspects and ten stages"*

The research concluded that the one-off local design workshop course is based on the "five aspects and ten stages" teaching structure, which includes the process from understanding, definition, creativity, prototyping to testing, combined with a short and efficient operation process, to provide stimulating and transformative learning opportunities. This structure is suitable for community situations with limited time resources and can quickly help community decision makers and participants identify problems, establish brand design perspectives, and develop preliminary solutions.

5.2 *The design learning process stimulates the aesthetic awareness and thinking transformation of community participants*

During the 3 to 6 hour intensive workshops, community participants demonstrated high learning motivation and expression skills. Through visual guidance, case studies and design discussions, participants can observe local product problems, think about brand packaging imagery and come up with creative and feasible ideas in a short period of time. The overall process not only improved their design perception and aesthetic quality, but also promoted the reconstruction of local knowledge and a shift in thinking.

5.3 *Local design teaching can serve as a strategic resource for sustainable community empowerment*

The design teaching cycle model constructed in this study has been proven to be highly operational and adaptable in many local practices. In the future, it can be expanded and applied to different topics and fields (such as elderly communities, indigenous tribes, small farmer brands, etc.). In addition, the study also recommends the establishment of a designer talent matching platform, cross-school resource sharing and design accompaniment system to achieve a sustainable teaching strategy of "one-time workshop launch and long-term support for implementation", as shown in Figure 4:

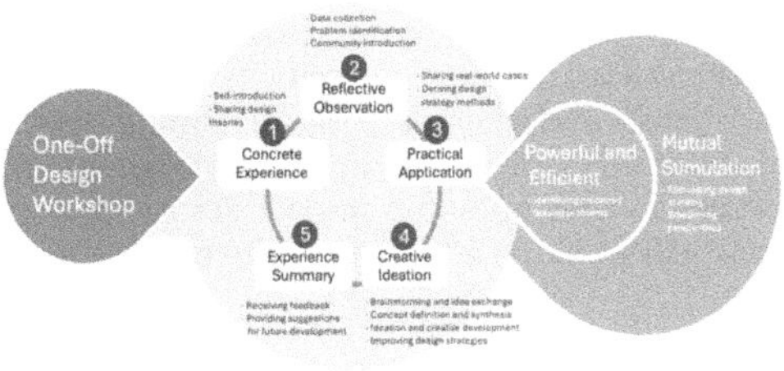

Figure 4. One-time design teaching workshop model (drawn in this study).

5.4 *Institutional design to promote sustainable operations still requires long-term support strategies*

Based on the experience of implementing one-off and short-term design workshops, they generally face challenges such as limited funding resources and lack of subsequent extended support. If local long-term design teaching programs can be promoted through institutionalization, it will help to effectively allocate resources and continuously improve community capabilities, and form a more in-depth and resilient local design support system. When localities demonstrate positive development intentions and results, they are more likely to obtain government subsidies and cross-domain cooperation resources, and gradually move towards the goal of local autonomy and sustainable development.

REFERENCES

Cai, Y. P. (2021). Local design: Extracting the charm of the land and tapping the value of the place, Japan's top design team reveals the secrets of operation, and creates a new moving economy! Guoli culture.

Du, M. H. (1999). The effect of health education on self-care behavior and blood pressure control among elderly veterans with hypertension. *Journal of Public Health*, 18(1), 54–65.

Duane Knapp. (2001). *Brand Thinking: Five Strategies for Building a Superior Brand*, translated by Yuan Shipei, McGraw-Hill, USA. Hill International Co., Ltd. Taiwan Branch.

Geoffrey Randall. (2000). *The Power of Branding*, translated by Cai Peijuan, Xiaozhitang Culture Enterprise Co., Ltd.

Gong, C. C. (1986). Develop a new style of overall community construction, the heart of the people-the idea and example of the overall construction of Japanese communities. *Taiwan Provincial Handicraft Industry Research Institute*, Nantou City, 27–32.

Gu, Y. L. (2007). The phenomenon of learning towns in the development of cultural industries. *City and Plan*, 34(2), 75–94.

Huang Fushun. (2008). *Adult education, adults' learning motivation*. Taipei: WuNan Publishing House, 110–3.

Huang, F. S. (2000). The humanistic meaning of local community leaders participating in the conservation of rural ancestral properties: Take Tainan Madou and Taipei Longpo as examples. Doctoral Dissertation, Institute of Geography, National Taiwan University, Taipei City.

Huang, F. S. (2008). *Adult Education: Learning Motivation Among Adults*. Wunan Publishing.

Hwang, S. H. (2012). Began to change from the community- The humanities and social practice opportunities for innovation. *Humanities and Social Sciences*, 14(1), 17–20.

Hwang, S. H., and Hwang, H. M. (2020). The Path Analysis of University Design Majors Infiltrating Indigenous Tribe: A Case Study of Social Practice in Laiji Tribe in Alishan Township. *Journal of Design*, 25(4), 65–88.

Hwang, S. H., and Su, H. T. (2017). Introspection on possibility of social practice from promotion of experiential learning in communities: A case study of design workshop in Laiji tribe in Alishan Township. *Journal of Design*, 22(3), 1–19.

Jhang, C. F. (2001). *The Formation and Significance of Local Culture-a Case Study of Anping Area*. Master's thesis of Institute of Rural Culture, Tainan Normal University, Tainan City.

JhangLi, S. J. (2009). Research on the revitalization policy of Japanese local industries. *Global Science and Humanities Journal*, 9, 103–123.

Jhuang, Y. S. (trans.). (2015). Community design: Rethink the definition of "community", not only to design space, but also to form "links between people". (Original author: Y. Ryo). Taipei: Faces. (Original work published 2011)

JSu, Z. Y. (2009). *Overall Community Construction*. Taiwan Encyclopedia, Ministry of Culture. Taken from: http://nrch.culture.tw/twpedia.aspx?id=3972

Knowles, M.S. (1980). *The Modern Practice of Adult Education: From pedagogy to Andragogy*. Englewood Cliffs: Cambridge Books.

Moran, J. J. (1991). Promoting cognitive development through adult education. *Education International*, 112, 186.

Ru, S. J. (2003). *A study on Brand Image for the Packaging Design of Regional Products*. Ming Chuan University, Taipei City.

Shih, S. W. and Chen, D. S. (2014). Introduction to the promotion and coordination of humanistic innovation and social practice projects. *Humanities and Social Sciences*, 15(4), 17–31.

Wei Huijuan. (2007). *Adult education program development, program development system model: conceptual framework*. Taipei: *WuNan Publishing House*, 65–7.

Wei, H. J. (2007). *Adult Education Program Development: Conceptual Framework of a Systemic Model*. Wunan Publishing.

Yang, Y. F. (1998). The cultural basis of design: design. symbol. *Communication*. Asia Pacific Book Publ.

Zheng, H. M. (2006). A study on the effectiveness of different types of self-directed learning on knowledge about hypertension prevention. *Journal of National Normal University*, 42, 95–111.

System Innovation for a Global Economy – Lam et al. (Eds)
© 2026 The Author(s), ISBN 978-1-041-10520-6

Dual-brain collaboration: A game-changing model to amplify AI's foresight and innovation

Yeong-Long Chen & Cenxi Wei
Interdisciplinary and Innovation Research Center, Zhaoqing University, Zhaoqing, Guangdong, China

ABSTRACT: This paper presents Dual-Brain Collaboration, an innovative framework that merges human creative-critical thinking with the computational power of artificial intelligence (AI). Aiming to overcome the limitations of current AI models in solving open-ended and cross-domain problems, we propose four original thinking models: (1) the Golden Ratio AI Value-Added Spiral Model (GRVAS), (2) the A+B Collision: 18 Thinking Models (AB-18), (3) the Multidimensional Thinking Funnel Model (MTF), and (4) the Divergent & Convergent Hybrid Moves (DCHM). These models are inspired by principles from cognitive science and design thinking, and are tested through structured innovation tasks including scenario design, concept generation, and interdisciplinary problem solving. In four rounds of experiments involving 13 questions, each model was benchmarked against mainstream AI outputs using criteria such as Knowledge Breadth, Knowledge Depth, Innovation Thinking, and Frontier Thinking. Results demonstrate statistically significant improvements in originality, contextual relevance, and anticipatory quality of solutions, highlighting the original thinking models' superiority in addressing open-ended and complex challenges. This study offers a practical and scalable path for human–AI collaboration, providing new tools for innovation management, strategic thinking, and knowledge integration. It lays the foundation for deeper cognitive-AI interaction, with potential impact across research, education, and applied innovation fields. Future research will explore adaptive deployment of these models in real-time decision-making environments.

1 INTRODUCTION

Artificial intelligence (AI) has rapidly evolved into a powerful tool for processing complex information across disciplines. Its strength in data computation and knowledge breadth has enabled transformative applications in science, business, and society. However, AI still faces significant limitations in innovative and frontier thinking, particularly when solving interdisciplinary problems or addressing scenarios requiring nonlinear, creative approaches. These limitations are largely due to AI's dependence on training data and algorithmic logic, which hinder its capacity for originality, insight generation, and foresight beyond established knowledge boundaries.

In contrast, the human brain excels in creative synthesis, critical analysis, and multidimensional reasoning—skills essential for generating novel ideas and envisioning future possibilities. This research addresses the central challenge: how can AI's logic-driven capabilities be meaningfully integrated with human cognitive strengths to enhance its innovation potential? To explore this, the study proposes a novel framework of dual-brain collaboration, which positions the human brain and AI brain as co-equal and complementary partners. Rather than treating AI as a mere tool, this model fosters dynamic interaction—where human insight frames the task and AI amplifies the exploration—enabling stronger innovation, adaptability, and problem-solving capacity. Four self-developed thinking models serve as the operational foundation for this dual-brain approach:

- GRVAS (Golden Ratio AI Value-Added Spiral): A knowledge enhancement framework integrating the aesthetic logic of the Golden Ratio with AI-assisted expansion. It follows Fibonacci stages (0,1,1,2,3,5,8,13) to deepen understanding, explore opposing views, apply 3D perspectives, connect relevant theories, and fuse expert wisdom—driving continuous intellectual augmentation and breakthrough innovation.

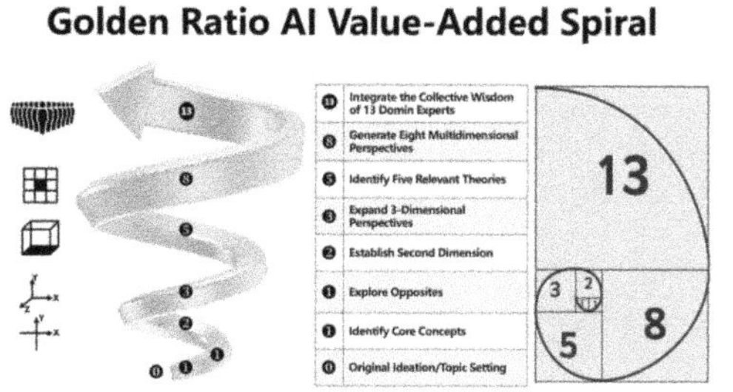

Figure 1. Golden Ratio AI Value-Added Spiral Model.

 DOI: 10.1201/9781003655534-34

- AB-18 (A+B Collision: 18 Thinking Models): A cross-innovation model that simulates the cognitive collision between Knowledge A and B through 18 structured thinking patterns, including intra-, extra-, multi-mode, and transdisciplinary techniques. It produces individualized and integrated innovation insights for short-term execution and long-term development.

- MTF (Multidimensional Thinking Funnel): A funnel-based model that harnesses AI to organize diverse thinking into structured layers of exploration and convergence. Through keyword generation and collision, it offers adaptive and personalized solutions to complex challenges, particularly useful for innovation bottlenecks or problem reframing.

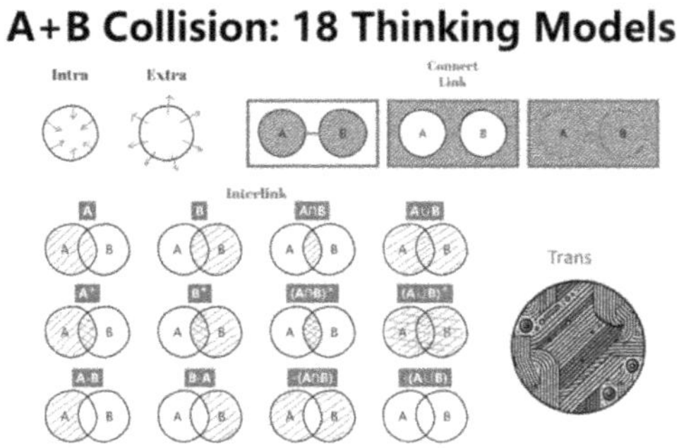

Figure 2. A+B Collision: 18 Thinking Models.

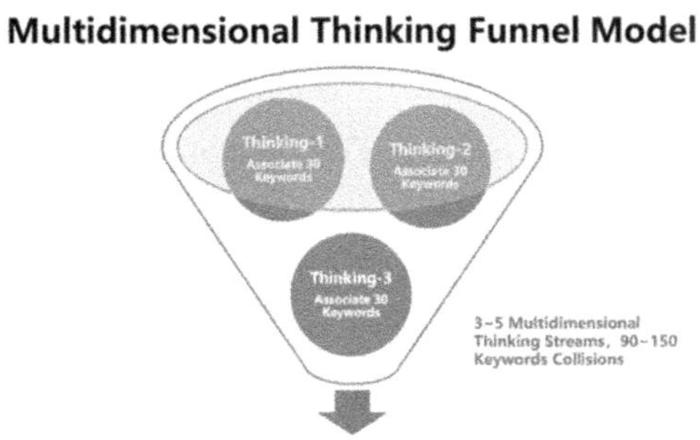

Figure 3. Multidimensional Thinking Funnel Model.

- DCHM (Divergent & Convergent Hybrid Moves): A creative thinking strategy combining free-flowing idea divergence with focused convergence. This model helps users escape mental constraints and refine breakthrough ideas through keyword expansion, collision thinking, and structured synthesis—ideal for foresight design and disruptive innovation.

The following comparative table summarizes the core advantages and optimal application scenarios of the four thinking models introduced above.

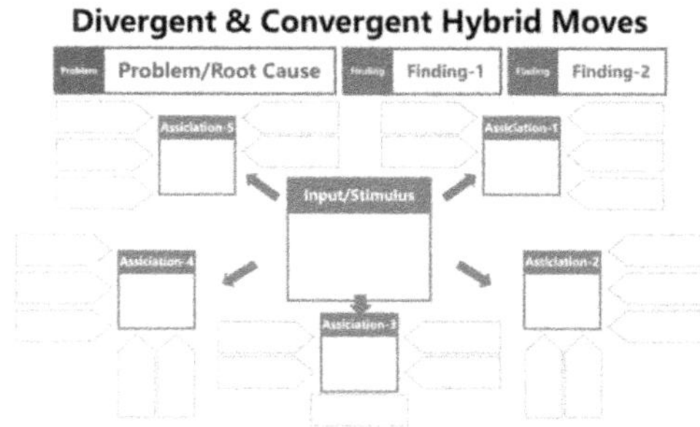

Figure 4. Divergent & Convergent Hybrid Moves.

Model Name	Key Advantages	Best Use Scenarios
GRVAS (Golden Ratio Value-Added Spiral)	■ Integrates Fibonacci sequence with AI reasoning ■ Expands into 3D thinking (width, height, depth) ■ Leverages collective wisdom of 13 domain experts	■ When deep knowledge value-added is needed ■ For multi-dimensional strategic planning ■ Ideal for developing innovation roadmaps and cross-domain frameworks
AB-18 (A+B Collision: 18 Thinking Modes)	■ Offers 18 structured modes of interdisciplinary collision ■ Generates short- and long-term strategies for both A and B ■ Fuses A and B into combined innovations	■ When two domains, technologies, or products need to interact ■ Useful for cross-functional collaboration ■ Ideal for designing new hybrid products or systems
MTF (Multidimensional Thinking Funnel Model)	■ Sparks ideas through diverse perspective collisions ■ Encourages iterative keyword expansions ■ Allows real-time dynamic adjustment via feedback	■ For complex, bottlenecked problems without clear solutions ■ Useful when idea diversity and novelty are required ■ Best for building new systems or concept models
DCHM (Divergent & Convergent Hybrid Moves)	■ Simple and fast to implement ■ Balances divergent ideation with convergent focus ■ Expands ideas from a single seed keyword into multi-layered directions	■ Ideal for quick creative breakthroughs ■ When working with unclear or abstract problems ■ Best for producing feasible ideas under time constraints

Figure 5. Comparative Table of Four Models: GRVAS, AB-18, MTF, DCHM.

These models were selectively embedded into the top-performing generative AI system—GPT-4o—identified through cross-evaluation by multiple AI reviewers. This strategic embedding approach aligns with current trends in academic literature, emphasizing depth integration with the most capable AI platform. The models were validated through four rounds of comparative experiments, each testing performance across knowledge breadth, knowledge depth, innovation, and frontier thinking—the core metrics of advanced cognition.

This study aims to build not only a validated operational pathway for human-AI collaboration but also a scalable model for enhancing AI's creative intelligence. The results demonstrate how targeted model design, question optimization, and interactive feedback loops can significantly improve AI's performance on complex, innovation-driven tasks. Ultimately, dual-brain collaboration represents a practical step forward in shaping the next generation of intelligent, co-creative systems.

2 LITERATURE REVIEW

The advancement of artificial intelligence (AI) has significantly improved data processing and automation across various industries (Brynjolfsson and McAfee 2014; Russell and Norvig 2016). AI's computational power supports complex decision-making, yet its limitations in innovation and cross-disciplinary creativity persist, particularly in addressing nonlinear problems. Scholars emphasize the need to integrate human creativity and AI efficiency to overcome these challenges (Amabile 2018; Shneiderman 2022).

In areas such as natural language processing and generative design, AI exhibits growing capability. Studies by Shafik (2024), Cheng (2024), and Kovari (2024) show that generative AI now excels in tasks like semantic modeling, predictive analysis, and content creation. However, its reliance on historical data restricts its ability to generate original, forward-looking ideas—a gap that dual-brain collaboration seeks to bridge. Theoretical foundations such as Csikszentmihalyi's "flow" theory and Sawyer's social creativity model underscore that innovation stems not only from individual insight but also from dynamic interaction and diverse cognitive input (Csikszentmihalyi 1997; Sawyer 2006). Hence, dual-brain collaboration—combining AI's logic and human intuition—has been proposed to optimize this synergy (Gartner 1988; Schumpeter and Swedberg 2021).

The three pillars of interdisciplinary innovation—Golden Ratio aesthetics, multidimensional thinking, and cross-domain integration—further reinforce the foundation of the self-developed thinking models used in this study (Amirante *et al.* 2022; Hadzieva and Bakreski 2020; Luria S. R. *et al.* 2017).

Importantly, recent research highlights the growing credibility of AI in academic peer review. Large language models like GPT-4 have performed at top human percentile levels in professional exams, confirming their potential in expert-level reasoning (Dhanvijay *et al.* 2023; OpenAI *et al.* 2024). Combined AI-human review systems are increasingly recommended to balance efficiency and fairness. For instance, Checco *et al.* (2021) demonstrate that AI can detect scoring patterns and reviewer bias in peer evaluations, while Giray (2024) argues that AI supports consistency in early-stage manuscript screening.

In this context, AI can be effectively used for preliminary scoring of academic papers on a 0–100 scale, but it should serve as an assistive tool rather than a final decision-maker. The primary objectives of AI-based scoring are to improve efficiency, standardize the review process, and safeguard academic integrity, yet critical aspects such as academic originality and research impact must still be evaluated by human experts (Doskaliuk *et al.* 2025).

Lastly, Woolley *et al.* (2015) and Landemore (2012) emphasize that optimal team sizes ($\approx$13 members) balance diversity and efficiency in collective intelligence. This principle informed the evaluative structure of the present study, combining multiple AI systems with human experts to achieve both rigor and balance.

3 RESEARCH METHODOLOGY

This study validates the dual-brain collaboration model through an empirical framework centered on four self-developed thinking models: GRVAS, AB-18, MTF, and DCHM. These models integrate theoretical insights with AI capabilities, each designed to address specific dimensions of innovation and frontier thinking. GRVAS builds knowledge using a Fibonacci-structured spiral for multi-perspective analysis. AB-18 fosters cross-domain idea generation through 18 structured collision patterns. MTF employs keyword-based funneling to resolve bottlenecks with layered thinking. DCHM merges divergent and convergent logic to produce creative yet grounded solutions.

The research includes four rounds of experiments, evaluated by four AI reviewers (Gemini, Copilot, GPT-4o, and Tongyi Qianwen) and benchmarked against mainstream models (GPT-4, GPT-4o) using four metrics: knowledge breadth, depth, innovation, and frontier thinking.

- Knowledge Breadth: The range and diversity of domains covered in responses, assessing the AI's cross-disciplinary knowledge capabilities.
- Knowledge Depth: The accuracy, rigor, and analytical capability of responses in specific fields, particularly in solving complex problems.
- Innovation Thinking: The novelty of viewpoints presented in responses and their unique contributions to problem-solving.
- Frontier Thinking: The AI's ability to provide insights into future trends or unexplored domains.

In Round 1, each model generated its own essay prompt to showcase its strengths, testing performance when aligned with model-specific capabilities. Results indicated that self-developed models significantly outperformed GPT-4o in most dimensions.

Round 2 introduced standardized essay questions for all models. Although the performance gap narrowed, self-developed models maintained competitive outcomes, validating their baseline innovation capacity.

In Round 3, prompts were modified according to each model's strengths before answering. This aimed to enhance response quality. While improvements were observed, gains were moderate, suggesting the need for more robust input customization mechanisms.

Round 4 implemented structured question templates tailored to each model's logic. By aligning user prompts with model-specific formats, performance in innovation and foresight metrics notably increased, reaffirming the importance of problem framing and template optimization in dual-brain synergy.

This staged methodology—model design, progressive testing, and evaluative comparison—confirms the potential of dual-brain collaboration to systematically enhance AI's creative and forward-thinking capabilities. This study did not involve any human subjects, personal data, or interventions requiring formal ethics approval. All evaluations were conducted by generative AI models (GPT-4, Gemini, Copilot, Tongyi Qianwen). No identifiable human data was collected. In cases where human experts provided informal qualitative insights (e.g., to validate scoring criteria), their input was non-invasive and anonymized. Therefore, institutional review board (IRB) approval was not required.

4 RESULTS AND DISCUSSION

This study conducted four rounds of experiments to evaluate the effectiveness of dual-brain collaboration models in enhancing AI's innovation and frontier thinking. Evaluated by four AI reviewers (Gemini, Copilot, GPT-4o, Tongyi Qianwen), each round provided insights into model performance under varying conditions.

In Round 1, models generated their own questions based on their strengths. Results were strongly favorable: self-developed models led with a score of 16:2 against GPT-4o. All four models excelled in innovation and frontier thinking.

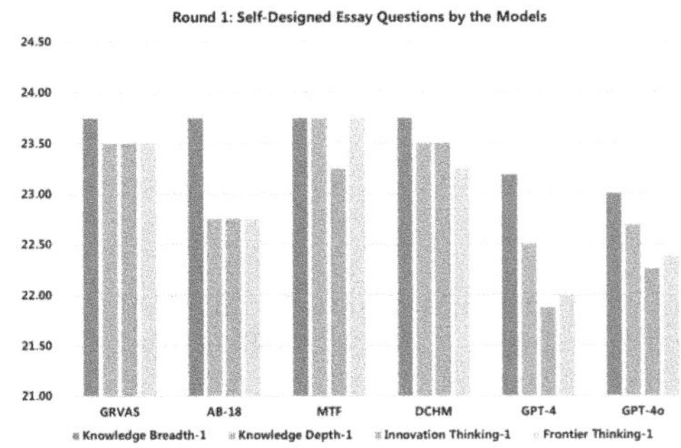

Figure 6. Scores for Model-Generated Essay Question Responses.

Execution Model	Knowledge Breadth-1	Knowledge Depth-1	Innovation Thinking-1	Frontier Thinking-1	Total Score	Lead Count
GRVAS	23.75	23.50	23.50	23.50	94.25	4
AB-18	23.75	22.75	22.75	22.75	92.00	4
MTF	23.75	23.75	23.25	23.75	94.50	4
DCHM	23.75	23.50	23.50	23.25	94.00	4
GPT-4	23.19	22.50	21.88	22.00	89.56	2
GPT-4o	23.00	22.69	22.25	22.38	90.31	2
Lead Count Ratio — Self-Developed Models : GPT-4o = 16:2						

Figure 7. Comparative Performance Metrics in Round 1.

Round 2 applied standardized questions. The performance gap narrowed (13:12), with models holding ground but without clear advantage. Innovation was still present but less prominent without tailored input.

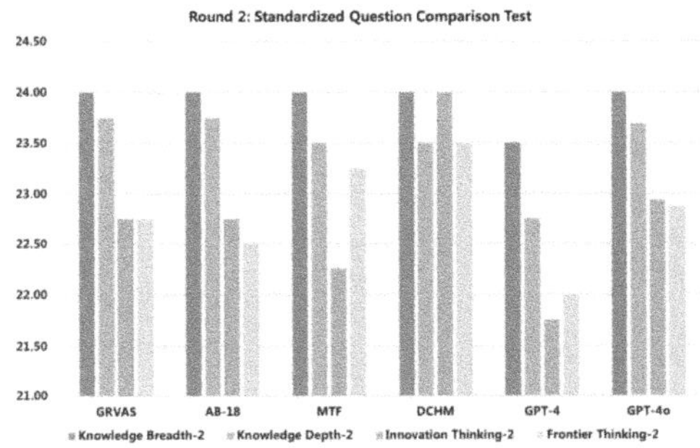

Figure 8. Scores for Standardized Question Comparison Test Responses.

Execution Model	Knowledge Breadth-2	Knowledge Depth-2	Innovation Thinking-2	Frontier Thinking-2	Total Score	Lead Count
GRVAS	24.00	23.75	22.75	22.75	93.25	4
AB-18	24.00	23.75	22.75	22.50	93.00	3
MTF	24.00	23.50	22.25	23.25	93.00	3
DCHM	24.00	23.50	24.00	23.50	95.00	3
GPT-4	23.50	22.75	21.75	22.00	90.00	0
GPT-4o	24.00	23.69	22.94	22.88	93.50	12
Lead Count Ratio — Self-Developed Models : GPT-4o = 13:12						

Figure 9. Comparative Performance Metrics in Round 2.

Round 3 tested question optimization. Models reformulated user questions based on their logic before answering. Results tied with GPT-4o (11:11), showing mixed improvements. Innovation was stronger than Round 2, but not to the level hypothesized—likely due to vague instructions on how to optimize prompts.

To address this, Round 4 required models to build problem templates first, then adapt questions accordingly. Results improved again (16:3). All models outperformed GPT-4o in innovation, and GRVAS, AB-18, and DCHM also exceeded it in frontier thinking. Template use, clarity in execution steps, and user confirmation loops significantly elevated outcomes.

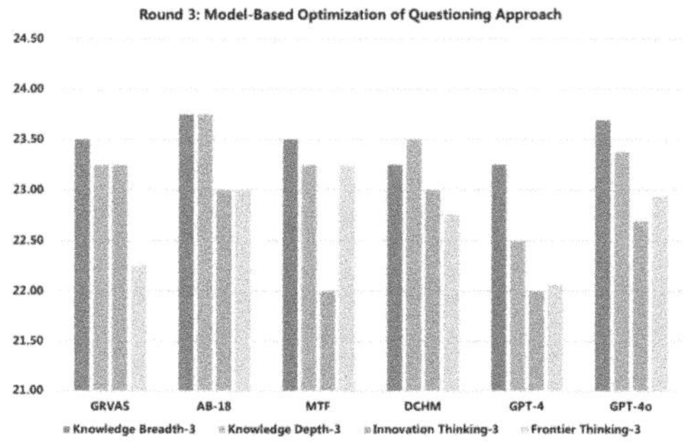

Figure 10. Scores for Model-Based Optimization of Questioning Approach Responses.

Execution Model	Knowledge Breadth-3	Knowledge Depth-3	Innovation Thinking-3	Frontier Thinking-3	Total Score	Lead Count
GRVAS	23.50	23.25	23.25	22.25	92.25	2
AB-18	23.75	23.75	23.00	23.00	93.50	3
MTF	23.50	23.25	22.00	23.25	92.00	4
DCHM	23.25	23.50	23.00	22.75	92.50	2
GPT-4	23.25	22.50	22.00	22.06	89.81	2
GPT-4o	23.69	23.38	22.69	22.94	92.69	11
Lead Count Ratio — Self-Developed Models : GPT-4o = 11:11						

Figure 11. Comparative Performance Metrics in Round 3.

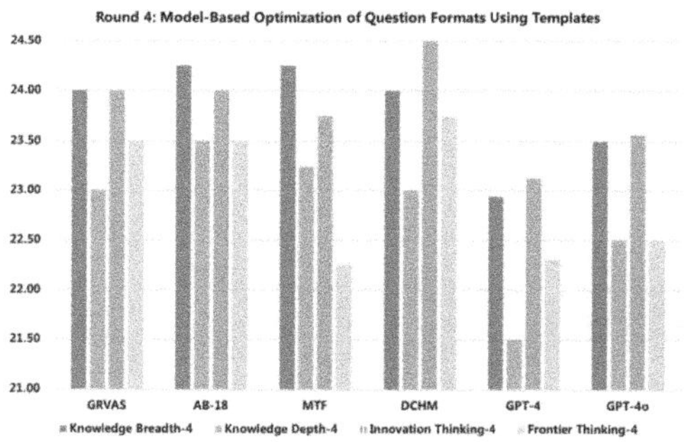

Figure 12. Scores for Model-Based Optimization of Question Formats Using Templates.

Execution Model	Knowledge Breadth-4	Knowledge Depth-4	Innovation Thinking-4	Frontier Thinking-4	Total Score	Lead Count
GRVAS	24.00	23.00	24.00	23.50	94.50	4
AB-18	24.25	23.50	24.00	23.50	95.25	4
MTF	24.25	23.25	23.75	22.25	93.50	4
DCHM	24.00	23.00	24.50	23.75	95.25	4
GPT-4	22.94	21.50	23.13	22.31	89.88	0
GPT-4o	23.50	22.50	23.56	22.50	92.06	3
Lead Count Ratio — Self-Developed Models : GPT-4o = 16:3						

Figure 13. Comparative Performance Metrics in Round 4.

Statistical validation supported these findings. Internal consistency was acceptable, with Cronbach's Alpha below 1. Inter-rater correlations all exceeded 0.7, with GPT-4o and Gemini scoring highest. While ANOVA (F-value: 2.495068, p-value: 0.069512) indicated no statistically significant difference in total scores, likely due to close overall performance, it did not diminish the practical innovation improvements observed.

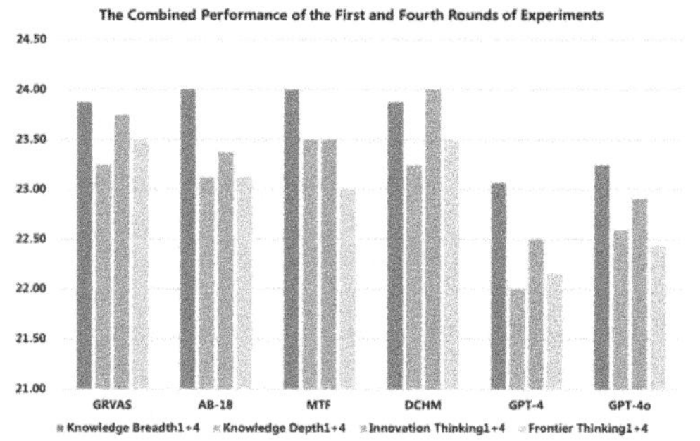

Figure 14. Combined Scores Across Four Performance Metrics.

Discussion reveals that success in Rounds 1 and 4 stems from aligning model output with their internal logic and strengths. Especially when equipped with structured input and interactive templates, models produce more creative and forward-thinking responses.

To enhance the effectiveness of dual-brain thinking models in AI-assisted cognitive tasks, we propose a structured guideline for model design and execution. First, the entire thinking process should be broken down into clear and concise instructions, treating natural language as executable prompts. Each step should be followed by a pause mechanism, allowing human users to assess outcomes and decide whether to proceed or revise prior outputs. This iterative control ensures alignment with design expectations. Once a model has demonstrated reliable performance, it can be instructed to generate question templates tailored to its strengths. These templates can then be integrated into the original instruction set, enabling automatic reframing of user queries. Conditional branching should also be embedded, defining when to return to previous steps or advance to later stages. Finally, designers should specify the desired output format for each step—such as text, tables, or structured lists—to maintain consistency and clarity throughout the process.

5 CONCLUSION

This study demonstrated that dual-brain collaboration models—GRVAS, AB-18, MTF, and DCHM—significantly enhanced AI's performance in innovation and frontier thinking. Particularly in the first and fourth experiment rounds, models utilizing self-generated or template-optimized questions outperformed GPT-4o. GRVAS and

DCHM showed strengths in foresight and systematic analysis, while AB-18 and MTF excelled in creative ideation and open-ended problem-solving.

Key findings include the importance of structured question templates, model-aligned input formats, and feedback mechanisms for boosting AI output quality. The four models have already been applied in over 35 interdisciplinary pilot-testing programs, such as education, 6G materials research, policy innovation, and cultural creativity, highlighting their adaptability and effectiveness in real-world settings.

This research contributes a validated operational framework for enhancing AI's cognitive capabilities via human-AI synergy. It establishes methodologies for model construction, question optimization, and interactive logic to support innovation-driven applications in knowledge management, interdisciplinary collaboration, and intelligent systems.

Despite its successes, the study notes several limitations including high model design thresholds, communication challenges between AI and users, and the need for clearer operational templates. Future research should focus on expanding model types, refining human-AI interfaces, incorporating next-generation AI platforms, and validating stability across broader task domains. Ultimately, dual-brain collaboration offers a scalable approach for enhancing AI intelligence, creativity, and adaptability—enabling it to function as a truly integrative assistant across diverse innovation ecosystems.

6 APPENDIX: ESSAY QUESTIONS EXPERIMENTAL ROUNDS 1 TO 2

Essay Questions – Round One

GRVAS: How can corporate sustainability strategies be redefined in the context of climate change? Please answer in Simplified Chinese, approximately 1000 words. (Scoring criteria: Knowledge Breadth, Knowledge Depth, Innovation, and Frontier Thinking each account for 25%, total score: 100 points) ; AB-18: How can a "health management system" be integrated with "social media platforms" to enhance users' health engagement and social interaction? Please answer in Simplified Chinese, approximately 1000 words. (Scoring criteria: Knowledge Breadth, Knowledge Depth, Innovation, and Frontier Thinking each account for 25%, total score: 100 points); MTF: How can more green energy solutions be introduced into urban transportation systems to reduce carbon emissions? Please answer in Simplified Chinese, approximately 1000 words. (Scoring criteria: Knowledge Breadth, Knowledge Depth, Innovation, and Frontier Thinking each account for 25%, total score: 100 points); DCHM: "How can cross-disciplinary design improve the adaptability and effectiveness of virtual reality (VR) in rehabilitation training for the elderly? Please answer in Simplified Chinese, approximately 1000 words. (Scoring criteria: Knowledge Breadth, Knowledge Depth, Innovation, and Frontier Thinking each account for 25%, total score: 100 points)".

Essay Questions – Round Two for all models

Under the empowerment of artificial intelligence, what are the new transformations in future education driven by interdisciplinary and technological innovation? Please explain separately from the perspectives of teachers and students in different contexts. Please answer in Simplified Chinese, approximately 1000 words. (Scoring criteria: Knowledge Breadth, Knowledge Depth, Innovation, and Frontier Thinking each account for 25%, total score: 100 points).

The optimized question texts used in the third round experiment (Model-Based Optimization of Questioning Approach) and the fourth round experiment (Model-Based Optimization of Question Formats Using Templates) are omitted from this appendix due to length constraints. A complete version will be presented in future journal publications.

REFERENCES

Amabile, T. M. (2018). *Creativity in Context: Update to the Social Psychology of Creativity* (2nd ed.). Routledge. https://doi.org/10.4324/9780429501234

Amirante, A., Tortorelli, L., and Veronesi, I. (2022). Mathematics, literature and art: Getting passionate about mathematics through the use of digital technologies. *In ICERI2022 Proceedings* (pp. 3877–3884). IATED. https://library.iated.org/view/AMIRANTE2022MAM

Brynjolfsson, E., and McAfee, A. (2014). *The second machine age: Work, progress, and prosperity in a time of brilliant technologies.* W. W. Norton & Company. https://books.google.com/books?id=WiKwAgAAQBAJ

Checco, A., Bracciale, L., Loreti, P., Pinfield, S., and Bianchi, G. (2021). AI-assisted peer review. *Humanities and Social Sciences Communications*, 8, Article 11.

Cheng, Z. (2024). Interpretable and generative AI for actionable insights from textual data [Doctoral dissertation, Boston University]. *OpenBU.* https://open.bu.edu/handle/2144/48748

Csikszentmihalyi, M. (1997). Flow and the psychology of discovery and invention. *HarperPerennial.*

Dhanvijay, A. K. D., Pinjar, M. J., Dhokane, N., Sorte, S. R., Kumari, A., and Mondal, H. (2023). Performance of large language models (ChatGPT, Bing Search, and Google Bard) in solving case vignettes in physiology. *Cureus*, 15(8), e43865. https://www.ncbi.nlm.nih.gov/pmc/articles/PMC10475852/

Doskaliuk, B., Zimba, O., Yessirkepov, M., Klishch, I., and Yatsyshyn, R. (2025). Artificial intelligence in

peer review: Enhancing efficiency while preserving integrity. *Journal of Korean Medical Science, 40(7), Article* e123. https://synapse.koreamed.org/articles/1516090023
Gartner, W. B. (1988). "Who is an entrepreneur?" is the wrong question. *American Journal of Small Business*, 12 (4), 11–32. https://doi.org/10.1177/104225878801200401
Giray, L. (2024). Benefits and Challenges of Using AI for Peer Review: A Study on Researchers' Perceptions. *The Serials Librarian*, 85(5–6), 144–154. https://doi.org/10.1080/0361526X.2024.2428377
Hadzieva, E., and Bakreski, Y. (2020). A mathematical concept in lens-based media: Revisiting the golden ratio. https://www.researchgate.net/publication/385379120
Kovari, A. (2024). Ethical use of ChatGPT in education—Best practices to combat AI-induced plagiarism. *Frontiers in Education*, 9, Article 1465703. https://doi.org/10.3389/feduc.2024.1465703
Landemore, H. (2012). *Democratic Reason: Politics, Collective Intelligence, and the Rule of the Many*. Princeton University Press. https://www.torrossa.com/gs/resourceProxy?an=5641701&publisher=FZO137
Luria, S. R., Sriraman, B., and Kaufman, J. C. (2017). Enhancing equity in the classroom by teaching for mathematical creativity. *ZDM–Mathematics Education*, 49(7), 1033–1039. https://doi.org/10.1007/s11858-017-0892-2
OpenAI, Achiam, J., Adler, S., Agarwal, S., Ahmad, L., Akkaya, I., Aleman, F. L., Almeida, D., Altenschmidt, J., Altman, S., ... and Zoph, B. (2024). GPT-4 technical report (No. arXiv:2303.08774). *arXiv.* https://doi.org/10.48550/arXiv.2303.08774
Russell, S. J., and Norvig, P. (2016). *Artificial intelligence: A modern approach (*3rd ed.). Pearson.
Sawyer, R. K. (2006). *Explaining Creativity: The Science of Human Innovation*. Oxford University Press.
Schumpeter, J. A., and Swedberg, R. (2021). *The Theory of Economic Development* (Reprint ed.). Routledge. https://doi.org/10.4324/9781003146766
Shafik, W. (2024). 2 Deep field of learning artificial impacts intelligence in the. In *Deep Learning Concepts in Operations Research* (Vol. 9).
Shneiderman, B. (2022). *Human-centered AI.* Oxford University Press. https://books.google.com/books?id=mSRXEAAAQBAJ
Woolley, A. W., Aggarwal, I., and Malone, T. W. (2015). Collective intelligence in teams and organizations. In T. W. Malone and M. S. Bernstein (Eds.), *Handbook of Collective Intelligence* (pp. 143–168). MIT Press.

System Innovation for a Global Economy – Lam et al. (Eds)
© 2026 The Author(s), ISBN 978-1-041-10520-6

On the numerical simulation and visualization of optical structures in solar cells: A TCAD approach for engineering education*

Zhiyou Jin, K-W.(G.H.)A. Chee, Liangxiao Ding & Yuxun Zheng
Next-Generation Intelligent Semiconductor Energy Engineering and Analysis Laboratory, Department of Electronic and Electrical Engineering, Kyungpook National University, Daegu, Republic of Korea

ABSTRACT: Technology Computer-Aided Design (TCAD) technology plays an important role in the design of modern semiconductor devices, and its quantitative analysis and visualization of the devices make it an essential tool for teaching and learning in the engineering field. In this paper, a simulation flow based on the Silvaco TCAD platform is designed around light-trapping structures in solar cells, which is used to guide the understanding of the relationship between structural design and device performance. Solar cell models with no anti-reflective coating (ARC), and with single- or double-layered ARCs, and combined with surface texturing, are constructed and compared through two modeling pathways, ATLAS and ATHENA, representing the device and process simulators, respectively. The simulation results show that the introduction of the modified surface structure can significantly improve photovoltaic conversion efficiency.

1 INTRODUCTION

With the continuous growth in global energy demand and the increasingly severe environmental challenges, solar energy—as a renewable and clean energy source—plays a critical role in the future energy landscape [1]. Enhancing the power conversion efficiency of solar cells has long been a central focus in the field of photovoltaics. To achieve higher efficiency, techniques such as anti-reflective coatings (ARCs) and surface texturing have been widely adopted to reduce front-surface reflection and enhance light absorption [2].

In conventional device development, research on novel structures or materials often relies on extensive experimental fabrication and measurement, which is both costly and time-consuming. With the advancement of semiconductor technology, TCAD has become an essential tool for assisting device design and analysis. By simulating semiconductor processes and device structures in a virtual environment, TCAD enables the prediction of device performance and optimization of structural parameters without the need for physical prototypes, thereby significantly accelerating the development cycle.

In addition, TCAD is increasingly being integrated into solar engineering education as a pedagogical tool to support teaching and learning. Through visualized simulations, students can intuitively observe key physical phenomena such as doping profiles and electric field distributions, thereby deepening their understanding of solar cell operation and structural evolution.

This study focuses on light-trapping structures in solar cells, specifically ARCs and surface texturing. Utilizing the Silvaco TCAD platform, a simulation workflow that integrates benefits for research and education is constructed and analyzed in terms of structure-performance optimization.

2 TCAD

In this paper, TCAD refers specifically to the Silvaco TCAD platform [3], which offers a comprehensive set of simulation functionalities. All TCAD components can be accessed through the integrated DeckBuild environment. For example, device structures can be generated using ATHENA or DevEdit, followed by device-level simulation using ATLAS, and finally visualized using TonyPlot2D or TonyPlot3D. The overall simulation workflow is illustrated in Figure 1.

ATHENA is capable of accurately and efficiently simulating all key fabrication steps, including ion implantation, diffusion, etching, deposition, photolithography, and oxidation. The ATLAS module, on the other hand, can model the electrical, optical, and thermal behaviors of semiconductor devices.

Both modules can be employed in the modeling of solar cells. Table 1 summarizes the key

*These authors contributed equally to this work and share first authorship

DOI: 10.1201/9781003655534-35

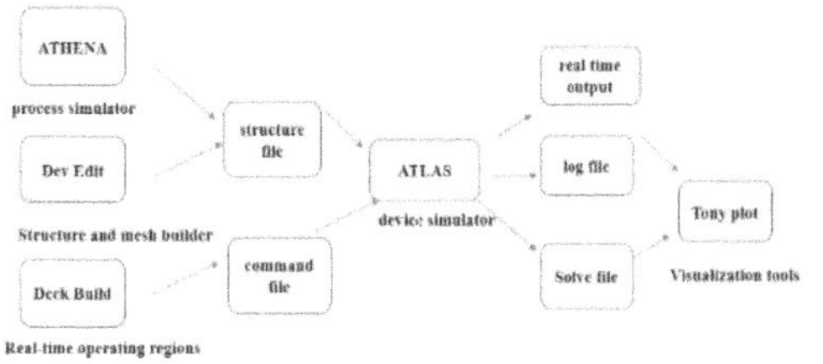

Figure 1. Schematic of process flow combining ATHENA and ATLAS modules [3].

Table 1. Constructional differences between ATLAS and ATHENA.

	ATLAS	ATHENA
Modeling Approach	Directly define structural layer parameters	Generate structure through actual process steps
Flexibility	High, suitable for rapid prototyping	Moderate, suitable for realistic process replication
Educational Value	Understanding of device structure	Understanding of fabrication processes
Typical Application	Prototype simulation, structural optimization	Teaching, process research

differences between using ATHENA and ATLAS in solar cell simulation workflows.

TCAD not only offers convenient tools for device structure definition and process flow control, but also solves the Poisson's equation and carrier continuity equations, enabling accurate simulation of internal electric field distribution, carrier concentration variations, and recombination mechanisms within the semiconductor. By comparing the external quantum efficiency (EQE) across different device architectures, the effects of various ARC materials (such as titanium dioxide, TiO_2, and magnesium fluoride, MgF_2) and their thickness combinations on light absorption performance were thoroughly evaluated.

3 BASIC PRINCIPLES OF SOLAR CELLS

An n-type semiconductor contains a significantly higher concentration of free electrons compared to holes, whereas a p-type semiconductor is characterized by a dominant hole concentration. At the interface between n-type and p-type semiconductors, a concentration gradient prompts the diffusion of electrons and holes toward regions of lower concentration, generating a built-in electric field directed from the n-type to the p-type region. This electric field opposes further majority carrier diffusion, ultimately achieving equilibrium when drift and diffusion currents balance [4].

When illuminated, photons absorbed by the solar cell's active layer excite electrons from the valence band into the conduction band, generating electron-hole pairs. Under the built-in electric field, these electron-hole pairs dissociate into free carriers. Electrons migrate toward the cathode, while holes flow to the anode, establishing a potential difference. Connecting the electrodes via an external circuit allows current flow, thus generating electric power.

4 ANTI-REFLECTIVE COATING (ARC)

The ARC is a crucial optical structure used to enhance the light absorption efficiency of solar cells by reducing surface reflection losses. Since silicon (Si) has a high reflectance of about 30% in the visible spectrum, a significant portion of incident sunlight would be lost without surface modification or treatment.

The ARC operates based on the principle of optical interference—by carefully designing the refractive index and thickness of the coating, destructive interference occurs at the surface, minimizing reflection. Common materials include silicon nitride (SiN_x), silicon dioxide (SiO_2), or TiO_2. A single-layer ARC is typically designed with an optical thickness of $\lambda/4$, while double- or multi-layer coatings extend anti-reflection performance across a broader wavelength range to match the solar spectrum. In addition to its optical function, SiN_x also provides excellent surface passivation, reducing minority carrier recombination and improving open-circuit voltage and overall efficiency. As such, the ARC has become an essential component in commercial crystalline Si solar cells [5].

5 TEXTURED SURFACE

Texturing is a typical light-trapping technique widely employed in crystalline Si solar cells [6]. By modifying the microscopic geometry of the cell surface—such as introducing pyramid, sawtooth, or random roughness features—the optical path of incident light is significantly extended within the Si absorber, thereby enhancing light absorption, particularly in the long-wavelength region.

Polished Si surfaces exhibit high reflectance, often exceeding 30 %, due to the large refractive index contrast between air and Si. A textured surface introduces micron-scale roughness that causes incoming light to undergo multiple angular reflections rather than a single bounce, increasing the probability of light being absorbed within the cell. This is especially beneficial in the near-infrared region, where Si's absorption coefficient is relatively low. As a result, more photogenerated electron-hole pairs are produced, contributing to higher short-circuit current density (J_{sc}).

Moreover, textured surfaces work synergistically with ARCs. While ARC minimizes single-pass reflection via optical interference, the textured geometry promotes multiple internal reflections. Together, they can reduce front surface reflectance to below 5%, resulting in significant improvements in light absorption and overall power conversion efficiency. Figure 2 shows the reflection of light within the texture structure.

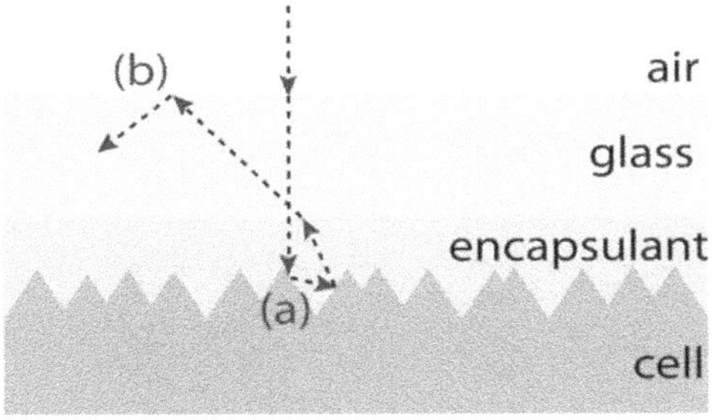

Figure 2. An incident light ray is reflected by multiple facets of the surface texture. (b) The reflected light ray is sometimes totaly internally reflected at the air–glass interface [7].

6 METHODOLOGY

Si solar cells are widely adopted, mainly based on their advantages of high technological maturity, and they are the mainstream products in the current photovoltaic market, with a standardized process and strong representation in industry. Since Si has been well studied and understood, TCAD platforms (e.g., Silvaco) have well-calibrated models of the electronic, optical and thermal properties of Si, allowing simulations of related devices to be carried out at high accuracy. Table 2 lists the modelling parameters used. At the same time, the structure of Si cells is clear and easy for understanding the core concepts of PN junction, reflectivity, composites, etc. Combined with the publicly available experimental data, Si solar cell modeling not only realizes theoretical validation, but also enhances engineering research and commercial development.

The following simulations were performed:

1. Baseline solar cell structure
2. Solar cells with single-layer ARC structure
3. Solar cells with double-layered ARC structure
4. Solar cells with double-layered ARC combined with a textured structure

An n-type Si wafer was used with graded boron doping on the front side to form a homojunction and phosphorus doping on the back side for free electron extraction. The doping distribution is shown in Figure 3. Next, a single-layer ARC of MgF_2 or TiO_2 was deposited on the front-surface, and the performance change was analyzed. The thickness of the ARC layer was also adjusted to observe the layer thickness variation effect on the device performance. Thereafter, an additional ARC layer was added to the front-surface structure, and the thickness of each layer was adjusted to study the effect of the different ARC layer thicknesses. The thickness was essentially adjusted at 10-nm intervals. Finally, a textured surface structure was added to the double-layer ARC and changes in solar cell performance were evaluated.

Table 2. Parameters for solar cell simulation.

Parameter	Value
Bandgap of Si	1.12 eV
Electron affinity of Si	4.10 eV
Optical intensity	0.1 Wcm^{-2}
Cathode material	Aluminum
Auger lifetime for electrons	1 μs
Auger lifetime for holes	1 μs
Refractive index of MgF_2	1.38
Refractive index of TiO_2	2.61
Si sample length	140 μm
Si sample width	50 μm
Cathode layer thickness	0.12 μm
Primary light source	AM1.5D spectrum
Wavelength range	0.3 to 1.2 μm
Temperature	300 K

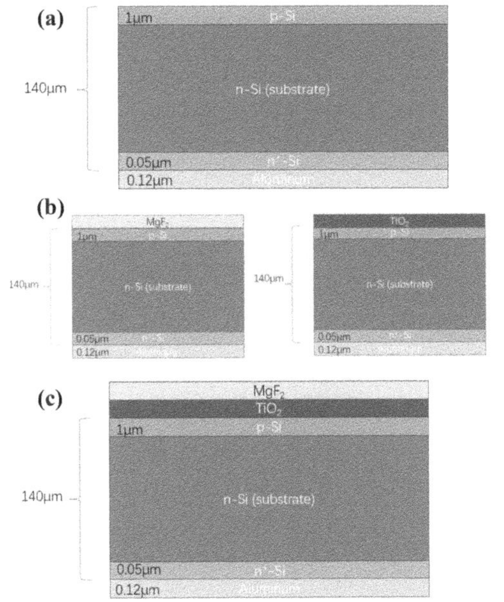

Figure 3. Basic schematic diagram of the modelled solar cell structure. (a) Baseline ARC-less solar cell, (b) solar cell with either MgF_2 or TiO_2 single-layer ARC, and (c) solar cell with double-layer MgF_2/TiO_2 ARC. The values indicate the fixed layer thicknesses.

7 RESULTS

Figure 4 illustrates the Gaussian doping profile in the p-type region of the baseline solar cell. This simulation output provides a clear visualization of the spatial distribution of doping concentration, which facilitates better understanding of the concept and practical application of Gaussian doping profile in semiconductor devices. Compared with a uniformly doped structure/junction, the graded junction offers multiple advantages: it extends the depletion region width, reduces the recombination probability of photogenerated carriers at the interface, and enhances the uniformity of the built-in electric field. These improvements contribute to more efficient carrier separation and result in an increase in the open-circuit voltage and the overall power conversion efficiency of the device.

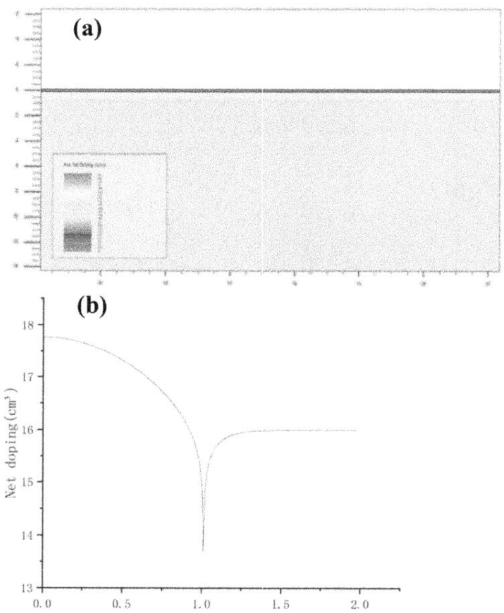

Figure 4. Doping structure of the baseline ARC-less Si solar cell. (a) 2D illustration of doping distribution. (b) Cross-sectional Gaussian dopant profile of the anode region as a function of depth below the front-surface. The n-substrate is blanket doped.

Figure 5 shows the spectral EQE for the baseline solar cell. The response is low in the short-wavelength region (<400 nm), likely due to surface reflection or recombination losses. In the mid-wavelength range (400–800 nm), the EQE reaches around 0.6, indicating efficient photon-to-current conversion. However, the EQE drops sharply beyond 900 nm, highlighting Si's weak absorption in the near-infrared region. This curve serves as a reference for evaluating the effectiveness of light management techniques such as ARCs and surface texturing, and illustrates how photon behavior varies with wavelength in solar cell devices.

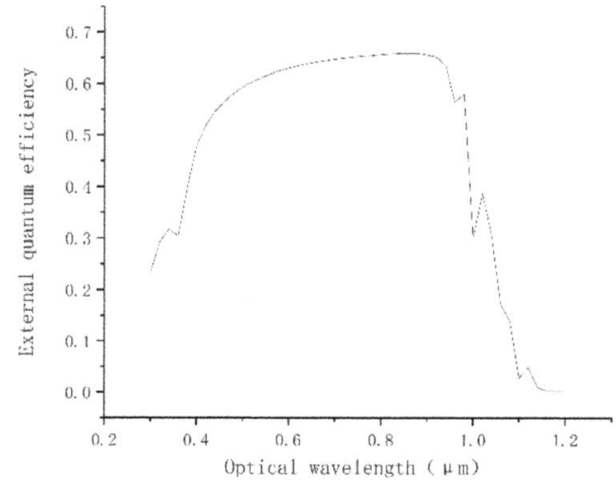

Figure 5. Spectral external quantum efficiency of the baseline ARC-less solar cell.

Figure 6 illustrates the spectral EQE of a solar cell with a single-layer ARC, based on different MgF_2 layer thicknesses ranging from 50 to 100 nm. As the layer thickness increases, EQE improves significantly across the visible spectrum (approximately 400–800 nm), with the best performance observed at 80–100 nm, where peak EQE exceeds 0.85. This indicates optimal destructive interference and enhanced light absorption. In contrast, thinner coatings (e.g., 50 nm) show weaker performance in the short-wavelength region due to inadequate reflection suppression. In the long-wavelength range (>900 nm), the EQE curves converge, suggesting that the ARC has limited influence in the near-infrared where Si's intrinsic optical absorption dominates. Overall, the results demonstrate that

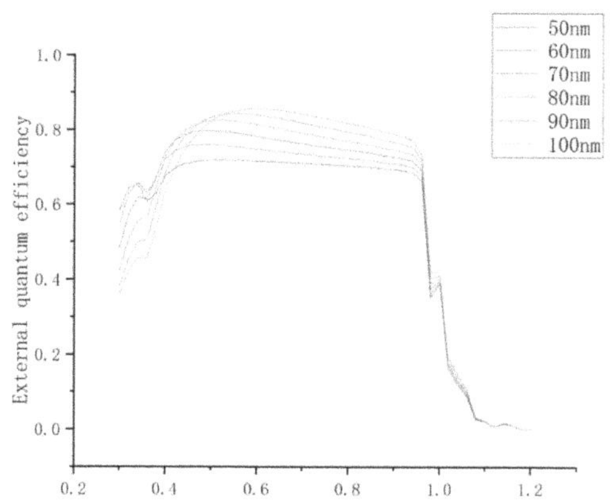

Figure 6. Spectral external quantum efficiency utilizing single-layer MgF_2 ARC thickness ranging from 50 to 100 nm.

properly optimizing the MgF_2 layer thickness can greatly enhance the optical response of the device.

Figure 7 illustrates the spectral EQE of a solar cell with different thicknesses of a TiO_2 single-layer ARC (ranging from 50 nm to 110 nm). As the film thickness increases, the EQE curves exhibit noticeable interference effects, with redshifts of the peak response. The optimal film thickness range for TiO_2 appears to be around 80–100 nm, where the device achieves high EQE values (close to 0.9) across the visible spectrum. Thinner or thicker coatings result in suboptimal performance due to mismatch in destructive interference conditions.

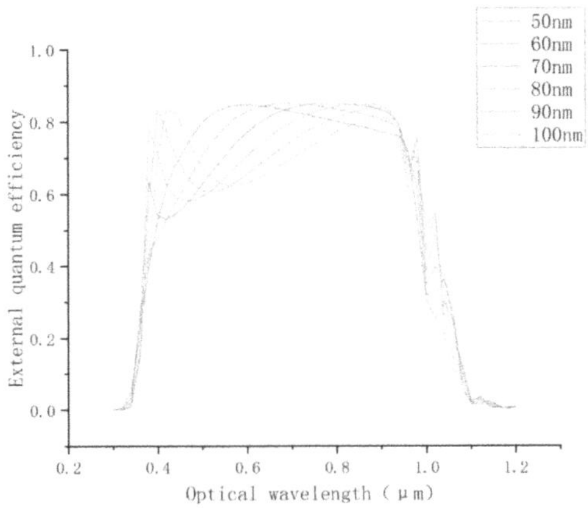

Figure 7. Spectral external quantum efficiency utilizing single-layer TiO_2 ARC thickness ranging from 50 to 100 nm.

Figure 8 presents the EQE performance of a dual-layer ARC composed of 80-nm-thick MgF_2 and varying TiO_2 thicknesses from 50 to 80 nm. The results show excellent broadband anti-reflection behavior across the 450–950 nm range, with EQE values reaching or exceeding 0.9. Notably, TiO_2 layer thicknesses of 70 and 80 nm yield the best performance, showing flatter EQE curves and enhanced short-wavelength response, indicating optimal interference conditions. Compared to single-layer ARC designs, this dual-layer structure achieves higher and more uniform light absorption across the spectrum, confirming the effectiveness of refractive index gradient engineering in solar cell light-trapping applications.

Figure 9 compares the EQE of the double-layered ARC-designed solar cells with uniform or random surface texturing. The performance of the baseline planar double-layer ARC-designed solar cell is also included for comparison, demonstrating a clear increase in optical absorption due to optimal surface texturing. The uniformly textured structure exhibits superior performance across the entire wavelength range under study, especially in

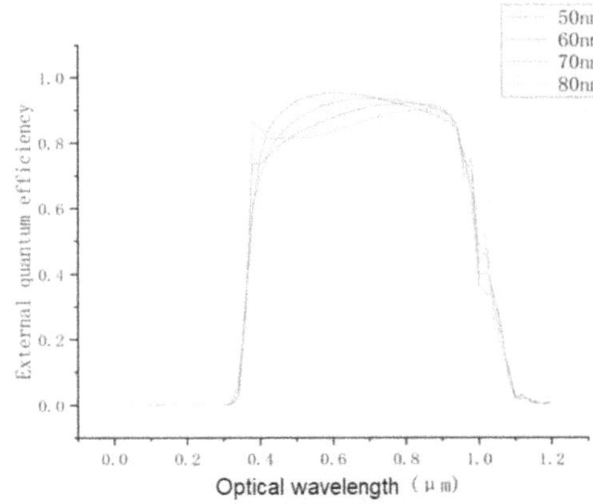

Figure 8. Spectral external quantum efficiency utilizing dual-layer ARC consisting of an MgF_2 layer thickness of 80 nm and TiO_2 layer thickness ranging from 50 to 80 nm.

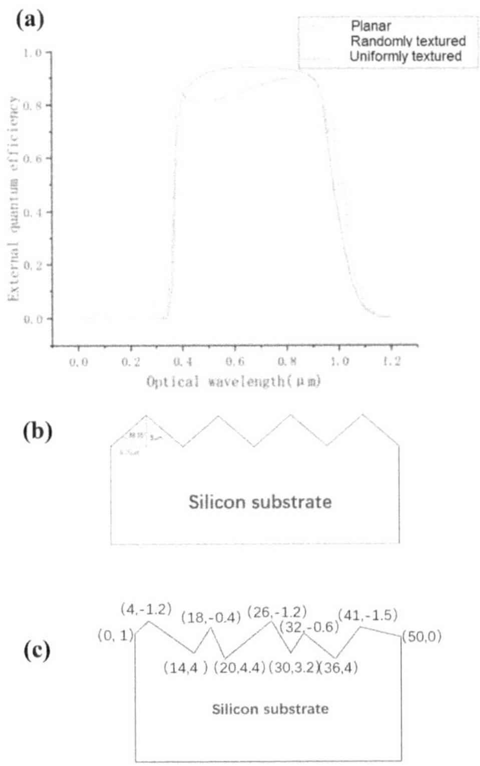

Figure 9. (a) Spectral external quantum efficiency for uniformly textured (b) and randomly textured (c) front-surface of Si solar cell. The baseline planar device is also included for comparison. The ARC consists of an 80-nm-thick MgF_2 layer stacked atop the 80-nm-thick TiO_2 layer.

the short-wavelength region (400–600 nm), where EQE exceeds 0.9. This improvement is attributed to the well-defined geometry of uniform textures, which enhances light trapping through controlled multiple reflections and extended optical path lengths. In contrast, random textures provide less effective light redirection due to irregular surface morphology. While uniform textures offer higher efficiency, random textures remain a viable, cost-effective option for large-scale fabrication.

8 CONCLUSION

This study focuses on the application of TCAD tools in solar cell engineering, establishing a complete simulation workflow from basic device modeling to optical structure optimization. Using the Silvaco platform, both ATLAS- and ATHENA-based approaches were employed to construct and analyze the electrical and optical behavior of solar cells, with a series of educationally oriented case studies designed—ranging from the baseline structure to single-layer and dual-layer ARCs, surface texturing, and their combined light-trapping effects.

Through EQE analysis, the influence of different ARC materials (*i.e.*, TiO_2 and MgF_2) and their film thickness variations on spectral response was investigated in detail. The results confirmed that well-designed dual-layer ARCs can significantly enhance light absorption, especially in the short and long wavelength regions, achieving EQE values above 0.95—outperforming single-layer solutions. Optimal surface texturing, *i.e.*, with a uniform textured surface structure, significantly enhances optical absorption and provides a further boost to EQE performance.

Overall, this work demonstrates that TCAD is not only a powerful engineering tool for device optimization but also an effective platform for providing mechanistic insights into the device performance. Indeed, this work aids visualization and understanding of the relationships between device structures, fabrication processes, and performance, offering a practical pathway for simulation-assisted teaching and learning in renewable energy curricula.

ACKNOWLEDGEMENTS

This work was supported by the BK21 FOUR project funded by the Ministry of Education, Korea (4199990113966) and Semiconductor Specialized College Support Project supported by the Ministry of Education, Korea, and the Korea Institute for Advancement of Technology.

REFERENCES

[1] Ranabhat, K., *et al.* (2016). An introduction to solar cell technology. *Journal of Applied Engineering Science*, **14**(4).

[2] Peter Amalathas, A. and M.M. Alkaisi, (2019). Nanostructures for light trapping in thin film solar cells. *Micromachines, 2019*. **10**(9): p. 619.

[3] Tang, L., (2014). *Silvaco TCAD Practical Tutorial for Semiconductor Process and Device Simulation Software*. 2014: Tsinghua University Press.

[4] Nelson, J.A., (2003). *The Physics of Solar Cells*. World Scientific Publishing Company.

[5] Raut, H.K., V.A. Ganesh, A.S. Nair, and S. Ramakrishna. (2011). Anti-reflective coatings: A critical, in-depth review. *Energy & Environmental Science*, **4**(10): p. 3779–3804.

[6] Kim, M.S., J.H. Lee, and M.K. Kwak, (2020). Surface texturing methods for solar cell efficiency enhancement. *International Journal of Precision Engineering and Manufacturing, 2020*. **21**(7): p. 1389–1398.

[7] Baker-Finch, S.C. and K.R. McIntosh, *Reflection of Normally Incident Light from Silicon Solar Cells with Pyramidal Texture. Progress in Photovoltaics: Research and Applications*, 2011. **19** (4): p. 406–416.

System Innovation for a Global Economy – Lam et al. (Eds)
© 2026 The Author(s), ISBN 978-1-041-10520-6

Analysis of pearl river delta university students' smartphone interaction and learning using the A^6 metric

Siu-Tsen Shen
Department of Multimedia Design, National Formosa University, 64 Wen-Hua Road, Hu-Wei, Yunlin, Taiwan

Stephen D. Prior
Aeronautics, Astronautics and Computational Engineering, The University of Southampton, Hampshire, Southampton, United Kingdom

Jia-Xiang Chai
Guangdong Literature and Art Vocational College, Panyu Campus, Panyu District, Guangzhou, China

ABSTRACT: This research used the A^6 Metric, created by the authors, to analyse Pearl River Delta University students' (based around Guangdong in Southern China) in terms of their smartphone interaction and use in the context of learning experiences. There was a total of 500 University students who participated in the survey during Jan-Feb 2025. The A^6 Metric uses six independent variables: (i) *Accessibility* that refers to the capacity of network technology; (ii) *Affordability* that refers to the cost of ownership of smartphones; (iii) *Adoptability* that refers to the individual's buying, downloading, installing, and starting to learn and use; (iv) *Adaptability* that refers to the individual who needs to be able to deal with the unexpected and that which is beyond their experience; (v) *Acceptability* that refers to individualistic acceptance and use of new technology; (vi) *Appropriateness* that refers to the course design model (Shen and Prior 2023*a*, 2024; Shen and Prior *et al.* 2024).

The overall results indicated that the Chinese participants are Neutral (60%) in their responses to the questions. Noting that the A^6 Metric has an inverse positivity scaling in that a lower overall score denotes higher positivity. It has been postulated that since the age group of the 500 participants falls almost entirely into the definition of Gen-Z, that this study group could represent the benchmark for the Neutral A^6 Metric. Future research will involve extending the research to other South East Asian countries, as well as Western countries, such as the Nordic block region, which consistently feature highly in the World Happiness Surveys, in order to compare and contrast this metric with that of the A^6 Metric.

1 INTRODUCTION

In 2025, China reportedly added 14 million more mobile internet users to its 1.1 billion internet population (79% penetration rate) (Kemp 2024; Statista 2025a, 2025b, 2025c).

In terms of Smartphone use, people worldwide spend an average of almost seven hours looking at a screen daily for internet connected activities (Moody 2024; Navarro 2024). The overall average screen time of Chinese people was three hours 32 minutes of their waking hours on their smartphones (Duarte 2025).

In this survey group, the average age of higher education student participants ranged from 18-22 years, and can therefore be classified as Generation Z (1997-2012). These users spend at least nine hours of screen time per day (Duarte 2025; Howarth 2024; Parker and Igielnik 2020). It is said that Generation Z is more pragmatic and analytical in terms of decision making compared to previous generations. A recent report stated that sixty-five percent of Gen Zers who are more aware of their ongoing circumstances and like being in control. They find it easier to absorb online information than learning in traditional institutions, because they have only seen the world through the technology lens (Francis *et al.* 2018, Rosalind JS and Ahmad 2021).

In this paper, the authors focused on University student perspectives in the Pearl River Delta of China, in terms of their smartphone screen time and usage by applying the A^6 Metric to measure their performance (Shen and Prior 2023b, 2023c, 2024, Shen, Prior *et al.* 2024). The Pearl River Delta Economic Zone (PRDEZ) including Guangzhou, Shenzhen, Zhuhai, Foshan, Jiangmen, Zhaoqing, Huizhou, Dongguan and Zhongshan, is one of the most dynamic and prosperous regions in China, known for its manufacturing and trade, and high levels of economic activity. The PRDEZ was often referred to as the "Factory of the World" (Wikipedia 2025). Despite its overall wealth, Guangdong

DOI: 10.1201/9781003655534-36

province has a significant gap between its prosperous coastal areas, particularly the Pearl River Delta, and its less developed northern and western regions such as Liannan and Lianshan, which are mountainous (Guo and You 2023). The income gap between urban and rural residents in Guangdong is significant, with a ratio of 2.6 in 2019 (Wu 2021). Therefore, it would be interesting to see the results of the A^6 Metric within such a diverse context.

Further, according to Hofstede's cultural dimension, Chinese had a high-power distance score (80%), which represents the unequal relationship between power holders and non-power holders, such as Teachers versus Students (TheCultureFactor 2025). Therefore, the goal of this research is to identify the A^6 criteria of University student experiences in the Pearl River Delta of China. Based on related literature reviews, the researchers will be keen to find key factors. Hopefully, the A^6 Metrics will reveal interesting findings for future cross-cultural research.

2 LITERATURE REVIEW

With regards to smartphone learning in higher education, several researchers have been active. Aubusson, Schuck, and Burden (2009) examined the role of smartphone learning in teachers' professional learning. They discussed that effective professional learning requires reflection and collaboration and that smartphone learning is ideally suited to allow reflection-inaction and to capture the spontaneity of learning moments. They also talked about the value of collaborations between teachers and students in professional learning. They suggested that authentic artefacts and anecdotes, captured through smartphone technologies, can enable the sharing, analysis and synthesis of classroom experiences by teachers and students.

Such analysis and synthesis helped to encourage collaborative reflective practice and is therefore likely to improve teacher and student learning as a result (Aubusson *et al.* 2009).

Giousmpasoglou and Marinakou (2013) discussed the concept of m-learning, the current developments and challenges related to the major stakeholders (educators and students) in higher education. M-learning shall be a part of the academic curricula and provide the potential to make learning more efficient, personal and culturally acceptable for learners (Giousmpasoglou and Marinakou 2013).

Ismail *et al.* (2016) carried out a quantitative study with 551 students to see if their University students were ready to adapt to the mobility of learning in Malaysia. The results showed relatively neutral and indicated that they were moderately ready for the educational use of smartphone technology. Furthermore, some thought of the smartphone cost which was not cheap. However, they showed their great interest in smartphone learning, but were not quite ready and uncertain about what it offers to assist their learning process. The authors recommended smartphone learning shall be employed widely in Malaysian higher education setting (Ismail *et al.* 2016).

Sönmez *et al.* (2018) reviewed related papers of smartphone learning, and argued that educational environments shall not be limited to schools. They analyzed 11 research articles published during that time in eight prominent peer-reviewed research journals between 2013 and 2017. The perceptions of learners in terms of smartphone technology, and acceptance of m-learning were proved to be the most popular topics (Sönmez *et al.* 2018). Ossiannilsson (2021) discussed some challenges in a post pandemic world for universities, the crucial implementation of the culture of open educational resources (OER), and issues of ethical sustainability, social justice and human rights to ensure the quality of accessible learning possibilities for all (Ossiannilsson 2021).

3 QUESTIONNAIRE SURVEY

The employment of the A^6 Metric that contains its six categories including Accessibility (A^1), Affordability (A^2), Adoptability (A^3), Adaptability (A^4), Acceptability (A^5), and Appropriateness (A^6) originally from Shen and Prior (2023) (Shen and Prior 2023a) aimed to compare the University students' smartphone learning experience in the Pearl River Delta of China in 2025.

There was a two-part questionnaire to discover University students' feedback on smartphone learning. A total of 500 University students responded. The gender balanced study group included 231 male students (46%) and 249 (50%) female students. Furthermore, there were 20 students (4%) who preferred not to reveal their gender.

The average age of the participants was 21.1 years and the ages ranged between 18-35 years. Almost 99% of the students fall under the category of Gen Zers, making then an interesting study group (See Figure 1).

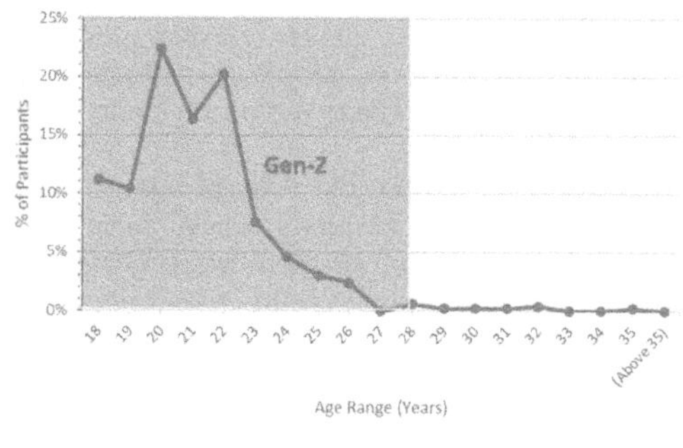

Figure 1. Age range of participants (n = 500).

4 RESULTS AND DISCUSSION

In terms of Accessibility (A^1), the participants internet speed (upload and download), which is one of the most important metrics when one considers satisfaction and the ability to undertake mobile learning, the results showed that 50% did not know their current network speeds.

When asked to measure this using a trusted online internet speed measurement tool, the average figures were: 78.4 Mb/s download speed and 29.8 Mb/s upload speed and the satisfaction was good (see Figure 2).

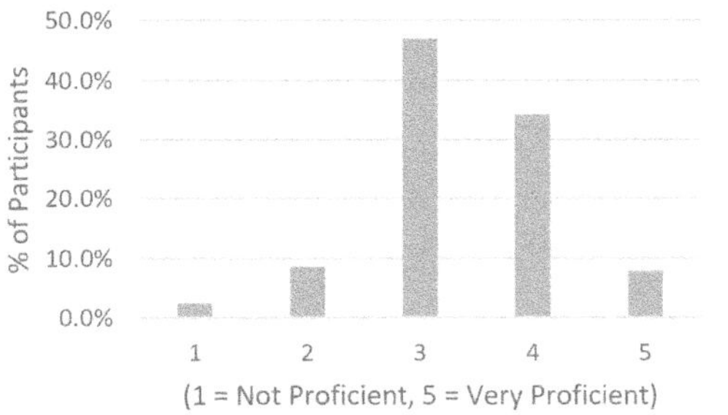

Figure 2. Satisfaction of the participants' in terms of their network speed (n = 500).

Whilst these numbers are regarded as quite good, there was considerable variability in the data, reflecting the divide between city dwellers (high speeds) and rural participants (low speeds), with roughly 20% of the participants in each of the five categories for speed.

This group of young people, who have grown up with mobile technology – the so-called smartphone generation, generally have the latest devices and regard themselves as highly proficient in the use of these (see Figure 3.)

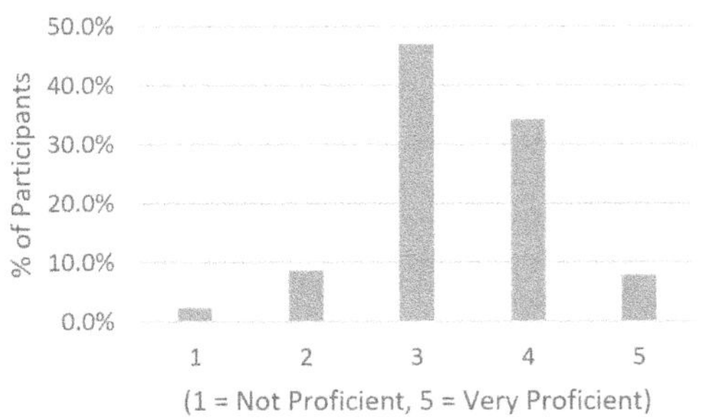

Figure 3. Proficiency of the participants' in terms of their smartphone use (n = 500).

In terms of Affordability (A^2), more than half of the participants (55%) had paid 2,801-8,000 RMB (383-1,094 US$) for their current smartphones, and 25% of them said they were willing to pay more than 5,001 RMB (684 US$) for a new up to date smartphone. This showed their strong purchasing power in this region.

In terms of Adoptability (A^3), two third of the participants were more positive about their higher adoptability such as downloading their study materials and relevant applications.

In terms of Adaptability (A^4), the majority of the participants (83%) considered that the modern smartphone had drastically changed their lifestyle, and 85% of the participants agreed with the overall usefulness of the smartphone. This suggested that they had higher adaptability.

In terms of Acceptability (A^5), more than half of the participants (56%) spend more than seven hours a day on their smartphones. More than 90% of the participants use their smartphones for four hours or more per day (see Figure 4).

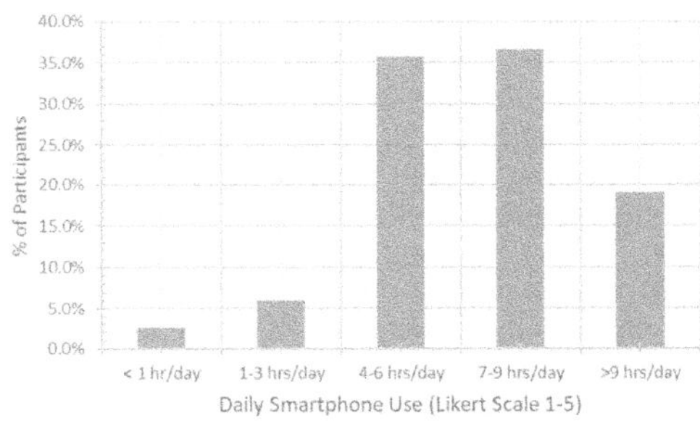

Figure 4. Daily smartphone use (n = 500).

There was 58% of the participants who preferred the real classroom setting environment than online learning. An overwhelming majority of the participants (94%) stated that they would feel unhappy if asked to switch on their camera during an online learning session.

In terms of Appropriateness (A^6), there was 74% of the participants that believed their cultural or racial background had an impact on their smartphone learning. The reasons included the tradition Chinese style with "cramming" which emphasizes memorization, rote learning, and a teacher-oriented approach, especially if it is not provided with their mother tongue language and if their teachers who come from the West are not familiar with their culture.

Furthermore, 72% of the participants agreed a religious belief had an impact on their smartphone learning style, while 62% of them felt gender issues had an impact on their learning. They thought that the role of religion can be important and included some teachers with their strong personal religious beliefs may be biased in their lectures. Some of the female participants reflected that their male lecturers made several inappropriate comments or jokes during the classes and made them feel uncomfortable, especially in certain subjects like science and engineering. In addition, some female participants preferred to look pretty or use their favourite filters before they switched on their own cameras. They all agreed with gender equity and equal inclusion.

Different religions may influence individual preferences for learning contents and affect individualistic attitudes towards learning. They believed good beliefs can have good influences such as Confucianism that is a unique tradition that blends philosophical and ethical principles with some religious elements including its emphasis on social order, ritual practices, and the veneration of ancestors. It also incorporates elements like ancestor worship, respect for elders, and a belief in a cosmic order or "Heaven," which are also found in various traditional religious systems (Society 2025).

5 CONCLUSION

China's Generation Z, one of the largest in the world, is a significant demographic, comprising 280 million people, or 19% of the nation's population. They are known for their digital nativism, focus on meaningful consumption, and influence on retail trends (Chhatwal 2024). A majority of Gen Zers reside in urban areas, reflecting China's urbanization trends, and they are more likely to have higher disposable incomes and access to digital technology than their rural counterparts (Booker 2024). Gen Z in China is characterized by their digital fluency, emphasis on experiences and quality, and a growing awareness of social issues and sustainability (Agency 2025).

In Figure 5, when compared with other South East Asian countries and regions i.e. Vietnam, Malaysia, Taiwan and Indonesia, we found that they showed roughly similar results, regarding to Accessibility (A^1) and Acceptability (A^5). It is worth noting that there was a difference between Indonesia and China in terms of Affordability (A^2). This could be explained by their per capital

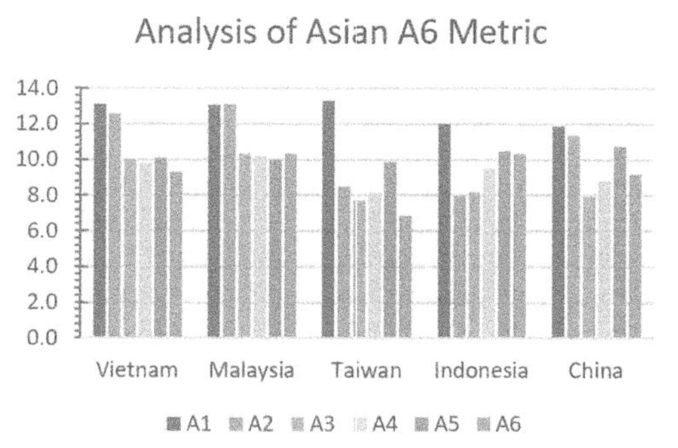

Figure 5. Overall A^6 Metric scores across five South-East Asian countries and regions.

GDP difference between the Pearl River Delta GDP per capital that was US$23,800 (China's GDP per capita that was US$13,000), and Indonesia's GDP per capita that was US$4,960 (China 2025; Statistik 2025; Textor 2024; Wikipedia 2025)(see Figure 5).

Figure 6 shows the overall A^6 scores from all five countries and regions: Malaysian (67%) and Vietnamese (65%) participants (slightly negative), the Pearl River Delta of China (60%) (Neutral), Indonesian (59%) and Taiwanese participants (54%) (slightly positive). This result indicated that the Pearl River Delta of China fitted well in the A^6 Metric. However, the Pearl River Delta cannot represent the whole of China, despite the fact that it is a relatively prosperous and wealthy region due to its geographical advantages.

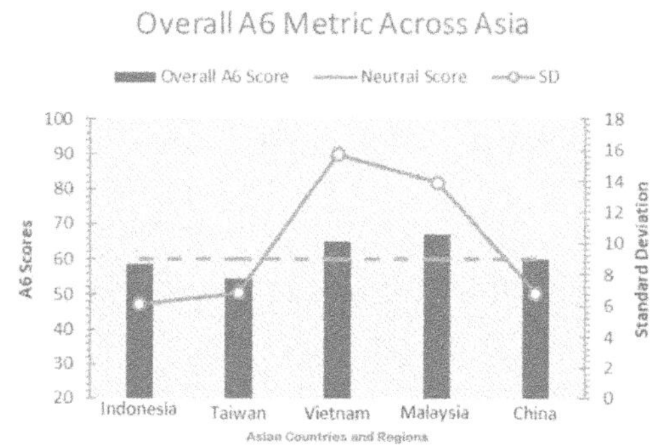

Figure 6. Overall A^6 Metric across five South-East Asian countries and regions.

The next stage of this research should extend and increase the number of Generation Z smartphone University students to other provinces in China. In order to understand the effect of A^6 Metric differences on the Generation Z's adoption behaviour of University students better, there is a need to recruit from Macao, Hong Kong, and Tier 1 and Tier 2 cities of China.

Future research will involve extending the research to other South East Asian countries, as well as Western countries, such as the Nordic block region, which consistently feature highly in the World Happiness Survey (Siu 2025), in order to compare and contrast this metric with that of the A^6 Metric.

REFERENCES

Agency, X. N. (2025). *How Gen Z Consumers are Shaping the Future of China's Retail Sector*. Retrieved April 11, 2025, from https://sponsorcontent.cnn.com/int/xinhua/how-gen-z-consumers-are-shaping-the-future-of-chinas-retail-sector/.

Aubusson, P., S. Schuck and K. Burden (2009). Mobile learning for teacher professional learning: benefits, obstacles and issues. *Journal of Association for Learning Technology* **17**(3): 233–247.

Booker, A. (2024). *Ambitious, educated, liberated but lonely, lethargic: a deep dive into China's Gen Z.* Retrieved April 11, 2025, from https://jingdaily.com/posts/ambitious-educated-liberated-but-lonely-and-lethargic-a-deep-dive-into-china-s-gen-z-what-can.

Chhatwal, G. (2024). *Gen Z consumers in China in 2024.* Retrieved April 11, 2025, from https://kadence.com/gen-z-consumers-in-china-in-2024/.

China, National Bureau of Statistics of China (2025). *Statistical Communique of The People's Republic of China on The 2024 Nathional Economic and Social Development.* Retrieved April 12, 2025, from https://www.stats.gov.cn/english/PressRelease/202502/t20250228_1958822.html#:~:text=The%20per%20capita%20GDP%20in,percent%20over%20the%20previous%20year.

Duarte, F. (2025). *Time Spent Using Smartphones (2025 Statistics).* Retrieved April 9, 2025, from https://explodingtopics.com/blog/smartphone-usage-stats#top-smartphone-stats.

Francis, T., F. J. M. Hoefel and Company (2018). *True Gen': Generation Z and its Implications for Companies. McKinsey & Company* **12**(2).

Giousmpasoglou, C. and E. Marinakou (2013). The future is here: m-learning in higher education. *2013 Fourth International Conference on e-Learning* Best Practices in Management, Design and Development of e-Courses: Standards of Excellence and Creativity, Manama, Bahrain, IEEE.

Guo, Q. and W. You (2023). Spatiotemporal changes of poverty based on the perspective of ecological poverty reduction: evidence from guangdong province, *China. Journal of Environmental Research Communications* **5** (11): 115003.

Howarth, J. (2024). Time Spent Using Smartphones (2024 Statistics). Retrieved September 28, 2024, from https://explodingtopics.com/blog/smartphone-usage-stats#top-smartphone-stats.

Ismail, I., S. N. Azizan and T. Gunasegaran (2016). Mobile learning in malaysian universities: are students ready? *International Journal of Interactive Mobile Technologies* **10**(3).

Kemp, S. (2024). Internet use in China in 2025. Retrieved April 9, 2025, from https://datareportal.com/reports/digital-2025-china#:~:text=Internet%20use%20in%20China%20in,the%20start%20of%20the%20year.

Moody, R. (2024). *Screen Time Statistics: Average Screen Time by Country.* Retrieved September 28, 2024, from https://www.comparitech.com/tv-streaming/screen-time-statistics/.

Navarro, R. (2024). *The Average Screen Time and Usage by Country.* Retrieved September 26, 2024, from https://www.electronicshub.org/the-average-screen-time-and-usage-by-country/.

Ossiannilsson, E. (2021). Some challenges for universities, in a post crisis, as Covid-19. *Radical Solutions for Education in a Crisis Context*, Springer: 99–112.

Parker, K. and R. Igielnik. (2020). *On the Cusp of Adulthood and Facing an Uncertain Future:* What We Know About Gen Z So Far. Retrieved September 28, 2024, from https://www.pewresearch.org/social-trends/2020/05/14/on-the-cusp-of-adulthood-and-facing-an-uncertain-future-what-we-know-about-gen-z-so-far/.

Proceedings of the IEEE 10th International Conference on Applied System Innovation (ICASI 2024), April 17-21, 2024, *Kyoto, Japan.* D. K.-T. Lam, S. D. Prior, S.-J. Young, S.-T. Shen and L.-W. Ji. Leiden, The Netherlands, CRC Press, Taylor & Franics Group: 392-396.

Proceedings of the IEEE 8th International Conference on Applied System Innovation (ICASI 2022), April 21–23, 2022, *Sun Moon Lake, Nantou, Taiwan.* A. D. K.-T. Lam, S. D. Prior, S.-T. Shen, S.-J. Young and L.-W. Ji. Leiden, The Netherlands, CRC Press, Taylor & Francis Group: 103-107.

Rosalind JS., and FS. Ahmad (2021). Gen-Z effect: New Opportunities of Employee Collaboration and Knowledge Sharing on Service Innovation in Malaysia. *Journal of Advanced Research in Business Management Studies* **25**(1): 6–16.

Shen, S.-T. and S. D. Prior (2023a). University lecturers' perspectives on the online learning environment during the COVID-19 pandemic: The Taiwanese context. *System innovation for a Troubled World: Applied System Innovation VIII.*

Shen, S.-T. and S. D. Prior (2023b). Mobile learning use of smartphones in the post-pandemic era. *System Innovation for a World in Transition: Applied System Innovation* IX. . D. K.-T. Lam, S. D. Prior, S.-J. Young, S.-T. Shen and L.-W. Ji. Leiden, The Netherlands, CRC Press, Taylor *& Franics Group*: 184–187.

Shen, S.-T. and S. D. Prior (2023c). Use of the A 6 metric to evaluate university students' online performance in Taiwan. *International Conference on Innovation, Communication and Engineering (ICICE 2023), Bangkok, Thailand, IET.*

Shen, S.-T. and S. D. Prior (2024). The Cross Cultural Difference in University Students' Mobile Learning Between Malaysian and Taiwanese by Using the A6 Metric. *System Innovation for a World in Transition: Applied System Innovation X.*

Shen, S.-T., S. D. Prior and P. M. Tuan (2024). *Analysis of Learning in Higher Education using the A6metric-a Vietnamese Perspective.* IET Conference Proceedings CP907, *IET.*.

Siu, E. (2025). *This Island is the Happiest Place in Asia, According to the 2025 World Happiness Report. Retrieved April 12, 2025*, from https://www.cnbc.com/2025/03/20/2025-world-happiness-report-taiwan-the-happiest-place-in-asia.html#:~:text=This%20island%20is%20the%20happiest,the%202025%20World%20Happiness%20Report&text=Taiwan%20ranked%20as%20the%20happiest,the%202025%20World%20Happiness%20Report.&text=Taiwan%20is%20the%20happiest%20place,Corruption.

Society, A. (2025). *Confucianism.* Retrieved April 11, 2025, from https://asiasociety.org/education/confucianism#:~:text=Confucianism%20is%20often%20characterized%20as,gods%20prevent%20the%20social%20upheavals?

Sönmez, A., L. Göçmez, D. Uygun and M. Ataizi (2018). A review of current studies of mobile learning. *Journal of Educational Technology Online Learning* **1**(1): 12–27.

Statista. (2025a). *Number of Internet Users in China 2005-2024.* Retrieved April 9, 2025, from https://www.statista.com/statistics/265140/number-of-internet-users-in-china/.

Statista. (2025b). *Number of Mobile Internet Users in China from 2007 to 2024*. Retrieved April 9, 2025, from https://www.statista.com/statistics/273973/number-of-mobile-internet-users-in-china/.

Statista. (2025c). *Penetration rate of internet users in China published by the state from 2005 to 2024*. Retrieved April 9, 2025, from https://www.statista.com/statistics/236963/penetration-rate-of-internet-users-in-china/#:~:text=Official%20penetration%20rate%20of%20internet%20users%20in%20China%202005%2D2024&text=As%20of%202024%2C%20about%2078.6,to%20a%20certain%20communication%20medium.

Statistik, B. P. (2025). Indonesia's Economic Growth 2024 was 5.03 Percent (C-to-C). Indonesia's Economic Growth in Q4-2024 was 5.02 Percent (Y-on-Y). Indonesia's Economic Growth in Q4-2024 was 0.53 Percent (Q-to-Q). Retrieved April 12, 2025, from https://www.bps.go.id/en/pressrelease/2025/02/05/2408/indonesia-s-economic-growth-2024-was-5-03-percent–c-to-c—indonesia-s-economic-growth-in-q4-2024-was-5-02-percent–y-on-y—indonesia-s-economic-growth-in-q4-2024-was-0-53-percent–q-to-q–.html.

Textor, C. (2024). *China's Greater Bay Area cities' per capita GDP 2023*. Retrieved April 12, 2025, from https://www.statista.com/statistics/1008540/china-per-capita-gdp-of-the-greater-bay-area-cities/#:~:text=China's%20Greater%20Bay%20Area%20cities'%20per%20capita%20GDP%202023&text=In%202023%2C%20the%20average%20per,in%20the%20Greater%20Bay%20Area.

TheCultureFactor. (2025). *Country Comparison Tool*. Retrieved April 9, 2025, from https://www.theculturefactor.com/country-comparison-tool.

Wikipedia. (2025). *Pearl River Delta*. Retrieved April 10, 2025, from https://en.wikipedia.org/wiki/Pearl_River_Delta#:~:text=Most%20of%20the%20region%20is,special%20economic%20zone%20of%20China.&text=The%20region%20is%20a%20megalopolis,Shenzhen%2C%20Guangzhou%2C%20and%20Macao.

Wu, J. (2021). Approaches to Eradicate Absolute Poverty in Guangdong Province, the People's Republic of China. *ADB East Asia Working Paper Series*. Philippines, Asian Development Bank. 45.

System Innovation for a Global Economy – Lam et al. (Eds)

Development of use of kit card toys as learning extensions in museums

Hong Y Pai
Department of Multimedia Design, National Formosa University, Yunlin, Taiwan

ABSTRACT: The museum's learning mechanism mainly focuses on interactive tours within the exhibition venue, and there is relatively little resource investment in continuing the learning after visitors leave. This limits the potential of museums to deepen consumers' awareness of brand values and consolidate learning outcomes to a certain extent. To solve this problem, we plan to launch a series of mini kit card toys specially designed for museums. These toys will be used as an innovative marketing tool to not only attract visitors, but also extend to the field of family education, improving the persistence and depth of learning. Through this strategy, we hope to enrich visitors' museum experience and extend the educational impact of museums into daily life. The detailed instructions that come with the toys are designed to guide the player or child through the assembly process in a fun and easy way and gain insight into the historical value of each piece. This not only enriches their knowledge, but also fosters interest in revisiting the museum through emotional investment, which in turn deepens loyalty to the museum. This way of learning makes knowledge inheritance more vivid and interesting, and effectively promotes the in- depth development of culture and education.

Keywords: kit card toy, museum learning, hands-on learning

1 INTRODUCTION

In the rapidly evolving digital era, the role of museums has significantly expanded beyond merely preserving cultural relics and showcasing history and culture. Hein (2006) and Bridal (2004) highlight museums as critical platforms for education and understanding diverse viewpoints [1] [2]. They serve not only to bridge knowledge and shape values and attitudes but also to foster cultural integration and moral development. Contemporary museums are dedicated to educational endeavors and cultural experiences while also promoting environmental protection. They have become multifunctional spaces that offer entertainment and facilitate social interaction. In this context of diverse interactions, museums face competition not only from various multimedia formats but also occasionally from theme parks. Consequently, museums must rethink their missions, exhibition strategies, and promotional approaches, which are essential for their ongoing development and success.

1.1 *Issue*

Hooper-Greenhill emphasized that educational methods engaging multiple senses are more effective than those relying on a single sense [3]. Museum learning offers these expectations. We acknowledge that the current museum experience has several shortcomings. For instance, the narrative content often lacks depth, leaving visitors feeling underwhelmed. Additionally, when information is too dense or complex, it can be difficult for the audience to comprehend and engage fully; there is also a noticeable lack of interest in participation among visitors. To address these issues, we have developed mini kit card toys. These innovative toys are designed for a range of museum display strategies including presentation, play, perspective, and zoom-in techniques, aiming to foster exploratory learning. We believe that this approach will allow users to engage in hands-on learning in a relaxed setting, enhancing their understanding of the educational functions and importance of museums, and improving overall engagement and learning outcomes.

1.2 *Motivation*

When exploring the gashapon (capsule toy) market, we discover that modern toys have transcended their roles as mere entertainment for children or as tools for creative stimulation. They have evolved into products with substantial brand value and the ability to resonate emotionally with consumers. In response to this trend, we plan to introduce a series of mini kit card assembly toys to broaden our brand presence, positioning them as a novel marketing strategy for museums. This innovative approach not only broadens the museum learning experience into family education but also

DOI: 10.1201/9781003655534-37

provides a pathway for the public to enhance their understanding of museum exhibits. Consequently, developing these mini assembly kit card toys will be crucial in boosting brand value and enriching the educational offerings of museums.

1.3 *Purpose*

We aim to highlight specific museum themes through the development of kit card assembly toys. This strategy serves not only as an innovative marketing tool but also enhances audience engagement by encouraging learning through practical activities and games, thereby drawing more visitors to the museum. For this project, we drew inspiration from the Railway Department Park collection of the National Taiwan Museum to design assemble-at-home toy models. The 3D files for these models are available for download and printing from our website, enabling users to construct the toys following step-by-step instructions. During the assembly process, participants deepen their understanding of the historical significance and value of each exhibit, engaging closely with every detail. This hands-on experience helps bridge learning gaps that might occur at the museum due to time restrictions or other challenges. Consequently, we believe these combination toy cards hold substantial promotional and educational value for museums.

2 METHODOLOGY

Developing mini kit card toys for museum learning involves a complex process that integrates creativity, design, education, and technology. These toys are not merely for entertainment; they are crafted to be educational tools that engage learners of all ages and impart knowledge engagingly. Throughout this development, we have embraced constructivism and exploratory learning to encourage active participation, deep thinking, and thorough exploration of the subject matter. Additionally, we have established a design framework geared toward hands-on learning, meeting the dual objectives of museum navigation and educational entertainment.

2.1 *Design framework*

Here are the key steps and procedures involved in developing this mini kit card toy:

- **Set Educational Objectives and Themes:** The design of the mini kit card toy is anchored in the museum's exhibition content or educational themes, ensuring alignment with clear educational goals. These may encompass history, culture, science, technology, or the arts, targeting K-12 students and beyond.
- **Incorporate Constructivism and Exploratory Learning:** Constructivism dictates that learners acquire knowledge through practical activities and experiences. Thus, the mini kit cards are designed for learning through assembly, operation, and interaction. Exploratory learning encourages learners to engage in problem-solving, promoting the flexibility to explore and learn independently [4].
- **Enhance Interactivity and Creativity:** The toys should be highly interactive to encourage user engagement with the exhibits, which can be facilitated through features like embedded prompts, movable parts, and modular components. Creativity is also crucial, with attractive design elements such as colors, shapes, and materials tailored to appeal to various age groups [5].
- **Prototype Design and Testing:** After establishing the concept, a prototype is developed and tested by various age groups to ensure it meets educational objectives and assess its operability, interactivity, and appeal. Feedback from this phase is used to refine and optimize the design.
- **Final Production and Educational Integration:** Following extensive testing and improvements, the final product is manufactured. It is then integrated with the museum's educational programs or guided tours, serving as a practical learning tool that complements and enhances the museum exhibits.
- **Provide Instructional Support and Resources:** To assist museum educators and visitors in maximizing the use of this toy, detailed instructional guides, user manuals, and additional resources are provided. These materials help users explore the educational possibilities of the mini-kit card both within and outside museum settings.

This meticulous development process ensures that the toys are not only educational and fun but also seamlessly integrated into the museum's learning environment. By incorporating these mini kit card toys into the museum's educational strategy, we enhance the learning experience, making it richer and more meaningful for all visitors.

2.2 *Modular structural design and publishing*

This summary outlines key aspects of 3D modular structural design and technology for marketing through 3D printing, online platforms, and user guides:

- **Modular Structural Design:** These toys, designed as interactive museum learning tools, feature a modular design that balances complexity and simplicity. The example model, a 1:100 scale Tze-Chiang Limited Express train from the Taiwan Railway Museum, consists of 20 component kits designed for third-grade elementary students and above.

- **Display Implications:** Accurate scale and proportions are essential for aligning with various display strategies such as detachable elements and internal visibility, simplifying complex details to enhance operability and focus on key features.
- **3D Printing Feasibility:** The designs are optimized for 3D printing using eco-friendly materials like PLA, suitable for flat-pack shipping and supporting "Industry 4.0" and digital manufacturing. This flexibility is ideal for small-scale production and educational purposes, enhancing problem-solving skills and parent-child interaction.
- **Mortise and Tenon Structures:** The design of the mortise and tenon joint ensures components can be easily assembled or disassembled without extra tools, with various latch structures providing stability and flexibility. Experiments indicate that a 0.01 mm gap ensures a tight fit, while a 0.02 mm gap allows for easy disassembly. The overall image of the bogie module is shown in Figure 1.

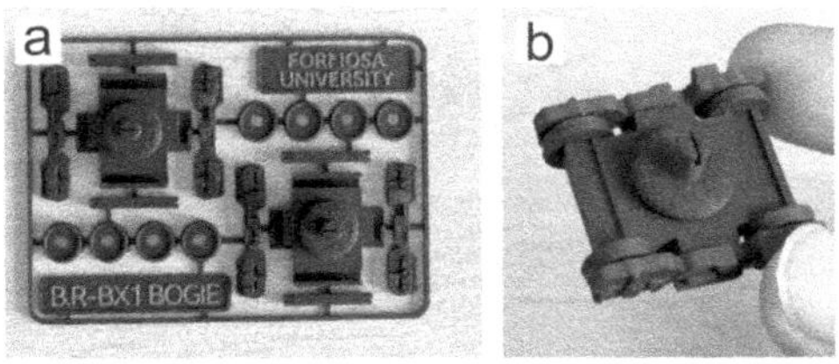

Figure 1. (a) kit card bogie module, (b) Assembled bogie model.

- **User Instructions:** A well-designed manual integrates assembly steps with museum-related knowledge, supported by visual charts to aid understanding and educational dissemination.
- **Online Marketing and Publishing:** The web platform facilitates easy access to 3D toy files, allowing the public to engage with museum content cost-effectively.

On-site initiatives like free toy distributions or gashapon machines enhance visitor interaction and loyalty.

3 RESULTS

From our development experience, we have discovered that museum guide toys are more than just a means to attract young audiences; they are also effective educational tools with multiple functions and benefits:

- **Educational Tools:** Toys serve both educational and entertainment purposes, particularly for younger visitors. Through play, children can learn about historical architectural styles or grasp scientific principles by assembling toys. This interactive approach boosts their understanding and interest in the exhibits. More than just a pastime, playing with toys supports children's mental health and fosters emotional relationships [6].
- **Enhanced Experience:** Toys can make the museum experience more hands-on and interactive, increasing audience participation. For instance, small models or role-play dolls that recreate historical events can deepen visitors' engagement with the exhibition themes.
- **Emotional Connection:** Toys often evoke childhood memories, and incorporating them into museum displays can trigger emotional responses from visitors. This emotional connection can enhance the retention of exhibition content.
- **Family Interaction:** Toys also facilitate interaction among family members. Incorporating family-friendly toy activities in museums can enhance the educational impact of family visits by encouraging exploration, learning, and knowledge sharing. Cooper [7] notes that families seek both fun and educational value from their museum visits.
- **Knowledge Bridge:** Using toys that relate to the exhibition theme as a prelude can help visitors establish a basic understanding before they explore the main exhibits. These pre-visit activities are particularly useful for preparing visitors mentally, enabling them to better absorb and understand complex information during their visit.

4 CONCLUSION

In summary, toys act as both a bridge and a medium in museum tours, significantly boosting the educational and entertainment value by facilitating education, enhancing interactivity, fostering emotional connections, promoting family interactions, and serving as an introduction to knowledge. The overall image of the train carriage modules is shown in Figure 2.

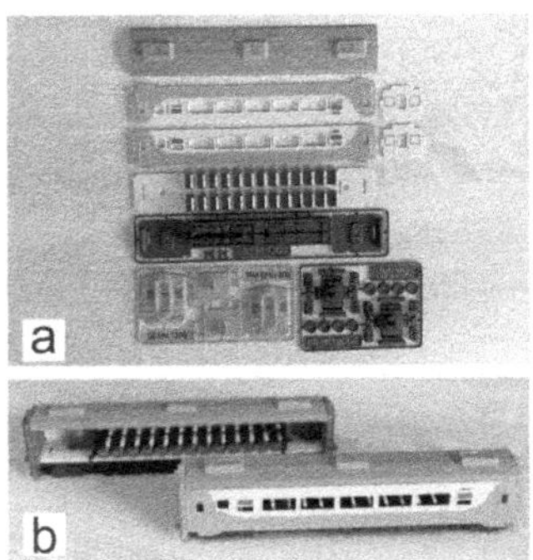

Figure 2. (a) All kit card modules for train carriage, (b) Assembled carriage model.

REFERENCES

[1] Hein, G. E. (2006). Museum education. *A Companion to Museum Studies, (Wiley Online Library)*. pp. 340–352

[2] Bridal, T. (2004). Exploring museum theatre. (Rowman Altamira Press)

[3] Hooper-Greenhill, E. (2020). *Museums and the Interpretation of Visual Culture*. (Routledge Press)

[4] Serrell, B. (1998). *Paying Attention: Visitors and museum Exhibitions. (American Association of Museums Press)*, pp. 59–63

[5] Jensen, N. (1994). Children's perceptions of their museum experiences: A contextual perspective. *Children's Environments* 1994, 11, (4),pp. 300–324.

[6] Önder, M. (2018). Contribution of plays and toys to children's value education. *Asian Journal of Education and Training*, 4, (2), pp. 146–149.

[7] Kanhadilok, P., and Watts, M. (2012). Family play-learning: Some learning outcomes from make-and-play activities with toys at a science museum. *Literacy Information and Computer Education Journal*, 2012, 1, (2), pp. 879–885.

System Innovation for a Global Economy – Lam et al. (Eds)
© 2026 The Editor(s), ISBN 978-1-041-10520-6

Author index

For Product Safety Concerns and Information please contact our EU
representative GPSR@taylorandfrancis.com
Taylor & Francis Verlag GmbH, Kaufingerstraße 24, 80331 München, Germany

www.ingramcontent.com/pod-product-compliance
Ingram Content Group UK Ltd.
Pitfield, Milton Keynes, MK11 3LW, UK
UKHW052049230926
475702UK00025B/981
* 9 7 8 1 0 4 1 1 0 5 2 0 6 *